HANDBOOK ON GLOBALIZATION AND HIGHER EDUCATION

T0314061

Handbook on Globalization and Higher Education

Edited by

Roger King

Visiting Professor, University of Bath, Visiting Professor, Open University, Research Associate, London School of Economics and Political Science, UK and Visiting Professor, University of Queensland, Australia

Simon Marginson

Professor of Higher Education, University of Melbourne, Australia

Rajani Naidoo

Director, Doctor of Business Administration in Higher Education Management, University of Bath, UK

Edward Elgar
Cheltenham, UK • Northampton, MA, USA

Published by
Edward Elgar Publishing Limited
The Lypiatts
15 Lansdown Road
Cheltenham
Glos GL50 2JA
UK

Edward Elgar Publishing, Inc.
William Pratt House
9 Dewey Court
Northampton
Massachusetts 01060
USA

This book has been printed on demand to keep the title in print.

A catalogue record for this book
is available from the British Library

Library of Congress Control Number: 2011924169

ISBN   978 1 84844 585 7 (cased)
       978 0 85793 765 0 (paperback)

Typeset by Servis Filmsetting Ltd, Stockport, Cheshire

Printed on FSC-certified paper

Printed and bound in Great Britain by
Marston Book Services Limited, Didcot

Contents

Figures and tables

FIGURES

TABLES

Contributors

Phillip Brown, Professor, School of Social Sciences, Cardiff University, UK

Vincent Carpentier, Senior Lecturer in History of Education, Institute of Education, University of London, UK

Qiongqiong Chen, PhD student in the Department of Educational Leadership and Policy at the State University of New York, Buffalo, USA

David D. Dill, Professor Emeritus of Public Policy, University of North Carolina, Chapel Hill, USA

Jürgen Enders, Professor and Director, Center for Higher Education Policy Studies (CHEPS), University of Twente, The Netherlands

Ellen Hazelkorn, Professor, Director of Higher Education Policy Unit, Dublin Institute of Technology, Ireland

Glen A. Jones, Associate Dean (Academic) and Ontario Research Chair in Postsecondary Education Policy and Measurement, University of Toronto, Canada

Sangeeta G. Kamat, Associate Professor, School of Education, University of Massachusetts, Amherst, USA

Terri Kim, Lecturer in Comparative Higher Education, Brunel University, London, UK

Roger King, Visiting Professor, University of Bath, Visiting Professor, Open University, Research Associate, London School of Economics and Political Science, UK and Visiting Professor, University of Queensland, Australia

Hugh Lauder, Professor of Education and Political Economy, Department of Education, University of Bath, UK

Yann Lebeau, Lecturer in Educational Research, University of East Anglia, UK

Mei Li, Associate Professor, Institute of Higher Education, East China Normal University, Shanghai, China

Alma Maldonado-Maldonado, Researcher at the Educational Research Department (Departmento de Investigaciones Educativas) of the Center for Advanced Research (Centro de Investigaciones Avazadas), Mexico

Simon Marginson, Professor of Higher Education, University of Melbourne, Australia

Ka Ho Mok, Professor of Comparative Policy and Associate Vice President, Dean of the Faculty of Arts and Sciences, The Hong Kong Institute of Education, HK China

Marcela Mollis, Associate Professor in History of Education and Comparative Higher Education, Head of the Comparative Higher Education Program, School of Philosophy and Letters, University of Buenos Aires, Argentina

Christine Musselin, CNRS Director and Senior Researcher, Sciences Po University, Paris, France

Rajani Naidoo, Director, Doctor of Business Administration in Higher Education Management, University of Bath, UK

Mark Olssen, Professor of Political Theory and Education Policy, University of Surrey, UK

Michael A. Peters, Professor of Educational Policy Studies, University of Illinois at Urbana-Champaign, USA

Ebrima Sall, Executive Secretary, CODESRIA (Council for the Development of Social Science Research in Africa), Africa

Peter Scott, Former Vice Chancellor, Kingston University and Professor of Higher Education Studies, Institute of Education, University of London, UK

Mala Singh, Professor of International Higher Education Policy, Centre for Higher Education Research and Information, the Open University, UK

William G. Tierney, University Professor and Wilbur Kieffer Professor of Higher Education, and Director of Center for Higher Education Policy Analysis, University of Southern California, USA

Elaine Unterhalter, Professor of Education and International Development, Institute of Education, University of London, UK

Jussi Välimaa, Professor, Institute for Educational Research, University of Jyvaskyla, Finland

Marijk van der Wende, Professor in Higher Education, Vrije Universitateit, Amsterdam, The Netherlands

Julian Weinrib, Doctoral candidate in the Higher Education Program at the Ontario Institute for Studies in Education, University of Toronto, Canada

Don F. Westerheijden, Senior Researcher, Center for Higher Education Policy Studies (CHEPS), University of Twente, The Netherlands

Christopher Ziguras, Associate Professor, School of Global Studies, RMIT University, Melbourne, Australia

Preface

It is difficult to imagine that this book could have been compiled ten or more years ago. With 29 chapters drawn from around the world, the volume has required extensive interactivity by editors and contributors. Before the Internet age, the whole enterprise would not only have been much more protracted, but also much more frustrating. Globalization, whatever its demerits, has aided global scholarship in ways unimaginable only a few years ago.

In one important sense the notion of time and space compression underpins almost every element of this book. But it does so only by being perceived as a platform for allowing wider imaginings and strategies for higher education institutions and systems. Moreover, although policy internationalization, competition and mimicry testify to the increasing importance of social networks globally – both as coordinating arrangements and as power arenas – it is how these networks are shaped by particular standards, norms and models that remains important; this continues to generate significant forms of difference as well as convergence for higher education systems.

The book is constructed as three parts: Generic; Case Studies; and Governance. Each part has an introduction to the chapters that follow. It is not necessary here to say very much about the chapters – except that the editors have sought to avoid a heavy bias in favour of western perspectives. The case studies in Part II in particular are designed to cover a diversity of interpretations and systems. The aim is not to conflate 'globalization' with 'westernization', although clearly considerable worldwide influence stems from the university systems of North America, the UK, Australia and Continental Europe. As the book highlights, however, alternatives to western forms of tertiary education are emerging globally, not least in the 'Confucian' countries of East Asia, where attitudes to family and private investment in higher education – and the role of the state – demonstrate key differences with Anglo-American traditions.

The changes taking place in global higher education can readily appear awesome, whether surveyed from high above or examined close at hand. Nevertheless, the book seeks to avoid grand generalizations based on excited enthusiasm for the speed of globalization processes in higher education. Clearly these processes have induced considerable change, but many of the chapters indicate quite forcibly that universities remain local and nationally regulated entities as well as becoming worldwide and informally shaped organizations. The university continues to occupy a multi-dimensional space where all the three planes of global, national and local operate – what Simon Marginson describes as 'glonacality'. Although this multi-level ranging by universities is not new, important accelerations in global perspectives, identities and strategies are apparent as well, and these are explored throughout the following chapters.

In their various ways the chapters examine and seek to explain the current epoch-changing eddies affecting our universities and in relation to which universities are important causal agents. They provide a diversity of terrains and a plurality of perceptions that highlight the continuing durability of universities and their enhanced cultural, political and economic centrality to contemporary nations in the current wave of globalization.

Roger King
Simon Marginson
Rajani Naidoo

Acknowledgments

The editors are very grateful to Blanca Torres of the University of Arizona, USA, for her help with translation services.

Roger King is grateful to Griffith University, Brisbane, Australia (and particularly Tony Sheil in the Vice Chancellor's Office, and Robyn Jorgensen, then Director of the Griffith Institute for Education Research) for arranging a Visiting Professorship at the Griffith Institute for Education Research, March–April 2009, when part of this book was written.

Simon Marginson is thankful to the Australian Research Council, whose Discovery Grant program underpinned the research that has informed his work on the book, colleagues at the Centre for the Study of Higher Education at the University of Melbourne, especially Richard James, and Vice Chancellor Glyn Davis.

Rajani Naidoo would like to thank Dr Dagmar Simon at the Social Science Research Centre in Berlin, and colleagues at the Center for Higher Education Policy Studies (CHEPS) at the University of Twente in The Netherlands for hosting her as a Visiting Scholar. Her interactions with doctoral candidates on the University of Bath's program in higher education management have greatly benefited her thinking.

Abbreviations

AACSB	Association to Advance Collegiate Schools of Business International
AAGR	average annual growth rate
AALL	American Association for Labor Legislation
AAU	Association of American Universities
ABET	Accreditation Board for Engineering and Technology
AERES	Agence d'Evaluation de la Recherche et de l'Enseignement Supérieur
AHELO	Assessment of Higher Education Learning Outcomes (OECD)
ANPED	Northern Alliance for Sustainability
APEC	Asia Pacific Economic Cooperation
APEX	Accelerated Program for Excellence (Malaysia)
APSC	Association of Private Schools and Colleges (Singapore)
ARWU	Academic Ranking of World Universities
ASEAN	Association of South-east Asian Nations
A*STAR	Agency for Science, Technology and Research (Singapore)
AUCC	Association for Universities and Colleges of Canada
BK21	Brain Korea 21
CAP	National Commission on Accreditation of Postgraduate Qualifications
CBO	Congressional Budget Office (USA)
CCCPC	Central Committee of the Communist Party of China
CCL	Canadian Council of Learning
CEO	chief executive officer
CEQ	Course Experience Questionnaire (Australia)
CERI	Centre for Educational Research and Innovation (OECD)
CERNET	Chinese Education and Research Network
CFI	Canadian Foundation for Innovation
CHE	Centre for Higher Education
CHE	Council on Higher Education (South Africa)
CHEPS	Center for Higher Education Policy Studies (Twente, The Netherlands)
CHERPA	Consortium for Higher Education and Research Performance Assessment (EU)
CIN	Inter-University National Council (Argentina)
CLA	Collegiate Learning Assessment (USA)
CMEC	Council of Ministers of Education, Canada
CNU	Conseil National des Universités (France)
CODESRIA	Council for the Development of Social Science Research in Africa
CONEAU	National Commission for University Assessment and Accreditation (Argentina)

CPC	Communist Party of China
CRC	Canadian Research Chairs
CRUP	Council of University Rectors of Private Universities (Argentina)
CSC	China Scholarship Council
CWTS	Center for Science and Technology Studies (University of Leiden)
DAAD	Deutscher Akademischer Austausch Dienst (German Academic Exchange Service)
DAC	Development Assistance Committee (OECD)
DGs	Directorates-General (EU)
DIUS	Department for Innovation, Universities and Skills (UK)
EAC	Education and Culture (an EU DG)
EAHE	European Area of Higher Education
EAP	Expert Assessment Panel
EC	European Commission
ECLAC	European Commission for Latin America and the Caribbean
ECTS	European Credit Transfer and Accumulation System
EDB	Economic Development Board (Singapore)
EDB	Education Bureau (Hong Kong)
EDUFRANCE	French Agency to Promote Internationally French Higher Education
EEA	European Economic Area
EEC	European Economic Community
EFMD	European Foundation for Management Development
EGM	emerging global model
EHEA	European Higher Education Area
EMU	Economic and Monetary Union (EU)
ENQA	European Association for Quality Assurance in Higher Education
EPO	European Patent Office
EPSRC	Engineering and Physical Sciences Research Council
EQAR	European Quality Assurance Register
EQIS	European Quality Improvement System
ERA	European Research Area
ERA	Excellence in Research for Australia
Erasmus	European Region Action Scheme for the Mobility of University Students
Erasmus Mundus	European Scheme for Scholarships and Academic Cooperation between Europe and the Rest of the World
ESG	European Standards Guidelines
ESIB	Student Unions in Europe, now ESU
ESU	Student Unions in Europe
EU	European Union
EUA	European Universities Association
EURATOM	European Atomic Energy Community
Eurostat	European Union Statistics Agency
EUs	electronic universities
EVA	Danish Evaluation Institute

FOMEC	Funding for the Improvement of University Quality (Argentina)
FP	Framework Program (EU)
FPCUs	for-profit colleges and universities
FT	*Financial Times*
FTA	free trade agreement
G20	Group of Twenty Nations
GATS	General Agreement on Trade in Services
GATT	General Agreement on Tariffs and Trade
GDP	gross domestic product
GEM	Gender Empowerment Measure
GER	gross enrollment ratio
GFC	global financial crisis
GPI	genuine progress indicator
GSA	Graduate Skills Assessment (Australia)
HE	higher education
HEEACT	Higher Education Evaluation and Assessment Council of Taiwan
HEFCE	Higher Education Funding Council for England
HEI	higher education institution
HEIPR	Higher Education Initial Participation Rate (UK)
HEQC	Higher Education Quality Committee (South Africa)
HEQCO	Higher Education Quality Council of Ontario
HERI	Higher Education Research Institute (USA)
HESA	Higher Education Statistical Agency (UK)
HKCAA	Hong Kong Council for Academic Accreditation
HKCAAVQ	Hong Kong Council for Accreditation of Academic and Vocational Qualifications
IAU	International Association of Universities
ICP	Indirect Costs Program (Canada)
ICTs	information and communication technologies
IDP	International Development Program (Australia)
IFEZs	International Free Economic Zones (South Korea)
IFWEA	International Federation of Workers' Educational Association
IHEP	Institute for Higher Education Policy
IIE	Institute of International Education
IIM	Indian Institute of Management
IIT	Indian Institute of Technology
IMBA	International Masters of Business Administration
IMD	Institute of Management Development (Switzerland)
IMF	International Monetary Fund
IMHE	Institutional Management in Higher Education (OECD program)
INEGI	Instituto Nacional de Estadistica y Geografia
INQAAHE	International Network for Quality Assurance Agencies in Higher Education
INSEAD	Institut Européen d'Administration des Affaires
INTOSAI	International Organization of Supreme Audit Institutions
IOSN	India Open Schooling Network

IP	intellectual property
IRAHE	Independent Regulatory Authority for Higher Education (India)
ISCED	International Standard Classification of Education
ISSC	International Social Science Council
ISTC	Industry Science and Technology Canada
IT	information technology
ITESM	Instituto Technologico de Estudios Superiores Monterrey
JPO	Japan Patent Office
KAIST	Korean Advanced Institute of Science and Technology
KEDI	Korean Educational Development Institute
KU	Korea University
LAN	National Accreditation Board (Malaysia)
LDSS	Library and Documentation Support System (China)
LRC	Lisbon Recognition Convention
MEFSS	Modern Equipment and Facilities Sharing System (China)
MEHRD	Ministry of Education and Human Resource Development (South Korea)
MEST	Ministry of Education, Science and Technology (South Korea)
MIT	Massachusetts Institute of Technology
MOE	Ministry of Education
MOHE	Ministry of Higher Education (Malaysia)
MOSST	Ministry of State for Science and Technology (Canada)
MQA	Malaysian Qualifications Agency
MQF	Malaysian Qualifications Framework
MQR	Malaysian Qualifications Register
NAFSA	NAFSA: Association of International Educators
NAM	Non-Aligned Movement
NCE	Networks of Centres of Excellence Program (Canada)
NCHE	National Commission on Higher Education (South Africa)
NGOs	non-governmental organizations
NICs	newly industrializing countries
NIH	National Institutes of Health (USA)
NKC	National Knowledge Commission (India)
NPM	new public management
NSB	National Science Board (USA)
NSERC	National Sciences and Engineering Research Council of Canada
NSS	National Student Survey (UK)
NSSE	National Survey of Student Engagement (USA)
NTU	Nanyang Technological University (Singapore)
NUFFIC	Netherlands Organization for International Cooperation in Higher Education
NURI	New University for Regional Innovation (South Korea)
NUS	National University of Singapore
NVAO	Netherlands–Flemish Accreditation Organization
NYU	New York University
OBC	other backward caste (India)

OBHE	Observatory for Borderless Higher Education
OCW	Open CourseWare (USA)
ODA	Official Development Assistance
OECD	Organisation for Economic Co-operation and Development
OMC	Open Method of Coordination (EU)
PBRF	Performance Based Research Framework (New Zealand)
PC	personal computer
PCT	public choice theory
PISA	Program for International Student Assessment
PKU	Peking University (China)
POSTECH	Pohang University of Science and Technology
P2P	peer-to-peer
QA	quality assurance
QAA	Quality Assurance Agency (UK)
QA-EHEA	Framework for Qualifications of the European Higher Education Area
QF	Qualifications Framework (Hong Kong)
QR	Qualifications Register (Hong Kong)
QS	Quacquarelli Symonds (university rankings)
RAE	Research Assessment Exercise (UK)
RCUK	Research Council UK
R & D	research and development
RECs	Regional Engineering Colleges (India)
REF	Research Excellence Framework
RICYT	Network on Science and Technology Indicators (Ibero-American and Inter-American)
RQF	Research Quality Framework (Australia)
RWTH	Rheinisch-Westfälische Technische Hochschule, Aachen University (Germany)
SAFEA	State Administration of Foreign Experts Affairs (China)
SAP	Structural Adjustment Program (World Bank and International Monetary Fund)
SAREC	Swedish Research Cooperation Agency
SC	scheduled caste (India)
SCI	Standard Citation Index
SES	Higher Education System
SET	science, engineering and technology
SIDA	Swedish International Development Cooperation Agency
SJTU	Shanghai Jiao Tong University
SJTUGSE	Shanghai Jiao Tong University Graduate School of Education
SKY	Seoul National, Korea and Yonsei universities (South Korea)
SMA	Singapore–MIT Alliance
SMU	Singapore Management University
SNI	National System of Researchers (Sistema National de Investigadores) (Mexico)
SNU	Seoul National University (South Korea)

SOCRATES	EU programme to encourage the European dimension of higher education, including languages, 1994–2006
SPU	Secretary of University Policies (Argentina)
SRHE	Society for Research in Higher Education
SSHRC	Social Sciences and Humanities Research Council of Canada
ST	scheduled tribe (India)
STIP	Status of Teacher for Irregular Professor (Korea)
TEAC	Teacher Education Accreditation Council (USA)
TFHES	Task Force on Higher Education and Society (UNESCO–World Bank)
THE	*Times Higher Education*
THES	*Times Higher Education Supplement*
TNCs	transnational corporations (or companies)
TUNING	Tuning Educational Structures in Europe Project
UCU	University and College Union (UK)
UGC	University Grants Committee (Hong Kong)
UGC	University Grants Committee (India)
UK	United Kingdom
UN	United Nations
UNAM	Universidad Nacional Autonoma de Mexico
UNCTAD	United Nations Conference on Trade and Development
UNDP	United Nations Development Program
UNESCO	United Nations Educational, Scientific and Cultural Organization
UNU	United Nations University
UniSIM	SIM University (Singapore)
UoA	unit of assessment
USA	United States of America
USM	Universiti Sains Malaysia
USNWR	*US News and World Report*
USPTO	United States Patent and Trademark Office
WASC	Western Association of Schools and Colleges (California)
WB	World Bank
WCU	World Class University (project; South Korea)
WIPO	World Intellectual Property Organization
WTO	World Trade Organization
WTO–GATS	World Trade Organization, General Agreement on Trade and Services
YU	Yonsei University (South Korea)

PART I

GENERIC

1 Introduction to Part I

Simon Marginson

Codified knowledge and higher education have always been, in one respect, essentially global. From their beginning in India (Tilak, 2008) they derived their meaning and value from the movement of ideas and people between place-bound centers of learning. No doubt cultural globalization of a kind has a long history, back to the radiation of farming in the Neolithic age and before, but the first global process we can identify with certainty is the spread of the Asian world religions, which began almost 3000 years ago. Centers of higher education were outgrowths of religious organization. Their distinguishing feature was that their main purpose became learning and scholarship, not worship. This enabled them to contribute to a variety of purposes, providing their local autonomy was sustained and they retained a recognizable position within larger networks of universal knowledge.

In the third century BCE the library and academy at Alexandria consolidated Greek and Persian learning under the Ptolemaic Dynasty in Egypt, becoming associated with path-breaking achievements in science, medicine and technology. In the sixth century CE in China the Sui Dynasty introduced written examinations of candidates for bureaucratic office to ensure they were steeped in Confucian attributes. In the Tang regime that followed, Wu Chao, China's only ruling empress, who reigned at the peak of the greatest of all China's dynasties, 'wished to further the formation of a new class of administrators recruited by competition' (Gernet, 1996, p. 257). She consolidated the civil service examination and grades of seniority, founded schools, and issued authorized versions of the classical writings. The number of meritocratically selected mandarins greatly expanded under the succeeding Song Dynasty (Ebrey, 1996).

Meanwhile learning flourished from the fifth to the twelfth centuries CE at the northeast Buddhist centre of Nalanda in India, which at its peak is said to have housed 10 000 students and a library with several hundred thousand volumes that was often visited by scholars from the Middle East and East Asia. Then there were the academies of Islam, including Al-Azhar, which began in the 970s as an attachment to the mosque of the same name and is maintained today in Cairo, the world's oldest center of higher education in continuous existence. The first of the medieval European universities was Bologna, founded in 1088 for the study of Roman law (University of Bologna, 2010). It was followed by more universities in Italy; by the University of Paris, which joined theology and philosophy; and later by Oxford. The first institutions were replicated across major cities within each culture in a wave of imitation. Thus began the mimetic pattern of development that still drives higher education and that embedded its differing forms within each regional domain. Eventually, in the era of science, the Humboldtian formula of the European/American university became the globally dominant model, and research the determinant of its mobile and universal value, as the University of California's Clark Kerr explained in the best of all the books on the modern institution, *The Uses of the University* (1963).

From the start these scholarly centers were all animated by a common principle – or rather they all rested on the common antinomy between place-bound identity and mobility. The early European universities combined an evolving sense of self-identity – partly grounded on site and partly derived from the surrounding cities, religious organizations and national cultures – with a characteristic openness to and engagement with a larger circuit of knowledge that stretched well beyond national borders. The illuminated books in the library, like the precepts of the Confucian classics in China, signified the universal mission of the institution, while its external engagement was continually renewed by traveling scholars and provided a material foundation for the mind's imagining of universal reach across a world without end. The universities (or their equivalents) rested on the intrinsic value of a set of common and portable ideas and ways of speaking that could be carried between the different centers of learning; and also carried between those centers and the sites of civil authority, commerce and the state–military world. The very *raison d'être* of the university lay in this paradoxical combination of place-bound concentrations of power based on localized resources and identity, with mobile and universal knowledge and discourse.

When scholarship was drawn to the center of the state, as under the Tang and in early imperial Rome, where the philosopher Seneca advised the emperor, and in the co-option of science to the aid of navigation in the European trading empires (Marginson, 2010), this betokened the need of rulers for a universalizing vision and technique to match their ambition and reach. The world was becoming wider. Knowledge lit the path ahead. When learning was forced back into itself in fragmented pockets, in isolated monasteries away from towns and off the beaten track, it was a sign that the spatial reach and mental horizons of state authority and commerce had shrunk.

All the great centers of learning founded before Al-Azhar were destroyed. They ran out of the conditions of existence that sustained them. The long history of universities shows that these institutions need states, never more so than in the modern nation-building period, as Peter Scott points out in his chapter; and increasingly, states also need universities. But universities are also troubled by states and their financial dependence on them (relations with cities are often happier). The coupling of power and knowledge is fecund but never easy, and is constantly renegotiated. Power always wants to bind universal knowledge to the agendas of the moment. Knowledge draws its authority from somewhere else and spills out from under all efforts to contain it. Nevertheless, both the potency and the vulnerability of knowledge are found in the places where it takes form as institutions.

A MORE GLOBAL ERA

This long antinomy between place and mobility, and the two different kinds of tensions associated with that antinomy, are more than ever evident today. The first tension is between local/national particularity and universal (global) knowledge. The second tension is between two different parts of local/national identity, between the autonomous identity of the institution and the requirements of external authority – whether church, or, increasingly as time went on, the nation-state. Arguably, in the absence of this antinomy and these two kinds of tension, the university as an institution would cease to exist.

If it severed its dependence on locality and the nation-state, not only would its resource base fragment; it would jettison much of its organic identity and potency. If its role as authoritative interpreter of universal knowledge was usurped by other entities, it would disappear. If it collapsed its local identity into the agenda of the nation-state, again it would vanish.

Although the antinomy between place and mobility was always integral to the university, it has undergone successive changes as higher education has moved to a more prominent role in human affairs, while human affairs have become more globalized. If the university's mission was always part-global, this aspect has been heightened – rendering the university more central because of its role in global networks that are becoming part of daily life, while also intensifying the tensions between the global and national missions of the university.

Contemporary globalization first followed in the wake of the European trading empires. It coincided with the spread of the modern nation-state across the world as the dominant political form (Bayly, 2004). In the nineteenth century higher education slowly shifted from the reproduction of knowledge to continuous change, to match the dynamism of the applications of knowledge in military and industrial technologies. In the twentieth century nations began to need mass higher education to meet their economic, social and cultural needs, including the needs of their own global engagement. And in the last generation education and research have been transformed by communicative globalization and the growing mobility of ideas, people and educational capital across borders.

Universities continue to source their authority in their traditional role of scholarship, but university-created knowledge is now accessed as a one-world library on the web. There every university in the world has become visible to every other. Some set up branches in foreign countries. Joint degrees abound. Student and staff mobility is commonplace. The global dimension can no longer be marginalized in relation to local and national-systemic affairs in higher education. It is now omnipresent – at least in research-intensive universities. Yet governments see the world in nation-bound terms, with themselves at the brightly lit center and the world beyond fading into a misty realm of opportunities and threats. The nation-state is focused on global reference points, but only in relation to its own competitive position. Research universities place themselves more modestly within the larger global setting, not only because it sets the standards they must achieve, but because the horizon of knowledge is, as it has always been, beyond the nation, at the world's very edge.

THE CHAPTERS

Part I of the Handbook considers globalization in higher education at the level of the world as a whole, although there is an inevitable focus on those institutions and parts of the world that are the most globally engaged. The chapters divide into two groups: three that provide world pictures of globalization and higher education (Simon Marginson, Rajani Naidoo and Peter Scott); and five that provide slices of the whole: Michael Peters on concepts of the knowledge economy; Chris Ziguras on cross-border movement of both students and programs; Marijk van der Wende on the global role of the Organization for

Economic Co-operation and Development (OECD) in higher education policy; Yann Lebeau and Ebrima Sall on the roles of UNESCO and the World Bank; and Vincent Carpentier and Elaine Unterhalter on globalization, higher education and inequality.

The global dimension of higher education and research is not a natural domain. It is one that humans make. It is formed by acts of imagining; by acts of practical strategizing and cross-border activity; and also by acts of formal and informal control, regulation and limits. All this generates the world patterns, institutional forms, and the openness, boundaries and constraints that make the global dimension. In Chapter 2 Simon Marginson looks at how we imagine global higher education and global strategy, and how path-breaking initiatives happen. He discusses partnerships, consortia, capacity-building in research, education 'hubs', knowledge cities, regionalization (especially in Europe), commercial education exports, offshore 'transnational' campuses, and virtual e-universities. There have also been two moves designed to shape the global space as a whole: global comparisons and rankings; and the WTO–GATS attempt to remake world higher education as a free trade zone. In these processes distances are reduced; place-based identity remains as important as it has always been; and universities have to be effective in all three dimensions of global, national and local activity at once. The chapter draws out the key ideas and ways of thinking that fashion approaches to cross-border higher education: the different subject-positions of university, national system, individual (student or researcher) and the global public good; and three 'world imaginaries': the global economic market, the world of university status competition, and the world of networks and 'flat' knowledge flows.

In Chapter 3 Rajani Naidoo explores the potentials of higher education systems in emerging nations, in the context of the 'new imperialism' with its international rivalries. The new imperialism works at the intersections of economic and territorial logics, and of knowledge, capital accumulation and discursive power. International borders are penetrated, not dissolved. The old international agency line that low-income countries should focus on universal basic education and postpone higher education and research has now been discarded. In its place is the new fetish with higher education as an instrument of the 'competition state' in the global setting, which combines too sanguine a view of the potentials of knowledge and communications technologies, with higher education as a means to global and regional cultural influence. These are joined to neoliberal marketization strategies and an open door to foreign capital in the developing world.

The orthodox policy prescriptions for low-income countries meet the interests of the education export nations, but fail to focus on collaboration and public goods, leaving developing countries without the full-blown infrastructures they need, and with access issues and, in some cases, a long tail of commercial 'diploma mills'. But for developing countries there are opportunities as well as limits. To see them as 'passive subjects of inter-hegemonic rivalry', as does much of the literature, misses the significance of the different adaptive strategies that have emerged.

A distinctive contribution of the chapter is the focus on China's capitalism and global trajectory, and its patterns of aid and investment, especially in Africa. China's globalization is led by state enterprises and World Bank prescriptions on higher education are ignored amid accelerated capacity-building. Other emerging nations operate effectively outside the formula, such as Cuba and the Gulf States.

'The university has always been an important mediator between local environments

. . . and global, or universal, cultures', says Peter Scott in Chapter 4. But the universalism or globalism of the university itself is continually evolving, and the 'national' and the 'global' do not always operate as separate categories. In a succinct and sweeping review of the university form across time, Scott corrects the too-easy assumption that universities are always and essentially 'global' and 'international'. As nation-builders and mass institutions they are embedded in localities and polities. The growth of cross-border international education mirrors the growth of mass participation as a whole. Knowledge itself and its applications are often locally manifest.

Even in their transcendent moments universities often exhibit particular national cultures rather than the mentality of an emerging world society. An earlier internationalism was expressed as imperialism. 'Even today the patterns established by empire still influence the flows of staff and students, as the links between anglophone and francophone countries demonstrate', Scott notes. But globalization has heightened the ambiguities of the university, which is positioned as both an agent of techno-scientific culture and universal modernism, general to part of but not to the whole of the world, and an agent of cultural definition and resistance. Globalization is also associated with tensions between global research communities and national innovation agendas. But the more contextualized research practices now apparent are not necessarily 'less global', as the global dimension is itself one of the arenas of directed research.

Since the Second World War different theorists have focused on a deep-seated transformation that appears to be moving capitalist society to a post-industrial economy focused on knowledge and symbolic goods. This transformation, which is both a cause and effect of accelerated globalization, is implicated in mass higher education and mass communications and the greater premiums attached to creativity and innovation across all fields. In Chapter 5, Michael Peters reviews three main strands of literature on the knowledge economy or information society. Each represents and points higher education, learning, pedagogy and knowledge formation in distinctive directions. The first is the 'learning economy', based on the work of Lundvall, in which the capacities to learn and innovate, and to do so on the basis of social interactions, determine the position of individuals, firms and nations. The second strand is the 'creative economy' of Richard Florida and others, which emphasizes the design and production of cultural goods in creative industries and institutions, along with intellectual property rights. In this imaginary, urban centers that have clustered the capacity for creative work – with intensive networks between artists, scientists and industries – are increasingly strategic in the global economy. The third strand is the 'open knowledge economy', a radically non-propertied form that combines work on open education and open science. Networked relations combine autonomy and community, as in the longstanding collegial relations in university scholarship, throwing into question neoliberal assumptions about self-interest.

In Chapter 6, Marijk van der Wende recounts how the Organization for Economic Co-operation and Development (OECD) has foregrounded, aided and abetted the connections between higher education and globalization in the minds of policy-makers – and describes the rise of the OECD itself as a distinctive multilateral policy space, joined to an active secretariat that has become a global policy actor. From the beginning, the OECD located the discussion of higher education and globalization in an economic policy setting – it positions higher education as a capacity-building sector essential in national responses to globalization – and it advocates the liberalization of educational trade. But one of the OECD's strengths is its acknowledgment of the social and cultural aspects. The OECD has developed a distinctive argument concerning the rationales for cross-border education and future global scenarios; and in its dealings with member governments it uses a number of different 'methods of persuasion' to advance its policy agenda: comparative education statistics, analysis of selected statistical trends, reviews of national higher education systems, the combined 'thematic reviews' of a large number of national systems enabling key criteria to be advanced, new data collection on comparative learning outcomes in higher education, and specific projects such as the work on higher education and globalization to the year 2030. It cooperates with other agencies and pays growing attention to the emerging economies and to the need for 'balancing globalization' in the light of global inequalities.

The focus of Chapter 7 by Chris Ziguras is the global mobility of teaching and learning in all their forms, from students who cross national borders to enroll in foreign systems to transnational education – the innovative movement of institutions and their programs onto foreign soil, which has grown rapidly in the last 15 years – to distance education and e-learning in all its forms. Ziguras provides data on student and program mobility, and analyzes the varied rationales for cross-border provision, noting the key roles played by global English and global communications in global higher education developments. The market-oriented philosophy of the Westminster countries, combined with the importance of the language factor in driving global demand, has enabled those countries to build large-scale export industries. He also dissects the respective cases for and against the growth of a global market in degrees, noting that globalization has brought with it both a tendency to unproductive political posturing and a set of difficult access and inequity issues. He suggests that these developments, and particularly institutional and program mobility, have begun to 'unravel' the national character of the university.

Other international agencies that have helped to shape worldwide higher education are the World Bank (WB) and the United Nations Educational, Cultural and Scientific Organization (UNESCO). In their historical account of agency thinking, Yann Lebeau and Ebrima Sall (Chapter 8) show that while UNESCO began with a humanist developmental agenda, one that respected self-determination and cultural diversity in the emerging postcolonial world, and while the World Bank has long operated a neoliberal economic agenda, from time to time the two approaches have achieved partial convergence – especially in the landmark Task Force Report, *Higher Education in Developing Countries: Peril and Promise* (Task Force on Higher Education and Society, 2000). The World Bank has dropped the argument that investment in basic education should take priority over tertiary education and has become (a little) more culturalist and developmental in its thinking, without repudiating its core concepts. On its side, UNESCO has partly adapted to the economistic notions of modernization such as human capital theory that are central to the World Bank and the OECD. The Bank and UNESCO agree about the importance of expanding tertiary participation, but differences remain on the meaning and forms of participation. Amid the emphasis of the Bank and the OECD on commercial international education as a strategy for capacity-building, UNESCO attempts to sustain an argument for higher education as a national and global public good.

In the final chapter in Part I, Vincent Carpentier and Elaine Unterhalter tackle the key issues of globalization and inequalities in and between higher education systems. The expansion of higher education has had limited success in fostering more equal provision of education, in part because inequalities are formed not simply by exclusion but also by the stratification of opportunities and institutions. Do global convergence and partial integration in higher education tend to exacerbate socioeconomic stratification and exclusions, and/or inequalities of opportunity and outcomes, on the basis of gender, ethnicity, disability and other factors? Are the dynamics of inequality in the global dimension different from those within national systems and do global transformations offer the potential to catalyze or correct national inequalities?

Carpentier and Unterhalter survey differences in participation rates across the world. They find that neoliberal policy-driven globalization enhances inequalities within and across borders, and that the benefits of globalization are unequally distributed. Yet there are also new freedoms. For example, from time to time global student mobility opens new doors for those excluded from their home-country systems. But again, what is missing is a global social justice agenda.

REFERENCES

Bayly, C. (2004), *The Birth of the Modern World 1780–1914: Global Connections and Comparisons*, Oxford: Blackwell.

Ebrey, P. (1996), *The Cambridge Illustrated History of China*, Cambridge: Cambridge University Press.

Gernet, J. (1996), *A History of Chinese Civilization*, 2nd edn, trans. J. Foster and C. Hartman, Cambridge: Cambridge University Press.

Kerr, C. (1963), *The Uses of the University*, Cambridge, MA: Harvard University Press.

Marginson, S. (2010), 'World', in P. Murphy, M. Peters and S. Marginson, *Imagination: Three Models of Imagination in the Age of the Knowledge Economy*, New York: Peter Lang, pp. 139–65.

Task Force on Higher Education and Society (2000), *Higher Education in Developing Countries: Peril and Promise*, Washington, DC: World Bank.

Tilak, J. (2008), 'Higher education: a public good or a commodity for trade?', *Prospects*, **38**, 449–66.

University of Bologna (2010), *Our History*, http://www.eng.unibo.it/PortaleEn/University/Our+History/default.htm, accessed 25 July 2010.

2 Imagining the global
Simon Marginson

INTRODUCTION

This chapter explores the global higher education space on a generic basis, spanning the different national systems and regions considered in Part II. The global dimension of higher education is not a sphere of nature. It is constituted by the actions of human beings and their organizations. It is formed by acts of imagining; by acts of practical strategizing and the productions and activities constituting cross-border higher education; and also by acts of formal and informal control, regulation and limits. Acts of imagining interplay with strategy-making. Together they generate the world patterns, institutional forms, openness, boundaries and constraints of the global dimension of higher education.

In sum, the global dimension is created by a combination of imagining, strategizing and ordering. This chapter and Chapter 23 in Part III provide a synthesis of these processes. The main emphasis of this chapter is on global imagining in higher education: on the manner in which time-space compression in a one-world knowledge system has changed what is possible and enabled more plural and more globally standardized human subjects and organizational forms.

The chapter begins by asking, 'What is the global in higher education?' It distinguishes the 'global' dimension of activity from the national and local dimensions. It lists the cross-border strategies and initiatives of institutions and systems; and reviews differing subject perspectives on the global dimension – those of individuals, higher education institutions, national systems, and the perspective of the world as a whole. It discusses the continuing importance of place, although place has become more mobile and multiple, and the ways that global subjects (individuals, institutions and national systems) shape themselves and invent and manage global space. It explores the world imaginaries, partly old and partly derived from more recent global potentials that human subjects use to conceive this new vast domain of education and knowledge. These imaginaries are the global market economy, worldwide status competition, and the world of networks and open source knowledge flows. Subjects often draw on more than one of these imaginaries.

Later the chapter in Part III will take the discussion further. It will look at how these increasingly global mentalities take shape in position-taking and strategy in higher education, at both institutional and national levels – how time-space compression, self-positioning by human subjects within the global 'space of positions' (Bourdieu, 1993), their creation and managing of space, and the contents of their world imaginaries, play out in real-life higher education. It will go on to consider the informal ordering and formal regulation of the global space, where some of the open possibilities are realized and others are not, and where there are contending possibilities for diversity/uniformity and inequality/common good. It will consider which global strategies work best, and why. The Part III chapter is about global strategizing and global ordering. The present chapter is about what comes first: global imagining.

INTERPRETATIONS

The global dimension is fast-moving and fluid. Global phenomena always burst out of the categories we use to trap or freeze-frame them in the terms of social science. In the most effective explanations global structures are partly open, changing, provisional and continually relativized by other parts of the field (Marginson, 2008). There is no closure. One element always at play, and a major source of this ontological openness, is the imagination and will of human subjects. The human imagination is the primary dependent variable in the mix. It is conditioned – and it can also trump everything else.

There is no lack of theories of globalization in the social science literature. A common limitation is that these theories were mostly developed for settings only marginally implicated in higher education, principally the financial economy. Yet even in economic terms, leaving aside its 'thick' involvement in cultural and social matters, higher education is an unusual beast. Knowledge is a public good in the economic sense, and this ensures that higher education is unable to function as a conventional market economy. Once disseminated, knowledge retains intrinsic value but cannot be owned by one subject or produced on the basis of scarcity, competition and market price. This affects both research and teaching/learning. While educational credentials can function as private goods, the learning that graduates take to work is a public good. Cultural theories of globalization such as those of Appadurai (1996) can be more suggestive of the specifics of universities and knowledge. But a full cultural theorization of global higher education has yet to emerge.

The other possible source of theories of global higher education is the higher education studies literature. But the main theorizations of higher education evolved prior to the communicative globalization of the 1990s and are mostly locked in national frameworks. They treat global or 'international' phenomena as epiphenomena of the national dimension, the conventional realm of policy, rather than as part of an autonomous world dimension of action. Yet in the global setting one of the variables at play is the nature and limits of the nation. For this reason alone it is essential to analyze the global from beyond the national.

In sum, we should be cautious in either transferring national interpretations into the global setting, or transferring a generic global theory into the study of higher education. There is no substitute for the painstaking but more rewarding process of composing an explanation distinctive to global higher education, one sufficiently open to a range of theory as to bring a broad range of phenomena under observation within an always moving frame. Rather than applying one pre-given theorization, this chapter draws on a plurality of insights. It discusses the global dimension of action in terms of more basic – and often empirically verifiable – categories such as practices, structures, subjects, capacity, flows, behaviors and freedoms (self-determining agency). It also acknowledges that there are many different perspectives on the global dimension, many standpoints for observation.

WHAT IS 'THE GLOBAL' IN HIGHER EDUCATION?

In the third volume of *Civilization and Capitalism* (1985) Fernand Braudel distinguishes the global or 'world' level from other dimensions of human activity such as the national, regional or local. The global dimension in higher education consists of world or part-world systems of knowledge and information flow, networks, and people movement between institutions and systems. It is constituted by worldwide or part-world thinking, activities, mobility and relationships. Global systems have two levels. There are individual, separable global systems such as, say, international law. There is also the meta-system, the sum of all global systems – the ecological imaginary, the perspective of the world taken as a whole.

Globalization is the process of forming the global dimension. It is marked by more extensive and intensive worldwide relationships and the quickening of global awareness (Held et al., 1999). It is the sum of all tendencies to convergence and integration across national borders. The global dimension lies across every nation-state, and also beyond all the nation-states. It does not dissolve each and every nation-state into itself, whether in higher education or elsewhere. But it has a life of its own while also affecting all nations.

Here there is debate about the order of magnitude of globalization – about the extent to which we are becoming one world and whether this is changing the potentials of the modern nation-state. David Held and colleagues (1999, pp. 2–10) distinguish between three positions. 'Hyper-globalists' privilege the one-world aspects and see the dissolution of nations as inevitable, with global culture and governance becoming dominant in the (near?) future. 'Sceptics' assert that there has been little change in the position of nation-states. 'Transformationalists' assert that global convergence and integration have partly modified the scope of nation-states – nations have been relativized by the global dimension but remain important. This chapter is closest to the transformationalist position. The nation-state is robust in governance and socioeconomic organization. Like all identities, national identities can be deeply entrenched (Marginson, 2010d). The question of which dimension, global or national, is decisive in human affairs is a case-by-case matter. It varies by sector: higher education may be more or less globalized than, say, finance. It varies by location: higher education in the USA may be more or less globalized than in, say, Japan or Singapore.

GLONACAL

Even at the level of the world the global is not 'everything'. We do not live our lives in continuing awareness of the world as a whole. Most of the time our horizon is closer and our systems more modest. Higher education systems and institutions, leaders and some personnel are active in each of three dimensions of life: local, national and global. Each dimension has its own mode of organizing life and has distinctive perspectives, imaginings and practices. Each dimension is affected by the others but irreducible to the others. People and organizations move in and out of the mentalities and practices associated with each dimension. They are not active in each dimension all the time – but often in more than one.

The local dimension is the day-to-day institution and its communities inside and

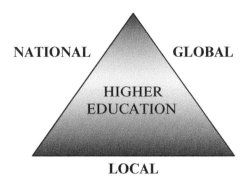

Source of concept: Marginson and Rhoades (2002).

Figure 2.1   Dimensions of higher education

outside the campus gate. The national dimension is about national culture and polity and policies, and the laws and regulations shaping higher education and research. Nation-states see higher education as one of their instruments, a provider of knowledge and skilled labor for the national economy and a structure of equitable social opportunity. As they always did, universities in this more global era continue to rest on locality in space and time, their place of being within a moving world. Most institutions need national government, which is the most important single source of funding. Universities insufficiently grounded in locality or nation will falter at all levels including the global level. (Universities whose sole identity derives in cyberspace have not done well.) This is an example of how activity in each of the three dimensions is affected by the others.

But what universities do in meeting the needs of governments is not always the same as what they do for their local stakeholders and students, or for their global partners and international students. The distinction between the three dimensions of action – global, national and local – is always there.

In short, we live in a 'glonacal' era of higher education (Marginson and Rhoades, 2002; Marginson and van der Wende, 2009a). Glonacal = *glo*bal + *na*tional + lo*cal*. Figure 2.1 provides a spatial description and identifies intersections between the dimensions. The glonacal framework allows us to differentiate and combine the activities of human subjects, whether persons, institutions and organizations, or governments. Figure 2.1 suggests that the global does not function as a universal container with the other dimensions inside it in descending order of size, regional to national down to local, like interlocking Russian dolls. A better metaphor is that of parallel and intersecting domains. Between them there are points of contact: gateways, portals and moments of synchrony when one inhabits more than one domain at the same time. Thus higher education calls up a capacity for multiple imaginings and flexible practices.

The focus in this chapter on an identifiable global dimension of higher education contrasts with studies (the majority) where global phenomena are considered primarily in terms of effects in the national dimension (especially) and in local higher education. Global phenomena in higher education are manifest in four different ways, as shown in Table 2.1: one-world, global systems, national effects, local effects.

Globalization has complex and multiple impacts in nations and localities. Following

Table 2.1   Global activity and impacts in higher education

Manifestations of global activity	Primarily showing in which glonacal dimension?	Examples in higher education
Global ecology: the world as one relational space (the sum of all global systems in higher education and research)	Global	• The combination of institutional classifications, worldwide comparisons, performance measures and rankings in relation to research, which together map the global sector • The WTO–GATS agenda of coordinated reform to national education systems, designed to create a one-world free trade zone in education
Global systems – formal and informal – in higher education	Global	• Internet and telecommunications • Publishing of academic journals and books • Export market as an informal global system of institutional/national economic competition • International law in intellectual property • Networks: university partnerships and consortia
Impacts of global systems and activities in national dimension	National	• Policy drive to improve national competitiveness on the basis of global comparisons in research and in tertiary education participation. Often associated with additional investment • Policies to increase international connectedness and activity ('internationalization') • National selectivity and concentration in research activity to lift comparative performance • Temporary migration in and out of each national system by mobile students • Regulation of export sector by nations • Regulation of foreign providers by nations • Education 'hub' and knowledge city strategies • Other national strategies to build research and to attract and hold global talent, such as 'fast-track' migration procedures, international scholarships
Impacts of global systems and activities in local dimension	Local	• Infrastructure investments to improve communications and global data monitoring • Policies to increase international connectedness and activity ('internationalization') • Selectivity and concentration in institutional research activity to lift comparative performance • Other reforms to lift research performance, e.g. incentive schemes via funding or promotion criteria designed to encourage more academic staff to publish in global English • Use of university ranking and research metrics to set targets and drive performance • Global catchment approach to recruitment • Entrepreneurial and marketing activity in global practices, e.g. fee-paying international education

Saskia Sassen (2006, pp. 42–3), Roger King notes that in the national dimension we find several spaces and sets of relations: some traditionally national, some becoming globalized, and some unequivocally global in form already (King, 2009, p. 3). The same kind of remark applies to the local dimension, which is populated by the irreducibly local; local elements subject to national colonization; national and local elements transforming via the global; and global and local elements transforming via the globalized national and so on. Nevertheless the emphasis in this chapter is on the first and second rows of the table. This creates a problem of selective perception. When activity in one glonacal dimension is illuminated brightly, the others are shadowed. When, as is mostly the case, we think exclusively in local or national terms, the global eludes us at the edge of our minds. When we consider global relations, the national and local dimensions become less vivid; they begin to fade. The focus of this chapter imparts a 'globalist' bias to the argument.

But the other dimensions remain important in their own right because they condition the global, and because global activity has little purchase unless it is manifest locally and/ or nationally.

GLOBAL ACTIVITIES IN HIGHER EDUCATION

During the 1990s the global dimension moved from the periphery of strategic vision in higher education, a main item only in research and knowledge, to become an external factor that required a central strategic response. Initially this response was often defensive, a matter of managing new outside pressures with the underlying goal of continuing as before. But increasingly the new possibilities of globalization and imperatives of competition demanded a more proactive approach. The global dimension passed from an external factor to an essential internal factor at the heart of research universities and (less consistently) of national 'competition states' (Naidoo, 2010).

In this process material globalization and global imagining fed each other. Synchronous communications brought a diversity of institutions into constant touch and opened wider mental and practical landscapes. The reflex of global comparison drove investment in research capacity and people mobility. Through these reciprocal changes globalization has become a primary form of modernization. 'Internationalization' strategies are designed to make systems and institutions more globally engaged and competitive.

This does not mean that universities or governments have 'become global' in the sense of adopting a one-world perspective. Rather, their institutional and national perspectives have altered. Institutions and systems find themselves thinking globally part of the time while building activities in the global dimension. There, to be globally effective, institutions and systems must establish global connectivity and global capacity. Connectivity is created by communications infrastructure, mobile personnel and programs, and networks. Global capacity is shaped in building research, the most important condition of global *gravitas* in higher education, by concentrating infrastructure, resources and marketing in global hubs and knowledge cities, and in education export industries and online platforms. Cross-national regionalization in higher education builds both capacity and connectivity.

The global dimension is not in equilibrium. It is constantly in motion, if not in flux.

The last 20 years have seen exceptionally dynamic growth in global higher education. Remarkable strategies have been envisioned and applied, a mixture of old and new but with significant innovations. The different global activities and their implications for the global, national and local dimensions are summarized in Table 2.2. Of course globalization is not driven solely by deliberate strategies and planned activities. As has been demonstrated by the rapid spread of Internet-mediated communication and open source knowledge, the global dimension also evolves spontaneously, accumulating in an unpredictable manner.

These strategies create new global systems, affect national system development, and lift individual universities into new trajectories. Some universities use their global activities to reposition themselves in the national system and their locality. The first two strategies, those of comparisons and rankings, and the WTO–GATS trade negotiations, are ecological strategies that set out to remake the global dimension as a holistic space in different ways.

1.   Multi-actor Strategy

Global comparisons, classifications and rankings

In the last decade global comparisons of the performance of institutions, and thereby of national systems, have become established, securing media prominence and growing effects in the choice-making of governments, institutions, employers, students and other stakeholders (Hazelkorn, 2008). These comparisons are often expressed in a single vertical hierarchy or 'league table' of institutions. Most global comparisons relate to research performance. The first and best-known data collection is by Shanghai Jiao Tong University Graduate School of Education (SJTUGSE, 2010). More specialized publication and citation counts (e.g. CWTS, 2010) affect decisions about research funding. The media public is impressed by omnibus rankings that summarize the global standing of universities by combining heterogeneous performances in a single number, as in the *US News and World Report* and in the *Times Higher Education*'s (2009) global ranking. More complex multi-purpose rankings are being developed in Europe supported by institutional classification of the type operating in the USA and China (van Vught, 2009).

A wide spectrum of agents is involved in classifications, comparisons and ranking: governments, including regulatory agencies as in Taiwan (HEEACT, 2010); publishing and media corporations; higher education research institutes; and Internet-based organizations such as Webometrics (2010). The OECD (2008b) is fashioning comparative measures of learning outcomes in higher education.

2. Nation-driven Strategies

Global higher education as a trading system (WTO–GATS)

The multilateral WTO–GATS negotiations emerged out of successive rounds of global trade talks. The objective is to create an open global trading regime in designated services sectors including education (OECD, 2004). Nations are expected to negotiate bilaterally to establish free trade in four designated areas: cross-border supply, for example online education; consumption abroad, such as international students; commercial presence, for example transnational education; and movement of natural persons, such as

Table 2.2   Practices forming the global dimension of higher education and knowledge

Strategy	Driven by	Description/examples	Glonacal dimensions
Global comparisons of institutions, and research performance	Many agents, including research institutes, publishing companies, governments	Comparisons of aspects of institutional performance and/or reputation, e.g. research publications and/or citations, peer academic standing, student surveys. May be based on classifications of institutions, often generate 'league tables', e.g. Shanghai Jiao Tong University, Leiden CWTS, Taiwan HEEACT rankings of research performance, Times Higher Education 'best universities' list	Institutional classifications and comparisons together form a holistic worldwide system of higher education, with subsystems (e.g. research metrics). Highly influential in shaping imagining of global higher education. Used to measure institutional performance: relativizes national competition and prompts local action to lift performance
WTO–GATS negotiation of global system of free trade in educational services	Government	Nations deregulate education systems to permit entry of foreign providers on the same terms as local providers. Most nations negotiate, few have adopted the more far-reaching changes except deregulation of online education. Full WTO–GATS vision not realized	Negotiation between nations to create a global higher education trading space – worldwide sector as economic market – by reforms in each nation to facilitate global systems and flows. Potentially remakes national dimension of higher education, with fallouts in local activity
Capacity-building in research	Government	Investment in research universities and institutes to lift quantity and quality of research to strengthen national innovation and/ or lift global rankings. May be joined to concentration of research in selected institutions, merger programs, etc., e.g. China, Taiwan, Germany, France	Action in national dimension that is designed to impact global dimension. At global level generates an 'arms race' in innovation (global system of continuing mimetic change). Nationally, entrenches global comparisons. Stimulates local activity in selected sites
Remaking of nation/city as a 'global hub' of education and research activities	Government	Investment in precinct and infrastructure, policy/ regulation to draw foreign providers, students and capital, building a global role for national education and research. May be joined to capacity building in research, and education export, e.g. Singapore, Qatar	Action takes place largely in national system, which is redesigned so as to pull global flows towards the nation, thereby positioned in the global dimension. Reshapes global dimension, transforms nature and capacity of national system, stimulates local activity in some sites

Table 2.2   (continued)

Strategy	Driven by	Description/examples	Glonacal dimensions
Knowledge cities	Government and higher education institutions	Investment by institutions, cities and governments in infrastructure to attract foreign education and research providers, students and investment capital. More modest version of hub strategy that is centered on a group of institutions, e.g. numerous cities around the world	Action in parts of national system that is designed to pull global flows of knowledge, people and capital to the chosen city center, thereby positioned in the global dimension. Can affect global flows and lift national capacity, stimulates local activity in selected sites
Commercial export of education	Government and higher education institutions	Higher education in a national system deregulated to enable full fee places for international students. Institutions set price and volume. Immigration regulation by export nations facilitates student visas and often, migration of some graduates, e.g. universities in UK and Australia, private colleges in Malaysia	Export industry capacity in national system designed to attract a growing share of global student flows. Export and import sectors together constitute a global education market (a global system). Changes national regulatory framework, policy and funding; and also local funding and activity
Regionalization in higher education and research	Government and higher education institutions	Regional (meta-national) cooperation between national higher education systems. May include research grant programs; alignment degree structures, curriculum contents and professional requirements; standard systems for recognizing institutions and qualifications; quality assurance; classification, comparison, ranking and evaluation on a regional basis, e.g. formation of the European Higher Education and European Research Areas via the Bologna reforms	Regional system building and partial convergence in higher education and research in Europe creates a meso-level of activity between global and national dimensions, designed to position Europe as a global player while modernizing its national and combined systems. The national dimension, relativized by regional elements, changes markedly, though global connections beyond the region may be retarded. Stimulates changes in the local dimension, which becomes more engaged outwards
Transnational campuses	Higher education institutions	Universities establish branch campuses in another country, with permission of national and local authorities, either in their own right by providing	Spatially complex and transformative in all three dimensions. Multiple in regulation, potentially in culture and identity.

Table 2.2   (continued)

Strategy	Driven by	Description/examples	Glonacal dimensions
		the premises, or in conjunction with an in-country partner that manages the site. Degrees are recognized in both nations, e.g. University of Nottingham (UK) in Malaysia and China, RMIT University (Australia) in Vietnam	Augments cross-border trade. Takes local institution into global space. Subjects it to two different systems of national regulation. Constitutes a global intervention in national systems. Brings other national and local influences back home to the parent institution
Partnerships between universities	Higher education institutions	Institutions sign agreements with parallel institutions in other countries; carry out cooperative joint activities, e.g. in personnel and student exchange, joint degrees, curriculum, research, university organization, benchmarking, etc., e.g. all research universities	Creates a lattice-like network around each institution as node. Some have more extensive and intensive global connectedness. All forms a semi-coupled global system of connections. Transmits global effects directly to local dimension. Bypasses national
University consortia	Higher education institutions	Formal networks of 15–40 institutions, although there are also some instances of intensive micro-consortia of 3–5 partners. Activities as for partnerships, e.g. Association of Pacific Rim Universities (42 members), League of European Research Universities (22)	Essentially a selective network, world-spanning or region-spanning in reach. Stimulates global flows of knowledge, messages, people, etc. but much activity also takes place outside consortia. Transmits global effects directly to local dimension. Bypasses national
Global 'e-universities' (eUs)	Higher education institutions	Virtual delivery of programs on the Internet, by established institutions or commercial providers. Curriculum, student assessment, credentialing and administration from a central location, e.g. NYU online (closed), U21 Global, University of Phoenix online	Passes from the local dimension straight to a global system of virtual institutions with one imagined global student constituency/market (or so is hoped). Individual e-universities intervene freely in all localities, bypassing the national dimension altogether

temporary migration as guest worker or education provider. But nations can exempt their education systems on grounds of 'national treatment'. Most governments continue to apply targeted subsidies to national higher education and protect them from competition in the form of market entry. Cross-border online education has a free hand because Internet-based activity cannot be regulated.

Capacity-building in research

Many national governments see investment in research as key to future economic competitiveness. Zones of accelerated investment include China (Li et al., 2008), Korea, Taiwan China and Singapore; parts of Europe including Germany and France (Salmi, 2009); and the USA, where the Obama Administration doubled funding for National Science Foundation and National Health Institute research programs in 2009. National systems expanding their research capacity are better positioned to attract global doctoral students, postdoctoral and senior researchers, and industry project monies. Investments in some nations generate a chain reaction of mimetic investments in others.

Global hubs

Global education and research hubs are designed to position the national system or city as attractive to foreign fee-paying students, and perhaps foreign educational institutions and investment capital. Some hubs also focus on research, industry innovation, and capital for R&D and commercialization. The idea is to enhance the nation/city as a global center of economic development, led by knowledge-related activities. Sponsoring governments invest in infrastructure and offer favorable terms to foreign providers. The first global knowledge hub was the Singapore Global Schoolhouse (Kong et al., 2006; Sidhu, 2009). Mauritius, the United Arab Emirates and Qatar have similar intentions. If successful, the hub strategy reshapes the global dimension, transforms the capacity of the national system by making it into a global actor, and stimulates local activity in some sites.

3. Strategies Driven by Nation and Institution

Knowledge cities

A more modest version of the hub strategy is often driven by universities in concert with local/municipal or provincial, sometimes national, government. This may involve infrastructure investment, precinct architectures, worldwide marketing, visa policies to facilitate mobile persons, and other conditions designed to make the city and its institutions attractive to talented people and investment capital.

Export of education

Commercial education exports of face-to-face education involve international students crossing borders into the export nation and paying full-price tuition (Bashir, 2007; Verbik and Lasanowski, 2007). This involves half the world's 3 million cross-border students, many enrolled in programs providing globally portable qualifications in business, technologies and English language. The estimated value of the global market is US$40–50 billion per year. This has the potential to transform local activity if international students enter in large numbers. Although US and Canadian doctoral universities subsidize many foreign students, the Westminster countries operate on a commercial basis, as do Singapore, Malaysia and China, and some programs in Europe. In the UK, Australia and New Zealand, international student tuition and enrollments are deregulated, though subject to visa policy. Many international graduates become skilled labor migrants. There is also a global doctoral 'market' associated with research competition and capacity-building, and driven by scholarship funding. About half of all mobile doctoral students attend US universities.

4. Region-building in Higher Education

Regionalization of capacity and people mobility, particularly in research, can build mutual global strength in small- or medium-sized higher education systems that lack the fire-power of the USA. It stimulates transformation of local activity and national systems, although there can be opportunity costs – an intense regional focus and interaction may retard other global connections. There are four conditions for success in regional organization: adequate national wealth and educational infrastructure; geographical proximity; some cultural commonality; and political will. Only Europe – currently pursuing the European Higher Education Area, and the European Research Area, via top-down intergovernment negotiations and the European Commission, and bottom-up in negotiations and exchange between institutions – fulfills all four conditions (Marginson and van der Wende, 2009b). There are extensive cross-border student flows and academic collaboration. There are more embryonic regional structures in South-east Asia and South America.

5. Institution-driven Strategies

Transnational education
Transnational education means the enrollment of students outside the home country of the institution (Verbik and Merkley, 2006; Ziguras and McBurnie, 2006). The institution, not the student, moves across borders, either via distance education or a branch campus in the student's home country, with the consent and often the assistance of the nation concerned – for example campuses of UK, Australian and US institutions in East and South-east Asia, Africa, India, Latin America and Western Europe. It takes two forms: (a) stand-alone campuses owned/rented and operated by the transnational institution; and (b) the more common but less transformative expedient, campuses managed by local partners. Offshore campuses are often joined to export market strategies, funneling students back to the export nation for later years. Some are designed to sustain a long-term presence, including research linkages. Like all institution-driven strategies, transnational education pushes beyond the nation-state. Mobile institutions are shaped by their own national rules, enter foreign jurisdictions, and are partly independent of both. Transnational education can change higher education in both nations. It may influence the system in the foreign nation by creating new norms; and when adapting curriculum and pedagogy for the local setting it develops a culturally plural approach that sometimes feeds back to the founding institution.

Partnerships and consortia
Cross-border partnerships engage all research universities and form a lattice of worldwide connections (Beerkens, 2004). The intensity of activity varies by institution and partnership. Although networks are not exclusive, they prioritize certain connections. Partnerships facilitate mutual learning and resource-sharing; benchmarking of administrative, service and promotional activities; staff exchange, student study abroad, joint

degrees and twinning programs across borders where students do part of the degree in each country. Some, such as the National University of Singapore, conduct many activities this way. In most countries short-term academic visits are growing (Enders and de Weert, 2004). Multi-agent networks or consortia are the extended family version of partnerships. The global framing of consortia is often consciously spatial, for example alliances with universities from all continents or reaching across a specific region such as the Pacific Rim.

Global e-universities
The delivery of programs via the Internet takes higher education straight from the local to the global dimension. There is an attractive if grandiose simplicity about the global e-university with its one-world classroom within a universe of virtual institutions paralleling the universe of face-to-face universities. Much was invested in e-university ventures, especially in the USA, in the late 1990s. These used low-cost business models and low-teaching intensity with curricula not varied for national or linguistic context. But they had little student take-up. E-degrees have limited appeal and are best for students working full-time or in remote locations. They lack status and the teaching and networking benefits of face-to-face delivery (OECD, 2005). Predictions that e-universities ('click') would supplant onsite universities ('brick') (Drucker, 2000) have failed. Online versions of place-based institutions and degrees are more attractive; for example the University of Phoenix, which uses a more teaching-intensive model tailored to specific markets in vocational education.

IMAGINING THE GLOBAL

The story of globalization in higher education is about how changing space and enhanced mobility transform vision, imagining and the self. There are four ways in which globalization fashions mentalities and is fashioned by those mentalities in return. The first is the forming and morphing of human subjects who act in the global dimension. The second way is the effects of space-time compression in the global imaginings of subjects. The third way is the imagined pictures of the world developed by global subjects in which their strategies are located. The fourth way (to be explored in Chapter 23 in Part III) is the self-positioning by global subjects within the global space of positions that they imagine and experience.

Global subjects position themselves at the same time in the two worlds that their experiences and imaginings – their outer and inner eyes – can see. Each eye is a prism for the other. Once positioned in landscapes they have made familiar to themselves, global subjects are freed for continuous action and re-imagination. They explore the visible potentials for exploiting or advancing their position, and envision new potentials. Yet when engaging globally, these subjects are always changing. They are continually altered in the environment. They deliberately form themselves. All people experience life as a double-reflexive process of external engagement and self-managed personal agency. What distinguishes global higher education is that this reflexivity is shaped by the antinomy of mobility and place, universality and identity.

GLOBAL SUBJECTS

Through these practices people, institutions and higher education systems become global subjects (part of the time), operating in the global dimension of higher education. But do they all perceive and practice the global dimension in common? What is a 'global subject'?

A study of the global dimension must consider the question 'from whose viewpoint?' The issue is basic but important. Global possibilities look different according to whether one is President of New York University, Minister for Education in Cambodia, a doctoral student from a teaching family in Sierra Leone, a software business in The Netherlands, or the World Bank higher education division. When analyzing global phenomena, most scholars and policy-makers skip over the issue of their own perspective. No doubt it is tactically smart to claim universality. Scholars want to align with the widest possible audience. Policy-makers like to speak broadly to the 'people'. But universality is always also a mask for something more specific, which determines what comes within the field of vision. What we see is limited to what we can see, what we need to see, and what we want to see.

Subject perspectives include those of individual persons (such as faculty, students); of institutions, professional organizations and companies; and of governments. We can also infer perspective in geospatial terms. Here the locality, the city, the region or the world as a whole also become subjects with a distinctive 'city' or 'global' perspective on higher education, although each person will have a different take on what this means. But only a few perspectives have a generic function in social discourse. These are of special interest.

In higher education two contrasting perspectives are dominant. They shape most of the literature and strategizing. These are the national system ('policy') perspective, and that of the institution, 'the university' (or 'university-as-corporation') perspective. Most research about higher education is directed as if fulfilling the objectives of either national government as understood by politicians or officials, or individual universities, mostly as understood by executive leaders. All see higher education as in tension between these two perspectives – as a binary, divided between the government national or 'public' interest and the interests of the institution. This binary frames the politics of higher education and drives much of the research and scholarship. Analysis is preoccupied by issues that lie on the fault line between the two perspectives, such as university autonomy and government funding.

In addition, two other perspectives are potentially foundational: the perspective of the individual in higher education, and the perspective of the world as a whole (the global public good). Figure 2.2 summarizes these possible perspectives on global higher education.

State versus University

It may seem odd to refer to a collective higher education system as a single 'subject'. But much imagining and action is framed by the policy perspective. What makes this possible is the centralized and hierarchical forms of national government, which create a point of discursive authority where the singular sovereign view is expressed; and also the characteristic reification of 'public' or 'people' or 'taxpayer' as a single interest defined

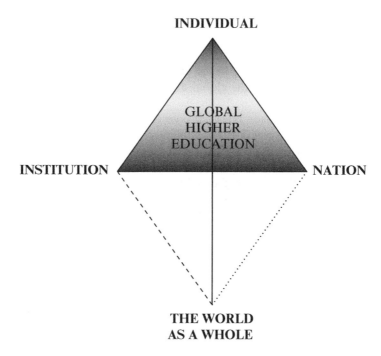

Source of concept: author.

Figure 2.2   Different subject perspectives on global higher education

by government. The normative logic of the national system or policy perspective is that what is good for the system as a whole is good for each of its component parts.

The complication for the national (system) perspective is that, despite this preten-sion, it does not cover everything. It struggles to control cross-border relations, which involve parties from outside the nation; and exerts less than full authority within the nation. The typical research university is partly decoupled or 'disembedded' (Beerkens, 2004) from the nation-state, via global activities such as research collaboration, partnership-building and foreign income-earning in teaching and research. Ironically these moves are encouraged by the new public management (NPM) policies of national governments, which model universities as firms and foster devolution of responsibility (Rose, 1999) and institutional entrepreneurship. The need of institutions to make a global splash in their own right is also rooted in the cross-border networks of knowl-edge that have long been essential to universities and integral to their status culture. This location in universal knowledge fashions for universities a measure of independ-ence (Marginson, 2010b). Universities are place-bound, as are states. But they are more mobile than states.

Like national system perspectives, institutional perspectives vary by location, being affected by nation, culture and local factors. Visions of the global mostly reflect white, masculine and Anglo-American and/or European perspectives (Luke, 2010, p. 45). Nevertheless some institutional perspectives embody postcolonial notions or the per-spectives of emerging East Asia systems, creating a more plural conversation.

The binary standoff in higher education is seen as inevitable and perhaps desirable. In the imaginings of higher education dominant in research, policy and the public mind, the university-as-firm is driven by competitive self-interest. This is seen to check the power of the state to overwhelm higher education. At the same time the national or system-level perspective provides an apparently objective basis for settling the competing claims of institutions. In the manner of all binaries, each half of the binary is necessary to and generates the other. And this binary, like all binaries, triggers a mental investment in synthetic unity that can never succeed. But in this endless ritual of war between two mighty forces, other perspectives that could contribute to a larger and richer whole are rendered invisible. Arguably the binary framing of global higher education, between national and institutional perspectives, blocks the larger possibilities of global creation.

THE GLOBAL PUBLIC GOOD

The perspective of the world as a whole is inherent in the universal forms of knowledge. This is the synthetic ecological perspective, that of the system of global systems. The planet is imagined as a single subject (Marginson, 2010c). This perspective lurks at the edge of much imagining of global higher education. In the form of interest or value, it is the global public good. Of course the notion of the global public good is open to many possible definitions, according to social values and cultural forms. Nevertheless the move from self-interest to the common and collective interest is always significant.

As indicated by the solid vertical line in Figure 2.2, individuals find it easier to make the leap of imagination from self-interest to the global public good than do institutions or nations. As indicated by the dashed line in Figure 2.2, institutions do this more readily than do nations, for example in collaborative research on common human problems. Governments can achieve the perspective of the global good in the face of shared issues of overwhelming importance such as climate change (part of the time). Europeanization in higher education represents a more sustained expression of common interest. Yet it draws part of its identity from a sense of Europe as the citadel of civilization walled against the outside world (File et al., 2005), including competition from the USA and East Asia and potential migration from Africa. This strengthens the sense of the common good within Europe by fracturing the global good, falling short of the ecological perspective.

There is more than one kind of individual perspective on the global. The most significant are those of student and scholar–researcher. (There are also many external stakeholders; university executives adopt the institutional perspective.) The perspective of the scholar–researcher shapes the behavior of both disciplinary communities and persons. It might seem surprising that the global scholar perspective does not play a more explicit part in literature on higher education. This perspective often enters theorizations but is less visible in empirical research, reflecting the domination of research funding by governments or institutions. The student perspective also falls short of its potential. It enters the separated decisions of millions about global mobility. But single students cannot contribute to holistic global relations – in contrast to nations, to very strong institutions, leading researchers and companies with interest in cross-border matters. It is only when collective student action spills across borders in a wave of global imitation, as in the 1960s, that the student perspective acquires a shaping influence. The global 'anti-globalization' protests against negotiations on trade deregulation are a reminder of this possibility (Drache, 2008).

SPACE-TIME COMPRESSION

It is often remarked that globalization facilitates time-space compression. When air travel replaces other transport it takes less time to cross the same geographical terrain. Although time as duration is not altered, distance seems to shrink. In electronic communication distance seems to disappear altogether. We are proximate with everyone in the network.

Time-space compression effects can be summed up in two words: 'de-severing' and 'synchrony' (Marginson, 2010a). 'De-severing' is the mental process whereby people bring remote locations close to them and eliminate physical distance in their minds (Heidegger, 1962, p. 139). Space and closeness are not simple functions of physical distance or the speed of messaging. De-severing is a state of mind. In *Being and Time*, Martin Heidegger (1962) noted that the logic of de-severing extends progressively outwards across the world. No place is now beyond our imagined proximity. There are places we may not wish to go. But all are within reach. We can imagine being there. We have reached the ends of the earth. Global engagement used to be episodic while local engagement was continuous. Many now find themselves constantly immersed in global community and universal knowledge, which is directly accessible. We oscillate freely between local and global. The global takes a growing part of our time. The early Soviet Russian psychologist Lev Vygotsky (1960) remarked that behavior is mediated by tools that facilitate thought. The Internet, whose essence is de-severing, is the principal tool with which we imagine global higher education. All this enhances the mobility side of the place/mobility antinomy.

Nevertheless, de-severing via the Internet has its limits. All is not one. Location-based identity continues. Distinctive, separated institutions remain. We can imagine the abolition of distance by seeing in our minds the end of the journey. Space is highly plastic to our perceptions of it. But our bodies move in space – and, in its materiality, space remains irreducibly 'there'. In movement through real space, time cannot be compressed to zero. We move with greater facility in the virtual universe than in the real one. But higher education is located in the real universe as well as in the virtual universe. Crucially the operations of institutions remain dependent on real people in real places. When university presidents discuss the ways they learn about what is happening in higher education, they acknowledge the utility of media and the Internet but they tend to place the greatest emphasis on the value derived from face-to-face meetings with each other (Marginson, 2011). Real-life meetings have an organic potency that de-severed communications lack. Fortunately the university retains a footing in both parts of the antinomy that founded it – fortunately and inevitably, because if it did not sustain its founding antinomy it would disappear.

'Synchrony' (or synchronism), the partner of de-severing, is concurrence at the same point in time. Global synchrony is the sharing of a common rhythm. Like de-severing, global synchrony is also a feeling. It is driven by the desire for sociability, for a sustainable connection with others across distances of space, nation and culture. A feature of both Internet-mediated talk and real-time academic association across borders is the affective power of those experiences. People want to connect, want to engage with difference on the basis of shared practices, whether they are scholar–researchers, doctoral students from a range of countries, or university executives out to make waves in the global setting. Global synchrony, especially in the form of electronically mediated communication, enables them to associate with each other in the low-risk form of multiple, loose and disposable ties.

At first we have to work at synchrony, but it becomes more familiar. People become adept in numerous partial encounters and many simultaneous options. Some synchrony takes the form of one-way adjustment: one person or one institution follows another. Other synchrony is the mutual evolution of a shared practice. To achieve this global synchrony is emotionally satisfying, like landing a fish in the fast-rushing mountain stream. Yet to secure synchrony does not presuppose emotional obligations. Unlike organic local relationships, global synchrony may work best without strong reciprocal emotions. The hallmarks of the universal communicator are openness, fluency, certainty of judgment and a capacity for disinterested friendship. Fast, loose and disposable ties based on apparent transparency – temporary synchrony with few obligations and no hidden dangers – are also ideal for business. The absence of ongoing obligations leaves options open. At the same time the satisfactions of synchrony should not be underestimated. There is power in the 'moral sentiments' (Smith, 1759) of encounters not just with fellows but with difference: pungency in the moment when difference turns into empathy, the world in its mysterious otherness becomes appropriated to the self, and the subject is like an Atlas standing astride the globe. Here the old conceit of imperial conquerors and oceanic explorers becomes a common and harmless property. How else can we explain the fact that without evidence all policy-makers believe that 'internationalizing' universities will generate a continuing flow of benefits?

The practice of synchrony has always been part of networked higher education. The point is that global communications and travel have greatly facilitated global de-severing and synchrony, rendered them more attractive, and expanded their strategic potentials. Meanwhile, in research and scholarly work, the effects of space-time compression have been akin to those of a supernova. Creative people readily adapt to electronically mediated synchrony with its flat low-risk relations and ease and speed of access, distribution and exit. We do not know how much open source knowledge flows have grown, but data on Internet usage (Webometrics, 2010; Internet World Statistics, 2010) suggest that they have expanded faster than commercial intellectual property, and much faster than either formal academic publishing or the size of the gross domestic product (GDP) economy and the global trade in goods.

The Importance of Place

David Harvey notes that in a global relational space, the role of place is reconfirmed:

> the more unified the space, the more important the qualities of the fragmentations become for social identity and action . . . The shrinkage of space that brings diverse communities across the

globe into competition with each other implies localized competitive strategies and a height-ened sense of awareness of what makes a place special and gives it competitive advantage. This kind of reaction looks much more strongly to the identification of place, the building and sig-naling of its unique qualities in an increasingly homogeneous but fragmented world. (Harvey, 1990, p. 271)

The global setting calls for a self both coherent and flexible – one that moves fluently in and out of places while grasping the total space in holistic fashion, while sustaining a sense of self. Mobility is now part of the normal conditions of higher education, not just for a few wandering scholars but for many persons. In a fast-changing world coherence is no longer naturalized by location or history and must come from within. That is true of institutions as well as of people (though less true of nations). Paradoxically, global open-ness and malleable identity confirm the function of place in defining the self – whether place is understood in terms of geographical location, group membership, cultural or institutional belonging, or social status and role. Subjects need a foundation from which to move and to which they return. Yet in the volatile global setting that foundation also shifts and changes.

MULTIPLE IMAGINING

Global subjects operate from more than one vantage point and are fixed and moving at the same time. The required attributes are those that facilitate not only mobility but also multiple imagining. For example, executive leaders in higher education see the relational space from two vantage points (two geo-perspectives) simultaneously, using double screening. They must grasp their immediate position from a point within local space. At the same time they position themselves above the relational space so as to see the whole. This perspective from above facilitates the synthetic imagining of the global and its space of positions. The switch between geo-perspectives also changes what can be seen. The close-up vantage, in which height relative to the observer is obvious, generates a hier-archical imagining of global relations. Strong universities, and national systems, tower over the others nearby. From the other vantage, above the global setting, the potential of flat networking is more apparent. This broadens the imagined scope for agency freedom and strategy-making.

Self-making

Synchronous global communications change people. Long-term travel for education is more transforming. We have seen how the individual and the institution observe the global setting from both within and above, and face the global setting as both local and national; and there can be tensions between these positions. In fact global subjects often identify with one primary place but move between several locations that vary in culture and language, values and politeness regimes. To meet these challenges requires more than flexibility. It requires the capacity to imagine plural selves and to remake oneself at choice and need.

International students are a good example of the self-changing self. There is much research on what happens to them during their sojourn. The primary conditions for self-managing the changes are the strength of agency, the capacity to communicate in the host-country language, and intercultural relationships (see, e.g., Church, 1982; Pedersen, 1991; Kashima and Loh, 2006; Yang et al., 2006; Montgomery, 2010; Marginson et al., 2010).

Mobile subjects use two strategies of self-formation in the global setting. The first can be called 'multiplicity'. Amartya Sen (1999, p. 120) remarks that 'we all have multiple identities, and . . . each of these identities can yield concerns and demands that can significantly supplement, or seriously compete with, other concerns and demands arising from other identities'. These complexities are especially apparent for those who cross borders. They continue to relate to the original home by electronic means or travel and return. They find themselves living more than one life. The bi-cultural self has been long identified in psychology (e.g. Berry, 1974, 1984; Pedersen, 1991). The fault line between sites (and selves) is often based on language of use. Languages are associated not only with varied social codes but differences in imaginings and possibilities for strategy.

Multiplicity in global relations in higher education plays out not just in the passage of students and scholar–researchers working offshore, but in transnational education where multiple and heterogeneous institutional sites, regulatory settings, groups of stakeholders and expectations about teaching and learning are built into institutional design.

The second strategy of self-formation can be called 'hybridity'. Here the globally active person synthesizes different cultural and relational elements into a new hybrid persona (Rizvi, 2005). This notion of synthesis or integration of different elements in the self-formation of identity, which, like multiplicity, is associated with a heightened reflexivity and sense of cultural relativism, often recurs in studies of intercultural relations. Rizvi cautions nevertheless that while hybridity is 'a useful antidote to cultural essentialism', it alone does not explain cultural relations (Rizvi, 2005, p. 338). Nor is it as neat as it sounds. Anderson suggests that for international students, identity exhibits 'ongoing movement, complexity and tension rather than endpoints and neat resolutions' (Anderson, 2006, p. 11).

When hybridity develops, often some multiplicity is maintained. Conversely a cross-border person with multiple cultural roles carries common elements from role to role: some integration takes place. Without any hybridity, multiple identities may be experienced as fragmentation and/or contradiction. Hybridity is associated with integrating, suturing, combining and recombining. Multiplicity is associated with dividing or differentiating. Both strategies are additive in different ways. Global subjects move between the two strategies. Does this make them conflicted and fraught? Not necessarily. Like all human beings, global subjects sustain identity through acts of will that hold together differing elements so that they can plot a coherent pathway. It all requires a robust sense of self and of the global project.

Flexible identity is not confined to individuals. In regional European higher education there are three different forms of identity at play. There are stand-alone national outlooks; there are systems and institutions operating within the European container as a multiplicity of separate nations; there are also the ways in which national practices have begun to combine, converge and synthesize in new degree structures, curriculum descriptors and research.

WORLD IMAGINARIES

Any individual, any institution and any system can secure a global presence providing the minimum condition is met: access to the means of cross-border communication. The capacity for global action is uneven. It is partly a matter of wealth, given the cost of communication, publications, travel and research. It is partly a matter of language, for it is a disadvantage not to be fluent in global English. It is partly determined by the stability of nation-states, for example in long-term research programs. Even so, prior inequalities do not close off all possibilities. The world imaginaries of global subjects also come into play. Creative understandings of the global setting that provide superior insight into objective conditions enable new global strategies.

Research literature and interviews with university presidents (Marginson, 2011) suggest that in higher education there are three primary world imaginaries. It is a momentous decision to invest in one or more of these world imaginaries, affecting not only position-making strategies but also identity and mission.

The first world imaginary is global higher education as a global economic market, whether in terms of the WTO–GATS vision or the universe of virtual higher education e-universities. The second imaginary is a global higher education sector patterned by comparisons and performance-based rankings, the imagining triggered by the first Shanghai Jiao Tong University rankings in 2003. The third world imaginary is that of a networked university world, patterned by linkages, partnerships, consortia and hubs.

We tend to interpret new phenomena in terms of the constructs of the past. None of these world imaginaries is entirely new. Each is grounded in a set of archetypal ideas about higher education, the economy and society. At bottom the three imaginaries rest on notions of the market economy, status competition and universal knowledge. They each have varied implications for power and social values. The first imaginary is global capitalism. The second imaginary is a largely vertical world that reflects and reproduces status and hierarchy in universities and in society. The third imaginary conjures up more open and horizontal relationships based in networks and flows. Each imaginary is associated with metaphors and myths about the human condition with mainstream plausibility. Each is linked to distinctive ideas in the social sciences. Each has its advocates. Each seems to explain certain practices in higher education. Each has a hold on the collective imagination.

Figure 2.3 sums up the contrasting world imaginaries, used and expressed in varying ways. Some global subjects imagine global higher education in terms of just one world imaginary, even a single bounded intellectual discipline – especially economics. The market vision inspires more single-minded devotion than ideas about status or knowledge. Others assemble a farrago of fragments with wider reach. Many global subjects, probably the majority, use hybrid pictures drawing on two or three of these imaginaries.

The Economic Imaginary

The idea of the world market dates from nineteenth-century economics but is strengthened by the partial global integration of finance and trade, and by neoliberal ideology in economic policy. In this imaginary higher education becomes a system for producing and distributing economic values and for augmenting economic values in other sectors. (The

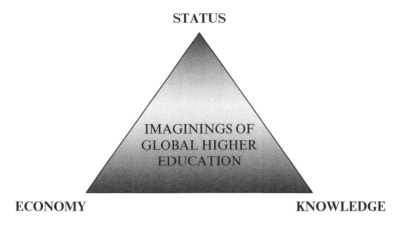

STATUS

IMAGININGS OF
GLOBAL HIGHER
EDUCATION

ECONOMY   KNOWLEDGE

Source of concept: author.

Figure 2.3   World imaginaries of higher education

relation between higher education as a revenue-creating economic actor and as hand-maiden of capital elsewhere is never made clear.) Some neoclassical economists remodel all erstwhile non-economic phenomena in economic terms (e.g. Becker, 1976). The core myth of the economics of education is the idea of students as investors in themselves, as human capital, thereby creating future private economic benefits subject to scarcity. This theorization has antecedents in Adam Smith (1776) and Alfred Marshall (1890), but was systematized in the 1960s (Becker, 1964; Blaug, 1970). It focuses on the individualized commodity value of education credentials rather than the formative contents of knowledge or the common benefits of a learned community. The notion is readily transferred to cross-border students, seen as investors in global mobility, but is unable to explain flat global networking and affective desires for synchrony, and falters in relation to research.

There is more than one possible economic imaginary. The critique of 'academic capitalism' (Slaughter and Rhoades, 2004) rests not on neoclassical economics but on critical political economy and goals about human emancipation and social justice (Pusser and Marginson, 2011). Martin Carnoy (1974) models the global education space in terms of economic imperialism and resistance. Some scholars emphasize the contribution of higher education to individual and collective human capability (Sen, 2000), or in advancing democratic social relations and critical social thought (Pusser, 2006). Others discuss higher education as a common public good and condition of other public good(s) (Marginson, 2007). Notions of 'publicness' connect to the universal aspects of mission and the economic nature of knowledge as a public good (see below), and affect institutions and some nation-states (Singh, 2001). Notions of capability and public goods are readily transferred to the global dimension. But these ideas are not dominant. Mainstream thought about higher education is led by neoliberalism, which emphasizes the market economy.

Neoliberalism is a political program couched in neoclassical economic language (Rizvi and Lingard, 2010). The program in education, first developed by Milton Friedman (1962), is a blueprint for remaking higher education systems as quasi-markets;

institutions as firms motored by scarcity, profit and competition; academic faculty as entrepreneurs or wage laborers; and students as full-cost consumers of educational services. Neoliberalism incorporates the anti-statism of classical liberalism but never seriously pursues this in national higher education systems. Nation-state controls are modernized, not withdrawn. 'There is greater functionality between the state and the market with the state establishing conditions for the quasi-market but also actively mobilizing market mechanisms to attain political goals' (Naidoo, 2010, p. 70). *Bona fide* deregulation takes place only in some global operations, where nations cannot fully regulate their own institutions offshore.

Neoliberalism underpins the new public management (NPM) reform programs. Here research-intensive universities never fit the template and are ongoing targets for reforms designed to remake them in the form of the market economy. In this framework knowledge generated in research is seen primarily as a source of new saleable commodities, while curiosity-driven research with no direct relation to the market economy is seen as wasteful. Neoliberal and NPM approaches have now spread through most of the higher education world.

In the 1990s the neoliberal reading of globalization in higher education was especially dominant, forming the outlooks of governments, many university leaders and many critics of the commodity approach. Both neoliberals and their opponents saw global convergence and integration as world markets at work; and the critics also explained globalization as another round of Anglo-American imperialism. This had some truth. The normative models of higher education institutions in neoliberal policy were (and are) based on US ideas of higher education as a market. Neoliberal reforms were pursued aggressively by US-dominated global institutions such as the World Bank. But the 1990s focus on the market aspects of globalization was too one-sided, missing the cultural transformations engendered by de-severing and synchrony, the new strategic potentials for all nations and institutions, and the continued salience of nation-states.

The imagining of global higher education as a world market is no longer hegemonic in research, though influential (e.g. Shin and Harman, 2009). On the other hand the imagining of a world university market is supported by, and supports, the growing role of rankings – although competition in higher education is more than an economic competition for resources and market share, as is now discussed.

Global Competition in Status

Although the vision of global higher education in terms of comparisons and rankings has been legitimated by neoliberalism, its foundations lie in older notions of social status. Here the modernist notion of meritocratic competition combines with the pre-modern university hierarchy.

Status is ubiquitous in higher education. First, there is higher education's role in producing and allocating social position. In the sociology of status, higher education is described as a 'positional good' (Hirsch, 1976; Marginson, 2006) or 'status good' (Frank and Cook, 1995). Second, there is the role of symbols of status in hierarchical academic affairs with their medieval forms of public display and their mostly male-god professors. Third, status positions universities in relation to each other. Here status is specified directly by rankings – where old leading universities still hold their places in all collections.

Few in higher education are untouched by the power of status to secure assent, define identity and compel action. Institutions display status conspicuously and continually, in the ancient form of gothic buildings, the modern form of science facilities and research outputs, and the corporate form of websites and global partnerships (Marginson, 2010b). Here the social joust for position or esteem is distinct from economic competition for capital. Success in one creates conditions for advance in the other. But in research universities the desire for status mostly outweighs the desire for resources, a necessary but not sufficient condition for the real objective – the timeless prestige and power of the university as an end in itself.

A positional education market incorporates competition not only between producers but between consumers. Universities compete for preferred customers, students with high entry scores. Student customers compete for entry to the preferred institutions. Prestige sustains high student scores, competition drives them higher, and scarcity reproduces the prestige of the elite universities in the kind of circular effect that sustains hierarchy. The social power of families often correlates to the academic standing of their student children; positional markets are a matching game in which the hierarchy of students/families is synchronized with the hierarchy of universities. Research plays a key role in defining the hierarchy of institutions, reproducing the status of elite university degrees, and maintaining the necessary revenue flows. Top research universities attract bright students and wealthy families. The prestige accumulated by student-magnet institutions is cashed in as tuition income – and leveraged to raise public and private monies to buy high-cost staff and research. Research performance is visible and measurable in ways generally understood, such as publications, citations, research-related revenues, number of doctoral students and so on; and research outcomes play the leading role in national and global systems of status ranking.

All of this transfers readily to the global level. Status power in universities is arbitrary, held in place by history, architecture and display. It is aristocratic in temper, as Bourdieu (1988, 1993) remarks. Like the marriages of European nobility in the nation-building era, it cuts across territorial boundaries and quickly makes global claims.

Universally circulating knowledge, and the status hierarchy in each nation, has always made parallel institutions abroad – like parallel royal families in Europe – appropriate comparators and partners. Now de-severing brings global competitors for status almost as close as in a national system. Universities and systems use networks as media for referred status, drawing advantage from the strongest members. They focus on attracting high-quality global staff and doctoral students: human capital that accumulates status 'capital'.

Here there are also differences between global status competition and national status competition. Global status is not as zero-sum as national status. The global university hierarchy is more open to upward mobility. But status remains the main measure of success. Although rankings are static, less dynamic than the global environment that they purport to describe, they draw local universities into the universal setting in a brilliant visual sweep. This was why global rankings were taken up so quickly – although they have become more deeply entrenched in nations where university hierarchy and/or competition are systematized and overt. There is always a hierarchy, whether formal or informal, but it is steeper in some systems than in others.

Networks and Open Source Knowledge

In social science the idea of networks pre-dates globalization; but today's network-based imaginary of 'flat' non-hierarchical relationships amid inequality is partly the product of communicative globalization and its theorists, such as Manuel Castells (2000) and Bruno Latour (2005). It is also sustained by open source knowledge practices in science, where in some disciplines networked cross-border groups are the dominant mode. The network imaginary reflects an epistemological logic of collaboration and an economic logic of economies of scale – for example, multilateral financing of large-scale facilities like particle accelerators. It is also sustained by changing practices. In most nations there has been a marked increase in cross-border research collaboration in the last two decades. In 2008 two-thirds of citations were international (NSB, 2010, p. 5.40) and in many nations a third or more of papers were internationally co-authored.

Imaginings based on networked relations and open knowledge flows are more readily embraced by institutions and individual scholar–researchers than by nation-states. In contrast with the economic market and the status imaginary, the world of networks is primarily collaborative rather than competitive. It can be annexed to competitive strategies. Networks are used to build status and are configured vertically as well as horizontally: 'networking up'. (Research universities are like sibling rivals, collaborating and competing with the same other institutions.) Nevertheless networks are intrinsically horizontal. Likewise, open source knowledge is not knowledge in the form of scarce parcels of status-producing research, or intellectual property (IP) bought and sold. It is freely available. Its benefits cannot be finally confined to one agent (Marginson, 2009). The benefits of knowledge can be annexed to private purposes but more than one party can do so. 'An idea is a thing of remarkable expansiveness, being capable of spreading rapidly from mind to mind without lessening its meaning and significance for those into whose possession it comes' (David, 2003, p. 3).

Paul Samuelson (1954) describes non-rivalrous and non-excludable products as 'public goods', noting that these are subject to market failure. It does not pay commercial firms to produce ideas with a natural price of zero that can be freely accessed by those who did not pay for their production (Stiglitz, 1999). Knowledge is a private good only at the moment of discovery, before it is broadly disseminated. This provides the single point of purchase for an IP regime based on knowledge, as distinct from knowledge-intensive artifacts. Once knowledge is disclosed it cannot be monopolized. If research were produced on a market basis, as neoliberalism suggests, it would be drastically undersupplied. Much of the research with practical ends in view nevertheless generates unforeseeable potentials.

Hence we find the 'public, collective character' and 'commitment to the ethos of cooperative inquiry and the free sharing of knowledge' in science (David, 2003, p. 3). 'Industry gets most of its benefits from academic science through open channels' (Nelson, 2004, p. 460). Open source knowledge is furthered by de-severing and synchronous networking. In this context IP holdings that block global flows of science tend to retard their contribution to innovation (OECD, 2008a). But open source knowledge also provides material for IP-based product innovations (David, 2003, pp. 4–6), persuading governments to fund basic science.

Hybrid Imaginings

The same knowledge is capable of many permutations and utilities. Here again is the potential for hybridity that explains the ubiquity of the university. But weightless hyper-abundant knowledge is scarcely compatible with any economy based on scarcity and bounded control. Appadurai (1996) suggests that the global mobility of cultural artifacts and ideas is less linear and more disjunctive than flows of economic capital. Tensions between IP and open science (Bok, 2003) vary by industry. There is more potential for commercial science in bioscience than elsewhere. Still, even biotechnology and pharma-ceutics can be annexed for the public good, for example in poorer nations where commer-cial products are out of reach. The market is not the only possible partner for bioscientific knowledge.

Likewise open source knowledge is both compatible and incompatible with status competition. Knowledge can play either role. Flat relations mediated by the sharing of knowledge have an ongoing potential to subvert status competition and hierarchy. Where cultural content becomes king and the imagination flows freely, content has an ability (alarming for some) to cut across everything else. Yet the knowledge disseminated in universities also dovetails with the world of status.

The hierarchy of universities decides which parcels of knowledge carry the most authority and value. Articles from Harvard are more likely to be cited because they are from Harvard. Research rankings and publication and citation measures express the status/knowledge relationship with precision (Marginson, 2009). If the university rests on both universal knowledge and place-based identity, relational status is part of defin-ing identity. Arguably knowledge achieves a better fit with the status hierarchy than with the economic market.

The knowledge system works like the classical gift economy (Kenway et al., 2006). Marcel Mauss (1954) notes how in the Pacific and North-west America a non-capitalist exchange of gifts reproduced individual and group/institutional/place-based status. Likewise in the modern university, freely distributed knowledge confers status ben-efits on its producers, while institutions disseminate teaching and research to magnify their status. Like all mass media, the Internet is a formidable engine in building status. Massachusetts Institute of Technology (MIT) placed its courseware online knowing the private positional value of an MIT degree would be enhanced, not diminished. In 2008 Harvard Faculty of Arts and Science placed its articles in the public domain – endorsing open source knowledge while also strengthening itself.

As this interplay of market economy, status competition and free knowledge suggests, real-life higher education cannot be confined to one way of seeing. It is populated by subjects with hybrid practices, motivated by economic interest, desire for status and the sharing of knowledge goods. Any attempt to impose a single master principle drawn from one world imaginary can 'succeed' only by eliminating everything else from view.

Some scholars of higher education produce hybrid theorizations. Bourdieu (1984, 1988, 1993) combines the logics of status competition and economic power. He models the university market as divided between two poles with different principles of institu-tional differentiation. At one pole, autonomous research universities engage in status competition. At the other, heteronomous mass institutions are driven by govern-ments or commercial markets. Bourdieu identifies interchangeable 'capitals', economic, social, cultural, symbolic, academic, scientific and so on in the exercise of power. The Bourdieuian schema is used to explain positional competition in national systems (Naidoo, 2004) and has salience at the global level (Marginson, 2008). When it comes to relationships of power, multidisciplinary reasoning works better than single disciplinary reasoning. Explanations of power, like systems of governance, management and regulation, invoke a range of phenomena including authority, ideology, instrumental power and agenda-setting (Ordorika, 2003); resource dependence and distribution (Slaughter and Leslie, 1997); hierarchy and inequality; center/periphery relations (Wallerstein, 1996); inclusion/exclusion; and domination/subordination. All are at play and a range of knowledges is needed to capture them.

Note, however, that the emphases within hybrid imaginings can shift. In the 1990s world-pictures held by executive university leaders, economic imaginings were often dominant. In the 2000s there was growing recognition of communicative globalization and research comparisons, terms of competition more specific to higher education. Many leaders also express a strong sense of hierarchies and inequalities in resources, research power and status (Marginson and Sawir, 2006; Marginson, 2011). No doubt university rankings reinforce these elements.

Neoliberal policies also use hybrid forms to strengthen their purchase. Quasi-markets in higher education combine the market economy and status competition. Commercial international education combines market revenues with the fostering of skilled migration and foreign relations, positioning institutions as both entrepreneurs and public policy actors (Unterhalter and Carpentier, 2010, p. 24). In research, NPM organization rests on the commodification of open source knowledge – so both elements are necessary to it.

From Imagining to Strategy

These then are primary elements that feed into the imaginings of global subjects in higher education. In the open global domain, with its wide range of potential visions and actions, global subjects create new possibilities and also new limits for themselves and others. Chapter 23 in Part III discusses how global imaginings become manifest in position-taking and position-making strategies, and the implications for global ordering and regulation.

REFERENCES

Anderson, V. (2006), 'Who's not integrating? International women speak about New Zealand students', paper presented at the 'ISANA International Education Conference, Educate, Advocate, Empower', University of New South Wales, Sydney, 5–8 December.
Appadurai, A. (1996), *Modernity at Large: Cultural Dimensions of Globalization*, Minneapolis, MN: University of Minnesota Press.
Bashir, S. (2007), 'Trends in international trade in higher education: implications and options for developing countries', Education Working Paper Series, No. 6, Washington, DC: World Bank.
Becker, G. (1964), *Human Capital: A Theoretical and Empirical Analysis, with Special Reference to Education*, New York: Columbia University Press.
Becker, G. (1976), *The Economic Approach to Human Behavior*, Chicago, IL: University of Chicago Press.
Beerkens, H. (2004), *Global Opportunities and Institutional Embeddedness: Higher Education Consortia in Europe and Southeast Asia*, doctoral thesis, Center for Higher Education Policy Studies, University of Twente, http://www.utwente.nl/cheps/documenten/thesisbeerkens.pdf, accessed 10 February 2006.

Berry, J. (1974), 'Psychological aspects of cultural pluralism', in R. Brislin (ed.), *Topics in Cultural Learning, Volume 2*, Honolulu, HI: Hawaii University, East–West Center, pp. 17–22.

Berry, J. (1984), 'Cultural relations in plural societies', in N. Miller and M. Brewer (eds), *Groups in Contact*, San Diego, CA: Academic Press, pp. 11–27.

Blaug, M. (1970), *An Introduction to the Economics of Education*, Harmondsworth, UK: Penguin.

Bok, D. (2003), *Universities in the Market-Place: The Commercialization of Higher Education*, Princeton, NJ: Princeton University Press.

Bourdieu, P. (1984), *Distinction: A Social Critique of the Judgment of Taste*, trans. R. Nice, London: Routledge and Kegan Paul.

Bourdieu, P. (1988), *Homo Academicus*, trans. P. Collier, Cambridge: Polity.

Bourdieu, P. (1993), *The Field of Cultural Production*, ed. R. Johnson, New York: Columbia University Press.

Braudel, F. (1985), *The Perspective of the World. Volume 3 of Civilization and Capitalism, 15th–18th Century*, trans. S. Reynolds, London: Fontana Press.

Carnoy, M. (1974), *Education and Cultural Imperialism*, London: Longman.

Castells, M. (2000), *The Rise of the Network Society, 2nd edn, Volume 1 of The Information Age: Economy, Society and Culture*, Oxford: Blackwell.

Centre for Science and Technology Studies Leiden University, CWTS (2010), *The Leiden Ranking*, http://www.cwts.nl/ranking/LeidenRankingWebSite.html, accessed 3 May 2010.

Church, A. (1982), 'Sojourner adjustment', *Psychological Bulletin*, **91** (3), 540–72.

David, P. (2003), 'The economic logic of "open science" and the balance between private property rights and the public domain in scientific data and information: a primer', revised version of paper presented to the National Research Council 'Symposium on The Role of the Public Domain in Scientific and Technical Data and Information', National Academy of Science, Washington, DC, 5–6 September 2002.

Drache, D. (2008), *Defiant Publics: The Unprecedented Reach of the Global Citizen*, Cambridge: Polity.

Drucker, P. (2000), 'Webucation', *Forbes*, 15 May.

Enders, J. and E. de Weert (eds) (2004), *The International Attractiveness of the Academic Workplace in Europe*, Frankfurt: Gewerkschaft Erziehung und Wissenschaft.

File, J., J. Huisman and D. Westerheijden (eds) (2005), *The European Higher Education and Research Landscape 2020: Scenarios and Strategic Debates*, Enschede: Centre for Higher Education Policy Studies, University of Twente.

Frank, R. and P. Cook (1995), *The Winner-Take-All Society: How More and More Americans Compete for Ever Fewer and Bigger Prizes, Encouraging Economic Waste, Income Inequality, and an Impoverished Cultural Life*, New York: The Free Press.

Friedman, M. (1962), *Capitalism and Freedom*, Chicago, IL: University of Chicago Press.

Harvey, D. (1990), *The Condition of Post-Modernity*, Cambridge, MA: Blackwell.

Hazelkorn, E. (2008), 'Learning to live with league tables and ranking: the experience of institutional leaders', *Higher Education Policy*, **21**, 193–215.

Heidegger, M. (1962), *Being and Time*, trans. J. Macquarie and E. Robinson, New York: Harper and Row.

Held, D., A. McLew, D. Goldblatt and J. Perraton (1999), *Global Transformations: Politics, Economics and Culture*, Stanford, CA: Stanford University Press.

Higher Education Evaluation and Assessment Council of Taiwan, HEEACT (2010), *Performance Ranking of Scientific Papers for World Universities*, http://ranking.heeact.edu.tw/, accessed 27 August 2010.

Hirsch, F. (1976), *Social Limits to Growth*, Cambridge, MA: Harvard University Press.

Internet World Stats (2010), *Internet and Population Statistics*, http://www.Internetworldstats.com/, accessed 27 August 2010.

Kashima, E. and E. Loh (2006), 'International students' acculturation: effects of international, conational, and local ties and need for closure', *International Journal of Intercultural Relations*, **30** (4), 471–85.

Kenway, J., E. Bulleen, J. Fahey with S. Robb (2006), *Haunting the Knowledge Economy*, London: Routledge.

King, R. (2009), *Governing Universities Globally: Organizations, Regulation and Ranking*, Cheltenham, UK and Northampton, MA, USA: Edward Elgar.

Kong, L., C. Gibson, L. Khoo and A. Semple (2006), 'Knowledges of the creative economy: towards a relational geography of diffusion and adaptation in Asia', *Asia Pacific Viewpoint*, **47** (2), 173–94.

Latour, B. (2005), *Reassembling the Social: An Introduction to Actor-network Theory*, Oxford: Oxford University Press.

Li, Y., J. Whalley, S. Zhang and X. Zhao (2008), 'The higher educational transformation of China and its global implications', NBER Working Paper No. 13849, Cambridge, MA: National Bureau of Economic Research.

Luke, A. (2010), 'Educating the other: standpoint and theory in the "internationalization" of higher education', in E. Unterhalter and V. Carpentier (eds), *Global Inequalities and Higher Education: Whose Interests are we Serving?*, London: Palgrave Macmillan, pp. 43–65.

Marginson, S. (2006), 'Dynamics of national and global competition in higher education', *Higher Education*, **52**, 1–39.

Marginson, S. (2007), 'The new higher education landscape: public and private goods in global/national/local settings', in S. Marginson (ed.), *Prospects of Higher Education: Globalization, Market Competition, Public Goods and the Future of the University,* Rotterdam: Sense Publishers, pp. 29–77.

Marginson, S. (2008), 'Global field and global imagining: Bourdieu and relations of power in worldwide higher education', *British Journal of Educational Sociology*, **29** (3), 303–16.

Marginson, S. (2009), 'University rankings and the knowledge economy', in M. Peters, S. Marginson and P. Murphy (eds), *Creativity and the Global Knowledge Economy*, New York: Peter Lang, pp. 185–216.

Marginson, S. (2010a), 'Space, mobility and synchrony in the knowledge economy', in S. Marginson, P. Murphy and M. Peters (eds), *Global Creation: Space, Mobility and Synchrony in the Age of the Knowledge Economy*, New York: Peter Lang, pp. 117–49.

Marginson, S. (2010b), 'Making space in higher education', in S. Marginson, P. Murphy and M. Peters (eds), *Global Creation: Space, Mobility and Synchrony in the Age of the Knowledge Economy*, New York: Peter Lang, pp. 150–200.

Marginson, S. (2010c), 'World', in P. Murphy, M. Peters and S. Marginson (eds), *Imagination: Three Models of Imagination in the Age of the Knowledge Economy*, New York: Peter Lang, pp. 139–65.

Marginson, S. (2010d), 'Nation', in P. Murphy, M. Peters and S. Marginson (eds), *Imagination: Three Models of Imagination in the Age of the Knowledge Economy*, New York: Peter Lang, pp. 225–325.

Marginson, S. (2011), 'Global perspectives and strategies of Asia-Pacific universities', in N. Liu, Q. Wang and J. Salmi (eds), *Paths to a World-Class University*, Rotterdam: Sense Publishers, pp. 3–27.

Marginson, S. and G. Rhoades (2002), 'Beyond national states, markets, and systems of higher education: a glonacal agency heuristic', *Higher Education*, **43** (3), 281–309.

Marginson, S. and E. Sawir (2006), 'University leaders' strategies in the global environment: a comparative study of Universitas Indonesia and the Australian National University', *Higher Education*, **52**, 343–73.

Marginson, S. and M. van der Wende (2009a), 'The new global landscape of nations and institutions', in OECD, Centre for Educational Research and Innovation, *Higher Education to 2030, Volume 2: Globalization*, Paris: OECD, pp. 17–62.

Marginson, S. and M. van der Wende (2009b), 'Europeanisation, university rankings and faculty mobility: three cases in higher education globalisation', in OECD, Centre for Educational Research and Innovation, *Higher Education to 2030, Volume 2 Globalization*, Paris: OECD, pp. 109–72.

Marginson, S., C. Nyland, E. Sawir and H. Forbes-Mewett (2010), *International Student Security*, Cambridge: Cambridge University Press.

Marshall, A. (1890), *Principles of Economics*, London: Macmillan.

Mauss, M. (1954), *The Gift,* trans. W. Halls, London: Routledge.

Montgomery, C. (2010), *Understanding the International Student Experience*, London: Palgrave Macmillan.

Naidoo, R. (2004), 'Fields and institutional strategy: Bourdieu on the relationship between higher education, inequality and society', *British Journal of Sociology of Education*, **25** (4), 446–72.

Naidoo, R. (2010), 'Global learning in a neoliberal age: implications for development', in E. Unterhalter and V. Carpentier (eds), *Global Inequalities and Higher Education: Whose Interests are we Serving?,* London: Palgrave Macmillan, pp. 66–90.

National Science Board, NSB, United States (2010), *Science and Engineering Indicators 2010*, http://www.nsf.gov/statistics/seind10/, accessed 18 April 2010.

Nelson, R. (2004), 'The market economy and the scientific commons', *Research Policy*, **33**, 455–71.

Ordorika, I. (2003), *Power and Politics in University Governance: Organization and Change at the Universidad Nacional Autonoma de Mexico*, New York: RoutledgeFalmer.

Organization for Economic Co-operation and Development (OECD) (2004), *Internationalization and Trade in Higher Education*, Paris: OECD.

Organization for Economic Co-operation and Development (OECD) (2005), *E-learning in Tertiary Education: Where do we Stand?,* Paris: OECD.

Organization for Economic Co-operation and Development (OECD) (2008a), *Tertiary Education for the Knowledge Society: OECD Thematic Review of Tertiary Education*, Paris: OECD.

Organization for Economic Co-operation and Development (OECD) (2008b), 'Roadmap for the OECD Assessment of Higher Education Learning Outcomes (AHELO): feasibility study', IMHE Governing Board, Document No. JT03248577, Paris: OECD.

Pedersen, P. (1991), 'Counseling international students', *The Counseling Psychologist*, **19** (10), 10–58.

Pusser, B. (2006), 'Reconsidering higher education and the public good: the role of public spheres', in W. Tierney (ed.), *Governance and the Public Good*, Albany, NY: SUNY Press, pp. 11–28.

Pusser, B. and S. Marginson (2011), 'The elephant in the room: power, global rankings, and the study of higher education organizations', in M. Bastedo (ed.), *Organizing Higher Education*, Baltimore, MD: Johns Hopkins University Press.

Rizvi, F. (2005), 'Identity, culture and cosmopolitan futures', *Higher Education Policy*, **18**, 331–9.

Rizvi, F. and B. Lingard (2010), *Globalizing Education Policy*, London: Routledge.

Rose, N. (1999), *Powers of Freedom*, Cambridge: Cambridge University Press.

Salmi, J. (2009), *The Challenge of Establishing World Class Universities*, Washington, DC: World Bank.

Samuelson, P. (1954), 'The pure theory of public expenditure', *Review of Economics and Statistics*, **36** (4), 387–9.

Sassen, S. (2006), *Cities in a World Economy*, 3rd edn, Thousand Oaks, CA: Pine Forge Press.

Sen, A. (1999), 'Global justice: beyond international equity', in I. Kaul, I. Grunberg and M. Stern (eds), *Global Public Goods: International Cooperation in the Twenty-first Century*, New York: Oxford University Press, pp. 116–25.

Sen, A. (2000), *Development as Freedom*, New York: Basic Books.

Shanghai Jiao Tong University Graduate School of Education, SJTUGSE (2010), *Academic Ranking of World Universities*, http://ed.sjtu.edu.cn/ranking.htm, accessed 21 August 2010.

Shin, J. and G. Harman (2009), 'New challenges for higher education: global and Asia-Pacific perspectives', *Asia Pacific Education Review*, **10**, 1–13.

Sidhu, R. (2009), 'The "brand name" research university goes global', *Higher Education*, **57**, 125–40.

Singh, M. (2001), 'Re-inserting the "public good" into higher education transformation', paper to Conference on 'Globalisation and Higher Education – Views from the South', University of Cape Town, March.

Slaughter, S. and L. Leslie (1997), *Academic Capitalism*, Baltimore, MD: The Johns Hopkins University Press.

Slaughter, S. and G. Rhoades (2004), *Academic Capitalism and the New Economy*, Baltimore, MD: The Johns Hopkins University Press.

Smith, A. (1759), *The Theory of Moral Sentiments* (2004), London: Barnes and Noble.

Smith, A. (1776), *An Inquiry into the Wealth of Nations* (1979), Harmondsworth, UK: Penguin.

Stiglitz, J. (1999), 'Knowledge as a global public good', in I. Kaul, I. Grunberg and M. Stern (eds), *Global Public Goods: International Cooperation in the Twenty-first Century*, New York: Oxford University Press, pp. 308–25.

Times Higher Education (2009), *World's Best Universities*, http://www.timeshighereducation.co.uk/Rankings2009-Top200.html, accessed 1 November 2009.

Unterhalter, E. and V. Carpentier (2010), 'Introduction: whose interests are we serving? Global inequalities and higher education', in E. Unterhalter and V. Carpentier (eds), *Global Inequalities and Higher Education: Whose Interests are we Serving?*, Basingstoke: Palgrave Macmillan, pp. 1–39.

van Vught, F. (ed.) (2009), *Mapping the Higher Education Landscape: Towards a European Classification of Higher Education*, Heidelberg: Springer.

Verbik, L. and V. Lasanowski (2007), *International Student Mobility: Patterns and Trends*, Report, London: The Observatory on Borderless Education, www.obhe.ac.uk [password protected], accessed 21 March 2008.

Verbik, L. and C. Merkley (2006), *The International Branch Campus: Models and Trends,* London: Observatory on Borderless Higher Education (OBHE).

Vygotsky, L. (1960), 'The instrumental method in psychology', in J. Wertsch (ed. and trans.), *The Concept of Activity in Soviet Psychology*, New York: M.E. Sharpe, pp. 134–43.

Wallerstein, I. (1996), *The Age of Transition: Trajectory of the World-System, 1945–2025*, London: Zed Press.

Webometrics (2010), *Ranking Web of World Universities*, http://www.webometrics.info/, accessed 2 March 2010.

Yang, R., K. Noels and K. Saumure (2006), 'Multiple routes to cross-cultural adaptation for international students: mapping the paths between self-construals, English language confidence, and adjustment', *International Journal of Intercultural Relations*, **30** (4), 487–506.

Ziguras, C. and G. McBurnie (2006), *Transnational Education: Issues and Trends in Off-shore Higher Education*, London: Routledge.

3 Rethinking development: higher education and the new imperialism

Rajani Naidoo

INTRODUCTION

Since the 1990s higher education has been positioned as one of the most important powerhouses for development in low-income countries. This signals a policy reversal on the part of powerful international organizations such as the World Bank, which for decades declared that there should be little investment in higher education because of low rates of social and economic return. In the context of the knowledge economy, the widely held view is that the ability to access, generate and transmit information rapidly across the globe has the potential to transform countries that are materially poor into countries that are 'information-rich' with the ability to utilize knowledge for economic development and leapfrog traditional developmental stages.

This chapter assesses the potential for building higher education systems that can contribute to development in low-income countries. Given the rapid development of a global higher education arena and the intensification of higher education relationships across borders, low-income countries cannot be researched in isolation but must be analyzed in the context of changing relations between capitalism and contemporary globalization, and the transformation of higher education systems worldwide. Drawing on scholarship related to the new imperialism, this chapter argues that rivalry between the most powerful nation-states is a key feature of contemporary globalization with considerable impact on higher education systems. Restructuring and cross-border interactions in higher education are increasingly characterized by governance mechanisms and rationales that aim to deploy higher education as a lever to enhance the competitive edge of the nation-state in the global economy and to assert political influence in the regional and global context.

The chapter begins by analyzing the global sociopolitical and economic contexts underlying the policy shift that has harnessed higher education so closely to the knowledge economy meta-narrative. It then presents an analysis of the new imperialism in the twenty-first century and explores how emerging powers such as China have the potential to impact on older hegemonic relations. Rather than conceptualizing low-income countries as passive subjects of inter-hegemonic rivalry, as much of the literature tends to do, the chapter explores the strategic interventions and actions taken by low-income countries themselves. The opportunities and the pitfalls for low-income countries under current global conditions are assessed before the chapter concludes with seminal issues for research and policy to enable genuine capacity-building in higher education systems with the potential to contribute to development.

HIGHER EDUCATION, GLOBALIZATION AND THE KNOWLEDGE ECONOMY

Transformations in higher education have occurred in the context of structural changes in western capitalism encapsulated under the term 'globalization' and the 'knowledge economy'. Wallerstein (1991) and Arrighi (1994) have persuasively demonstrated that globalization is not a recent phenomenon but may be understood as an articulation of economic, social and political processes that have evolved over the past five centuries. While there is a great deal of contestation over the term, there is some common agreement that globalization is associated with the actions and interests of transnational corporations, the workings of global financial and labor markets, the development of new forms of production based on new technologies, and the compression of time and space resulting in an ascendancy of real time over clock time (Harvey, 1989; Held et al., 1999). The current context has also seen the rise of the knowledge economy. This too has a history stretching back to the end of the Second World War with disagreements between scholars from different disciplinary traditions and political orientations (see Peters, Chapter 5 in this volume). However, there is little argument that economic advantage is seen to accrue from the production and consumption of knowledge. Political, intellectual and economic strategies as well as a wide range of government policies are therefore framed by hegemonic discourses linking knowledge and global competitiveness (Jessop, 2008).

Although globalization has resulted in new forms of capitalist production beyond the confines of the nation-state, the premise of this chapter is that power in the nation-state has not been hollowed out and depleted. Instead, the state has transformed itself into what Cerny (1990) has termed the 'competition' state in which the government's primary objective is to foster a competitive national economy. Policies are shaped to promote, control and maximize returns from market forces in international settings while abandoning some of the core discourses and functions of the welfare state. State capacities, functions and partnerships with non-governmental stakeholders including the governance of cyberspace are reorganized territorially and functionally on subnational, national, supranational and transnational levels (Jessop, 2008). Furthermore, as well as pulling in different directions, there is also increasing articulation between national and global markets as well as network, state and other modes of coordination.

In addition, nation-states themselves form a specific arrangement around a world order relating to the hierarchical nature of both the international state system and global capital flows. A theory of interstate rivalry or what commentators have called the new imperialism therefore remains indispensable for understanding both the contemporary world order and the place of low-income countries in that order as the context in which higher education interactions across nation-states take place. Political analysts have noted that while relations between the major powers have changed significantly since the end of the Cold War, inter-imperialist rivalries have nevertheless continued. Theories relating to the new imperialism have continuity but also show significant differences from classical theories of imperialism such as those developed by Bukharin (1972 [1917]) and Hobsbawm (1987). Contemporary analysts such as Harvey (2003) and Callinicos (2009) exemplify this continuity by describing the new imperialism as the intersection of, and tensions between, 'territorial and economic logics of power' through which dominant states search for new areas for capitalist accumulation. 'Territorial power' refers to the political and military strategies invoked by a state or collection of states to assert influence worldwide while economic power refers to the ways that economic power flows across and through continuous space and towards or away from territorial entities (Harvey, 2003, p. 26). Their work is supplemented by cultural theorists such as Edward Saïd (1993), who refer to the importance of culture and discursive formations in maintaining and legitimating imperialism. The new imperialism therefore presents a framework for understanding the actions of powerful states through an analysis of the intertwined logic of economic competition and struggle for hegemony involving complex networks of economic, military, political and discursive power.

The new imperialism, however, also differs from previous phases of imperialism in a number of ways. First, as Hardt and Negri (2000) show, while the power of dominant nation-states is still highly visible, states exist in complex relationships with supranational institutions and major capitalist corporations. Second, in general, the direct annexation of territory is not a widespread practice as existed under classical imperialism. The new imperialism respects notionally the principle of national sovereignty, although, as Tikly (2004) shows, military intervention and illegal occupation can easily override the principle of national sovereignty with the rationale that global security is threatened. In general, however, the exercise of power is more subtle and exercised more by 'economic' or 'political' rather than military means (Went, 2002; Kiely, 2007). Borders, particularly those in developing economies of the South and in Eastern Europe, are penetrated without being dissolved through fashioning economic and political environments that are open to global market forces and the commodities and capital of foreign firms. This occurs through the implementation of a system of global economic regulation such as trade liberalization measures to open new markets in low-income countries as well as through systems of debt patronage (Hoogvelt, 1997; Kiely, 2006). These strategies give access to markets, raw materials, and strategic geopolitical positions for regional and global influence. Finally, classical imperialism was legitimated by a view of biological racism and sexism with its origins in the eugenics movement (Willensky, 1998; Tikly, 2004). In the current context, culture and religion have been included as a basic category for explaining difference and conflict. Western values and market-based democracy are expected to provide the norm against which other cultural forms and political and economic regimes are measured (see, e.g., Huntingdon, 1998).

Finally, the rise of India and particularly China as emerging powers is likely to create what Henderson (2008) has termed a 'critical disruption' in the hierarchical order of inter-hegemonic rivalry. China is a one-party state in which the Communist Party retains control of the state apparatuses and is therefore a dramatically different sociopolitical formation. It has a giant economy and an unusual form of capitalism. A combination of developments, including its capacity to move into higher valued-added, more technology-intensive products such as nanotechnology (Appelbaum and Parker, 2008) and the dramatic expansion of the graduate labor force particularly in subjects such as engineering, has led the World Bank to state that the shock that China is administering to the world is unprecedented (Winters and Yusuf, 2007, p. 11). Relatedly, it is the only political economy where state-owned companies are utilized as drivers of globalization.

The implication of this, as Henderson (2008) notes, is that the primary concern of major corporations will not be purely profit-driven but will also be driven by China's strategic interests and its national development strategy. Henderson concludes that as a consequence the logic of the present phase of globalization and the impact on countries absorbed into it could be dramatically different from previous phases of globalization (see also Cerni, 2006). In addition, China is likely to forge a very different relationship with low-income countries. China's perceived sense of injustice associated with what it terms its '100 years of humiliation' as a result of being subjected to attack at various times in its history by Britain, the USA, France, Belgium, Germany and Japan (Chang, 2001) is likely to influence its relations with both hegemonic powers and with the developing world. China's influence is also likely to increase in developing countries as a result of its active role in global governance and aid (Guerrero and Manji, 2008). Finally, China is re-entering the global political economy at a moment when geopolitical relations are fragile. Political violence, the financial crisis, climate change and increasing levels of poverty appear as insoluble problems. China's rise as an emerging power therefore has the potential to challenge dominant hegemonic powers and the associated economic and political world order.

HIGHER EDUCATION AND INTER-HEGEMONIC RIVALRY

While the governance and funding terrain for higher education has undergone dramatic changes in the last decades, the state in general has not withdrawn from its role as overseer of higher education. In fact, as Green (1997, p. 4) notes, with the declining legitimacy of other central components of the welfare state, national governments have 'come to regard education as one of the most effective remaining instruments of national policy'. While state funding and academic self-steering are diminishing worldwide and various forms of market competition are emerging, including the entry of private and for-profit institutions, the state nevertheless retains crucial elements of overall control. The particular combination and power of state-steering, national and global market competition, and university self-autonomy differs across countries and in relation to university status, resources and prestige (Marginson, 2010a).

In the UK the highly stratified higher education system is steered by a combination of audit and market mechanisms with differing consequences for universities at the top and the bottom of the hierarchy (Naidoo, 2008). In China, expansion has been accompanied by fundamental reform tied to China's development strategy and its attempt to enhance its position in the order of nation-states. In a major ideological shift, quasi-marketization elements have been introduced. These include fees, a diversification of institutions, internal competition and revenue-generating activities (Vidovich et al., 2007). Mok (2005) has referred to China as a 'market-accelerationist' state that pursues regulation for competition and uses the market to further state goals. Marketization may therefore be interpreted as a pragmatic strategy to strengthen the state's capacity rather than an ideological shift to neoliberalism. Indeed, the Communist Party Secretary serves as Chair of the University Council, which is responsible among other responsibilities for appointing senior university managers such as deans and vice presidents (Halachmi and Ngok, 2009).

Higher education therefore continues to play an important role in the economic and political rivalries between nation-states. The dependence on knowledge, especially scientific and technological knowledge, and on innovation to enhance each country's comparative advantage in the global economy has led to the positioning of higher educa-tion as a crucial engine for economic development (Castells, 2001). Second, in a rapidly changing, uncertain and multipolar world higher education is also increasingly deployed to assert sociopolitical and cultural influence in regional and global contexts. The next sections will address each of these functions in turn, although it must be noted that in practice there are considerable overlaps, contradictions and tensions between the various ways in which higher education is deployed.

Global Economy

The expected contributions of higher education to enhancing a country's edge in the global economy are manifold. First, government policy advisors have argued that the emphasis on value-added production through innovation and changes in technology requires a configuration of skills that is at a substantially higher level and of a more generic kind than the technical competences required to perform specific occupational roles (Brown et al., 2001). Skill-formation strategies are therefore expected to lift the national skills base rather than limit the opportunity for high-level education to a small elite cadre of workers. These developments have resulted in significant pressures on national higher education systems to move from elite to mass institutions and to train the new 'knowledge workers' with the technical, personal, social and managerial skills to take their place in the knowledge economy (Gibbons et al., 1994).

The scenario of knowledge-driven capitalism has also resulted in the repositioning of universities in low-income countries. The late 1980s marked a dramatic overturning of the view, long held by the World Bank and powerful western governments, that invest-ment in higher education would bring limited social and economic benefits to developing countries. The new orthodoxy in the context of the knowledge economy is that the ability to generate, utilize, access and transmit information rapidly across the globe will enable developing countries to utilize knowledge to 'leapfrog' over intermediate developmental stages and improve their positions in the global economy (Castells, 2001). Universities have therefore become the new developmental actors and higher education has been positioned as a crucial motor for development. According to the World Bank, 'Higher education has never been as important to the developing world as it is now. It cannot guarantee rapid economic development but sustained progress is impossible without it' (Task Force on Higher Education in Developing Countries, 2000, p. 19).

These factors have led to the exponential expansion of higher education as countries benchmark themselves against competitor nations. Developed economies such as the USA, Canada, Japan and countries in Western Europe which achieved participation rates of 50 percent and over have been caught up or indeed overtaken by countries like South Korea. In addition, higher education expansion is extending beyond the rapidly growing economies of Brazil and Russia to emerging economies such as Lithuania and Hungary, and to resource-rich Middle Eastern countries like Saudi Arabia and the United Arab Emirates (Brown et al., 2010). The rise of emerging powers such as India and China has intensified this competition (Wildavsky, 2010). In the post-Mao era of the 1980s China's integration into the global economy was accompanied by the positioning of higher education as an important driver for economic development. The government embarked on an ambitious plan for higher education reform and development. Figures from 2006 show that in one decade China tripled its share of gross domestic product spent on higher education, that the numbers of institutions more than doubled, and the numbers of students enrolled in higher education increased five times (Zhong, n.d.). The Indian government has also planned an enormous expansion of its national system of higher education, including the aim to build 30 new comprehensive universities and 40 new institutes specializing in science, technology and management by 2012 (Brown et al., 2010).

Changes in state funding and steering that have applied pressure on universities to generate surplus income have also resulted in universities crossing borders in competition for large numbers of students in other countries. In the UK and Australia the dominant rationale for attracting increasing numbers of international students is primarily to boost income at the institutional level and trade surpluses at the national level. In Continental Europe and the USA, these revenue-generating aims are supplemented by the aim to attract, develop and retain talent to produce innovation and generate longer-term value for the economy. In Europe, reforms such as the Bologna Process can be seen as strategies to align national study programs and regulations across European countries to develop a competitive European market to attract international students. As Robertson (2009) has indicated, the aims of Bologna include the desire to increase Europe's overall market share of higher education as well as to attract the world's best minds to motor the European economy. While national governments respond in a variety of ways to the momentum of the Bologna reforms, including resisting as well as incorporating elements to further their own political aims, Hartmann (2008) has nevertheless illustrated how Bologna has at the same time been deployed to challenge hegemonic relations in higher education. She shows how a series of strategic moves such as the inclusion of some countries, and the exclusion of others including the USA simultaneously challenged its hegemonic role as standard-bearer in higher education.

Robertson's work (2009) also demonstrates the interaction of the Bologna Process with national reform in other regions of the world; this has given Europe the status for normative leadership in higher education. Bologna is therefore viewed as a potential threat in the USA and Australia, as a model for domestic restructuring in Brazil, and as the basis for new regional projects in Africa and Latin America. Europe has also reached over to Asia to counter the perceived threat of China and to make itself as visible in the Asian policy horizon as the USA. A number of initiatives that blur the boundaries between trade and aid with China and India and with Asian regional organizations have been developed (Robertson, 2008). Attempts by organizations such as the European Commission to persuade Asian countries of the gains of progressive liberalization through the World Trade Organization illustrate that these interactions go beyond a preferred model of higher education and include a preferred model for a political and economic world order.

Sociopolitical and Cultural Competition

While various forms of competition have always existed across university systems, the linking of universities to global competitivity has accelerated the race for prestige and world-class status primarily through jostling for position in systems of global university rankings. China has declared its intentions to join this race, which has historically been dominated by a global super-elite of prestigious American and British universities (Marginson, 2009). Min Weifang, the party secretary of Peking University, has argued that since universities are a major factor affecting a country's competitive ability, 'creating and running world-class universities should be one of the strategic foci of building up a country' (Min, 2004, p. 8). The implementation of the 985 scheme in 1998, which began with Peking and Tsinghua universities receiving US$225 million, followed in 1999 by the inclusion of a number of other institutions, indicates strong intent on the part of the Chinese government (Halachmi and Ngok, 2009). However, the influence of global rankings is not limited to elite institutions in high or rapidly growing economies. As Marginson (2009) and King (2009b) argue, the global templates that result from world rankings, which align closely with the characteristics of elite American and European institutions, exert an influence on all institutions, including non-elite institutions in low-income countries that have little capacity to feature in such rankings.

Thus, at the same time as pursuing economic aims, higher education is also increasingly deployed to assert sociopolitical influence worldwide, including persuading students to adopt particular values and political and economic models. In the UK a variety of funding and policy levers has been developed to encourage universities to become more business-friendly and to teach employability skills, including the dispositions and attitudes to be successful knowledge workers in global labor markets (Middleton, 2000). These values are also transported into other countries through both explicit and 'hidden' curriculum strategies that include the kinds of learning derived from the nature and organizational design of the institution and curriculum as well as from the behavior and attitudes of faculty (Wells, 1993). In the USA, following the 9/11 World Trade Center and Pentagon attacks, there have been various laws to link institutions of higher education to attempts to rebuild national security. The Patriot Act of 2001, for example, has increased government oversight of university education and research through expanding the definition of classified and sensitive information, restricting the movement and work of foreign-born students and scholars, and initiating surveillance of academic conferences and other research and teaching activities (Tannock, 2007). In the USA the role of higher education is also seen to be crucial in spreading influence. Wesley Clark, a retired four-star general in the US Army and former National Atlantic Treaty Organization Supreme Allied Commander, has stated:

> China could change the very nature of America as we know it, just by virtue of its sheer scale. It is essential that leaders in higher education participate in crafting a new strategy for America. They must consider the larger context of their decisions and actions, both at home and abroad . . . How, in an age of global competition, do we optimize our activities and international relationships so they are good for universities, good for students, and good for the country? (Clark, n.d., p. 7)

Richard Riley, a former US Secretary of Education, has coined the term 'education diplomacy' with reference to the deployment of higher education to pursue the country's diplomatic interests with the rest of the world (NAFSA, 2003). These sentiments have been endorsed by a range of higher education constituencies, including the Association of American Universities and the National Association of International Educators (see Tannock, 2007).

China's deployment of higher education to assert influence may still be at an early stage. According to commentators, China's use of 'soft power' in spreading its influence must be seen in the context of its desire to manage its image and contain perceptions of the rise of China as a threat to the west (Humphrey and Messner, 2006). The government has set up the Confucius Institutes, which aim to promote Chinese language and culture and a better understanding of the country in general. These institutes have emerged in around 272 higher education institutions in 88 countries. Their potential for worldwide influence may be indicated by the level of opposition in some western contexts, which view the Institutes as propaganda tools of the government.

China's influence is also likely to increase in developing countries as a result of its active role in global governance and aid. China has criticized western countries for compelling low-income countries to open up to global markets while maintaining protectionist stances themselves. These types of position-taking may have implications for the General Agreement on Trade and Services (GATS) and higher education in the near future. As part of China's increased involvement in Africa, China and 49 African countries have agreed on a three-year action plan to establish partnerships to promote knowledge-based sustainable development. Twenty higher education institutions in Africa and China will engage in one-to-one inter-institutional cooperation, including funding for 100 joint R&D projects over the next three years (Sawahel, 2009). These developments clearly have the potential for incorporating emerging economies that were previously subjected to older forms of European and American power into new and shifting multipolar regimes of power.

In addition, while universities from the USA and the UK are attracted by the large numbers of revenue-generating students in rapidly growing economies, governments such as those in China and India are increasingly shaping such interactions through policy and regulation in order to avoid low-quality providers and to leverage university partnerships for knowledge transfer to build indigenous research and teaching capacity. As Brown and colleagues show, this conception of knowledge transfer has been likened by Chinese officials to a country that is crouching, watching and learning before leaping to a position of global advantage (Brown et al., 2010). Singapore too has invited a number of the world's elite universities to set up centers of excellence and research through its Global Schoolhouse project, including Harvard and Wharton Business Schools, INSEAD, Johns Hopkins Medical School, and the Massachusetts Institute of Technology (Gopinathan, 1999; Sanderson, 2002). These universities have been invited on Singapore's terms and in strong articulation with its national development strategy. Singapore has embarked on a major marketing and recruitment drive to attract students from the region and worldwide by requiring a fee of only 10 percent more than domestic students pay. Singapore also requires students to stay on in Singapore and enter employment for three years. While this creates little extra revenue, the intention, according to Sanderson (2002), is that the development of a global alumni body that has lived and worked in Singapore will be an important strategic asset for the future.

However, it is also important to avoid characterizing low-income countries as passive subjects of inter-hegemonic rivalry. As is shown in Part II of this volume, while developing countries are influenced by global templates of higher education, at the same time particular aspects of such templates are also transformed, excluded and adapted in line with each country's own historical trajectories, cultural influences and sociopolitical milieus. An important recent initiative has been the development of regional hubs by countries in the Middle East that are trying to position themselves as regional centers of excellence in education. Dubai in the United Arab Emirates has created a Knowledge Village and more recently the Dubai International Education City in which foreign education institutions and companies are co-located in an economic zone with financial and tax benefits. In Qatar, the Qatar Foundation has invited six US institutions and one UK university to offer their full degree programs and qualifications to national and regional students. These initiatives aim to recruit international students, prepare domestic students for employment in the knowledge economy, increase revenue, and build an international profile and geopolitical status in the region (see Knight, 2010). The partnerships embrace a model of internationalization that employs western expertise and technology while eschewing aspects of western culture and values in favor of 'Asian' values that are taught explicitly as part of the higher education curriculum.

There are also examples of models in countries such as Cuba that are an alternative to dominant American and Western European templates. Cuba is an important example as it is a developing country that has succeeded in less than half a century in creating a mass, high-quality higher education system. The higher education system boasts internationally renowned schools in disciplines such as medicine and a critical mass of reputable scientists (Sabina, 2003; Cabrera, 2008). Cuban higher education analysts have argued that knowledge in neoliberal political systems is placed at the service of economic competition and is submerged in a legal, economic and military web that cancels its role in contributing to the public good (Cárdenas et al., 2008, p. 1). In contrast, Cuba has developed a 'social policy of knowledge' that consists of implementing strategies for the wider production, appropriation, diffusion and application of knowledge. Institutional bases for knowledge development and implementation are strengthened and knowledge is linked to positive social and economic impact (Cárdenas et al., 2008, p. 3).

The Cuban higher education system is characterized by the absence of internal market competition, open source publishing, and strong articulation between productive and national innovative systems. In addition there is a focus on social inclusion to include mature learners and marginalized youth who are not in employment or in education. The curriculum encompasses training in the humanities, science and technology, political ideology and community development (Cárdenas et al., 2008). Cuba has also engaged in higher education interaction with other countries. In the last 40 years Cuba has accepted disadvantaged students from developing countries in Africa, Latin America and the Caribbean, particularly in the medical sciences. Since 2007, bilateral agreements have also been signed with Nicaragua, Bolivia, Ecuador, Venezuela, Argentina and Mexico. While socioeconomic and political transformations are occurring in the country, the Cuban model of higher education, as well as aspects of its political and economic system, has the potential to become influential in certain parts of the world.

In the next section I turn to the consequences of these changing global conditions for higher education systems in low-income countries. These conditions may be seen to offer both important opportunities as well as potential dangers.

IMPLICATIONS FOR LOW-INCOME COUNTRIES

One of the most important advantages of the current context is the reversal of the idea that higher education is a luxury that developing economies can ill afford. This sea change has occurred in an increasingly multipolar world. The development of the European Higher Education Area, for example, poses challenges to US hegemony and differing models of higher education interaction may result. The emerging powers of India and China may also affect world relations of power (Bach et al., 2006). China in particular participates actively in a variety of global governance bodies such as the World Trade Organization and the International Monetary Fund (Wang and Rosenau, 2009). China has responded to the accusation that core countries have developed international rules that in effect kick out of the reach of developing countries the ladders that were so useful in their own historical development (Chang, 2002). China has put forward its own vision of global governance under the concept of a 'harmonious world' (see Wang and Rosenau, 2009). The principle is that each country has the right to choose its own development model and political system. Ramo (2004) has suggested that a 'Beijing Consensus' may emerge to oppose some elements of the 'Washington Consensus', which currently dominates institutions of global and national governance. These developments have the potential to give developing countries greater freedom of maneuver amidst the struggle of more powerful countries to push forward their own strategic interests.

In the context of rising demand for higher education in developing countries and the limited resources available to governments, trends that encourage the provision of higher education through external means have the potential to provide a number of benefits. Foreign providers may help alleviate pressures for access in countries where there is limited domestic capacity to meet growing demand and may provide access to groups not provided for by government as a result of ethnic or religious affiliation (Naidoo, 2010). External providers may also respond more readily to the needs of prospective students by linking programs more directly to the labor market or providing convenient class times and locations for working adults (Levy, 2003). In some countries such as India and China, research-focused public institutions may be best able to succeed if the goal to provide certain levels of higher education on a mass scale can be met by other providers, including private and transnational ones.

In a more sector-wide sense commentators have indicated that transnational higher education may help build capacity in higher education and help stem brain drain (Vincent-Lancrin, 2005). Developments in the Chinese and Indian national economies and higher education systems have resulted in the retention of an increasing proportion of their graduates. The initiative by governments in some developing countries to develop partnerships with reputable foreign providers in order to become regional hubs of learning is also an important development for world regions. Most importantly, as Marginson's work indicates, many of the major problems faced by the world today, such as rising levels of poverty, the financial crisis, environmental degradation on a planetary scale, and the escalation of conflict around ethnic, political and religious differences can only be solved by countries and universities collaborating across national, cultural and ideological boundaries (Marginson, 2010b).

However, it is also important to recognize the dangers. One concern is that the revitalization of higher education has occurred within the straitjacket of what Jessop (2008) has termed the 'master economic imaginary' of the knowledge economy. By this he means a hegemonic discourse linked to the idea of global competitiveness that frames political, intellectual and economic strategies as well as a wide range of government policies. This discourse results in the tight coupling of higher education to the needs and requirements of the knowledge economy, which in turn poses many dangers for developing countries. First, it is not clear to what extent the interests of developing countries are served by an uncritical acceptance of the prescriptions encapsulated within this discourse. A number of analysts have argued that the rise of the knowledge economy to the status of master narrative was at least in part a response to the 1970s crisis of the post-Second World War model of economic growth. An economic strategy based on knowledge and intellectual property as a new source of competitive advantage was needed to enlarge and protect the dominance of US capital for the next long wave of capitalist development (Jessop, 2008; Robertson, 2009). If this analysis is accepted, then the advantage that powerful countries already have, as well as continuing unequal power relations and structural barriers, are likely to impede the development prospects of the majority of low-income countries.

A further difficulty is that the faith in higher education as a motor of development relies on the high-skills thesis, which states that for nation-states to remain competitive in current economic conditions a change in the nature of skills and its relationship to productivity is required. Higher levels of skill within the workforce in advanced economies are perceived to be a prerequisite for economic activity to shift into a new high-skills mode of working. However, this thesis, which is intimately linked with the role of higher education in development, has come under criticism by researchers who have pointed out that even in high-income countries, high-performance production systems and high-skills regimes are not widely distributed (see, e.g., Kraak, 2004). Ashton (2004) has pointed out that contrary to the high-skills mantra, the incorporation of a low-skills development strategy may be viewed positively in developing countries since it could lead to labor-intensive forms of employment and help alleviate mass unemployment (Ashton, 2004). A development strategy built around the interlocking potential of low, intermediate and high skills to allow for greater variability and unevenness is thus a persuasive one (Kraak, 2004) and has implications for a mixture of investment strategies in higher and other levels of education, including vocational training.

As I have shown in previous work (Naidoo, 2010), the deployment of higher education to enhance trade surpluses and its transformation into a global commodity raises concerns for quality as well as social inclusion in low-income countries. There is some evidence to indicate that the proliferation of for-profit institutions, particularly in countries with weak regulation, may lead to an increasing number of low-quality 'diploma mills' (Knight, 2003). In India it is estimated that about three-quarters of private higher education institutions do not meet minimum standards and indulge in malpractices relating to admissions and fees (Anandakrishnan, 2006). McCowan (2004) has indicated that in Brazil institutions regarded as of low quality have achieved growth simply because there is no geographical or financial alternative for large numbers of the population.

In addition, publicly funded universities in high-income countries that are being financially squeezed may also devise strategies to protect their core on-campus provision in their home countries while viewing developing countries with weak regulation as mass markets for lower-cost learning (see, e.g., Noble, 2002; Altbach, 2002). The reduction of costs may be achieved primarily by focusing on scale rather than quality, and the temptation will therefore be to produce standardized products and generic content that are more easily and cheaply transferable across borders. In addition, foreign providers who may be primarily motivated by profit are likely to offer programs in disciplines that are profitable rather than disciplines that are expensive or difficult to teach (Nussbaum, 2007). Since comprehensive universities often function on the basis of cross-subsidization, where expensive courses like medicine are taught alongside cheaper ones such as business studies, indigenous universities may lose students to the new providers, especially in the very disciplines that generate important revenue for cross-subsidization (Teixeira and Amaral, 2001). Moreover, little interest has been shown in offering programs to build indigenous research capacity such as research degrees at postgraduate level or doctoral-level work.

Policy instruments borrowed from high-income countries to steer higher education in low-income countries may also impact on social inclusion. Mechanisms that require universities to privilege research output and demonstrate rapid rates of student progression militate against widening participation since students from non-traditional constituencies are time- and resource-intensive (Naidoo, 2000). These developments, when combined with an influx of foreign and private providers in relatively unregulated environments, have the potential to lead to a university sector in which status and resources are likely to be inversely proportional to institutional and student disadvantage. De Cohen (2003), for example, has noted that in Argentina public higher education traditionally served as a vehicle of upward occupational and social mobility, albeit in a limited manner. However, the growth of an elite private sector, along with restricted student financial aid and problems of overcrowding, has threatened to undermine the role of public higher institutions as facilitators of social mobility. In the context of technological education in India, Kamat and colleagues (2006) have argued that the state has provided a high-quality technological education for an elite while technology education for the masses is left to unregulated private providers. These providers have abandoned a broad-based education and instead focus on a narrow set of skills condensed into short certification programs. According to the authors, this strategy has led to the reproduction of caste and class inequality.

KNOWLEDGE IMPERIALISM

The potential of education and research to contribute to development in low-income countries is also compromised by a particular hegemonic view of research. The master narrative of the knowledge economy combines with policy templates favored by dominant countries to lay down the criteria for what is meant by high quality and relevant research. In this model what is valued is the generation and dissemination of knowledge that can be utilized for national competitive advantage (Slaughter and Rhoades, 2004). Furthermore, as Jessop (2008) has shown, the growing commodification of knowledge intensifies contradictions between the circulation of knowledge as a collective resource and its appropriation as a source of private profit. Knowledge is increasingly commodified, subjected to closure, and treated as intellectual property, as shown by pressures for the privatization and patenting of publicly financed research in higher education.

However, it is also important to note that the inherent public-good character of knowledge ensures that appropriation and commodification can never be fully realized.

Researchers from developing countries have also argued against the imposition of scientific-innovation models such as the 'triple helix', which developed in the context of high-income countries and advocates strong relations between universities, industry and government. They suggest that in many developing countries industries are unwilling to fund research and training, and may not have sufficient capacity to utilize research findings or high-skilled knowledge workers.

Universities will therefore face pressures to perform low-level, routine, consultancy-type activities with the aim of generating income (Arocena and Sutz, 2005). Research conducted in Malawi has also indicated that in a national context where Mode 1 knowledge was never thoroughly institutionalized, high market demand for knowledge for narrow utilitarian purposes has already constrained research and education to the point of squeezing out explanatory questions (Holland, 2008). Such analyses indicate that universities can more appropriately correspond to the developmental goals of their countries by developing strong relationships with a variety of stakeholders including government, the public sector and community organizations. Moreover, an important additional mission of the university that is often excluded is the aim of linking high-level knowledge production with the problems affecting the most vulnerable sectors of the population (see, e.g., Subotzky, 1999; Arocena and Sutz, 2000).

There are also concerns that transnational higher education is guilty of cultural imperialism. Xiaoming and Haitao (2000, pp. 101–13), in their chapter on China's response to internationalization, express the concern that in the context of the dominance of western culture and differences in national resources, transnational education may begin to eliminate cultural difference and lead to the erosion of indigenous values and culture. Escobar (1995), in considering Latin America, has illustrated how indigenous knowledge has been largely erased from the intellectual field, while Connell (2007) has persuasively argued that social theory from peripheral societies is often marginalized and discredited by the metropole. These studies are substantiated by research into the evolution of knowledge, which indicates that the growth of intellectual fields has always been characterized by power struggles and specific interests (Collins, 1998) and that knowledge can and has been utilized as an ideological device for protecting privilege. At the same time, as Muller (2000) and Young (2007) warn, there are also dangers with an uncritical acceptance of these conceptions of knowledge. For example Moore and Muller (1999) show that it is all too easy to reach the point where academic knowledge can be perceived as being unable to make an epistemological claim to validity since it can only ever be an ideological device for maintaining positions of dominance. In addition, as Appadurai (1996) has indicated, in an increasingly interrelated world in which there is simultaneously greater homogeneity as well as greater heterogeneity, it is extremely difficult to demarcate indigenous from non-indigenous knowledge. A binary logic contrasting a homogeneous perception of US and European culture with 'non-western' cultures; modernity with tradition; and technology with agrarian production is therefore unlikely to be helpful. There is also the danger that equating knowledge in a simplistic manner with ideology or culture may result in the detachment of new knowledge emerging out of different national contexts from epistemologically powerful knowledge structures and from procedures for generating better knowledge. There needs to be a wider acknowledgment that while knowledge is not entirely reducible to the conditions of its production, at the same time it is not entirely independent of the conditions of its production. Conceptual frameworks to bring power and knowledge back into a non-reductionist dialogue are urgently required.

A RESEARCH AND POLICY AGENDA

In the following section some key issues are presented that may contribute to the development of a research agenda on higher education and its role in development.

Greater research attention is required to understand inter-hegemonic relations between countries and the effect on higher education and its contribution to development in low-income countries. In this context there is the need to scrutinize what Gindin (2004) has termed 'the fetish of competitiveness', which, when applied to higher education, pits universities against other universities in a global race to achieve goals that exclude important questions such as how a university contributes to the national and global public good. In addition, conceptual frameworks and empirical investigations are required to understand the impact of the rapidly growing economies of India and China on low-income countries. Africa's traditional relationships with the USA and Europe are being challenged by competing relationships with India and, to a greater extent, with China (Kaplinsky, 2006). Research on the relationship between China and Africa has tended to veer between two opposing and oversimplified arguments. The first, supported by many western commentators in what may be termed a self-serving manner, argues that the engagement by the emerging powers in Africa is purely exploitative. Their conclusion is that China is a new imperial power involved in a second scramble for Africa that will perpetuate Africa's underdevelopment. The opposing argument asserts that China will work in solidarity with African states to achieve development objectives. A more nuanced analysis of the multifaceted relationship between China and Africa is required that goes beyond blind endorsement or prejudice. This type of scholarship is currently emerging (see, e.g., Guerrero and Manji, 2008; Strauss and Saavedra, 2010) but excludes an analysis of higher education. Research also needs to include an analysis of alternative models of higher education emerging in Latin America and other regions of the world. Here again the debate has been unhelpfully polarized, and more balanced analyses will be helpful in understanding the relationship between higher education, development and democracy.

Given research findings that indicate that the orientation and effectiveness of the state are critical variables in explaining successful development, it is also important to develop more in-depth analyses of different types of relationships between higher education, states and markets. There are many examples of erstwhile developing countries, such as South Korea, Singapore, China and India, where higher education has been invested in as a major component of economic growth and development. However, as shown in previous sections, this is not necessarily a straightforward relationship or one of direct correlation. As Cloete et al. (2007) have indicated in the context of Africa, the link between higher education and development has become highly politicized in many developing countries. They argue that rather than formulating development frameworks, governments have tried to force higher education into undemocratic political agendas, resulting in antagonistic relations between higher education institutions and governments. In addition, as Lundvall (2007) and Arocena and Sutz (2008) show, merely tying universities to the developmental path of the state is not sufficient. Higher education policy needs to be embedded within an analysis of the national innovation system in order to coordinate it with a wider set of policies. An important area for research consideration is whether the liberalization of higher education is itself conducive to the development of high-quality systems and under what conditions. Research has shown that liberalization can have the effect of undermining stability and the prospects for state policies that are designed to promote dynamic comparative advantage. As the work of King (2009a) illustrates, a close analysis of emerging trends in higher education regulation as well as subsequent impacts is highly instructive. (See also Chapter 24, Part III of this volume.) Research analysis and policy development in relation to strategies that enhance collaboration and competition between public, private and foreign providers in higher education is also vital.

Even more fundamental is how development and developmental strategies are defined. In general, economic growth has been prioritized as an end in itself and other activities are justified in so far as they foster growth. In this framework, human capital preparation becomes a major responsibility of the university and it is assumed that, once growth is assured, basic needs such as food, heath and security will trickle down to the most vulnerable sections of the population. However, these dominant ideas about development have been severely tested by food and fuel crises, and alternative visions, in which economic development is seen as important but in the service of other goals such as security, freedom from fear, more secure livelihoods, and political and cultural freedoms, have begun to emerge (Deneulin and Shahani, 2009).

The most promising of these is the 'Wellbeing Regimes' framework that grew out of an analysis of the limitations of Esping-Andersen's model of welfare regimes when applied to developing countries (Esping-Andersen, 1991). 'Wellbeing' refers to an individual's right to health, autonomy, security and other fundamental aspects to achieve quality of life. The theoretical framework has been developed and applied in a variety of national contexts by a multidisciplinary group of researchers from economics, social policy and international development (Wood and Gough, 2006; Copestake, 2007). The framework is relational and broadens the concept of welfare to include subjective as well as objective dimensions. It conceptualizes the aim of development strategies to achieve the 'wellbeing' of the population. 'Wellbeing' is not just as an end in itself, but also a process and experience that relies heavily on cultural factors such as motivation for personal and collective agency (Copestake, 2007).

The framework also gives more emphasis to political instability and the challenges of societies undergoing rapid change. It includes the position of the state in the global world order as well as the relationship between state and non-state actors such as social movements, religious organizations and non-governmental organizations (NGOs). It also recognizes the importance of empowering poor, marginalized and vulnerable people themselves. The development of a framework that brings together macro and micro analysis and that takes account of the position of the state in the world order and in relation to other international and national organizations, that expands the conception of development beyond the relationship between human capital and economic development, is a major breakthrough. However, what is highly significant is the lack of linkage between this emerging body of research from research and policy on higher education in developing countries. This separation results in the exclusion of a key institutional site from the wellbeing regime framework and constrains the development of research and policy on the potential of higher education to contribute to development. If development theory and practice are undergoing change, it is imperative that higher education research should be both encapsulated as well as contribute to this field.

ACKNOWLEDGMENTS

I would like to acknowledge gratefully the insights that I have gained from conversations with High Lauder.

REFERENCES

Altbach, P. (2002), 'Knowledge and education as international commodities?', *International Higher Education*, **28**, 2–5.
Anandakrishnan, M. (2006), 'Privatization of higher education: opportunities and anomalies', paper presented at a seminar on 'Privatisation and Commercialisation of Higher Education', organized by the National Institute of Educational Planning and Administration, New Delhi, India, May 2006.
Appadurai, A. (1996), *Modernity at Large: Cultural Dimensions in Globalization*, Minneapolis, MN: University of Minnesota Press.
Appelbaum, R. and R. Parker (2008), 'China's bid to become a global nanotech leader: advancing nanotechnology through state-led programs and international collaboration', *Science and Public Policy*, **35** (5), 319–34.
Arocena, R. and J. Sutz (2000), 'Interactive learning spaces and development policies in Latin America', DRUID Working Chapter No. 00-13, available at www.druid.dk/wp/pdf_files/00-13.pdf accessed 17 August 2010.
Arocena, R. and J. Sutz (2005), 'Latin American universities: from an original revolution to an uncertain transition', *Higher Education*, **50**, 573–92.
Arocena, R. and J. Sutz (2008), 'Uruguay: higher education, national system of innovation and economic development in a small peripheral country', *Uruguay UniDev Discussion Paper Series:* Paper No. 3, available at http://developinguniversities.blogsome.com/, accessed 20 July 2010.
Arrighi, G. (1994), *The Long Twentieth Century*, London: Verso.
Ashton, D. (2004), 'High skills: the concept and its application to South Africa', in S. McGrath, A. Badroodien, A. Kraak and L. Unwin (eds), *Shifting Understandings of Skills in South Africa: Overcoming the Historical Imprint of a Low Skills Regime,* Pretoria: Human Science Research Council Press, pp. 98–115.
Bach, D., A. Newman and S. Weber (2006), 'The international implications of China's fledgling regulatory state: from product maker to rule maker', *New Political Economy*, **11** (4), 499–518.
Brown, P., A. Green and H. Lauder (2001), *High Skills: Globalisation, Competitiveness, and Skill*, Oxford: Oxford University Press.
Brown, P., H. Lauder and D. Ashton (2010), *The Global Auction: The Broken Promises of Education, Jobs and Incomes*, Oxford: Oxford University Press.
Bukharin, N. (1972 [1917]), *Imperialism and World Economy*, London: Merlin Press.
Cabrera, L. (2008), 'Knowledge creation and knowledge creators within the Cuban higher education system', *The International Journal of Cuban Studies*, **1** (1), 1–10.
Callinicos, A. (2009), *Imperialism and Global Political Economy*, Cambridge and Oxford: Polity Press.
Cárdenas, J., D. Gutiérrez and A. González (2008), 'Universal higher education and sustainable social development: the Cuban model', *The International Journal of Cuban Studies*, **1** (1), 1–12.
Castells, M. (2001), 'Information technology and global development', in J. Muller, N. Cloete and S. Badat (eds), *Challenges of Globalisation: South African debates with Manuel Castells*, Cape Town: Maskew Miller/Longman.
Cerni, P. (2006), 'Imperialism in the twenty-first century', *Theory and Science*, available at http://theoryand science, icaap.org/content/vol8.1 /cerni.html, accessed 20 July 2010.

Cerny, P. (1990), *The Changing Architecture of Politics: Structure, Agency and the Future of the State*, London/ Newbury Park, CA/New Delhi: Sage.

Chang, H. (2002), *Kicking Away the Ladder: Development Strategy in Historical Perspective*, London: Anthem Press.

Chang, M. (2001), *Return of the Dragon: China's Wounded Nationalism*, Boulder, CO: Westview Press.

Clark, Wesley (n.d.), 'Higher education in a global era: challenges and prospects', available at http://net.edu- cause.Edu/ir/library/pdf/ff0601S.pdf, accessed 22 July 2010.

Cloete, N., T. Moja, J. Nkata, L. Brito and E. Sutherland Addy (2007), 'Concept document: establishing a higher education expertise network in Africa', available at http://chet.org.za/papers/establish-higher- education-expertise-network-africa-heena-research-teaching-data-and-advocacy, accessed 20 August 2010.

Collins, R. (1998), *The Sociology of Philosophies: A Global Theory of Intellectual Change*, Cambridge, MA: Belknap Press of Harvard.

Connell, R. (2007), *Southern Theory: Social Science and the Global Dynamics of Knowledge*, Cambridge and Oxford: Polity Press.

Copestake, J. (2007), 'Poverty and exclusion, resources and relationships: theorising the link between social and economic development', in I. Gough and J.A. McGregor (eds), *Well-being in Developing Countries: From Theory to Research*, Cambridge: Cambridge University Press, pp. 178–98.

De Cohen, C. (2003), 'Diversification in Argentine higher education: dimensions and impact of private sector growth', *Higher Education*, **46**, 1–35.

Deneulin, S. and L. Shahani (2009), *An Introduction to the Human Development and Capability Approach: Freedom and Agency*, London: Earthscan.

Escobar, A. (1995), *Encountering Development: The Making and the Unmaking of the Third World*, Princeton, NJ: Princeton University Press.

Esping-Andersen, G. (1991), *The Three Worlds of Welfare Capitalism*, Cambridge and Oxford: Polity Press.

Gibbons, M., C. Limoges, H. Newtony, S. Schwartsman, P. Scott and M. Trow (1994), *The New Production of Knowledge: The Dynamics of Science and Research in Contemporary Societies*, Thousand Oaks, CA: Sage Publications.

Gindin, S. (2004), 'Globalization and labor: defining the problem', Speech given at Brandeis University, 24 April 2004.

Gopinathan, S. (1999), 'Preparing for the next rung: economic restructuring and educational reform in Singapore', *Journal of Education and Work*, **12** (3), 295–308.

Green, A. (1997), *Education, Globalisation and the Nation State*, Basingstoke: Palgrave Macmillan.

Guerrero, D. and F. Manji (2008), *China's New Role in Africa and the South: A Search for a New Perspective*, Cape Town, Nairobi and Oxford: Fahamu and Focus on the Global South.

Halachmi, A. and K. Ngok (2009), 'Of sustainability and excellence: Chinese academia at a crossroads', *Public Administration Review*, December, 513–20.

Hardt, M. and T. Negri (2000), *Empire*, Cambridge, MA: Harvard University Press.

Hartmann, E. (2008), 'Bologna goes global: a new imperialism in the making?', *Globalisation, Societies and Education*, **6** (3), 207–20.

Harvey, D. (1989), *The Condition of Postmodernity*, Oxford: Basil Blackwell.

Harvey, D. (2003), *The New Imperialism*, Oxford: Oxford University Press.

Held, D., A. McGrew, D. Goldblatt and J. Perraton (1999), *Global Transformations: Politics, Economics and Culture*, Cambridge and Oxford: Polity Press.

Henderson, J. (2008), *China and the Future of the Developing World: The Coming Global Asian Era and its Consequences*, New York: United Nations University and World Institute for Development Economics.

Hobsbawm, E. (1987), *The Age of Empire: 1875–1914*, London: Weidenfeld and Nicolson.

Holland, D. (2008), 'Discipline in the context of development: a case of the social sciences in Malawi, Southern Africa', *Higher Education*, **55**, 671–81.

Hoogvelt, A. (1997), *Globalization and the Postcolonial World: The New Political Economy of Development*, Basingstoke: Macmillan.

Humphrey, J. and D. Messner (2006), *Unstable Multipolarity? China's and India's Challenges for Global Governance*, Berlin: German Development Institute.

Huntington, S. (1998), *The Clash of Civilizations and the Remaking of World Order*, London: Simon & Schuster.

Jessop, B. (2008), 'The knowledge-based economy', article prepared for Naked Punch, available at eprints, lancs.ac.uk/ 1007/1/ Microsoft_Word_-_I-2008_Naked_Punch.pdf accessed 10 June 2010.

Kamat, S., A. Mir and B. Matthew (2006), 'Producing hi-tech: globalization, the state and migrant subjects', in H. Lauder, P. Brown, J.-A. Dillabough and A. Halsey (eds), *Education, Globalization, and Social Change*, Oxford: Open University Press, pp. 341–54.

Kaplinsky, R. (2006), 'Revisiting the terms of trade revisited: will China make a difference?', *World Development*, **34** (6), 981–95.

Kiely, R. (2006), 'United States hegemony and globalisation: what role for theories of imperialism?', *Cambridge Review of International Affairs*, **19** (2), 205–21.

Kiely, R. (2007), *The New Political Economy of Development: Globalization, Imperialism, Hegemony*, Basingstoke: Palgrave Macmillan.

King, R. (2009a), *Governing Universities Globally: Organizations, Regulation and Rankings*, Cheltenham, UK and Northampton, MA, USA: Edward Elgar.

King, R. (2009b), 'Institutional rankings and regulation: universities and the growth of global private authority', paper presented to the Society for Research in Higher Education South West Region Seminar Series, University of Bath, 13 November 2009.

Knight, J. (2003), 'GATS, trade and higher education: perspective 2003 – where are we?' London: The Observatory on Borderless Higher Education, May, http://200.229.43.1/imaged6/documents/DOC_DSC_NOME_ARQU120060214115610, accessed 15 August 2010.

Knight, J. (2010), 'Regional education hubs: rhetoric or reality?', *International Higher Education*, **59**, Spring, 20–21.

Kraak, A. (2004), 'The national skills development strategy: a new institutional regime for skills formation in post-apartheid South Africa', in S. McGrath, A, Badroodien, A. Kraak and L. Unwin (eds), *Shifting Understandings of Skills in South Africa: Overcoming the Historical Imprint of a Low Skills Regime*, Pretoria: Human Science Research Council Press, pp. 116–39.

Levy, D. (2003), *Expanding Higher Education Capacity through Private Growth*, London: The Observatory on Borderless Higher Education Report, January.

Lundvall, B.-Å. (2007), 'Higher education, innovation and economic development', paper presented at the World Bank's Regional Bank Conference on Development Economics, Beijing, 16–17 January.

Marginson, S. (2009), 'University rankings and the knowledge economy', in M. Peters, S. Marginson and P. Murphy, *Creativity and the Global Knowledge Economy*, New York: Peter Lang, pp. 185–216.

Marginson, S. (2010a), 'Making space in higher education', in S. Marginson, P. Murphy and M. Peters, *Global Creation: Space, Mobility and Synchrony in the Age of the Knowledge Economy*, New York: Peter Lang, pp. 150–200.

Marginson, S. (2010b), 'World', in P. Murphy, M. Peters and S. Marginson, *Imagination: Three Models of Imagination in the Age of the Knowledge Economy*, New York: Peter Lang, pp. 139–65.

McCowan, T. (2004), 'The growth of private higher education in Brazil: implications for equity and quality', *Journal of Education Policy*, **19** (4), 453–72.

Middleton, C. (2000), 'Models of state and market in the modernisation of higher education', *British Journal of Sociology of Education*, **21** (4), 537–54.

Min, W. (2004), 'Address regarding first-class universities', *Chinese Education and Society*, **37**, 8–20.

Mok, K.-H. (2005), 'Globalization and educational restructuring: university merging and changing governance in China', *Higher Education*, **50**, 57–88.

Moore, R. and J. Muller (1999), 'The discourse of "voice" and the problem of knowledge and Identity in the sociology of education', *British Journal of Sociology of Education*, **20** (2), 189–206.

Muller, J. (2000), *Reclaiming Knowledge: Social Theory, Curriculum, and Education Policy*, London: RoutledgeFalmer.

NAFSA (2003), *Securing America's Future: Global Education for a Global Age. Report of the Strategic Task Force on Education Abroad*, available at http://www.nafsa.org/ uploadedFiles/NAFSA_Home /Resource_Library_Assets/Public_Policy/securing_america_s_future.pdf?n=3894, accessed 15 August 2010.

Naidoo, R. (2000), 'The third way to widening participation and maintaining quality in higher education: lessons from the United Kingdom', *Journal of Educational Enquiry*, **1** (2), 24–38.

Naidoo, R. (2008), *The Competitive State and the Mobilised Market: Higher Education Policy Reform in the United Kingdom (1980–2007)*, Paris: Critique Internationale/Presses de Sciences Po.

Naidoo, R. (2010), 'Global learning in a neo-liberal age', in E. Unterhalter and V. Carpentier (eds), *Whose Interests Are We Serving?: Global Inequalities and Higher Education*, Basingstoke: Palgrave Macmillan, pp. 66–90.

Noble, D. (2002), 'Rehearsal for the revolution', in K. Robins and F. Webster (eds), *The Virtual University*, Oxford: Oxford University Press, pp. 282–300.

Nussbaum, M. (2007), 'Education for global citizenship: the importance of the humanities', paper at a 'Conference on the Future of the Humanities', Center for Philosophical Studies, Pontifical Catholic University of Peru, Lima, 27–9 August.

Ramo, J. (2004), *The Beijing Consensus*, London: Foreign Policy Centre.

Robertson, S. (2008), *Europe/Asia Regionalism, Higher Education and the Production of World Order*, Bristol: Centre for Globalisation, Education and Societies, University of Bristol.

Robertson, S. (2009), 'The EU, "regulatory state regionalism" and new modes of higher education governance', paper for the panel on 'Constituting the Knowledge Economy: Governing the New Regional Spaces of Higher Education', International Studies Association Conference, New York.

Sabina, E.M. (2003), 'Higher education in Cuba in the 2000s: past and future', paper presented at the 'Comparative and International Education Society Conference', New Orleans, USA, 12–16 March, available at http://www.eric.ed.gov/PDFS/ED482068.pdf, accessed 20 June 2010.

Saïd, E. (1993), *Culture and Imperialism*, London: Chatto and Windus.

Sanderson, G. (2002), 'International education developments in Singapore', *International Education Journal*, **3** (2), 85–103.

Sawahel, W. (2009), 'China–Africa: three year partnership plan announced', *University World News Africa*, Edition 29, 42, November.

Slaughter, S. and G. Rhoades (2004), *Academic Capitalism and the New Economy: Markets, State and Higher Education*, Baltimore, MD: Johns Hopkins University Press.

Strauss, J. and M. Saavedra (eds) (2010), *China and Africa: Volume 9: Emerging Patterns in Globalization and Development*, Cambridge: Cambridge University Press.

Subotzky, G. (1999), 'Alternatives to the entrepreneurial university: new modes of knowledge production in community service programs', *Higher Education*, **38** (4), 401–40.

Tannock, S. (2007), 'To keep America number 1: confronting the deep nationalism of US higher education', *Globalisation, Societies and Education*, **5** (2), 257–72.

Task Force on Higher Education in Developing Countries (convened by UNESCO and the World Bank) (2000), *Higher Education in Developing Countries: Peril and Promise*, available at http:///www. tfhe.net/report/overview.htm accessed 20 June 2010.

Teixeira, P. and A. Amaral (2001), 'Private higher education and diversity: an exploratory survey', *Higher Education Quarterly*, **55** (4), 359–95.

Tikly, L. (2004), 'Education and new imperialism', *Comparative Education*, **40** (2), 173–98.

Vidovich, L., R. Yang and J. Currie (2007), 'Changing accountabilities in higher education as China "opens up" to globalisation', *Globalisation, Societies and Education*, **5** (1), 89–107.

Vincent-Lancrin, S. (2005), *Building Capacity through Cross-border Tertiary Education*, London: Observatory on Borderless Higher Education, April.

Wallerstein, I. (1991), *Geopolitics and Geoculture: Essays on the Changing World-system*, Cambridge: Cambridge University Press.

Wang, H. and J. Rosenau (2009), 'China and global governance', *Asian Perspective*, **3** (3), 5–39.

Wells, M. (1993), *The Export of Education: Exploitation or Technology Transfer?*, Sydney: Research Institute for Asia and the Pacific, University of Sydney.

Went, R. (2002), 'Globalization in the perspective of imperialism', *Science and Society*, **66** (4), 473–97.

Wildavsky, B. (2010), *The Great Brain Race: How Global Universities are Reshaping the World*, Princeton, NJ: Princeton University Press.

Willensky, J. (1998), *Learning to Divide the World: Education at Empire's End*, Minneapolis, MN and London: University of Minnesota Press.

Winters, L. and S. Yusuf (eds) (2007), *Dancing with Giants: China, India and the Global Economy*, Washington, DC: World Bank and Singapore: Institute of Policy Studies.

Wood, G. and I. Gough (2006), 'A comparative welfare regime approach to global social policy', *World Development*, **24** (10), 1696–1712.

Xiaoming, Z. and X. Haitao (2000), 'Internationalisation: a challenge for China's higher education', in *Current Issues in Chinese Higher Education*, Paris: OECD, pp. 101–13.

Young, M. (2007), *Bringing Knowledge Back In: From Social Constructivism to Social Realism in the Sociology of Education*, London: Routledge.

Zhong, Y. (n.d.), *Globalization and Higher Education Reform in China*, available at http://www.aare.edu.au/05pap/zho05780.pdf, accessed 22 June 2010.

4 The university as a global institution
Peter Scott

INTRODUCTION

The university is generally regarded as an international, if not global, institution – in terms both of its historical development and of its future trajectory. This supposedly fundamental characteristic is accepted as a 'given', too easily perhaps because it tends to emphasize one element in the formation of the modern university (the international, or global) at the expense of other, arguably more significant, elements (the local and the national); and also because it may also place too much emphasis on a single strand, however important, in its future direction, leading to the adoption of a single-path model of development.

The purpose of this chapter is not to debunk but to problematize this idea that the university is (or should be) first and foremost a global institution. The intention is to lead to a more rounded and more nuanced account of the university's global role.

Both aspects of the claim – the historical and the developmental – require careful investigation. The historical development of the university is a complex phenomenon. It is true that the first universities emerged in a recognizable form in the Middle Ages before nation-states had properly formed, although it may be significant that two of the earliest examples, Paris and Oxford, were established and flourished in France and England, which were perhaps the most advanced territories in terms of state formation (and went on to become the two most developed nation-states in Europe in later centuries). But, rather than regarding the medieval university as an international institution, it is perhaps better described as a pre-national institution. Even then it was clear that national institutions, most obviously strong monarchies, were waxing while universal institutions, such as the Catholic Church, were waning; the victors in this long revolution in government were already plain. The medieval university belonged in both worlds, as an expression of universalism in its structures (e.g. the mobility of scholars and students and the organization of its curriculum) but also as an agent of state formation (because these university-trained scholars staffed the emerging national, or royal, bureaucracies) (Pedersen, 1997; de Ridder-Symoens, 2003).

In the early modern period and the ages of political and industrial revolutions the national orientation of the university became even more pronounced. The establishment of universities was indeed often a key element within state formation, certainly in terms of the consolidation of bureaucratic structures but also in the development of national consciousness (and of elite solidarities). Scotland is perhaps a good example: although the Scottish state had been forged in wars with England in the Middle Ages, the establishment of its four ancient universities in the fifteenth and sixteenth centuries powerfully helped to articulate the idea of Scottish nation. There are many other examples elsewhere in Europe. This practice continued into the nineteenth and twentieth centuries, especially in colonial regimes and their successor independent states, and also in the settler societies of the New World (and Australasia). Until late in the nineteenth century the link between universities and state formation was explicit; the most celebrated example remains the establishment of the University of Berlin in 1810 as part of the engineered revival of the Prussian state following the disastrous defeat at the battle of Jena at the hands of Napoleon. The one interesting counter-example is provided by France itself, where the universities, already in decline on the eve of the Revolution, were deliberately left for much of the nineteenth century to atrophy as loose collections of faculties while republican elites gravitated to the *grandes écoles.*

Only in the final decades of the nineteenth century and into the twentieth century did the universities, most decisively in the recently united Germany, begin to engage more directly with the emerging industrial society, with its insatiable demand for scientific, technical and professional expertise – and, in many countries, only reluctantly. In much of Europe non-university institutions, less exclusive higher vocational schools as well as the elite *grandes écoles*, continued to be more open to such engagement. In the USA the establishment following 1864 of the land-grant universities, which in the following century became the powerhouses of the USA's world-class research university and mass higher education system, marked a significant shift towards social and economic engagement on a wider plane – although the 'college' with its more intimate and more elite values remained a prominent feature of US higher education. In one sense this engagement could be said to represent a shift beyond the national, because science (almost entirely) and technology (predominantly) were universal domains and because social trends and market economies transcended national frontiers. But in another sense this engagement was – and is – still very much channelled through national priorities as economic competition has succeeded earlier forms of struggle between states.

In the course of the twentieth century almost everywhere the scope of universities was enlarged to form the leading elements in more extensive higher education systems. As such they became more closely embroiled in movements of social reform and in processes of democratization. Again the archetype is the US system, which from the 1950s onwards took on many of the characteristics of a social movement – within which, however, the drive towards scientific and scholarly excellence, and the wider development of a research culture, sat comfortably (Kerr, 1963). Most other higher education systems have followed a similar trajectory, as closer articulations have been established between the development of universities, the evolution of broader policies for the whole of education, and the wider (and deeper) social changes. Some of these changes have been nationally determined, often steered by the ambitious social policies of assertive welfare states (in many European countries it was not unreasonable to regard the university as a 'welfare state' institution, albeit with rather archaic and rigid characteristics); others have links to more fundamental cultural shifts, such as changing attitudes to the status of women, which were common to many countries (although not perhaps sufficiently pervasive to be categorized as global). It remains, therefore, a matter for debate whether the contemporary university is a less national institution than its nineteenth- and twentieth-century, early modern or medieval, predecessors.

The second aspect of the claim that the university is a global institution – the developmental – demands equally careful investigation. The conventional argument is that the future of the university is inexorably bound up with the development of a global 'knowledge' economy, or, for those who prefer a wider – and more humane

– representation, the emergence of a world society in which national particularities are increasingly subsumed within a multicultural future. However, the apparent interchangeability of terms such as 'international', 'global' and 'world' presents an immediate difficulty. The contrast between internationalization and globalization is already well appreciated. The former describes a process of intensifying exchange between nations (or other, securely institutionalized organizations and agencies), most of which occurs within the public domain. The latter describes rather different processes, the progressive integration of economic structures within global (but also volatile) arrangements and the homogenization (but also hybridization) of distinctive national cultures, both of which occur largely in the private domain (in a double sense, the market economy and individual responses). Seen in this light, many of the non-national activities of universities appear more international than global.

But in recent years the concept of globalization has itself fragmented. Although a particular form of globalization, neoliberal in economic terms and hegemonic in geopolitical and cultural terms, remains dominant, it has been challenged by rival and antagonistic forms as the twenty-first century has unfolded. The most virulent is fundamentalism, usually associated with more extreme strands within Islam (unfairly so, because equally virulent forms of fundamentalism can be observed within the heartlands of the Judaeo-Christian 'west'), which is expressed through a backlash against supposedly 'universal' social and cultural norms derived from the Enlightenment, or even through terrorist acts. However, a more pervasive alternative form of globalization is represented by the rise of new social movements, of which the best examples are the various movements to sustain the environment. This alternative form of globalization has emerged from within the Enlightenment tradition; indeed the commitment to scientific rationality is arguably a more powerful strand within these movements than within the dominant neoliberal free market form. This alternative form also reignites some of the social altruism and cultural idealism characteristic of more traditional twentieth-century social movements denominated in terms of class struggle.

If globalization is an appropriate term to describe the international activities of universities, it is clear that it cannot be easily aligned with just one form of globalization, the dominant neoliberal form; rather the international activities of universities touch all forms – for example, fundamentalism through the academic appreciation, and also practical application, of cultural 'difference'; or the new social and environmental movements through the diversity of its research practice (in particular, its generation of rival experts) and also through the alignment of academic and social values.

These preliminary remarks already indicate the complexities of the categorization of the university as a global institution. Its historical development displays the tensions, but also the synergies, between its many roles, national, international (and global?). It also demonstrates that simple and exclusive contrasts between the national and the universal, or global, are not convincing: nation-building, to which universities often decisively contributed, often contained within it universal claims (France and the USA are the most obvious examples, but even England's more pragmatic values are not without aspiration to much wider applicability). As a result, for much of its history, the university could justly claim both to be serving national needs and transcending purely national frames of reference – without contradiction. The future trajectory of universities is marked by the similar complexities, by the same confusion (or elision) between the national and the universal, but also by the rivalry between different forms of globalization to all of which the university makes important contributions and by which it is powerfully influenced – although maybe not without contradiction.

The rest of this chapter will pick up and further explore these themes – first, the degree to which the core values of the university can be said to reflect global norms rather than simply national frameworks; next, the various strands within the discourse of globalization, in terms of concepts and of policy; third, and more concretely, the extent to which the global dimensions of the university can be identified in terms of shared scientific and intellectual norms and communities (to reflect the university's all-important research mission – or, more broadly, its status as a knowledge organization); and finally, more concretely still, the realization of the university's global ambitions through staff exchanges, research collaboration and cross-border flows of students.

CORE VALUES IN THE CONTEXT OF GLOBALIZATION

The university has passed through various stages in the course of its evolution and its core values, and principal functions have undergone significant shifts as a result. To simplify what is a complicated story three broad historical types of university, and their values and functions, will be discussed here: the classical university that flourished in the nineteenth century; the modern (or, better, mass) university that developed in the course of the twentieth century and reached its apogee between the 1960s and the 1980s (Scott, 1995); and the entrepreneurial university that is emerging the early years of the twenty-first century (Clark, 2001). Earlier types of university in its long historical evolution – the scholastic university of the Middle Ages and the dynastic and confessional universities that prevailed during the sixteenth and seventeenth centuries, only to crumble before the advance of the scientific revolution, the culture of the Enlightenment, and revolutionary politics – are important in understanding the evolution of these later types. But they are not considered here because they are perhaps too remote from the subject of this chapter, the university as a global institution.

It is important to recognize that these are ideal types – and also composites. The modern/mass university incorporated many of the features of the classical university, and the entrepreneurial university has incorporated elements from both its predecessors. As a result there has been an accumulation of values, in ways that tend to undermine a clear distinction between core or fundamental values and other values apparently more contingent and supposedly more peripheral.

Alongside this confusion of values an increasing complexity of function can be observed. However, the most striking differences are ones of scale. The total number of students, the number of universities, and their size have increased exponentially. The demographic of the university has been transformed – from catering for small and stable elites, through more dynamic and extended elites to mass student populations (or from aristocracy through meritocracy to democracy, to apply a metaphor derived from politics). For all its assumed antiquity, the university is also a novel institution. The majority of universities, even those that have adopted a classical form, are recent creations; more than one-third of Europe's universities have been established since 1945 and three-quarters since 1900. But the changes in organizational scale, and character, are perhaps the most dramatic of all. The largest universities today enrol as many students as whole national systems did less than a century ago. It is this quantitative growth that has driven qualitative change, including shifts in core values and extensions of function – including the university's international character and global engagement.

It is hardly surprising that the internationalism of the university has undergone significant modifications over the last two centuries. As has already been argued, the classical university was a strongly national institution, despite the discourses and forms inherited from earlier phases of university history when national identifications were more fluid and conditional (although it is important to recognize that the 'universalism' of the medieval and pre-modern university had strict geographical limits, being confined largely to Europe, with little engagement with institutions of higher learning in India, China or – after the fourteenth century – the Arab world). Although the classical university was largely a product of nineteenth-century nationalism (and an agent, and beneficiary, of state-building), it became a global institution at the same time – and as part of the same dynamic. Indeed the national and the global were linked by the 'expansion' of Europe to other continents through the establishment of settler states and of colonial empires.

However uncomfortable such a conclusion may be, the initial expression of the contemporary university's global role of the contemporary university was through imperialism. Even today the patterns established by empire still influence the flows of staff and students, as the links between anglophone and francophone countries demonstrate. In the twenty-first century the dynamic between metropolitan centres (London and Paris) and cultural peripheries echo older imperial subordinations. Even when the influence of metropolitan centres has been weakened, linguistic solidarities still shape the organization of universities into international blocs – most notably in Latin America, whether positive (in the form of the Spanish or Portuguese language they share) or negative (in suspicions of anglophone advance).

The modern, or mass, university inherited many of these patterns of internationalization. Indeed, the dismantling of colonial empires intensified these patterns as the links between higher education and state-building that had been so pronounced in nineteenth-century Europe were reproduced in newly independent states in Africa and Asia in the second half of the twentieth century. The need to expand local elites, and to train technical experts, was much greater than during the colonial period – and, by definition, could not be satisfied with local resources. It was no accident that decolonialization was followed by large increases in the number of students being educated in the universities of the former colonial powers. The closer identification of mass higher education systems with social justice and democratic entitlement at home reduced the dissonance of this continuing, and even increasing, dependence. International students from former colonies and home students from less privileged social backgrounds could be said to have much in common, in particular the same focus on emancipation. In this sense the core values of mass higher education underpinned its drive towards even greater internationalism.

A second element that shaped the international character of the mass university was the Cold War, which had a similar effect. The expansion of higher education, notably in the USA but also in Western Europe, and the persistence of the Cold War were closely linked – from the imperatives in weapons research, a key trigger for the much wider explosion of university research after 1945, to the promise of democracy, because widening participation could be seen as a powerful assertion of human rights and individual liberties in the face of totalitarianism. Revealingly, the mass university and widening participation were much less pervasive phenomena in the former Soviet Union, Central and Eastern Europe, and China (Scott, 2000). Cold War rivalry shaped the characteristics of international higher education in the second half of the twentieth century. Ideological struggle was a decisive element, not only in the indirect sense that the recruitment of international students was a competitive game as the USA in particular and the former Soviet Union sought to co-opt national elites, but also directly because the development of mass higher education in the west was a social project, designed to demonstrate the compatibility of collective social reform with individual self-realization (and, therefore, the west's moral as well as material superiority).

The internationalism of the entrepreneurial university, the third ideal type, has incorporated a new twist. The increasing emphasis on higher education as individual (and national) investment, and on universities as quasi-commercial organizations within a global knowledge economy, has highlighted the importance of international activities. The knowledge 'industry' is regarded as global business, as potentially global as financial services. One effect has been to remove the inhibitions once created by the alleged 'exploitation' of international students when, as in the UK, they are charged much higher fees than home students. Because higher education is seen as a 'market' game rather than as a social project (as was in the case of the era of the mass university), universities no longer have to apologize for treating international students as 'customers' who represent a significant 'income stream'; indeed they are now urged to regard all students in a similar light. Another effect is that the recruitment of international students, whether by individual universities or by countries, can now be justified as a simple quest for 'market share' rather than within a complex web of concerns about capacity-building on the one hand and cultural hegemony (and political and commercial advantage) on the other; to the extent that these other considerations are still current, it is as rhetorical justifications akin to public relations. A third effect is that research collaboration between universities in different countries is no longer justified so much in terms of the shared values, and endeavours, of scientific communities 'without frontiers' but more in terms of innovation strategies, national R&D, and wealth generation (and, more occasionally, social improvement).

The core values exhibited by these three ideal types of university – the classical university that emerged in the nineteenth century; the modern (or mass) university that succeeded it in the second half of the twentieth century; and the entrepreneurial university that is now struggling to become the dominant form in the early years of the twenty-first century – have had important implications for how universities have regarded themselves as global institutions. In the first period the emphasis on state-building and international rivalry encouraged universities to align themselves with colonial and imperial ambitions, by no means always with negative effects because the development of higher education in large parts of Africa and Asia was initiated as an imperial project. Many of the basic patterns of recruitment of students, researchers and staff still conform to these imperial connections three or four generations after the dismantling of the old colonial empires. In the second period the development of mass higher education systems with their overtly social objectives was an important weapon in the ideological struggles of the Cold War. Competition among the principal combatants for global influence focuses attention on international higher education with a new intensity, stimulating its development. As a result, the university became an even more global institution. In the final, and present, period the growth of the entrepreneurial university has offered new justifications for the development of international education, not always welcome but often dynamic in their effects. International higher education has been incorporated, conceptually at any rate, within a much wider global knowledge 'industry'.

However, it is important to avoid any impression of teleological analysis. One type of university has not displaced another within an inevitable sequence leading to the triumph of the entrepreneurial university. Instead each type has added new layers of complexity as older values and practices have been modified, sometimes complemented, and at other times compromised, by new ones. In very many ways the entrepreneurial university has incorporated most of the features of the modern (or mass) university, just as the modern university in its time took over many of the characteristics of the classical university. Continuities are important. To take one example, the role of the classical university in state-building during the nineteenth century has been continued into the twenty-first century in Europe, as universities work through the Bologna Process to establish the European Higher Education Area (EHEA) – but at the same time the establishment of the EHEA is also an attempt to improve the competitiveness of Europe's universities and so is a manifestation of the entrepreneurial university (Waechter, 2004).

THEORIES AND DISCOURSES OF GLOBALIZATION

In considering the status of the university as a global institution it is necessary not simply to discuss the degree to which the core values of the university (in its successive historical phases) engage with international (or global) themes, but also to examine how the university – and, more broadly, higher education and research systems – is positioned within theories of globalization (and the policy discourses that flow from these theories). In other words the question needs to be considered from the 'outside' as well as the 'inside'. Globalization theory has become a luxuriant academic field in the past two decades (Friedman, 2002). It has sought to explain, and integrate, a range of developments, such as the growth of global economic structures that transcend (and dissolve?) national frontiers, the end of the Cold War with its bipolar geopolitical formation (and the apparent 'triumph' of democratic capitalism), the acceleration of science, technology and all kinds of expert systems (especially in information and communication technologies), and the gathering strength and also hybridization of world cultures that has given new force to notions of 'difference'. But two global phenomena in particular have influenced the role, and perceptions, of the university. The first is the emergence of a knowledge economy and information society. The second is the emerging dialectic between mass-media-engineered world cultures and cultures of 'difference' (even resistance).

The emergence of a knowledge economy and information society has been a complex phenomenon. One dimension, of course, has been the development of economic forms in which 'knowledge' itself has become a primary resource. This idea goes back to at least the 1970s and was first expounded by Daniel Bell and others in their work on 'post-industrial society' (Bell, 1973). At that time the emphasis was more on transition, from industrial societies based on manufacturing output to post-industrial societies based on services – in one sense a commonplace analysis. By the last decade of the twentieth century the focus had shifted to more febrile services, especially in the financial sector but also in the media and creative industries; and the label 'post-industrial' had fallen into disuse, switching the emphasis from linear and orderly development to non-linear and potentially more disruptive novelty with an increasing emphasis on risk (Beck, 1992).

A second dimension has been the emergence so-called 'techno-society' in which individuals, institutions and indeed whole communities have become increasingly dependent on expert systems, developed through scientific research and technological application. But, once again, what was perceived to be a generation ago a comparatively benign and progressive phenomenon is now sometimes regarded in more apocalyptic terms. A third dimension is the development of new cultural forms as time and space have been reconfigured, or, the more adventurous would argue, 'abolished' (Urry, 1998; Nowotny, 1994). The idea of an information society has come to emphasize the substitution of traditional forms of communication such as books, newspapers, and network radio and television by novel forms based on increasingly powerful, and both intrusive and individualizing, new technologies – especially information and communication technologies, and the now ubiquitous 'social networking'.

Two issues are worth exploring. The first is the assumption, too easily made, perhaps, that the knowledge economy and information society are a global phenomenon. 'Knowledge', whether defined in terms of science and its dependent technologies or of mass-media culture, is typically regarded as a global product. But interesting counter-currents can be observed. The ugly word 'glocalization' suggests that knowledge is often the product of complex negotiation between global 'theory' and local 'practice'; the more emphasis is placed on 'knowledge' as the driving force within contemporary societies, the more multidimensional and reflexive, even problematical, becomes its constitution (Robertson, 1995). Indeed the pervasiveness of 'knowledge' makes it more likely that expert technologies are increasingly distanced from their normative roots in science (ends, if you like) and become technical artefacts (means).

The second issue is the implications for the mission of the university. Even if the knowledge economy and information society are defined as essentially global phenomena, their complexity undermines the very idea of single-path development. While universities must clearly produce global experts and act as conduits through which global science flows to national, regional and local environments, universities must also create a curriculum that enables the mass of its students to cope with the, perhaps forbidding, phenomena of techno-society and mass-media culture – whether as citizens or as consumers.

These dilemmas become more acute if the second phenomenon is considered, the dialogue (or dialectic) between mass-media-engineered world cultures and potentially antagonistic cultures of 'difference'. As with theories of post-industrialism, the emphasis was once predominantly on transition, because the adoption of significant elements of 'western' culture was regarded as an inescapable component of modernization. Perhaps arrogantly, the superiority of the culture rooted in the values of the scientific revolution, of the Enlightenment, and of social and political reform (and, occasionally, revolution) was regarded as superior – or, at any rate, as easily combined with more traditional cultures. This symbiosis had been successful in Europe and North America – why not elsewhere? Over the past two decades theories of hybridization became more popular.

So-called 'creole' cultures were no longer simply regarded as primitive and distorted responses to modernization, but as more complex adaptations; at a higher level it was increasingly recognized that, in literature for example, both creativity and sophistication were as likely to be found in once peripheral communities as in metropolitan centres. Now there has been a further shift. Science, Enlightenment and reform appear to have been taken over by a manipulative mass-media culture that is now an integral part of a late-capitalist political economy. As a result, concepts of 'tradition', largely passive or at any rate defensive, have been superseded by more active (and even aggressive) ideas of 'difference' – and even resistance.

Mass higher education systems are delicately poised. As higher education systems they are deeply implicated in processes of modernization and as research systems they are potent transmitters of scientific culture; but as mass systems they are also more deeply embedded in their societies. In other words the development of globalization has posed new dilemmas for the university. In one sense these dilemmas can be overcome. Intellectual criticality and scientific methods can be applied to a wide range of concepts and contents. The proliferation of 'experts' on environmental questions, with their competing conclusions, is a demonstration of the strength of scientific culture, not of its weakness. But, in another sense, these dilemmas are more difficult to resolve. At times the university may appear to be 'taking sides', especially between the values and practices of techno-science and the cultural resistances provoked by its advance. So globalization theory demonstrates the complexity, and ambiguities, of the university's position. However, more populist discourses of globalization too often lack the sophistication of the theory from which they are derived – and point instead to simplistic policy prescriptions, neoliberal and technocratic, that compound the university's difficulties.

SCIENTIFIC CULTURES AND ACADEMIC COMMUNITIES

The university's strongest claim to be regarded as a global institution is often supposed to be its allegiance to a shared – and, therefore, arguably 'global' – scientific culture. Even if mass higher education systems are rooted in national, even local and regional, environments with respect to teaching, in the context of research they operate on a more elevated, and global, plane. The evidence of global university rankings, of international journals, of research communities that transcend national frontiers appears to support this view. Revealingly, in successive Research Assessment Exercises (RAEs) in the UK the highest grade of research performance has always been denominated in terms of 'international' standing and competitiveness, literally so in some fields (most of the natural sciences) and notionally so in fields where the actual degree of international correspondence has been less easy to demonstrate (typically the humanities) (Barker, 2007).

However, this supposed proof has to be carefully interrogated. The first, and most obvious, qualification is that the production of 'global' science is confined to particular regions of the world – most especially the USA but also Europe (mainly Western Europe since the collapse of Soviet science), Canada, Australia and, increasingly, South and East Asia. Africa, the Middle East and Latin America make only modest contributions. So, although universal in its claims (and quality), it is markedly regional in its actual distribution. 'World-class' perhaps, but hardly global.

To a large extent this distribution may be explained in terms of resources and relative rates of development. But it is difficult to exclude entirely more social and cultural explanations that are interwoven with resource levels, as both causes and effects – and that, in turn, may compromise the universal, or global, claims of science. It is possible to argue, without abandoning the field to either relativism or social constructivism, that the institutional frameworks within which so-called 'world-class' science is produced, and its intellectual values and social practices, reflect the national and cultural environments in which it has developed over the past two centuries, and that this may partly explain the apparent constraints on its reproducibility. In other words, it is about more than resources. Certainly this would mirror the long-running debate about the necessary links between modernity and modernization referred to in the previous section of this chapter.

A second qualification is that paradoxically the emergence of a global 'knowledge economy', certainly in its current neoliberal late-capitalist mode, may itself have compromised the present constitution of 'world-class' science – in other words, its self-organization into global research communities motivated by scientific curiosity rather than competitive advantage, except in the competition for esteem and reputation. Certainly one effect of the global 'knowledge economy' has been to promote the idea that science must be subordinated to innovation in order to maintain national competitiveness (Hicks and Katz, 2002). In many countries curiosity-driven research has been subordinated first to wider institutional strategies (designed to strengthen research performance, as measured by nationally determined assessment tools, and so to maximize institutional resources), which themselves have been increasingly steered by – or even incorporated into – wider research and development strategies, and most recently still, wider innovation strategies. Of course, this has been a complex and reflexive process, which has always relied heavily on grass-roots scientific creativity and, as a result, may often have reinforced rather than weakened the scientific base. Certainly it cannot be crudely described as a shift in emphasis from 'basic' to 'applied' science. Perhaps it is better described as one version of universal (or global) science, in essence 'owned' by scientists themselves organized in their own borderless and 'virtual' communities, being replaced, or complemented, by another version of global (rather than universal) science, with multiple stakeholders and focused more clearly on outcomes of identifiable commercial or social benefit.

This shift is perhaps neatly summed up in the UK in the change from 'esteem', which was measured within successive Research Assessment Exercises (RAEs), to 'impact', which will be measured in the forthcoming Research Excellence Framework (REF).

There is a third reason why the international scope and standing of (most) research supports the claim of the university to be regarded as a global institution. This is the growing belief that traditional models of research production are no longer appropriate in the context of the increasingly heterogeneous, more open, and more distributed knowledge systems that now characterize advanced societies. In these traditional models the primacy of basic science is asserted and, therefore, the hegemony of self-organizing scientific communities is seen as a fundamental principle, while other forms of knowledge production are regarded as secondary (and sequential). However, these models have come under sustained challenge – for two main reasons.

First, there has been an 'external' challenge. As has already been pointed out, institutional research strategies (and wider R&D and innovation strategies) have come to qualify the intellectual norms and social practices of discipline-based research communities as the source of authoritative advice, and decisions, about scientific priorities. The emergence of research systems, often with explicit performance measures and targets, is itself a threat to the self-organization of science.

Second, there has been an 'internal' challenge. More open and reflexive models of knowledge production have complemented, and partly replaced, traditional models of scientific research. These new models have been articulated in a number of different ways. One example has been an emphasis on what has been called 'Mode 2' knowledge production. This new mode of knowledge production, while not replacing traditional models (labelled 'Mode 1'), has a number of new characteristics – its wider social distribution, its proliferation of research actors, the growth of new and novel sites of knowledge production, the increasing reflexivity between its various components, radical forms of interdisciplinary (even anti-disciplinary?) enquiry (Gibbons et al., 1994; Nowotny et al., 2001). Another example is the so-called 'triple helix' of the university, government and industry (Etzkowitz and Leydesdorff, 1997; Etzkowitz, 2008).

These new formulations have themselves been challenged. Traditional critics have argued that they potentially undermine the integrity, independence and quality of research – if not in their argument at any rate in their likely application (Ziman, 2000). More radical critics have argued that these formulations are too timid and their authors are reluctant to push them to their logical conclusions, perhaps for fear of being labelled relativists and/or social constructivists. For example, in a recent article the case for articulating ideas of 'Mode 3' knowledge production and of a 'quadruple helix' was strongly argued, developing both ideas to give greater weight to sociocultural dimensions (Carayannis and Campbell, 2009).

However, the relevant consideration for the purposes of this chapter is whether these new models of knowledge production, including university-based research, strengthen or weaken the university's claim to be regarded as a global institution. In one sense the greater emphasis on various forms of contextualization of research, whether in terms of society or of the market, may appear to weaken older, and more idealistic, notions of universally applicable knowledge. To that extent the university as a global institution is diminished. But, in another sense, these new linkages themselves are often to global agendas – for example, the prevention of disease or the protection of the environment. In other words the contextualization of research operates at all levels – local, regional, national, international and global. It is perhaps a mistake to argue that universities that are deeply embedded in socially distributed knowledge systems are more 'local' and inherently less global in their orientation – as it may be a mistake to argue that universities that continue to pursue more traditional forms of research practice are inherently more 'global'.

The fourth reason for believing that the university's research mission does not – automatically – support the claim that the university is naturally a global institution is that such an association is more difficult to make in the case of the humanities and many of the social sciences. The criteria for research assessment in the UK have been careful to distinguish between research of 'international standing' and internationally focused research (which, of course, may be of lower quality). The core humanities disciplines such as history and literature are inevitably deeply embedded in different national cultures in their choice of topics and methods, and in their underlying values. In the case of the social sciences the prevalence of national labels – the 'Austrian School' in economics, the 'French School' in philosophy – indicates that national provenance remains significant even when the ideas themselves transcend national frontiers. Categorization of disciplines reflects national preferences that can be explained not simply in terms of the contingencies of their particular development but also in terms of more profound currents of intellectual history. For example, in France, history is typically regarded as the queen of the social sciences, despite the significance of cultural history in the French historiographical tradition, while in England, despite the importance of social and economic history, history has remained a predominantly political and literary pursuit. As a result, although separated by only a narrow sea, France and England regard history and the social sciences differently. Indeed the vitality and creativity of the humanities are rooted in notions of 'difference' – temporal, geographical and cultural.

The status of the university as a global institution, therefore, cannot be derived from its research mission without significant reservations and qualifications. Both the inner lives of particular disciplines, especially but not exclusively the humanities, and the political dynamics of modern research systems, which are often closely linked to national innovation agendas, tend to undermine the claim that research can simply be regarded as a global enterprise. But it may be misleading to suggest that the entrepreneurial university of the twenty-first century therefore has less intense global engagements. In fact the reverse could be true. The reason for this apparent inconsistency may be that globalization itself is not one phenomenon but many – some, as has already been discussed, antagonistic to each other. Globalization is also highly fluid, having an impact at multiple levels. For example, Richard Florida's 'clever cities' are both local environments, physical spaces in which researchers, developers, entrepreneurs, critics and artists meet and interact, and also the cutting edge of global change (Florida, 2005). The safest conclusion perhaps is that the university's engagement with research, and its stake in global science, provides complex evidence of the heterogeneity of globalization rather than simple confirmation of its status as a global institution.

THE INTERNATIONALIZATION OF HIGHER EDUCATION

Whatever the status of the university as a global institution, international education is an increasingly significant activity in (most) modern higher education systems. It is significant in a number of different senses: quantitatively, because international flows of students (and staff) have increased, are increasing, and are expected to continue to increase; financially, because the recruitment of international students represents an important income stream for universities in those countries, including the UK, that charge tuition fees (and usually higher fees for international than home students); organizationally, because new cross-border institutional arrangements are being developed (e.g. joint courses and other forms of shared educational provision) and in-country campuses established, although only 7000 of the 197000 students following courses leading to UK qualifications were enrolled on such campuses in 2007–08 (HESA, 2009); and academically, because new initiatives are being taken to internationalize the curriculum, new research partnerships are being forged and, especially at the doctoral and postdoctoral level, scientific talent is being imported to sustain higher education and research systems.

The growth of international education has been a remarkable phenomenon, at any rate as measured by the number of international students. Precise data are not always easy to obtain because definitions of international students are not consistent. In some countries, such as the UK, the defining characteristic is not citizenship but fee status (whether a particular student is eligible to be treated as a 'home' student or not depending on prior residence), while in other countries, such as Germany, it is nationality. But the broad picture is clear. Between 1970 and 2007 the number of international students worldwide increased from 0.8 million to 2.8 million, an increase of 350 per cent (UNESCO, 2009). In the UK between 1996–97 and 2008–09 the number more than doubled, from 117 290 to 251 310 (HESA, 1998, 2009). Major increases have also taken place over the same period in the USA, which still remains the favourite destination for international students despite the legacy of the Bush presidency in terms of unpopular foreign policies and more restrictive admissions regimes; in Australia, although the aggressive recruitment policies characteristic of the late 1980s have been moderated; and in the rest of Europe, notably France and Germany, which have benefited from charging low fees and the spin-off of the success of the Bologna Process – from which the UK has benefited to a lesser degree because it is seen as less engaged.

However, this spectacular growth in the number of international students does not necessarily mean that universities have become more international, let alone global, institutions.

First, in most countries there has been an equally spectacular growth in the number of all students. The proportion of all tertiary-level students who are international students has not changed significantly over the past two decades. In the UK, for example, despite the incentive provided by high fees to recruit more international students and the disincentive offered by declining unit-cost funding, and occasional restriction on the number of home students universities have been allowed to recruit, the proportion of international students in the overall student population increased between 1996–97 and 2008–09 from 6.3 to 10.5 per cent, a rather more modest increase than might have been supposed given the impressive growth in actual numbers (HESA, 1998, 2009). Worldwide, the percentage of mobile tertiary-level students actually declined from 2.7 per cent in 1970 to 2 per cent in 2005 (UNESCO, 2009). In other words, the internationalization of higher education as measured by the growing number of international students is perhaps better seen as an epiphenomenon of the development of mass higher education systems at home than as a separate phenomenon.

Second, important shifts are taking place within the overall pattern of international student recruitment. Some of these shifts have been generic. For example, the emphasis has shifted from undergraduate to postgraduate students, which reflects successful efforts to build capacity for undergraduate education in countries that previously lacked that capacity (and which may also pose a longer-term threat if they are also successful in building the capacity for postgraduate education as well – except perhaps in a dwindling number of more specialist subjects).

Other shifts have been more specific. For example, the decline in the scale of post-colonial (or neocolonial) recruitment has been masked by the new sources of international students, notably China, which now accounts for 400 000 international students, although there are already early signs that this growth has stalled – and the longer-term prospects must be of reversal in the light of China's impressive investment in building up its higher education system.

One reason for distinguishing between the internationalization and massification of modern higher education systems is that the former is regarded as essentially a 'market' phenomenon, characterized by competition between nations and universities, while the latter remains a domain of public policy, characterized by political direction, public funding of universities, and no or subsidized tuition fees. It is assumed, therefore, that the two processes have different and distinctive dynamics. Much has been written about the potential impact of the General Agreement on Trade in Services (GATS) on international education. To the extent that the two processes are seen as linked, it has often been by categorizing internationalization as a trailblazer for the development of market-based policies within countries.

But, as has already been argued, the patterns of development in these two processes, internationalization and massification – at any rate, in terms of growth – are sufficiently similar to suggest that they have a great deal in common. This, exaggerated, contrast may tend also to focus too much attention on 'market' mobility among students at the expense of 'sponsored' mobility. For example, various European programmes such as Erasmus, Leonardo and Tempus have sponsored large-scale mobility. Indeed, in some European countries with a much more limited stake in 'market' mobility they account for the bulk of student mobility. Nor are these European mobility programmes an exception; many state-sponsored regional mobility programmes also exist, of which the Nordplus programme among Scandinavian countries is a good example. Mobility among academic staff is also perhaps more accurately described as sponsored; although the long-term recruitment of international staff is clearly a market process the bulk of staff mobility is accounted for by short-term exchanges and sabbaticals.

The role played by the university's research mission in establishing its claim to be a global institution has been discussed in the preceding section. However, research collaboration is clearly an important element within the internationalization of higher education. It is even more difficult than in the case of international student flows to quantify either the scale of research collaboration or its growth trajectory. Yet indirect evidence is available. For example, the number of journal articles and research papers with authors in more than one country has increased substantially – although, as with student growth, this increase has to be seen in the context of a worldwide explosion in scientific and scholarly production, which reflects not only the dynamism of modern research systems but also the behavioural impact of new accountability and assessment regimes. Another novel phenomenon is the development of global rankings of universities, which are largely denominated in terms of comparative research performance and, as a result, promote international competition if not international collaboration. An associated phenomenon is the emergence of research-oriented associations of universities such as Universitas 21 and the Association of European Research Universities. These associations, although predominantly established to promote their high-status 'brands', also promote international research collaboration.

The internationalization of higher education provides strong but not decisive evidence of the status of the university as a global institution. Within higher education there is a natural inclination to see universities as the primary agents of internationalization, which is often regarded as one of the most significant attributes of the entrepreneurial university. The increase in the number of international students, of transnational education, and of cross-border research collaboration appears to support higher education's claim of prime agency. But it is important to give proper weight to other forces outside the academic system that are also promoting the internationalization of higher education, the most obvious of which is the emergence of a global knowledge economy and perhaps even more so of a 'world' society in which the immediacies of global brands and instant communication coexist with the persistence (even the proliferation) of 'difference'.

It is also important to acknowledge the wider context in which the internationalization of higher education is taking place. This wider context is made up of many, occasionally discordant, elements – the (false?) intimacies of mass-media culture that elide the exotic and the familiar; the development of multicultural societies (and, in particular, of world cities such as New York, Paris and London, which are often key sites for the internationalization of higher education); the lure of high-status though rootless global careers; and mass migratory flows, which, incidentally, help to fill up the academic – and, more broadly, professional – workforces in many developed countries, as well as obliging universities to play a key role in the integration of the displaced and the dispossessed. Many of these elements directly affect the university: in terms of student composition, the explosion of so-called 'minority' students, as well as the recruitment of international students; their curriculum, the advance of business and management is closely linked to the development of global careers; their workforce, especially in terms of research through the recruitment of international PhD and postdoctoral students; and their engagements, to the global knowledge economy, mediated perhaps through their pivotal situation in the world's 'clever cities'.

CONCLUSION

The starting point of this chapter was to question two 'givens', the twin beliefs that the university has always been an international institution and that its future destiny is to become a global institution – in two senses. First, the quality and reputation of individual universities are now linked directly to the intensity of their global involvement; the more global, the more successful and higher status. Second, that the global 'market' represents the most advanced stage of development for universities and higher education systems, superseding the national 'public service' model that prevailed in the last century and is still dominant. This questioning has been undertaken not in a spirit of negative scepticism but of genuine enquiry. The aim has been not to debunk but to problematize these beliefs, too often perhaps regarded as self-evident and requiring no sustained proof. The counter-argument presented here has been that, by questioning these beliefs, a deeper and more developed understanding of the university's status as a global institution can potentially be gained, reinforcing rather than eroding that claim.

Neither claim is necessarily invalidated by such examination. The first indeed is largely sustained, although it also needs to be revised. At issue is not the international character of the university but rather the implied assumptions that 'national' and 'global' are separate categories and that the university is becoming (or should become) more international in its focus in some (naively?) deterministic and teleological manner. It is not simply the university's status as a global institution that needs to be examined – as has been done in this chapter, in terms of its historical evolution and present situation, of its core values, of its engagement with science and scholarship on the international plane, with the global knowledge economy, and of the internationalization of higher education in more concrete terms. The nature of globality must also be examined with equal attention because it has been constantly shifting. The universalism of the medieval church in the infancy of the university was very different from the universalisms of the Enlightenment and the scientific revolution, of global capitalism, of urbanism, industrialism and secularism, and of the totalizing ideologies of the nineteenth and twentieth centuries when the modern university came of age – and very different again from the multiple strands of globalization in the twenty-first century (global markets and global resistances, world brands but also hybrid cultures) with which the entrepreneurial university must engage.

The university has always been an important mediator between local environments and global, or universal, cultures. Local environments clearly determine some of its key characteristics such as governance, funding, organization and – largely – the composition of the student body. Global, or universal, cultures are embodied in scientific research and, more broadly, widely acknowledged intellectual values. It has always helped to interpret these global cultures in the context of local environments, and also to contribute local values and experiences to the definition of global cultures – in other words, a two-way process. The elevation of the essentially local cultures of the 'west' to the status of global, or universal, culture over the past two centuries has to some extent obscured this dialogic process, especially in Europe and North America. It has been easier to assume that the universities of the 'west' are inevitably also global institutions, an equivalence that is more difficult to make in the case of universities in the rest of the world.

This dialogue between national and global, local and universal, is not novel but has been a constant feature of the university's history. What have changed are the terms of exchange as both the values and practices of the university and the characteristics of globality have evolved. These complex interactions between the university, its local environments, and global cultures – all in a state of constant evolution that is highly reflexive and non-linear – make it more difficult fully to sustain the second claim, that the global 'market' is a more advanced stage of university development than the national 'public service' model. It has been argued in this chapter that the universal and the local, the global and the national, 'market' and 'public service' models, cannot readily be distinguished. These categories conceal too many complexities within them and synergies between them. It follows that, if these categories cannot be clearly separated, a stage of development based on the belief that they can be cannot properly be described as more advanced. The analysis and arguments here offer a more nuanced – but, inevitably, less prescriptive and definitive – account.

To the simple question 'Is the university a global institution?' the answer can only be – yes, but . . . The potential of the university resides as much in the 'but' as in the 'yes'.

REFERENCES

Barker, K. (2007), 'The UK Research Assessment Exercise: the evolution of a national research evaluation program', *Research Evaluation*, **16** (1), 3–12.

Beck, U. (1992), *Risk Society: Towards a New Modernity*, London/Newbury Park, CA: Sage.

Bell, D. (1973), *The Coming of Post-industrial Society: A Venture in Social Forecasting*, New York: Basic Books.

Carayannis, E. and D. Campbell (2009), '"Mode 3" and "Quadruple Helix": towards a twenty-first century fractal innovation ecosystem', *International Journal of Technology Management*, **46** (2/3), 201–33.

Clark, B. (2001), *Creating Entrepreneurial Universities: Organizational Pathways of Transformation*, Oxford: Pergamon.

Etzkowitz, H. (2008), *The Triple Helix: University–Industry–Government Innovation in Action*, Abingdon and New York: Routledge.

Etzkowitz, H. and L. Leydesdorff (eds) (1997), *Universities and the Global Knowledge Economy: A Triple-helix of University–Industry–Government Relations*, London: Pinter.

Florida, R. (2005), *Cities and the Creative Class*, London: Routledge.

Friedman, B. (2002), *Globalization and Its Discontents*, New York: Norton.

Gibbons, M., C. Limoges, H. Nowotny, S. Schwartzman, P. Scott and M. Trow (1994), *The New Production of Knowledge: The Dynamics of Science and Research in Contemporary Societies*, London/Newbury Park, CA: Sage.

Hicks, D. and S. Katz (2002), 'Science policy for a highly collaborative science system', *Science and Public Policy*, **23**, 39–44.

Higher Education Statistics Agency (HESA) (1998), *Students in Higher Education Institutions 1996–97*, Cheltenham: HESA.

Higher Education Statistics Agency (HESA) (2009), *Students in Higher Education Institutions 2007–08*, Cheltenham: HESA.

Kerr, C. (1963), *The Uses of the University*, Cambridge, MA: Harvard University Press.

Nowotny, H. (1994), *Time: The Modern and Post-modern Experience*, Cambridge: Polity Press.

Nowotny, H., P. Scott and M. Gibbons (2001), *Re-Thinking Science: Knowledge and the Public in an Age of Uncertainty*, Cambridge: Polity Press.

Pedersen, O. (1997), *The First Universities: Studium Generale and the Origins of University Education in Europe*, Cambridge: Cambridge University Press.

de Ridder-Symoens, H. (ed.) (2003), *A History of the University in Europe: Universities in the Middle Ages*, Cambridge: Cambridge University Press.

Robertson, R. (1995), 'Glocalization: time-space and homogeneity–heterogeneity', in M. Featherstone, S. Lash and R. Robertson (eds), *Global Modernities*, London: Sage, pp. 25–44.

Scott, P. (1995), *The Meanings of Mass Higher Education*, Buckingham: Open University Press.

Scott, P. (2000), *Ten Years On: Higher Education in Central and Eastern Europe*, Bucharest: UNESCO–CEPES.

UNESCO (2009), http://www.uis.unesco.org/publications/GED2009.

Urry, J. (1998), 'Contemporary transformations of time and space', in P. Scott (ed.), *The Globalization of Higher Education*, Buckingham: Open University Press, pp. 1–18.

Waechter, B. (2004), 'The Bologna Process: developments and prospects', *European Journal of Education*, **39** (3), 265–73.

Ziman, J. (2000), *Real Science: What it is and What it Means*, Cambridge: Cambridge University Press.

5 Three forms of the knowledge economy: learning, creativity and openness

Michael A. Peters

INTRODUCTION

This chapter outlines and reviews three forms and associated discourses of the 'knowledge economy': the 'learning economy' based on the work of Lundvall; the 'creative economy' based on the works of Landry, Howkins and Florida; and the 'open knowledge economy' based on the work of Benkler and others. Arguably these three forms and discourses represent three recent related but different conceptions of the knowledge economy, each with clear significance and implications for education and education policy. The last provides a model of a radically non-propertied form that incorporates both 'open education' and 'open science' economies.

Distinguishing a number of different strands and readings of the 'knowledge economy' provides a history of a policy idea and charts its ideological interpretations.[1] The different strands of this discourse are radically diverse and include attempts to theorize not only 'knowledge economy' but also the parallel term 'knowledge society', and also the attempts to relate these terms to wider and broader changes in the nature of capitalism, modernity and the global economy. Early attempts by von Hayek (1937, 1945) to define the relations between economics and knowledge were followed by the economic value-of-knowledge studies of the production and distribution of knowledge in the USA by Fritz Machlup (1962). Both of these scholars were associated with the Austrian School of economics. Gary Becker (1964), a prominent member of the Chicago School, analyzed human capital with reference to education while Peter Drucker (1969), the management theorist, developed an emphasis on 'knowledge workers'. He coined the term in 1959 and founded the field of 'knowledge management'. In a different vein, Daniel Bell's (1973) sociology of post-industrialism emphasized the centrality of theoretical knowledge and the new science-based industries, and Alain Touraine's (1971) *The Post-Industrial Society* hypothesized students as a new social movement and predicted the 'programmed society'.

In the 1970s, 1980s and 1990s there were various attempts by theorists from different disciplines to theorize aspects of the emerging economy. There is no space to discuss their work here, but only to mention examples of the diverse literature. Granovetter (1973) theorized the role of information in the market based on weak ties and social networks. Porat (1977) defined 'the information society' in a series of publications for the US government, and Alvin Toffler (1980), the futurist, talked of knowledge-based production in the 'Third Wave economy'. The French philosopher Lyotard (1984) defined *The Postmodern Condition* as an age marked by the contingency, complexity, dispersal and distribution of knowledge. The Marxist geographer David Harvey (1989) analyzed large-scale shifts from Fordist to flexible accumulation in contemporary capitalism.

Coleman (1988) analyzed how social capital creates human capital and Pierre Bourdieu (1986) and Robert Putnam (2000) further developed the notion, providing distinctive notions of cultural and social capital. The Stanford economist Paul Romer (1990) argued that growth is driven by technological change arising from intentional investment decisions where technology as an input is a non-rival, partially excludable good. The OECD (1996), basing its work on Romer and endogenous growth theory, provided an influential model of the 'knowledge-based economy'. Meanwhile Joseph Stiglitz (1999b) developed the World Bank's 'Knowledge for Development' and 'Education for the Knowledge Economy' programs based on the notion that knowledge is a global public good.[2]

In the wake of these reports employers called for new workforce skill sets (Partnership for 21st Century Skills, 2008), and public policy applications and developments of the 'knowledge economy' concept began to appear in authoritative policy anthologies at the end of the decade (Hearn and Rooney, 2008).

This demonstrates that since the Second World War theorists from different perspectives and disciplines have simultaneously tried to analyze and describe certain deep-seated and structurally transformative tendencies in western capitalism, society and modernity to move to a form of post-industrial economy that focuses on the production and consumption of knowledge and symbolic goods as a higher-order economic activity that encompasses and affects the entire economy and society (Foray, 2000). While they differ on its societal effects and impacts, these theorists agree on the epochal nature of this deep economic transformation and the way in which it represents an ongoing automation and technologization of processes of scientific communication, including access, distribution and dissemination that lie at the heart of knowledge creation.

What this brief history reveals is the different stages in the evolution of a discourse with parallel streams in economics and sociology, often contradictory or opposing, different ideological sources, separate conceptual histories, and different visions of economy and society. We can no longer simply hold that 'knowledge economy' or 'knowledge society' are neoliberal notions and ignore their descriptive and analytical force. They are complex and openly contested policy descriptions that have emerged to describe the trajectory of the rich liberal capitalist states and now function as a generalized world policy framework that permits local applications and forms of indigenization of associated concepts and policies, depending on location, the geopolitical climate, state actors, and a range of other factors. Rather than discuss the origin and ideological basis of the knowledge economy, which I have done elsewhere (see Peters and Besley, 2006), I want to focus on recent developments and applications of the concept that depend directly on processes of education and learning.

The term 'knowledge economy' is a concept undergoing further conceptual development. In the following sections I have detailed three forms of the knowledge economy: the 'learning economy'; the 'creative economy'; and the 'open knowledge economy'. Each of these has a special relationship to education and pedagogy, and highlights the significance of learning processes within these larger policy frameworks. What this analysis demonstrates is the increasing and dynamic differentiation of the concept and progressive new developments that distinguish and refine elements of the general concept. What is also clear is that the main strands of the analysis of the knowledge economy draw on overlapping literatures in economics, sociology and philosophy, and share some underlying general concepts concerning economic, social or epistemic shifts that characterize modes of economy and social organization and large-scale global, geopolitical historical periodizations – agricultural–industrial–post-industrial–knowledge 'economy' and 'society' – that map onto more general debates concerning European 'modernity' and 'postmodernity' and that more recently mention global or historical 'multiple (post) modernities', and a set of broader philosophical debates that employ the terms 'modernism', 'postmodernism' and 'antimodernism'.

THE LEARNING ECONOMY

The concept of the learning economy was first coined and has been championed by Bengt-Åke Lundvall, a Swedish economist from Aalborg University, who uses the term to talk about a new context for European innovation policy.[3] Lundvall (2003; Lundvall and Johnson, 1994) first used the concept in the mid-1990s in a series of working papers to discuss technological change, innovation and institutional learning, directly applying it to the learning society and economy, to universities, and to education more generally in the 2000s. This culminates in *How Europe's Economies Learn* (Lorenz and Lundvall, 2006), which focuses on diversity in European competence-building systems, organization, labor markets and corporate governance, and the links between education and science–industry. The concept and theory of the learning economy is a refinement of the 'knowledge economy' concept based on the way a set of interlocking forces (ecologies) in information/ knowledge intensities, distributed new social media, and greater computer networking and connectivity have contributed to the heightened significance of human capital formations, mode of social production, and an emphasis on learning processes. Lundvall (1996, p. 1) argues, for instance, that the growing frequency of so-called paradoxes in economic theory and of unsolved socioeconomic problems reflects that neither economic theory nor policy has been adapted to the fact that we have entered a new phase: the 'learning economy'.

In the learning economy it is the capacity to learn that increasingly determines the relative position of individuals, firms and national systems, and Lundvall claims that the growing polarization in the OECD labor markets is explained by the increasing importance of learning and the acceleration in the rate of change. Sustainability of these learning economy tendencies ultimately depends on the distribution of capabilities to learn. The OECD highlights the importance of skills and learning, focusing on lifelong learning becoming the central element in a high-skill, high-wage, jobs strategy. Lundvall distinguishes between information and knowledge: the former is logical, sequential, and easily broken down into bits and transmitted by computer, whereas the latter is associated with learning that is often a form of know-how with competencies based on tacit knowledge. An information or knowledge economy is quite different from a learning economy in that it is not tied to formal knowledge institutions and goes beyond formal propositional forms of knowing to the arena of routinized learning based on 'learning by doing' or 'learning by using'. Such a definition allows us to consider the types of learning associated with the process of working that emphasizes tacit, practical and embodied knowledge generated during the work process. One might also argue in a broader sense that the learning economy focuses on learning processes that are responsible for the production of knowledge.

Lundvall et al. (2008) argue that innovation is crucial to economic competitiveness and learning is crucial to innovation. They argue that knowledge is becoming obsolete more rapidly than before, and that therefore firms and employees constantly have to learn and acquire new competencies, mostly through experience. Lundvall and his colleagues argue that traditional schooling, isolated from society and organized according to traditional disciplines and educational cultures focusing on collaboration, interdisciplinarity and engagement with real-life problems, are required to produce flexible workers who can successfully participate in the new economy. Learning in this conception is not an end in itself but only in the service of innovation policy, and is focused on processes of institutional learning within firms, which it is assumed can easily be applied and transferred to schools. Lundvall is influenced by Pasinetti's (1981) work and his distinction between *producer learning,* linked to productivity growth, and *consumer learning,* which is connected to consumers' adoption of new consumption goods, in an attempt to understand value creation. Lundvall also emphasizes 'learning by doing' and 'learning by using', following Arrow (1962), to talk about the need for firms and the workforce to engage in building new competencies in order to survive global competition. To this he adds 'learning by interacting' (Lundvall, 1988), which purportedly has the effect of transforming local learning into general knowledge. In the context of the EU's emphasis on creativity and innovation Lundvall has focused on innovation as an interactive learning process and the relation of the national innovation system to science and technology policies, with a focus on knowledge-management design and strategies. This provides an interesting and useful macroeconomic context for understanding the centrality and significance of various forms of 'organizational learning' for the national economy as a whole but with limited application to formal systems of education or to understanding the nature of academic knowledge and its transformation from propositional learning to learning by doing. Lundvall's formulations have proved influential and helpful, and have also given greater profile to the significance of 'learning processes', but fail to link with the considerable literature in education on learning theory or to view learning processes as central to broader visions of society and politics.

THE CREATIVE ECONOMY[4]

The conception of the creative economy emphasizes the creative industries and institutions as an interlocking sector producing cultural goods and services as a rapidly growing and key component of the new global knowledge economy. It refers to those broadly defined design industries and institutions that draw on the individual and increasingly collective resources of creativity, skill and talent that have strong potential for the generation of wealth and job creation through the development and exploitation of intellectual property. Both the idea and policies associated with it originate in the late 1990s and early 2000s in the work of Landry, Howkins and Florida. Increasingly the notion has been applied to education at all levels, in terms of the development of creative minds, the creative curriculum and universities as creative institutions. This section provides a broad conceptual understanding of the creative economy and its relation to education.

Today there is a strong renewal of interest by politicians and policy-makers worldwide in the related notions of creativity and innovation, especially in relation to terms such as 'the creative economy', 'knowledge economy', 'enterprise society', 'entrepreneurship' and 'national systems of innovation' (Baumol, 2002; Cowen, 2002; Lash and Urry, 1994). In its rawest form the notion of the creative economy emerges from a set of claims that suggests that the industrial economy is giving way to the creative economy based on the growing power of ideas and virtual value – the turn from steel and hamburgers to software and intellectual property (Florida, 2002; Howkins, 2001; Landry, 2000).

In this context, policy increasingly latches on to the issues of copyright as an aspect of intellectual property (IP), piracy, distribution systems, network literacy, public service content, the creative industries, new interoperability standards, the World Intellectual Property Organization (WIPO), the development agenda, WTO and trade, and means to bring creativity and commerce together (Cowen, 2002; Shapiro and Varian, 1998; Davenport and Beck, 2001; Hughes, 1988; Netanel, 1996, 1998; Gordon, 1993; Lemley, 2005). At the same time this focus on creativity has exerted strong appeal on policy-makers who wish to link education more firmly to new forms of capitalism, emphasizing how creativity must be taught, how educational theory and research can be used to improve student learning in mathematics, reading and science, and how different models of intelligence and creativity can inform educational practice (Blythe, 2000). Under the spell of the creative economy discourse there has been a flourishing of new accelerated learning methodologies together with a focus on giftedness – the design of learning programs for exceptional children.[5] One strand of the emerging literature highlights the role of the creative and expressive arts, of performance, of aesthetics in general, and the significant role of design as an underlying infrastructure for the creative economy (Caves, 2000; Frey and Pommerehne, 1989; Ginsburgh and Menger, 1996; Heilbrun and Gray, 2001; Hesmondhalgh, 2002).

There is now widespread agreement among economists, sociologists and policy analysts that creativity, design and innovation are at the heart of the global knowledge economy: together creativity, design and innovation define knowledge capitalism and its ability to continuously reinvent itself.[6] Together and in conjunction with new communications technologies they give expression to the essence of digital capitalism – the 'economy of ideas' – and to new architectures of mass collaboration that distinguish it as a new generic form of economy different in nature from industrial capitalism.

The fact is that knowledge in its immaterial digitized informational form as sequences and value chains of 1s and 0s – ideas, concepts, functions and abstractions – approaches the status of pure thought. Unlike other commodities it operates expansively to defy the law of scarcity that is fundamental to classical and neoclassical economics and to the traditional understanding of markets. A generation of economists has expressed this truth by emphasizing that knowledge is (almost) a global public good; it is non-rivalrous and barely excludable (Stiglitz, 1999a; Verschraegen and Schiltz, 2007). It is non-rivalrous in the sense that there is little or marginal cost to adding new users.

In other words, knowledge and information, especially in digital form, cannot be consumed. The use of knowledge or information as digital goods can be distributed and shared at no extra cost, and the distribution and sharing is likely to add to its value rather than to deplete it or use it up. This is the essence of the economics of file-sharing education; it is also the essence of new forms of distributed creativity, intelligence and innovation in an age of mass participation and collaboration (Brown and Duguid, 2000; Tapscott and Williams, 2006; Surowiecki, 2004).

The United Nations *Creative Economy Report* (2008, p. 3) views the creative economy as a new development paradigm that is able to link all aspects of the economy together in a way that provides new growth opportunities for developing countries.

> A new development paradigm is emerging that links the economy and culture, embracing economic, cultural, technological and social aspects of development at both the macro and micro levels. Central to the new paradigm is the fact that creativity, knowledge and access to information are increasingly recognized as powerful engines driving economic growth and promoting development in a globalizing world. The emerging creative economy has become a leading component of economic growth, employment, trade and innovation, and social cohesion in most advanced economies. Unfortunately, however, the large majority of developing countries are not yet able to harness their creative capacity for development. This is a reflection of weaknesses both in domestic policy and in the business environment, and global systemic biases. Nevertheless the creative economy offers to developing countries a feasible option and new opportunities to leapfrog into emerging high-growth areas of the world economy.

This is a comprehensive report by a group that was set up by the Secretary General of the United Nations Conference on Trade and Development (UNCTAD) in 2004 in the context of preparations for the high-level panel on creative industries and development held during the UNCTAD XI Ministerial Conference, and it provides a useful introduction to the concept and context of the creative economy, including its development dimension, as well as focusing on its analysis and measurement, its role in international trade, and the importance of intellectual property. Curiously, it has little to say directly about education as such or its link with development, which is a major weakness.

Much of the literature concerning education and the creative economy emphasizes the role of the arts in economic development and the need for building forms of cultural, social and public entrepreneurship. The problem is that beyond the formulation of concepts such as 'creative industries', 'creative cities' and 'creative class', little analysis has been made of creativity in schools apart from fostering instrumental versions of creativity or simply regarding 'education, training and skills' as one aspect of the creative economy. There is still a long way to go in theorizing and developing policies that encourage creativity in schools, predicated on new forms of social media and better understanding of new media and knowledge ecologies that democratize access to knowledge, decentralize organizational and authority structures, encourage a greater personalization and autonomy of learning, while promoting new forms of 'collective intelligence' and peer learning based on a new ethic of participation and collaboration (Lave and Wenger, 1991; Caron and Caronia, 2007; Ito, 2006, 2008; Peters, 2010).[7]

THE OPEN KNOWLEDGE ECONOMY

Bill Gates (2006, p. 3) uses the term 'information democracy' to signal the public world of information available globally that ordinary citizens can access through a personal computer (PC). Gates says: 'While information wants to be free, knowledge is much "stickier" – harder to communicate, more subjective, less easy to define.' And he indicates that as software gets smarter it will help people synthesize and manage knowledge. He mentions a range of technologies like OneNote that promote consilience and just-in-time information – 'technologies that infuse online data with meaning and context'.

Gates's argument is another demonstration of a kind of technological determinism, yet the general point he raises – the changing relationship between democracy and information – has a venerable past in democratic theory and plays a strong role in educational theory and practice. In some quarters the term has come to mean no more than 'information-sharing', with attention directed towards different models – dictatorship, anarchy, democracy, embassies – that might be employed in businesses to enhance productivity and in education to foster participation and collaboration.

At the 2007 World Economic Forum at Davos, Switzerland, the participants – among them Gordon Brown and Rupert Murdoch – acknowledged that the ground rules for democratic societies have been permanently altered by an 'explosion of self-expression' (Murdoch) and a changed economy of information (Brown) that favors the individual active consumer–citizen or 'prosumer' who through the Internet accesses or creates blogs and bypasses much of the media mainstream. This new media thrives on a constant torrent of opinion with millions of 'information transactions' that break stories, circulate endless commentaries and opinions, but also 'gets the facts out there' (Murdoch) via a kind of public scrutiny that acts as a source of constant feedback. No government, no state, is now immune to information; what is more, no state or government can police or control information borders although state and corporate surveillance remains a real threat not only to privacy but also to basic democratic rights. The 'information state' is thus the first politically porous state that, with all its contradictions, mutations and imperfections, looks the most likely model for a world public space.

Information and knowledge have always been central to accounts of democracy from its early modern formulations where the emphasis was placed on the necessity of an informed or educated citizenry through to more recent movements like that of open government, which began in the 1960s. Open government opposed reason of state, state secrecy and national security, often popularized as 'big brother' and 'faceless bureaucracy', with a system of public accountability based on principles of freedom of information. The presumption of openness, political transparency, and the demand for public scrutiny at all levels found favor with a range of groups pressing for democratic freedoms in the 1960s first in the USA, with countries in Europe and Australasia following in the 1970s and 1980s. Much of this demand and struggle found its way into legislation designed to enact 'freedom of information' that regulates and controls public access to government records.

'Freedom of information' is sometimes tied to the historic right, enshrined in Article 19 of the Declaration of Human Rights, to the universal right to freedom of opinion and expression without interference. Generally such legislation became part of the establishment of an ombudsman office that represents the interest of the public against government departments.

Even before the movement for open government, democratic theory held a special place for the free press and assumed a benign relationship between the media, democracy, citizenship and education. On some accounts processes of media globalization have diminished the public sphere as the centralization of media control and the intensification of ownership and commercialization has led to the growth of the media transnational conglomerates. Media outputs are trivialized through 'edutainment' and also commoditized, thus serving market rather than citizenship needs.

With the democratization of media, a new paradigm of communication has emerged that seems to facilitate individual interactivity and enhance democracy, autonomy and justice. Yochai Benkler (2003, 2006) has been at the forefront of a movement that argues that the political economy of the sphere of liberal communication has now changed with the radical decentralization of information production. The new paradigm of social production in the networked global information economy has diminished the significance of the corporate and transnational media conglomerates to create meaning, to influence the public agenda, and to control the format (sound-bites) of news discussions. This is part of Benkler's argument for an enhancement of democracy and education. It is an argument that also places strong emphasis on the logic of decentralization such that no individual actor (person or corporation) can exercise control over the totality and allows individuals to 'build their own window on the world' (2003, p. 1247) and to invent the pathways, the sequences, the topics, and the logic of performance that determines the next link. In Benkler's terms individual access and user (inter)activity alleviates the 'autonomy deficit by an exclusively proprietary communications system' (ibid., p. 1267).

Finally, Benkler (ibid., p. 1271) identifies the third leg of his argument concerning 'justice', where he states succinctly:

> Commons in information and communications facilities are no panacea for inequality in initial endowments, but they do provide a relatively simple and sustainable way of giving everyone equal access to one important set of resources. Second, commons in communications infrastructure provide a transactional setting that ameliorates some of the inequalities in transactional capabilities that Ackerman identifies as a focus for liberal redistribution.

Benkler and Nissenbaum (2006) go a step further to develop an argument concerning the relationship between commons-based peer production and virtue, combining two lines of inquiry – commons-based peer production and philosophy of technology – where moral and political values can be seen to be inherent in technical design (Flanagan et al., 2005).

Commons-based peer production challenges not only the traditional basis of hierarchical economic management but also neoliberal theories based on the revival on *homo economicus* with its controlling assumptions of rationality, individuality and self-interest. It is the self-interest assumption that they problematize. Benkler and Nissenbaum (2006, pp. 394–5) suggest that

> the emergence of peer production offers an opportunity for more people to engage in practices that permit them to exhibit and experience virtuous behavior. We posit: (a) that a society that provides opportunities for virtuous behavior is one that is more conducive to virtuous individuals; and (b) that the practice of effective virtuous behavior may lead to more people adopting virtues as their own, or as attributes of what they see as their self-definition. The central thesis of this paper is that sociotechnical systems of commons-based peer production offer not only a remarkable medium of production for various kinds of information goods but serve as a context for positive character formation.

A range of initiatives and movements, including free and open source software, open access and Wikipedia, now tends to throw into question neoliberal assumptions within the global network information economy. The empirical fact is that self-interest is an inadequate explanation for the active engagement of millions of users worldwide who contribute without monetary reward to these projects and many thousands of smaller ones. The implications of this changed political economy for education has barely been registered.

Benkler (2006) theorizes fundamental changes to liberal society and economy in *The Wealth of Networks*. Benkler develops a vision of the good society based on access and distribution of information goods in a networked global information economy that places a high value on individual autonomy, where within the public information space of the Internet and the information commons people have the individual means to pursue their own interests.[8] He indicates that a set of related changes in the information technologies entailing new social practices of production has fundamentally changed how we make and exchange information, knowledge and culture, and he envisages these newly emerging social practices as constituting a new information environment that gives individuals the freedom to take a more active role in the construction of public information and culture. The emergence of the globally networked information economy made possible by increasingly cheaper processors linked as a pervasive network has created an information economy based on the production of information and culture that enables social and nonmarket or peer-to-peer production and exchange to play a, perhaps even *the*, central role.

Benkler's arguments chime with a number of others who have been working in the same area of the intellectual commons as a newly defined public space or laid the groundwork for doing so: Richard Stallman, John Perry Barlow, Larry Lessig, James Doyle and Pamela Samuelson. Stallman's (2002) collected essays in *Free Software, Free Society*, originally written a couple of decades ago, provide a discussion of the philosophy underlying the free software movement, including the GNU's Not Unix (GNU) project and manifesto, the difference between 'free' and 'open' software, the concept of copyleft and the GNU General Public License. As Larry Lessig (2002, p. 10) writes: 'Every generation has its philosopher . . . who captures the imagination of a time.' The philosopher who best captures our time, Lessig asserts, is Richard Stallman, who began as a computer programmer designing operating systems and came to define the freedom of code as the central pressing issue confronting a computer society. Free software is Stallman's answer to the question of control – 'free' as in 'free speech', that is, free from control, transparent, and open to further development, change and innovation. Such freedom, then, is the basis of 'free laws', an economy of free code and the 'free society'. The principles demand openness and transparency that form the basis for control of code, for laws that guarantee this freedom and for government itself. Stallman argues that copyright is not defined as a natural right in the US Constitution and he seeks to reduce it, arguing also for the distribution of scientific publishing in non-proprietary formats.

The fact is that the accumulated canon of patent and copyright law applies well to things but faces insuperable difficulties when applied to non-material goods. Information increasingly separates itself from the material plane to exist merely in the ideational form as pure ideas. Digital technologies tend to eliminate the distinction between the idea and its expression in some physical form, also 'erasing the legal jurisdictions of the physical world'. Lessig (2004), building on earlier work (e.g. Lessig, 2001), argues for an underlying conception of freedom and its protection as the basis for 'free culture', at the same time warning of the dangers of 'big media' in colonizing public media space. He emphasizes the way the Internet makes possible the efficient spread of content through peer-to-peer (p2p) file-sharing in a way that does not respect traditional copyright and he warns us of the dangers to the kind of creativity that is the basis of cultural innovation. In *The Future of Ideas* (Lessig, 2002) he describes how the Internet counterculture has encouraged an explosion of innovation and creativity, and the legal architecture protecting it as a public space is now under threat.

In the same context we can also talk of James Boyle and Pamela Samuelson. Boyle is a law professor at Duke University and the co-founder of the Center for the Study of the Public Domain,[9] established in 2002 with the mission to promote research and scholarship on the contributions of the public domain to speech, culture, science and innovation, to promote debate about the balance needed in our intellectual property system, and to translate academic research into public policy solutions. Boyle (1997) argues that that we need a political economy of 'intellectual property'. Likening the Net to an environment and drawing on the politics of environmentalism, he suggests that our intellectual property discourse has structural tendencies towards overprotection, rather than underprotection. He claims that the 'public domain' is disappearing in an IP system built around the interests of the current stakeholders and the notion of the original author, around an overdeterministic practice of economic analysis, and around a 'free speech' community that is undersensitized to the dangers of private censorship.

He argues that a pay-as-you-read architecture will be inefficient and that such a system will 'lead to extraordinary monopoly and concentration in the software industry, as copyright and patent trump antitrust policy' and possibly legitimize the extension of 'intellectual property rights even further over living organisms, including the human genome, transgenic species and the like' as well as privatizing 'words, or aspects of images or texts that are currently in the public domain, to the detriment of public debate, education, equal access to information . . .' (Boyle, 1997, n.p.). Boyle is one of a number of scholars working in this area, including Michael Carroll, Molly Shaffer Van Houweling and Larry Lessig, along with the filmmakers Eric Saltzman and Davis Guggenheim, the computer science expert Hal Abelson, and CEOs like Jimmy Wales (founder of Wikipedia), Laurie Racine (founder of dotSUB), Joi Ito (founder of Neotony), and John Buck (founder of Magnatune.com) (and all members of Creative Commons[10]). Pamela Samuelson is another scholar working on intellectual property and the public space. Samuelson (1996) in Wired's 'The Copyright Grab'[11] warned that President Clinton's White Paper on intellectual property was a sellout of the public and a reward of supporters in the copyright industry.

'Henry' in the 'Crooked Timber' seminar[12] in Benkler's *The Wealth of Networks* indicates how this recent literature maps onto 'a broader tradition of thought; that of people like Jane Jacobs, James Scott, Richard Sennett and Iris Marion Young'. He acknowledges that the Internet enables us to engage with each other in new creative ways and to form networks of collaboration and of conversation, creating possibility conditions for the kinds of diversity and critical thinking that democratic theorists prize. The essential point emphasized here, especially for the political Left, is that these newly enabled forms of 'community' or 'conversation' are non-constraining and occur without central planning or the heavy-handed agency of the state. Henry suggests that three key norms – linking, attribution and authenticity – structure the blogosphere, creating an economy built on 'gift exchange', and contemplates how even self-regulatory solutions tend to rigidify over time, reducing spontaneity and introducing more formal rules and hierarchies.

To summarize: information is the vital element in a 'new' politics and economy that links space, knowledge and capital in networked practices. Freedom is an essential ingredient in this equation if these network practices develop or transform themselves into knowledge cultures. The specific politics and eco-cybernetic rationalities that accompany an informational global capitalism comprising new multinational edutainment agglomerations are clearly capable of colonizing the emergent ecology of info-social networks and preventing the development of knowledge cultures based on non-proprietary modes of knowledge production and exchange.

Complexity as an approach to knowledge and knowledge systems now recognizes both the development of global systems architectures in (tele)communications and information, with the development of open knowledge production systems that increasingly rest not only on the establishment of new and better platforms (sometimes called Web 2.0), the semantic Web, new search algorithms and processes of digitization. Social processes and policies that foster *openness* as an overriding value are evidenced in the growth of open source, open access, and open education, and in their convergences that characterize global knowledge communities that transcend borders of the nation-state. Openness seems also to suggest political transparency and the norms of open inquiry, indeed even democracy itself as both the basis of the logic of inquiry and the dissemination of its results (Peters and Britez, 2008; Peters and Roberts, 2011). This is increasingly evident in forms of open science economy based on large-scale, international science portal systems that themselves are aimed at addressing large-scale natural systems attrition, rapid industrial depletion of natural ecosystems, and environmental collapse and debasement.

THE PROMISE OF OPEN EDUCATION

Open education develops around a successive series of utopian historical moments based on a set of similar ideas stemming from core Enlightenment concepts of freedom, equality, democracy and creativity.[13] The early history of open education consists of political and psychological experiments conducted in special schools established in the early twentieth century (Neil, 1960; Rogers, 1969; Illich, 1972). The movement from the very beginning was thus shaped by contemporary political and psychological theory that attempted to provide alternatives to the mainstream, connected to and exemplified a form of society and set of institutions that was seen as politically desirable. These early ideas also significantly involved an analysis of space and the architecture of schools, and the associated idea of freedom of movement underwent considerable refinement and development over the course of the twentieth century.

An important aspect concerned not only the analysis of architecture but the overcoming of distance in a form of distance education that began in the late nineteenth century through correspondence and progressed through various media eras including that of radio and television. Open education consisted of several strands and movements that often coalesced and overlapped to create a complex skein that, despite its complexity, was able to rapidly avail itself of new communication and information technologies in the last decade of the twentieth century, and to identify itself more broadly with the new convergences among open source, open access and open courseware movements. It was as though the open education movement in its infancy required the technological infrastructure to emerge as a major new paradigm rather than a set of small-scale and experimental alternatives or a form of distance education.

The model of technology-based distance education really received its impetus in the 1960s when the Open University in the UK was established, founded on the idea that communications technology could extend advanced degree-learning to those people who for a variety of reasons could not easily attend campus universities. It has been immensely influential as a model for other countries; distance education flourished in the 1970s and picked up new open education dimensions with the introduction of local area network environments.[14]

Open courseware (OCW) is very much a feature of the twenty-first century. Massachusetts Institute of Technology (MIT), one of the first universities to introduce OCW, announced its intention in the *New York Times* in 2001, formed the OpenCourseWare Consortium in 2005, and by 2007 published virtually all its courses online.[15] MIT is only one example of the OpenCourseWare movement, an important player, but nevertheless only one institution among many.[16] Most recently The Cape Town Open Education Declaration mentions the variety of openly licensed course materials, including lessons, games, software and other teaching and learning materials that contribute to making education more accessible and help shape and give effect to a 'participatory culture of learning, creating, sharing and cooperation' necessary for knowledge societies. It goes on to provide a statement based on a three-pronged strategy designed to support 'open educational technology, open sharing of teaching practices and other approaches that promote the broader cause of open education'.[17] The open education movement and paradigm has arrived: it emerges from a complex historical background and its futures are intimately tied not only to open source, open access and open publishing movements but also to the concept of the open society itself (Peters and Britez, 2008; Iiyoshi and Kumar, 2008).

THE OPEN SCIENCE ECONOMY

Openness has become a complex code word for a variety of digital trends and movements that has emerged as an alternative mode of 'social production' based on the growing and overlapping complexities of open source, open access, open archiving, open publishing and open science. Openness in this sense refers to open source models of scientific communication, knowledge distribution and educational development, although it has a number of deeper registers that refer more widely to government ('open government'), society ('open society'), economy ('open economy') and even psychology (openness as one of the five traits of personality theory). The concept and evolving set of practices have profound consequences for education at all levels. 'Openness' has become a leading source of innovation in the world global digital economy increasingly adopted by world governments, international agencies and multinationals, as well as leading educational institutions as a means of promoting scientific inquiry and international collaboration.

It is clear that the free software and open source movements constitute a radical non-proprietary (that is, social) alternative to traditional methods of text and symbolic production, distribution, archiving, access and dissemination. This alternative non-proprietary model of cultural production and exchange threatens traditional models of intellectual property and it challenges the major legal and institutional means such as copyright currently used to restrict creativity, innovation and the free exchange of ideas. The OpenCourseWare (OCW) Consortium advertizes itself in the following terms, emphasizing one aspect of alternative educational globalization – the distribution and free exchange of course content and also potentially a major source for the internationalization of curriculum:

> An OpenCourseWare is a free and open digital publication of high quality educational materials, organized as courses. The OpenCourseWare Consortium is a collaboration of more than 200 higher education institutions and associated organizations from around the world creating a broad and deep body of open educational content using a shared model. The mission of the OpenCourseWare Consortium is to advance education and empower people worldwide through opencourseware. (http://mindsecret1.blogspot.con/2009/09/open-courseware.consor tium.html, accessed 12 September 2010)

On 14 February 2008 Harvard University adopted a policy that requires faculty members to allow the university to make their scholarly articles available free online. The new policy makes Harvard the first university in the USA to mandate open access to its faculty members' research publications and marks the beginning of a new era that will encourage other US universities to do the same. The Harvard policy is a move to disseminate faculty research and scholarship and to give the university a worldwide license to make each faculty member's scholarly articles available globally. In effect the new policy establishes a global scholarly publishing system that allows scholars to use and distribute their own work, giving them greater control over these aspects of scholarly production. Harvard's open access repository makes scholarly research available worldwide for free, while the faculty member retains the copyright of the article.

Harvard University is not alone; both the National Institutes of Health (NIH) and the European Research Council have recently adopted similar open access mandates, putting pressure on other government agencies in the USA and governments abroad to do the same. In a clear sense this is the beginning of a mega-trend that will make intellectual research and teaching resources freely available worldwide and encourage forms of education based on open source, open access, open archiving and open publishing models as well as supporting burgeoning initiatives like the Creative Commons project,[18] the P2P Foundation,[19] the Public Knowledge Project[20] that supports Open Journal Systems, and the Open Knowledge Foundation,[21] to mention only a few.

Openness is a new mode of social production that has become a leading source of innovation in the world global digital economy. It constitutes a radical non-propertied alternative to traditional methods of text production, dissemination and distribution. In terms of a model of communication there has been a gradual shift from content to code in the openness access, use, reuse and modification, reflecting a radical personalization that has made these open characteristics and principles increasingly the basis of the cultural sphere. Open source and open access have been developed and applied in open publishing, open archiving and open music, constituting the hallmarks of 'open culture'.

I would argue that 'openness' seems also to suggest political transparency and the norms of open inquiry, indeed, even democracy itself as both the basis of the logic of inquiry and the dissemination of its results. In other words, certain institutional forms are required to promote the organization of knowledge that enhance its free flow, the mode of open criticism, testing and validation characteristic of science-based institutions, and the non-ideological replication, trial-and-error ethos that typifies the scientific method consonant with an open community of inquiry.

New models of open science are rapidly developing based on Mode 2.0 with greater interdisciplinarity and 'flattening' of geocentric science centers and knowledge flows toward global teams. Correspondingly there is a reversal from close-conduit peer review to open source public scrutiny and increased use of open source data analysis, management of large databases and sharing (bioinformatics). Science publishing has undergone a sea-change with changes in creation, production and consumption of scholarly resources – 'creation of new formats made possible by digital technologies, ultimately allowing scholars to work in deeply integrated electronic research and publishing environments that will enable real-time dissemination, collaboration, dynamically-updated content, and usage of new media'; and 'alternative distribution models (institutional repositories, pre-print servers, open access journals) have also arisen with the aim to broaden access, reduce costs, and enable open sharing of content' (Ithaka Harbors, Inc., 2007, p. 4).[22]

The new models of open science are to some extent in opposition or conflict with expanded protection of IP. Open source initiatives have facilitated the development of new models of production and innovation. The public and non-profit sectors have called for alternative approaches dedicated to public knowledge redistribution and dissemination. Now distributed peer-to-peer knowledge systems rival the scope and quality of similar products produced by proprietary efforts where speed of diffusion of open source projects is an obvious advantage. The successful projects occur in both software and open source biology. Open access science has focused on making peer-reviewed, online research and scholarship freely accessible to a broader population (including digitized back issues).

Open science demonstrates an exemplar of a compound of a 'private–collective' model of innovation that contains elements of both proprietary and public models of knowledge production (von Hippel and von Krogh, 2003). Rhoten and Powell (2007) ask whether the expansion of a patenting culture undermines the norms of open science and whether the intensification of patenting accelerates or retards the development of basic and commercial research.

As Waldrop (2008), writing in *Scientific American*, acknowledges, the emergence of Science 2.0

> generally refers to new practices of scientists who post raw experimental results, nascent theories, claims of discovery and draft papers on the Web for others to see and comment on. Proponents say these 'open access' practices make scientific progress more collaborative and therefore more productive. Critics say scientists who put preliminary findings online risk having others copy or exploit the work to gain credit or even patents. Despite pros and cons, Science 2.0 sites are beginning to proliferate; one notable example is the OpenWetWare project started by biological engineers at the Massachusetts Institute of Technology.

Waldrop (2008) demonstrates that the rich-text, highly interactive, user-generated, and socially active Internet (Web 2.0) has seen linear models of knowledge production giving way to more diffuse open-ended and serendipitous knowledge processes.

Open science economy plays a complementary role with corporate and transnational science, and implies a strong role for governments. Increasingly portal-based knowledge environments and global science gateways support collaborative science (Schuchardt et al., 2007; see, e.g., Science.gov and Science.world). Cyber-mashups of very large data sets let users explore, analyze and comprehend the science behind the information being streamed. The World Wide Web has revolutionized how researchers from various disciplines collaborate over long distances, especially in the life sciences, where interdisciplinary approaches are becoming increasingly powerful as a driver of both integration and discovery (with regard to data access, data quality, identity and provenance) (Sagotsky et al., 2008). National science reviews and assessments focus on developing distributed knowledge systems based on quality journal suites in disciplinary clusters with an ever finer mesh of in-built indicators. Meanwhile economists argue that open source software can be an engine of economic growth (see Garzarelli et al., 2008; Etzkowitz, 1997, 2003, 2008; David, 2003) and clearly the notion of open science economy has the strong potential to become one of the leading sectors of the knowledge economy.

CONCLUSION

Higher education debates need to be centered on the changing concepts of the knowledge economy. They need to systematically address questions in three domains. First, that of the 'learning economy', in a way that links education to national innovation without embracing a crude economic instrumentalism. Second, that of the 'creative economy', without reducing either creativity to innovation and/or higher education to questions of enhanced productivity, and in a way that recognizes and utilizes the prospects of new social media and learning ecologies that promote greater personalization, participation and peer collaboration. Third, the 'open knowledge economy', which understands the public benefits of open knowledge production for sustainable higher education, science and democracy.

These questions have become pressing at a time when the prevailing neoliberal policy credo has been discredited and policy-makers look for a new development paradigm that is sustainable in the long term. The three forms of the knowledge economy that I have presented under the headings 'learning', 'creativity' and 'openness' offer three interrelated concepts and practices that define the future of higher education in the twenty-first century.

NOTES

1. This list is based on Peters et al. (2009) as it was compiled for *New Learning: a charter for change in education*, at http://education.illinois.edu/newlearning/.
2. These two World Bank programs have been very influential. For both associated websites, see http://web.worldbank.org/WBSITE/EXTERNAL/WBI/WBIPROGRAMS/KFDLP/0,,menuPK:461238~pagePK:64156143~piPK:64154155~theSitePK:461198,00.html and http://web.worldbank.org/WBSITE/EXTERNAL/TOPICS/EXTEDUCATION/0,,contentMDK:20161496~menuPK:540092~pagePK:148956~piPK:216618~theSitePK:282386,00.html.
3. For Lundvall's publications see his webpage at http://www.business.aau.dk/ike/members/bal.html.
4. This section is based on my entry in *New Learning: a charter for change in education*, at http://education.illinois.edu/newlearning/ – but see Peters et al. (2009).

5. See The Center for Accelerated learning at http://www.alcenter.com/; see, for example, *The Framework for Gifted Education* at http://education.qld.gov.au/publication/production/reports/pdfs/giftedandtalfwrk.pdf.

6. For innovation theory see the Swedish economist Bengt-Åke Lundvall's webpage at http://www.business.aau.dk/ike/members/bal.html, and especially his concept of 'the learning economy' (above).

7. See also the education section of the P2P Foundation at http://p2pfoundation.net/Category:Education.

8. See Benkler's homepage at http://www.benkler.org/, where he outlines his research in terms of a set of general theoretical problems, including: cooperation and human systems design (how we understand the dynamics of human cooperation through work in many disciplines, from experimental economics, evolutionary biology, and computer science, to organizational sociology and anthropology, and how we can synthesize this body of work into an approach to designing human systems: be they technical platforms, business processes, or law); commons-based information production and exchange (sustainability and comparative efficiency); and freedom, justice, and the organization of information production on nonproprietary principles (normative analysis of the implications of commons-based production and exchange of information and culture). Many of his papers are available online.

9. See http://www.law.duke.edu/cspd/.

10. See http://creativecommons.org/.

11. See http://www.wired.com/wired/archive/4.01/white.paper_pr.html.

12. See http://crookedtimber.org/category/benkler-seminar/.

13. This section is based on my entry in *New Learning: a charter for change in education,* at http://education.illinois.edu/newlearning/.

14. See, for example, the Indian Open Schooling Network (IOSN) at http://www.nos.org/iosn.htm, the National Institute of Open Schooling at http://www.nos.org/, and Open School BC (British Columbia) at http://www.pss.gov.bc.ca/osbc/.

15. See http://www.ocwconsortium.org/index.php?option=com_content&task=view&id=15&Itemid=29.

16. See the OpenCourseWare Consortium for the full list of participating countries and list of courses at http://www.ocwconsortium.org/.

17. The full declaration can be found at http://www.capetowndeclaration.org/read-the-declaration.

18. See http://creativecommons.org/.

19. See http://p2pfoundation.net/The_Foundation_for_P2P_Alternatives.

20. See http://pkp.sfu.ca/.

21. See http://www.okfn.org/.

22. See, for instance the *Journal of Visualized Experiments* at http://www.jove.com/.

REFERENCES

Arrow, K. (1962), 'The economic implications of learning by doing', *Review of Economic Studies*, **29**, 80.

Baumol, W.J. (2002), *The Free-Market Innovation Machine: Analyzing the Growth Miracle of Capitalism*, Princeton, NJ: Princeton University Press.

Becker, G. (1964, 1993, 3rd edn), *Human Capital: A Theoretical and Empirical Analysis, with Special Reference to Education*, Chicago, IL: University of Chicago Press.

Bell, D. (1973), *The Coming of Post-Industrial Society: A Venture in Social Forecasting*, New York: Basic Books.

Benkler, Y. (2003), *Freedom in the Commons: Towards a Political Economy of Information*, at http://www.law.duke.edu/shell/cite.pl?52+Duke+L.+J.+1245.

Benkler, Y. (2006), *The Wealth of Networks: How Social Production Transforms Markets and Freedom*, New Haven, CT: Yale University Press.

Benkler, Y. and H. Nissenbaum (2006), 'Commons-based peer production and virtue', *The Journal of Political Philosophy*, **14** (4), 394–419.

Blythe, M. (2000), *Creative Learning Futures: Literature Review of Training and Development Needs in the Creative Industries*, http://www.cadise.ac.uk/projects/creativelearning/New_Lit.doc.

Bourdieu, P. (1986), 'The forms of capital', trans. R. Nice, in J. Richardson (ed.), *Handbook of Theory of Research for Sociology of Education*, Westport, CT: Greenwood Press, pp. 241–58.

Boyle, J. (1997), *A Politics of Intellectual Property: Environmentalism for the Net?*, http://www.james-boyle.com/.

Brown, J. and P. Duguid (2000), *The Social Life of Information*, Boston, MA: Harvard Business School Press.

Caron, A. and L. Caronia (2007), *Moving Cultures: Mobile Communications in Everyday Life,* Montreal, Kingston, London and Ithaca, NY: McGill-Queens' University Press.

Caves, R. (2000), *Creative Industries: Contracts between Art and Commerce*, Cambridge, MA: Harvard University Press.

Coleman, J. (1988), 'Social capital in the creation of human capital', *American Journal of Sociology*, **94** Supplement, S95–S120.

Cowen, T. (2002), *Creative Destruction: How Globalization is Changing the World's Cultures*, Princeton, NJ: Princeton University Press.

Davenport, T. and J. Beck (2001), *The Attention Economy: Understanding the New Economy of Business*, Cambridge, MA: Harvard Business School Press.

David, P.A. (2003), 'The economic logic of "open science" and the balance between private property rights and the public domain in scientific data and information: a primer', at http://129.3.20.41/eps/dev/papers/0502/0502006.pdf.

Drucker, P. (1969), *The Age of Discontinuity: Guidelines to our Changing Society*, New York: Harper and Row.

Etzkowitz, H. (1997), 'The entrepreneurial university and the emergence of democratic corporatism', in H. Etzkowitz and L. Leydesdorff (eds), *Universities and the Global Knowledge Economy: A Triple Helix of University–Industry–Government Relations*, London: Continuum, pp. 141–54.

Etzkowitz, H. (2003), 'Innovation in innovation: the triple helix of university–industry–government relations', *Social Science Information*, **42** (3), 293–337.

Etzkowitz, H. (2008), *The Triple Helix: University–Industry–Government Innovation in Action*, London: Routledge.

Flanagan, M. and H. Nissenbaum (2005), 'Embodying values in technology: theory and practice', http://www.nyu.edu/projects/nissenbaum/papers/Nissenbaum-VID.4-25.pdf.

Flanagan, H., D. Howe and H. Nissenbaum (2005), 'Values at play: design tradeoffs in socially oriented game design', presented at Conference on Human Factors in Computing Systems, *Proceedings*, pp. 751–60.

Florida, R. (2002), *The Rise of the Creative Class*, New York: Basic Books.

Foray, D. (2000), *The Economics of Knowledge*, Cambridge, MA: The MIT Press.

Frey, B. and W. Pommerehne (1989), *Muses and Markets: Explorations in the Economics of the Arts*, Cambridge, MA: Blackwell.

Garzarelli, G., Y. Limam and B. Thomassen (2008), 'Open source software and economic growth: a classical division of labor perspective', *Information Technology for Development*, **14** (2), 116–35.

Gates, B. (2006), 'The road ahead', *Newsweek*, 25 January, http://www.msnbc.msn.com/id/11020787/.

Ginsburgh, V. and P.-M. Menger (eds) (1996), *Economics of the Arts*, Amsterdam: North-Holland.

Gordon, W. (1993), 'A property right in self-expression: equality and individualism in the natural law of intellectual property', 102 *The Yale L.J.*,1533, 1568–72.

Granovetter, M. (1973), 'The strength of weak ties', *American Journal of Sociology*, **78** (6), 1360–80.

Harvey, D. (1989), *The Condition of Postmodernity*, Oxford: Blackwell.

Hayek, F. von (1937), 'Economics and knowledge', Presidential address delivered before the London Economic Club, 10 November 1936, reprinted in *Economica IV* (new ser., 1937), 33–54.

Hayek, F. von (1945), 'The use of knowledge in society', *The American Economic Review*, **35** (4), 519–30.

Hearn, G. and D. Rooney (eds) (2008), *Knowledge Policy: Challenges for the Twenty First Century*, Cheltenham, UK and Northampton, MA, USA: Edward Elgar.

Heilbrun, J. and C. Gray (2001), *The Economics of Art and Culture*, 2nd edn, New York: Cambridge University Press.

Hesmondhalgh, D. (2002), *The Cultural Industries*, Thousand Oaks, CA: Sage.

von Hippel, E. and G. von Krogh (2003), 'Open source software and the "private-collective" innovation model: issues for organization science', *Organization Science*,**14** (2), 209–23.

Howkins, J. (2001), *The Creative Economy: How People Make Money from Ideas*, London: Allen Lane.

Hughes, J. (1988), 'The philosophy of intellectual property', 77 *GEO. L.J.* 287, 337–44.

Iiyoshi, T. and V. Kumar (2008), *Opening Up Education: The Collective Advancement of Education through Open Technology, Open Content, and Open Knowledge*, Cambridge, MA: MIT Press.

Illich, I. (1972), *Deschooling Society*, Harmondsworth, UK: Penguin.

Ithaka Harbors, Inc. (2007), *University Publishing in a Digital Age*, at http://www.ithaka.org/strategic-services/university-publishing, accessed 14 October 2008.

Ito, M. (2006), 'Japanese media mixes and amateur cultural exchange', in D. Buckingham and R. Willett (eds), *Digital Generations*, London: Lawrence Erlbaum, pp. 49–66.

Ito, M. (2008), 'Mobilizing the imagination in everyday play: the case of Japanese media mixes', in K. Drotner and S. Livingstone (eds), *International Handbook of Children, Media, and Culture*, draft manuscript available at: http://www.itofisher.com/mito/.

Landry, C. (2000), *The Creative City: A Toolkit for Urban Innovators*, London: Earthscan.

Lash, S. and J. Urry (1994), *Economies of Signs and Space*, London: Sage Publications.

Lave, J. and E. Wenger (1991), *Situated Learning: Legitimate Peripheral Participation*, New York: Cambridge University Press.

Lemley, M. (2005), 'Property, intellectual property, and free riding', 83 *Tex. L. Rev.* 1031.

Lessig, L. (2001), *Code: And Other Laws of Cyberspace*, New York: Basic Books.

Lessig, L. (2002), *The Future of Ideas: The Fate of the Commons in a Connected World*, New York: Random House.

Lessig, L. (2004), *Free Culture: How Big Media Uses Technology and the Law to Lock Down Culture and Control Creativity*, New York: Allen Lane.

Lorenz, E. and B.-Å. Lundvall (eds) (2006), *How Europe's Economies Learn*, Oxford: Oxford University Press.

Lundvall, B.-Å. (1988), 'Innovation as an interactive process – from user–producer interaction to national systems of innovation', in G. Dosi et al. (eds), *Technical Change and Economic Theory*, London: Pinter Publishers, pp. 349–69.

Lundvall, B.-Å. (1996), 'The social dimension of the learning economy', Druid Working Paper 96-1, at http://www3.druid.dk/wp/19960001.pdf, accessed 12 September 2010.

Lundvall, B.-Å. (2003), 'Why the new economy is a learning economy', *Economia e Politica Industriale: Rassegna trimestrale diretta da Sergio Vaccà/Vaccà*, Sergio, Milano: FrancoAngeli s.r.l., **117**, 173–85.

Lundvall, B.-Å. and B. Johnson (1994), 'The learning economy', *Journal of Industry Studies*, **1** (2), 23–42.

Lundvall, B.-Å., P. Rasmussen and E. Lorenz (2008), 'Education in the learning economy: a European perspective', *Policy Futures in Education*, **6** (6), 681–700.

Lyotard, J.-F. (1984), *The Postmodern Condition: A Report on Knowledge,* trans. G. Bennington and B. Massumi, Manchester: Manchester University Press.

Machlup, F. (1962), *The Production and Distribution of Knowledge in the United States*, Princeton, NJ: Princeton University Press.

Neil, A. (1960), *Summerhill: A Radical Approach to Child Rearing*, 'Preface', by Erich Fromm, New York: Hart Publishing.

Netanel, N. (1996), 'Copyright and a democratic civil society', *106 Yale L.J. 283*, 347–62.

Netanel, N. (1998), 'Asserting copyright's democratic principles in the global arena', *51 Vand. L. Rev. 217*, 272–6.

OECD (1996), *The Knowledge-Based Economy*, Paris: OECD.

Partnership for 21st Century Skills (2008), at http://www.21stcenturyskills.org/index.php?Itemid=40&id=82&option=com_content&task=view.

Pasinetti, L. (1981), *Structural Change and Economic Growth*, Cambridge: Cambridge University Press.

Peters, M.A. (2010), 'Creativity, openness and user-generated cultures', in D. Araya and M.A. Peters (eds), *Education in the Creative Economy: Knowledge and Learning in the Age of Information*, New York: Peter Lang, pp. 203–24.

Peters, M. and T. Besley (2006), *Building Knowledge Cultures: Education and Development in the Age of Knowledge Capitalism*, Boulder, CO; Lanham, MD and Oxford: Rowman and Littlefield.

Peters, M. and R. Britez (eds) (2008), *Open Education and Education for Openness*, Rotterdam and Taipei: Sense Publishers.

Peters, M. and P. Roberts (2011), *The Virtues of Openness: Education and Scholarship in a Digital Age*, Boulder, CO and London: Paradigm Publishers.

Peters, M., S. Marginson and P. Murphy (2009), *Creativity and the Global Knowledge Economy*, New York: Peter Lang.

Porat, M. (1977), *The Information Economy*, Washington, DC: US Department of Commerce.

Putnam, R. (2000), *Bowling Alone: The Collapse and Revival of American Community*, New York: Simon and Schuster.

Rhoten, D. and W. Powell (2007), 'The frontiers of intellectual property: expanded protection versus new models of open science', *Annual Review of Law and Social Science*, **3**, 345–73.

Rogers, C. (1969), *Freedom to Learn*, New York: Merrill.

Romer, P. (1990), 'Endogenous technological change', *Journal of Political Economy*, **98**, 71–102.

Sagotsky, J.A., L. Zhang, Z. Wang, S. Martin and T. Deisboeck (2008), 'Life sciences at the web: a new era for collaboration', *Molecular Systems Biology*, **4**, 201.

Samuelson, P. (1996), 'The Copyright Grab', *Wired*, retrieved from http://www.wired.com/wired/archive/4.01/white.paper_pr.html.

Schuchardt, K., C. Pancerella, L. Rahn, B. Didier, D. Kodeboyina, D. Leahy, J. Myers, O. Oluwole, W. Pitz, B. Ruscic, J. Song, G. Von Laszewski and C. Yang (2007), 'Portal-based knowledge environment for collaborative science', *Concurrency Computation Practice and Experience*, **19** (12), 1703–16.

Shapiro, C. and H. Varian (1998), *Information Rules: A Strategic Guide to the Network Economy*, Cambridge, MA: Harvard Business School Press.

Stallman, R. (2002), *Free Software, Free Society: Selected Essays of Richard M. Stallman*, Boston, MA: GNU Press, at http://www.gnu.org/philosophy/fsfs/rms-essays.pdf.

Stiglitz, J. (1999a), 'Knowledge as a global public good', at http://www.worldbank.org/knowledge/chiefecon/articles/undpk2/.

Stiglitz, J. (1999b), 'Knowledge for development: economic science, economic policy, and economic advice', Keynote Address, *Proceedings from the Annual Bank Conference on Development Economics 1998*, Washington, DC: World Bank, pp. 9–58.
Surowiecki, J. (2004), *The Wisdom of Crowds: Why the Many are Smarter than the Few and How Collective Wisdom Shapes Business, Economies, Societies and Nations*, New York: Anchor.
Tapscott, D. and A. Williams (2006), *Wikinomics: How Mass Collaboration Changes Everything*, New York: Penguin.
Toffler, A. (1980), *The Third Wave*, New York: Bantam Books.
Touraine, A. (1971), *The Post-Industrial Society: Tomorrow's Social History; Classes, Conflicts and Culture in the Programmed Society*, trans. L. Mayhew, New York: Random House.
United Nations (2008), *The Creative Economy Report*, retrieved from http://www.unctad.org/en/docs/ditc 20082cer_en.pdf.
Verschraegen, G. and M. Schiltz (2007), 'Knowledge as a global public good: the role and importance of open access', *Societies without Borders*, **2** (2), 157–74.
Waldrop, M.M. (2008), 'Science 2.0: is open access science the future?', *Scientific American*, **298** (5), at http://www.sciam.com/article.cfm?id=science-2-point-0-great-new-tool-or-great-risk, accessed 18 October 2008.

6 Global institutions: the Organization for Economic Co-operation and Development
Marijk van der Wende

INTRODUCTION

'Higher education drives and is driven by globalization. It trains the highly-skilled workers and contributes to the research base and capacity for innovation that determine competitiveness in the knowledge-based global economy' (OECD, 2009, p. 13). This clause summarizes the vision of the Organisation for Economic Co-operation and Development (OECD) on the relationship between globalization and higher education. Higher education's contribution to economic competitiveness is at the center, and the OECD emphasizes a conceptual link between the knowledge base and the global character of the economy in the twenty-first century.

From the 1960s onwards neoclassical economists conceived of higher education as a producer of human capital. This defined and legitimated the notion of 'education as an investment' in economic development. It became central to the OECD's involvement in the sector and its support for countries modernizing and expanding their national systems of higher education. In the 1990s the notion of globalization as a major contextual factor – not only characterizing changing economic realities but shaping the higher education sector itself – became more explicit. This introduced questions about competitiveness at a global level, the role of nations and cooperation between them (including regionalization), of cross-border flows, and about the role of new technologies therein. As the OECD saw it, higher education delivery and quality assurance had to be considered in a cross-border perspective. It suggested that supply and demand at a global level could be framed by global trade agreements based on privatization, (market) liberalization and deregulation. This put a range of policy questions on the agenda for common discussion.

With globalization and the intensification of the knowledge base of the economy, global flows of education ideas and policies have also grown. The OECD has been a central actor in initiating policy debates, and a decade after the first main emphasis on globalization it is closely monitoring how global higher education will evolve and how governments and institutions are meeting the challenges and exploiting the opportunities. It is above all in relation to global matters that the OECD as an institution positions itself as a global intergovernmental actor, and that its own role as a globalizing agency can be analyzed.

This chapter focuses on the role the OECD plays as a global institution in higher education policy, both through its own analysis and by providing a setting where national governments compare policy experiences, seek answers to common problems, identify good practice, and coordinate domestic and international policies.[1] The chapter also considers how the OECD contributes to globalization processes by guiding the policy debate or setting the agenda and shaping educational policies, both through and beyond its core activities, such as producing comparative statistics and economic and social data; by monitoring trends; and analyzing and forecasting economic developments.[2] The chapter will look at how the global nature of the organization itself is evolving; how globalization affects the coordinating role and steering capacities of its members, that is, national governments; and alters the playing field of higher education institutions. The chapter will go on to discuss OECD cooperation with other major global institutions, such as UNESCO and the World Bank, and regional bodies such as the European Commission. The final section of the chapter will address critical perspectives on these developments, with some attention to yet another global phenomenon: the financial and economic crisis that began in 2008.

FROM INTERNATIONALIZATION TO GLOBALIZATION

During the last decades of the twentieth century the internationalization of higher education gradually became a widespread and strategically important phenomenon (Teichler, 1999). Higher education trends were increasingly analyzed at the international level. In such work a growing part was played by international and intergovernmental organizations such as the OECD and by international comparative higher education research, such as that carried out by the Center for Higher Education Policy Studies (CHEPS) at the University of Twente in The Netherlands. There was increasing recognition of the need to address internationalization in national governmental policies and to develop policy initiatives at international level (van Vught et al., 2002).

In the early 1990s the OECD's Centre for Educational Research and Innovation (CERI) initiated a study on 'Education in a new international setting', leading to its first comprehensive publication on the internationalization of higher education (OECD, 1996b). Among the 'new developments' was 'the globalization of the economy' (p. 3). At this stage internationalization was mainly understood as expanding international student mobility, and changing curricula for domestic students with a view to the cross-border mobility of qualifications. The OECD's program on Institutional Management in Higher Education (IMHE) carried out a range of regional case studies, which provided a framework to assist institutions in designing and reviewing their own internationalization strategies and policies. At the same time the internationalization of quality assurance systems, still generally based at national level, was explored.

Various rationales for institutional approaches to internationalization were identified in order to guide policy development: political, economic, cultural and academic. It was found that the economic rationale for internationalization had gained importance as a result of economic globalization. Growing interdependence was forcing countries to focus on their economic, scientific and technological competitiveness, and the need for a highly skilled workforce (OECD/IMHE, 1999).

At the start of the twenty-first century CERI undertook further conceptual work in relation to internationalization policy. It conceived four rationales for internationalization. Mutual understanding was seen as related to the social, cultural and linguistic aspects of regional integration, international diplomacy, the creation of international networks of elites and the enhancement of human capital. The main policy instrument of this approach was student mobility programs, which were still largely publicly funded. Capacity-building referred to the growing demand for higher education in developing countries and emerging economies. This demand could be met by study abroad and return, but was also addressed by transnational foreign providers: higher education institutions from abroad offering programs and services either on their own or in cooperation with domestic institutions. A more market-oriented model emerged, with imports and exports. In this context, internationalization could also involve a revenue-generating approach, in which revenues from exports were used to finance the domestic higher education sector. Full-cost tuition fees for international students and for-profit overseas branch campuses emerged. Global competition meant not just educating domestically for national competition but also attracting highly skilled foreign people for the knowledge economy, especially in fields where there were national shortages. Skilled migration became another form of internationalization. The attraction of foreign graduate students and academic staff enhanced the competitiveness of higher education and R&D in the host country, provided that internationalization policies were coordinated with immigration regulation (OECD, 2004).

Various studies demonstrated that, overall, economic rationales for internationalization had become more dominant (van der Wende, 2001; van Vught et al., 2002; Teichler, 2004). As noted, the OECD linked this clearly to globalization and its impact on higher education, especially through the global competition for talented students and highly skilled workers, which took the form of a cross-border market. At the turn of the century this worldview was underlined by two important developments: the Bologna Declaration of 1999 which explicitly focused on enhancing the global attractiveness and competitiveness of European higher education; and the 2000 launch of the World Trade Organization (WTO) agenda on further liberalization of trade in services (GATS), including cross-border trade in educational services. The former was initially interpreted in terms of routine cooperation between nationally defined (and mainly public) systems of higher education. The latter introduced the new interpretation of higher education institutions and systems in terms of exporters and importers with the relationship between them designed and regulated through global trade agreements.

This new interpretation fitted better with the OECD's ideological framework than with a range of other organizations and actors. Within the OECD there were exchanges of ideas between experts from higher education and those from the OECD Directorate for Trade; in other circles there were heated debates and much criticism of the conception of higher education as a tradable commodity on the grounds of its role as a (national) public good. At the same time the OECD acknowledged the need to develop a regulatory framework for the emerging global markets, developing in cooperation with UNESCO a set of *Guidelines on Quality Provision of Cross-Border Higher Education* (OECD/ UNESCO, 2005).

During the first decade of the twenty-first century the global competitiveness rationale became more prevalent. In the European context the Bologna Process became increasingly interwoven with the economically oriented Lisbon Strategy of the European Commission, which aimed to make Europe the most competitive and dynamic knowledge economy in the world by 2010 (van der Wende, 2009). A growing range of OECD countries developed policies to attract foreign students in the spirit of the revenue-generating and skilled-migration approaches, although the so-called Doha Round of the

WTO including the GATS negotiations did not lead to substantial conclusions. Trends in overseas campuses and programs were less impressive than some predicted. E-learning (virtual universities) did not emerge as a significant global market. The complex possibilities of international e-learning were typically left to small-scale, department-led experiments (OECD, 2005).

This account illustrates how the internationalization of higher education became increasingly contextualized by economic globalization, and conceptualized in its framework. However, this does not imply any straightforward or linear relationship between the two concepts, as will be discussed in the next section. Nor does it mean that globalization has impacted merely the international dimension of higher education. It shows itself in a range of areas, including governance and management; and through the processes of global comparisons, benchmarks and best-practice models – in which, as is explored below, the OECD itself has played a key role as a global intergovernmental actor.

THE OECD'S FIELD OF ACTION AND ITS MAIN STAKEHOLDERS

Globalization cannot be regarded simply as a higher form of internationalization. The relationship between the two concepts is not linear or cumulative but of a different order. Scott (1998, p. 122) argues that the relationship is a dialectical one. 'Not all universities are (particularly) international, but all universities are subject to the same process of globalization – partly as objects, victims even, of these processes, but partly as subjects, or key agents of globalization.' Globalization and internationalization in higher education can be potentially conflicting or rival while at the same time interactive, mutually generative and continually reinforcing each other.

Globalization is generally understood as the widening, deepening and speeding up of worldwide interconnectedness (Held et al., 1999). This is related not only to economic convergence and interdependence and the liberalization of trade and markets but has an important cultural dimension. Globalization goes directly to the economic, cultural and political core of nations while also refashioning the larger higher education environment. In a networked environment in which every higher education institution is visible to every other, and the weight of the global dimension is increasing, it is no longer possible for nations or for individual institutions to seal themselves off from global effects. In this respect internationalization can be seen as one possible response to globalization, that is, as a way to make higher education institutions more effective in response to the globalization of societies, cultures, economies and labor markets. By definition, internationalization is a process more readily steerable by governments than is globalization. By the same token single governments have only a partial purchase on global developments through the medium of internationalization (Marginson and Van der Wende, 2009).

All the changes related to globalization have the potential to impact higher education in its various capacities in research, teaching and service, including even in its regional and local roles. At the same time globalization plays out very differently according to the type of institution and its profile, mission and locality. Not all higher education institutions are directly globally active. Yet no nation or individual institution can seal itself off completely from changing global realities. How then does this affect the playing field of the OECD, in terms of the behavior of and the relationships with and among its major stakeholders?

First, the nation-state still matters. This is of prime interest for an intergovernmental organization such as the OECD with national governments as it main stakeholders. Despite earlier predictions that the nation-state would fade away as a consequence of globalization, it remains significant, especially in higher education. Despite deregulation and the growth of the private sector, the main legislative and legitimating powers still rest with national government.[3] The nation remains the principal financer of higher education in nearly all OECD countries. European studies confirm the continued importance of national policy-making and the viability of national steering, even when global and (supra) regional influences such as the Bologna Process, GATS and the formation of international university consortia are taken into account (Beerkens, 2004; Vlk, 2006; Witte, 2006). This position is also held by Henry et al. (2001, p. 20), who nevertheless note the reconstitution of the nation-state; and by Marginson (1997), who underlines mutually reinforcing effects.

National regulation can hinder higher education institutions in their international operations. It may even work against their ambitions to become independent global players. At the same time most national policy-makers want institutions to be more competent for the global era. In a global knowledge economy the higher education sector represents potential leverage for the competitiveness of the nation, maximizing its knowledge capacity and research performance at global level and optimizing the benefits from global flows – for example by attracting highly skilled workers. These global orientations have consequences for strategy-making by nations and higher education institutions. In the past nearly all action was undertaken between the nation-state and the institution(s) at national and local levels. Now the same agents pursue change also at global level. Global strategy-making is important to both nations, through intergovernmental negotiations, and institutions, where individual universities function as global actors.[4]

Second, both cooperation and competition hold major strategic options for higher education institutions and governments. For example the European Union (EU), in the form of the European Higher Education Area and the European Research Area, can be understood as a space in which internal cooperation provides a strategic pathway to the global competitiveness of the EU as a whole. The same applies at a smaller but still regional scale in the Nordic countries through the creation of their Nordic Research and Innovation Area; and at national (or even subnational) levels, where governments stimulate cooperation in order to make higher education institutions and systems more competitive in the global context.

Yet at the same time, and with the same aim of enhancing global competitiveness, the device of national or regional competition may be used – for example through competitive research funding, which is increasingly concentrated at supranational level, for example in the creation of the European Research Council. It seems that at this point both kinds of strategy are seen as potentially beneficial and mutually reinforcing. As yet little is known of their combined effectiveness or the interface between the abundance of options and levels.[5] But major strategic questions cannot be ignored, however. Governments must consider what is the best way to make the national higher education system more globally competitive, whether national or international cooperation or competition, or (more likely) an effective mix of these options. Overly simplistic or one-sided competitive models can enhance vertical differentiation by building strength in certain institutions or areas but weakening others. This can suppress diversity. It is essential to devise an effective division of labor and a good balance between global competitiveness and national and regional priorities and interests. Intergovernmental consultation is a *sine qua non* in this process.

The increasing focus on intergovernmental negotiation as a zone for strategy-making, and on international cooperation as a strategic option for enhancing global competitiveness, underlines the OECD's role in the field of higher education. Perhaps, also, the growth in the roles of individual higher education institutions as global actors has the potential to enhance their interest in membership of the OECD's program on Institutional Management in Higher Education (IMHE).

THE OECD AND TOOLS FOR GLOBAL IMAGINING

As an intergovernmental forum with limited instrumental power, the OECD has a mostly discursive role in global transformations. By developing world pictures, tools for imagining, conceptual models and categories of phenomena, the OECD frames higher education policy discourses at intergovernmental level and with an increasing flow-on to national level (Henry et al., 2001, p. 128). As more and more governments start to use and adapt these methods, this process in itself tends to advance global convergence. One example of these tools for imagining is global scenario-building.

In the first decade of the twenty-first century, the OECD through CERI developed four scenarios for the future of higher education. Scenarios are analytical and conceptual tool images with the potential to structure policy debate. The two variables differentiating the OECD scenarios were the extent of globalization (global–local) and the amount of coordination influence exercised by government (administration–market) (OECD, 2006b). The four scenarios were as follows:

1. *Open networking*   In this scenario the key driver of change is the further harmonization of higher education systems and expanding the impact of the Bologna Process beyond Europe, leading to increased trust and understanding as a basis for ease of recognition of degrees. Lower costs of communication and transportation greatly facilitate cooperation and mobility, and the civic society ideal of open knowledge (open source) allows sharing of knowledge and data resources. This scenario is based more on collaboration than on competition, yet there is a strong hierarchy among higher education institutions, with some having more research funding and higher prestige than others.
2. *Serving local communities*   This scenario is driven by a public opinion backlash against globalization and growing skepticism about internationalization, due to terror attacks and wars, problems with immigration, outsourcing and perceptions of threatened national identity. Higher education institutions (re)focus on national and local community missions with a strong emphasis on teaching and lifelong learning. Only a very small number of 'elite' institutions link to international networks and conduct leading-edge research.

3. *New public management*   The main driving forces here are the mounting budget pressures created by the aging society, which in most countries lead to cost-shifting and -sharing. There is more use of new public management tools, including market forces, financial incentives (competitive funding), increased autonomy and accountability, and deregulation. Higher education institutions are active in foreign education markets and have taken advantage of the deregulation of tuition fees. On the research side there is more competition for national funding. Only a small amount of funding comes from international sources, with the exception of the funds coming from the European Research Council. There is a division of labor between institutions with specialized missions within each country. An institution's research reputation defines its ability to attract the best (international) students and its level of tuition fees.

4. *Higher education Inc.*   This scenario is strongly driven by trade liberalization in education, through WTO–GATS or on the basis of bilateral free trade agreements. Low transportation and communication costs, the increasing migration of people, and the rise of private funding and private provision of higher education further facilitate the emerging international marketplace. Higher education institutions compete globally and on a commercial basis. Research and teaching are increasingly disconnected. Institutions and even whole higher education systems concentrate on specific missions (core business strategy), leading to an international division of labor. Some countries earn reputations for high-quality undergraduate education while others are competitive in postgraduate studies and research. International rankings play an important role and English has become the language of research and postgraduate studies.

These scenarios overlap to a large extent, while also varying in the extent of cooperation as distinct from competition and whether a division of labor is achieved at national or international level. There is varied scope for intergovernmental negotiation and international cooperation (and hence for the role of the OECD as an intergovernmental organization).

The scenarios are a good example of how the OECD has contributed to the construction of the policy context for globalization and higher education.[6] Through this and other methods the OECD has foregrounded more commercially driven, competitive approaches in which higher education is imagined as a good tradable in global markets, heightening the need for institutions to prepare their students for the global economy, thereby putting the human capital paradigm in a global context (Henry et al., 2001, p. 129).

Another example of the OECD's discursive intervention in relation to the global context – and another expression of what is generally perceived as neoliberal ideology – is the promotion of the new public management (NPM) as an organizational model for the public sector and a means of ensuring global competitiveness (as mentioned in the third scenario). The OECD has been an important vehicle for embedding this approach in management and governance. In nations throughout the world the responses of higher education systems and institutions to globalization have been conditioned by national reforms that draw on NPM techniques (Marginson and Considine, 2000). Facing global competition for talent and an international market in cross-border students, nations have responded by modeling national systems as economic markets with government-steered competition between institutions. In this framework, institutions ideally enjoy considerable autonomy and are encouraged to become entrepreneurial in the international higher education market.

THE OECD'S 'MECHANISMS OF PERSUASION'

The promotion of the NPM as a response to global competitive pressures is a good example of how global transformations are taking place. This can be viewed as the diffusion of a reform template, tending to produce convergence and probably some interconnectivity between national systems (although this is more directly apparent in reforms that touch the connections between systems, such as the changes to degree structures implied in the Bologna Process). With the increasing cross-national flow of policy concepts and emergence of a global policy community, international and supranational organizations such as the OECD take on an enhanced policy role. For some time the OECD has seen itself as a key player in this global policy community, with national system impacts:

> OECD has evolved greatly in the globalizing world economy. It has been 'globalizing' itself, notably through new Members and dialogue activities . . . Analyzing the many facets of the process of globalization, and their policy implications, has become the central theme in OECD's work, as the challenges and opportunities of globalization have become a high priority of policy-makers in OECD countries. (OECD, 1996a, p. 15, cited in Henry et al., 2001, p. 19)

The OECD uses a range of functions to secure its influence. It should be noted that it has no regulatory mandate over its member countries. It rather seeks to operate through a process of peer pressure and consensus-building, and by monitoring, analyzing, and forecasting policy trends and issues. This includes its work on:

- comparative statistics on education indicators, especially the yearly publication of *Education at a Glance*, which provide overviews of performance standards and benchmarks for countries;
- further analysis and specific study of these data (*Education Policy Analysis*, also yearly), sometimes in specific key areas, notably higher education (OECD, 2006a);
- reviews of national policies for (higher) education; prepared at the request of OECD member states, and sometimes also reviews of non-members;
- occasional topically oriented or thematic reviews, for example those on higher education in 1998 and 2008 (see below); and
- specific projects, such as the development of future scenarios for higher education (OECD, 2006b); other forecasting studies like the project on *Higher Education to 2030* (OECD, 2008a, 2009); or feasibility studies such as the one on the assessment of learning outcomes (again, see below).[7]

It might appear that the production of comparative statistics, policy analysis and the search for consensus are technical features of the OECD's work. But the effective and combined use of these 'mechanisms of persuasion' enables the OECD to engage in actual agenda-setting. It can be viewed as a kind of think tank, able to take up issues that are not necessarily a priority of its member states, and initiating analysis and formulating alternative strategies that do not necessarily reflect the views of those states (Sadlak and Hüfner, 2002, p. 95). In this manner the OECD can place new issues on national policy agendas. Henry et al. (2001) confirm that although the organization describes itself as a place for reflection and discussion, and as offering research and analysis that may help governments shape policy, it has increasingly assumed the role of policy actor. This interpretation is especially apparent in the thematic reviews, where, as admitted by the organization itself, the 'descriptive, analytic, and normative are combined' (p. 129). But even in the work on comparative indicators, Henry and colleagues observe 'a global politics of comparison' that constitutes supranational agenda-setting (p. 57).

The examples that follow show these mechanisms at work.[8] Policy discourses are shaped and reshaped, and translated into messages for governments. The examples touch particularly on the theme of higher education in the global context and responses to globalization. The succession of OECD interventions also enables the evolution of the OECD's own policy position to be traced, as is later discussed.

Comparative Educational Indicators

The comparative data in *Education at a Glance* include clusters of higher education indicators with direct relevance for the role of higher education as an investment in and producer of human capital in the context of global competition. These indicators include the number of students who access and complete higher education, the socioeconomic backgrounds of those students, and their contribution to economic growth via the transition to the labor market. There is an increasing focus on the public–private division in higher education, in relation to both the costs (including costs-sharing and -shifting) and the benefits, such as relative earnings and other returns on educational investment. Another cluster of indicators concerns the patterns in student mobility, that is, study abroad, distinguishing between the origins and destinations of these flows.

Time series for these indicators reveal that while there has been an impressive expansion of tertiary education enrollment worldwide, from 68 million in 1991 to 132 million in 2004 (94 percent growth in 13 years at 5.1 percent per annum), the expansion of international student enrollment has been even more impressive: from 600 000 in 1975 to 1.8 million in 2000 and 2.7 million in 2005 (annual growth of 7.3 percent worldwide). This trend has provided the OECD with a credible platform for further exploring and developing its internationalization agenda.

Policy Analysis: Setting New Directions for the Policy Agenda

In 2006 the OECD conducted a further policy analysis of the comparative data. That year also saw the first ever OECD ministerial meeting exclusively focused on higher education, in Athens in June, and the arrival of Angel Guria as the new Secretary General of the OECD.

In Athens the Secretary General confirmed the increasingly international character of the policy debate on higher education and the role of the OECD within it (OECD, 2006a). He noted that discussion of higher education at the international level had grown because of its implications for the capacity of nations to participate successfully in the global knowledge economy; the growing mobility of students and researchers; and the emergence of international policy instruments such as the Bologna Process, GATS and the OECD/UNESCO guidelines on quality provision in higher education. He also noted a number of emerging challenges. First, the funding of higher education: many countries, especially in Europe, could not finance the expansion of higher education from the public purse alone without endangering quality and/or equity in access. Second, he proposed to shift the policy focus from making higher education systems bigger – on average in OECD countries about 50 percent of young people were enrolled – to making them better. He sought a mandate to engage in measuring learning outcomes in higher education in the same way that the OECD was doing successfully at the secondary school level with its PISA program.[9] He hoped that the OECD could provide member countries with evidence of the quality of their higher education systems. Third, he advocated an NPM approach to governance, in which greater autonomy of institutions in relation to government was coupled with performance-based accountability. He also argued for greater diversity at system level, on the grounds that in a competitive global market institutions should focus on their strengths and only some exceptional institutions could offer world-class basic research along with teaching, learning and service activities.

The Secretary General also emphasized the uneven effects of globalization. He noted the downsides for some nations in relation to poverty, limited access to public services and the negative effects of migration. He underlined the wide disparities between the winners and the losers under globalization within OECD countries and between OECD countries and developing countries. He also announced intensified cooperation with UNESCO. Subsequently 'Balancing Globalization' became a slogan of the organization.

The next period saw these new directions implemented. The themes of funding, governance, equity and internationalization were addressed in the OECD's second thematic review of tertiary education. Wider trends in demography and globalization were taken up in further work on the future of higher education by CERI. The idea of developing a 'PISA for Higher Education', which was met with many questions and much skepticism, took shape in consultation with the higher education sector through IMHE. IMHE also integrated the theme of diversification of institutional profiles and mission into its work program, and undertook an ambitious project on the role of higher education in regional development (OECD, 2007). These follow-up steps, and the various 'mechanisms of persuasion' they entailed, are now discussed.

Thematic Reviews of Tertiary Education

The OECD introduced thematic reviews in 1995 to provide a horizontal view of key educational issues across countries. Henry et al. (2001) analyze this mechanism in the context of the changing relationships between nations and the OECD. They see it as a sign of the enhanced role of the OECD as a policy actor (p. 129). Thematic reviews provide scope for direct comparisons and for the organization to select issues for analysis. The first thematic review of higher education (OECD, 1998) introduced the definition of higher education as 'tertiary education', including both university and non-university types of institutions and programs.[10]

The second thematic review (OECD, 2008b) encompassed 24 countries and was probably the most comprehensive analysis ever undertaken in higher education. Its framework was again the recognition of tertiary education as a major driver of economic competitiveness in an increasingly knowledge-driven global economy. The main concerns were to simultaneously raise participation rates, improve quality and achieve or maintain a sufficient level of funding. There were sustained messages on the need for cost-sharing based on recognition of the private benefits of tertiary education; on NPM-type models of institutional governance and management with enhanced autonomy and strategic leadership; and on a shift in the role of the government – from providing subsidies to steering via performance-based funding, accountability and quality assurance mechanisms, and increasing diversity and competition within the sector. The importance of internationalization was underlined, with emphasis on economic and market-oriented rationales.

The review (OECD, 2008b) describes globalization as one of the major contextual factors driving the sector. At the same time it makes clear that the unit for building and defining global competitiveness is the nation-state. Despite their enhanced autonomy, higher education institutions are expected to align their priorities with the national agenda and respond to the demands of stakeholders that are (more or less implicitly) positioned at the national level, as the public interest seems (again implicitly) bound to this level. Internationalization policies are also defined at the national level. This seems to suggest that of the four scenarios developed by OECD for the future of higher education, the NPM scenario (still) clearly represents for the OECD the current framework for higher education policy. It also suggests that despite the OECD's argument for enhanced institutional autonomy, institutions are still seen as agents of national policies, not as independent global players. Strategy-making and negotiation are positioned in the national context rather than a global zone of global strategy-making and intergovernmental negotiation. But perhaps the limited scope for globalization that this suggests is also due to the methodology applied in the thematic reviews: a parallel compilation of national reviews with multiple cross-case analysis on particular themes. In the same sense, international comparative higher education research is not the same as the study of the dynamics of internationalization and globalization in and around higher education (van der Wende, 2002).

Forecasting the Future: Higher Education to 2030

CERI's most recent work on the future of higher education (OECD, 2009) focuses on globalization as a contextual factor. It examines the elements that frame possible global trajectories of national systems and individual institutions, including geographical and economic position, national history, system organization, resources and competence in English. It addresses global power relations in higher education and research and the unbalanced global flows of knowledge, including cross-border faculty mobility. This emphasizes the hegemonic role of higher education and research in the USA, the global magnet for doctoral and postdoctoral work. It reflects on the emergence of China and India as powers in the global setting. Performance in scientific research is rising throughout Eastern Asia and Singapore. The OECD analysis argues that the global setting offers much scope for varied and inventive strategy-making, for example in the EU with the Bologna Process and the Lisbon Strategy.

The OECD discusses the respective roles of competition and cooperation at institutional level, especially in research. Competition is fueled by global rankings that tend to be biased towards research, the natural and medical sciences, and the English language. Global rankings suggest there is only one model with global standing, that of the large comprehensive research university. In many countries the effects of global competition and the enhanced visibility of research performance have been to drive a greater concentration of research resources in centers of excellence. This concentration model has a longer tradition in the USA and the UK than in most countries. It tends to improve brand image and lift the institution's position in rankings, in turn attracting more international funding. We now have a global reputation race (van Vught, 2006).

On the question of public goods, the report remarks on the manner in which these are mostly imagined only in the national context.

Correspondingly, the international sphere is automatically associated with private goods. However, there is a need to recognize both private goods within national systems and public goods at global level (Marginson, 2007). Global public goods such as international recognition systems, exchange schemes, cross-border student security and knowledge flows should be recognized as such and will become more important in a more globalized context.

The OECD also further develops its scenarios for cross-border higher education in this work. In the first scenario internationalization continues, the diversity of national systems is preserved, and there are varied strategies across countries – for example, revenue-generating approaches in English-speaking countries, subsidized foreign student recruitment in Europe, and mutual understanding strategies for countries in need of resources. The second scenario is a liberal model of commercial trade in the higher education sector, installed with internationally coordinated recognition and quality assurance systems. The third scenario depicts 'the triumph of the (former) emerging economies' with strongly developed systems in countries such as India and China, able to retain their domestic students and to attract foreign students themselves – creating difficulties for economically advanced countries dependent on revenue generation and/ or skilled migration through internationalization.

The Assessment of Learning Outcomes in Higher Education

At the 2006 Athens conference the ministers of higher education agreed that greater attention should be paid to the quality and relevance of higher education. This led to the OECD's decision to initiate a major international project on the Assessment of Higher Education Learning Outcomes (AHELO). It was recognized that there is no reliable information enabling comparative judgments about the competence of students or graduates in different countries and institutions, or teaching quality. The reputations of institutions are largely based on (historical) research performance, reflected in rankings, which may distort decision-making by students and other stakeholders. The project aims to assess whether it is possible to measure on a comparative basis what students know and can do at the end of a Bachelor degree program. It is a study of the scientific and practical feasibility of assessing learning outcomes across institutional, system, national, linguistic and cultural boundaries.

The project is controversial. Stakeholders' concerns focus on whether the diversity that characterizes most higher education systems, with respect to the type of students accepted (selectivity, demographics) and the different institutional profiles and missions (e.g. research versus teaching intensiveness), will be taken sufficiently into account. As a lack of data on the differences among these settings would bias the validity of obtained results, result in unintentional rankings, and inhibit the use of results for improvement of learning outcomes, as part of AHELO the OECD is developing work on the contextual dimension of a system for situating learning outcomes assessment in the case-by-case institutional context.

Experts from quality assurance recognize that learning outcomes assessment encompasses both a dimension of accountability, leading to the publication of better data on what students actually learn, and a new means or diagnostic tool for institutional self-improvement. There is a need to move beyond the assessment of inputs and processes. AHELO could be very relevant in deepening the appraisal of outcomes and can be complemented by the Tuning approach.

In the EU-funded Tuning project, intended learning outcomes were formulated across numerous countries for a range of disciplinary degrees at bachelor and master levels, including the definition of generic skills. By putting Tuning and AHELO together it becomes possible to aim to move from intended to achieved learning outcomes, provided that issues related to linguistic and cultural biases in assessment are effectively addressed. Success would enhance the practices of mutual recognition of higher education credits and degrees. Success in AHELO could also improve university rankings by supplementing them with the element missing up until now: sound data on the quality of learning. However, AHELO itself explicitly rejects the idea of rankings and any notion that higher education can be reduced to a handful of criteria that leaves out more than it includes. Instead AHELO sets out to identify and measure as many factors as possible influencing higher education, with emphasis on teaching and learning. Its creators are nevertheless aware that AHELO, or part of its results, could be used by others for ranking purposes.

Although the emphasis on learning outcome assessment is growing at international level, it is not uncontested. In particular the notion that standardized testing[11] is the appropriate way to assess learning outcomes at the university level has not been universally accepted. For example, in 2007 the University of California explicitly rejected this, noting that 'using standardized tests on an institutional level as measures of student learning fails to recognize the diversity, breadth, and depth of discipline-specific knowledge and learning that takes place in colleges and universities today' (Thomson and Douglass, 2009, p. 2).

THE GLOBAL NATURE OF THE OECD: WIDENING HORIZONS, INTENSIFYING PARTNERSHIPS

In the post-Cold War environment, with the developing idea of the world as a 'global village', the OECD started to extend relations beyond its member countries. A deputy-secretary post was created with responsibility to coordinate activities with non-member countries, focusing on 'economies in transition' in Central and Eastern Europe and the 'economic tigers' in Latin America and Asia. Cooperation with other regional, international and supranational organizations such as the EU, UNESCO, the World Bank and APEC was intensified.

As noted above, the arrival of the new Secretary General from Mexico in 2006 introduced more emphasis on 'balancing globalization'. Although the risks for social cohesion of large divergences in economic growth had been addressed before (in education, mostly in terms of social inclusion and exclusion), recognition of the potential social and economic costs now became more explicit. It was also recognized that, in future, economic power was likely to become less concentrated within the existing OECD membership. In 2007, OECD countries agreed to invite Chile, Estonia, Israel, Russia and Slovenia to open discussions for membership of the organization; and they offered enhanced engagement with a view to possible membership, to Brazil, China, India, Indonesia and South Africa. Chile became a member of the OECD in early 2010.

Countries on their way to accession may participate in certain activities for member countries. China took part in the 24-country wide thematic review (see above). This was coordinated by the OECD's Directorate for Education and its program for Co-operation with Non-Member Economies, and co-funded with support from the World Bank. This cooperation has been extended into the development of a 'Chinese Higher Education at a Glance' by a leading Chinese higher education research center.

Since the 1990s there has been more frequent cooperation between the OECD and the World Bank, especially in transition countries and emerging economies. The policy assumptions of both organizations are based on a human capital approach to higher education, which is seen as an important engine of economic growth in a knowledge society (World Bank, 2002). Henry et al. (2001) note that ideologically speaking the OECD occupies a position midway between the World Bank and UNESCO, although these positions are not static. The OECD, however, does not have the financial clout of the World Bank (p. 17). Their agendas and action programs have different orientations in that the World Bank focuses on developing countries and the OECD on industrialized countries. But globalization effects also require combined attention. The basis of international cooperation between developed and developing nations has changed. Next to the traditional 'aid paradigm', the 'trade paradigm' has been introduced. But what is their combined result? For example, how do skilled migration and revenue-generating models for internationalization work out in developing countries? How can the detrimental effects of cross-border mobility such as brain drain be avoided or addressed? Can the cross-border mobility of programs and institutions contribute to capacity-building in developing countries? If so, how and under what conditions? These questions are explored in a joint publication by OECD and the World Bank on *Cross-Border Tertiary Education* (OECD/World Bank, 2007).

There is long-term cooperation between the OECD and UNESCO in the collection of international comparative statistical data. There has been almost continuous interaction regarding the development and adjustment of the International Standard Classification of Education (ISCED). The extent to which the two organizations' stances with respect to (higher) education's role in society differ is by and large explained by their different charters and constituencies. UNESCO's position is inspired by mostly humanitarian values and the paragraphs of the UN Universal Declaration of Human Rights on higher education, which emphasizes that 'Higher education shall be equally accessible to all on the basis of merit' (Article 26, paragraph 1). As its constituency includes many developing countries and its mission is educational–scientific and cultural, UNESCO's concerns are by nature strong in areas such as equality of opportunity and cultural and linguistic diversity in education.

Yet there is some convergence of policy rhetoric and agendas, for instance through the lifelong learning agenda, which holds that higher education is a means to a further end, which can be personal, social or economic, depending on whether humanitarian or utilitarian positions are taken (Henry et al., 2001). Combining various concerns in a pragmatic way, the two organizations cooperated significantly on the regulation of cross-border education, as noted above (OECD/UNESCO, 2005). The final communiqué of the second World Conference on Higher Education demonstrates a pragmatic position on the nature of higher education as a public good. It recognizes that public funds are limited, private contributions may be needed, and private higher education pursuing public objectives has an important role to play (UNESCO, 2009).

With two-thirds of its member countries[12] and its headquarters located in Europe, it is almost inevitable that the OECD should be widely seen as Eurocentric. But while there has been longstanding cooperation between OECD and Eurostat on statistical indicators, other types of cooperation on higher education only became feasible after the European Commission obtained a stronger mandate[13] in this field when the Lisbon Strategy was launched in 2002. The introduction of the Open Method of Coordination[14] led to greater similarity in approaches and messages. The European Commission found its concerns on access and funding paralleled those of OECD. 'While most of Europe sees higher education as a "public good", tertiary enrollments have been stronger and grown faster in other parts of the world – mainly thanks to much higher private funding', stated the European Commission (2005, p. 3). 'Despite the strong social values, the EU is performing much weaker when it comes to access and equity than the US', stated an OECD official. A recent report of the Lisbon Council displays an OECD-style message about the economic returns to investment in education as a key to crisis recovery strategies: 'If, for instance, all OECD countries in Europe could raise their educational performance to Finland's level, the result could be an aggregate GDP increase of US$200 trillion – an important conclusion as the EU is pondering next steps in its EU 2020 strategy.'[15]

CONCLUDING REMARKS

The OECD is criticized both for its ideological stance and what is seen as undue influence on national policy. The organization is seen as an advocate of a predominantly neoliberal reading of globalization and a narrow paradigm of education as a human capital investment in economic development and competitiveness. Thus Henry and colleagues (2001, p. 175) conclude: 'Such a paradigm serves to legitimate a set of education values feeding off and feeding into the broader culture of rampant individualism and consumerism . . . and for a commodification of what was once regarded as "the public sphere".' Some critiques of the OECD's national policy effects focus on its interpolation of a universalizing western norm against which the performance and values of individual countries, including developing countries, are benchmarked (ibid., p. 57). Martens (2006, p. 3) refers to a 'Trojan Horse' and an 'eventual takeover', noting how 'intergovernmental governance arrangements serve as instruments for national executives to withdraw decisionmaking control from domestic actors or institutions and to manipulate the domestic context'.

Its critics are firing at a moving target. The OECD's policy paradigm is not static. In the second half of the 1990s, when destabilizing outcomes from economic globalization were becoming apparent – such as high unemployment, widening income disparities, persistent poverty and social exclusion – social cohesion became an important concept. The organization talked of complementary social and economic goals. Later 'Balancing Globalization' was put on the agenda and some priority was given to the development of indicators on the social benefits of education. This work has since been intensified.[16]

The global financial and economic crisis that began in 2008 suggests the need for further reflection. It highlights the renewed importance of the nation, including protectionist measures; and the integration of new parties at global negotiation tables, for example at the G20 and International Monetary Fund (IMF). The WTO Doha Round has failed to deliver significant results so far. This suggests that trade liberalization is not now a burning agenda item. In higher education shifting patterns of supply and demand, including enhanced capacity-development in rising economies (notably China) and reduced purchasing powers in others (for example South Korea), with consequent shifts in international mobility flows, will all have effects (Douglass and Edelstein, 2009).

A recent IMHE seminar on *Higher Education at a Time of Crisis*[17] revealed that not only will the crisis spur the demand for higher education; it will do so in the context of stagnating or reduced budgets. Many institutions consider attracting more international students (the revenue-generating form of internationalization) to compensate for lower domestic per capita funding. This becomes even more important in countries where student numbers are declining because of demographic changes, such as Japan. However, it remains to be seen how the domestic and international markets will respond to all this, and sudden shifts into new forms of revenue-raising have their dangers.

> In almost all countries, the drive to recruit foreign students is based on the lure of money. Cash-strapped institutions faced with declining government support have turned to exporting education as a revenue-generating business. The danger is that too heavy a reliance on foreign fees can leave universities open to budgetary crises should student numbers start to fall. (*University World News*, 2010; Douglass, forthcoming)

Existing scenarios will need to be reconsidered (van der Wende, 2007). For example, should we expect to see more scope for the 'serving local communities' scenario as described above than for the 'higher education Inc.' one? Or will the 'triumph of the (former) emerging economies' scenario predominate? Should the new situation be interpreted as a backlash against globalization, or as a lighter or probably temporary form of de-globalization? In any case, we have learnt that the world is *not* flat.[18] But does the situation also indicate that globalization is less irreversible than often suggested, a position defended from historical analyses of reversing globalization periods (James, 2001)? Is the great era of globalization over? Has the global free market economy been a utopian project, so that global multilateral frameworks and agreements will struggle and transnational institutions that have built the global free market have to accept a more modest role, as argued for some time by globalization skeptics such as Gray (2002)? Or is it that globalization itself is reversing, in other words, that globalization is in retreat (Altman, 2009)?

In any case, balancing globalization is the main challenge. Global imbalances represent serious threats to the stability of many national (and regional) economies. Perhaps it will not be the 'Washington Consensus' of free markets but a 'Beijing Consensus' of stronger state direction that will define the new geopolitical order. If so, the OECD with its outreach strategy has already positioned itself adroitly. It seems to be well placed to continue to play a pivotal global role.

NOTES

1. For information about the OECD as an organization and its history refer to http://www.oecd.org/home.
2. See also the comprehensive study on globalization and OECD's role by Henry et al. (2001).
3. With notable exceptions in federal contexts such as the USA and Germany, where the major responsibilities are positioned at the state (or *Länder*) level.
4. See Marginson and van der Wende (2009, p. 27) for a more complete depiction of the conceptual model on zones of strategy-making.
5. See van der Wende (2007) for a more complete conceptual model of strategic options for enhancing global competitiveness.
6. These scenarios were discussed in an informal session with ministers of higher education, preceding the OECD ministerial meeting on higher education in June 2006 in Athens.
7. See www.oecd.org/edu/ahelo.
8. The examples do not include the OECD's role in reviews of national policies, and the impacts of such reviews, but see Henry et al. (2001).
9. PISA is the OECD's Programme for International Student Assessment.
10. Referring to programs at ISCED levels 5A, 5B and 6.
11. Such as through the Collegiate Learning Assessment (CLA).
12. Eighteen out of the now 31 OECD countries are located in the EU and 21 in the European Economic Area (EEA).
13. This mandate was of a political rather than a legal nature (see van der Wende, 2009, p. 320).
14. The European Union's Open Method of Coordination (OMC) is a method that in principle assumes that coordination of policies can be achieved without the use of 'hard law' (Gornitzka, 2005). The use of indicators and comparative statistics is quite central to it and was sometimes referred to as the 'OECD-ization' of the EC.
15. http://www.lisboncouncil.net/news-a-events/152-highcostloweducation.html, retrieved 27 January 2010.
16. See OECD's *Education at a Glance* (2009), http://www.oecd.org/dataoecd/41/25/43636332.pdf.
17. Copenhagen, June 2009. See http://www.oecd.org/document/10/0,3343,en_2649_35961291_43253066_1_1_1_1,00.html.
18. The globalization thesis that the 'world is flat' was generated by Thomas Friedman (2005).

REFERENCES

Altman, R. (2009), 'Globalization in retreat: further geopolitical consequences of the financial crisis', *Foreign Policy*, July/August, accessed 30 January 2010 at http://www.foreignaffairs.com/articles/65153/roger-c-altman/globalization-in-retreat.

Beerkens, H. (2004), *Global Opportunities and Institutional Embeddedness: Higher Education Consortia in Europe and Southeast Asia*, doctoral dissertation, Center for Higher Education Policy Studies (CHEPS), University of Twente, accessed 20 January 2010 at http://www.utwente.nl/cheps/documenten/thesisbeerkens.pdf.

Douglass, J. (forthcoming), 'Higher education budgets and the global recession: tracking various national responses and their consequences', Research and Occasional Paper Series, CSHE.x.10, Berkeley: University of California Berkeley.

Douglass, J. and R. Edelstein (2009), 'Whither the global talent pool?', *Change*, July–August, 38–44.

European Commission (2005), *Mobilising the Brainpower of Europe: Enabling Universities to Make their Full Contribution to the Lisbon Strategy*, Communication from the Commission, COM (2005) 152 final.

Friedman, T. (2005), *The World is Flat: A Brief History of the Globalized World in the 21st Century*, New York: Farrar, Straus and Giroux.
Gornitzka, A. (2005), 'Coordinating policies for a Europe of Knowledge – emerging practices of the "open method of coordination" in education and research', Arena Working Paper no. 16/2005.
Gray, J. (2002), *False Dawn: The Delusions of Global Capitalism*, London: Granta Books.
Held, D., A. McGrew, D. Goldblatt and J. Perraton (1999), *Global Transformations: Politics, Economics and Culture*, Stanford, CA: Stanford University Press.
Henry, M., B. Lingard, F. Rizvi and S. Taylor (2001), *The OECD: Globalization and Education Policy*, Oxford: IAU Press/Pergamon.
James, H. (2001), *The End of Globalization: Lessons from the Great Depression*, Cambridge, MA: Harvard University Press.
Marginson, S. (1997), *Markets in Education*, Sydney: Allen and Unwin.
Marginson, S. (2007), 'The public/private divide in higher education: a global revision', *Higher Education*, **53**, 307–33.
Marginson, S. and M. Considine (2000), *The Enterprise University: Power, Governance and Reinvention in Australia*, Cambridge: Cambridge University Press.
Marginson, S. and M. van der Wende (2009), 'The new global landscape of nations and institutions', in OECD, *Higher Education to 2030, Volume 2: Globalization*, Paris: OECD, pp. 17–57.
Martens, K. (2006), *Boomerangs and Trojan Horses: The Unintended Consequences of Internationalizing Education Policy through the EU and the OECD*, European University Institute, 2006–07 European Forum Series.
Organization for Economic Co-operation and Development (OECD) (1996a), *Globalization and Linkages to 2030: Challenges and Opportunities for OECD Countries*, Paris: OECD.
Organization for Economic Co-operation and Development (OECD) (1996b), *Internationalization of Higher Education*, Paris: OECD.
Organization for Economic Co-operation and Development (OECD) (1998), *Redefining Tertiary Education*, Paris: OECD.
Organization for Economic Co-operation and Development (OECD) (2004), *Internationalization and Trade in Higher Education: Opportunities and Challenges*, Paris: OECD/CERI.
Organization for Economic Co-operation and Development (OECD) (2005), *E-learning in Tertiary Education: Where do we Stand?* Paris: OECD.
Organization for Economic Co-operation and Development (OECD) (2006a), *Education Policy Analysis: Focus On Higher Education*, Paris: OECD.
Organization for Economic Co-operation and Development (OECD) (2006b), *Four Future Scenarios For Higher Education*, accessed 29 January 2010 at http://www.oecd.org/dataoecd/22/22/38073691.pdf.
Organization for Economic Co-operation and Development (OECD) (2007), *Higher Education and Regions: Globally Competitive, Locally Engaged*, Paris: OECD.
Organization for Economic Co-operation and Development (OECD) (2008a), *Higher Education to 2030, Volume 1: Demography*, Paris: OECD.
Organization for Economic Co-operation and Development (OECD) (2008b), *Tertiary Education for the Knowledge Society, Vols 1 and 2*, Paris: OECD.
Organization for Economic Co-operation and Development (OECD) (2009), *Higher Education to 2030: Vol 2. Globalization*, Paris: OECD.
Organization for Economic Co-operation and Development (OECD/IMHE) (1999), *Quality and Internationalization in Higher Education*, Paris: OECD.
Organization for Economic Co-operation and Development (OECD/UNESCO) (2005), *Guidelines on Quality Provision of Cross-Border Higher Education*, Paris: OECD.
Organization for Economic Co-operation and Development (OECD)/World Bank (2007), *Cross-Border Tertiary Education: A Way Towards Capacity Development*, Paris: OECD.
Sadlak, J. and K. Hüfner (2002), 'International governmental organization and research on higher education', in J. Enders and O. Fulton (eds), *Higher Education in a Globalizing World: International Trends and Mutual Observations*, Dordrecht: Kluwer, pp. 87–102.
Scott, P. (1998), Massification, internationalization and globalization', in P. Scott (ed.), *The Globalization of Higher Education*, Buckingham: Society for Research into Higher Education/Open University Press, pp. 108–29.
Teichler, U. (1999), 'Internationalization as a challenge for higher education in Europe', *Tertiary Education and Management*, **5** (1), 5–23.
Teichler, U. (2004), 'The changing debate on internationalization of higher education', *Higher Education*, **48**, 5–26.
Thomson, G. and J. Douglass (2009), *Decoding Learning Gains: Measuring Outcomes and the Pivotal Role of the Major and Student Backgrounds*, Research and Occasional Paper Series: CSHE.5.09, Berkeley, University of California Berkeley.

United Nations Educational, Scientific and Cultural Organization (UNESCO) (2009), *2009 World Conference on Higher Education: The new dynamics of higher education and research for societal change and development*, UNESCO, Paris, 5–8 July 2009, Communiqué, 8 July.

University World News (2010), **108**, 24 January.

Vlk, A. (2006), *Higher Education and GATS: Regulatory Consequences and Stakeholder's Response*, doctoral dissertation, CHEPS, University of Twente, accessed at http://www.utwente.nl/cheps/documenten/thesisvlk.pdf.

Vught, F.A. van (2006), 'Higher education system dynamics and useful knowledge creation', in J. Duderstadt and L. Weber (eds), *Universities and Business: Towards a Better Society*, New York: Economica, pp. 103–21.

Vught, F.A. van, M. van der Wende and D. Westerheijden (2002), 'Globalization and internationalization: policy agendas compared', in J. Enders and O. Fulton (eds), *Higher Education in a Globalizing World: International Trends and Mutual Observations*, Dordrecht: Kluwer, pp. 103–21.

Wende, M. van der (2001), 'Internationalization policies: about new trends and contrasting paradigms', *Higher Education Policy*, **14** (3), 249–59.

Wende, M. van der (2002), *Higher Education Globally,* Inaugural lecture, University of Twente, Enschede: Twente University Press.

Wende, M. van der (2007), 'Internationalization of higher education in the OECD countries: challenges and opportunities for the coming decade', *Journal on Studies in International Education,* **11** (3–4), 274–90.

Wende, M. van der (2009), 'European responses to global competitiveness in higher education', in J. Douglass, J. King and I. Feller (eds), *Globalization's Muse: Universities and Higher Education Systems in a Changing World*, Berkeley, CA: University of California Berkeley Public Policy Press, pp. 317–41.

Witte, J. (2006), *Change of Degrees and Degrees of Change: comparing adaptations of European higher education systems in the context of the Bologna Process,* doctoral dissertation, CHEPS, University of Twente, The Netherlands, accessed at http://www.utwente.nl/cheps/documenten/thesisvlk.pdf.

World Bank (2002), *Constructing Knowledge Societies: New Challenges for Tertiary Education,* Washington, DC: The World Bank.

7 Extra-national provision
Christopher Ziguras

INTRODUCTION

This chapter considers education provided by institutions outside the student's home country, focused on the provision of whole programs of study rather than short courses. Cross-border education might involve students traveling beyond national borders to enroll in a foreign institution, or might involve staying in the home country but enrolling in a program offered by a foreign institution. The chapter explores the ways in which students access higher education that originates outside their national borders and considers different ways of understanding the growth of extra-national provision since the 1990s.

The earliest universities were established in Europe before the first nation-states in the modern sense. We might say that extra-national provision of higher education was once the norm. The Middle Ages witnessed the creation of a network of universities, with a common curriculum (theology, medicine, law), a common language of instruction (Latin), and a common mission (to promote a universalizing intellectual transcendence of the cultural and linguistic diversity of the continent across which the network was overlaid). Students and scholars often traveled considerable distances to early universities, but they did not cross national borders as we know them. The origins of higher education were extra-national because they were pre-national, little affected by the changing fortunes of the empires, kingdoms and principalities on whose lands the campuses were located.

Since then the world has been delineated into a system of sovereign states, each with jurisdiction over its own higher education institutions. During the last century the massification of higher education in the advanced economies took place under the control of states that had a previously unparalleled command of their citizens, their national economies and their borders. The modern university was a vehicle for national development with very high proportions of students, staff and funding sourced within the nation-state. Over the past two decades the national character of the university has begun to unravel, as the chapters collected in this volume demonstrate.

INTERNATIONAL STUDENT MOBILITY: AID AND TRADE

Between the end of the Second World War (1945) and the end of the Cold War (1990), student mobility across borders occurred on a much smaller scale than today, and was normally coordinated by governments. In communist states governments cooperated to foster the movement of students between politically allied states, both to build greater social connections between states but also to facilitate the transfer of knowledge and skills to foster economic and social development. (The last bastion of this model is Cuba, which continues to host significant numbers of international students, particularly in medicine, as part of the nation's efforts to build relationships of solidarity with politically friendly states.) In these states overseas travel was normally highly restricted, and participation in such state-sponsored overseas studies was one of the few means for a young person to travel legitimately.

In the west, international travel was less politically restricted, but as in the communist states most extra-national study was government-sponsored. The USA and former European colonial powers sponsored students from politically aligned developing countries to study in their universities. In most western receiving countries a significant proportion of the cost of tuition of international students was borne by the host government.

However, alongside the government-sponsored students were growing numbers of self-funded or 'private' students. For example, between 1950 and 1975 the Australian government sponsored around 18000 students, with the largest numbers of students coming from Indonesia, Malaysia, South Vietnam and Thailand. During the same period, however, Australia hosted an additional 45000 private international students, with the largest numbers from Malaysia, Hong Kong and Singapore. By 1975 less than a quarter of the 12500 international students in Australia were in government-sponsored programs (Cleverley and Jones, 1976, pp. 26–9). During the 1970s and 1980s, in the UK, Australia and New Zealand successive government inquiries debated whether subsidizing the tuition of private international students was an effective way of targeting international development assistance. Private international students tended to be affluent, urban and well connected in business and government circles, and were hardly the most needy recipients for development assistance.

Foreign aid for tertiary education continues today. France, Germany and Japan are currently the world's leading international aid donors in tertiary education, contributing between them US$2.7 billion in 2004, which represents 80 percent of the global total of official development assistance spending on tertiary education (Bashir, 2007). In 2007 these three countries enrolled 21 percent of the world's internationally mobile students who studied abroad for a year or more (UNESCO, 2009b). Most countries where English is not the language of instruction in higher education to some extent subsidize international students tuition in public institutions, through tuition-free or heavily subsidized places and through scholarships to cover living expenses.

In the mid-1980s the UK, Australia and New Zealand shifted from an aid to a trade orientation. This involved removing government subsidies for private international students and allowing institutions to autonomously determine tuition fees and enrollment levels for international students. This created a bifurcated student market in these countries. Universities could charge a premium for programs for which there was significant international demand, and were free to promote these programs and spend the resulting tuition income as they saw fit. Meanwhile governments continued to exercise tight control over the domestic student market, with regulated tuition income and enrollment levels. Understandably many institutions developed an entrepreneurial approach to the international education market. Enrollments in all three countries grew rapidly through the 1990s and 2000s. Since that time the proportion of international students in these university systems, and consequently the proportion of funding generated by their export activities, has risen steadily (Marginson and van der Wende, 2009).

As noted, this chapter focuses on the provision of whole programs by institutions based in one country to students from another country. This usually involves extended studies overseas. But intensive short courses, often for language studies or professional development, appear to be increasingly common. Data for short courses are difficult to come by as these students usually travel on tourist visas and enroll in programs that tend not to be included in national statistics. Several other forms of short-term international student mobility serve to add an international dimension to a national qualification. Study tours are organized as part of the student's program of studies in their home country and sometimes involve collaboration with an overseas educational institution. Exchange programs involve students spending one or two semesters at an overseas partner institution for credit to their program of studies in their home country, while paying their usual tuition fees at the home institution and studying free at the host institution. Study abroad involves students spending one or two semesters at an overseas institution for credit to their program of studies in their home country, while paying tuition fees at the host institution but none at their home institution. These students are often sometimes referred to as 'free movers' in Europe.

These forms of international mobility are popular with students from affluent societies, who prefer to study in local universities but seek to enhance their program with an overseas experience. Such mobility is usually supported by governments in affluent societies through schemes such as University Mobility in Asia and the Pacific, and the European region action scheme for the mobility of university students (the Erasmus program). More than 4000 institutions in 33 countries participate in Erasmus, which has sponsored the international exchange of 2.2 million students since it started in 1987 (European Commission, 2010).

GROWTH OF STUDY ABROAD

One of the most striking features of the globalization of higher education has been the rapid growth in the number of students studying abroad. Globally the number of students enrolled for a year or more outside their country of origin more than doubled from 1.3 million students in 1995 to 2.8 million in 2007 (OECD, 2007; UNESCO, 2009b). The number of students in higher education has also grown rapidly, with global tertiary enrollments up by 51.7 million between 2000 and 2007. In OECD member states enrollments were up by 44.3 percent between 1995 and 2003, with faster rates of growth across developing countries, which are starting from a significantly lower base (WTO, 2010). Globally the proportion of tertiary students who study for a year or more outside their home country has remained constant at just under 2 percent (1.9 percent in 1999 and 1.8 percent in 2007) (UNESCO, 2009b). As tertiary participation rates in developing countries continue to grow, the number of mobile students is projected to rise accordingly.

Compared with those who study in their home country, internationally mobile students are more commonly enrolled in those fields of study that offer portable qualifications and salaries that provide a return on investment for self-funded students: business and administration, science, engineering, manufacturing and construction, and humanities and the arts. They are less likely to be enrolled in health, welfare and education programs, where foreign qualifications are less commonly recognized and salaries are lower.

Internationally mobile students are also more commonly enrolled in higher-level tertiary studies than are those who study in their home country (UNESCO, 2009b).

The destination countries are highly concentrated but less so now than a decade ago. In 2007, 62 percent of students studied in just six countries – the USA, the UK, France, Australia, Germany and Japan. The core–periphery pattern of students moving from across the globe to study in North America and Western Europe has a long history, and is integrally connected with broader economic and cultural relationships between the world's established industrial powers and developing and emerging economies. This pattern is deeply embedded and, as Altbach (1981) showed, the inequalities in access to knowledge and resources that underlie this pattern are very resistant to change. However, more students now study in another country in the same region than was the case in 1999. Students are now traveling shorter distances in greater numbers, usually to nearby countries with more developed education systems and higher per capita incomes (UNESCO, 2009b).

TRANSNATIONAL EDUCATION

While student mobility is the most visible and established form of extra-national provision of education, in recent decades we have seen the birth of large-scale program and institutional mobility. This phenomenon is usually referred to as 'transnational' education, a term that encompasses education delivered by an institution based in one country to students located in another. Such programs proliferated in the 1990s in Malaysia, Singapore and Hong Kong as demand for higher education rapidly outstripped the capacity of local institutions, and new private providers in partnership with extra-national anglophone universities could quickly develop new offerings to appeal to a student body proficient in English. Since then transnational education includes many other countries.

Although few governments collect data on higher education programs delivered across borders, we can reasonably estimate that on a global scale there are several thousand such programs currently on offer, enrolling around 500 000 students (Bashir, 2007; McBurnie and Ziguras, 2007). Of the countries that do publish data on offshore enrollments, the most recent available data show that the UK enrolled 196 640 students offshore (2007–08), Australia enrolled 125 987 (2008), and New Zealand enrolled 1385 (2004) (Banks et al., 2010; Catherwood and Taylor, 2005; HESA, 2009).[1] No data are available for the other major provider of transnational education, the USA.

The leading importers of cross-border education are mostly middle-income countries in which the growth in secondary school completions and labor market demand for graduates has outstripped the capacity of the domestic higher education system. Transnational programs make a significant contribution to the total supply of higher education in some countries, most notably Singapore. By the middle of the last decade, after 20 years of continued growth, 32 percent of Singapore's 250 000 tertiary students were enrolled in transnational education programs, compared with 23 percent in national universities, 34 percent in institutes and polytechnics, and 11 percent in private colleges (based on data from Lee, 2005, p. 15; Statistics Singapore, 2010, table 19.1).

In terms of total student numbers, China appears to be the largest importer of transnational education, just as it is the largest source country for internationally mobile students. Foreign programs started to be offered in the mid-1990s and by 2003 there were over 712 approved teaching partnerships between Chinese and foreign institutions, according to the Ministry of Education. The USA was involved in the highest number of partnerships, followed by Australia, Canada, Japan, Singapore, the UK, France and Germany (Garrett, 2004). By 2006, 352 British collaborative programs were being offered by 82 UK universities in collaboration with 223 Chinese higher education institutions and organizations in 2006 (QAA, 2006).

Distance education, delivered online or in print without face-to-face instruction, accounts for 51 percent of UK universities' offshore enrollments, but only 13 percent of those in Australian universities (Banks et al., 2010; HESA, 2009). The UK has a small number of very large specialist distance education providers, including the UK Open University and the University of London External System, which both have a global reach.

Most transnational education provided by the three countries for which data are available is delivered through a partnership between one institution that awards the qualification (usually an anglophone university) and a local partner institution. Local partner institutions may be private colleges, commercial arms of public universities or professional associations. The awarding university usually provides the curriculum, overseas local teaching staff sometimes in conjunction with fly-in-fly-out lecturing staff, and controls assessment. Local partners provide a campus and teaching staff, administer programs, and recruit and support students. In some cases there is a 'twinning' arrangement, whereby the first part of the course is conducted in the host country and students travel to the home campus to complete their qualification. The models of collaboration between the extra-national and national institutions vary widely, and the division of labor between the parties often changes over time as the relationship matures.

A branch campus involves a bricks-and-mortar presence in the host country, fully or jointly owned by the extra-national institution. Courses are taught in a similar manner to other campuses of the institution and usually involve higher proportions of face-to-face teaching from more highly qualified teaching staff than is the case in partner-supported transnational education. The Observatory on Borderless Higher Education in a report by Becker (2009) defines a branch campus as an entity trading directly as a branch of the parent institution, recruiting primarily local students, and attempting to replicate breadth of function of the parent institution (e.g. research as well as teaching). The Observatory identified 162 such international branch campuses globally in 2009, double the 82 identified in 2006. Only 35 of the currently existing branch campuses (22 percent) have been in operation for more than a decade, indicating a very rapid rate of growth. Their locations are concentrated in the Middle East and South-east Asia, with more being developed currently in India, China and Central Asia. US and Australian universities have the largest number of branch campuses, with smaller numbers operated by institutions based in the UK, Malaysia and Singapore. In recent years enrollments in Australian universities' branch campuses have been growing while enrollments in distance education and partner-supported programs have been declining (Banks et al., 2010).

CROSS-BORDER INVESTMENT IN HUMAN CAPITAL DEVELOPMENT

Through the forms of extra-national provision outlined above, over the past two decades we have witnessed the advent of a global education market. In addition to local higher education options, students are able to access a range of foreign programs that is increasingly diverse in terms of field of study, location, language of instruction, price of tuition, student experience and prestige. On this point, it seems, everyone is in agreement. However, opinions are very divided over the positive and negative consequences of the growth of this global market in higher education. In most respects those who favor global economic integration focus on what they see as the positive dimensions of extra-national provision while those who are wary of economic globalization focus on the negatives.

The pro-globalization camp comprises governments of the major education exporting countries, particularly the USA, the UK, Australia and New Zealand, and international organizations that are dedicated to fostering greater economic integration of national economies, the most prominent of which are the Organization for Economic Co-operation and Development (OECD), the World Trade Organization (WTO) and the World Bank (WB). These governments and agencies see cross-border education as a positive means of connecting consumers and producers of education in different countries. They seek to grow the scale of international trade in education through analyzing the factors affecting demand and supply for foreign educational services. There is a high level of cooperation and sharing of resources between these international agencies, resulting in a Washington–Paris–Geneva consensus on cross-border education (Bashir, 2007; OECD, 2004; Vincent-Lancrin, 2007, 2009; WTO, 2010).

Demand for international education is spurred by several factors, including rapid industrialization, increased affluence, the lag between local demand and local supply of tertiary education, the role of English as the international business language, and the ready employability of business and IT graduates in the industrial and knowledge economies. Globally governments have invested heavily in secondary education, leading to more secondary-school graduates who are qualified for tertiary study. As we saw earlier, in many rapidly industrializing economies both national and extra-national higher education provision grew strongly across the past two decades.

In many developing countries the adoption of government policies aimed at fostering greater integration into the global economy has clearly spurred demand for international education, and this is perhaps most clearly evident in the Asia-Pacific region. Rapid industrialization by many countries in the region has been spurred by the adoption of export-oriented industrialization policies, which were pursued first by Japan, followed by the 'Asian tiger' economies – Hong Kong, Taiwan, South Korea and Singapore – and more recently by China and Vietnam. The resulting economic transformations created growing labor market demand for tertiary graduates. At the same time increased affluence fuelled student demand for higher-level educational qualifications.

Simultaneously, rising incomes have increased the affordability of foreign study, although study overseas is usually a far more expensive option than studying in the home country. Viewed in economic terms, many families are willing to invest a significant amount of money in foreign education in expectation of a 'higher rate of return on internationally-recognized qualifications (through higher earnings and migration possibilities)' (Bashir, 2007, p. 51). Students and their families see the higher cost of overseas study as being worthwhile given the preferences of many employers in low- and middle-income countries for foreign qualifications, and the pathway to migration that international education has become.

Foreign direct investment and export-oriented development create a demand for qualifications in business, information and communications technology, and English-language skills, all of which play a role in facilitating international engagement. International student mobility can be seen as one means of transferring skills from high-income countries to emerging economies, alongside those transfers facilitated by the relocation of manufacturing operations and the outsourcing of business services. The adoption of such technologically advanced processes requires high levels of skills, and student demand for international study can be seen as a response by millions of families to the premium paid for such skills in Asian labor markets. International students are thus, in effect, buying their way into the global knowledge economy (Gürüz, 2008). In short, students can be seen as making rational decisions to invest in their own human capital development through international education, which offers a higher return on investment during a period of globalization.

The English language is now clearly one of the most significant determinants of choice of host country. Of the 2.8 million students studying overseas for one year or more, around half (1.38 million) are studying in ten countries with English-language higher education systems.[2] The English-language dominance of transnational higher education is even more striking, with very few examples of offshore programs or campuses in languages other than English.

On the supply side, technological developments in both transportation and communications have greatly simplified the process of studying in foreign institutions. In transportation the gradual reduction in the cost of air travel has made overseas study much more affordable. Ease of travel also reduces the isolation felt by international students, by allowing many to return home during breaks in their studies and making it more affordable for parents to visit during their studies. The greatest development in communication has been the use of the Internet by prospective students who are able to investigate study options online, using institutional websites directly or by exploring options through various portals operated by national authorities such as Japan's Student Services Organization[3] and Education New Zealand,[4] as well as those operated by a wide and variable range of private marketing agencies, the most established of which is Australia's IDP.[5]

These portals allow students to access information about a range of study options in a particular country, as well as information about immigration, work rights, cost of living and other related logistical issues. Students usually draw upon a range of resources in making such a big decision, including advice from family and friends, former teachers and recruitment agents. An increasing proportion of students use online resources to research options and communicate with prospective institutions. Students are able to apply for enrollment directly with a foreign institution, and can expect to receive an offer of enrollment in a matter of days or weeks rather than the months required in the past for postal application processes. Once students have received an offer from an institution, they can access student visa application forms online and may be able to submit a visa application online. During their studies international students can maintain contact with family and friends back home much more easily through various online channels.

Similarly the transnational provision of programs is made possible by low-cost and rapid international travel, which allows lecturers to undertake short 'fly-in-fly-out' teaching stints and allows managers to visit distant partner institutions to establish and monitor collaborative programs more quickly and cheaply. Information and communication technology advances have led to the weightless portability of curriculum materials, which can now be shared by student cohorts distributed across the globe (for case studies, see Ziguras, 2000).

As a result of the importance of language in driving demand, combined with a market-oriented philosophy in anglophone nations, English-language higher education systems and institutions almost always charge international students tuition that covers the full cost of provision, whereas nearly all international students in non-English-speaking institutions and countries are subsidized and pay significantly less that the full cost of provision. In some anglophone countries, such as Australia, public educational institutions are not allowed to charge below the full cost of provision of education to international students, a rule intended to ensure that international students are not cross-subsidized by funding intended for domestic students. In English-language higher education systems the enrollment of domestic students is often more highly regulated in terms of both student numbers and tuition fees. Many anglophone universities therefore have limited capacity to grow their size or income by appealing to domestic students, and must instead recruit globally where they are much less restricted by national governments. By contrast, in non-anglophone systems where governments subsidize international students to a much greater extent, there are usually caps on international student numbers, commonly around 5 to 10 percent of enrollments, to limit the displacement of local students who are competing for publicly funded places.

CHALLENGES OF ACCESS AND EQUITY

Concerns about the growth of the global education market are often expressed as opposition to the commodification of education. It is common for international forums on higher education to become preoccupied with debates between those on the political Left who see education as a public good that should be provided primarily or solely by the state, and economic liberals who see education as serving both public and private needs to be provided by a mix of government, not-for-profit and for-profit institutions. At the 2009 UNESCO World Conference on Higher Education much energy was devoted to a single line in the introduction of the conference's final communiqué. Over five days of negotiations Latin American countries lobbied for the text 'Higher education is a social public good and a human right', while the USA lobbied against the use of the term 'public good', but in the end accepted the description of higher education 'as a public good' rather than 'is a public good' (Maldonado-Maldonado and Verger, 2010). The final communiqué stated, 'As a public good and a strategic imperative for all levels of education and as the basis for research, innovation and creativity, higher education must be a matter of responsibility and economic support of all governments' (UNESCO, 2009a).

Such posturing is common but ultimately unproductive. It is clear that extra-national education generates both public goods (the global spread of expert knowledge, higher levels of productivity, mutual understanding, and so on) as well as private benefits to individuals and organizations. It is also clear that extra-national higher education is provided by state institutions (which account for the majority of extra-national enrolments globally) as well as private not-for-profit institutions and commercially oriented providers (particularly in language and preparatory programs, and testing services). For all the heat in these debates there is surprisingly little discussion of practical solutions to the limitations of market-driven extra-national provision. Below we consider the most pressing political challenge for the global education market, which is its tendency to reinforce the privilege of the rich while neglecting the needs of the poor.

The majority of students who are internationally mobile or study in transnational programs are self-funded, and in many cases families make a substantial investment in their education. Self-funded students are overwhelmingly drawn from the wealthier social strata of developing and middle-income countries. Many receiving countries have financial tests as preconditions for obtaining a student visa, requiring students to show that they have sufficient funds to cover the costs of their studies held in a bank account or a letter from a sponsor such as an employer or scholarship program. Students from less privileged backgrounds are dependent on scholarships and support from host institutions, but there are still two types of barriers. First, scholarships awarded on the basis of academic merit alone often reward prior educational privilege, since students from wealthy areas or who attend expensive secondary schools generally achieve higher academic results. Second, most forms of financial support for international study do not cover the full costs of studying and living abroad. Students from less wealthy families, who do manage to excel academically and are eligible for financial assistance, may still be deterred by the difficulty of raising funds to cover these additional costs.

It is easy to draw attention to the resulting inequalities, but much more difficult to know how to render extra-national provision more equitable. In the past some governments addressed this inequity by putting in place measures to restrict the mobility of self-funded students. In countries where citizens required exit permits to travel abroad, as was the case in most socialist countries until the late 1980s or early 1990s, a permit was usually only available to those whose overseas study was organized and sponsored by the sending and receiving governments. The Indian government also endeavored to stop self-funded students from leaving the country, but through currency-exchange restrictions that prevented the use of funds from India to pay for study overseas. (Indian citizens were free to leave the country but they were not free to take their money with them.) Many Indian students managed to bypass this requirement in one way or another, or relied on financial support from overseas relatives. Both of these restrictive approaches have fallen out of favor in all but a few states.

Some governments try to redress the unequal access to overseas study by providing financial support targeted at poorer students who are more dependent on loans to finance their study. Many countries now provide government-backed loans (usually on considerably better terms than other forms of finance). These are sometimes awarded on the basis of academic merit, such as national examination results, and sometimes are means-tested to specifically support students who would not be able to obtain family support or private sector loans. Norway has gone the furthest in this direction, introducing a voucher-type system of tuition funding that is portable to national and extra-national institutions.

Host governments have considerable influence over the affordability of study in their country for foreign students. After scholarships for tuition and living expenses, the most obvious way to support international students is for the host government to subsidize the tuition of foreign students, as is the case in France and Germany, for example, making these countries the world's leading international aid donors in higher education (Bashir, 2007). The Japanese government subsidizes the tuition of most international students to varying degrees. There are obviously limits on the capacity and will of host governments to fund foreign students, especially if it is perceived that international students are displacing deserving local students through direct competition for places.

In recent years the most important policy initiatives for broadening access to international education have been to provide international students with easier access to labor markets in the host country rather than direct government funding. Australia and New Zealand have seen huge growth in enrollments in lower-cost vocational education and training programs that are popular with students from poorer backgrounds (Baas, 2006). These programs respond to international students for whom education and employment in the host country are mutually dependent. Many education-exporting countries now allow international students to work up to 20 hours per week during term-time and sometimes more during breaks, and this has allowed many students to fund their overseas study with part-time work. In addition, many anglophone countries have been making it easier for larger numbers of international students to remain in the host country to work after completion of their studies, which enables students to recoup the cost of their studies sooner after graduation – an especially appealing prospect for students from low-income countries. Since around 2000 Australia and New Zealand have been bestowing permanent residency rights on a significant proportion of international students, up to a third of completing international students in Australia's case.

In the past few years these policies dramatically expanded the accessibility of international education in Australia for poorer students, particularly those from South Asia. One unforeseen consequence was the vulnerability of these students to exploitation in the labor market, and to violence. Poorer students are more dependent upon income from shift work, such as driving taxis, stacking supermarket shelves, and working in convenience stores and as security guards. Because students are legally permitted to work only 20 hours per week, many work in undocumented jobs with substandard wages and conditions. They are more likely to be living in outer suburbs with cheaper housing and using public transport late at night in areas where street violence is more common. Several much-publicized violent attacks against Indian students in Australia are attributable to their vulnerability and exposure to entrenched pockets of violence in Australia's large cities, although some cases were clearly racially motivated assaults by groups of teenagers of various ethnic backgrounds (Ziguras, 2009). The Indian tabloid press and 24-hour news channels featured blanket coverage of a series of assaults on Indian students, which were portrayed as evidence of Australian racism, while nationalist politicians called for the cutting of cultural, economic and sporting relationships between the two countries.

The Australian government responded by stepping up policing in dangerous areas of capital cities, by making it much more difficult for international graduates of vocational programs to obtain permanent residency, by enhancing the regulation of private colleges, and by tightening student visa requirements for those categories of students who appeared to be most at risk. As an experiment in broadening access to extra-national higher education, this approach clearly failed. Rather than being remembered for allowing tens of thousands of less affluent international students to study in a high-income country and then achieve permanent residency, this period will be remembered more for a small number of assaults on Indian students who were unfortunately targeted by thugs while traveling on public transport to work in fast-food restaurants late at night.

As well as exacerbating inequalities between poor and affluent students, extra-national provision is often criticized for exacerbating inequalities between institutions. Altbach and Knight (2007, p. 291), for example, argue that 'Globalization tends to concentrate wealth, knowledge, and power in those already possessing these elements. International academic mobility similarly favors well-developed education systems and institutions, thereby compounding existing inequalities.' The danger is that staff and students will choose to invest their careers and their tuition fees in more highly developed extra-national institutions, threatening the further development of national institutions with a commitment to public service. Clearly high-income countries, particularly the anglophone countries, have benefited enormously from their ability to recruit students and staff globally, which further strengthens their institutions. There is also a more direct economic benefit from tuition income and living expenditure, which in 2007 generated US$34 billion in educational export income for the top three exporters, the USA, Australia and the UK (WTO, 2010, p. 14). Again, this is an easy observation to make but a difficult problem to solve.

BUILDING CAPACITY

So how can extra-national provision contribute to building the capacity and quality of institutions and systems in developing countries? One way is through the provision of doctoral programs to international students, since doctoral graduates are essential for building a modern higher education system but are in short supply in most developing countries. This is one aspect of extra-national provision where governments are the major purchasers of education. Developing countries from China to Chile that are seeking to grow their higher education systems are sending large numbers of doctoral students abroad through scholarship schemes, and host countries also fund a high proportion of international doctoral students, through government scholarships, research project funds or teaching assistantships.

The international mobility of educational programs and campuses has the potential to build and supplement domestic institutions in a much more far-reaching manner than overseas movements of students. Transnational education has been attractive to some governments as a way to rapidly supplement and assist in building the capacity of the domestic higher education system.

'Pro-globalization' economic development policies of host countries have also played a significant role in boosting demand. In this sense the patterns of development of international education services in newly industrializing countries have strong parallels with other service sectors that are crucial for successful integration into the global economy, including financial services, transportation and logistics. Those countries in Asia where transnational education first developed were those that first adopted export-oriented growth strategies. Employers, both in the multinational corporations attracted to countries that encouraged foreign direct investment early on, and in domestic firms that had their eyes on foreign markets, were willing to pay a premium for graduates with foreign qualifications and English-language proficiency. Rapid rates of economic growth in the Asian tiger economies fueled rapid increases in participation in domestic universities and in outward mobility, and in this context transnational programs played an important demand-absorbing role. As a second wave of larger and previously more inwardly focused Asian economies such as China, India and Vietnam have adopted similar export-oriented economic development strategies, they too have seen demand for foreign programs escalate rapidly, and much of the current growth in numbers is in these economies.

Typically countries in the Asia-Pacific region that have experienced rapid growth in demand for higher education that cannot be met by local providers establish relatively 'light-touch' regulatory frameworks, aiming to expand the volume of transnational provision and increase the capacity of the system. With rapid economic development, demand for higher education quickly outpaced the capacity of local public universities to respond, particularly in those fields in demand in increasingly globalized economies. In this first phase the number of students traveling abroad to study grows dramatically. Taiwan, Singapore, Malaysia and Hong Kong experienced this growth of outward mobility in the 1980s and 1990s, and currently numbers are growing from those countries whose economic growth has come later, such as China, India and Vietnam.

Some governments were initially wary of cross-border supply through collaborations between domestic private colleges and foreign universities because these collaborations were designed to bypass domestic regulatory frameworks that restrict the ability of un-authorized local providers to confer degrees. Private colleges that were not able to confer their own degrees could instead offer foreign degrees. In most countries, governments are moving away from restricting the type of institutions able to enter into cross-border supply and instead to establish common quality assurance processes that can be applied to public, private not-for-profit, private for-profit, domestic and foreign institutions equally. This is a shift broadly from protection of existing domestic providers to protection of students as consumers through quality assurance and accreditation measures (McBurnie and Ziguras, 2001).

Host-country governments sometimes encourage the development of transnational programs as a way to reduce the number of students traveling abroad to study and to broaden access to extra-national higher education. This usually goes hand in hand with efforts to rapidly grow domestic institutions. In some countries, such as China, the growth of local institutions is funded primarily by governments through public universities; while in others, such as South Korea, the growth has been largely in the non-government sector. Foreign universities can play important capacity-building and demand absorption roles, chiefly in partnership with local private providers and public institutions. When students study locally in a foreign program rather than studying overseas, they take less money out of the country, support the growth of the domestic education system, and are less likely to emigrate after completing their studies. While governments may be relaxing market-entry restrictions for overseas-based education providers, few have extended the principle of national treatment (treating foreigners and locals equally) to foreign providers. Rarely are government student loans or subsidies available to students enrolled in foreign providers. Even in Australia, which has been a leading proponent of removing barriers to free trade in higher education, government loans are restricted to students studying in providers that have their 'central management and control in Australia' (Norton, 2008).

Governments' wariness about foreign providers stems from widely held concerns about potential for new foreign providers to harm existing providers and to widen socio-cultural divisions, especially in developing countries. First is the potential to exacerbate socioeconomic inequalities by further favoring the privileged who are able to pay fees. This may diminish the capacity of the public system in the host country by luring away local academics by offering higher salaries, and luring middle-class students by offering higher-quality facilities and educational experiences. This is exacerbated by the tendency for foreign providers to 'cherry-pick', offering only those profitable programs (such as business and information technology) for which there is demand from fee-paying students but where the cost of delivery is low, while leaving less profitable programs (nursing, education and engineering, for example) for domestic providers, thereby reducing the public institutions' ability to cross-subsidize less popular or high-cost courses. The additional academic employment provided by transnational education may be geared only to a limited range of teaching programs and without provision of time and resources for staff to carry out research – staff may be treated as semi-skilled workers in a 'teaching factory'.

The profit-seeking focus of these programs may result in substandard provision of education if appropriate quality measures are not in place and enforced. Governments in education-exporting countries may be concerned that new substandard foreign providers seeking to recruit international fee-paying students damage the national 'brand'. An unregulated open market with high levels of unmet demand may be inundated with low-quality providers, ranging from underresourced shop-front operations with under-qualified staff to 'degree mills' offering unearned qualifications or outright bogus degrees in return for a fee.

Many governments remain wary of the motives of partner-supported programs and are concerned that commercially oriented partnerships threaten quality and undermine domestic providers, and may try to restrict cross-border supply once capacity shortages begin to be overcome. For example, the Chinese Ministry of Education has recently decided to more actively vet foreign program applications, announcing in April 2007 that if a proposed program is 'already popular and concentrated among those Chinese institutions, or if its proposed tuition and other charges are significantly higher than the cost, the proposal will not be accepted or approved' (quoted in Mooney, 2007, p. A32). Such policies may be attractive to governments that feel that student demand can and should be met primarily by domestic providers, and that may tolerate an open education market if required to quickly boost supply but seek to restrict the ability of foreign providers (and often also domestic private providers) to enter that market once domestic supply has begun to catch up with demand. One much-discussed way of doing this would be to restrict the market entry of foreign universities that are not highly ranked in one of the major international rankings of universities. Another way to restrict cross-border provision is to allow private colleges to confer their own degrees on condition that they no longer partner with foreign universities to award foreign degrees at the same level, which provides a seamless means of reducing supply of foreign programs as domestic capacity comes on stream (McBurnie and Ziguras, 2009).

CONCLUSION

The number of students studying in extra-national educational institutions has been growing rapidly over the past two decades, in line with rapid growth in national enrollments. International student mobility is split between anglophone exporters (the USA, the UK and Australia), the aid donors (France, Germany and Japan), and a growing list of countries with smaller but significant numbers of foreign students. The current period of austerity in high-income countries will affect these host countries quite differently. In education-exporting countries constraints on national funding for universities will lead many universities to heighten their efforts to recruit international students, especially those from developing countries that are for the moment the world's engines of economic growth. The aid donors will face the opposite pressure. Governments in France, Germany and Japan, looking for ways to cut public expenditure and debt, may seek to constrain public funding of international students (who are not eligible to vote).

The scale of extra-national provision by mobile programs and institutions has increased considerably over the past two decades, especially in Asia. The forms of delivery vary interestingly between the three major exporting countries. UK institutions reach across borders through a combination of distance education and partner-supported delivery, with small numbers enrolled in branch campuses. Australian universities are seeing a shift from distance education and partner-supported delivery to branch campuses, which are proliferating in number and growing in scale. US universities' overseas branch campuses appear to be proliferating also. In-country provision of extra-national education has the potential to assist in the building of education systems in developing and middle-income countries, but these are very new types of institutions and it will be interesting to watch the extra-national branch campus come of age.

NOTES

1. The figure for Australia includes 69 733 offshore students in universities, 55 332 in public vocational education and training providers, and 922 in non-university higher education providers.
2. Including (in order of number of international students) the USA, the UK, Australia, Canada, South Africa, New Zealand, Malaysia (where nearly all international students study in English-language institutions or programs), Ireland, India and the Philippines. All data are from UNESCO for 2007, except for India, where the data are for 2006. No data are available for Singapore.
3. www.jasso.go.jp.
4. www.newzealandeducated.com.
5. www.idp.com.

REFERENCES

Altbach, P. (1981), 'The university as centre and periphery', *Teachers College Record,* **82** (4), 601–21.
Altbach, P. and J. Knight (2007), 'The internationalization of higher education: motivations and realities', *Journal of Studies in International Education,* **11** (3–4), 290–305.
Baas, M. (2006), 'Students of migration: Indian overseas students and the question of permanent residency', *People and Place,* **14** (1), 9–24.
Banks, M., P. Kevat, C. Ziguras, A. Ciccarelli and D. Clayton (2010), *The Changing Fortunes of Australian Transnational Higher Education,* London: Observatory on Borderless Higher Education.
Bashir, S. (2007), *Trends in International Trade in Higher Education: Implications and Options for Developing Countries,* Washington, DC: World Bank.
Becker, R. (2009), *International Branch Campuses: Markets and Strategies,* London: Observatory on Borderless Higher Education.
Catherwood, V. and L. Taylor (2005), *Offshore Education: Stocktake and Analysis,* Wellington: Education New Zealand.
Cleverley, J. and P. Jones (1976), *Australia and International Education: Some Critical Issues,* Hawthorn: Australian Council for Educational Research.
European Commission (2010), The Erasmus Programme, accessed 26 June 2010 from: http://ec.europa.eu/education/lifelong-learning-programme/doc80_en.htm.
Garrett, R. (2004), 'Foreign higher education activity in China', *International Higher Education,* Winter, 21–3.
Gürüz, K. (2008), *Higher Education and Student Mobility in the Global Knowledge Economy,* Albany, NY: State University of New York Press.
HESA (2009), Press Release 133: 'HESA Students in Higher Education Institutions 2007/08 reveals 197 000 students studying overseas for UK HE qualifications', accessed 26 June 2010 at: http://www.hesa.ac.uk/index.php/content/view/1398/161/.
Lee, S. (2005), 'Educational upgrading through private educational institutions', *Singapore Statistics Newsletter,* September, 15–17.
Maldonado-Maldonado, A. and A. Verger (2010), 'Politics, UNESCO, and higher education: a case study', *International Higher Education,* **58**, 8–9.
Marginson, S. and M. van der Wende (2009), 'The new global landscape of nations and institutions', in *Higher Education to 2030, Volume 2: Globalization,* Paris: OECD, pp. 17–62.
McBurnie, G. and C. Ziguras (2001), 'The regulation of transnational higher education in southeast Asia: case studies of Hong Kong, Malaysia and Australia', *Higher Education,* **42** (1), 85–105.
McBurnie, G. and C. Ziguras (2007), *Transnational Education: Current Issues and Future Trends in Offshore Higher Education,* London: RoutledgeFalmer.
McBurnie, G. and C. Ziguras (2009), 'Trends and future scenarios in programme and institution mobility across borders', *Higher Education to 2030, Volume 2: Globalization,* Paris: OECD, pp. 89–108.
Mooney, P. (2007), 'China to increase scrutiny of foreign degree providers', *Chronicle of Higher Education,* **53** (48), A32.
Norton, A. (2008), 'Protectionist ploy a blast from past', *The Australian,* 11 June, accessed at: http://www.theaustralian.news.com.au/story/0,25197,23843249-25192,00.html.
OECD (2004), *Internationalization and Trade in Higher Education: Opportunities and Challenges,* Paris: OECD.
OECD (2007), *Education at a Glance 2007,* Paris: OECD.
QAA (2006), *UK Higher Education in China: An Overview of the Quality Assurance Arrangements,* Mansfield, UK: The Quality Assurance Agency for Higher Education.
Statistics Singapore (2010), *Yearbook of Statistics Singapore 2009,* Singapore: Statistics Singapore.
UNESCO (2009a), *Communiqué of the 2009 World Conference on Higher Education: The New Dynamics of Higher Education and Research for Societal Change and Development,* Paris: UNESCO.
UNESCO (2009b), *Global Education Digest,* Paris: UNESCO Institute for Statistics.
Vincent-Lancrin, S. (2007), *Cross-border Tertiary Education: A Way Towards Capacity Development,* Paris and Washington, DC: OECD and The World Bank.
Vincent-Lancrin, S. (2009), 'Cross-border higher education: trends and perspectives', *Higher Education to 2030, Volume 2: Globalization,* Paris: OECD, pp. 63–88.
WTO (2010), *Education Services: background note by the Secretariat (S/C/W/313),* Geneva: WTO.
Ziguras, C. (2000), *New Frontiers, New Technologies, New Pedagogies: Educational Technology and the Internationalization of Higher Education in South East Asia,* Clayton: Monash Centre for Research in International Education.
Ziguras, C. (2009), 'Indian students in Australia: how did it come to this?', accessed 26 June 2010, at: http://globalhighered.wordpress.com/2009/08/11/indian-students-in-australia-how-did-it-come-to-this/.

8 Global institutions, higher education and development
Yann Lebeau and Ebrima Sall

INTRODUCTION

Influential global organizations such as the World Bank (WB), UN Educational, Scientific and Cultural Organization (UNESCO), the Organisation for Economic Co-operation and Development (OECD) and the World Trade Organization (WTO), along with bilateral-aid agencies, major private foundations and more recently regional organizations such as the European Union (EU) have had a pronounced impact on higher education institutions (HEIs) and shaped higher education landscapes in the developing world. The expansion of higher education systems on the basis of the formats of western countries has always raised questions about the relevance of those systems, particularly universities, to the developmental needs of the nations concerned.

This chapter highlights the roles played by international agencies in framing higher education policy agendas in developing countries. In order to show how such roles have been influenced by a complex array of contextual factors – some local and others global – the chapter combines historical and institutional perspectives. The main focus of the chapter is on the reflections and policies of two major players in the field since the Second World War, the WB and UNESCO, on the relation between higher education and development. These organizations have dominated the conceptualization of higher education and development, and influenced the main initiatives taken. The WB and UNESCO have exercised more or less influence on other global, regional or local stakeholders. In tracing evolving policy paradigms the chapter outlines the periodization of the initiatives of these agencies: successive, parallel, often convergent, and at times divergent.

Neither of these two organizations ever had a specific mandate to govern higher education systems around the world, nor did they ever treat this sector of education as a policy priority. The WB has long been accused of overlooking higher education in its development strategies – and although UNESCO's mandate predisposes it to take a serious interest in higher education and in science, its campaign for access to general education for all has been much more important to the organization than any interest in higher education. Karen Mundy and Megan Madden have even argued that UNESCO's work in higher education has always operated at the margins of its education program (Mundy and Madden, 2009). When in the 1980s and 1990s the WB pushed for developing countries to prioritize basic education, this resonated well with UNESCO's campaign for access to basic education.

Nevertheless, these two organizations have so far produced, for good or for bad, the most influential reflection on the articulation of higher education and economic development.

UNESCO AND THE DEVELOPMENTAL UNIVERSITY IN THE POSTCOLONIAL CONTEXT: AN OPPORTUNE AGENDA IN THE COLD WAR ERA

Since its establishment in 1946, UNESCO has played a significant role in attempting to anchor higher education in national educational policies, to relate the establishment of universities to the overall objective of social and economic change, and to connect research institutions and researchers around the world (UNESCO, 1997). Its interest in the higher education sectors has also always emphasized the issue of access, enshrined in the 'right to education' of the Universal Declaration of Human Rights.

The Tananarive Conference

In the 1950s and 1960s the organization sent advisory missions around the developing world. It also organized a number of regional conferences on the development of higher education, for example in Tananarive in 1962 and San José in 1966, which led to the establishment of regional networks and university associations.

Let us look more closely at the Tananarive forum. The Conference on the Development of Higher Education in Africa, held in Tananarive, Madagascar under the auspices of UNESCO from 3 to 12 September 1962, was convened to:

1. Identify possible solutions to (a) problems of choice and adaptation of the higher education curriculum to the specific conditions of African life and development, and the training of specialized personnel for public administration and economic development techniques; (b) problems of administration, organization, structure and financing encountered in the creation or development of institutions of higher education both from the point of view of the institutions themselves and from the wider angle of national policy.
2. Provide data to the United Nations, its Specialized Agencies, and to other organizations and bodies concerned with international co-operation and assistance, for the development of their programmes in aid to and use of institutions of higher education in Africa. (UNESCO, 1997, p. 168)

The African delegates at the conference adopted a resolution in which they stated that 'African universities must go beyond the traditional role of giving a broad liberal education' and, instead, aim to equip the African people with 'skills that will enable them to participate fully in the economic and social development of their continent' (Lawi, 2008, p. 12).

The Developmental University

UNESCO spear-headed the creation of the International Association of Universities (IAU, established in 1950), of the International Social Science Council (ISSC, established in 1948), and the United Nations University (UNU) in Tokyo in 1975. In the aftermath of the Second World War and in the decolonization context, the UNESCO paradigm – multicultural in expression, promoting a culture of peace associated with the establishment of UNESCO Chairs around the world, and focused on official development assistance at national and regional levels – aimed to shape higher education institutions according to the development needs of newly formed nations.

The 1960s saw the emergence of the notion of the 'developmental university' in the Third World. This promoted a curriculum organized around learning that could be productively applied immediately. This notion of higher education's role in national development attracted international support not only from international organizations but also major foundations (Samoff and Carrol, 2004a; Balán, 2009).

The consensus around this project might have been created by its origins: on the one hand in the US land-grant colleges (a problem-solving university for 'new' nations), and on the other in the Soviet model, which promoted a 'rigorous fit between the university product and manpower requirements projected in successive five-year plans, and the use of the university as an instrument both to right inequalities in society and to socialize students into the ideology of the regime' (Coleman, 1986, p. 479). Within this broadly economistic concept of development universities were meant to serve the following core functions:

- Teaching: making the entire university learning experience more relevant to the indigenous culture and the practical problems of development.
- Research: establishment of organized applied research units and government-commissioned applied research projects on concrete problems of, and technological constraints upon, development.
- Service: encouragement and facilitation of members of the professoriate to participate in public policy formulation at national, regional, and local levels. Establishment and operation of programs in community health outreach, agricultural extension, adult education, and so on (Coleman, 1986).

In the context of newly independent African countries 'development' was part of a broader and more political nation-building project. The university's role in both processes was seen as central. This drew the link between the state and the university much closer. In supporting this agenda, and in the context of the Cold War, foundations and international organizations closed their eyes to the authoritarian nature of the developmental university project. But this form of support to higher education institutions declined in the 1970s. There was a decline of donor confidence in the roles of government in national development and the introduction of structural adjustment initiatives (Balán, 2009). In the 1990s the notion of a development university regained some currency, as in some of the new public higher education institutions established in Senegal (e.g. Gaston Berger University in Saint-Louis), Ghana and elsewhere. These institutions were meant to address the problems of the crisis bedevilling the higher education sector through programs thought to be 'more relevant' to the development needs of those countries.

'Technical–Scientific' Modernization

Even where universities were already in place, the 'university for development' model required profound modernization reforms, justifying an international mobilization:

Modernization tenets were relatively simple and in most cases shared by significant segments of the local academic communities: professionalization of the academic work along disciplinary lines, the unity of research and teaching within graduate education, a public mission drafted within a developmental model, and a more centralized, managerial model for academic and financial administration. (Balán, 2009, p. 238)

The 'technical–scientific' approach to educational multilateralism fitted the Cold War context by placing the largely apolitical concept of national economic modernization at the heart of a strategy 'solvable through the provision of technical, depoliticized forms of western expertise and the more limited transfer of technology and capital to the South' (Mundy, 1999, p. 36).

Focused only on the developmental agenda, development agencies exhibited a general complacency towards authoritarian regimes. In Latin America under the military regimes of the 1960s and 1970s little space was left for universities to formulate their own teaching and research agendas and for academics to contribute to formulating policy. De Figueredo-Cowen (2002, p. 477) notes that in Brazil, for example, 'the university became extremely vulnerable to ideological control', and lived under the constant threat of 'ministerial acts of dismissal and early retirements of academic staff'. Similarly in Argentina, under post-Peronist military rule, institutional autonomy was denied to the universities. In Chile, vice chancellors nominated by the Pinochet government were given absolute power within the university (ibid.). Paradoxically, higher education developed rapidly under these military regimes. The agenda of institutional modernization was supported by local industrialists and international development agencies alike. In many cases the developmental university was assigned a special function of political socialization into the ideology of the governing regime. Coleman notes in relation to the mid-1980s that:

> President Suharto is attempting this in Indonesian universities. President Mobutu made an abortive effort to introduce his ideology of *authenticity* and later 'Mobutuism' in the National University of Zaire, but it was received with derision. Under the pressure of a group of nine entirely expatriate Marxist staff members at the University of Dar es Salaam in Tanzania, a conference was held in March 1967 which recommended that it was the responsibility of the university 'to impart political education . . . [and] the emphasis should be on the teaching of Tanzanian socialism as seen against the African and international background'. It also recommended that the university should ensure that 'the majority of its academic staff and all its teachers of the social sciences are sympathetic to Tanzanian socialism'. (Coleman, 1986, p. 487)

Up to the mid-1970s there were many examples of rapid consolidation of higher education systems in the developing world. However, after an initial, relatively short period of post-independence euphoria, during which the university communities and the state sought to work together to build the new nation, there developed almost everywhere a climate of mistrust between academic communities and state authorities as a result of the political sphere's intrusions into academia. There was a rapid erosion of the ideal of universities serving the development needs of their host societies on their (the universities') own terms, rather than as defined by governments. This generated the first waves of academic migration towards western universities, particularly from Latin America and Africa. In Africa, refugee scholars also found an intellectual home in CODESRIA (Council for the Development of Social Science Research in Africa), a regional social science research council set up in the early 1970s by the deans of social science and humanities faculties, and directors of social research centers and institutes of public universities around the continent, as an autonomous space for research. CODESRIA was positioned at a critical distance from the state.

Public institutions of the developing world became gradually marginalized as a result of tensions and conflicts, and therefore increasingly non-accountable, despite still benefiting from reasonable financial assistance. Often they developed into uncontrollable 'mega institutions' unable to absorb the surge in higher education demands resulting from the uncoordinated expansion of access to primary and secondary education.

UNESCO'S IDENTITY CRISIS: FROM 'THIRD WORLD SUPPORT' TO WORLD BANK ALIGNMENT

Marginalized within their nations and experiencing erosion in donor confidence, after the mid-1970s public universities in the developing world were hit by an irreversible crisis and decline. Donor reappraisals found that universities and their outcomes did not demonstrably relate to development, as defined by western countries, and had failed to adapt themselves so as to realize their developmental potential. This led to major revisions in donor policy, as found for example in the 1975 UK government White Paper entitled *The Changing Emphasis in British Aid Policy: more help for the poorest.* According to Coleman,

> By the mid-1970s the pendulum had shifted to this new emphasis in the policies of virtually all members of the donor community, as well as the World Bank, as reflected in its 1974 Education Sector report. The Rockefeller Foundation, the donor agency which most single-mindedly concentrated upon university development over a two-decade period, finally decided in 1977 to phase out its Education for Development Program over the following five years. (Coleman, 1986, p. 481)

Support dropped and became more selective. It was usually directed to those institutions, departments and research centers that offered promise of a developmental orientation (Coleman, 1986). The earlier model championed by UNESCO, that of unconditional national or regional support, had served its time. Countries were no longer seen as policy-making domains by the international financial institutions. These institutions were now surpassing the most powerful countries as principal enforcers of global dictates (Samoff, 2003).

As we shall see below, this crisis coincided with the emergence of new paradigms on the relation between education and development that favored support for basic education. But the change of mood among the international donors did not necessarily affect their instrumental (and developmentalist) conception of higher education for emerging economies. However, UNESCO's unconditional support for what was now the increasingly criticized model of the national developmental university, combined with the dominance of the WB and the International Monetary Fund (IMF) over the conceptualization and financing of multilateral assistance to higher education, started to weaken UNESCO's legitimacy and weight in higher education matters. Besides, UNESCO's position as a forum for increasingly radical Third World demands eroded its support among western powers, particularly the USA. This generated disagreements within the organization, and a long identity crisis, further marginalizing its higher education work.

Its work in education had become at once more ambitious, diverse, fragmented, and diffuse. It continued to face exceedingly sharp budgetary constraints. Overall the organization had entered what Haas has characterized as a period of 'turbulent non-growth,' in which it searched unproductively for a core rationale or set of goals with which to bridge the radical demands of developing countries and the liberal, developmentalist ideologies. (Mundy, 1999, p. 39)

In this context the importance of the WB in education increased spectacularly. By the early 1980s 'the World Bank's combined disbursements have been almost double those of the UN and its organizations' (Torres and Schugurensky, 2002, p. 429). The Bank not only overshadowed all other forms of development assistance with its loans, but created its own expertise in assessing needs and planning. This developed into a complex blending of financing and research, with longstanding effects on bilateral and multilateral institutions' reading of, and support of, higher education in developing countries (Mundy, 1999; Torres and Schugurensky, 2002; Samoff, 2003).

HIGHER EDUCATION AND THE NEOLIBERAL AGENDA

The non-compulsory tertiary level of education remained a long-term absentee in the WB's economic and human development strategy. Not that the WB failed to pay attention to universities and the higher education sector in developing countries; until the mid-1990s higher education was more often targeted as obstacle than as catalyst for economic recovery within the WB's poverty eradication agenda. Higher education was defined as a high consumer of public subsidies for a poor rate of return. It was also seen as a source of political instability and contestation of the WB's recovery strategies. Seen as part of the problem rather than part of the solution, universities were on the receiving end of the structural adjustment policies of the 1980s.

The World Bank's Reading of Human Capital Theory

From the late 1950s economists such as Gary S. Becker and Jacob Mincer claimed that, other things being equal, personal incomes varied according to the amount of investment in human capital. This investment was understood as the education and training undertaken by individuals or groups of workers. Widespread investment in human capital was seen as creating in the labor force the skills base required for economic growth. The theory was consistent with the dominant ideologies of democracy and economic liberalism that characterized most western societies. It was based on a broad conception of development in which 'human resources constitute the ultimate basis of the wealth of nations' (Psacharopoulos and Woodhall, 1997, p. 102).

The appeal of human capital lay in the presumption of economic returns to investment in education, at both the macro and micro levels:

The benefits of education are both direct and indirect. They accrue to society and to individuals. An important private direct benefit for educated individuals is their higher incomes over the less-educated throughout their working lives; the corresponding social benefit consists in the increased productivity of the educated who make higher contributions to national income for the period of their employment. Thus the higher lifetime earnings of the educated may serve as a measure of the direct benefits of education. (Menon, 2003, p. 375)

Efforts to promote investment in human capital were seen to result in rapid economic growth – which fitted perfectly within the ideology of state-led development discussed above. Countries such as Hong Kong, Korea, Singapore and Taiwan were (and are) frequently cited as examples of the coupling of economic growth and large investments in education (Olaniyan and Okemakinde, 2008). From the 1960s onwards human capital theory consistently dominated the WB's approach to education, even though its theoretical shortcomings and lack of empirical evidence had been repeatedly exposed and despite the fact that two decades of huge public investments in education were followed in the early 1980s by a deep recession in most developing economies. For many years the WB's particular reading of human capital theory also limited its priorities within education.

The most commonly cited critique of human capital theory is known as the credentialist or 'screening' hypothesis. According to this line of reasoning, employers mainly use education as a screening device or filter to sort job applicants. Thus

> Earnings differentials in favor of the more educated do not result from the content of the education received or the skills imparted, but by the signal or message received by employers through the qualification or credential obtained. Employers use credentials such as university degrees in order to identify candidates with superior natural ability or personal qualities. They reward them on the basis of the ability suggested by the credential. (Menon, 2003, p. 373)

Another major problem in the application of the theory to developing economies has been its failure to account for a growing gap between people's increasing knowledge base and the level of qualification, and the diminishing number of corresponding jobs in local markets (Olaniyan and Okemakinde, 2008, p. 160).

The WB's economists nonetheless informed the international community that 'public investments in education should be dominated by primary education, the proportion of public investments in education ideally declining as one proceeded up the education ladder' (Jones, 1997, p. 122). This was because the human capital equations showed that rates of return were highest for primary education. From the late 1980s onwards the WB introduced cost-sharing and cost-recovery strategies as a response to the crisis, but it did not depart fundamentally from its interpretation of rates of return on higher education (Jones, 1997; Woodhall, 2007).

The WB Changes its Mind

In contrast with this era of mutual mistrust, the WB today is said to place higher education at the heart of its anti-poverty and development strategy. It is encouraging bilateral donors to likewise place priority on tertiary education (Salmi et al., 2009). Why, when and how did such a pendulum swing occur? This section will consider three factors that fed the WB's apparent U-turn: its changing conception of the importance of human capital and human development; the evolution of its mandate and its changing relations with other international organizations and donors interested in higher education and development; and the concomitant transformation of the higher education sector and the status of universities in developing countries.

The 1994 report *Higher Education: The Lessons of Experience* (World Bank, 1994) is often seen as a landmark in the WB's U-turn on higher education. The title of the report hints at an acknowledgment of the negative impact of more than a decade of systematic undermining of the higher education sector in the context of soaring demands for higher education across the developing world.

As predominantly public institutions, universities in the developing world inevitably paid a high price for the implementation of structural adjustment policies and for the 'Washington Consensus' development strategies based on market fundamentalism, which involved emphasizing privatization, liberalization and macroeconomic (usually meaning price) stability, and downscaling and minimizing the role of government (Stiglitz, 1999). In their resulting state of dereliction and confinement, universities were hit by a second wave of brain drain and a process of informalization as survival strategies took over all aspects of academic development. All of this was already well documented by 1994 when the WB published its report. In Africa in particular, academic unions and other bodies had often reported on the consequences of structural adjustment policies and authoritarian polities. These reports had criticized the roles of the WB and of key bilateral donors (Federici et al., 2000).

On the face of it, the diagnosis offered by the 1994 report did not differ significantly from other studies. Higher education systems around the world were suffering from a compression of public finances. The decrease in resources from the early 1980s has been particularly acute in Sub-Saharan Africa, the Middle East and Latin America at a time when 'higher education has been the fastest-growing segment of the education system' (World Bank, 1994, p. 16). As a result, and without expanding on the specific pressures affecting public resources in the developing world (no direct reference to the consequences of the structural programs, for instance), the WB offered the following description of the situation in low- and middle-income countries:

> With continued enrollment expansion accompanied by steadily declining real resources, public institutions have become overcrowded. Higher education managers are increasingly concentrating on meeting immediate operating needs and neglecting the maintenance requirements of the physical plant. Instructional and living conditions have deteriorated in many institutions. Examples of infrastructure decay and insufficient pedagogical resources in classrooms, laboratories, and libraries can be found in all regions. (World Bank, 1994, p. 19)

The WB saw the drivers of the problem as a combination of low-quality, rapid enrollment growth under conditions of limited resources, excessive and inappropriate use of public resources ('a large share of the public higher education budget is devoted to non-educational expenditures in support of student grants and subsidized student service', ibid., p. 20), high dropout rates and program duplication. In his comparison of WB and UNESCO readings of the crisis, Rollin Kent notes that the WB emphasized 'that without serious attention to the institutional level – that is, management, leadership, the use and accountability of public resources, and so on – little progress can be expected in higher education reform' (Kent, 1996, p. 3). It is little surprise that the 1994 report should focus on internal responsibilities, and failures of states and institutions, rather than international pressures and inequalities.

The key policy prescriptions of the 1994 report – to be implemented at a varying pace, 'depending on specific country circumstances such as the level of income and the degree of educational development' – emphasized cost-sharing and income generation. The WB urged the greater differentiation of institutions, including the development of private institutions. It proposed that public institutions should be provided with incentives to diversify sources of funding, including cost-sharing with students. It suggested that government funding should be linked closely to performance. It proposed to redefine the role of government in higher education. It also recommended policies that were explicitly designed to give priority to quality and equity objectives (World Bank, 1994, p. 4).

These prescriptions sat comfortably in the market-oriented policy framework of the 'Washington Consensus'. They were fed into the lending portfolios for the poorer countries. But from the late 1990s the continuing failure of developing countries to 'establish the institutional infrastructure required to make markets work' (Stiglitz, 1999, p. 587) led to a reorientation of the WB's approach to higher education and development. It began to acknowledge that 'what separates more-developed from less-developed countries is not only a scarcity of capital, but a disparity in knowledge' (ibid., p. 588).

BRIDGING THE KNOWLEDGE DIVIDE

Terms such as 'globalization' and 'knowledge economy' did not feature in the 1994 report. But eight years later they entirely framed the strategy for higher education in *Constructing Knowledge Societies* (World Bank, 2002). During this same period there was a more systematic commissioning of studies as part of the knowledge-sharing strategy of the WB (Salmi et al., 2009, p. 106), combined with a redirection of lending 'to those sectors and those countries that did not have easy access to the market' (Stiglitz, 1999, p. 589). These developments together helped to shape one of the most prominent of the commissioned studies, *Higher Education in Developing Countries: peril and promise*. This was prepared by a Task Force on Higher Education and Society (TFHES) co-convened by the WB and UNESCO and published in 2000 (TFHES, 2000). Drawing on 18 months of research, it offered a new diagnosis of higher education in developing countries. It reiterated certain weaknesses outlined in the 1994 report (outmoded teaching methods, favoritism and patronage, politicization and lack of merit-based selection) in a language critical of local political systems and cultural values.

Elsewhere, however, the new report touches timidly on the negative impacts of WB-supported neoliberal measures on access for underrepresented groups, and on the funding of public universities (TFHES, 2000). 'Peril and Promise' also introduced a new strand of reflection on higher education and development that situated knowledge at the heart of development strategy:

> The expansion and differentiation of higher education is occurring at the same time as the pace of knowledge creation is dramatically accelerating. The categories into which new knowledge falls are becoming increasingly specialized, and a revolution has occurred in people's ability to access knowledge quickly and from increasingly distant locations. (TFHES, 2000, p. 32)

Building on this new conceptualization, and on the acknowledgment of knowledge development as a central tool in poverty reduction in the *World Development Report 1998/1999* (World Bank, 1999), *Constructing Knowledge Societies* (World Bank, 2002) noted the need to 'expand the higher education sector to meet rapidly growing demand, inequality of access and outcomes, quality assurance concerns, and the need for more effective and relevant governance and management structures' (p. 102).

The main messages of the report were summed up as follows:

● Social and economic progress is achieved principally through the advancement and application of knowledge.
● Tertiary education is necessary for the creation, dissemination, and application of knowledge and for building technical and professional capacity.
● Developing and transition countries are at risk of being further marginalized in a highly-competitive world economy because their tertiary education systems are not adequately prepared to capitalize on the creation and use of knowledge.
● The state has a responsibility to put in place an enabling framework that encourages tertiary education institutions to be more innovative and responsive to the needs of a globally-competitive knowledge economy and the changing labor market requirements for advanced human capital.
● The World Bank Group can assist client countries in drawing on international experience and mobilizing the resources needed to improve the effectiveness and responsiveness of their tertiary education systems. (World Bank, 2002, p. 6)

In addition, the report saw the WB as 'uniquely positioned to work with its partners in the international community' – international organizations, bilateral donors, and foundations – to help facilitate or create a discussion platform and promote an enabling framework for the global public goods that are crucial for the future of tertiary education in the developing world (ibid., p. 122).

While some have seen in this statement an 'openness to debate about the World Bank's mission and the method of its achievements' (Kotecha, 2004, p. 120), the convergence sought by the WB around its proposed new role in higher education could also be seen as framing a more worrying multilateral agenda. Susan Robertson argues that the promotion of the knowledge-based society and knowledge-economy discourses 'not only legitimates the Bank's policy reversal on the value of higher education, but it has enabled an articulation with capacity discourses and projects that provide a platform for trade agendas to be prioritized' (Robertson, 2009, p. 120). Robertson and others have demonstrated the importance of the convergence of international agency discourses (the WB, OECD, WTO and EU) and key bilateral donors on the role of higher education in so-called knowledge-led economic development. These discourses provide policy researchers with analytical concepts that give international agencies the legitimacy they need to interfere more directly and more openly in national higher education matters.

Market-led reforms such as the encouragement of private provision, cross-border supply, or the introduction of student fees were always going to be appealing to cash-strapped states, with or without a 'knowledge-economy' glossing. But it is less clear the extent to which nation-states anticipated that these new policy reforms would further undermine the sovereignty of those same states in relation to educational matters and development strategy.

BYPASSING THE DEVELOPMENTAL STATE AND PUBLIC UNIVERSITIES

However, what is certain is that the institutionalization of international influence through these reforms generated tensions between international control and national implementation. These tensions hampered reform processes. In 2003 Joel Samoff observed in Sub-Saharan Africa: 'For the international agencies, the challenge in this setting is to find strategies for exercising influence while encouraging national commitment to and implementation of the recommended reform strategy' (Samoff, 2003, p. 11).

The WB is doing exactly that with its latest report on higher education in Africa. The argument concerning the need for more and improved higher education still relies on the development equation of *Constructing Knowledge Societies*:

> Human capital affects growth through multiple channels: by increasing allocative efficiency and the efficiency with which assets are managed, utilized, and maintained; through entrepreneurship; and through innovation, which raises productivity, unlocks new investment opportunities, and enhances export competitiveness. The spread of information and communication technology (ICT) is further strengthening the demand for skills and, in particular, for skills of higher quality. (World Bank, 2009, p. xxiv)

Likewise the suggested strategic approach sticks to the neoliberal new public management (NPM) agenda, with a 'strategic orientation' that 'provides the basis for tertiary policy attention to institutional differentiation, quality assurance, system oversight bodies, competitive funding, externally accountable governance, and more businesslike management' (ibid., p. 81). The report then introduces the imperative of a regional dimension:

> Some difficulties in equilibrating the market for tertiary-level skills might be most effectively dealt with through regionally coordinated interventions that shape the supply of graduates and the demand for skills. In view of the small size of many of the countries and the limited resources at their disposal, regional partnerships among groups of countries would be both cost-effective and more likely to help build institutions that have the scale and the finances to provide specialized training and conduct strategic research. (Ibid., p. xxiv)

While complimenting African states on facilitating an unprecedented period of economic growth in the first half of the decade, the report pushes the now familiar agenda of diversification, privatization and regionalization of tertiary education provision with particular emphasis on the non-university sector (more easily manageable outside state control). In the process, the state becomes the instrument of its own de-capabilization. This is far from the empowering perspectives that were championed by UNESCO 40 years ago. But where does UNESCO stand in relation to these twenty-first-century policies on higher education and development?

BEYOND THE ECONOMY: UNESCO DIALOGUES AT THE TURN OF THE CENTURY

In the post-'Washington Consensus' era much of UNESCO's work on higher education has been centered on successive World Conferences on higher education, held for the first time in 1998, and the World Conferences on Science that began in Budapest in 1999. Holding a World Conference on higher education is no doubt a sign that higher education is being taken seriously. For an organization that has 'education', 'science' and 'culture' at the heart of its mandate and in its very name, this should not come as a surprise.

The World Declaration on Higher Education

The 1998 conference led to a World Declaration on Higher Education. Among its most important points were:

1. Higher education shall be equally accessible to all on the basis of merit.
2. The core missions of higher education systems (to educate, to train, to undertake research and, in particular, to contribute to the sustainable development and improvement of society as a whole) should be preserved, reinforced and further expanded.
3. Higher education institutions and their personnel and students should preserve and develop their crucial functions, through the exercise of ethics and scientific and intellectual rigour in their various activities . . . For this, they should enjoy full academic autonomy and freedom, while being fully responsible and accountable to society.
4. Relevance in higher education should be assessed in terms of the fit between what society expects of institutions and what they do.
5. Higher education is part of a seamless system, starting with early childhood and primary education and continuing through life.
6. Diversifying higher education models and recruitment methods and criteria is essential both to meet demand and to give students the rigorous background and training required by the twenty-first century.
7. Quality in higher education is a multidimensional concept, which should embrace all its functions and activities: teaching and academic programs, research and scholarship, staffing, students, infrastructure and the academic environment.
8. A vigorous policy of staff development is an essential element for higher education institutions.
9. Institutions should educate students to become well-informed and deeply motivated citizens, who can think critically, analyze problems of society, look for solutions to the problems of society, apply them and accept social responsibilities.
10. Measures must be taken or reinforced to ensure the participation of women in higher education.
11. The potential of new information and communication technologies for the renewal of higher education by extending and diversifying delivery, and by making knowledge and information available to a wider public, should be fully utilized.
12. Higher education should be considered as a public service. While diversified sources of funding, private and public, are necessary public support for higher education and research remains essential to ensure a balanced achievement of its educational and social missions.
13. The international dimension of higher education is an inherent part of its quality. Networking, which has emerged as a major means of action, should be based on sharing, solidarity and equality among partners.
14. Regional and international normative instruments for the recognition of studies and diplomas should be ratified and implemented, including certification of skills, competencies, and abilities of graduates, making it easier for students to change courses, in order to facilitate mobility within and between national systems.
15. Close partnership amongst all is required in order to set in train a movement for the in-depth reform and renewal of higher education. (UNESCO, 1998)

The insistence of some of UNESCO's funders, particularly the Nordic countries, and the criticisms of scholars around the world prompted UNESCO to engage the WB more actively in relation to higher education. As noted above, by the mid-1990s the WB itself had begun to change its position on higher education. The convergence between the higher education policies of UNESCO and those of the WB was best illustrated by the creation, shortly after the 1998 World Conference on Higher Education and the 1999 World Conference on Science, of the joint UNESCO–WB Task Force on Higher Education and Society (TFHES), whose report was published as *Higher Education in Developing Countries: Peril and Promise* (see above).

The 2004 UNESCO Forum

Following the publication of the report of the TFHES, UNESCO, in collaboration with the government of Sweden, created the UNESCO Forum on Higher Education, Research and Knowledge. The Forum was a follow-up activity to the first World Conference on Higher Education and to the World Conference on Science. Swedish government support for the UNESCO Forum on Higher Education went beyond the provision of funds for the operation and global activities of the Forum, to include the secondment of a Swedish government official to head the small secretariat of the Forum at the UNESCO headquarters building in Paris. The Forum initiated a new, regular annual global meeting on higher education, science and research, the first of which was held in December 2004, as well as regional forums on higher education science and research. It also generated many studies on all these matters.

One of the ambitions of the Forum was to restore a plurality of perspectives on higher education, including those of the higher education communities of the global South. It was hoped thereby to create a departure from the monolithic, neoliberal policy perspective on higher education that had become dominant in many regions of the world, including Africa – despite the rapid and profound differentiation evident within the worldwide higher education sector (and in social research worldwide as well). Arguing along lines similar to those in the report of the TFHES, the promoters of the Forum tried to make a case for strong national 'systems and structures of higher education and research'. If knowledge was seen as important a factor of production as land and labor, as the Task Force report had argued, universities – as places where much of the research and knowledge production is carried out – should be given the importance that they deserve. The Task Force report had argued for each country in the world to have at least one research university. The 'rationale' of the December 2004 UNESCO Forum stated:

> As the twenty-first century begins, the research sector is undergoing many profound changes associated with global social and economic forces. In the OECD countries, it is widely expected that this will result in a markedly different research landscape over the next 20 years. In this process of change, perceived priorities can be both diverse and numerous, as various lobbies seek to achieve their objectives. Decisionmakers – both national and institutional – tend to face many appeals to channel human and financial resources earmarked for higher education elsewhere. However, despite the fierce competition for higher education funding, countries and institutions cannot ignore the need to strengthen their systems and structures of higher education and research.

In many countries across all regions, regardless of socioeconomic and cultural context, recognition of the need to revive, renew, and strengthen higher education systems and structures is manifest. This recognition confirms that higher education should contribute more effectively to meeting both the objectives of development policies and educational and training needs.

The current dynamic to renew the higher education sector has created two particular imperatives:

1. The need to widen the understanding of, to enhance access to, research on systems and structures of higher education, research and knowledge – that is, to follow trends in these areas and to analyze and advise on aspects of national and institutional policy on the basis of up-to-date information and research. Both efforts aim at reinforcing higher education as an academic discipline and at providing enhanced advisory services to policymakers, should be undertaken.
2. The need to collate and make available data and analysis of the research mission in higher education. Through research the sector has traditionally contributed to the generation and dissemination of advanced knowledge. Research is considered the necessary part of academic higher education. However, due to major changes in knowledge production, research function needs to be analyzed and adjustments considered, to ensure quality.

It is thus essential to reaffirm the importance of research development in all countries, industrialized and developing, and to secure wide support and improve conditions for strengthening the development of research. (UNESCO, 2005a)

The promotion of *Education for All* and 'lifelong learning' already constituted a slight departure from the exclusive emphasis on basic education implied in the campaign for *Universal Primary Education*. However, neither the *Education for All* campaign, nor the campaign for 'lifelong learning', had left important space for higher education. The return to a more systematic defense and promotion of higher education, comparable to the kind of engagement UNESCO had with higher education in the 1950s and 1960s, really occurred with the World Conference on higher education – that is, towards the end of the 1990s.

The UNESCO Forum was short-lived. It was folded up in 2009 while its parent organization was busy organizing its second global Forum on higher education. The reasons behind the folding up of the Forum are unclear. But it seems that, beyond the bureaucratic explanations (UNESCO was unable to raise funds to sustain the Forum),[1] the more fundamental reasons have to do with shifts in the higher education policies of global institutions, including UNESCO. There was increasing recognition of the importance of higher education for the achievement of the global goals of the international campaigns and, more generally, for the sustainability of the information and knowledge societies.[2] With UNESCO running World Conferences on Higher Education, the Forum became less of a necessity as a medium for promoting more positive policies towards higher education. It remains to be known to what extent the Forum was successful in promoting alternative perspectives and policies on higher education in its different global and regional forums and committees. At the onset of the second decade of the new millennium, the need for diverse, culturally sensitive and context-sensitive perspectives in global debates on higher education, research and knowledge is probably as great as it was ten years earlier when the Forum was created.

In 2005, UNESCO published a World Report titled *Towards Knowledge Societies*. The report could be seen as part of UNESCO's efforts to deal with the growing internationalization of higher education (Mundy and Madden, 2009). In this report UNESCO's take on the concept of knowledge societies seems slightly different from that of the WB. The report seems to signal UNESCO's intent to distance itself from narrow economistic and technologically deterministic discourses on knowledge and information societies (Leye, 2007). There was a return to the traditional UNESCO advocacy of cultural pluralism and diversity:

> The idea of the information society is based on technological breakthroughs. The concept of knowledge societies encompasses much broader social, ethical and political dimensions. There is a multitude of such dimensions which rules out the idea of any single, ready-made model, for such a model would not take sufficient account of cultural and linguistic diversity, vital if individuals are to feel at home in a changing world. Various forms of knowledge and culture always enter into the building of any society, including those strongly influenced by scientific progress and modern technology. It would be inadmissible to envisage the information and communication revolution leading through a narrow, fatalistic technological determinism – to a single possible form of society. (UNESCO, 2005b)

It has also been argued that UNESCO was then struggling to counterbalance the rising influence of the discourse on the 'information society' discussed above, and that 'through its allegiance to knowledge-based economy reasoning (concerning education and learning; globalization and development), UNESCO in this report actually endorses and helps to construct the discourse on the information society' (Leye, 2007, p. 73).

FROM PUBLIC TO PRIVATE GOOD: THE MOVE AWAY FROM DEVELOPMENT DEBATES?

Policies proposed by, or in some cases imposed by, the WB have been particularly challenging for the capacity of states to regulate the provision of educational opportunities. In the context of increased liberalization of the sector, higher education has been increasingly perceived as a service generating international demands and huge profits, notably through student mobility and transborder course provision. Besides, the decreasing public support for tertiary education at a time of unabating demand has prompted the growth of a private sector that today enrolls more than 60 percent of the student population in countries such as Brazil, India, Colombia, Indonesia, South Korea and the Philippines. Some countries have deliberately liberalized their higher education systems to position themselves as regional hubs in the international market of higher education services, operating an interface role between, on one hand, massive unsatisfied demands in the developing world, and on the other hand, the marketization of higher education in the most developed economies, plus the globalization of such markets through ICT and the inclusion of educational services in the regulations of the General Agreement on Tariffs and Trade (GATT).

According to Sajitha Bashir (2007, p. 10), 'the annual value of exports of higher education services from the five main exporting countries exceeds annual bilateral and multilateral Official Development Assistance (ODA) for postsecondary education by a factor of ten'. An interesting trend is reflected in the high number of recently acceded members to the World Trade Organization – all of whom are from the least developed part of the world – with GATS commitments in higher education[3] (Lim and Honeck, 2009). At the same time, the status of public education and the prevailing perception that states should retain their sovereignty over the regulation of the higher education sector are posing problems in the ongoing negotiations (the Doha Round) aimed at liberalizing educational services in order to facilitate the market penetration of transborder provision.

In the context of these developments, the 2009 World Conference on Higher Education appears – in some respects at least – as a last desperate attempt by UNESCO to rescue and restore the notion of public good in higher education, even while trying to keep pace with the rapid development of internationalization and the strong infusion of free trade rules in higher education. The conference's final Communiqué, a compromise document as always, emphasizes the public-good dimension of higher education and the importance of paying particular attention to the ethical challenges and the specific developmental needs of each region of the developing world. It also discusses the advantages and risks associated with cross-border provision of higher education. With specific reference to the current economic downturn, the Communiqué stresses the importance of the social responsibility of higher education institutions (promotion of critical thinking and active citizenship, equity and intercultural dialogue, the provision of skills) through their core functions of research teaching and service to the community. But also, and perhaps more importantly, it reiterates 'the responsibility of all stakeholders, especially governments' (UNESCO, 2009, p. 2) for higher education as a public good at a time when governments and aid agencies alike were considering their funding priorities in development strategies.

The question that remains is whether and to what extent UNESCO can function as a strong and effective counterweight to the WTO and the WB. To perform this role, UNESCO needs to ensure that it benefits from continued (if not enhanced) support from the USA, whose policies tend to be more supportive of the neoliberal agenda of the WB and the WTO.

CONCLUSION

Global institutions have contributed to the shaping of the higher education landscape in developing countries in a very significant way. In addition to the WB and UNESCO – for a long time perhaps the two most influential global institutions in the higher education field – the policies of the WTO are also reshaping the global higher education landscape.

However, it is important to note that the evolution of the higher education policies of the global institutions was in part shaped by the transformation of the field, with the growing internationalization that has occurred with deregulation and the ICT revolution, and in part by the responses from the global South – and, in some instances, the resistance encountered. In Africa national policy-makers always tried to resist the injunctions of the WB towards an exclusive focus on basic education, arguing that Africa needed both basic education and higher education (Samoff and Caroll, 2004b). The excessive commodification and overemphasis of the application of market principles and free trade rules to the higher education sector also met with resistance from some bilateral donors and the liberal private US foundations supporting African universities – in part because universities are where local elites and leaders are groomed.

We have argued that the higher education policies of UNESCO and the WB have often converged, and occasionally diverged. These days there is a global consensus around the importance of higher education for economic growth, development and good governance. However, development and governance paradigms have changed, and with them the role of the state and the place and role of higher education in development. So long as UNESCO continues to be a platform where developing countries can articulate their views and voice their concerns, there will be meaningful differences between UNESCO and the WB in their approaches to global higher education. The recently published UNESCO–ISSC *World Social Science Report* (2010) shows that despite its rapprochement with the WB on many issues, UNESCO still has space within it for critical thinking on questions of development and of ethics. The report highlights the expansion of the social sciences in the global South, particularly in India, Brazil and China, and shows that this expansion is closely related to the growth of higher education in developing countries.

On the other hand, although its policies have moved away from a narrow focus on growth, the WB's approach to higher education is still largely informed by a concern for human capital development. The knowledge that it seeks to promote is what in some strands of the literature is referred to as 'Mode 2' type knowledge, that is, technical, and 'usable' for one purpose or another. In contrast, UNESCO emphasizes the need to sustain the diversity of cultures and perspectives, albeit within a common 'universal' set of values. In practice, the dominance of one or the other of these approaches has direct consequences for the kind of higher education institutions and programs provided, and the disciplines and research programs promoted or sidelined. Higher education is a strategic component of the reproductive system of modern society. It is an engine for social mobility and change, and for the empowerment of both individual citizens and social groups such as women. If the concept of a knowledge society is to be meaningful for both the countless numbers of poor people around the world, and for those seeking investment opportunities, it is in the transformative potential of higher education that this meaning is embedded.

NOTES

1. We are grateful to Dr Berit Olsson, former Director of the Swedish Research Cooperation Agency (SAREC) of the Swedish International Development Cooperation Agency (SIDA), for sharing her views on the experience of the UNESCO Forum in a series of discussions, the latest of which was held in Dakar on 13 March 2010.
2. For instance, article 11 of the final Communiqué of the 2009 World Conference on Higher Education claims: 'Our ability to realize the goals of *Education for All* is dependent upon our ability to address the worldwide shortage of teachers. Higher education must scale-up teacher education, both pre-service and in-service, with curricula that equip teachers to provide individuals with the knowledge and skills they need in the twenty-first century' (UNESCO, 2009, p. 3).
3. The GATS entered into legal force in 1995, covering 12 services sectors including education. Overall, as noted by Lim and Honeck (2009, p. 137), 'out of the 12 services sectors covered by GATS, educational services ranks amongst the sectors with the fewest number of commitments, together with health services'.

REFERENCES

Balán, J. (2009), 'American foundations and higher education in developing countries: shifting rationales and strategies for support', in R. Bassett and A. Maldonado-Maldonado (eds), *International Organizations and Higher Education Policy: Thinking Globally, Acting Locally?* New York: Routledge, pp. 231–50.

Bashir, S. (2007), 'Trends in international trade in higher education: implications and options for developing countries', Education Working Paper Series, 6, Washington, DC: World Bank.

Coleman, J. (1986), 'The idea of the developmental university', *Minerva*, **24** (4), 476–94.

De Figuerido-Cowen, M. (2002), 'Latin American universities, academic freedom and autonomy: a long-term myth?', *Comparative Education*, **38** (4), 471–84.

Federici, S., G. Caffentzis and O. Alidou (2000), *A Thousand Flowers: Structural Adjustment and the Struggle for Education in Africa*, Trenton, NJ: Africa World Press.

Jones, P. (1997), 'On World Bank education financing', *Comparative Education*, **33** (1), 117–30.

Kent, R. (1996), 'The World Bank and UNESCO on higher education', *International Higher Education*, **4**, 3–5.

Kotecha, P. (2004), 'A bridge too far? Constructing knowledge societies: new challenges for tertiary education', *Journal of Higher Education in Africa*, **2** (3), 115–22.

Lawi, Y. (2008), 'The idea of university', in I. Kimambo, B. Mapunda and Y. Lawi (eds), *In Search of Relevance: A History of the University of Dar es Salaam*, Dar es Salaam: University of Dar es Salaam Press.

Leye, V. (2007), 'UNESCO's road towards knowledge societies', *Javnost – The Public*, **14** (4), 73–88.

Lim, A. and D. Honeck (2009), 'GATS and education services: current commitments and future prospects', in R. Bassett and A. Maldonado-Maldonado (eds), *International Organizations and Higher Education Policy: Thinking Globally, Acting Locally?*, New York: Routledge, pp. 132–52.

Menon, M. (2003), 'An evaluation of four decades of rate of return analysis in higher education policy making: weaknesses and future prospects', *Higher Education Policy*, **16**, 369–84.

Ministry of Overseas Development (1975), *Overseas Development: the Changing Emphasis in British Aid Policies: More Help for the Poorest*, Cmnd 6270, London: HMSO.

Mundy, K. (1999), 'Educational multilateralism in a changing world order: UNESCO and the limits of the possible', *International Journal of Educational Development*, **19**, 27–52.

Mundy, K. and M. Madden (2009), 'UNESCO and higher education: opportunity or impasse?', in R. Bassett and A. Maldonado-Maldonado (eds), *International Organizations and Higher Education Policy: Thinking Globally, Acting Locally?*, New York: Routledge, pp. 46–63.

Olaniyan, D. and T. Okemakinde (2008), 'Human capital theory: implications for educational development', *European Journal of Scientific Research*, **24** (2), 157–62.

Psacharopoulos, G. and M. Woodhall (1997), *Education for Development: An Analysis of Investment Choice*, New York: Oxford University Press.

Robertson, S. (2009), 'Market multilateralism, the World Bank group, and the asymmetries of globalizing higher education: toward a critical political economy analysis', in R. Bassett and A. Maldonado-Maldonado (eds), *International Organizations and Higher Education Policy: Thinking Globally, Acting Locally?*, New York: Routledge, pp. 113–31.

Salmi, J., R. Hopper and R. Bassett (2009), 'Transforming higher education in developing countries: the role of the World Bank', in R. Bassett and A. Maldonado-Maldonado (eds), *International Organizations and Higher Education Policy: Thinking Globally, Acting Locally?*, New York: Routledge, pp. 99–112.

Samoff, J. (2003), 'Institutionalizing international influence', *Safundi*, **4** (1), 1–35.

Samoff, J. and B. Carrol (2004a), 'The promise of partnerships and continuities of dependence: external support to higher education in Africa', *African Studies Review*, **47** (1), 67–199.

Samoff, J. and B. Carrol (2004b), 'Conditions, coalitions, and influence: the World Bank and higher education in Africa', prepared for presentation at the Annual Conference of the Comparative and International Education Society, Salt Lake City, 8–12 March 2004, accessed January 2011 at http://www.eldis.org/vfile/upload/1/document/0708/DOC17679.pdf.

Stiglitz, J. (1999), 'The World Bank at the millennium', *The Economic Journal*, **109** (November), 577–97.

TFHES (Task Force on Higher Education and Society) (2000), *Higher Education in Developing Countries: Peril and Promise*, Washington, DC: World Bank.

Torres, C. and D. Schugurensky (2002), 'The political economy of higher education in the era of neoliberal globalization: Latin America in comparative perspective', *Higher Education*, **43** (4), 429–55.

UNESCO (1997), *UNESCO: 50 Years for Education*, Paris: UNESCO.

UNESCO (1998), *Summary of the World Declaration on Higher Education*, accessed June 2010 at http://www.unesco.org/education/educprog/wche/summary.htm.

UNESCO (2005a), 'The need for renewal and renovation', UNESCO Forum on Higher Education, Research and Knowledge, accessed January 2001 at http://portal.unesco.org/education/en/ev.php-URL_ID-21047&URL_DO-DO_TOPIC&URL_SECTION-201.html.

UNESCO (2005b), *Towards Knowledge Societies*, Paris: UNESCO.

UNESCO (2009), *World Conference on Higher Education: The New Dynamics of Higher Education and Research for Societal Change and Development*, Final Communiqué, UNESCO, Paris, 8 July 2009, accessed June 2010 at http://www.unesco.org/fileadmin/MULTIMEDIA/HQ/ED/ED/pdf/WCHE_2009/FINAL%20 COMMUNIQUE%20WCHE%202009.pdf.

UNESCO–ISSC (2010), *World Social Science Report 2010: Knowledge Divides*, International Social Science Council (ISSC) and UNESCO, accessed June 2010 at http://www.unesco.org/new/en/social-and-human-sciences/resources/reports/world-social-science-report/.

Woodhall, M. (2007), 'Funding higher education: the contribution of economic thinking to debate and policy development', Education Working Papers Series No. 8, Washington, DC: World Bank.

World Bank (1994), *Higher Education: The Lessons of Experience,* Development in Practice series, Washington, DC: World Bank.

World Bank (1999), *World Development Report 1998/1999: Knowledge for Development*, New York: Oxford University Press.

World Bank (2002), *Constructing Knowledge Societies: New Challenges for Tertiary Education*, Washington, DC: World Bank.

World Bank (2009), *Accelerating Catch-up: Tertiary Education for Growth in Sub-Saharan Africa*, Washington, DC: World Bank.

9 Globalization, higher education and inequalities: problems and prospects
Vincent Carpentier and Elaine Unterhalter

INTRODUCTION

At the end of the twentieth century, globalization was associated with new and enormously expansive forms of capitalist growth. For higher education it offered many opportunities for innovation and networking. However, from the beginning of the twenty-first century, globalization has become as much associated with danger, threat and crisis – for example in relation to the financial system and climate change – as with opportunity and endeavour. The 'dark' side of globalization is seen as both cause and effect of global and local social division. For higher education institutions these processes of inequality entail a complex intermingling of opportunity, risk and social injustice (Unterhalter and Carpentier, 2010).

Problems of global inequality require both transnational and subnational responses. But higher education institutions and systems find it difficult to respond in both registers. Global inequalities present both problems and prospects for higher education. They constitute a distinctive location for research, teaching, learning and organizational formation. In this chapter we consider global inequalities as a major site of injustice that confronts higher education institutions, and we attempt to assess the prospects for change that the sector offers.

Much of the scholarship on inequality and higher education discusses the topic in relation to national contexts (Archer and Leathwood, 2003; Bourdieu and Passeron, 1964; Duru-Bellat et al., 2008). However, as we show below, a number of drivers of inequality have long been associated with global processes. Nationally located higher education institutions reproduce practices associated with global inequality – either unwittingly, because these practices are often taken for granted, or through strategies that promote the practice of particular nations or socioeconomic or cultural groups. The first part of this chapter examines this historically. From the 1990s a range of new forms of higher education emerged that entailed changes in higher education institutions' relationship with the nation-state and with each other. The second part of the chapter considers the ways this process is enmeshed with both national and global inequalities. The third part reviews problems associated with inequalities and the prospects of achieving justice.

DIMENSIONS OF INEQUALITY

Definitions

Before we discuss global higher education and inequalities, it is necessary to consider definitions of inequality and their global dimensions. Jacob and Holsinger (2008, p.

4) define equality 'as the state of being equal in terms of quantity, rank, status, value or degree'; while equity 'considers the social justice ramifications of education in relation to fairness, justness, and impartiality of its distribution at all levels of educational subsectors'. A wide-ranging debate exists on how to understand aspects of equality in education: in relation to school choice; the treatment of children in school; and gender, disability and cultural identity. This work discusses the salience of childhood, family life and the conditions of learning (e.g. Lynch and Lodge, 2002; Brighouse, 2000; Swift, 2003; Ball, 2006; Eisenberg, 2006; Gereluk, 2006; Terzi, 2008; Unterhalter, 2007). Much of the literature on equality in higher education has focused on widening participation, bringing into play questions of equity and fairness (Burke, 2005; Reay et al., 2005; David, 2009). However, like the literature on equality and schooling, virtually all these studies consider equality and equity in terms of national processes of distribution or appraisal. There are few works that define equality and equity in relation to global processes.

In a recent work co-edited by this chapter's authors (Unterhalter and Carpentier, 2010) some pieces start to do so (Naidoo, 2010; Luke, 2010; Unterhalter, 2010). Similarly Marginson (2006, p. 35) argues that 'global hierarchy in higher education is not fixed for all time but subject to continual movement and flux', while Currie and Newson (1998, p. 1) analyse the impact on higher education of a narrow 'conception of globalization that combines a market ideology with a corresponding material set of practices drawn from the world of business'. Inequalities are a feature of both opportunities and outcome. Individuals, groups and countries do not have the same histories, contemporary social relations or prospects. Inequality is one feature of diversity but inequity partly lies in processes that do not recognize this diversity or attempt to change its unjust consequences. Inequity can entail reproducing, exacerbating or extending inequalities associated with one historical period, a particular region or field of educational work into another. Within a 'capabilities' approach, inequalities can be defined in the 'space' of opportunities or outcomes and in their interconnections (Sen, 1993; Robeyns, 2006). In the analysis that follows our understanding of inequity partly draws on Harvey's (2005) account of neoliberalism and the use of both coercive and discursive forms.

This chapter also partly builds on the distinctions used by Unterhalter in writing about equity (Unterhalter, 2009, 2010). This work highlights different processes to establish equity – but similar points can be made about structures and actions associated with inequity. Forms of inequity may be established 'from above' through structures of political economy and institutional formation. These processes are somewhat different but connected to inequity maintained 'from below', for example research or pedagogy that fails to engage equitably with issues of poverty or injustice. Unterhalter also suggests that there is a third form of inequity, associated with processes that flow 'from the middle'. These last processes may be particularly salient to global increases in the speed, range, and mobility of ideas and people, and the discourses associated with programmes and institutions that make claims about partnership (which often mask continued inequities). In considering problems and prospects for change in global higher education we shall touch on all three forms of inequity: from above, from below and from the middle.

Indicators of Inequality

Manifestations and 'measures' of inequalities in higher education are multiple. Perceptions about these have evolved across space and time. While initially the focus of much research and action on inequalities was on access, there is now increasing awareness of inequalities relating to participation and academic achievements. The ways in which higher education does or does not translate into socioeconomic benefits include social networks, labor market advantages, and the nature of employment and pay. There have been gradual changes in the way inequalities have been defined, and this is reflected in the indicators used. The current indicators used to frame, drive and monitor higher education policies and practices tend to give inadequate insight into the multidimensionality of inequality.

The most widely used indicator of access seeks to estimate the ratio of students to the population: the gross enrolment ratio (GER) for higher education. This indicator is traditionally used to estimate expansion of higher education systems across the world. It enables the mapping of inequalities between countries and trends over time. More refined indicators compare enrolment by age group. For example, in the UK, the Higher Education Initial Participation Rate (HEIPR) measures the number in the age group of 18–30 years who entered a higher education course. This reached 43 per cent in 2006 (DIUS, 2008). The Labour government aimed to increase the HEIPR to 50 per cent by 2010, but this target was not met. Such aggregate indicators are less useful in understanding inequalities between groups, for example the ways that an overall GER enrolment may not translate into engaged participation or valued outcomes for some groups. They focus on access and do not provide data on processes in relation to retention, outcomes and experience. Brennan and Naidoo (2008, p. 299) stress the 'need for greater attention to be given to the end products of higher education. Does greater equity at the point of entry to higher education necessarily provide greater equity at exit?' Another limitation of aggregate participation indicators is they do not offer information on the social structuring of access and the inclusion/exclusion of particular groups. We need to understand how social divisions shape each other in patterns of enrolment, and to explore inequalities and unpack the crucial difference between expansion and democratization of higher education.

International Comparisons

In a summary overview of the global picture, Philip Altbach and colleagues (Altbach et al., 2009, p. iv) note that worldwide 'the percentage of the age cohort enrolled in tertiary education has grown from 19 per cent in 2000 to 26 per cent in 2007 . . . There are some 150.6 million tertiary students globally', about a 53 per cent increase since 2000. However, 'the most dramatic gains' have been in 'upper middle- and upper-income countries'. Further:

> In low-income countries tertiary-level participation has improved only marginally, from 5 per cent in 2000 to 7 per cent in 2007. Sub-Saharan Africa has the lowest participation rate in the world (5 per cent). In Latin America, enrolment is still less than half that of high-income countries.

Table 9.1 summarizes the worldwide picture. As Altbach and colleagues note, quantitative analysis offers a mixed picture of inequalities in higher education. There has been overall worldwide progress, but inequalities between nations have persisted.

Table 9.1 *Comparative worldwide tertiary participation (GER) and progress indicators (GPI), by region*

	Gross enrolment ratio (GER)		Genuine progress indicator (GPI)	
	1999	2007	1999	2007
World	18	26	0.96	1.08
Highest	North America/ W. Europe (61)	North America/ W. Europe (70)	North America/ W. Europe (1.23)	North America/ W. Europe (1.33)
Average	Central Asia (18)	East Asia/the Pacific (26)	Central Asia (0.93)	Central Asia (1.10)
Lowest	Sub-Saharan Africa (4)	Sub-Saharan Africa (6)	Sub-Saharan Africa (0.67)	Sub-Saharan Africa (0.66)
Arab states	19	22	0.74	1.05
Highest	Egypt (37)	Lebanon (54)	Qatar (3.82)	Qatar (2.87)
Average	UAE (18)	UAE (24)	Morocco (0.71)	Jordan (1.1)
Lowest	Mauritania (5)	Djibouti (3)	Yemen (0.28)	Yemen (0.37)
Central and Eastern Europe	38	62	1.18	1.25
Highest	Slovenia (53)	Slovenia (86)	Latvia (1.65)	Latvia (1.8)
Average	Hungary/Moldova (33)	Estonia (65)	Croatia (1.16)	Ukraine (1.24)
Lowest	Albania (15)	Macedonia/ Turkey (36)	Turkey (0.68)	Turkey (0.76)
Central Asia	18	24	0.93	1.1
Highest	Georgia (36)	Mongolia (48)	Mongolia (1.88)	Mongolia (1.56)
Average	Azerbaijan (16)	Tajikistan (20)	Uzbekistan (0.82)	Georgia (1.12)
Lowest	Uzbekistan (14)	Uzbekistan (10)	Tajikistan (0.35)	Tajikistan (0.35)
East Asia and the Pacific	14	26	n.a.	1
Highest	Australia (65)	New Zealand (80)	Palau (2.35)	Brunei (1.88)
Average	Micronesia (14)	China (23)		China (1.01)
Lowest	Cambodia/Laos (2)	Cambodia (5)	Cambodia (0.35)	Cambodia (0.56)
Latin America/ the Caribbean	21	34	1.12	1.19
Highest	British Virgin Islands (60)	Cuba (109)	Cayman Islands (2.79)	British Virgin Islands (2.28)
Average	Cuba (21)	Ecuador/Peru (35)	Colombia/Nicaragua (1.11)	Ecuador/El Salvador (1.22)
Lowest	Trinidad and Tobago (6)	Saint Lucia (9)	Chile/Mexico (0.91)	Mexico (0.93)
North America/ W. Europe	61	70	1.23	1.33
Highest	Finland (82)	Finland (94)	Iceland (1.69)	Iceland (1.86)
Average	Belgium/UK (60)	Iceland (73)	Finland (1.23)	Israel (1.32)
Lowest	Luxembourg (11)	Andorra/ Luxembourg (10)	Switzerland (0.73)	Liechtenstein (0.49)

Table 9.1   (continued)

	Gross enrolment ratio (GER)		Genuine progress indicator (GPI)	
	1999	2007	1999	2007
South Asia/ West Asia	n.a.	11	n.a.	0.77
Highest	Iran (19)	Iran (31)	Iran (0.8)	Iran (1.15)
Average	n.a.	Nepal (11)	n.a.	India (0.72)
Lowest	Bhutan (3)	Bhutan/Pakistan (5)	Nepal (0.4)	Bhutan (0.51)
Sub-Saharan Africa	4	6	0.67	0.66
Highest	South Africa (14)	South Africa (15)	Lesotho (1.65)	South Africa (1.24)
Average	Congo (4)	Ghana/Namibia (6)	Angola (0.63)	Nigeria (0.69)
Lowest	12 countries (1)	5 countries (1)	Chad (0.18)	Chad (0.14)

Source: UNESCO (2009).

HISTORICAL CONTEXTS AND DRIVERS: CONSTRUCTING FORMS AND SITES OF INEQUALITIES

Historically, global political economy and associated sociocultural divisions (colonialism, slavery and the diversity between states) have shaped inequalities in higher education within and between nations. Inequalities of class, race, ethnicity and gender intersect and map onto divisions between higher education institutions. From the eighteenth century onwards the most well-endowed and prestigious universities were located in countries that formed the centres of empires, benefited from slavery, and imposed sharp social divisions in access to what was deemed by ruling elites to be the most powerful forms of knowledge.

In the dominated countries the colonial powers did not have an interest in expanding higher education much beyond training a small elite (Saïd, 1993). In the African context Teferra and Altbach (2004, p. 23) note that 'colonial authorities feared widespread access to higher education. They were interested in training limited numbers of African nationals to assist in administering the colonies'. The elitist higher education models of the nineteenth century (Lowe, 2008) were reproduced in countries subject to colonial rule. Limited access to study, preference for the language of the colonial ruling group, and limited freedom of association and freedom of curricula (Teferra and Altbach, 2004, p. 24) rendered higher education complicit in the imperial project. It was not well placed to generate change. Britain's will to shape and monitor higher education across its empire was symbolized by 'the creation of the Asquith Commission which prepared a seminal report on the future of higher education in the colonies' (Whitehead, 2003, p. 192). In Indonesia in the 1950s:

> The teaching and learning methods were entirely based on the Dutch or continental style of higher education, characterized by emphasis on the education of a few individuals with little

attention given to the need for a more systematic approach to mass education. The teaching staff was primarily Dutch professors but included also a few Indonesians educated in the Dutch tradition. (UNESCO, 1991, p. 39)

When Algeria gained independence from France in 1962, in the University of Algiers there were only 557 Muslims to 4548 Europeans (Gordon, 1985, p. 137).

From the late 1940s decolonization provided an opportunity for higher education institutions to reshape themselves as projects associated with newly formed governments. But particular local challenges, combined with the changing form of the global relationships between countries, meant that the expansion and democratization of higher education was not easy to achieve. Political independence, whether absolute or relative, has not solved economic dependence. Unequal economic development, which was for many countries a by-product of colonialism, survived in the postcolonial era and has exacerbated inequalities between higher education systems worldwide. Post-Second World War strategies of growth based on the development of educational systems depended on the financial might of particular countries (Schultz, 1961; Denison, 1967). This led to significant differentials in investment in human capital and brought further inequalities in the development of higher education systems, exacerbating the economic gaps between countries established in the colonial era. Most developed countries benefited from the knowledge-driven postwar economy. These outcomes were felt in a few developing countries: 'Higher education has expanded well in the east Asian tiger economies and a few central and west Asian countries, the gross enrolment ratio being comparable to that in some of the developed countries' (Tilak, 2003, p. 155). But for many developing countries knowledge-driven catching up was not translated into practice (Jomo and Fine, 2006; Wallerstein, 1976). Global inequalities inherited from the colonial era imposed a mode of expansion of higher education that reproduced local inequalities and severely constrained newly formed institutions in closing gaps in relation to research and teaching. Why did this happen?

MAPPING DRIVERS, SITES AND FORMS OF INEQUALITY: THE CONNECTIONS BETWEEN THE GLOBAL AND THE LOCAL

A first site of inequality is the world order at the global level. Education reflects inequalities between and within countries. However, it is also important to recognize that education not only reflects social, political and economic inequalities, but also reproduces and sometimes accentuates national inequalities according to class (Ball, 2006), race or ethnicity (Gillborn, 2008), gender (Unterhalter, 2007) and disability (Barton and Armstrong, 2008). National inequalities are often, at least in part, the outcome of global processes associated with the form of the labor market, ideas about national competition and assumptions about processes of decision-making. Policies and practices in compulsory education explain a great deal of the inequalities in higher education. But unequal opportunities of access, participation and success in higher education between and within countries are not just a backwash from these practices in schools, but also reflect policies and practices that avoid challenging the existing structures of inequality.

Limited or ineffective government legislation is found in mechanisms to widen participation (Greenbank, 2006), efforts to reduce unfair or inadequate practices on admission and recruitment (Leathwood, 2004), and support for the most vulnerable students (Burke, 2005).

Understanding higher education as a site of inequality necessitates a shift of focus from 'whose' access to 'what kind' of access. The segmentation of higher education systems within countries and between countries is an important determinant of the inequalities that stratify access, experience, achievement and the capacity to transfer a qualification socially and economically. Worldwide expansion of higher education has been filtered by the construction of tier systems and unequal access to institutions of higher education. Sites of inequalities emerge across institutions (elite–non elite/academic–vocational/research–teaching/public–private) and of course between countries (elite universities in the global North/poorly equipped universities in the global South). However, there are subtle layers of inequalities within particular sites. Thus elite institutions in the global North have long been the setting for the education of minorities from higher professional and ruling groups in the global South. Depending on the country, elite higher education institutions may be public and private, as in the USA (Bastedo and Gumport, 2003), or highly competitive public institutions, as in France (Albouy and Vanecq, 2003) and China (Ding, 2007). In countries like Brazil, some private providers target the richer parts of the population while others may enrol the less wealthy parts of the society unable to access the free but highly selective public system of higher education (McCowan, 2007).

The main features of elite higher education include the staff resources provided – both the experience of staff and the level of student access to staff – and the quality of libraries, laboratories and research communities. Hassim (2009, p. 71) notes in the case of South Africa 'massive imbalances in resource allocations by government to different institutions intensified disadvantage historically as well as into the contemporary era'.

Consequently there are many forms of inequality in higher education. What follows cannot be exhaustive. Inequality characterizes social division along lines of gender, social class, disability, nationality and ethnicity, political belief, religion and so on. Studies show that inequalities shape each other. Archer and Leathwood (2003, p. 175), for example, commenting on the UK, underline 'the importance of recognizing how multiple identities and inequalities of race, ethnicity, social class, and gender (amongst others) affect the way in which people construct, experience, and negotiate different educational opportunities and routes'. Expansion of higher education has historically been the result of a gradual and hierarchically inflected process. Expansion admits the previously excluded, such as lower-income groups, women, ethnic minorities or castes, but many national studies offer a mixed story: the expansion of higher education is based on widening participation together with persistence of inequalities (Volkman et al., 2009). This exclusion is associated with global as well as national processes of class formation that are difficult to disentangle.

The expansion of universities has only partially affected the strong relationship between social class and access, participation, experience and achievement in higher education. For example, in the UK and France one can observe growing numbers of working-class students entering higher education from the 1960s onwards, but differences in participation rates have persisted (Bourdieu and Passeron, 1964; Reay et al., 2005; Archer et al.,

2003). Since the 1980s the proportion of UK students from the lowest social group has only slightly increased compared to higher-income groups (Galindo-Rueda et al., 2004, p. 86). Similar gaps are confirmed in most developing countries. Altbach and colleagues (2009, p. v) note that 'despite many policy initiatives in recent years broader postsecondary participation has not benefited all sectors of society equally. A recent comparative study of 15 countries shows that despite greater inclusion, the privileged classes have retained their relative advantage in nearly all nations.'

When assessing the expansion of higher education, gender inequalities cross-cut class. The expansion of higher education in many developed countries in the postwar era has been largely driven by the integration of middle-class women (Dyhouse, 2006). Global gender parity in higher education was reached in 2003 but there remain important differences between countries. In Sub-Saharan Africa in 2007 the tertiary GER for men was 6.8 per cent, 1.5 times higher than that for women (4.5 per cent). Women were also strongly disadvantaged in terms of access to tertiary education in South and West Asia, where in 2007 the GER for men (13 per cent) was one-third higher than that for women (10 per cent) (UNESCO, 2009, p. 15). In other regions like the USA, Europe, Latin America and the Arab states, participation rates are higher for women. Unterhalter argues that the politics of inclusion, whereby numbers of women students and staff have increased, should be complemented by concerns with 'the relations of power, both overt and covert, that exclude women from realising their full potential' (Unterhalter, 2006, p. 623). Morley and Lugg's (2009, p. 46) research on Tanzania shows that when gender and class are taken together, gender inequality is greater within groups that are already underrepresented. Thus, in some countries women's access to higher education has expanded but this is by no means universal, and in many countries, even those that enrol large numbers of women students, explicit and implicit forms of gender inequality persist.

Nationality, race and ethnicity shape inequalities. Given that much global injustice has been associated with these factors, it is no surprise that their traces are found in higher education throughout the world. 'In many countries, racial, ethnic, or religious minorities play a role in shaping higher education policy. Issues of access will be amongst the most controversial in debates concerning higher education', notes Altbach (1998, p. 15). Across the world substantial inequalities on the basis of nationality, ethnicity or caste remain. These are sometimes associated with particular explicit forms of discrimination, such as apartheid in South Africa, or, more often, simply with a lack of commitment to social justice (Reay et al., 2005). The participation figures for ethnic groups in a particular country reveal differences between minorities. For example, Tomlinson (2005, p. 163) notes that in the UK, 'Indian, Chinese and black African groups are well represented in higher education. African-Caribbean men, Pakistani and Bangladeshi women are represented least well.' In India, where caste and class intersect, notwithstanding governmental policies of reserved spaces (Carpentier et al., forthcoming), in higher education 'there has been modest improvement in the participation of lower castes; rural populations and Muslims lag behind the general population while lower castes tend to be clustered in less expensive programs' (Altbach et al., 2009, p. iv).

The increase in the numbers of disabled students hides the fact that in OECD countries their participation rates are still far lower than those of non-disabled students (Ebersold and Evans, 2003). In the UK it was recently estimated by government that 'by age 19, the proportion of disabled people that have participated in HE courses is around 30 per cent, as opposed to 45 per cent of those without disabilities' (DIUS, 2009, p. 13). Similar problems exist in developing countries such as South Africa (Matshedisho, 2007).

Across the world, some progress has been made in addressing some forms of social inequality. But many inequalities persist. These manifest themselves in patterns of participation as well as assumptions about the nature of the university and its reflection on and engagement with global inequalities.

International Pressure from Economic Globalization

One way of understanding the persistence of inequalities and the inability to close the gap within and between countries is to look at the connection (or rather the clash) between funding and access policies that followed from the response of neoliberal globalization to the 1970s structural crisis of the economy (Carpentier, 2010). While funding does not explain everything, there is a good case to be made that the public funding constraints that arose in the 1970s affected the mission of higher education, including its attitude to discriminated groups. This was a global trend in the sense that it was intensified by international pressure on funding and policy borrowing.

Those historical inequalities which survived – and to a certain extent shaped – the 'golden age' of the postwar higher education expansion became more of a problem after the 1973 structural crisis of the capitalist economy (Carpentier, 2006b; Fontvieille and Michel, 2002). In many countries the sustained public investment which drove post-Second World War higher education was brought to a halt by the 1970s crisis. Spending per student was caught between, on one side the expectation of continuous expansion of enrolment to feed the knowledge economy, and on the other the reluctance to increase public funding in the context of neoliberal anti-taxation policies (Carpentier, 2010). The tensions between these conflicting agendas led to intense political debates across the globe on questions of funding and equity. Who benefits from higher education? Who should pay for it? The neoliberal response to the 1970s crisis was not necessarily based on a return to a minimal state but rather on a reorientation of the role of the state in favor of market expansion and individual choice-making. In this ideological framework higher education was considered a semi-public or even semi-private good and its funding an individual rather than a state responsibility. This neoliberal strategy overlooked social groups and the inequalities between them.

These austerity policies preceded globalization but were strengthened by it. The policies were exported from high-income countries to developing countries under the banner of imposed structural adjustment policies. 'The development of higher education in low-income countries has been framed in general by a neoliberal paradigm' (Naidoo, 2010, p. 66). This led to changes in higher education funding policies at national and global levels.

Funding austerity led governments to tough choices: should they roll back their enrolment and inclusion policies? Should they maintain access with shrinking budgets and jeopardize quality? Should they increase private funding (fees)? Should they welcome new providers? The responses to these dilemmas strongly impacted access, student experience and student achievement. They also affected individuals and their families differently according to socioeconomic background. Affordability readily led families and governments to consciously or unconsciously prioritize the access of certain groups over others (e.g. by gender, age, and so on). If for most countries the reduction of public funding meant big tensions between access and funding policies, these were felt more strongly in developing countries whose higher education systems were generally smaller and at an earlier stage of development (Tiyambe Zeleza and Olukoshi, 2004). For example, structural adjustment policies particularly hit disadvantaged socioeconomic groups in Chile (Espinoza, 2008) and 'eroded the opportunities for the higher education of many women' in Nigeria (Obasi, 1997, p. 171). Decreasing public resources led to quality shortcomings and/or the uneven spread of spending across institutions, with strong implications for equal access, student experience, retention and outcomes from higher education. One consequence of globalization was diminishing public resources. This led some countries to opt for sending more students abroad rather than developing a national higher education system.

Many countries sought to solve underfunding while building capacity and while welcoming in new providers (Altbach, 1999). These providers could be domestic private providers, but also foreign (private or public) providers, so driving the internationalization of higher education (see next section). King (2003, p. 4) observes that the fastest-growing segment of higher education worldwide is private higher education. According to Levy (2003, p. 3), this 'adds enrolment capacity to the higher education system, mostly escaping the constraints about public expenditures that now restricts public expansion'. While most of these factors relate to all countries, the pressure was (and is) more pronounced for developing countries. The effect is often to exacerbate rather than dissolve older social divisions. Altbach (2004, p. 22) states that while growth of enrolment 'has slowed in many industrialized countries, expansion continues in the developing nations, and will remain the factor in shaping academic realities in the coming period'. This is confirmed by Banya (2001, p. 1), who, although he recognizes the achievement of state universities in Sub-Saharan countries, argues that 'increased enrolments, fiscal challenges, quality issues, and rising graduate unemployment make the recourse to private higher education necessary'.

That private institutions are interested in profit has raised questions about access in relation to quality, and generated concerns about the overall impact on host countries' social structure. Welch (2007, p. 681) notes with regard to Indonesia that 'if funding to public-sector higher education institutions continues to be seriously constrained over the next few years and, at the same time, high-quality private institutions are restricted to the wealthy, this will likely lead to a significant decline in equitable access to higher education'. McCowan (2007) notes that in Brazil many private higher education providers for students from lower social backgrounds are increasing inequalities by offering study of dubious quality. However, a concomitant trend is that in many countries state universities are also working with private sector organizations closely linked with global corporations. As remarked by Altbach (1999, p. 1), 'with tuition and other charges rising, public and private institutions look more and more similar'. Ball (2010, p. 21) notes of public institutions that many 'are no longer in any straightforward sense national public universities, they are transnational, corporate, profit-oriented, and they are positioned on the boundaries between academia and business – they are hybrids'. In many countries public universities are acting as international providers and, outside their own countries, work in ways that are indistinguishable from private institutions.

Global pressure on resources has also led many countries to develop fee policies in public universities based on cost-sharing, with students and their family contributing to the cost of their studies in order to make up for declining public funding. The impact of these policies on inequalities depends on the balance between fees, grants and loans (Teixeira et al., 2006). It is therefore crucial to have sufficient grants and scholarships from government and institutions to ensure fair access. The ongoing debates in the UK about the increase in fees and its potential impact on inequalities address issues that were already generated by the increasing contribution of non-EU international students since the 1980s (Carpentier, 2010). But rather than raising concerns about inequality, fee-paying international students have been seen increasingly in developed countries as an income-generating opportunity. All of these policies together are exacerbating concerns about equity: increased private funding and provision; marketization; higher fees; inadequate student support; and international education (Carpentier, 2006a). Countries are at varying stages of the process of public/private substitution, with more or less impact on inequalities; and they also vary in the extent to which they benefit or suffer from global higher education – whether they are importers or providers.

Economic globalization is implicated in the shrinking base of public funding and the marketization and commodification of higher education. The question, however, is whether the construction of global higher education arenas simply accelerates global inequalities or also has the potential to offer alternatives.

GLOBAL HIGHER EDUCATION AND INEQUALITIES

Universities have from their creation been worldwide institutions with international activities, including highly mobile staff and students (Geuna, 1998). However, international activities have often been seen as complementing other activities and driving political and cultural interests. Historically they have not necessarily been considered as ways to solve financial problems. However, economic globalization, with its stress on free trade and low taxation, has offered a new space for internationalization. A convenient marriage has occurred. Pressures for private-income generation in some advanced higher education systems have coincided with the need for capacity-building in higher education from other countries.

The quantitative intensification of international exchanges under pressure from economic globalization has been complemented by a qualitative change in the forms of global higher education. The sites of inequity are thus not only associated with economic decisions at the top, but with shifts concerning pedagogic and administrative practices in the middle. Changes include those following the implementation of the Bologna Process (a roadmap towards a European Higher Education Area), and the World Trade Organization's adoption in 2000 of the General Agreement on Trade in Services (GATS) (a driver of global free trade including education). New practices and actors include the acceleration of older forms of student and staff mobility, the emergence of new forms of institution – franchises, satellite campuses and e-learning. Global developments in higher education constitute a space for institutions where national systems attempt to solve their domestic problems concerning funding, quality and access. This provides very little ground on which to address problems of national or global inequity.

Globalization and Inequalities

Analysis and criticisms of the current model of global higher education are prompted by its uncritical acceptance of neoliberal discourses and practices. The state is being used to promote the market in all spheres of society including public services. In the last 20 years globalization has been driven by market competition on a global scale. As Galbraith (2002, p. 11) puts it, 'the doctrine of globalization as it is understood in elite circles contains the curious assumption that the global market is itself beyond reproach'. However, the positive story of economic globalization and the belief in the superiority of the market over public sector practices has been undermined by recurrent global crises in the capitalist economy. The 1991 financial crisis in East Asia, referred to as the first crisis of globalization, was surpassed by the strength and speed of propagation of the global financial crisis that started in 2008. This socioeconomic crisis has been the biggest challenge to the current model of globalization (though not necessarily to the idea of globalization itself). It questions the assumption that globalization necessarily alleviates inequalities, and raises serious concerns about the ways we produce and distribute wealth (Carpentier, 2009) at both national and global levels.

Connections, or rather disconnections, between production and redistribution were being debated well before the recent global financial crisis. Debates over the impact of globalization on inequalities within and between countries echo many earlier debates on industrialization. The hypothesis of a Kuznets curve (1955) – the idea that the development process initially produces greater income inequalities but these eventually reduce – has generated intense discussions since the observation of a resurgence of international inequalities from the 1980s onwards. This debate has been linked with sharply different positions on globalization (Aghion and Williamson, 1998; Held and Kaya, 2007). So does globalization increase or reduce inequalities? Basu (2006) reminds us that we need to take into account both inequality between countries as measured by GDP per head, and inequalities within countries as measured by the Gini Index, and between the two it is hard to trace the impact of globalization. The dimension of time is important as well. Looking back to the 1820s, Lindert and Williamson (2005, p. 228) conclude that 'world incomes would still be unequal under complete global integration, as they are in any large integrated national economy. But they would be less unequal in a fully-integrated world economy than in one fully segmented.'

The neoliberal 'Washington Consensus' that has driven economic globalization at the policy level largely overlooks the question of inequality. This is seen to be automatically resolved by global free trade (Serra and Stiglitz, 2008). Growing income inequality observed worldwide (Atkinson and Piketty, 2007) suggests that neoliberal policies are associated with increased, not reduced inequalities. In response, Krugman argues that 'distribution deserves to be treated as an issue as important as growth' (2008, p. 33). Could we consider the global economic downturn that started in 2008 as the decisive moment of a crisis of the model of globalization and an opportunity to address the disconnections between wealth production and redistribution?

The tensions between globalization and economic inequalities have dominated the public debates, but it is also important to consider the impact of globalization on other categories of inequalities. Global processes have differentially affected women across the world, depending on country and social class. Globalization has increased the feminization of the labor force, leading to different outcomes: in some cases emancipation, in others low-skilled work and pay (Benería, 2003). Other studies have shown that neoliberal policies on the social safety net particularly disadvantage women (Seguino and Grown, 2006). Clarke and Thomas (2006, p. 1) note that 'because globalization today is facilitated by the transmission and reproduction of deeply embedded social prejudices rooted in a past characterised by territorial concepts of belonging that both generated and were generated by racial inequalities, the contemporary redistribution of wealth has exacerbated historically entrenched racial hierarchies'. Moreover, in some cases economic globalization in particular has contributed to the development of ethnic strains in developing states and regions (Held and McGrew, 2007, p. 63).

All this suggests that the benefits of economic globalization have not been equitably distributed and have tended to reinforce inequalities along the lines of social class, gender and ethnicity. Similar questions need to be asked about the impact of globalization in relation to higher education and inequalities. Can global higher education increase or redress inequalities created by economic globalization? Will global higher education benefit from free trade and deregulation? Or will the disconnections observed in other sectors appear? Will this increase or reduce inequalities within and between higher education systems?

From International to Global Higher Education

While internationalization is generally used to define increasing links or exchanges between nations, globalization tends to refer to practices adopted across nation states (Held and McGrew, 2002). In the context of higher education similar differences are expressed between internationalization and globalization. We consider here that internationalization is based on a particular nationally situated higher education institution, while globalization entails a range of practices across and between differently situated higher education institutions. This represents a shift in the practices and relations that construct the nation states. According to Knight (2006, p. 209), globalization includes 'the knowledge society, information and communication technologies, the market economy, trade liberalization and changes in governance structures'. It entails a shift in practices and forms of regulation in higher education. Altbach and Knight (2007, p. 290) define globalization as 'the economic, political, and societal forces pushing twenty-first century higher education towards greater international involvement'. They see internationalization as the policies and practices of higher education that have been developed to deal with this. Globalization can thus be seen as a process entailing particular socioeconomic practices and forms of (de)regulation, which in turn require and drive an intensification of internationalization of higher education.

The transition to global higher education involves new sites, new actors, and new policies and practices. These shifts present many challenges in relation to inequalities within and between countries. Scott (1998, p. 111) underlines the difficulty for universities of articulating equity at the national level with equity at the international level. New actors are emerging through the open market for private or public foreign providers of higher education. In this context new practices must be carefully assessed as to whether they reproduce existing inequalities within countries or are associated with the process of transformation.

Contemporary globalization has a different relationship with nation-states and higher education systems. The global trend to limit public funding of universities and promote institutional autonomy preceded global higher education but generated numerous opportunities for its development. In a context of funding pressure, the transition from international to global higher education is a shift from political and cultural rationales to an economic one. This mirrors the wider pre-eminence of economic globalization over political, geopolitical and social justice.

Some shifts from international to global practices in higher education are closely linked to free trade policies. For example, controversies exist over GATS, which includes education as a domain. Debates about the liberalization of higher education mirror those on the impact on globalization. Economic globalization and global higher education are subject to criticisms about their exclusive economic dimension and the focus on free trade, and the deregulation of nation-states' prerogatives with potential impacts on inequities. Robertson (2006a, p. 14) notes that 'when member states allow education to be included and traded in global agreements like GATS, member states' ability to ensure that education is a right for all, rather than a commodity to be purchased by the well off, is considerably diminished. There are no global structures ensuring legal requirements for equality.'

Under the frame of global higher education, some countries become importers of global higher education while others with developed higher education systems but also under public funding constraints become exporters. Both are responding to fiscal austerity. The increased demand for and supply of global higher education has been generated by the global agendas of the knowledge economy – the need to educate the workforce at higher levels to compete internationally – and also the need to top up public funding. Resources from global higher education potentially accelerate the trend to public/private substitution in funding. It is possible that extra international resources will merely substitute for public funding, changing the structure of funding and provision without raising total resources available to higher education, and with the risk of increasing levels of inequalities even further (Carpentier, 2010).

NEW TRENDS, NEW FORMS AND NEW ACTORS IN GLOBAL HIGHER EDUCATION AND THEIR IMPACT ON EQUITY

Global higher education is associated with an acceleration of old practices, such as student and staff mobility. According to UNESCO (2009, p. 36), in 2007 more than 2.8 million students enrolled in educational institutions outside of their country of origin, an increase of 53 per cent since 1999. Student mobility moves mostly in one direction. A total of 68 per cent of mobile students are registered in universities from North America and Western Europe. The USA with 21 per cent and the UK with 12 per cent are the major host countries. Australia is a leading host if one considers the number of international students as a proportion of total enrolment. There is a strong intra-mobility within western countries, and an increasing number from outside the western sphere. A total of 15 per cent of students come from China, followed proportionally by India and Korea. This trend corresponds to the old political and cultural rationales for internationalization that have long led students worldwide to study in developed countries. It also increasingly reflects the emergence of the income-generation rationale. For example, in the UK from the 1970s 'the share of enrolment by overseas students doubled while their contribution to income grew eightfold' (Carpentier, 2010, p. 158).

The growing contribution of international students through fees raises numerous problems with respect to public–private funds substitution and inequalities in connection to the host countries. Is the importation of global higher education part of a strategy from host governments to externalize funding in higher education? How does this fit with national strategies of fair and widening participation in quality higher education? Can new providers destabilize existing institutions of higher education? Does substitution put domestic and home students into competition with each other? Substitution raises the issue of sufficient and adequate funding for teaching and learning support for an increasing number of international students (Luke, 2010). Scarcity of public resources available for scholarships combined with higher fees also raise global social justice issues in relation to the reproduction of a worldwide elite of mobile students (Carpentier, 2010). Brooks and Waters (2009) have shown that UK students going abroad are from the most advantaged socioeconomic categories. This suggests that internationalization in this form does not reduce inequalities.

While worldwide student mobility has reached gender parity (UNESCO, 2009, p. 36), it is still difficult to assess the extent to which student mobility offers opportunities to groups that could not have enrolled in their own countries for socioeconomic or discriminatory reasons. In terms of inequalities between countries, one question to consider is whether student mobility leads to capacity-building or brain drain. Studies report some positives (remittances) and some negatives (loss of skills) for the country of origin (Spring, 2008; Robertson, 2006b). The capacity of student mobility to address inequalities at national and global levels depends in part on financial practices.

Global higher education also involves new kinds of mobility such as offshore and franchise activities, which are developing quickly. Many institutions are opening 'subsidiaries abroad or offering their educational programmes or qualifications via partnership with host-country institutions' (Larsen and Vincent-Lancrin, 2002, p. 21). There are important debates about whether borderless higher education represents an opportunity for capacity-building or a return to academic, cultural, political and economic neo-imperialism which could increase further inequalities within and between nations (Chan and Lo, 2008). There are questions about whether a purely mercantile activity ranging from very expensive to low-cost forms of higher education could ultimately lead to increase or reduce inequalities within host nations.

A recent study identified 162 international branch campuses in the world in 2009, compared to 24 in 2002 and 82 in 2006 (Becker, 2009, p. 6). Nearly 70 per cent of these offshore campuses are from anglophone nations (48 per cent from the USA, 9 per cent from Australia, 8 per cent from the UK and 7 per cent from France). India is a strong provider (7 per cent) followed by several other countries, including Mexico, The Netherlands, Malaysia, Canada and Ireland. Interestingly, since 2006 new international branch campuses have been created by institutions from Lebanon, Malaysia, South Korea and Sri Lanka. There were 51 host countries in 2009 but most institutions are located in the United Arab Emirates (25 per cent), China (9 per cent), Singapore (7 per cent) and Qatar (6 per cent). The flows are still dominated by South to North mobility (51 per cent), but North to North provision has increased (30 per cent). South to

South provision constitutes 16 per cent, a fivefold increase since 2006. North to South is lagging behind at 3 per cent. A third of Malaysian students are enrolled in transnational programmes. On the providers' side, it is important to note that these programmes are costly and it is difficult to make a profit. There are doubts as to whether it contributes to solving inequalities as 'cross border higher education tends to only be affordable for students from affluent families, particularly if it is provided on revenue-generating basis' (Vincent-Lancrin, 2007, p. 101).

Another aspect of global higher education is virtual learning. This has also been presented as an opportunity to reduce inequalities at national and global levels. However, some studies argue that the move towards information and communications technologies in higher education should be driven by pedagogic, not economic concerns (Clegg et al., 2003). Paradoxically, Carnoy (2004) observes that distance learning is not as cost-effective as often assumed. Some research questions the impacts on equity between nations. Gulati states:

> Although these developments aim for equitable and extended educational opportunities that extend to disadvantaged and poor populations, the lack of educational and technology infrastructures, lack of trained teachers, negative attitudes towards distance learning, social and cultural restrictions imposed on girls and women, and inappropriate policy and funding decisions, have all resulted in furthering the gap between the rich and poor, rural and urban, and between genders. (Gulati, 2008, p. 11)

Ekundayo and Ekundayo (2009) consider the barriers to e-learning in Nigeria as being associated with unequal access to technology among students and involving the cost of Internet connectivity; inconsistent power supplies; and the limited expertise of technical staff.

CONCLUSION

Inequalities in higher education are multidimensional. They result in substantial differences in access, participation, completion and success between different groups (gender, social class, caste, disability and religion) within and among countries. These differences should not be understood only as the reflection of entrenched inequalities within and between societies. They are also produced by the problematic higher education policies and practices of governments and institutions. Political and economic imbalances between and within nations are not new, but have been enhanced by neoliberal economic globalization. The pressure on public resources has produced tensions between funding policies and access policies, and redefined the role of the state in relation to the funding, organization and regulation of higher education.

This has also shifted the internationalization agenda in higher education from traditional political and cultural rationales to a growing economic one. In a context of declining public funding, the demand for global higher education from countries seeking to build capacity is met by institutions searching for income generation. This has accelerated old forms of internationalization such as student mobility, but generated new global practices and rules (such as GATS), new activities (such as offshore and programme mobility, and distance education) and new actors (such as private providers). There are polarized debates about the impact of these components of global higher education on the different forms of inequality. It remains to be seen whether global higher education can be separated from the economic globalization agenda (GATS) and integrate other global values such as social justice. It is notable that in many respects global higher education has developed in response to national problems rather than in terms of the global challenges ahead.

In a recent book we engaged with colleagues in a reflection on how higher education systems and their institutions could address these multiple global challenges. The fight for social justice in higher education was seen as crucial to aspirations for combining economic growth, equity, democracy and sustainability (Unterhalter and Carpentier, 2010). We argued that changes in higher education policies and practices towards social justice could contribute to making these goals – which too often in the world of policy-making became conflicting agendas – into complementary objectives. This will require new thinking in the way global higher education is constructed, beyond solely responding to economic globalization. The question about 'education as a public good and/ or a private commodity' should be placed in 'a different analytical framework which is not only based on economic theory and has at its core the breadth of contribution that higher education makes to both society as a whole and to the individual' (Knight, 2008, p. 185). This will also require new structures and organizations. While global legislation and agreements such as GATS have a strong impact on the organization and funding of higher education, there is lack of global organizations concerned with quality and equity.

Another area of change is related to policies and practices. This will require a shift in the ways forms of equity are constructed (Unterhalter, 2010) and in changes to pedagogic practices (Walker, 2010). Sometimes this takes place in small initiatives. The challenge is to understand this better and connect up practices so that global inequality in higher education is not just reproduced by default, but is clear-sightedly confronted with a view to effecting change.

REFERENCES

Aghion, P. and J. Williamson (1998), *Growth, Inequality and Globalization: Theory, History and Policy*, Cambridge: Cambridge University Press.

Albouy, V. and T. Vanecq (2003), 'Les inégalités sociales d'accès aux grandes Écoles', *Économie et Statistique*, **361**, 27–52.

Altbach, P. (1998), *Comparative Higher Education: Knowledge, the University and Development*, Greenwich, CT: Ablex.

Altbach, P. (ed.) (1999), *Private Prometheus: Private Higher Education and Development in the Twenty-first Century*, Westport, CT: Greenwood Press.

Altbach, P. (2004), 'Globalization and the university: myths and realities in an unequal world', *Tertiary Education and Management*, **1**, 3–25.

Altbach, P. and J. Knight (2007), 'The internationalization of higher education: motivations and realities', *Journal of Studies in International Education*, **11**, 290–305.

Altbach, P., L. Reisberg and L. Rumbley (2009), *Trends in Global Higher Education: Tracking an Academic Revolution: A Report Prepared for the UNESCO 2009 World Conference on Higher Education*, Paris: UNESCO.

Archer, L. and C. Leathwood (2003), 'Identities, inequalities and higher education', in L. Archer, M. Hutchings and A. Ross (eds), *Higher Education and Social Class: Issues of Exclusion and Inclusion*, London and New York: RoutledgeFalmer, pp. 175–91.

Archer, L., M. Hutchings and A. Ross (eds) (2003), *Higher Education and Social Class: Issues of Exclusion and Inclusion*, London and New York: RoutledgeFalmer.

Atkinson, A. and T. Piketty (2007), *Top Incomes over the Twentieth Century: A Contrast between European and English-speaking Countries*, Oxford: Oxford University Press.

Ball, S. (2006), *Education Policy and Social Class: Selected Works*, London: Routledge.

Ball, S. (2010), 'Global education, heterarchies and hybrid organizations', in K.H. Mok (ed.), *The Search for New Governance of Higher Education in Asia*, New York: Palgrave Macmillan, pp. 13–28.

Banya, K. (2001), 'Are private universities the solution to the higher education crisis in Sub-Saharan Africa?', *Higher Education Policy*, **14** (2), 161–74.

Barton, L. and F. Armstrong (2008), *Policy, Experience and Change: Cross-cultural Reflections on Inclusive Education*, Dordrecht: Springer.

Bastedo, M. and P. Gumport (2003), 'Access to what? Mission differentiation and academic stratification in U.S. public higher education', *Higher Education*, **46**, 341–59.

Basu, K. (2006), 'Globalization, poverty, and inequality: what is the relationship? What can be done?', *World Development*, **34** (8), 1361–73.

Becker, R. (2009), *International Branch Campuses: Markets and Strategies*, London: The Observatory on Borderless Higher Education.

Benería, L. (2003), *Gender, Development and Globalization: Economics as if All People Mattered*, London: Routledge.

Bourdieu, P. and J. Passeron (1964), *Les Héritiers, les étudiants et la culture*, Paris: Editions de Minuit.

Brennan, J. and R. Naidoo (2008), 'Higher education and the achievement (and/or prevention) of equity and social justice', *Higher Education*, **56**, 287–302.

Brighouse, H. (2000), *School Choice and Social Justice*, Oxford: Oxford University Press.

Brooks, R. and J. Waters (2009), 'International higher education and the mobility of UK students', *Journal of Research in International Education*, **8** (2), 191–209.

Burke, P. (2005), 'Access and widening participation', *British Journal of Sociology of Education*, **26** (4), 555–62.

Carnoy, M. (2004), *ICT in Education: Possibilities and Challenges*, Inaugural Lecture of the Universitat Oberta de Catalunya 2004–5 Academic Year.

Carpentier, V. (2006a), 'Funding in higher education and economic growth in France and the United Kingdom, 1921–2003', *Higher Education Management and Policy*, **18** (3), 1–26.

Carpentier, V. (2006b), 'Public expenditure on education and economic growth in the USA in the nineteenth and twentieth centuries in comparative perspective', *Paedagogica Historica*, **42** (6), 683–706.

Carpentier, V. (2009), 'The credit crunch and education: an historical perspective from the Kondratiev cycle', *London Review of Education*, **7** (2), 193–6.

Carpentier, V. (2010), 'Public–private substitution in higher education funding and Kondratiev cycles: the impacts on home and international students', in E. Unterhalter and V. Carpentier (eds), *Global Inequalities and Higher Education*, Basingstoke: Palgrave Macmillan.

Carpentier, V., S. Chattopadhyay and B. Pathak (forthcoming), 'Funding and access to higher education in the context of globalization', in M. Lall and G. Nambissan (eds), *Education and Social Justice in the Era of Globalisation: India and the UK*, [New Delhi]: Routledge.

Chan, D. and W. Lo (2008), 'University restructuring in east Asia: trends, challenges and prospects', *Policy Futures in Education*, **6**, 641–52.

Clarke, K. and D. Thomas (2006), *Globalization and Race: Transformations in the Cultural Production of Blackness*, Durham, NC: Duke University Press.

Clegg, S., A. Hudson and J. Steel (2003), 'The Emperor's new clothes: globalisation and E-learning in higher education', *British Journal of Sociology of Education*, **24** (1), 39–53.

Currie, J. and J. Newson (eds) (1998), *Universities and Globalization: Critical Perspectives*, Thousand Oaks, CA and London: Sage.

David, M. (2009), *Improving Learning by Widening Participation in Higher Education*, London: Routledge.

Denison, E.F. (1967), *Why Growth Rates Differ: Post-war Experience in Nine Western Countries*, Washington, DC: The Brookings Institution.

Department for Innovation, Universities and Skills (2008), *Full-time Young Participation by Socioeconomic Class*, London: DIUS.

Department for Innovation, Universities and Skills (2009), *Disabled Students and Higher Education, Higher Educational Analysis*, Research Report 0906, London: DIUS.

Ding, X. (2007), 'Expansion and equality of access to higher education in China', *Journal Frontiers of Education in China*, **2** (2), 151–62.

Duru-Bellat, M., A. Kieffer and D. Reimer (2008), 'International patterns of social inequalities in access to higher education in France and Germany', *Journal of Comparative Sociology*, **49**, 347–68.

Dyhouse, C. (2006), *Students: A Gendered History*, London: Routledge.

Ebersold, S. and P. Evans (2003), *Disability in Higher Education*, Paris: OECD.

Eisenberg, A. (2006), 'Education and the politics of difference: Iris Young and the politics of education', *Educational Philosophy and Theory*, **38** (1), 7–23.

Ekundayo, M. and J. Ekundayo (2009), 'Capacity constraints in developing countries: a need for more e-learning space? The case of Nigeria', *Proceedings ascilite Auckland*, pp. 243–55.

Espinoza, O. (2008), 'Creating (in)equalities in access to higher education in the context of structural adjustment and post-adjustment policies: the case of Chile', *Higher Education*, **55**, 269–84.

Fontvieille, L. and S. Michel (2002), 'Analysis of the transition between two successive social orders: application to the relation between education and growth', *Review*, **25** (1), 23–46.

Galbraith, J.K. (2002), 'A perfect crime: inequality in the age of globalization', *Daedalus*, 11–24.

Galindo-Rueda, F., O. Marcenaro-Gutierrez and A. Vignoles (2004), 'The widening socioeconomic gap in UK higher education', *National Institute Economic Review*, **190**, 75–88.

Gereluk, D. (2006), *Education and Community*, London: Continuum.

Geuna, A. (1998), 'The internationalization of European Universities: a return to medieval roots', *Minerva*, **36**, 253–70.

Gillborn, D. (2008), *Racism and Education: Coincidence or Conspiracy?*, London: Routledge.

Gordon, D. (1985), 'The Arabic language and national identity: the cases of Algeria and of Lebanon', in W. Beer and J. Jacob (eds), *Language Policy and National Unity*, Totowa, NJ: Rowman and Allenheld, pp. 134–50.

Greenbank, P. (2006), 'The evolution of government policy on widening participation', *Higher Education Quarterly*, **60** (2), 141–66.

Gulati, S. (2008), 'Technology-enhanced learning in developing nations: a review', *International Review of Research in Open and Distance Learning*, **9** (1), 1–16.

Harvey, D. (2005), *A Brief History of Neoliberalism*, Oxford: Oxford University Press.

Hassim, A. (2009), 'South Africa: justice and disadvantage in a new democracy', in T. Volkman, J. Dassin and M. Zurbuchen (eds) (2009), *Origins, Journeys and Returns: Social Justice in International Higher Education*, New York: Social Science Research Council.

Held, D. and A. Kaya (2007), *Global Inequality: Patterns and Explanations*, Cambridge: Polity.

Held, D. and A. McGrew (2002), *The Global Transformation Reader*, 2nd edn, Cambridge: Polity.

Held, D. and A. McGrew (2007), *Globalization/Anti-Globalization*, London: Polity.

Jacob, W. and D. Holsinger (2008), *Inequality in Education: Comparative and International Perspectives*, Dordrecht: Springer.

Jomo, K. and B. Fine (2006), *The New Development Economics: After the Washington Consensus*, London: Zed Books.

King, R. (2003), *The Rise and Regulation of For-Profit Education*, London: Observatory on Borderless Higher Education.

King, R. (2004), *The University in the Global Age*, Basingstoke: Palgrave Macmillan.

Knight, J. (2006), 'Internationalization: concepts, complexities, and challenges', in J. Forest and P. Altbach (eds), *International Handbook of Higher Education*, Dordrecht: Springer, pp. 207–28.

Knight, J. (2008), 'The role of cross-border education in the debate on education as a public good and private commodity', *Journal of Asian Public Policy*, **1** (2), 174–87.

Krugman, P. (2008), 'Inequality and redistribution', in N. Serra and J. Stiglitz (eds), *The Washington Consensus Reconsidered*, Oxford: Oxford University Press, pp. 31–41.

Kuznets, S. (1955), 'Economic growth and income inequality', *American Economic Review*, **65**, 1–28.

Larsen, K. and S. Vincent-Lancrin (2002), 'International trade in educational services: Good or bad?', *Higher Education Management and Policy*, **14** (3), 9–45.

Leathwood, C. (2004), 'A critique of institutional inequalities in higher education', *Theory and Research in Education*, **2** (1), 31–48.

Levy, D. (2003), *Expanding Higher Education through Private Growth: Contributions and Challenges*, London: The Observatory on Borderless Higher Education.

Lindert, P. and J. Williamson (2005), 'Does globalization make the world more unequal?', in M. Bordo, A. Taylor and J. Williamson (eds), *Globalization in Historical Perspective*, Chicago, IL: The University of Chicago Press, pp. 227–76.

Lowe, R. (2008), *The History of Higher Education*, London: Routledge.

Luke, A. (2010), 'Educating the other: standpoint and theory in the "internationalization" of higher education', in E. Unterhalter and V. Carpentier (eds), *Global Inequalities and Higher Education*, Basingstoke: Palgrave Macmillan, pp. 43–65.

Lynch, K. and A. Lodge (2002), *Equality and Power in Schools*, London: RoutledgeFalmer.

Marginson, S. (2006), 'Dynamics of national and global competition in higher education', *Higher Education*, **52**, 1–39.

Matshedisho, K. (2007), 'Access to higher education for disabled students in South Africa: a contradictory conjuncture of benevolence, rights and the social model of disability', *Disability and Society*, **22** (7), 685–99.

McCowan, T. (2007), 'Expansion without equity: an analysis of current policy on access to higher education in Brazil', *Higher Education*, **53** (5), 579–98.

Morley, L. and R. Lugg (2009), 'Mapping meritocracy: intersecting gender, poverty and higher educational opportunity structures', *Higher Education Policy*, **22** (1), 37–60.

Naidoo, R. (2010), 'Global learning in a neoliberal age: implications for development', in E. Unterhalter and V. Carpentier (eds), *Global Inequalities and Higher Education*, Basingstoke: Palgrave Macmillan, pp. 66–90.

Obasi, E. (1997), 'Structural adjustment and gender access to education in Nigeria', *Gender and Education*, **9**, 161–77.

Reay, D., M. David and S. Ball (2005), *Degrees of Choice: Class, Race, Gender and Higher Education*, Stoke-on-Trent: Trentham Books.

Robertson, S. (2006a), *Globalisation, GATS and Trading in Education Services*, Centre for Globalisation, Education and Societies, University of Bristol, Bristol at: http://www.bris.ac.uk/education/people/academicStaff/edslr/publications/04slr/.

Roberston, S. (2006b), 'Brain drain, brain gain and brain circulation', *Globalisation, Societies and Education (Special Issue)*, **4** (1), 1–5.

Robeyns, I. (2006), 'Three models of education: rights, capabilities and human capital', *Theory and Research in Education*, **4** (1), 69–84.

Saïd, E. (1993), *Culture and Imperialism*, New York: Knopf.

Schultz, T. (1961), 'Investment in human capital', *The American Economic Review*, **51** (1), 1–17.

Scott, P. (ed.) (1998), *The Globalization of Higher Education*, Buckingham: Society for Research into Higher Education and Open University Press.

Seguino, S. and C. Grown (2006), 'Gender equity and globalization: macroeconomic policy for developing countries', Working Paper, University of Vermont, Levy Economics Institute.

Sen, A. (1993), *Development as Freedom*, Oxford: Oxford University Press.

Serra, N. and J. Stiglitz (2008), *The Washington Consensus Reconsidered: Towards a New Global Governance*, Oxford: Oxford University Press.

Spring, J. (2008), 'Research on globalization and education', *Review of Educational Research*, **78** (2), 330–63.

Swift, A. (2003), *How Not to Be a Hypocrite*, London: Routledge.

Teferra, D. and P. Altbach (2004), 'African higher education: challenges for the 21st Century', *Higher Education*, **47**, 21–50.

Teixeira, J., B. Johnstone, M. Rosa and H. Vossensteyn (2006), *Cost-Sharing and Accessibility in Higher Education: A Fairer Deal?* Dordrecht: Springer.

Terzi, L. (2008), *Justice and Equality in Education: A Capability Perspective on Disability and Special Educational Needs*, London: Continuum.

Tilak, J. (2003), 'Higher education and development in Asia', *Journal of Educational Planning and Administration*, **17** (2), 151–73.

Tiyambe Zeleza, P. and A. Olukoshi (2004), *African Universities in the Twenty-First Century: Knowledge and Society*, South Africa: CODESRIA.

Tomlinson, S. (2005), 'Race, ethnicity and education under New Labour', *Oxford Review of Education*, **31** (1), 213–30.

UNESCO (1991), *Trends and Issues Facing Higher Education in Asia and the Pacific*, Report of Regional Conference, University of New England, Armidale, NSW, Australia, 14–18 October 1990.

UNESCO (2009), *Global Education Digest*, Paris: UNESCO.

Unterhalter, E. (2006), 'New times and new vocabularies: theorising and evaluating gender equality in Commonwealth higher education', *Women's Studies International Forum*, **29**, 620–28.

Unterhalter, E. (2007), *Gender, Schooling and Global Social Justice*, London: Routledge.

Unterhalter, E. (2007), 'What is equity in education? Reflections from the capability approach', *Studies in Philosophy and Education*, **28** (5), 415–24.

Unterhalter, E. (2010), 'Considering equality, equity and higher education pedagogies in the context of globalization', in E. Unterhalter and V. Carpentier (eds), *Global Inequalities and Higher Education*, Basingstoke: Palgrave Macmillan, pp. 91–113.

Unterhalter, E. and V. Carpentier (2010), *Global Inequalities and Higher Education: Whose Interests are we Serving?*, Basingstoke: Palgrave Macmillan.

Vincent-Lancrin, S. (ed.) (2007), *Cross-border Tertiary Education: A Way Towards Capacity Development*, Paris: OECD and World Bank.

Volkman, T., J. Dassin and M. Zurbuchen (2009), *Origins, Journeys and Returns: Social Justice in International Higher Education*, New York: Social Science Research Council.

Walker, M. (2010), 'Pedagogy for rich human being-ness in global times', in E. Unterhalter and V. Carpentier (eds), *Global Inequalities and Higher Education*, Basingstoke: Palgrave Macmillan, pp. 219–40.

Wallerstein, I. (1976), *World Systems Analysis: Theory and Methodology,* Beverly Hills, CA: Sage Publications.

Welch, A. (2007), 'Blurred vision? Public and private higher education in Indonesia', *Higher Education*, **54**, 665–87.

Whitehead, C. (2003), *Colonial Educators: The British Indian and Colonial Education Service 1858–1983*, London: I.B. Tauris.

PART II

CASE STUDIES

10 Introduction to Part II

Rajani Naidoo

In Part II the focus is on the positioning strategies of national systems and institutions within the realm of global imaginings and universities operating at the intersection of the global, national and local. Authors point to the influence of powerful but fluctuating global influences that are mediated by specific economic arrangements, geopolitical positions, and the nature, structure and governance of national higher education systems. As we see from the rich array of perspectives and localities in this part, such strategies result in the mimicry, recontextualization and displacement of global templates as well as convergences and divergences across nation-states. New models of higher education internationalization that are emerging in certain regions also reveal that the globalization of higher education cannot be simply conflated with hegemonic models that are dominant in Western Europe and the USA. These chapters taken together offer a diversity of interpretations of the changing relationships between the global, national and local, and provide important analyses of the consequences of the enhanced positioning of higher education in relation to political, economic and cultural change.

The opening chapter by Ka Ho Mok (Chapter 11) compares the initiatives of governments in Singapore, Hong Kong and Malaysia to develop their societies into regional hubs of education. He illustrates how, in this context, transnational education has become increasingly popular since the expansion of higher education not only improves the quality of national populations but also helps to assert each country's influence in the global context.

Mok's chapter illustrates how the quest to become a regional hub leads to a diversification of educational programs, which in turn leads to new terrains of governance. Singapore and Malaysia are classified as 'market-accelerationist states' while Hong Kong is classified as a 'market-facilitating state'. The factors encouraging transnational higher education, the diversity of organizations and organizational linkages that have emerged, and the attendant problems of coordination, accountability and transparency are closely examined. Mok argues that while the rise of transnational and private dimensions of higher education has resulted in shifts away from centralized models of governance, state capacities do not necessarily fade away but result in a variety of regulatory regimes encapsulating the dialectical conflicts between market efficiency and state capacity.

One of the conclusions of the chapter is that after roughly two decades, the conflicts between market efficiency and state capacity have led to similar directions of reform in these countries. Singapore and Malaysia may be required to reduce strong state intervention in order to maintain the vitality and efficiency of their sectors of transnational higher education, while the Hong Kong government may be required to deploy state capacity more proactively in order to further industrialize the sector. The policy implications that follow from this analysis include the need for research on regulatory regimes to assure the quality of newly emerging education programs, an understanding of the complexity of the heterarchies and hybrid organizations that are developing, as well as an acknowledgment of the difficulty of sustaining conventional public–private distinctions.

In Chapter 12, Mala Singh explores the development of an external evaluation system for higher education in the context of the interplay between quality assurance as a regulatory strategy in global higher education reform and national policy imperatives such as social justice arising in the context of post-apartheid transformation. The strategic choices that were made for the new external evaluation system out of local conjunctures and global policy frameworks and how these choices were conceptualized, legitimated, negotiated and given expression are analyzed.

The local–global interface is examined through a conceptual framework that includes how the meanings, powers and effects of globalization were understood, the nature of the context and policy regime where transnational policy influence was evident, understandings of the nature of the global template for quality, the nature of policy influence mechanisms, and the connection between policy symbolism and policy implementation. By outlining the political and policy setting for higher education reform in South Africa in the first decade of the transition amidst the presence of globally resonant change principles, she illustrates how spaces for local agency to modify global imperatives were made possible. At the same time she acknowledges the structural and ideological limits in the work of policy localization.

In the final sections, the possibilities, limits and contradictions are presented. While space was created to argue that the interfaces between quality, equity and social transformation could be evaluated as a legitimate dimension of quality assurance, limitations included the framing of notions of quality and accountability by a new public management (NPM) framework in a context where social transformation imperatives required a broader framing of both. The chapter concludes by arguing that while the trumping of local transformation imperatives by global templates raises concerns about the fate of the country's emancipatory social project, greater research attention is required to analyze the nature and scope of policy influences, and the content of the convergences between global and local policy in South Africa.

In Chapter 13, Jones and Weinrib focus on the impact of, and resistance to, globalizing pressures in Canada. The three policy areas of internationalization, research and innovation, and quality assurance are selected to illustrate key features of the Canadian context. The authors note that internationalization of higher education is not a national priority and that policy developments are frequently stymied by Canada's federal arrangements that assign the responsibility for education to the provinces, but responsibility for foreign affairs to the national government. In addition, concerns about national cultural sovereignty and brain drain to the USA and the racial and ethnic diversity of immigrants have mediated internationalization strategies based on global templates.

The policy area of research and innovation is analyzed through a focus on federal initiatives aimed at steering university research outputs and developing closer links between higher education and industry. The authors reveal, however, that Canadian federal arrangements and the lack of a centralized coordinating unit for higher education policy have resulted in fragmented efforts to create and operationalize these new public policy options.

With regard to quality assurance, the authors argue that Canada has historically been characterized by a highly decentralized, province-based higher education landscape that has abdicated responsibility for substantive policies and programs to institutions. They note, however, that the new pressures of a globalized higher education arena have challenged the decentralized Canadian model while at the same time the strong sense of higher education autonomy as a cornerstone of policy has served to avoid some of the more draconian quality assurance measures found in other parts of the world.

The authors conclude that while there are common themes, it is the variations that are linked to Canada's historic concerns about US political, economic and cultural domination, the decentralized approach to higher education policy under Canada's federal arrangements, and Canada's highly diverse, multicultural and multi-ethnic population that are truly interesting.

Chapter 14 by Li and Chen examines major strategies deployed by government and universities in mainland China in response to globalization, with a specific focus on the building of world-class universities. The chapter begins with an overview of changes related to the internationalization of higher education in China regarding the mobility of students and faculty; cross-border collaboration; and the internationalizing of the curriculum.

The government's policy of developing world-class universities is presented, and government-directed programs such as Project 211, Project 985 and graduate scholarship programs are shown to be attempts to support selectively key disciplines, institutions and scholars as a priority for the twenty-first century. The analysis of Tsinghua and Peking universities gives interesting insights into the experience of two top universities vying for world-class status. The authors analyze the universities' strategic responses such as the internationalization of staff, students, and the curriculum and the building of international networks and illustrate the link to national priorities.

The final section of the chapter offers a critical reflection on the ongoing 'world-class university movement' in China. Barriers such as the lack of academic freedom and strong government regulation of universities are identified. Consideration is also given to the contributions that Chinese universities might bring to a reshaping of global intellectual culture. Li and Chen argue that there is a danger that the consideration of 'world class' within China is largely imitative rather than creative, and that China should for example retain independence in the soft sciences such as the humanities, which are culturally bounded and ideologically relevant. Their conclusion is that Chinese universities need to reflect on how to balance and integrate the complexity and significances of localization, nationalization and internationalization with a creative vision based on specific cultural and political environments, and equal dialogue between Chinese universities and other universities worldwide.

In Chapter 15, Välimaa argues that the EU plays the role of a globalizing regional actor that aims to create a European Area of Higher Education through the implementation of processes such as Bologna and the Lisbon Strategy. He reveals how these dynamics aim to strengthen Europe as a knowledge-based economy in competition with other regions of the world. He suggests that the interplay between the different actors in the EU can best be understood through a historical analysis of the processes of integration between European nations.

An analysis of the nature and the political structures of the EU is followed by a focus on three periods, from the 1950s to the present through which higher education has grown in importance as a policy domain. Välimaa undertakes a detailed analysis of the Lisbon, Bologna and Erasmus strategies. He indicates that while the Lisbon Strategy supported important developments such as the European Research Council, it nevertheless suffered from incoherence and inconsistencies. The author indicates that the Bologna Process, which aimed to construct a European Area of Higher Education and to promote it worldwide by, for example, establishing a system of credits for cross-border mobility and European cooperation in quality assurance, had some measure of success. The Erasmus program, which aims to enhance student and staff mobility, is also analyzed in its relationship to Bologna and as a strategy to build a European identity.

Reflecting on how the EU promotes globalization in and for European higher education institutions, Välimaa notes that the process is highly interactive, comprising multi-level exchanges between national and regional levels, horizontal integration represented by intra-governmental cooperation, and vertical integration represented by processes led by the European Commission. The author concludes that the 'EU 2020' strategy will in all probability result in new social innovations in the context of attempts to resolve tensions between the European Commission and sovereign European states.

Kamat, in Chapter 16, notes that higher education has become central to India's national economic reform progress. She contrasts an earlier period after independence of pride and achievement in higher education (and where state policy provided the groundwork for India's success in the IT sector in the 1990s by regarding science and technology as keys to modernization) with a current sense of deep unease and concern at its global uncompetitiveness. A present-day repositioning of higher education in India is accompanying a wider shift in national economic policy toward a less state-regulated and more liberalized economy, including expanding the role of private sectors. In higher education increasing private but often dubious provision has been a marked feature of the sector, and the task is to ensure that such provision (including from abroad) plays a properly regulated role in the future expansion and quality enhancement of the system.

Kamat focuses especially on the role of the government-appointed National Knowledge Commission in 2005. Reporting in 2009, the Commission recommended a substantial increase in the budgetary allocations for higher education and argued for a much tighter set of relationships between the public institutions and the market economy. This involves increased university autonomy in areas such as student fees, utilizing existing resources such as land holdings, the use of incentives for productive staff, and developing joint activities with business. As part of equipping higher education for global competition with China and other nations, the Commission also recommends establishing 50 national universities (10 quite quickly) that would form elite research universities, and also an additional 1500 universities including public and private entities and high-performing colleges granted university or university college status, plus a range of two-year community colleges.

Kamat notes a conspicuous lack of detailed analysis on the global knowledge economy and how the reforms will meet its challenges. In particular it is not clear how the expanded number of graduates will match India's employment demands in the future. Nonetheless, despite all the 'private talk', it is clear that the drive to a neoliberal competition state will involve strong state and public regulatory drivers that cast some doubt on the substantive nature of the autonomy reforms for higher education institutions.

Chapter 17 by Terri Kim offers a critical review of the current state of South Korean higher education in the context of globalization. Kim begins by articulating the distinctive characteristics of the South Korean developmental model and the ways in which the state has met the global challenges of the Asian economic crisis and neoliberal market restructuring.

The distinctive characteristics of government–university relations and higher education reform in Korea are presented. These include the dominance of the private sector and the unique combination of strong governmental regulation and the power of the *chaebol* (the large conglomerates equivalent to the *zaibatsu* in Japan) in relation to university governance and management. Kim outlines a number of policy reforms, including the 'Brain Korea 21 Project', which aims to bring selected major university research projects to a 'world-class' level and to increase the competitiveness of local universities.

At the same time Kim illustrates the implementation of a new public management process that has included the encouragement of competition, mergers and acquisitions. Kim argues that despite the number of higher education reforms in South Korea, assumptions about the university and its pragmatic and subordinate relations to the national government and the *chaebol* have not changed. Since the implementation of the government's 'deregulation' policy in 1995 the role of government seems to have become more refined as regulator and assessor, but it has not weakened. Kim argues that, despite the official focus on internationalizion, the internal features of the university in South Korea are still very local in practice and rest on a culture based on Confucian patriarchal relationships and principles. She suggests that Korean higher education is now at a crossroads, with one route leading to ethnocentric internationalization and the second route leading to commercialization. She warns of global commercialization leading to homogeneity and commodification of knowledge by means of nominally multicultural and intercultural higher education marketing. However, she concludes that despite these difficulties, given the strong culture of learning, the new internationalization in Korean universities may eventually be successful.

Mollis in Chapter 18 addresses the topics that were rendered invisible in Argentina in the debate on higher education policy during the recent neoliberal decade of global reforms. The first topic is the link between the national education system and the capitalist nation-state that financed the university while protecting its privileges. The university in turn was entrusted with the mission of shaping citizens. Mollis indicates that the current crisis of modern reason has led universities to replace their contribution to a democratic citizenry in favor of reproducing global capitalism and training competent workers for a restricted labor market.

The second invisible topic identified by Mollis is the dialectic between knowledge and power. Transnationalization in universities is conceptualized as a cornerstone of the neoliberal project, with the geopolitics of knowledge and power dividing the world into countries that consume the knowledge produced by countries that are culturally and economically dominant. The third topic focuses on the neoliberal transformation of the mission of the university while the fourth topic refers to the institutionalization of international influence that has occurred through agreements between the state and multilateral agencies such as the World Bank.

Mollis draws on a range of data to present the fifth theoretical topic, which is the privatization of the educational public interest, represented by developments such as diminishing state subsidies for science and culture, and the expansion of private institutions. She notes that one of the consequences is the existence of two disarticulated subsystems of higher education that result in costly fragmentation and overlap. Mollis explains how the crisis of the structural model of the public university has led to the development of various myths, including the myth of universal access. The chapter concludes by identifying crucial elements of a diagnostic framework that is at the same time transformative and that includes the need to rebuild institutional missions, to focus on the value of knowledge, to recognize the crisis of the representative collegiate bodies, and to project research towards the satisfaction of local cultural and social issues.

In Chapter 19, Maldonado-Maldonado discusses the complex relationships between globalization, the knowledge-based economy, and higher education in Mexico. She illustrates how globalization encapsulates highly uneven consequences across world regions by presenting figures for global income distribution and the use of ICT. The knowledge economy too is problematized. Knowledge production is shown to be related to world socioeconomic disparaties, reflected in global university rankings, the geographical concentration of student mobility, and the central role of the USA in academic collaboration.

Mexico is characterized as medium-globalized and is ranked 71 in the KOF Globalization Index. Some of the main indicators of a knowledge-based economy, such as the gross domestic expenditure on R&D as a percentage of GDP, are the lowest of the countries reported by the OECD. Maldonado-Maldonado also notes that two of the most important characteristics of Mexico are its inequalities and contradictions. She highlights the problem of young adults who are neither in employment nor in education because the state can provide neither.

As an illustration of how universities can contribute to the shaping of globalization, Maldonado-Maldonado analyzes the discourses and policies of 25 Mexican institutions on globalization and internationalization. Her analysis reveals that their responses can be grouped into four types. One group considers globalization to be a challenge and opportunity; a second group perceives it as mostly positive and as naturally occurring; a third group perceives globalization as a threat; and a fourth group does not express a particular opinion.

The problems of data gathering in Mexico are presented, together with analyses of dimensions such as faculty mobility and international cooperation agreements. The current situation of Mexican universities facing globalization, such as the lack of incentives for institutions to internationalize and institutions perceiving internationalization as the main outcome rather than a step towards the process of Mexico's greater integration into the knowledge economy, are highlighted. The chapter concludes with a call for a national debate on the role of higher education in Mexico and its relationship to the global knowledge race.

Chapter 20 by Tierney challenges the assumptions that globalization is a synonym for US imperialism, that the USA is uninfluenced by globalization, and that globalization is the next logical stage in the country's development. Since the USA has a diversified system, Tierney focuses on California's post-secondary system, which is the largest system in the country and which represents a microcosm of issues that are being played out on a national level, albeit in different ways from state to state.

After discussing conceptions of higher education as a public good, Tierney turns to a discussion of the relationship between the state and higher education by focusing on key areas such as public higher education, inequality and access, privatization, regulation, and knowledge-based economies and research. He draws on California as a case study by considering how the impact of globalization has changed interpretations in the areas specified above. He shows how throughout much of the twentieth century California's research universities were thought of as among the best in the world, the system served more students than any other state system, and higher education received significant government funding.

He argues that the impact of globalization has resulted in the state maintaining an ideology that higher education should be openly available for its citizens. However, the underlying philosophy has changed. The state does not see its role as providing higher education but rather assuring that different organizations exist in the marketplace, that consumers are provided with some form of funding, and that providers are regulated. While research remains important, the focus is less on research policy than on political and fiscal imperatives. In this context, academic staff and administrations of the public universities have seen their wages decrease, their numbers decline while class sizes have increased, and their pensions threatened. Basic services such as telephones and janitorial services have been cut back.

The largest concerns over privatization are that the university is becoming a glorified trade school and that when donors 'buy' departments through naming rights there is a concern that academic freedom has been compromised. The chapter concludes by describing potential trends that lie ahead and argues that critical judgment, rather than the simple advocacy or rejection of higher education reform, is urgently required.

In the concluding chapter (Chapter 21), Olssen analyzes how changes to higher education in the UK in the early 1980s were constituted by a strain of liberal thought referred to as 'neoliberalism'. He notes that, unlike classical liberalism, neoliberalism contains a positive role for the state in creating the conditions for markets to operate and in developing individuals as enterprising and competitive entrepreneurs. Public choice theory is identified as one of the major neoliberal models attempting to extend market approaches to public sector restructuring. In essence the notion of the public good is asserted as a fiction, and the fact that civil servants serve the public interest is disputed. Olssen notes that on this basis education reforms have restructured the basis of accountability through individually attached incentives and targets, and periodic monitoring and assessment.

The chapter indicates that research was the first area to be subjected to increased accountability. The UK's Research Assessment Exercise (RAE), which was implemented in 1986, became a model for other countries. Australia implemented the Research Quality Framework (RQF) from 2004 to 2007, followed by the Excellence in Research for Australia (ERA) strategy from 2008, while New Zealand implemented the Performance Based Research Framework in 2006. Olssen notes that while benefits such as the sharpening of the quality and focus of research have been identified, negative consequences for research productivity, rising levels of anxiety and stress, and the deprofessionalization of the sector have been reported.

Olssen describes the replacement of the RAE with the Research Excellence Framework (REF) in the UK, with some of its justification unjustly drawn from the ERA, as changing matters 'from bad to worse'. He argues that the effect of assessing the non-academic impact of research (a new ingredient) has the potential to erode two of the central roles of the liberal university. First, the pressures over the nature of what is researched and the resulting decline of academic freedom are likely to alter the nature of knowledge production. Second, by governmental authorities insisting that research must be evaluated according to its impact on end-users, the separation of universities and higher education from the market is further undermined. For Olssen, the determining of such specific indicators at central levels of society potentially undermines the very preconditions of openness and freedom essential for discovery and innovation. The chapter concludes with a plea for the re-professionalization of academics and the institutions of academic self-governance and collegiality.

11 Regional responses to globalization challenges: the assertion of soft power and changing university governance in Singapore, Hong Kong and Malaysia
Ka Ho Mok

INTRODUCTION

Aspiring to become world cities in Asia, together with the strong intention to enhance the global competitiveness of their higher education systems, attract more overseas students and create increased educational opportunities for their citizens, the governments of Singapore, Hong Kong and Malaysia have sought to develop their societies into regional hubs of education. Realizing that the expansion of higher education would not only improve the quality of their populations, these Asian governments also consider that exporting education services strengthens their international 'soft power' and helps to assert their global influence. It is in this context that transnational education has become increasingly popular in these Asian societies, although its development leads to a new terrain of governance and triggers concerns about problems of coordination, accountability and transparency. This chapter compares and contrasts the governance and regulatory models that the governments of Hong Kong, Singapore and Malaysia have adopted for their growing provision of transnational education programs. It examines particularly the policy implications that follow from the proliferation of providers and the diversification of funding.

THE RISE OF TRANSNATIONAL HIGHER EDUCATION IN THE ASIA PACIFIC

The pressing need for transformation to a knowledge economy has exceeded the capacity of many states to rapidly expand their public higher education institutions (HEIs) to meet growing demand. The proliferation of providers, coupled with the global trends of marketization and privatization in higher education, subsequently have created a much more diversified ecology of national systems while fundamentally blurring the line traditionally drawn between the public and private sectors. 'Transnational education' as a term here is applied to denote education in which the learners are located in a country different from the one where the awarding institution is based (UNESCO/Council of Europe, 2001). It could therefore include both collaborative and non-collaborative transnational arrangements across borders, such as franchising, twinning and joint-degree programs in the former, and branch campuses in the latter.

The rise of transnational higher education in the Asia-Pacific region undeniably reflects the growing pace of globalization and the subsequent pressures imposed by it. Singapore, Malaysia and Hong Kong, among others, are three notable cases of states that explicitly and individually have declared their intentions to become a regional hub of education. This has led to a rather dramatic expansion of transnational higher education as a means of achieving such strategies. This chapter critically examines changing governance and regulatory reforms in Singapore, Malaysia and Hong Kong as transnational higher education has developed. Policy backgrounds and governance strategies adopted by these countries respectively will be initially considered, followed by a more specific comparative analysis, particularly of the regulatory regimes set up to assure the quality of higher education offered by various transnational arrangements.

GLOBALIZATION AND TRANSNATIONALIZATION

In recent decades the internationalization of higher education has become a more discernible trend in Asia as a result of the growing impact of globalization. Although globalization and internationalization are related, they are not the same (Altbach, 2004). One of the major features associated with globalization is the breakdown of national/local barriers to free trade and the open movement of people, information and capital. Communication and knowledge travel afar across oceans and mountains with the click of the mouse as new technology rapidly compresses distances, leading to a 'flat world' (Friedman, 2005). Against this background, coupled with pressing demands for more and better higher education for the knowledge-based economy, transnational higher education has developed quickly in Asia, particularly with the emergence of international education hubs in Malaysia, Singapore, China and India (Fahey, 2007).

It is fueled further by the inclusion of higher education as an industry under the WTO–GATS (World Trade Organization–General Agreement on Trade in Services) framework (Knight, 2002). The processes of liberalization and privatization of higher education undergone in the Eastern Asian societies considered here during the last two decades are dramatic and highly impressive. All these states are readjusting their role from the principal provider of higher education to something more like a facilitator. Private institutions have been encouraged enthusiastically to establish and expand, particularly through various transnational arrangements. Under GATS, higher education is developing as a tradable service in Asia (Mok, 2010).

Although it is difficult to exactly pinpoint the financial gains from the rise of transitional higher education in Asia, recent estimates suggest that at least US$50–60 billion is being generated (Welch, 2010). As universities expand their provision across domestic borders, not only economic gains but also the enhancement of human capital and the mobility of talent are achieved. More importantly, the rise of transnational higher education and the quest for regional hubs has created a platform for Asian states to assert their global leadership by strengthening their 'soft power' through the importation and exportation of education services. However, due to the diverse politico-economic contexts of these societies, a variety of governance and regulatory systems for these developments is found. The discussion below touches on each case individually before moving to a more integrative comparison. The role of the state as well as its related capacity will be the focus. The theoretical framework of analysis basically will be drawn from Mok (2008).

A broad categorization of four types of states, namely the market-accelerationist state, the interventionist state, the market-facilitating state and the market-coordinating state, is identified. In the Asia-Pacific region the strong developmental states of the 1970s and 1980s have undergone a number of decentralization and deregulation processes to become more competitive and entrepreneurial to face the growing challenge of globalization. This may not result in a weakening of state influence. A close scrutiny of states' capacity, not least in their governance of transnational higher education, reveals new possibilities that could sustain the pivotal role of the state.

Overall the fundamental impetus behind the prosperity of transnational higher education in these three country cases may well be economic. Although initially domestic demand for higher education could be the catalyst for the state to introduce or allow the advancement of transnational higher education (as in the case of Malaysia, where non-Malays are discriminated against in their access to public universities), it finally boils down to 'the competitive rush for international students and their money' (Chan and Ng, 2008, p. 291). In this sense, regardless of the nuances between the grand strategies/initiatives of the so-called 'Global Schoolhouse' or 'Regional Hub of Education' (see later), higher education as an exportable product of services requires strict quality control to achieve sustainability and competitiveness in such a booming yet fiercely competitive market. Thus, as McBurnie and Ziguras (2001) point out, South-east Asia is now akin to a laboratory for the development and regulation of transnational education. The region combines high demand and keen competition among service providers, and the regulatory regimes in host countries range from relatively *laissez-faire* to strongly interventionist.

THE RISE OF TRANSNATIONAL EDUCATION: POLICY CONTEXTS AND RECENT DEVELOPMENTS

Singapore: From Deregulating Public Universities to the 'Global Schoolhouse' Initiative

The Singapore government has long been aware of the importance of higher education not only in fostering economic growth but also in nurturing human capital more generally. In the last decade, HEIs in Singapore have experienced different types of reforms, including government-introduced competition to drive the public universities to perform more like private corporations. Based on recommendations of the 'Steering Committee to Review University Autonomy, Governance and Funding', published in 2005, the government granted the National University of Singapore (NUS) and Nanyang Technological University (NTU) further autonomous powers by incorporating them as not-for-profit companies, similar to how the Singapore Management University (SMU) is run currently (Ministry of Education, 2005). When asked about the major rationale behind this reform, Perry Lim, the then Director of Higher Education at the Ministry of Education, made it very clear that the incorporation of national universities in Singapore was not financial- but management-driven, since all the incorporated universities are still heavily funded by the government. While the Ministry previously controlled almost every detail of university governance, incorporated universities now would negotiate with the Ministry on 'key performance indicators' and would be held accountable for achieving them (interview by the author with Perry Lim, May 2008).

Yet policies of quality assurance and the corporatization of public universities alone may be far from sufficient instruments for achieving a regional hub strategy. More opportunities for higher education participation, in terms of both the number of places and variety of institution and program, have to be delivered to domestic Singaporeans as well as attracting foreign learners from elsewhere in the region. The mid-1980s school-leaver boom saw the beginnings of transnational higher education in Singapore and, as Garrett (2005, p. 9) points out, this school-leaving cohort (20–24-year age group) continues to rise until around 2010. However, by 2003 Singapore's public universities and polytechnics had enrolled only around 40000 and 56000 students respectively. On the other hand, 119000 students were studying with broadly 170 private tertiary providers, in which 140 offered programs in collaboration with foreign institutions and enrolled 75 percent of the total student population in this section (ibid., pp. 9–10). The importance of transnational education provision in Singapore has therefore become increasingly apparent.

In order to tap into the lucrative education market more aggressively, the Singapore government launched its 'Global Schoolhouse' initiative in 2002. Ever since 1998, the government, through efforts taken by its Economic Development Board (EDB) rather than its Ministry of Education, has strategically invited 'world-class' and 'reputable' universities from abroad to set up their Asian campuses in the city-state. As a result, Singapore is today home to 16 leading foreign tertiary institutions and 44 pre-tertiary schools offering international curricula. The prestigious INSEAD (Institut Européen d'Administration des Affaires) established its Singapore branch campus in 2000. The University of Chicago Booth School of Business (2000), S.P. Jain Center of Management (2006), the New York University's Tisch School of the Arts (2007), and DigiPen Institute of Technology (2008) also are among the list of other foreign tertiary institutions, ranging impressively in curricula across business, management, arts, media, hospitality, information technology, biomedical sciences and engineering.

In 2003 a further and more integrated step was taken by the government to promote Singapore as a premier education hub through 'Singapore Education', a multi-government agency initiative led by the EDB and supported by the Ministry of Education. According to the official website of Singapore Education, EDB is responsible for attracting internationally renowned educational institutions to set up campuses in Singapore, whereas of the other agencies involved, the Tourism Board is tasked with overseas promotion and marketing of Singapore education, and International Enterprise Singapore is in charge of helping quality local education institutions (such as the Anglo-Chinese School International and Raffles Education) to develop their businesses and set up campuses overseas. Another participating agency, SPRING Singapore, has the role of administering quality accreditation for private education institutions in the city-state.

One point that deserves attention here is that the Singapore government not only endorses the growth of local private education, but also coordinates a wide range of private education programs in order to cater to the needs of both local and overseas students. The Association of Private Schools and Colleges (APSC) in Singapore has received government funding to help assure the overall academic standards and governance of its member organizations, confirming the government's strong encouragement for more private schools/colleges, provided that high-quality programs can be assured, so as to encourage more students from overseas. International cooperation has also been widely sought by these private education providers, as shown in the development of Singapore's first and only private university, SIM University (UniSIM, established in 2005), which is dedicated to the upgrading and learning needs of working professionals and adult learners. With the government's support for continuing education and training initiated in July 2008, students enrolling in adult learning programs are able to receive up to a 40 percent subsidy, thus making UniSIM's degree programs more affordable to local adults.

Another significant strategy adopted by the government in promoting transnational higher education is the joint-degree program arranged between local universities and overseas partners. Local Singapore universities are actively collaborating with peer universities across the world on a diversified spectrum of academic programs. Students are granted the freedom to study at both campuses, and receive supervision and teaching by faculty from both universities. A representative example is the Singapore–MIT Alliance (SMA), an innovative engineering education and research enterprise jointly founded in 1998 by the National University of Singapore, the Nanyang Technological University, and the Massachusetts Institute of Technology (MIT). This alliance has so far developed five graduate degree programs and has created a leading-edge distance-learning environment.

There is no sign of weakening ambition by the Singapore government. Following the recent recommendations made by the *Report of the Committee on the Expansion of the University Sector*, a fourth publicly funded university is planned for 2011 to provide a more integrated and interdisciplinary approach to learning, to offer real-world experience by allowing students to apply classroom learning in a practical context, and to encourage an entrepreneurial spirit among its students. In addition, a small liberal-arts college is projected in affiliation with one of the existing public universities, and with a select intake of the brightest local and foreign students (Ministry of Education, 2008).

Finally, as part of its policy to support transnational higher education, the Singapore government also offers a comprehensive package of financial aid to international students through several public channels (Cheng et al., 2009). Tuition fees are only 10 percent above the local rate and such students can apply for whatever financial assistance schemes are open to local students. These include scholarships provided by the 'Singapore Scholarship' fund and tuition grants conditional on agreeing to work for a Singapore-registered company for at least three years upon graduation. Moreover, numerous bursaries are provided by individual tertiary institutions and student loans are also available at favorable interest rates. Recent immigration policies that aim to attract talented and skilled individuals more generally to live and work in Singapore also have facilitated the development of its transnational education industry.

Malaysia: From Liberalization of Higher Education to the Ambitious Goal of Regional Hub of Education

As in the case of Singapore, reforms in Malaysia also began with the process of incorporation of the public universities as statutory bodies. Starting in January 1998, the University of Malay, the oldest university in Malaysia, was incorporated along with eight other public universities. According to the original policy objectives, these public universities were to become more self-financing through instruments such as the freedoms to borrow money, enter into business ventures, establish companies and consultancy firms, and to acquire and hold investment shares. In short, these incorporated universities were expected to raise funds through a variety of channels (Lee, 1999b).

Under the favorable framework set out by the Private Education Act and the Universities and University College Act amendments, public universities began to franchise their programs to local private colleges. For example, from 1996 to 1999 University Putra Malaysia expanded its franchising programs from 1 to 33 with local private colleges, while they increased from 11 to 32 at University Tekonologi Malaysia (Tan, 2002). Alongside the development of other flexible teaching, learning and research arrangements, public universities in Malaysia do indeed appear to be becoming more entrepreneurial. However, to date, it seems that the strategy of incorporation does not really remove longstanding issues of over-bureaucratic and powerful state intervention over the governance of these public universities. The establishment of the Ministry of Higher Education (MOHE) in 2004 is to some yet another sign of the failed promise made by the government to endow more operational autonomy to public universities (Abdul Razak, 2008; Morshidi, 2009b).

The country's ambition to become a regional education hub was first sketchily noted in the grand development blueprint of 'Wawasan 2020' (Vision 2020) initiated by the Mahathir Administration in 1991. According to Vision 2020, the government was establishing a policy target of having 40 percent of youth aged 19–24 admitted into tertiary education. By 2020 it is expected that 60 percent of high-school students will be admitted into public universities, with the rest going to private colleges and universities. The publication of the *National Higher Education Strategic Plan 2020* and the *National Higher Education Action Plan 2007–2010* (both launched in August 2007) are the most recent responses to the changing socioeconomic and sociopolitical circumstances in Malaysia. Given that the global higher educational environment has significantly changed in recent years, the *National Higher Education Strategic Plan 2020* outlines seven major reform objectives: widening access and enhancing quality; improving the quality of teaching and learning; enhancing research and innovation; strengthening institutions of higher education; intensifying internationalization; enculturation of lifelong learning; and reinforcing the MOHE's delivery system.

In December 2008 the Malaysian government again revealed its seriousness in pursuing ambitious goals by amending the Universities and University Colleges Act significantly in order to further improve governance and reduce bureaucracy. Among other changes, it introduced more prominent professionals into the public university board of directors. Selection committees are to be established by the MOHE to appoint every vice chancellor of the public universities, while the vice chancellors will have the authority to extend the services of academic staff beyond retirement age on a contractual basis. Nevertheless, as pointed out in a World Bank report, the current governance regime of Malaysian public higher education is still restrictive, particularly with regard to three critical decision-making capacities for universities: the ability to select their students on their own terms; the freedom to offer competitive remuneration packages to attract the most talented faculty internationally; and the authority to appoint a highly qualified and capable university leader (World Bank, 2007, pp. 35–6).

With regard to transnational higher education in Malaysia, the *Report by the Committee to Study, Review and Make Recommendations Concerning the Development and Direction of Higher Education in Malaysia (Halatuju Report)* was published in July 2005 and contained 138 recommendations. Although this report was controversial (Wan Abdul Manan, 2008), central to it was the recommendation that local higher education institutions should engage in self-promoting activities in the outside world. In addition, the report also recommended that the government should invest more in international student and staff exchange programs that would promote more collaboration between local and transnational education institutions. Based on inputs from the Cabinet, another report entitled the *Transformation of Higher Education* was issued in July 2007 to combine the relevant elements in the Ninth Malaysia Plan and recommendations from the *Halatuju Report*. Subsequently the latest publication for this long-term strategy, the *National Higher Education Strategic Plan*, was put together in August 2007. According to the Plan, the Malaysia government aims to attract 100000 students from overseas by 2010.

Twinning programs between local and foreign institutions have had a long and successful history in Malaysia ever since the mid-1980s. Yet the establishment of international branch campuses became possible only after the construction of a new legal framework in 1996. Various forms of transnational higher education have since swiftly emerged in Malaysia, especially in the Klang Valley, where Kuala Lumpur is a major component. The development of international branch campuses here is particularly impressive. In Malaysia, branch campuses of foreign universities can be established only following an invitation from the Ministry of Education or the Ministry of Higher Education (since 2004). The invited foreign universities, however, need to establish themselves as Malaysian companies with majority Malaysian ownership in order to operate their campuses. The University of Nottingham, for example, has run its programs at its Malaysia campus since 2000 and added a further campus at Semenyih, Negeri Sembilan in 2005. The other three international branch campuses in Malaysia, to date, are all Australian universities, namely Monash University (Petaling Jaya campus, since 1998), Curtin University (Miri campus, since 1999) and Swinburne University of Technology (Kuching campus, since 2000). According to the Observatory on Borderless Higher Education (2002), Monash University cooperates with the Sunway Group – a pioneer of twinning arrangements in the field of education as early as the late 1980s – and the latter provides funding for its Malaysia campus. Similarly, the local partner of Swinburne University of Technology in Malaysia is the Sarawak state government, which cooperates indirectly with the university through its Yayasan Sarawak (Sarawak Foundation) and Sarawak Higher Education Foundation.

Malaysia's increasing cooperation with foreign universities has coincided with increased regulation for transnational provision (Lee, 1999a; McBurnie and Ziguras, 2001). After establishing partnerships with local corporations, foreign university campuses in Malaysia have done well. For instance, Monash University was the first to build an overseas branch campus in Malaysia. With its five faculties including medicine and health sciences, engineering, information technology, business, and arts and sciences, the Monash University–Malaysia now offers various undergraduate and graduate programs to almost 4000 students. A purpose-built campus was opened in 2007 and provides a high-tech home for the university. The Nottingham Malaysia campus has also successfully recruited more than 2700 international students from more than 50 countries. According to the Malaysian Qualifications Agency, by April 2009 there were four branch campuses (one set up by a UK university and three by Australian universities) running 84 programs.

Official statistics also indicate that the private sector has played an increasingly important role in enhancing access to higher education in Malaysia. In 2004, 32 percent of students were enrolled in private higher education institutions in Malaysia. Furthermore, 27 731 international students were studying in Malaysian private HEIs. The Malaysian Qualifications Agency confirmed to the author in April 2009 that 19 UK universities were running 110 twinning programs accredited in the list of the Malaysian Qualifications Register (MQR), while 18 Australian universities were offering 71 programs of this kind. Institutions from other countries such as New Zealand, the USA, Egypt and Jordan are also offering twinning programs in Malaysia.

Finally, the government has also initiated a general regulatory framework for quality assurance of higher education. The private education sector was initially the only focus. The Lembaga Akreditasi Negara (National Accreditation Board) was established under the Lembaga Akreditasi Negara Act of 1996 as a statutory body to accredit certificate, diploma and degree programs provided by the private institutions of higher learning. Yet by 2002 the Ministry of Education had also set up its own quality assurance division to coordinate and manage the quality assurance system in public HEIs. With the rise of transnational education programs and the rapid expansion of private higher education, the government eventually decided to streamline these existing regulatory frameworks in 2003 and adopted the unified Malaysian Qualifications Framework (MQF) the following year. This became governed by the newly established Malaysian Qualifications Agency (MQA) established in 2007 to accredit qualifications awarded by all institutions of higher education.

Hong Kong: From the Quest for Quality Education to an Exporter of Higher Education Services

As in Singapore and Malaysia, higher education in Hong Kong has also experienced significant transformations. A specifically commissioned review report in 2002, entitled *Higher Education in Hong Kong* (or the *Higher Education Review 2002*), raised controversial recommendations for the reform of Hong Kong's higher education system. Among other proposals it recommended the government to strategically identify a small number of institutions for the focus of support from both the public and private sectors. The aim was to assure their capacity for competing at the highest level internationally. The report also proposed detaching the pay scale of academic staff from that of the civil service to enable universities to possess greater freedom and flexibility in determining their own terms and conditions of service. Additionally the existing system of quality assurance should be strengthened, and a proportion of the public funding allocated for research based on the evaluations of Research Assessment Exercises (RAEs) (University Grants Committee (UGC), 2002).

A further restructuring of higher education was done after the UGC released two other review reports in 2004 (UGC, 2004a, 2004b). Their essence was the advocacy of more articulated role differentiation between the existing universities while at the same time encouraging greater collaboration as well. Thus each institution under this 'differentiated yet interlocking system' (UGC, 2004a, p. 7) would have its own role and mission but yet be committed to extensive collaboration with the others to enable a greater variety of programs. The vision was that the Hong Kong higher education sector – basically the publicly funded sector – should aspire to be 'the education hub of the region' (UGC, 2004a, p. 5). According to the UGC, the strong competitive edge of the Hong Kong system over its regional competitors was predominantly 'its strong links with Mainland China' (ibid.), followed by other elements, such as its geographical location and cosmopolitan outlook, plus its internationalized and vibrant higher education sector (although these latter characteristics are also frequently claimed by Singapore for its 'Global Schoolhouse' strategy).

As for transnational higher education, it was initially regarded by the government as a supplementary means to help meet domestic demand as part of the broader massification of higher education (Chan and Lo, 2007) rather than anything more ambitious. With limited resources due to its low-tax policy and particularly after the Asian financial crisis of the late 1990s, the Hong Kong government has come to rely more on non-state financial sources and providers (including overseas academic institutions) to cater for the further development of its higher education system.

Institutional collaborations between Hong Kong and Mainland China seized much of the attention from policy-makers throughout the first decade of post-handover Hong Kong. This has resulted in a growing population of non-local tertiary students consisting mainly of Mainland Chinese. Not until 2007 did Donald Tsang, the chief executive of Hong Kong, explicitly state his intention to expand the population of international students by 'increasing the admission quotas for non-local students to local tertiary institutions, relaxing employment restrictions on non-local students, as well as providing scholarships' (Tsang, 2007, p. 40). More recently (June 2009), based on recommendations made by the Task Force on Economic Challenges set up after the onset of the global financial crisis, the government has declared its resolution to develop six economic areas where Hong Kong still enjoys clear advantages, including 'educational services'.

Compared to Malaysia and Singapore, transnational education in Hong Kong is mainly provided in the form of joint programs and distance learning as well as twinning programs. In the context of financial constraint, all the local publicly funded HEIs are required to develop more self-financing programs or joint programs with their overseas partners in order to recover costs and to generate income (Chan, 2008; Yang, 2006). Consequently continuing education units as well as community colleges have been established by these institutions and the full-time self-financing local programs that they offer have steadily increased from 41 in 2001/02 to 347 in 2008/09. Academic qualifications cover higher diploma (128), associate degree (161) and bachelor degree (58).

As for the non-local higher education and professional courses, the expansion of their numbers is even more impressive. While to date no foreign university has been approached and invited by the Hong Kong government to set up a branch campus in the territory, by the end of August 2009 a total of 1230 non-local courses had become available to both local and overseas students (405 registered courses and 825 exempted courses). Among these, 49 percent and 66 percent respectively are offered by institutions from the UK, while Australian institutions take up another 30 percent and 20 percent correspondingly.

Recognizing that Hong Kong can offer very good market conditions for transnational higher education, especially its geographical proximity to Mainland China, overseas institutions have become increasingly proactive in setting up their academic programs in Hong Kong during the last few years to attract Mainland students (Yang, 2006). Similarly, top universities from Mainland China have also begun to offer programs in Hong Kong and are expanding their market share (currently offering 5 percent of registered courses and 7 percent of exempted courses). This reflects the closer ties between both sides, particularly after agreement on a memorandum of mutual recognition of academic degrees in higher education was signed in 2004. For example, Tsinghua University and Peking University, in collaboration with Hong Kong University and Hong Kong Shue Yan University, offer academic programs ranging from professional certificates to master's degrees in law, economy, literature and architecture. Likewise, universities in Hong Kong have also started to export their education programs to the Mainland.

Despite the rapid development of non-local courses, the Hong Kong government has to date set out only a code of practice for their regulation of courses (HKCAAVQ, 2007), which is a moderately 'light' step. Foreign universities can easily enter or exit Hong Kong's market. Currently all courses conducted in Hong Kong leading to the award of non-local higher academic qualifications (that is, associate degree, degree, postgraduate, or other post-secondary qualifications), or professional qualifications, must be properly registered or be exempted from registration. Overseas institutions are required to obtain accreditation or other formal permission from the Education Bureau (EDB) prior to operation. However, this is rather a broad provision, ranging from compulsory registration to the formal assessment of academic criteria. The EDB will normally seek the independent expert advice of the Hong Kong Council for Accreditation of Academic and Vocational Qualifications (HKCAAVQ) as to whether a course can meet the criteria for registration or be exempted from registration. Yet again the relevant requirements are considered to be straightforward and non-burdensome.

Overall it would appear that the Hong Kong government does not tend to directly curb and regulate the quality, content, level and cost of courses offered by foreign educational institutions. Rather, the government relies heavily on market mechanisms, with its main role reduced to simply providing sufficient information for consumers (Yang, 2006, pp. 41–2). That is, its regulatory mechanism is largely about quality assurance in order to protect customers.

Continuing global economic turbulence led the Hong Kong government in 2008 to seek to diversify its economy further, and education was identified as an important sector. It was an instrument able to position Hong Kong as a regional hub for exporting services to Mainland China and the rest of the region (Tsang, 2009).

CHANGING GOVERNANCE AND REGULATORY REGIMES: A COMPARISON

Singapore: Market-accelerationist State with Highly Proactive and Systematic Regulation

Analyzing the regulatory measures adopted by the Singapore government in driving its agenda of becoming a regional hub of education, it is clear that it resorts to a fairly systematic, controlled and measured approach towards transnational higher education. With the grandiose objective 'to make Singapore a Global Schoolhouse providing educational programs of all types and at all levels from pre-school to post-graduate institutions, and that attracts an interesting mix of students from all over the world', the government not only maintains its guidance over the developmental path of public universities through certain forms of 'decentralized centralism' (Tan and Ng, 2007), but also handpicks prestigious foreign universities for invitation to set up campuses in Singapore. Under the current GATS framework, the government is supposed to relinquish some of its ability in picking and choosing foreign universities, as GATS is against such restrictions on market entry. Consequently a clearer and more transparent framework may need to be worked out in order to treat foreign universities 'no less favorably' than it treats the local universities in the city-state (Ziguras, 2003).

The government also actively regulates transnational higher education. Online courses and other forms of distance education that do not have a local presence in Singapore appear to be exempted from approval processes, although foreign programs offered by a local partner institution must obtain permission from the Ministry of Education and both the awarding university and its local partner must provide detailed information to convince the Ministry that they are capable of delivering their programs to the equivalent standard of those offered in the home institution (Ziguras, 2003, p. 100). Moreover, in order to make clear the division of labor and responsibilities between the local partners and overseas degree-awarding institutions, the Ministry only allows the local agents/partners to offer administrative support instead of engaging in teaching and learning activities. Yet despite this prohibition it is still difficult to know whether it is upheld in practice. As Ziguras suggests, local tutors have been employed by overseas institutions to teach tutorials and provide lectures.

Consequently no clear guidelines are available for regulating external programs. No central authority in Singapore assesses or grants recognition for degrees obtained from overseas universities; the Ministry of Education does not have a list of accredited overseas universities. This decentralized approach is based on a rationale that employers should decide whether a degree-holder has the qualities and qualification desired for the job. Professional overseas degrees, such as those in engineering, medicine, law and accountancy, are expected to rely on inspection and accreditation by the respective local professional bodies. For courses offered by overseas universities in Singapore through their local agents, the Ministry regards the institutions concerned and their agents as responsible for all aspects of the programs.

Nevertheless the proactive role played by the state in the formation of Singapore's transnational higher education arrangements is exemplified in its highly selective process of inviting overseas partners to set up branch campuses, as well as by its strategic master plan to guide and orchestrate various sectors in the city-state towards the goal of promoting Singapore as a major exporter of higher education in the region. The government does intervene in the market by deciding who the partners are and what programs can be launched to fulfill its nation-building agenda. In terms of resources, while the government has offered attractive financial incentives (including land) to lure top foreign universities, in return the latter are also expected to live up to expectations (Chan and Ng, 2008). A recent example in this vein is the closure of the Division of Biomedical Sciences of Johns Hopkins University in Singapore in July 2006. It was ordered by the government-affiliated Agency for Science, Technology and Research (A*STAR) on the grounds that the Division failed to achieve several key performance indicators, including the recruitment of doctorate degree students and also internationally reputable scholars into its Singapore campus (Lee and Gopinathan, 2008, pp. 579–80). In short, the rise of transnational higher education in Singapore has shown a rather successful operation of the state-corporatist regulatory regime, in which the state makes use of various pro-competition instruments to accelerate market forces towards its desired developmental model.

Malaysia: Market-accelerationist State with an Undecided Regulatory Regime of Simultaneous Centralization and Decentralization

Comparatively the integrative framework constructed by the Malaysian government for the quality assurance of transnational education is arguably the most comprehensive among the three cases. As mentioned previously, the Lembaga Akreditasi Negara (LAN or National Accreditation Board) was established in 1996 with the limited function of accrediting only programs offered by the private institutions of higher learning. Under this regulatory structure the latter were obliged to apply for approval directly to the Minister of Education (not just the Ministry collectively) to conduct a program based on the recommendation of LAN. Various guidelines for the criteria and standards of programs at different levels or in different modes were to be met. LAN was even authorized to conduct site audit visits to ascertain the compliance of these institutions to minimum standards. Moreover, LAN had also built a database on these private institutions, which included evaluation of their staff qualifications and facilities, as well as their student–teacher ratios.

A unified quality assurance structure that covers both the private and public HEIs, the Malaysian Qualifications Framework (MQF) was adopted in 2004 and the framework has become even more centrally controlled after the founding of the Malaysian Qualifications Agency (MQA, or Agensi Kelayakan Malaysia), on 1 November 2007. MQA is a merger of LAN and the Quality Assurance Division of the Ministry of Higher Education, and is now responsible for the implementation of the MQF. Nevertheless MQA is still a subordinate agency placed directly under the Ministry of Higher Education. In terms of accreditation, a new feature worth noting is that under the MQA Act 2007 there is now the possibility of the conferment of 'self-accrediting status' for those mature HEIs that already have well-established internal quality assurance mechanisms. However, to be so conferred, the institution concerned needs to undergo an institutional audit, and, if successful, all qualifications it offers will then be automatically registered on the Malaysian Qualifications Register (MQR).

The MQA claims that these processes are further supported by continuous monitoring in order to consistently ensure the quality of programs offered by HEIs. Moreover, unlike its Singapore counterpart, the Ministry in Malaysia does have a list of accredited overseas universities or, in some cases, a list of accredited programs of certain universities. In other words, the state is involved in the assessment not only of all the domestic public and private tertiary programs in Malaysia (transnational programs included) but in overseas programs as well. Yet this seemingly impeccable framework obviously entails a powerful, significant and centralized bureaucracy to act as its administrative support, and a powerful bureaucracy may adversely imply more hassles than benefits in its outcomes. Moreover, in terms of execution, the lackluster track record of the concerned Ministry of Education/Higher Education during the past few decades may also worry some observers regarding the effectiveness of the framework.

The strong tendency for state intervention is found in aspects of the governance of transnational higher education in Malaysia other than quality assurance. While a series of decentralized policies, including the drastic liberalization of the private higher education sector and corporatization of public universities, have been pushed forward since the mid-1990s, the Malaysian government on the other hand has also paradoxically strengthened its own governance – though in some cases indirectly – of higher education, particularly for public institutions. Academics in Malaysia, for instance Sirat Morshidi, remark that the Malaysian higher education system is still very much dominated by the state and that it is virtually part of the government bureaucracy. The establishment of the Ministry of Higher Education in 2004 clearly reveals the state's intention to retain its centralized control in this respect. These newly developed, superfluous bureaucratic procedures would certainly reduce the efficiency in administration (interview with Morshidi, September 2009).

The Malaysian government has confronted the paradox with the development of transnational education. The rather undecided regulatory regime of simultaneous centralization and decentralization for higher education governance is epitomized in the recent conferment of the privileged position of 'Apex University' on Universiti Sains Malaysia (USM) and in subsequent events. The Malaysian government designated four public universities in 2006 as 'Research Universities' based on their satisfactory track records in research. From these, the USM was further selected in 2008 as the first university to participate in the government's Accelerated Program for Excellence (APEX). As a result, the University is considered to be adequately endowed and empowered to achieve world-class status and be included as one of the top 100 in global university rankings by 2013 and a member of the top 50 by 2020. However, as Morshidi and Razak (2010, pp. 4, 9) worryingly point out, the government has yet to show its political will in offering a bold and liberal new legal and regulatory framework that is 'radically' different from the current framework shaped under the 1996 Universities and University Colleges Act. Admittedly, as far as the private and transnational higher education providers are concerned, it is, to date, still evident that the state's regulatory approach is comparatively liberal. However, the insistence of the Malaysian government in keeping a broad reserve role for the protection of the 'national interest' is equally evident, impacting legally even upon private and transnational higher education (Morshidi, 2009b). Morshidi (2009a) argues that the Malaysian government adopts 'selective decentralization', which is clearly reflected in oscillating education policy and management.

Hong Kong: Market-facilitating State with Comparatively Much Liberal Regulation

As noted before, the Hong Kong government initially tended to see transnational higher education as simply a supplement to the operations of the local universities. It was therefore a sector allowed to generate its own revenue and operate under a free market mechanism with hardly any public resources or proactive regulation affecting its development. Since 2007, particularly since the 2009 Task Force on Economic Challenges pinpointed 'educational services' as one of the key industries for Hong Kong's future development, the government has become increasingly committed to the progress of transnational higher education. Nonetheless it still refrains from any direct intervention or regulation on either the content or quality of courses offered by foreign educational institutions.

The reliance on the market mechanism implies a regulatory regime for transnational higher education that focuses primarily on providing sufficient market data for the consumers to choose in a well-informed manner, as well as on defending their interests through quality assurance of the 'products'. Nevertheless, ever since the restructuring of the Hong Kong Council for Academic Accreditation (HKCAA) and thereafter the establishment of a more inclusive accreditation authority, HKCAAVQ, on 1 October 2007, a similar quality assurance mechanism to that in Malaysia has been constructed. Although HKCAAVQ is still not as inclusive and versatile as its Malaysian counterpart (MQA), a more rigorous – at least as regards formality – Qualifications Framework (QF) and its associated Qualifications Register (QR) is now in place and administered by the HKCAAVQ. This brand new structure is made possible through the provision of the Accreditation of Academic and Vocational Qualifications Ordinance (Chapter 592), which has become fully operative only as recently as May 2008. One of the functional differences between HKCAAVQ and MQA is that the former assesses only academic and vocational programs conducted by non-self-accrediting institutions. The exempted list of self-accrediting institutions is significant and includes all the eight UGC-funded institutions and the Open University of Hong Kong.

This new quality assurance framework, though rigorous as far as it goes, is still a fairly moderate approach as far as the non-local higher and professional education courses are concerned. These courses are regulated by the Non-Local Higher and Professional Education (Regulation) Ordinance (Chapter 493) through a system of registration, yet the registration criteria set for non-local higher academic qualifications, for instance, are rather lenient and consist of only two points:

(1) The awarding institution should be a non-local institution recognized in the home country;
(2) Effective measures should be in place to ensure that the standard of the course is maintained at a level comparable with a course conducted in the home country leading to the same qualification. As such it should be recognized by that institution, by the academic community in that country, and by the relevant accreditation authority there (if any).

Moreover, non-local courses conducted in collaboration with all the eight UGC-funded institutions and several other local institutions are exempt from registration. Similarly, in respect of the standing of these courses in local society, the Hong Kong government has taken a similar view as its Singapore counterpart, namely that it is a matter of discretion for individual employers to recognize any qualification to which this course may lead. Thus, as McBurnie and Ziguras (2001) originally observe, the Hong Kong government is adopting a relatively liberal approach in dealing with transnational education. Unlike its Singapore and Malaysian counterparts, it simply performs the role of a 'market facilitator' instead of 'market generator'. The rationale behind this civil society regulatory regime is closely related to the tradition of the free market economy to which the government has long been committed. Hence the objective of the Ordinance, as claimed by the official website of Education Bureau, is 'to protect Hong Kong consumers by guarding against the marketing of substandard non-local higher and professional education courses conducted in Hong Kong'.

Further elaboration of this neoliberal approach came from Nigel French, the then secretary general of the Hong Kong University Grants Committee, when he suggested in 1999 that a key function of the regulatory regime was to provide Hong Kong consumers with detailed information from providers regarding their offerings. Once this information is made publicly available, the government leaves individual consumers to decide, providing that their choices are informed ones (French, 1999).

DISCUSSION: DIALECTICAL CONFLICTS BETWEEN MARKET EFFICIENCY AND STATE CAPACITY

Analyzing the recent developments of transnational higher education and the growing privateness in higher education in these three Asian societies, we can easily realize that they are experiencing fundamental changes in their governance and regulatory models, shifting to an interactionist focus with a growing sense of government–society interdependences (Kooiman, 1993). With heightened expectations from their citizens for more and better higher education, it is obvious that depending upon the provision of the states alone is no longer sufficient to meet demand, particularly after most Asian states experienced economic setbacks after the Asian financial crisis in 1997. Public universities in these societies have been encouraged to diversify their funding sources from non-state actors or sectors, and the market, the community, as well as the civil society at large, have subsequently been revitalized by governments in Singapore, Malaysia and Hong Kong to engage in higher education financing and provision. The rise of transnational higher education, coupled with the growing importance of privateness in higher education, has suggested a shift to some degree from the conventional centralized model of governance and regulation in these Asian states. Nevertheless. while they no longer monopolize the provision, financing and regulation of higher education, these three cases demonstrate that, paradoxically, the states' capacity may not necessarily fade away and that there are varieties of regulatory regimes encapsulating the dialectical conflicts between market efficiency and state capacity.

While governments in Singapore and Malaysia have played a 'market generator' role not only in setting out strategic directions but also proactively orchestrating developments in transnational higher education to meet their national agendas, the Hong Kong government is, conversely, far more committed to free market economic principles and thus performs the role of 'market facilitator'.

The Singapore government is particularly effective and systematic in promoting transnational higher education as part of a larger project of nation-building. Yet significant state intervention and proactive guidance, though carefully modulated to ensure a well-managed and regulated hub of higher education, means that institutional autonomy and vitality, and academic freedom, remain at risk in the long run. The Malaysian government, in similar vein, has also adopted a similar path in boosting its transnational higher education, yet the lack of strategic and philosophical consistency in its planning has created a regulatory regime of simultaneous centralization and decentralization, which is a paradox shared also by its Singapore counterpart but comparatively less noticeable.

Overall, the highly selective approach adopted by both the Singapore and Malaysian governments in directing developments of transnational higher education clearly shows that these two Asian economies are not altogether market-embracing states. Rather, they are market-accelerationist states that operate with the logic of the market but intervene in order to remove inefficiencies there. This new form of market-accelerationist state demonstrates that the developmental states in Eastern Asia have not entirely given way to neoliberal globalization. The Singapore and Malaysian governments are now pursuing regulation-for-competition rather than regulation-of-competition, aiming at enhancing the state's competitiveness through regulation in order to achieve its goals of economic nationalism (as highlighted, for example, in Malaysia's Master Plan, Vision 2020).

On the other hand, while in comparison the governance and regulatory approach taken by the Hong Kong government towards transnational higher education is the most liberal, several significant changes, as mentioned earlier, are also found more recently. These recent reforms all point in the direction of stronger state regulation and for a more proactive role to be played by the state. For instance, apart from the very new efforts of constructing a more inclusive qualifications framework, the government has also become more aggressive in providing financial incentives to lure international students with talent and expertise while at the same time relaxing immigration policies to facilitate their stay in Hong Kong. It also intends to raise the international student proportion in Hong Kong to beyond the current 10 percent threshold and actively promotes the business-related programs that are most popular with Asian students.

It is thus intriguing to see that as far as the governance and regulatory regimes of transnational higher education are concerned, both the market-accelerationist states (Singapore and Malaysia) and the market-facilitating state (Hong Kong), after roughly two decades of experiencing and adjusting to the rapid development of transnational higher education in their societies, have gradually approached a similar direction of reform: Singapore and Malaysia may have to reduce their strong flavor of state intervention in order to maintain the vitality and efficiency of their sectors of transnational higher education; while on the other hand the Hong Kong government may be forced to wield its state capacity more proactively in industrializing the same sector so as to make it more supportive of the territory's economy. After all, it is not easy either in theory or in practice to strike a balance between a market economy and a strong regulatory state.

CONCLUSION

This chapter has discussed the growing proliferation of providers in higher education, especially as transnational higher education has become increasingly popular in Singapore, Malaysia and Hong Kong. The quest to become a regional hub of education has inevitably diversified educational programs in these Asian societies, and this development has also changed the relationship between the state and the market in educational provision and financing. In addressing the increasing complexity of the organization and delivery of transnational education, comparative education researchers and analysts have to critically examine the changes taking place in the governance and management of transnational higher education, with particular reference to the regulatory regimes governing and assuring the academic quality of the newly emerging transitional education programs. A consideration of the changing governance and regulatory regimes for transnational higher education in Singapore, Malaysia and Hong Kong indicates the complexity of the heterarchies and hybrid organizations that are found when global education is rapidly expanding. The proliferation of higher education providers, coupled with the mobility of students and the diversification of educational services, tends to render conventional public–private distinctions inappropriate.

REFERENCES

Abdul Razak, A. (2008), 'The university's governance in Malaysia: re-examining the role of the state', paper presented at the symposium on 'Positioning University in the Globalized World: changing governance and coping strategies in Asia', University of Hong Kong, Hong Kong, 10–11 December 2008.

Altbach, P. (2004), 'Globalization and the university: myths and realities in an unequal world', *Tertiary Education and Management*, **10**, 3–25.

Chan, D. (2008), 'Global agenda, local response: changing university governance and academic reflections in Hong Kong's higher education', paper presented at the symposium on 'Positioning Universities in the Globalized World: changing governance and coping strategies in Asia', University of Hong Kong, Hong Kong, 10–11 December 2008.

Chan, D. and W. Lo (2007), 'Running universities as enterprises: university governance changes in Hong Kong', *Asia Pacific Journal of Education*, **27** (3), 305–22.

Chan, D. and P. Ng (2008), 'Developing transnational higher education: comparing the approaches of Hong Kong and Singapore', *International Journal of Educational Reform*, **17** (3), 291–307.

Cheng, Y., S. Ng and A. Cheung (2009), *A Technical Research Report on the Development of Hong Kong as a Regional Education Hub*, Hong Kong: Hong Kong Institute of Education.

Fahey, S. (2007), 'Rethinking international education engagement in the Asia-Pacific region', Keynote address at the 'Pacific Economic Cooperation Council Conference', Sydney, April.

French, N. (1999), 'Transnational education – competition or complementarity?: The case of Hong Kong', *Higher Education in Europe*, **24** (2), 219–23.

Friedman, T. (2005), *The World is Flat: A Brief History of the Twenty-First Century*, New York: Farrar, Straus and Giroux.

Garrett, R. (2005), 'The rise and fall of transnational higher education in Singapore', *International Higher Education*, **39**, 9–10.

Hong Kong Council for Accreditation of Academic and Vocational Qualifications (HKCAAVQ) (2007), *Code of practice for non-local courses recommended by the Hong Kong Council for Accreditation of Academic and Vocational Qualifications*, December.

Hong Kong Council for Accreditation of Academic and Vocational Qualifications (HKCAAVQ) (2008), *Guidelines on four-stage quality assurance process under the qualifications framework: QF Levels 1–3 (Version 1.0)*, May.

Knight, J. (2002), 'Trade talk: an analysis of the impact of trade liberalization and the general agreement on trade in services on higher education', *Journal of Studies in International Education*, **6** (3), 209–29.

Kooiman, J. (1993), 'Sociopolitical governance: Introduction', in J. Kooiman (ed.), *Modern Governance: new government-society interactions*, London: Sage, pp. 1–8.

Lee, M. (1999a), 'Corporatization, privatization, and internationalization of higher education in Malaysia', in P. Altbach (ed.), *Private Prometheus: Private Higher Education and Development in the 21st Century*, New York: Greenwood Press, pp. 137–60.

Lee, M. (1999b), *Private Higher Education in Malaysia,* Penang, Malaysia: School of Educational Studies, Universiti Sains Malaysia.

Lee, M. and S. Gopinathan (2008), 'University restructuring in Singapore: amazing or a maze?', *Policy Futures in Education*, **6** (5), 569–88.

McBurnie, G. and C. Ziguras (2001), 'The regulation of transnational higher education in southeast Asia: case studies of Hong Kong, Malaysia and Australia', *Higher Education*, **42**, 85–105.

Ministry of Education (MOE), Singapore (2005), *Autonomous Universities – Towards Peaks of Excellence* (preliminary report of the Steering Committee to review University Autonomy, Governance and Funding), January.

Ministry of Education (MOE), Singapore (2008), *Report of the Committee on the Expansion of the University Sector: Greater Choice, More Room to Excel*, August.

Mok, K.H. (2008), 'Varieties of regulatory regimes in Asia: the liberalization of the higher education market and changing governance in Hong Kong, Singapore, and Malaysia', *The Pacific Review*, **21** (2), 147–57.

Mok, K.H. (2010), 'Global aspirations and strategizing for world class status: new modes of higher education governance and emergence of regulatory regionalism in East Asia', paper presented at the conference, 'The Global University: past, present and future perspectives', 5–6 February, University of Wisconsin, Madison, WI.

Morshidi, S. (2009a), 'Internationalization and the commercialization of research output of universities: emerging issues in Malaysian higher education 2006–2010', paper presented at the 'Regional Conference on Comparative Education and Development in Asia', 24–25 September, National Chung Cheng University, Taiwan.

Morshidi, S. (2009b), 'Strategic planning directions of Malaysia's higher education: university autonomy in the midst of political uncertainties', *Higher Education*, DOI 10.1007/s10734-009-9259-0.

Morshidi, S. and A. Razak (2010), 'University governance structure in challenging times: the case of Malaysia's first APEX university (Universiti Sains Malaysia)', in K.H. Mok (ed.) *The Search for New Higher Education Governance in Asia*, New York: Palgrave, pp. 125–38.

Observatory on Borderless Higher Education (2002), *International Branch Campuses: Scale and Significance*, London: OBHE.

Tan, C. and P. Ng (2007), 'Dynamics of change: decentralized centralism of education in Singapore', *Journal of Educational Change*, **8** (2), 155–68.

Tan, J. (2002), 'Education in the early 21st century: challenges and dilemmas', in D. da Cunha (ed.), *Singapore in the New Millennium*, Singapore: Institute of Southeast Asian Studies.

Tsang, D. (2007), *The 2007–2008 Policy Address: The New Direction for Hong Kong*, Hong Kong: Government Printer.

Tsang, D. (2009), *The 2009–2010 Policy Address*, Hong Kong: Government Printer.

UNESCO/Council of Europe (2001), *Code of Good Practice in the Provision of Transnational Education*, Riga, Latvia: UNESCO–CEPES.

University Grants Committee (UGC) (2002), *Higher Education in Hong Kong: Report of the University Grants Committee*, Hong Kong: UGC.

University Grants Committee (UGC) (2004a), *Hong Kong Higher Education: To Make a Difference, to Move with the Times*, Hong Kong: UGC.

University Grants Committee (UGC) (2004b), *Hong Kong Higher Education Integration Matters: A Report of the Institutional Integration Working Party of the University Grants Committee*, Hong Kong: UGC.

Wan Abdul Manan, W. (2008), 'The Malaysian national higher education action plan: redefining autonomy and academic freedom under the APEX experiment', paper presented at the ASAIHL Conference, 'University Autonomy: interpretation and variation', Universiti Sains Malaysia, Penang, 12–14 December.

Welch, A. (2010), 'Contributing to the southeast Asian knowledge economy? Australian offshore campuses in Malaysia and Vietnam', paper to the WUN Conference, 'The Global University: past, present and future perspectives', 5–6 February, University of Wisconsin, Madison, WI.

World Bank (2007), *Malaysia and the Knowledge Economy: Building a World-class Higher Education System (Report No. 40397-MY)*, New York: Human Development Sector, East Asia and Pacific Region, the World Bank.

Yang, R. (2006), 'Transnational higher education in Hong Kong: an analysis', in F. Huang (ed.), *Transnational Higher Education in Asia and the Pacific Region*, Hiroshima, Japan: Research Institute for Higher Education, Hiroshima University, pp. 35–58.

Ziguras, C. (2003), 'The impact of the GATS on transnational tertiary education: comparing experiences of New Zealand, Australia, Singapore, and Malaysia', *The Australian Educational Researcher*, **30** (3), 89–109.

12 Global 'toolboxes',[1] local 'toolmaking': the contradictions of external evaluation in South African higher education reform

Mala Singh

INTRODUCTION

In considering the implications and effects of globalization on education policy in the developing world, issues of trade-off between risk and opportunity for local agendas loom large. Concerns about 'control, autonomy and agency' (Mittelman, 2001, p. 1) arise in exploring the ambivalent and changing relationships between the local and the global, as do questions of possibility, constraint and contradiction in the tracking of policy interfaces of global paradigms and national imperatives. Analysts have pointed to the increasing power of global models to influence local systems as nation-states become less able to shape policy priorities according to national reference points alone (Dale, 2007; Ozga and Lingard, 2007; Scott, 1998; Rizvi and Lingard, 2010, p. 22). In this regard the attraction and influence of transnational and trans-regional trends on national education policy are evident, not only as a recent phenomenon (Phillips, 2002), nor only across the divide between the global North and South. Rhoades and Sporn (2002, p. 355) illustrate the latter in their analysis of the 'diffusion of quality assurance models and practices' between Europe and the USA. However, the challenges of mediating and modifying global models to make them fit for contextual purpose or engaging in the more difficult task of thinking about local 'solutions' outside global 'toolboxes' become more acute in developing-country contexts, especially where structural asymmetries of power, poor capacity and limited resources come together to constrain local agency (Obamba and Mwema, 2009; Singh, 2010).

This chapter seeks to explore the interplay of global paradigms for higher education reform and the emergence of locally purposed education policy systems in a developing-country setting. Drawing on the post-1994 higher education policy reform in South Africa, it focuses on the development of an external evaluation system for higher education as a key instrument of that reform and an instructive arena for understanding the dynamic between global and local imperatives in shaping the identity of reform strategies. The context for the analysis is, on the one hand, the use of quality assurance as a globally ubiquitous regulatory strategy in higher education reform in the developed and developing world alike, and on the other the emergence of new governance regimes and steering levers in the construction of a transformed post-apartheid higher education system in South Africa. How and why did the fates of these different political projects intersect?

The chapter examines the strategic choices that were made for the new external evaluation system out of both a compelling local conjuncture and a persuasive global policy 'toolbox', and how these choices were conceptualized, legitimated, negotiated and given expression. It also looks at the convergences and dissonances between global and local reference points in the attempt to construct a new quality assurance system within the trajectory of post-apartheid higher education reform. The focus in the chapter is on the political, normative and conceptual factors at work in the interplay of policy internationalization and policy localization in the new quality assurance system. More specifically the analysis centers on the initiative to conceptualize and implement a contextually appropriate quality assurance system, based on rethinking quality and accountability as well as the purposes of quality assurance through the lens of the social justice and social transformation[2] imperatives of the local political project (Phillips and Ochs, 2004, p. 16), which is somewhat different from how these are conventionally framed within the global template. This is not an account of the operational details of the system, nor is it an in-depth empirical study of the positive and negative effects of the approach.[3]

Ranging over issues relating to 'travelling policy' (Ozga and Lingard, 2007, p. 69), higher education regulation through evaluation and ideologically contending reform imperatives in higher education, the chapter consists of four sections. The first sets out a conceptual frame of reference for thinking about the relationship between globalizing education policy models and 'vernacular' (Appadurai, 1996) applications and uses of them. The second outlines the political and policy setting for higher education reform in South Africa in the first decade of the transition and the emerging presence of globally resonant change principles and instrumentalities. The third elaborates on the mix of global influences and local imperatives in the construction of a new external evaluation system, especially the resort to a different kind of 'optic' (Giroux, 2008) for evaluation beyond its predominantly economic- and 'consumer'-oriented accountability parameters. And the fourth reflects on the possibilities, limits and contradictions of this particular 'hybrid' system that brought together the differing as well as overlapping political projects of the local and the global (Lingard, 2000).

CONCEPTUAL FRAME OF REFERENCE

The environmental setting for an exploration of the policy nexus between global paradigms and local imperatives is the current positioning of higher education within the political and economic discourses of globalization, described by Held et al. (1999, p. 2) as 'the widening, deepening and speeding up of worldwide interconnectedness'. Less neutral in its framing of higher education is the influence of knowledge-economy discourses in prioritizing the relationship between higher education and economic growth, and of new public management (NPM) policy approaches in shaping structural and behavioral changes within higher education, especially in respect of norms, agendas and goal-setting. For the purposes of this chapter, Marginson and van der Wende's summary of the defining elements of the latter is useful:

> The templates of the new public management include the modelling of national systems as economic markets; government-steered competition between institutions, and executive-steered competition between academic units; part-devolution of responsibility for administering and often for raising finances; incentives to reduce costs per unit and to engage in entrepreneurial behaviour; new or augmented price signals; incentives to link with business and industry; performance measures and output-based funding; and relations with funding agencies and

managers based on quasi-corporate forms such as contracts, accountability and audit. (2009, p. 55, note 3)

The impacts of globalization, knowledge-economy discourses and NPM approaches on higher education have shaped the predominant senses in which a relevant and good-quality education is understood and has influenced the ideological, normative and policy identities of quality assurance systems. The role and purposes of quality assurance in evaluating and attesting to the accountability of higher education in delivering quality within the above paradigms (accompanied by a less emphasized focus on quality improvement) is now a familiar feature of higher education regulation in many OECD and non-OECD countries alike. Quality assurance systems are a key constituent element of national higher education frameworks, and their regulatory weight has become a marker of reform and progress towards the achievement of commonly advocated policy goals in different countries. Among these well-known goals are the development of more efficient, effective and stakeholder-responsive higher education systems although, as Marginson and van der Wende point out, their content, even within NPM approaches, is likely to be 'nationally nuanced' (2009, p. 21).

How do these globalization-linked reform templates play themselves out in the shaping of new or changing policy frameworks, especially in developing-country contexts? Arguments about the influence of global models on local policy systems range from the position that globalization templates have a reductively homogenizing effect on education policy, irrespective of contextual histories and settings (which subordinate local agency and limit it to mimicry) to the view that 'vernacular' mediations are possible and even necessary (which opens up spaces for local agency to reorient and modify global imperatives). The approach to the relationship between global and local policy interactions outlined here falls within the latter position. It does not presume, however, that national agency is unconstrained by structural and ideological limits in its work of policy localization (Ball, 2006, p. 48), or that the locally beneficial outcomes of its reorientation of global templates outweigh other, possibly negative, globalization-linked outcomes, or that initially beneficial outcomes do not become more uncertain or contested over time.

What are relevant dimensions in a conceptual frame of reference for elucidating the local–global interfaces in the South African higher education evaluation system? In order to have a clearer sense of what spaces exist for choice-making by local agency and what limits prevail in a global–local policy connection, it may be useful to construct an analytical baseline as outlined below.

1. The Meanings, Powers and Effects of Globalization

The argument that the meanings and effects of globalization are not homogeneous, universal or singular is made by many analysts (Dale, 2007, p. 50; Marginson and van der Wende, 2009, p. 20; Scott, 1998). Lingard (2000, p. 103) points out that the effects of globalization, especially in relation to education policy and politics, can account for both convergence and divergence in context, rather than convergence only. Rizvi and Lingard (2010, p. 42) maintain that the 'neoliberal view of education has become a dominant social imaginary of globalization . . . through . . . processes which include: the global circulation of ideas and ideologies; international conventions and consensus that steer educational policies in a particular direction and formal bilateral and multilateral contracts between systems'. They challenge the ostensible inevitability of this trend and assert the possibility and necessity of alternatives to it. Emerging from these analytical positions is a picture of globalization as nuanced in its meanings, powers and effects, with potential openings for local maneuver.

This is a useful antidote to a totalizing view of globalization and its presumed power to produce uniform effects in different historical and political settings. Building on these insights for an analysis of the local–global policy interplay in South African higher education, the working premise of this chapter is that globalization's forces and influences can be mediated by local actors; that templates with globalization-linked lineages can be translated into contextually applicable policies and systems (although within limits); that the policy outcomes of the interaction are neither predetermined nor inevitable but involve choice and agency; that local structural, political and resourcing conditions are important mediating factors; and that global policy influence does not automatically make for local isomorphism along all key dimensions but produces similarities as well as differences in dimensions spanning policy goals, strategies, instruments, processes and outcomes.

2.   The Nature of the Context and Policy Regime where Transnational Policy Influence is Evident

According to Marginson and van der Wende (2007, p. 5), 'nations and institutions bring varying capacities and agendas to global exchange'. Dale (2007, p. 49) argues that 'while globalization does represent a new set of rules, there is no reason to expect all countries to interpret those rules in identical ways, or to expect them all to play to the rules in identical ways'. His observations about the importance of whether the locus of origin for the initiation of policies is external or internal and about the difference between policy imposition and other non-coerced forms of policy influence are also instructive for understanding what possibilities exist within local conjunctures to shape policies that could privilege contextual imperatives.

Rizvi and Lingard (2010, p. 42) point out that 'global processes do not affect all educational systems in the same way. They are filtered through particular national and cultural traditions, as well as the specific ways in which policymakers engage with global pressures.' Change agendas, even within national systems, are not uniformly understood, nor are they uncontested, especially where there are multiple levels and layers of policymakers, policy translators and implementors at work. Directions and choices are often shaped by different 'networks of actors' (Bleiklie in Kogan et al., 2000, p. 62) who are involved in managing the processes of local–global policy interactions. The post-1994 context in South African higher education was characterized by a relatively non-coerced embrace of international paradigms and benchmarks by national policy-makers at the same time as the priority of local imperatives was being asserted. The policy imaginary in relation to the quality reform agenda presumed that local and global policy imperatives in higher education could be hybridized in a credible and sustainable way and made to serve nationally determined purposes, and that the disjunctures between global and local imperatives could be managed through reorienting the former or privileging the latter as required.

3. The Nature of the Global Model or Template

Roger King, in his analysis of 'policy internationalization' in Chapter 24 in Part III of this book points to the generalizability and transposability of global models[4] that allow solutions to similar problems worldwide but that also 'undergo specific critiques and nuanced modifications of form and content in processes of substantive application' (p. 416). King goes on to speak of '"situated agents" at a concrete level [who] accomplish outcomes that rest on a view of their capabilities and resources to resist, shape, or regulate globalizing schemas and models' (ibid.). Such a view allows for local agency to seek to mediate global models and to shape them into appropriate contextual translations in different historical and political settings.

The quality assurance template has become generalized not only at the level of accountability symbolism, but also in terms of operational modalities (accreditation, audit) and more recently in relation to processes (self-evaluation, site visit, published report, agency follow-up). However, the overall purposes of quality assurance, the specificities and weightings of criteria, the ways in which 'evidence' from evaluations is interpreted, and the consequences of judgments remain open to contextual nuance. In the South African case it was presumed that the accountability symbolism and rationales for quality assurance from the global template were not tied to NPM thinking in an essentialist way and, therefore, permeable to modification by local need. At the same time a number of other generalized elements from the global template, including the methodologies of audit and accreditation, did form part of the new quality assurance system, with the intention that the methodologies would incorporate a social transformation lens in the assessment of arrangements for quality.

4. The Nature of the Policy Influence Mechanisms

The issue of policy influence across borders, within both bilateral and multilateral arrangements, has been analyzed under different rubrics. These include policy borrowing and lending, policy learning, cross-national policy attraction, policy transfer, policy diffusion, policy emulation, as well as 'pinching' and 'copying' (Bennett, 1997, p. 213). Many analytical frameworks and models have been developed to investigate and interpret the phenomenon of 'policy transfer' and 'policy convergence' across countries in the northern hemisphere but also across the North–South divide (Spreen, 2004; Steiner-Khamsi, 2004; Phillips and Ochs, 2004). Important cautions have also been expressed about the vagueness and lack of concrete content in the way many of these rubrics are used. Dale (2007, pp. 58–62) proposes a multidimensional and differentiated frame of reference for thinking about the diversity of globalization effects, identifying five different types of policy transfer mechanisms at work under globalization, in addition to the more traditional forms of policy borrowing and learning. Bennett (1991, p. 225) argues for greater precision and clarity in the different 'labels' used to indicate policy influence, since the labels 'obscure more important differences in emphasis relating to who learns, what is learned and with what effect'. Such approaches make for a more complex and sophisticated view of policy-influence mechanisms than a monocausal account of globalization-induced convergence and assumptions of simple policy isomorphism. Drawing on them holds good promise for a multi-layered and analytically richer account of globalization effects in South African education policy reform.

5. The Connection between Policy Symbolism and Policy Implementation

In his assessment of post-1994 education policy and practice in South Africa, Jansen (2001) argues that the purpose and logic of early education policy-making in South Africa was more about political symbolism to mark the shift from apartheid to a post-apartheid order than about educational change 'on the ground'. For Jansen this first period (1994–99) was about 'establishing the ideological and political credentials of the new government' with an ostensible shift to more pragmatic implementation realities in the next period between 1999 and 2004 (ibid., pp. 272–3).

Many White Papers were produced in the period up to 1999, including one for higher education transformation, which flagged the necessity for a new quality assurance system within a larger canvas of commitments to social justice and social transformation. Jansen's periodization of the new education policy regime may be somewhat overstated, but it is a sober reminder of the vulnerability of an emancipatory political agenda at the interface of the politics of symbolic policy-making and the politics of implementation in South Africa. For the quality assurance project, it raises questions about the pathways from the policy commitments of the quality agency to its implementation systems and procedures. It puts the spotlight on the nature and extent to which the policy symbolism of translation was translated (or translatable) into the operational systems of audit and accreditation, and its normative and operational fit with the NPM elements of the global template. In this regard the questions raised by Phillips and Ochs (2004, p. 11) in their four-stage framework to analyze educational borrowing are also useful, in focusing attention on how 'foreign' practices become absorbed and synthesized' within local contexts.

THE POST-1994 POLITICAL AND POLICY SETTING IN SOUTH AFRICAN HIGHER EDUCATION

Systemic reform initiatives came to South African higher education only in the last decade of the twentieth century. The national reform project followed in the wake of a negotiated political settlement in the country, whose terms set the broad parameters for the nature, possibilities and limits of change and transformation in social policy. The post-1994 political project in South Africa demonstrates the ambition of social policy reform in a developing country that was seeking to transcend its apartheid-era isolation through international benchmarking of its policies.

What explains the attraction to international reform trends and the influence of global policy models in the post-1994 policy change processes? In his look at the literature on 'diffusion analysis', Bennett (1997, p. 214) distinguishes between the 'relative explanatory power of contextual explanations where policy responses are hypothesized to be the by-product of socioeconomic or technological developments, and "diffusion" explanations where policy is shaped through processes of transnational communication and learning'. Both explanations are reflected in South African higher education policy-making, with the watershed transition creating a changed sociopolitical environment that was both local- and global-facing, and within which participation in and communications with transnational networks were accelerated. The perceived benefits of benchmarking with global paradigms were connected to a self-projected 'coming-of-age' status from apartheid 'backwardness' into a globalizing world. Inclusion into global networks was deemed necessary for a national 'modernization' and 'development' agenda, the ideological boundaries and policy choices of which did not necessarily coincide. Jansen's analysis of post-apartheid policy-making indicates the *realpolitik* behind the new government's decision to seek incorporation into the prevailing global political and economic order so as to be able to 'maximize economic gains' (including expectations of foreign direct investments) rather than risk 'continued marginalization' (Jansen, 2004, p. 201), which was regarded as the fate of 'non-adopters' of the dominant policy paradigms of that order.

The change processes included entry into a globalizing world order resonant with ubiquitous discourses about the 'fundamentals' of sociopolitical development and economic growth, and about 'best practice' in relation to governance, accountability and efficiency. Insertion into a range of global networks at the same time as the construction of new policy frameworks for domestic reform brought both policy similarities as a result of the influence and/or adoption of key principles, models and instruments of reform derived from global policy paradigms as well as disjunctures in respect of the local priorities of social justice and democratic reconstruction. The elements of convergence did not necessarily clear the way for the almost automatic triumph of 'neoliberal globalization' over local imperatives (Bundy, 2006; Singh, 2006; Lange, 2006), but they undoubtedly sharpened tensions in relation to what constituted the nature and content of transformatory policy and strategy. They also raised troubling questions about the risks and limits of accommodating potentially contending reconstruction imperatives.

The post-transition reform project in higher education was formally launched in 1995 with the setting up of the National Commission on Higher Education (NCHE), which was tasked with drawing up recommendations for the restructuring of the higher education system. Its comprehensive scope of work was both locally focused and internationally referenced. The NCHE's recommendations were based on a series of analyses of the local conjuncture as well as a global reconnaissance of developments and trends in higher education in both OECD and non-OECD countries. By this stage quality assurance was already becoming visible as a higher education reform strategy in the international policy arena, especially within the UK and European contexts.[5] The power of local social-transformation imperatives was unmistakable in the NCHE's recommendations for increased participation (especially of those who had been historically excluded), greater societal responsiveness, and increased cooperation and partnerships in South African higher education.

The influence of the global was evident in the NCHE's methodology of benchmarking its policy work internationally through the involvement of higher education experts[6] from different countries in all its task teams, the NCHE study visits to higher education systems abroad, and a final discussion at a Salzburg Seminar in 1996 with international participants. A set of debates in the early 1990s about the need to think of policy development in the face of the tensions between equity (social justice with its links to national human rights and democratization goals) and development (economic growth with its links to global macroeconomic models for efficiency and competitiveness) prefigured the inward- and outward-facing dimensions of the NCHE's work (Bundy, 2006, p. 16). This 'Janus-faced' theme was to become a common challenge in the policy development and implementation work that was to follow.

The key policy framework for higher education, the 1997 Education White Paper, located itself consciously within the pressures and demands of globalization as the country pursued a national agenda of 'political democratization, economic reconstruction and development, and redistributive social policies aimed at equity . . . The policy challenge is to ensure that we engage critically and creatively with the global imperatives as we determine our national and regional goals, priorities and responsibilities' (Department of Education, 1997, pp. 1.7–1.8).

The White Paper's own content covered both sides of the tension. There was a package of elements familiar from global reform lexicons (public accountability to those outside of academe; goal-oriented and performance-related public funding; cost-sharing between the public and private beneficiaries of higher education; the reduction of wasteful expenditure, improvement of efficiency and enhancement of quality; national and institutional planning using performance indicators and time-frames, and so on). There was also a strong and explicitly asserted equity and social justice thread. The key principles for the transformation of higher education included equity, redress and democratization as much as effectiveness, efficiency and public accountability.

It was not long into the first decade of reform that critical questions began to surface about the narrowing of the policy agenda and lack of attention to on-the-ground transformation needs. Concerns were raised about whether the right balances were being struck between the global paradigms and local imperatives in order to ensure that the latter did not remain largely symbolic. A number of critics argued that, as the implementation processes unfolded, the global neoliberal reform templates had, in fact, trumped the social justice and transformation agendas contained in the policy agendas. The clearer disjunctures between equity and efficiency discourses in the 2001 *National Plan for Higher Education* and the growing power of the latter were cited as indicators of this trend (Jansen, 2001; Cloete and Maassen, 2002; Bundy, 2006).

The lexicon of NPM thinking was beginning to find its way among the ordering principles for higher education reform. However, concerns about system inefficiencies also had more complex origins relating to social-justice considerations. The apartheid higher education regime had been hugely inefficient as a result of racially based duplication of provision and extremely low participation and throughput rates of students from the majority black population. This had exacerbated the scope and depth of exclusion and inequity, not only in the higher education system but in all societal activities requiring graduate knowledge and skills, including the labor market. From the point of view of access and success in relation to quality education, the equity and efficiency discourses were not conveniently on opposite sides of a neoliberal divide. The continuing trend of negative differences in the equity and efficiency profiles of white and African students was a powerful influence in shaping understandings of quality and the requirements of quality assurance as part of the new reform dispensation.

Enrollment in the public higher education system had almost doubled in the period between 1990 and 2005, and showed a steady increase in the proportion of African and women students[7] (CHE, 2004, p. 62). The expansion in African and female participation rates, however, concealed a number of continuing disparities. In 2004 the national overall participation rate of 20–24-year-olds in higher education was 16 percent, with 61 percent white participation and 12 percent African (Scott et al., 2007, p. 10). The overall participation of Africans who constitute more than 90 percent of the country's population, and especially African and female participation rates in the fields of science, engineering and technology, and business and commerce, remained low a decade after the political transition. The situation in relation to efficiency in delivering graduate outcomes was as bleak. A 2006 study of the cohort in the year 2000 showed that throughput rates were not only low in general but also highly differentiated in terms of race. Only 30 percent of first-time-entry students enrolled in 2000 had graduated within five years and a staggering 56 percent had dropped out (Scott et al., 2007, p. 12).

When these data are further disaggregated in terms of fields of study, race and level of study, the failure of the higher education system to address issues of access or to manage the relationship between equity and quality becomes even more telling. The pattern for graduation in all universities (except for the distance education institution, the University of South Africa) after five years in a professional bachelor degree in subjects that are in high demand in the labor market indicates graduation rates of 83 percent for whites compared to 33 percent for blacks in business/commerce, 64 percent for whites compared to 32 percent for blacks in engineering, and 48 percent for whites compared to 21 percent for blacks in law (Scott et al., 2007, p. 16). A similar situation can be seen in relation to the general academic first bachelor degrees with graduation rates for whites around double those for blacks.

In seeking to address the racially skewed patterns of enrollments and graduation rates in higher education, it was not surprising that efficiency concerns and social justice objectives converged in defining quality and setting the parameters for the scope of quality assurance processes.[8] Although there was consensus on the need for policy interventions to address the low rates and patterns of participation and throughput in higher education, there were differences in the discursive framing of the rationales for such interventions. On the one hand, interventions to grow enrollments and graduations were represented as necessary to the production of the high-level human resources required for the achievement of social and economic growth targets set for the country. This was in line with a globally dominant human capital approach to the relationship between higher education, economic development and employment. In another vein the interventions were also understood as a massive human rights and social justice challenge that required targeted equity and redress strategies to increase the participation and success rates of students from the majority population of the country, given the legacies of longstanding patterns of discrimination and exclusion.

The associations between quality (with graduation rates as one proxy for quality) and racial exclusion/racial advantage were painfully clear. The need to engage with this legacy was both a political and an educational task, translating into the connection between social transformation and quality in the new evaluation system. At one level change was a quantitative matter of growing the numbers of black and women graduates. However, even within a human rights approach to increasing African and female participation, the question had to be addressed as to what constituted quality education in a transforming dispensation. Was it to be the same only writ large, with its access and success benefits more fairly redistributed to a larger number of the previously excluded, or did it require

alternative conceptualizations and approaches relating to the new political and normative aspirations for social transformation? The convergences and dissonances in the
policy discourses between globally resonant human capital and locally insistent human
rights approaches to social change and transformation in higher education brought to
the fore questions about the scope and content of a transformation-framed quality education and how it was to be assessed.

The tension between economic efficiency and social justice approaches in addressing
issues of widening participation and enhanced social inclusion is by no means specific to
the South African policy setting, but prevails in many educational systems, as pointed
out by Rizvi and Lingard (2010, p. 140). The specific South African challenge, nevertheless, was to ensure that both efficiency and social justice goals were part of a combined
policy package that continued to reflect the political and normative principles of the
larger transformation project, especially within the politics of implementation.

The political and policy setting in South Africa at the time when quality assurance was
proposed as one of three steering instruments for higher education reform and when the
details of the system were being developed reflected a country looking to deal with past
legacies and future identities through assembling a number of system elements into a
policy *ensemble* that would have both local legitimacy and international comparability.
Constructing a transformed post-apartheid higher education system meant incorporating both locally referenced transformation imperatives as well as international models
(especially from OECD countries) in policy 'solutions' that were framed in response to
the problems of fragmentation, inequitable funding and quality gaps in the apartheid
inheritance. Some analysts saw the predominant impetus in the new education policies as
coming from outside the country. Jansen (2004, p. 199) argues that the 'emergence of a
whole suite of higher education policies – from institutional mergers to quality assurance
to performance-based funding – can be attributed to a range of cross-national influences
on both sides of the Atlantic'. By the time the new South African evaluation system was
launched in 2004, quality assurance had morphed into a key element of global strategy
for higher education regulation through the advocacy and initiatives of multilateral
organizations such as the OECD, UNESCO and the World Bank.

The manner and extent to which the globally templated quality assurance 'solution'
was 'indigenized' (Phillips and Ochs, 2004, pp. 9–15) and implemented in South Africa in
order to take on the strong equity and democratization imperatives of the local context
is addressed in the next section.

THE SOUTH AFRICAN QUALITY ASSURANCE SYSTEM

The dualism between local transformation demands and global templates for higher
education regulation manifested itself in the task of developing a new quality assurance
system as part of the higher education reform. Quality assurance has become a powerful,
almost self-evident part of the global regulatory armoury for higher education. Equity
and transformation demands were compelling moral, political and economic reference
points in the reform of South African higher education and, as such, informed the thinking of the quality agency about the purposes of quality assurance in a transforming
higher education system. How were these impulses made to coexist, given that the values

and orientations of the global templates for quality assurance regulation typically do not reference issues of social justice in definitions of quality or conceptions of regulatory accountability?

In the development of the post-apartheid quality assurance system, the global–local identity challenges for the South African quality agency tasked with the responsibility for quality regulation can be divided into four types. These are: the policy environment and legislative mandate of the agency and what these made possible but also what they foreclosed; the international quality assurance setting and its direct and indirect influences on the emerging system; the premises about the scope and goals of quality assurance that underpinned the new system; and the translation of the symbolic commitments to social justice and social transformation into operational strategies and procedures.

1. Policy Content and Mandate

The *National Plan for Higher Education* (2001) reiterated the position of the earlier policy documents that the higher education system would be steered through the three instruments of planning, funding and quality. Planning and funding were in the hands of the government department in charge of higher education. Regulatory oversight for quality was vested in a new independent statutory body, the Council on Higher Education (CHE), set up in 1999 to provide advice to the Minister of Education and to take responsibility for quality assurance through a Higher Education Quality Committee (HEQC). The combination of planning, funding and quality assurance was a policy package for steering reform that was familiar from the global reform lexicon but again infused with the White Paper vision of social transformation and its goals and targets relating to equity and redress.

Issues of social justice and social transformation were strongly embedded in all areas of post-1994 social policy formation – in the Constitution of the country, in new legislation in all fields, and in public policy and implementation frameworks. Indicators and proxies for evaluating social progress in a post-apartheid dispensation also referenced equity and social transformation. Within higher education the social justice objectives had been flagged in various legal frameworks and policy documents, finding expression in educational targets set by the government (*National Plan*, 2001) and informing planning and resource allocation strategies at the institutional level. The connections between quality and social justice and social transformation were made in a number of legislative and policy frameworks. In the government's *Education White Paper 3: A Programme for the Transformation of Higher Education*, which formed the basis for the Higher Education Act of 1997, quality is identified as a guiding principle for the transformation of higher education in a package that includes equity, redress and democratization, in addition to effectiveness and efficiency, academic freedom, institutional autonomy and public accountability. The Higher Education Act, the South African Qualifications Authority Act, and the Skills Development Act flag the role of quality assurance in 'delivering key national objectives of equity and development' (HEQC, 2001, p. 1). On the basis of this legislative trail, the *Founding Document* of the HEQC was able to make formal connections between social justice, quality and quality assurance. It thus signalled as a guiding principle for the work of the quality agency the intention to link the achievement of quality to equity.

The stipulation from the Higher Education Act of 1997, based on the earlier White Paper, was that the HEQC would have the functions of program accreditation, audit of the quality assurance mechanisms of institutions, and quality promotion without specifying how these functions were to be discharged. Halpin and Troyna (1995, p. 304) argue that, since cross-national policy 'borrowing' has less to do with the success of policies in their originating countries than with 'legitimating other related policies', governments are 'more interested in the borrowed policy's political symbolism than its details'. In this case the task of developing the detail was the responsibility of the independent statutory agency to which the quality assurance function had been assigned. Not only were there no directives for system goals, implementation strategies or operational procedures from the government; at the time the advisory mandate of the CHE also included the possibility of providing advice to government on matters of quality promotion and quality assurance.

This left the agency relatively free to conceptualize the relationship between higher education reform goals and the goals and purposes of quality assurance, as well as to consider an enlargement of the notions of accountability and quality in relation to equity and transformation challenges within a restructured higher education system. However, the national systemic choices and stipulations from the topmost policy-making layer in government did mark out a particular policy trajectory for the work of the quality agency, bearing out Ball's observation (Ball, 2006, p. 49) that one of the effects of policy is the fact that it 'changes the possibilities we have for thinking "otherwise", thus it limits our responses to change . . .'. The situation also reflected the complexities of policy-making for quality assurance at different levels in the system – by government at one level and the quality agency at another. The policy decision of government was to mandate the role of quality assurance as a regulatory tool for higher education governance (system-steering) rather than as a national education improvement strategy designed in the first instance to tackle grave quality problems on the ground. This was accompanied by the stipulation that audit and accreditation would constitute the main methodologies of quality assurance instead of a multidimensional suite of targeted capacity development and quality improvement interventions (accompanied by relevant accountability arrangements). Such a starting point rendered the new quality assurance system more vulnerable to the NPM dimensions of the global template, although not entirely trapped within or paralyzed by them.

2.   International Quality Assurance Links and Influences

The White Paper positioning of quality assurance as a principal lever in the restructuring and steering of South African higher education signalled a role and status for it that was different from the function of pre-1994 quality assurance in the national system. Its appearance as a reform strategy was in line with the global spread of external evaluations of higher education institutions and their academic programs as part of the overarching arrangements for national higher education governance and regulation. However, the growing phenomenon of formalized requirements for external evaluation in higher education was not only familiar from international practice but also known and experienced in the country through local evaluation systems that had been in place before and soon after 1994. Institutional audits were undertaken in the UK at the time that the South

African NCHE was conducting its work but had also been initiated in South Africa in 1996 as a voluntary improvement-oriented activity by the universities' Vice Chancellors' association. Program accreditation was familiar from US higher education but also as an established part of mandatory system-level evaluations of the *technikons*[9] since 1988.

These local pre-HEQC systems also had sought to benchmark their systems internationally through participation in the work of the International Network for Quality Assurance Agencies in Higher Education (INQAAHE). The HEQC itself tracked international trends in quality assurance in the process of developing its own systems, but also sought to reference existing local systems through drawing on findings from a CHE evaluation of them commissioned in 2000.[10] The search for information and benchmarks for quality assurance focused on countries such as the UK, the USA, The Netherlands and Australia, but also India, Nigeria and Hong Kong in order to be able to draw on Northern and Southern perspectives and experiences. Cooperation agreements with the agencies in the UK, Australia and India formalized a variety of interactions with those countries, including the use of their institutional auditors. The HEQC became a member of the INQAAHE and the agency's senior staff served on its board and participated in its activities and debates. This range of international involvements contributed to the diffusion of influence from global quality assurance models and not only directly through the work of the agency. Interlocutors and implementers from the higher education institutions also had their own readings, not only of national policy but also of international discourses, reinforced through participation in the professional activities of international quality assurance networks. Both within the national system and also within individual institutions, the circulation and diffusion of quality assurance discourses and understandings of 'good practice' between the global and the local increased the exposure to the powerful shaping influence of global benchmarks for quality assurance while at the same time deepening the challenges of giving substance and effect to the local transformation agenda in the quality assurance system.

3. Premises

As is familiar from the global march of quality assurance,[11] the rationales for and anticipated impacts of increased regulatory evaluation are often strongly associated with economic and consumer interests that have become pre-eminent in framing the social purposes of higher education at the same time as non-economic goals have become increasingly symbolic in the process of measuring higher education's achievements. Although external evaluation is part of higher education governance and regulation in many countries where multiple social inequalities are prevalent and various struggles for social change under way, issues of social justice and social transformation rarely have a direct and explicit focus within evaluation rationales and systems. They are not among the dimensions of what counts as quality or excellence in the assessment of performance and achievement in and through higher education. Attesting to achievements in relation to them is, therefore, not included in the lists of purposes drawn up for external quality assurance.[12]

This absence is what the national quality agency sought to address. Despite the tensions and contradictions between the global lineages of quality accountability regimes and the social justice imperatives that underpinned the post-apartheid restructuring of higher education, the working premise of the quality agency was that the available policy development and implementation spaces would be utilized to mediate the market and consumer models of quality assurance with a broader underpinning vision of equity and social transformation.[13] Given the historical legacies of exclusion and the human rights and democratization agenda of the reform, the key notions of accountability and quality were reframed using an equity and transformation lens. It was assumed that in a society that was striving to democratize and become more just, higher education in general and the sphere of evaluation in particular was a legitimate arena for the pursuit of transformative goals.

A strong emphasis on the role of higher education in nurturing employment skills has shaped assessment criteria for institutional effectiveness (e.g. the responsiveness of institutional program planning to labor market needs) and educational effectiveness (e.g. the relevance of graduate competencies to the world of work). What the appropriate educational quality outcomes and student competencies would be in advancing social transformation and public-good goals and how one could assess institutional and program effectiveness in this regard became a strong normative consideration in the work of the quality agency. However, this interest was viewed more as a basis for dialogic engagement with institutional role-players than a matter of quantitative measurement given the immense difficulties in developing appropriate 'indicators' in this regard.

The human rights and democratization themes in the new social policy frameworks made it possible to think beyond the connection, familiar from the global template, between evaluation and predominantly economic and consumer interests. It was assumed that such concerns formed only one dimension of the social setting of higher education and that other dimensions relating to local transformation struggles were equally valid imperatives of which to take account. It was also assumed that the connection between quality assurance and neoliberal values was not essentialist but reflected particular policy choices and challenges, and that other choices based on wider interpretations of the social purposes of higher education were possible in considering evaluation goals and methods.

A recent analysis seeking to theorize the interrelationships between equity, access, success and quality argues in similar vein for the 'uncoupling' of quality 'from the necessity of a neoliberal framing allowing broader interpretations arising from more inclusive ideologies' (Gidley et al., 2010, p. 123). The often simultaneous role of higher education in both reproducing and undercutting asymmetries of power and social inequality is a challenge for policy planners engaged in higher education reform, as evident in analyses of the relationship between higher education and social transformation (Brennan et al., 2004). Despite the difficulties of assessing such shifts, it was assumed by the agency that the inclusion of social transformation requirements in higher education evaluation systems was a legitimate public policy choice whose effects were intended to help tilt the balance in South African higher education in the direction of social transformation over the gravitational pull of social reproduction.

4. System Details

How was the symbolic policy commitment to equity and transformation translated into operational detail within the mandated audit and accreditation systems? Before addressing this, it is necessary to clarify how the quality agency understood the connection and difference between social justice and social transformation. At the time of its establishment in 2004, faced with the quality-related legacies of social exclusion, the HEQC consciously invoked the idea of social justice in its quality assurance system primarily in relation to race and gender equity and redress. This included looking at institutional policies for access and success in respect of both staff and students, including affirmative policies for redressing demographic imbalances and capacity development interventions. Here it was taking its cue from documents such as the *White Paper on Higher Education*, which had postulated equity and redress as guiding principles for the restructuring of higher education. However, the HEQC also invoked the idea of social transformation, which had a broader set of philosophical and political connotations for thinking about change in higher education, including but going beyond compensatory justice and demographic representation for the formerly excluded. Lange and Singh (2010, p. 54) point out that 'Issues of equity in South Africa encompass dimensions of race, class, gender, disability, the urban/rural divide, and adult access'. Despite the multidimensionality of exclusion, the demands of race and gender equity had been strongly asserted in many struggles. However, the notion of transformation as a more complex metaphor for social and educational change was invoked in order to ensure that the equity challenges would be addressed within a framework that took account of, for example, curriculum reform, changes in institutional culture, innovative scholarship, academic freedom, and public-good engagement as much as it did race and gender diversity (ibid., p. 57).

Issues of class have become more prominent within the equity challenges as demographic shifts have altered race and gender balances more positively in higher education. Correspondingly, social transformation goals have become even more crucial in a period of policy consolidation, especially where the 'pragmatism' of implementation has begun to subdue and even displace the emancipatory intent in the political project of higher education reform.

One of the first steps of the agency in its early systems development was to add the crucial function of quality-related capacity development to its already existing legislated responsibilities for audit, accreditation and quality promotion. This was an important signal about the necessity to support all institutions, but especially those that had been historically disadvantaged, in the task of improving quality and developing mechanisms to safeguard quality. The HEQC included all three core function areas in its evaluation system, though with differing degrees of focus. It 'did not separate the work of higher education institutions, that is, teaching and learning, research, and community engagement from broader processes of social transformation. On the contrary the HEQC argued that the fitness for purpose of higher education institutions, that is, what institutions do in relation to the three core functions, was a "site" of transformation' (Lange and Singh, 2010, p. 59). The inclusion of community engagement in its evaluation framework was particularly important since this bestowed formal recognition for the first time on concrete higher education–community linkages beyond mission rhetoric and steered it towards becoming part of institutional planning, quality assurance and social responsiveness frameworks.

QUALITY

The definition of quality used by the HEQC encompassed 'fitness *of* purpose' *apropos* national goals and priorities as well as the requirements of social development. This was in addition to the standard elements familiar from other quality assurance systems – 'fitness for purpose', value for money, and the development of individual capabilities. The 'fitness-of-purpose' issue was viewed as the point of connection to the national imperatives of social transformation facing all higher education institutions in the post-1994 reconstruction.[14]

To the development of individual student capabilities was added the social transformation dimension. This was inevitable in a context where the fate of individual advancement was so closely tied to necessary large-scale societal change, but it was also a signal of the importance of the larger societal good over and above private individual benefits. The applicability of the 'value-for-money' element, a powerful component of the global template, was not spelled out very clearly except for a concern about arpartheid wastefulness on the one hand and the need for increased investments in quality improvement on the other. It has not had as strong a focus as the transformation issues in the first quality assurance cycle of the HEQC.

The HEQC included the transformation imperative in its definition of quality, in its criteria and operational procedures for all its functions (institutional audits, program accreditation and national reviews), and in its recommendations for quality improvement. Questions were posed and 'evidence' required on the alignment between institutional transformation mission, planning, resource allocation and quality improvement; on new curricula and pedagogies; on new research themes and community partnerships that were responsive to the needs and priorities of an emerging democracy; and on addressing the negative effects of power and prejudice in institutional cultures. Institutions were required to address the quality–social justice–social transformation interface in their self-evaluation documents. Institutional leadership, academics, students, and other internal and external constituencies were interviewed on issues of institutional mission and social transformation. Recommendations for action were made by the evaluation panels and the agency on the implications of transformation issues for educational processes and achievements.

Taking demographic diversity into account in relation to peers and experts meant a change in the race and gender profiles of the evaluation panels. The provision of joint-training programs for experienced and new evaluators sought to professionalize their work in general but in particular to equip them with common understandings of the quality–transformation nexus and how to assess it in different institutional contexts.[15] The issue of social transformation in higher education was not defined in an unequivocal way by the HEQC, but used in a dialogic manner to engage institutional interlocutors on issues of demographic fairness, curriculum reform, institutional culture, new research directions and new social partnerships. The transformation issues within evaluation findings, especially within the context of institutional audits, were intended to be developmental recommendations rather than 'make-or-break' judgments that would carry sanctions, loss of public funds or rewards. Although the agency view was that it was seeking a balance among the potentially conflicting aspects of the 'statutory requirements of quality assurance, the transformation requirements of social development, and safeguarding the integrity of the academic enterprise' (HEQC, 2001, Foreword, p. iv), there were concerns and criticisms when the system was first implemented that the transformation focus was a political stipulation rather than one about education quality and that it threatened the academic autonomy of institutions (Luckett, 2007).

In discharging its policy development and implementation responsibilities, the quality agency did make the shift beyond policy symbolism (Jansen, 2001, p. 252). The symbolic commitments to social justice and social transformation were translated into the implementation systems of the agency, although there remain differing views about the nature and efficacy of that translation in respect of both transformational progress and quality improvement. The use of a transformation lens in the quality assurance system made for a contextually nuanced application of a global regulatory template. But it also posed sharp questions about the possibilities for equity and transformation imperatives to be given substantial effect within a quality assurance system that operated, in many respects, as a conventional evaluation regime. Could the dialogic and managerialist dimensions of a hybrid quality assurance system be held in balance, coming as they did from different ideological strands in the local and global environments?

POSSIBILITIES, LIMITS AND CONTRADICTIONS

Possibilities

The current contours of formal quality assurance according to global templates are well known. They are tied to requirements for the demonstration and verification of accountability, often linked to public funding (value for money), external stakeholder demands and 'consumer' confidence in educational provision. Calhoun (2006, p. 8) refers to this as the 'instrumental evaluation of universities as providers of private goods'. The post-1994 political transition and the reform spaces that it opened up enabled the quality assurance agency to act on different premises.

The paradigms and policy frameworks of an economically overdetermined conception of higher education were deemed to be an insufficient basis for a new quality assurance system in a context where the social purposes of higher education were being defined across a spectrum of issues relating as much to democratic development as to economic development. The powerful steering lever of external regulation was used to address quality issues with an equity and transformation lens. Operating on the premise that global paradigms could be negotiated and reoriented for local purposes allowed the agency to argue that the interfaces between quality, equity and social transformation could be evaluated as a legitimate dimension of quality assurance.

This starting point also made it possible to explore the knowledge and skill competencies required to equip graduates to live and work in a transforming society, and contribute to struggles within them for greater levels of democratic participation and social justice. The effectiveness of the transformation take-up within institutional-level quality assurance depended to a large extent on institutional histories and their capacities to make a meaningful connection between quality and transformation (beyond demographic representativeness). But the agency was able to use its regulatory authority to make the quality–transformation connection into an essential and acknowledged part of the national quality assurance system, a connection with whose requirements all institutions had to engage.

Conceptions of quality and excellence in South Africa had already been politicized through their strong associations with racially based access and success within higher education. Conceptualizing the purposes and goals of quality assurance anew in such a context made it possible to explore questions about different measures of quality in higher education. What spheres of activity and what achievements can or should be taken into account when making a judgment about quality in education or about the enabling conditions for educational quality to be achieved? Input measures like staff credentials and output indicators like graduation rates and research outputs are familiar proxies for quality in many systems. The approach taken by the HEQC made it possible to explore the question as to whether the contribution of an institution or program to the advancement of social transformation goals could count as one measure of a quality education, especially in light of the fact that the goals set for higher education often include the advancement of the public good, citizenship readiness and so on.

The insertion and use of a global regulatory template (infused with NPM norms) in a social and educational context rich with social justice and social transformation challenges required a mediation of both the symbolic as well as the operational dimensions of conventional external quality assurance. The mediation was successful in giving a contextual distinctiveness and a normative identity connected to local imperatives to the new quality assurance system. It is not so clear, however, that even the use of a transformation lens within a global template for regulation could keep at bay some of the worst of the NPM influences in higher education.

Limits

Although the reform spaces opened up the possibility for reframing the goals and purposes of quality assurance as well as understandings of quality, the power of the global model continued to exert influence at various levels within the higher education system. So, for example, although local quality agencies have regulatory authority to require higher education institutions to give attention to specified contextual priorities, how institutions do so and what other considerations they take into account in quality reputation-building are not within the jurisdiction or control of the agency. The post-1994 context opened up the global policy arena for system level policy-makers to draw upon. It also enabled South African higher education institutions to become part of wider international networks and to articulate reputational aspirations influenced by, for example, global ranking systems, OECD indicators, and good practice benchmarks from INQAAHE and other international quality assurance organizations. The issue of the transnational mobility of professionals and students, premised on the comparability of quality and qualifications across institutions and systems in a globalizing higher education world, also meant that institutionally preferred definitions of quality sometimes privileged global trends rather than nationally self-referential priorities.

The limits of local modification were also becoming clearer as the implementation unfolded. As indicated earlier, although the goals of quality assurance were interpreted using a social transformation optic and translated into criteria that allowed for an exploration of the link between quality and social transformation, this had to be undertaken through the methodologies of audit and accreditation. The South African system remains a recognizable quality assurance system from the point of view of widespread quality assurance practice in other countries.[16] The social justice–social transformation optic helped to nuance but did not necessarily alter the core identity of the system as a quality assurance regime.

This poses the question of how far down the local road a national initiative in reorienting quality assurance can go in the face of the power of the global paradigm to steer towards conformity and convergence with what is regarded as 'global good practice'. This is even more salient when national agencies and individual higher education institutions seek the benefits of membership of global networks through demonstrating their professional credentials and seeking international recognition for achievements measured against the global templates (in addition to local requirements).

It was also to be expected that differences in policy translations and implementation emphases among the different networks of actors responsible for the three steering instruments of planning, funding and quality assurance (government and independent statutory body), and the absence within implementation politics of an integrated system-wide engagement with the meanings and content requirements of social transformation, would set limits to the power of the transformation impetus in the quality assurance system.

In the global–local interplay, a further set of limits on how far the localization initiative could go in reconfiguring the goals and processes of a quality assurance system derives from the hybridity of the model itself. How could a policy package, which sought to graft together approaches to quality and accountability from two different genealogies – one from the global template informed by NPM understandings of efficiency and cost-effectiveness and the other from a local setting informed by strong equity and transformation imperatives – hold the different contending elements together in an operational system? The industrial, management and financial accounting roots of higher education evaluation are often held up by critics as 'proof' of its identity as a neoliberal instrument for higher education reform. The premises and practices of the 'evaluative state' represent what is ostensibly a 'natural' evolution from such roots to a legitimating quality assurance philosophy and policy package for ensuring the value-for-money, efficiency and consumer responsiveness of higher education. This has become standard fare in a range of historically different implementation contexts around the world.

Such a lineage has given quality evaluation an ideological orientation somewhat at odds with an emancipation agenda of social justice and social transformation. In the face of such a dominant conception of external evaluation as evident in the global template, was it possible to graft a social transformation agenda onto what is usually regarded as an NPM strategy? The broader, more progressive intent that is linked to the transformation agenda is potentially vulnerable to serious compromise by the origins, lineages, values and effects of current quality evaluation systems and approaches.[17] It was possible to overlay 'world model' notions of quality and accountability with social justice and social transformation imperatives, but was this enough to redeem the rest of the system elements and their potentially negative effects? Equally, it could be argued that ceding notions of quality and accountability to an NPM frame of reference, in a context where social transformation imperatives required a broader framing of both, was not an option in the construction of a new quality assurance system. However, the preconditions for and limits of a successful hybridization were insufficiently interrogated at the time, given the euphoria of the transition and the prevailing sense of 'exceptionalism' among the policy elites in the country (Mamdani, 1996).

Contradictions

The accountability imperative is, as indicated earlier, a powerful driver of external quality assurance. Critiques of this emphasis on higher education accountability are well known: it is economically overdetermined; it shifts the focus from academic self-regulation to accountability by external stakeholders and internal 'clients' (students); and it signals a loss of trust and confidence in academe (Trow, 1994; Morley, 2003). It may also be the case that quality assurance helps to strengthen accountability requirements more than it has positive effects on educational quality. Brennan and Shah (1997, p. 164) highlight research on external quality assurance that shows only 'an indirect and fairly limited effect on quality improvement' but a clear role in relation to accountability.

Harvey (1997, p. 134) argues that the perceptions of quality and its value among academics have been colored by the 'politicization of quality' through the pressures of external accountability as well as the 'intrusive paraphernalia of quality monitoring'. It could be argued that inserting social transformation objectives into higher education evaluation further strengthened the accountability dimension in South African higher education (albeit in relation to a public-good imperative). Moreover, although there are indications that some institutions and programs are using the external systems reflectively to direct attention to internal quality issues beyond compliant behaviors, the quality improvement gains are as yet unclear, especially in making the move from setting up institutional systems for quality assurance to actually improving quality outcomes.

The enlargement of quality assurance accountability to include social transformation concerns reflects a further contradiction relating to the regulatory relationship between the state and higher education. Despite the shift from a state control to a state steering model in European higher education in the mid-1980s, Neave (1998) points out that one of the effects of the hegemony of the 'evaluative state' is steering higher education closer to national priorities. Such priorities include social transformation in South Africa just as much as economic competitiveness in global markets is an explicit national priority in OECD countries. Adding social justice and social transformation to the evaluation slate does not diminish or weaken the trend of using evaluation to steer higher education towards priorities set by the state. It only widens the net to include national priorities more directly relevant to the public good. This may help to make the notion of the public good more concrete and less symbolic within higher education. However, it could also become an extension of an already powerful state-driven accountability net over higher education.

The quality assurance agency stressed the importance of strengthening academic agency within formal evaluations and the necessity for dialogic engagement with academics on the quality–social transformation interface. However, the intensified levels of institutional planning required for managing complex institutional and systemic transitions within the comprehensive restructuring of the higher education system, including the setting up of institution-wide quality assurance systems, has contributed to power imbalances between academe and managers, evident in many reforming higher education systems across the globe (Clark, 1983). The agency was not able to control the downstream institutional interpretations and translations of quality assurance into managerialist systems, a familiar outcome of audit requirements in many higher education systems (Kogan, 2004, pp. 2–3). The likely appeal for academics in including a social transformation lens in external evaluation is uncertain, despite the opportunity it poses for examining the connections between their education and training work and the conditions of social inequality in their work settings. This is because of the potential added workload, increased reporting and possibly higher levels of intrusive surveillance of what may be considered to lie in the arena of private political views and/or academic freedom. A social transformation optic in quality assurance, intended as a progressive change strategy in a society seeking greater levels of justice and democracy and premised on an open-ended dialogic notion of transformation, could turn into a rigid and doctrinaire approach, thus becoming a threat to academic freedom and institutional autonomy.

Probably the most potent structural contradiction for the quality agency relates to its ambition to facilitate a system-wide environment for quality improvement within which access and achievement are more fairly distributed in a transforming society through the collective capacities of all institutions. The introduction of formal evaluation mechanisms, even with a transformation focus, into a landscape that has been reconfigured but is still characterized by historically shaped differences in institutional capacities to internalize and benefit from quality assurance and quality improvement strategies, carries the potential of deepening or maintaining the quality divide between different parts of the higher education system.

CONCLUSION

Despite the limits of a negotiated settlement, the post-1994 sociopolitical environment in South Africa was not a 'steady-state' context for policy change where the outcomes were only modifications and readjustments of existing policy as a result of ongoing cross-national interactions in a globally networked world. The historic reconfiguration of the political system created the opportunity to rethink the very foundations of social policy. Unsurprisingly, this opened up the policy-making processes to the influences of international policy discourses while simultaneously taking on local demands for social justice and social transformation. Policy learning was unavoidable not only in relation to the messages from the global templates, but also in grappling with the translation of transformation norms and ideals into implementable policy frameworks. What were the effects of the influence of the global templates and were they sufficiently mediated by the local imperatives relating to social justice, social transformation and democratization?

The critique that global templates in their NPM incarnations trumped local transformation imperatives, especially as policy implementation got under way, is important as an indicative concern for the fate of the country's emancipation social project. It may, however, be in need of greater analytical and empirical specificity in relation to higher education policy-making in order to provide a more detailed understanding of the nature and scope of the policy influences as well as the content and impact of the convergences and divergences between global and local policy in South Africa.

One of the critical distinctions made by Dale (2007, p. 52) is whether globalization policy effects apply only to policy programs and organization or extend more substantially (and problematically) to include policy goals as well. A detailed look at convergences and dissonances between local and global policy imperatives across the full continuum of policy goals, strategies, instruments, processes and outcomes could provide a more substantial basis for assessing the success of local mediations of global templates or the trumping effects of those same templates. The quality agency's postulation of goals for quality assurance that were different from the global template must be juxtaposed against its use of instruments from that same template and judged, most importantly, against the quality–transformation linked outcomes relating to these different goals. This is a task that remains to be undertaken as the impacts of the first cycle of quality assurance begin to show themselves more clearly.

For the quality agency, opting to use a locally referenced transformation lens to mediate a global template for higher education regulation was to choose to operate in a constant struggle mode in managing different orders of contradiction so as not to let the values of the global template predominate. So, for example, the requirements of accountability, efficiency and stakeholder interests familiar from the global quality assurance template were not absent from the agency's concerns. However, in the South African context, these requirements could be ambivalently read, both as a legitimate set of tasks for the social transformation agenda within higher education but also as a neoliberal regulatory formula for higher education governance. The greater degree of transparency about educational processes and outcomes, which is now associated with quality assurance, could be read as a contribution to strengthening public access to information in a country where the institutionalization of democratic structures was still at an early stage, but it could also be considered, as in other countries, as an instrument of the 'evaluative state' (Bennett, 1997, p. 220). The initiatives to benchmark quality assurance approaches internationally was about recognition and credentialing within new global networks, but it did not exclude the possibility of relevant learning about what works and does not work in cross-national experience, especially from other countries in the global South. Rizvi and Lingard (2010, p. 185) point out that ostensibly contradictory values like 'efficiency' and 'equity' are generally part of public policies everywhere. The decisive issue in relation to the power of NPM paradigms has to do with 'how these values are assembled and allocated . . . politically mediated by particular national traditions . . . [and] discursively formed within particular social imaginaries'.

Having chosen a transformation lens for quality assurance as a founding principle of its work leaves the quality agency with the ongoing struggle to keep present, in its own work of implementation as well as in institutional understandings of external evaluation, the idea that the quality assurance system is a hybrid project seeking constantly to absorb a global template for higher education regulation into the social imaginary of the transformation project.[18] How much potential there is for tipping the balance in a long-term and sustained way in the direction of the latter remains an open question.

NOTES

1. Stephen Ball (2006, p. 43) cites Foucault's view of his books as toolboxes and the possibilities for elements from them to be used as tools with chosen intent. 'All my books . . . are little tool boxes . . . if people want to open them, to use this sentence or that idea as a screwdriver or spanner to short-circuit,

discredit or smash systems of power, including eventually those from which my books have emerged . . . so much better!' Ball himself argues that what is needed in policy analysis 'is a toolbox of diverse concepts and theories', so as to cope better with 'the complexity and scope of policy analysis' (ibid.). I have drawn on this idea to characterize the predominant global policy-change package as a 'toolbox' from which quality assurance has emerged as a strategic tool for deployment in different national and regional settings.

2. Since the early 1990s in South Africa, the notion of transformation has been used to signify social change more generally and within higher education in particular. The expectation about these changes is that they are not only all-encompassing and deep-rooted, but also have a clear emancipation intent, aligned to the values and aspirations of a society that is more inclusive, egalitarian and democratic. This is despite substantially different understandings of and contestations over what democracy, justice or equality entail. The notion has evolved in political strategy and policy content from its usages in the pre-1994 anti-apartheid struggle, through the early days of public policy development soon after 1994 to more recent versions a decade and a half later. Enver Motala's unpublished paper – 'Transformation revisited' (2004) – provides a comprehensive conceptual, political and historical analysis of the term in South Africa and the nuances and shifts in its use. It remains a contested multidimensional term whose key points of reference include initiatives to change race, class and gender profiles, especially in leadership positions; to alter hugely unequal distributions of income and asset wealth and asymmetries of institutionalized power; to construct and strengthen democratic institutions and practices in the country; and to increase public and citizen participation in democratic decision-making. The scope and content of the quality agency's use of it is indicated in the body of the chapter.

3. The new system commenced in 2004 and the first cycle of quality assurance is yet to be completed. The agency had a formal evaluation of its work in 2009, see www.che.ac.za. An in-depth analysis of the impact of the quality assurance system, especially of its social justice–social transformation ambitions, is still to be undertaken.

4. The perception that global higher education models are generalizable often obscures the fact that 'global' is in effect consonant with 'Anglo-American–European' ideas and imperatives, and that it reflects processes of problem identification and solution finding that are geopolitically specific but globally influential (Marginson and van der Wende, 2007, p. 8).

5. See Sursock (2010); INQAAHE was established in 1991; external quality assurance in countries such as the UK and The Netherlands has undergone several reconfigurations (Lewis, 2009).

6. Bennett's view about issues entering domestic policy debates as 'objective evidence' (1997, p. 229) is useful in order to understand the role of both international and local experts in influencing the direction of policy debates.

7. This section draws heavily on Lange and Singh (2010).

8. See Sayed's analysis (Sayed, 2004, pp. 247–65) of teacher education in South Africa for a similar argument about convergences in efficiency and equity rationales for reform interventions.

9. These are polytechnic-type institutions that were renamed universities of technology as part of the reform and restructuring of higher education in South Africa.

10. See CHE Evaluation of SERTEC (Certification Council for Technikon Education) and the Quality Promotion Unit, 2000, at www.che.ac.za.

11. See as a proxy indicator the membership growth and spread in INQAAHE from eight members in 1991 to more than 200 in the current period.

12. See Evalsed, in Brennan and Shah (1997), p. 158.

13. The HEQC in South Africa was not the first in attempting to insert social justice issues into external evaluation systems in higher education. In the USA there had been a history of policy interventions to increase higher education access to those historically excluded on grounds of race, ethnicity and gender. The response to such inequalities had, since the Civil Rights Act of 1964, been couched in the language of 'affirmative action' and later 'diversity', and had manifested itself in changed policies and practices relating to student access, financial aid, faculty hiring, curriculum reform, changes in pedagogy and so on. In some instances diversity had also been an explicit component of accreditation systems that evaluated institutional and program effectiveness and student achievements and outcomes, such as the approach of the Western Association of Schools and Colleges (WASC) operating in California. Diversity issues in WASC systems dates back to the early 1980s as a response to the changing demography in California and within its HEIs, and ending in 2006 with Proposition 209, a piece of state legislation that outlawed any initiative to give due consideration to matters of race and ethnicity in public education and other public sector activities, including the evaluation work of WASC.

14. See Criterion One of the *Criteria for Institutional Audits*, CHE publication, 2004: 6, at www.che.ac.za.

15. See Lange and Singh (2010) for a more detailed account of the HEQC's systems, and especially the equity and transformation challenges in implementation.

16. A recent external evaluation of the HEQC (with international participants), in addition to using local

reference points in the evaluation, also took into account the agency's compliance with the INQAAHE *Guidelines for Good Practice in Quality Assurance*, intended for use by agencies worldwide to benchmark their work (www.inquaahe.org).
17. See the responses in Lange (2006) and Singh (2006) to Bundy (2006).
18. Here I draw on Spreen's instructive analysis (Spreen, 2004, pp. 221–36) of the phenomenon of concealment of the international origins of borrowed policies in relation to school education policymaking in South Africa.

REFERENCES

Appadurai, A. (1996), *Modernity at Large: Cultural Dimensions of Globalisation,* Minneapolis, MN: University of Minnesota Press.
Ball, S. (2006), 'What is policy: texts, trajectories and toolboxes', *Education Policy and Social Class,* Oxford and New York: Routledge, pp. 43–53.
Bennett, C. (1997), 'Understanding ripple effects: the cross-national adoption of policy instruments for bureaucratic accountability', *Governance, 10* (3), 213–33.
Bleiklie, I. (2000), 'Policy regimes and policy making', in M. Kogan, M. Bauer, I. Bleiklie and M. Henkel (eds), *Transforming Higher Education: A Comparative Study,* London: Jessica Kingsley, pp. 53–87.
Brennan, J. and T. Shah (1997), 'Quality assessment, decisionmaking and institutional change', *Tertiary Education and Management, 3* (2), 157–64.
Brennan, J., R. King and Y. Lebeau (2004), 'The role of universities in the transformation of societies', *Synthesis Report,* London: Centre for Higher Education Research and Information, The Open University www.open.ac.uk/cheri.
Bundy, C. (2006), 'Global patterns, local options? Changes in higher education internationally and some implications for South Africa', *Kagisano: Ten Years of Higher Education under Democracy,* Issue 4, Pretoria: Council on Higher Education, pp. 1–20.
Calhoun, C. (2006), 'The university and the public good', *Thesis 11,* **84,** 7–43.
Clark, B. (1983), *The Higher Education System: Academic Organization in Cross-national Perspective,* Los Angeles, CA: University of California Press.
Cloete, N. and P. Maassen (2002), *The Limits of Policy in Transformation in Higher Education: global pressures and local realities in South Africa,* Cape Town: Juta Press.
Council on Higher Education (CHE) (2004), *South African Higher Education in the First Decade of Democracy,* Pretoria: CHE, www.che.ac.za.
Dale, R. (2007), 'Specifying globalization effects on national policy', in B. Lingard and J. Ozga (eds), *RoutledgeFalmer Reader in Education Policy and Politics,* London: Routledge, pp. 48–64.
Department of Education (1997), *Education White Paper 3: A Programme for the Transformation of Higher Education, 1997,* Government Gazette, Pretoria, South Africa.
Department of Education (2001), *National Plan on Higher Education,* Pretoria, South Africa.
Gidley, J.M., G.P. Hampson, L. Wheeler and E. Bereded-Samuel (2010), 'From access to success: an integrated approach to quality higher education informed by social inclusion theory and practice', *Higher Education Policy,* **23,** 123–47.
Giroux, H. (2008), 'Beyond the biopolitics of disposability: rethinking neoliberalism in the new gilded age', *Social Identities,* **14** (5), 587–620.
Halpin, D. and B. Troyna (1995), 'The politics of education policy borrowing', *Comparative Education,* **31** (3), 303–10.
Harvey, L. (1997), 'Quality is not free!', *Tertiary Education and Management, 3* (2), 133–43.
Held, D., A. McGrew, D. Goldblatt and J. Perraton (1999), *Global Transformations: Politics, Economics and Culture,* Stanford, CA: Stanford University Press.
Higher Education Quality Committee (2001), *Founding Document,* Council on Higher Education, Pretoria, at www.che.ac.za.
Jansen, J. (2001), 'Explaining non-change in education reform after apartheid: political symbolism and the problem of policy implementation', in Y. Sayed and J. Jansen (eds), *Implementing Education Policies: The South African Experience,* Landsdowne, SA: University of Cape Town Press, pp. 271–92.
Jansen, J. (2004), 'Importing outcomes-based education into South Africa: policy borrowing in a post-communist world', in D. Phillips and K. Ochs (eds), *Educational Policy Borrowing: Historical Perspectives,* Oxford: Symposium Books, pp. 199–220.
Kogan, M. (2004), 'Framework Paper: the issues', *Managerialism and Evaluation in Higher Education,* Paris: UNESCO Forum Occasional Paper Series, **7,** 2–10.

Kogan, M., M. Bauer, I. Bleiklie and M. Henkel (2000), *Transforming Higher Education: A Comparative Study*, London: Jessica Kingsley.

Lange, L. (2006), 'Symbolic policy and "performativity": South African higher education between the devil and the deep blue sea', in *Kagisano: Ten Years of Higher Education under Democracy*, Issue 4, Pretoria: Council on Higher Education, pp. 39–52.

Lange, L. and M. Singh (2010), 'Equity issues in quality assurance in South African higher education', in M. Martin (ed.), *Equity and Quality Assurance: A Marriage of Two Minds*, Paris: IIEP/UNESCO, pp. 37–73.

Lewis, R. (2009), 'Quality assurance in higher education: its global future', in *Higher Education to 2030, Vol. 2: Globalisation*, Paris: CERI, OECD, pp. 323–55.

Lingard, B. (2000), 'It is and it isn't: vernacular globalization, education policy and restructuring', in N. Burbules and C. Torres (eds), *Globalization and Education: Critical Perspectives*, New York: Routledge, pp. 79–108.

Luckett, K. (2007), 'The introduction of external quality assurance in South African higher education: an analysis of stakeholder responses', *Quality in Higher Education*, **13** (2), 97–116.

Mamdani, M. (1996), 'Centre for African Studies: some preliminary thoughts', *Social Dynamics*, **22** (2), 1–14.

Marginson, S. and M. van der Wende (2007), 'Globalisation and Higher Education', *Education Working Paper 8*, Paris: CERI, OECD.

Marginson, S. and M. van der Wende (2009), 'The new global landscape of nations and institutions', in *Higher Education to 2030, Vol. 2: Globalisation*, Paris: CERI, OECD, pp. 17–62.

Ministry of Education (2001), *National Plan on Higher Education*, Pretoria, South Africa.

Mittelman, J. (2001), 'Globalization: captors and captives', in J. Mittelman and N. Othani (eds), *Capturing Globalization*, London: Routledge, pp. 1–16.

Morley, L. (2003), *Quality and Power in Higher Education*, Buckingham: Open University Press.

Motala, E. (2004), 'Transformation revisited', unpublished paper.

Neave, G. (1998), 'The evaluative state reconsidered', *European Journal of Education*, **33** (3), 265–84.

Obamba, M. and J. Mwema (2009), 'Symmetry and asymmetry: new contours, paradigms, and politics in African academic partnerships', *Higher Education Policy*, **22** (3), 349–71.

Ozga, J. and B. Lingard (2007), 'Globalization, education policy and politics', in B. Lingard and J. Ozga (eds), *Routledge Falmer Reader in Education Policy and Politics*, London: Routledge, pp. 65–82.

Phillips, D. (2002), 'Reflections on British interests in education in Germany in the nineteenth century', *Educa*, Lisbon.

Phillips, D. and K. Ochs (2004), *Educational Policy Borrowing: Historical Perspectives*, Oxford: Symposium Books.

Rhoades, G. and B. Sporn (2002), 'Quality assurance in Europe and the US: professional and political economic framing of higher education policy', *Higher Education*, **43** (3), 355–90.

Rizvi, F. and B. Lingard (2010), *Globalizing Education Policy*, London: Routledge.

Sayed, Y. (2004), 'Teacher education in post-apartheid South Africa', in L. Chisholm (ed.), *Changing Class: Education and Social Change in Post-apartheid South Africa*, Cape Town: HSRC Press, pp. 247–65.

Sayed, Y. and J. Jansen (eds) (2001), *Implementing Education Policies: The South African experience*, Cape Town: University of Cape Town Press.

Scott, I., N. Yeld and J. Hendry (2007), 'A case for improving teaching and learning in South African Higher Education', *Higher Education Monitor*, No. 6, Council on Higher Education, Pretoria, at www.che.ac.za.

Scott, P. (ed.) (1998), *The Globalization of Higher Education*, Buckingham: SRHE and Open University Press.

Singh, M. (2006), 'Bundy blues: contradictions and choices in South African higher education', *Kagisano: Ten Years of Higher Education under Democracy*, Issue 4, Council on Higher Education, Pretoria, pp. 64–75.

Singh, M. (2010), 'Re-orienting internationalisation in African higher education', *Globalisation, Societies and Education*, **8** (2), 267–80.

Spreen, C. (2004), 'The vanishing origins of outcomes-based education', in D. Phillips and K. Ochs (eds), *Educational Policy Borrowing: Historical Perspectives*, Oxford: Symposium Books, pp. 221–36.

Steiner-Khamsi, G. (ed.) (2004), *The Global Politics of Educational Borrowing and Lending*, New York: Teachers College Press.

Sursock, A. (2010), 'Accountability in Western Europe: shifting quality assurance paradigms', in B. Stensaker and L. Harvey (eds), *Accountability in Higher Education: Global Perspectives on Trust and Power*, London: Routledge, pp. 111–32.

Trow, M. (1994), 'Managerialism and the academic profession: quality and control', *Higher Education Report No. 2*, London: Quality Support Centre, Open University.

13 Globalization and higher education in Canada
Glen A. Jones and Julian Weinrib

INTRODUCTION

Our objective in this chapter is to critically analyze globalization and higher education in Canada by focusing on the impact of, and resistance to, globalizing pressures in selected policy areas within the Canadian context. Canada is an interesting case study because of the highly decentralized structure of its higher education policy environment and the country's historic preoccupation with maintaining cultural and political sovereignty from its powerful neighbor to the south (USA), while benefiting from its close economic ties with it. We begin by providing a brief introduction to the structure of higher education in Canada followed by a discussion of three selected policy areas: internationalization, including student and faculty mobility; research and innovation; and evaluation and quality assurance. While it is impossible to provide a comprehensive analysis of the Canadian case in a single chapter, we believe that a discussion of globalization in relation to these three policy areas illustrates key features of the Canadian context.

HIGHER EDUCATION IN CANADA

Canada is a highly industrialized nation that forms the top half of the North American continent above the USA and Mexico. The second-largest (geographically) nation on earth (after Russia), Canada has a population of just over 34 million (Statistics Canada, 2010). It is one of the world's most sparsely populated countries and it has the lowest population of any G8 nation.

The aboriginal populations that resided in the area that was later to become Canada were first invaded by European colonial powers in the seventeenth century. Competing French and English colonial interests were resolved in favor of the English under the Treaty of Paris of 1763. While England would have a major influence on Canada well into the twentieth century, one could also argue that the USA has had a dramatic influence on the northern territories since the American Revolution. The War of Independence led to a large migration of United Empire Loyalists into the remaining English colonies and the War of 1812–14 strengthened concerns about US imperialism and the political and military weaknesses of the independent colonies.

The British North America Act of 1867 created the Dominion of Canada as a federation of some of these independent colonies, and it provided a framework under which other colonies would join the federation and new provinces would be created out of the western territories. The structure of the federation was originally designed to create a strong federal government under a constitutional monarchy in order to avoid the jurisdictional conflicts associated with the Civil War that had just ended in the USA. The federal government was assigned responsibility for major policy areas such as trade, shipping, banking and the military. The provincial governments were assigned responsibility for policy areas of local interest, including hospitals and education (Jones, 1997).

The federal government exhibited some early interest in the higher education policy area through the creation of a military college (1877), a research council (1916), and a collaborative arrangement with the provinces for the support of student loans (1939). Yet it was really only following the Second World War that higher education came to be viewed as a policy issue of national importance, and the government of Canada played a major role in supporting the massification of higher education in the 1950s and 1960s by providing direct grants to universities. Concerns that the federal government was intervening in an area of provincial responsibility led to a shift in funding mechanisms in favor of conditional transfers from the federal government to the provinces to support post-secondary education in 1967, later evolving into ostensibly unconditional transfers to the provinces in 1977 (Cameron, 1991).

Canada's ten provinces and three territories have come to assume the major role in the legislation, regulation and operating support of higher education. Each province has developed a unique regulatory and institutional framework for education and higher education. Perhaps the key characteristic of Canadian higher education relevant to the discussion of globalization is decentralization. The fact that there is no minister or ministry of education or higher education, and no national legislation or regulation focusing explicitly on higher education, has important implications that we address in detail below.

While the government of Canada has no explicit constitutional role in higher education, it has come to assume a major role in a variety of policy areas that are enormously important to Canada's universities, community colleges and institutes, including research, student financial assistance, and the support of language and culture. The importance of the federal government's indirect role in higher education policy was reinforced during the 1990s when the government of Canada made major reductions in provincial transfers to the provinces as a function of deficit reduction, and then, at the turn of the century, made major reinvestments in higher education under the guise of a national strategy for innovation through R&D (Shanahan and Jones, 2007). These changes have had an enormous impact on Canadian higher education and will be described in a later section of this chapter.

Each province has developed its own higher education policies and structures, although a number of common characteristics emerged during the 1960s. Provincial higher education 'systems' include universities, almost all of which are relatively autonomous, government-supported comprehensive institutions, and community colleges, an umbrella term used to describe a range of different non-university institutional types (Dennison, 1995). The decentralized nature of the Canadian approach can also be found at the provincial level, where universities have historically enjoyed high levels of autonomy (Anderson and Johnson, 1998).

Canadian participation rates in tertiary education are among the highest in the world, although a number of other OECD countries have higher university participation rates. Maintaining or increasing access to post-secondary education has been the cornerstone of most provincial policies since the 1960s, although Canada's actual track record of providing equitable access to higher education is far from exceptional and, in the case of Canada's aboriginal populations, embarrassingly poor (Jones et al., 2008).

FEDERALISM AND INTERNATIONALIZATION

Canadian higher education has long benefited from international academic connections and labor flows, though Canada's modest network of universities was predominantly influenced by its Anglo-Saxon and, in the case of French-language universities, Parisian, connections until the massive expansion of higher education following the Second World War. While the influence of Oxbridge and the American state universities was strong (Falconer, 1930), Canadian universities were slow to adopt the German research model; the first doctoral degree was awarded at the University of Toronto in 1900, and Toronto and McGill University were responsible for more than half of all doctoral degrees awarded in Canada before 1939 (McKillop, 1994).

Most Canadians traveled south or east for higher degrees, and immigration played a large role in staffing Canadian universities, just as it played a large role in almost every other aspect of Canadian society. Between 1896 and 1914 more than 2.5 million people immigrated to Canada; the Canadian population increased by over one-third during the decade from 1901 to 1911 (Careless, 1963). The federal government undertook an active immigration recruitment policy to expand the settlement of western farmland, and the Canadian population became increasingly diverse to include populations from a broad range of European countries in addition to the traditional flows from the British Isles.

During the massive postwar expansion of Canadian higher education, universities turned increasingly to international academic labor pools. Canadian universities awarded only 306 doctoral degrees in 1960, a small fraction of the number of junior scholars required to staff what Duckworth (2000) referred to as an expanding higher education empire in which the concrete never sets. Canadian universities employed qualified (or almost qualified) faculty from anywhere they could find them, but the largest numbers continued to arrive from the USA and the UK.

As a new wave of Canadian nationalism washed over the country in the late 1960s, a number of educational research studies noted that schools were dominated by US textbooks (Hodgetts, 1968) and that Canadian social sciences and humanities were not receiving the attention they deserved within universities staffed by US or English-born professors (Jones, 2009a; Mathews and Steele, 1969; Symons, 1975). The response was an increasing interest in 'Canadianization' within higher education, including the development of Canadian Studies programs, strengthening academic publishing in Canada including funding new national journals, and a desire to expand doctoral programs so that a larger number of Canadian graduates would be available for Canadian academic positions. The number of doctoral graduates increased from 1680 in 1970 to 3660 in 2001 (Williams, 2005). National policies under Trudeau had reinforced the importance of strengthening Canadian media and cultural industries, while at the same time treating foreign policy as an extension of domestic interests and building stronger connections with other francophone countries and developing new linkages with China and Southeast Asia.

Rather than develop an internationalization strategy, the federal government's approach during most of the 1970s and 1980s was to strengthen international economic linkages while ensuring that the 'international' did not displace the 'local'. Canadian immigration policies prevented universities from hiring professors from other countries unless they could demonstrate that there were no qualified Canadian applicants.

Until the turn of the century, the visas awarded to foreign students studying in Canada prevented them from working outside the university, based on the fear that they would take jobs from domestic students. At the provincial level governments and institutions agonized during the 1980s and 1990s over the question of whether Canadian taxpayers should continue to subsidize foreign students, or whether these students should be charged a higher fee than domestic students. As Jones (2009a) has noted, during the same time period when Australia was reforming higher education with a view to generating revenue through an international student industry, the Canadian conversation focused on the appropriate level of government subsidy for international students.

This history framed what generally became a provincial- or institution-level discussion of internationalization in the late twentieth century, and continues today. Canada has never had a national policy or strategy on internationalization, in part because there is no national education or higher education policy. But there has also been relatively little national discussion of internationalization as a domestic policy issue – certainly nothing comparable to the discussions taking place in Europe, China, Australia and the USA (Shubert et al., 2009). As Trilokekar (2009, p. 99) has noted:

> The literature on the internationalization of higher education in Canada is critical of the Canadian approach and numerous reports elaborate the many ways the Canadian federal government could take a lead by substantially increasing fiscal allocations for international education activities, developing a flagship program and establishing a national coordinated initiative, thus enhancing a strategic approach towards the internationalization of Canadian higher education.

There are no major national programs supporting international student mobility, the development of international curriculum, or, until quite recently, the development of international research partnerships or linkages (Jones and Oleksiyenko, 2011). In the absence of a clear national strategy or policy, the Canadian approach to internationalization has been highly decentralized with a few provinces (especially Quebec and Ontario) developing initiatives but with most policy development taking place at the institutional level. As Shubert et al. (2009) have noted, the discussion of internationalization in the context of Canadian higher education has been heavily influenced and framed by a number of key themes.

First, Canadian universities continue to be viewed as 'public' institutions and higher education continues to be viewed as a public good, but these perceptions are discordant with the economic imperative attached to globalization and the view of international students as revenue generators. Second, it is impossible to disentangle the discussion of internationalization from the Canadian discussion of multiculturalism, cultural diversity and inclusion. Changing immigration patterns have led to an extremely diverse Canadian population and it is difficult to separate the discussion of developing inclusive curriculum within institutions of higher education in order to address the needs of an increasingly multiracial, multicultural population, from the discussion of developing an international curriculum and 'global' institutions. In some respects one might argue that it is immigration, rather than explicit strategies of internationalization, that has been the major global driver of institutional policy change. Roughly 7 percent of students in tertiary type A institutions in Canada are international, a figure that is comparable to the OECD average, but well below the average of other jurisdictions where English is a major language. On the other hand, the majority of individuals holding doctorates in Canada were born outside the country (54 percent in 2001), a much higher percentage than in Australia, the USA or Germany (Auriol, 2007).

Issues of student and faculty mobility, the cornerstones of US, Chinese, and European internationalization efforts, are largely navigated at the institutional level since there are no significant national programs and only a few provinces have developed modest mechanisms to support international experiences for domestic students. Graduate scholarship programs supported under the federal government's R&D initiatives generally encourage national, rather than international, student mobility by offering high-status competitive awards for the best Canadian students to study at the top Canadian universities.

Individual institutions have developed student mobility initiatives, but without significant government funding these programs are modest and poorly subscribed. There has perhaps been greater success in Quebec, where both institutions and government have come to view internationalization as an important objective (Picard and Mills, 2009). Internationalization has become a mechanism for the Quebec government to assert some element of autonomy over international activities through bilateral relationships, and government-supported student mobility programs provide a mechanism to promote international experiences for francophone students beyond the Anglo-centric domination of the North American research university.

The internationalization of higher education is not a national priority in Canada, and policy initiatives in this area are frequently stymied by Canada's federal arrangements that assign the responsibility for education to the provinces but with responsibility for foreign affairs reserved to the national government. Canadian federalism, however, is only part of the story. Concerns about national cultural sovereignty and more recently 'brain drain', in a country lying next door to the USA, have had an impact on internationalization strategies. Canada's historic reliance on immigration and, more recently, the tremendous racial and ethnic diversity of immigrants to Canada has meant that the pressures of globalization on curriculum are frequently mediated by pressures to respond to increasingly diverse citizens and address local inequities in participation. The pressures of globalization look a little different when, as in some Canadian universities, more than half of the domestic student population was not born in Canada.

INNOVATION, SCIENCE, TECHNOLOGY AND R&D: INTEGRATING WITH THE GLOBAL KNOWLEDGE ECONOMY/KNOWLEDGE SOCIETY

Higher education in the late twentieth and first decade of the twenty-first centuries has been revitalized by the rise of a global knowledge economy that sees innovation, science, technology and R&D as cornerstones of national economic development and competitiveness agendas (OECD, 1996, 2008). As other authors have established, the current wave of globalization processes incorporates higher education institutions in the global marketplace, specifically through knowledge society and knowledge-based economy discourses and practices (Ozaga, 2007; Olssen and Peters, 2005; Marginson, 2006, 2007; Välimaa and Hoffman, 2008). This has resulted in changing conceptions and expectations of publicly funded institutions of higher education as potential mechanisms of national economic development throughout OECD countries (Marginson, 2006, 2007).

However, analysts also contend that globalization is limited by regional, national and local mediating forces that are capable of articulating global transformations in context-specific ways (Marginson and Rhoades, 2002; Välimaa and Hoffman, 2008). While the impetus for higher education institutions to increase their global position and contribute to national economic competitiveness is at unprecedented heights, Canadian contextual variables drastically affect the way these forces manifest in Canadian public research institutions. This section will map out how the Canadian context has mediated the global push for institutions of higher education to be more responsive to national economic needs and global market forces by analyzing federal initiatives directed at steering university research outputs in the twentieth and twenty-first centuries.

As in many other nations, higher education institutions in Canada have historically acted as a mediator between the demands and needs of federal and provincial governmental bodies and the broader society, negotiating ideas of public and private goods through their professional and disciplinary expertise and judgments. While ministries, funding agencies, intermediary bodies and institutional boards of governors attempt to interpret the needs of Canadian society through their organizational mandates, Canadian universities have maintained relatively strong autonomy through the setting of admissions, curricula and examining standards, and the preservation of academic freedom to determine matters of research and teaching (Rajagopal and Buchbinder, 1996, p. 283). The current instantiation of globalization, with its focus on intellectual capital as a tradable and marketable commodity, has shifted many ministerial and agency mandates and cultures towards increasing Canadian competitiveness through more market-oriented universities. However, the lack of a centralized planning authority for Canadian higher education relegates the federal government to arm's-length interventions in public policies and institutional activities, primarily through line agencies and ministries, in order to create a high-skill knowledge class and market-oriented public research sector that can raise Canadian competitiveness (Wolfe, 2005; Jones, 2009a; Metcalfe and Fenwick, 2009).

FEDERAL INVOLVEMENT IN HIGHER EDUCATION RESEARCH: 1916–88

The federal government's drive to get industry more involved in publicly funded research institutions is not a new phenomenon. As early as 1916, with the creation of the Honorary Advisory Council (later the National Research Council), the federal government sought to influence the planning, coordination and direction of research towards meeting 'practical and pressing problems indicated by industrial necessities' (Atkinson-Grosjean et al., 2001, p. 8). At the end of the Second World War Canadian universities were drawn into the generation of knowledge for industrialization projects in Canada, as well as helping in the reconstruction of Europe and sections of South-east Asia affected by the war (Tudiver, 1999). While industrial interests and pressures were increasingly factored into higher education research, the role of the state in economic development and the resulting belief in state investment in higher education remained a defining characteristic of the postwar Keynesian state.

In the post-Second World War era higher education in Canada, as in most other western nations, experienced rapid massification that drastically altered the mission and role of universities in society and the economy, and as such, the federal government continually reviewed the role that higher education played in social and economic development. The Glassco Commission of the late 1950s and the Lamontage Special Committee on Science Policy, which spanned the 1960s, were both established to review Canada's R&D expenditures. Each respectively called for increased coordination and interpenetration of university and industry research activities and outputs in order to produce more economically relevant research (Atkinson-Grosjean et al., 2001, pp. 6–8). The 1968 Science Council of Canada Report, *Towards a National Science Policy for Canada*, advocated 'greater collaboration between university, government and industry . . . it also suggested government laboratories work closely with industrial and university sectors' (Science Council of Canada, 1968, p. 26, quoted in Atkinson-Grosjean et al., 2001). However, due to the tepid reception of the aforementioned councils and commissions by university leaders and faculty, and the difficulties of organizing and coordinating national research initiatives in Canada due to the challenges of social and physical geography, it was not until the early 1980s and the rise of the current wave of globalization dynamics that the federal government more forcefully and directly intervened in higher education research policies and activities.

With the global economic crisis of the late 1970s, the election of Conservative governments in many western nations, including Canada, during the 1980s and the resulting ideological shift in public organizations towards increased privatization and market-based economic activities, the government mandate to reform and restructure public higher education institutions in Canada was at a critical mass, especially in regard to their research functions (Rajagopal and Buchbinder, 1996; Buchbinder, 1993). In conjunction with the rise of information and communication technologies that radically changed the dynamic and intensity of the global market, the Canadian federal government began to envision knowledge production as an increasingly important facet of national economic development and competitiveness, while simultaneously reducing funding to institutions of higher education due to the increasing perception of higher education as a private good (Shanahan and Jones, 2007).

During the 1980s the federal government implemented Canada's first national science and technology policy (in 1987), allocating US$1.5 billion in funding and merging the Ministry of State for Science and Technology (MOSST), already in charge of the major natural and social science research councils, NSERC and SSHRC, with the Department of Regional Industrial Expansion in order to create a new super-ministry: Industry Science and Technology Canada (ISTC) (Atkinson-Grosjean et al., 2001, p. 18). The result of this process was the centralization of control over major national granting processes and the establishment of an arm's-length intermediary body that could more directly intervene in the steering and direction of Canadian higher education research activities. This new intermediary was capable of pressing market relations and the power of capital into public-research organizations, where previously non-market or quasi-market models were in operation (Burchell, 1996).

FEDERAL INVOLVEMENT IN HIGHER EDUCATION RESEARCH IN THE GLOBAL KNOWLEDGE ECONOMY: 1989–PRESENT

The federal government has developed a number of policies and initiatives designed to steer university research practices and strengthen ties between universities and industry. It can be argued that these initiatives and activities represent attempts to intervene in the autonomy and direction of Canadian universities by encouraging public–private partnerships and the commodification of knowledge production in response to global market forces and pressures. New federal policies for R&D raise important questions regarding the extent to which institutions of higher education should act as vehicles for legitimating and privileging certain types of knowledge in the drive to build national knowledge capacities, rather than as institutions promoting broader societal needs and more diverse types of knowledge (Ozaga, 2007).

The Networks of Centres of Excellence Program (NCE), established in 1989, represented the first major initiative promoted by the federal government to directly steer university research to increase industry relations in the new era of globalization. Although 'centers of excellence' were a rising phenomenon in global research-oriented policies in the late 1980s, the Canadian implementation of the NCE program was innovative in that it established a national network aimed at building interdisciplinary research capacity in response to Canadian geography and varying provincial jurisdictions and scientific resources (Atkinson-Grosjean et al., 2001, p. 18). Billed as 'the only program that engages researchers, partners, and institutions in nationwide networks, and that works with users in industry and government to create commercial opportunities and develop public policy based on sound evidence' (NCE, 2004, p. 2), the NCE represented a drastic shift in federal policy towards the autonomy of universities. Under the 'parasitic' structural arrangement (Atkinson-Grosjean et al., 2001, p. 18), universities provide all the indirect costs, researcher and administrator salaries, support for network administration, and the graduate students and postdoctoral fellows required to undertake the research projects, and the physical infrastructure and facilities (NCE, 2004, p. 3) for research that is directly correlative to industry pressures and needs. The NCE program has developed regional systems of innovation that distribute research capacity and enable significant start-up activities across Canada.

However, it comes at a cost to publicly funded research universities with only minimal private buy-in; between 1990 and 2000 the private sector contributed roughly 10 percent of the $730 million (ibid., p. 19). A second major initiative of the federal government is the Canadian Foundation for Innovation (CFI), an independent, not-for-profit Crown Corporation directed to 'strengthen the capacity of Canadian universities, colleges, research hospitals, and non-profit research institutions to carry out world-class research and technology development that benefits Canadians' (CFI, 2008, p. 5). Promoting the 'optimal use of research infrastructure' (ibid., p. 5), the CFI potentially 'alters and builds the very foundation of Canadian HE and its research capacities, leaving physical legacies to its research policy ideology that will likely long outlast the organization itself' (Metcalfe and Fenwick, 2009, p. 215).

As Metcalfe argues in her detailed outline of the program, the CFI provides only 40 percent of project funding, with the rest being found by institutions and provincial governments, and it is allocated directly to institutions rather than to individual research-ers. As such, institutions of higher education are forced to look beyond their walls to industry in order to effectively operate high-level research in the increasingly competi-tive landscape. One outcome of this trend is a decrease in institutional and professional autonomy and an increase in industry and government influence over research agendas (ibid.). With a reported $3.65 billion in federal investment since 1997 (CFI, 2008, p. 13) and as the largest source of research infrastructure in Canada (Shanahan and Jones, 2007), the CFI represents a key mechanism from which the federal government can influ-ence the direction of Canadian university R&D. With the ability to override provincial policies and mandates in order to create a research environment that is more responsive to the global knowledge economy, CFI represents a substantial threat to the ability of institutions to respond to more diverse societal needs.

The Canadian Research Chair Program (CRC), established in 2000 with the intent of raising the competitiveness of Canadian universities in attracting and retaining top researchers, represents a more indirect means of federal intervention in institutional research planning than either the CFI or NCE. As Shanahan and Jones (2007, p. 34) contend, 'for the first time (in Canada), institutions were required to develop and submit an institutional research plan in order to obtain support'. Chairs are allocated to univer-sities based on a formula that emphasizes institutional success in competitive research grant mechanisms, but they are also assigned to broad areas of scholarship correspond-ing to Canada's three research-granting councils; as of 2006–07, 80 percent of the chairs were in the health sciences, natural sciences or engineering, leaving only 20 percent in the humanities and social sciences (ibid., p. 8). The program also distinguishes between two levels of chairs (Tier 1, which focuses on senior research stars, and Tier 2, which pro-vides status to junior rising stars), and between new appointments (to increase Canada's research capacity) and chairs awarded to existing professors (to retain capacity and avoid 'brain drain'). In conjunction with other federal programs in operation, the CRC has become another vehicle for the federal government to fund more globally competi-tive and market-oriented researchers and programs.

A final area of research that has been often overlooked in Canadian higher educa-tion discussions, but that helps to develop a broader conceptualization of how deeply the impact of the global knowledge-based economy has infiltrated national policies, is through the increased reliance on grants for university researchers and the effect this has had on the various levels of academic culture. Over the last 20 years the adoption of neoliberal economic policies at both federal and provincial levels has led to consider-able budget cuts in public support for Canadian higher education. Between 1988 and 2006 the total federal transfer (both cash and tax points) for Canadian institutions of higher education in 1988 dollars decreased by 40 percent (Fisher et al., 2006, Chart 6 and Appendix 1). One effect of this trend is that researchers are increasingly dependent on federal research funding through the major granting councils. In 1992 sponsored research comprised 15.6 percent of university revenues, and by 2003 it had risen to 23.5 percent (CAUT, 2004, p. 3 in Polster, 2007, p. 602).

One significant alteration that the federal government has made to supporting federal research initiatives is the recognition that hosting high-level research programs carries indirect and hidden expenses for Canadian institutions. As a result, in 2003 the federal government established a permanent program, the Indirect Costs Program (ICP), to provide Canadian universities and colleges with annual grants to help pay a portion of their indirect research costs. Indirect costs may be physical resources, such as lighting and heating research offices, or human resources, such as administrative support salaries, and administrative costs of getting a patent. The first indirect cost payment was made to 79 institutions in 2001–02 and totaled $200 million. The program currently has a budget of $325 million for 2009–10 and is directed at 125 institutions (Circum and Malatest, 2009).

The increasing reliance on federal grants for institutional research, the impact that institutional success or failure can have on the ability of an individual researcher to secure future research funding, and the rising importance of institutional reputation in both national and global marketplaces have serious implications for the Canadian researcher. While publishing has historically been the litmus test for western academics, grants are increasingly becoming a condition for some academics not only to perform their research, but to continue their professional development and remain employed (ibid., p. 602). As a result, increased competition within and between institutions for federal grants may result in a more effective corporatization of academic culture than the aforementioned CFI, CRC and NCE programs. Researcher dependencies on acquiring research grants may result in a willing adoption, or at least tacit acceptance, of many of the broader ideological shifts that increase the vulnerability to external influences and propagate a national system based more on competitive relationships with other researchers and institutions than on collaborative networks engaged with broader societal actors.

As such, the majority of the western nation-states, and growing sections of the less-industrialized nations, are striving to better integrate their national economies with global trends in the production, management and marketization of knowledge through increased relations between industry and public research organizations. Canada is no exception to this trend. However, as outlined above, the Canadian federal arrangements and the lack of a centralized coordinating unit for higher education policy have resulted in fragmented efforts to create and operationalize new public policy options for higher education institutions and their research activities. Interventions and steering mechanisms directed at increasing national competitiveness in higher education have come through indirect means, primarily through federal and provincial ministries, and various funding initiatives.

EVALUATION AND QUALITY ASSESSMENT

Increased global interaction and competition in the higher education sector has resulted in the rise of new discourses and practices for system management and evaluation. Issues of quality assurance, degree and program accreditation, and the recognition of academic and professional qualifications have become central to the construction and operation of globally engaged and publicly accountable national higher education systems (van Vught, 1994; van Vught et al., 2002; Knight, 2003; Marginson, 2006; OECD, 2008). As Harvey (2008, p. 1) contends, 'from the late 1980s through to the middle of this decade, higher education has been characterized by a headlong rush to introduce quality assurance processes geared primarily to accountability. The underlying principle was that accountability will generate improvement, or at the very least a sense of responsibility within the academy'.

The marketization and commodification of education as a tradable good, the need for governments to increase access to post-secondary education and the impact that globalization processes have had on increasing the worldwide interconnectedness of the competitive market for both knowledge and 'knowledge workers' have increased the perceived need to differentiate institutional hierarchies, accommodate more fluid and robust student mobility, and refine institutional and degree accreditation, and quality assurance processes (OECD, 2008). However, as articulated throughout this chapter, 'the spread, velocity, and intensity of global transformations undergo many permutations, and are articulated through differing national and local zones' (Marginson, 2006, p. 2). In this section we describe and analyze how Canada has responded, or failed to respond, to the global impetus for increased quality assurance mechanisms and accreditation systems for various reasons that reflect the country's unique governance structures and historical context.

Issues of quality assurance and degree accreditation have historically been situated at the periphery in Canadian debates around post-secondary education, not because they have been viewed as unimportant, but because quality assurance (QA) processes have been firmly embedded at institutional and provincial levels (Jones, 2009c; Knight, 2003). The Canadian system is characterized by provincial and territorial legislative autonomy over the establishment of new degree-granting institutions and the issuing of baccalaureate degrees. Under this framework governments have historically acted as *de facto* accreditation bodies that maintain a relatively homogeneous two-sector system: a university sector with a tight monopoly on the baccalaureate degree, and a community college sector with a sufficient amount of differentiation to meet the demands of students and local industry (Jones, 2009c; Marshall, 2004). While each province and territory operates under different sets of legislative processes and local needs, until recently quality had not been defined as a core issue for debate and action, primarily due to the assumed homogeneity of Canadian university standards, especially at the undergraduate level. The absence of a strong private for-profit sector in Canada meant that there were few external challengers to the system. In addition the variation between each of the provinces has never been considered so great that it could disrupt the 'tacitly accepted framework of Canadian degree-granting postsecondary education' (Marshall, 2004, p. 74).

Over the last 20 or more years the diffused federalist model of Canadian post-secondary education quality assurance and accreditation has increasingly been challenged by a number of pressures impacting the global post-secondary landscape: increased demand for baccalaureate degrees; higher levels of system differentiation; increased competition for internationally mobile students and faculty; and growing consumer markets for educational services. In Canada, as in other countries with mature post-secondary education systems, these developments have led to a heightened sensitivity and responsiveness of legislative bodies and post-secondary institutions to issues of quality and accreditation, not merely in terms of the national context, but in an outward-looking conceptualization of the problem in response to institutional competition and expansion.

As a result of these global pressures many countries have seen quality assurance and accreditation processes and discourses become more powerful, professionalized, publicized and permeable within their national contexts and within broader regional and global conversations (Stensaker, 2007). Stensaker, in his examination of global quality assurance processes, remarks that common reactions to increased accountability, new managerialism and global competition between institutions and systems has resulted in increased pressure for national systems to centralize quality systems, processes and information; increase the number and presence of written routines, scripts and rule-driven handbooks to make tacit knowledge transparent; use quality processes as marketing and branding tools for institutions and national systems, and at a more basic level increase the proliferation of information regarding higher education institutions, programs and processes (Stensaker, 2007, pp. 60–61).

Brennan and Shah (2000) argue that we probably know more about higher education than ever before, and this has led to more informed decision-making processes where data and information about performance, relevance and quality are used more systematically. For many countries, Canada included, the shifting emphasis towards more formalized quality control and accreditation systems has meant that these processes can no longer be based on a combination of 'quality' as embedded in elite institutions and tight governmental regulation (ibid.). In the Canadian context, the legacy of the federalist system, the relative homogeneity of institutional types and functions across the provinces, and the coupling of extremely strong institutional autonomy and weak provincial higher education policy capacity have all limited the ability of Canada to operationalize public transparency, establish comprehensive data collection and analysis systems regarding the post-secondary sector, set national standards and practices around QA and accreditation, and market its institutions globally in a comprehensive manner.

Canada's federalist system has historically been the greatest obstacle to establishing national quality assurance processes and accreditation frameworks. Despite the national massification of post-secondary education that occurred after the Second World War, which increased enrollments, the number and diversity of post-secondary institutions, degrees and programs, and the amount of public financial support to the post-secondary sector, the Canadian system has maintained a decentralized governance structure that facilitates high levels of institutional autonomy and provincial control over key higher education decision-making processes (Shanahan and Jones, 2007; Jones, 2009b; Marshall, 2004). The federal government has maintained a strong presence in research and financial assistance sectors, as well as affecting post-secondary institutions indirectly through immigration, labor, innovation and provincial transfer policies. As such, it has all but abdicated its direct influence on institutional governance. While other nations have marshaled the central role of post-secondary education in key national economic and social dynamics to increase public accountability measures over the sector, Canada's federal government has been unable or unwilling to extend its reach in a similar manner (Jones, 2009a). In Canada economic and social development have been couched in provincial terms and measures, allowing the provinces to develop locally driven policies that ensure their systems, institutions and programs are meeting provincial needs and quality standards, as opposed to engaging with broader national priorities and discourses.

The result of this fragmented and hands-off national system is the relegation of national policy dialogue to secondary bodies – organizations that are limited in their ability to set national standards due to their lack of institutionalized authority. The Council of Ministers of Education, Canada (CMEC), a formal grouping of provincial and territorial ministers, has been one of the strongest proponents of stimulating pan-Canadian dialogue and trying to establish a national framework for quality and accreditation. In 2007 the CMECs Quality Assurance Sub-committee published a report detailing provincial and territorial QA practices and a *Ministerial Statement on Quality Assurance of Degree Education in Canada* that presented guidelines for a Degree Qualifications Framework, Procedures and Standards for New Degree Program Quality Assessment, and Procedures and Standards for Assessing New Degree-Granting Institutions (CMEC, 2007). However, given the limited influence that pan-Canadian initiatives have over provincial and institutional accountability, CMEC ministers 'recognize the primary responsibility for academic and institutional quality assurance rests with postsecondary institutions themselves' (ibid., p. 1).

A second body that deals with issues of institutional quality standards is the Association for Universities and Colleges of Canada (AUCC). While not formally engaged in a state-sanctioned accreditation process, membership in the Association has historically been used as a benchmark in a number of quality-assurance-related activities, including research, information services and international cooperation (Knight, 2003, p. 4). This informal quality assurance role has even reached to the federal level where privileges such as federal grants and student aid have at times been tied to membership in the AUCC (Marshall, 2004, pp. 88–9). A third organization attempting to stir conversations about pan-Canadian quality assurance and accreditation is the Canadian Council of Learning (CCL), which has on occasions advocated for a national discussion of higher education. However, these have manifested at a basic and general discussion level and have had minimal, if any, policy implications (Jones, 2009a).

A byproduct of this decentralized structure and the lack of intra-provincial policy coordination and dialogue is the absence of a robust federal data collection system directed at supporting public policy formation in post-secondary education (Jones et al., 2008). While the accumulation of data has implications for all areas of higher education system development, it is extremely significant for issues of quality as the evaluation of new and previously existing institutions and programs in most cases requires historical benchmarks for comparison (ibid., p. 27). There is a consensus within Canada and abroad that Canadian national data collection systems are inadequate in comparison to its western peers. The CCL (2007, p. 1) argues that 'Canada has no clear picture of how our post-secondary education is faring on the international stage due to a striking absence of key information' and advocates 'a comprehensive plan for gathering and utilizing information', while the OECD has highlighted the continued limitation of Canada's national data infrastructure with 'huge delays associated with obtaining what data are available' (Jones et al., 2008, p. 27). While issues of data collection and analysis have fostered the development of national quality assurance bodies in many western countries, this has been noticeably absent from Canadian conversations and can be partially attributed to the lack of intra-provincial dialogue and harmonization, as well as the uniquely high number of organizations in quality assurance processes, and a deficit in provincial policy capacity.

The issue of policy capacity in provincial governments is a direct offshoot of the absence of quality assurance and accreditation discourse throughout the Canadian context. Since the provincial governments have acted as *de facto* accreditation bodies and institutional autonomy has historically been viewed as central to the Canadian post-secondary landscape, 'the majority of provinces have come to assume only a modest role in monitoring and regulating the sector' (Jones, 2009c, p. 47). The majority of the provinces have focused their policy work on student assistance programs and operating grant mechanisms, resulting in the lack of infrastructure capacity in most governments to deal with more complex policy initiatives in the post-secondary sector. As Jones argues, 'for the most part, governments have trusted universities to do the right thing, and there has been little interest in making major investments in the creation of a new government infrastructure to deal with issues of quality or accountability' (ibid.). Some provinces, specifically Ontario, British Columbia, Quebec and Alberta, have been more active in developing policy capacity around quality, particularly through arm's-length government initiatives such as the Higher Education Quality Council of Ontario (HEQCO), which is mandated with providing policy-based advice to the provincial government around issues of quality, and provincial quality assessment boards that review applications for new degree programs.

The primary reason that the above four provinces have been at the front of developing more robust quality assurance systems is tied to the final key feature of the Canadian system that is slowly being challenged: institutional homogeneity. Since the end of the massification process in Canada, the national system, while slightly varied at provincial levels, has consisted of two sectors: relatively homogeneous, baccalaureate-degree-granting universities; and a highly diverse network of diploma-(non-degree)-granting community colleges meant to complement the activities and programs associated with the university sector (Dennison, 1995; Marshall, 2004; Jones, 2009b). Over the last 50 years the fact that the universities have been considered roughly equal in quality and standards has been a defining characteristic of the Canadian post-secondary landscape. However, since the early 1990s increased demands for access, an increasingly mobile population, demands for high-skill laborers and 'knowledge workers' who can interface with the global knowledge economy, and the encroachment of private providers and foreign institutions have resulted in the need for many provinces to expand and differentiate their systems (Marshall, 2004; Beaudin, 2009). Distance and cross-border higher education provision are also becoming more prevalent in the Canadian marketplace, offering new quality assessment challenges for provincial legislatures (Beaudin, 2009).

As different territories respond to changing local demands and global pressures, the national quality and credential environment has become increasingly opaque. As examples of regional responses, Ontario and Alberta have established new types of applied baccalaureate degrees that can be offered by the community college sector; British Columbia has created a hybrid University College model (Dennison, 2006; Levin, 2003); Alberta and British Columbia have allowed a select group of colleges degree-granting privileges for complete foundational BA and BSc degrees, with the exception of graduate-level programming (Marshall, 2004); Alberta, British Columbia, New Brunswick and Ontario legislators have permitted the presence of foreign providers (Beaudin, 2009); Alberta, Ontario and Quebec have allowed degree-granting institutions to provide 'distance degrees' (Marshall, 2004, p. 83); and in Alberta and British Columbia the private sector has begun to entrench itself as a strong post-secondary player.

Each of these initiatives has been implemented by provincial legislatures in part to facilitate system expansion in order to meet demands. However, the implication for national standard-setting is a blurring of the two-sector system, where institutional types no longer directly correlate to degree-granting status. As a result, the systems of quality assurance and accreditation are being forced to reconcile an increasingly differentiated and varied post-secondary sector, one that has challenged provincial-level accreditation as both a concept and a process, and as requiring increases in provincial quality and accreditation infrastructure (Marshall, 2004, pp. 86–7).

The Canadian context has historically been characterized by a highly decentralized, province-based higher education landscape that has abdicated responsibility for substantive quality, accreditation, and accountability policies and programs to the institutions. Even when pan-Canadian dialog has been raised at the ministerial level, institutional autonomy and authority have been assumed cornerstones of any initiative. This 'Canadian' system has also been marked by provincial and territorial differentiation of post-secondary systems, whereby the national landscape has maintained a relatively homogeneous two-sector framework of universities and community colleges. However, over the last 15 years, new pressures for expansion and differentiation have increasingly challenged provincial quality and accreditation frameworks and infrastructures.

The lack of systematic data collection systems and coordinated national frameworks, despite the interest of certain pan-Canadian organizations, has resulted in a highly fragmented national response to issues of quality and accreditation, including matters of accountability and degree transfer, that does not appear to be at fundamental risk. While this system has worked in Canada for the last 50 years, the new pressures of a globalized higher education arena, with increased student and faculty mobility, marketization of and competition between institutions and systems, and the need for globally attuned high-skill laborers will continue to challenge the decentralized Canadian model, and as provinces continue to adapt in highly differentiated ways, the relative harmony of the Canadian system may be under threat of disruption.

CONCLUSIONS

In their 1997 book *Academic Capitalism*, Slaughter and Leslie analyze higher education policy in the USA, Australia, the UK and Canada, and argue that there were clear trends as governments, institutions and individual professors responded to globalizing forces associated with the growth of global markets and the repositioning of the university and university research in relation to national economic development. While they noted similar trends in three of the four countries, they wondered whether Canada was an outlier or a partial resistor to international pressures. Fourteen years later, with the advantage of hindsight, the answer is no – and yes. As their book was going to press, Canada's federal government was reducing the level of support to post-secondary education provided through unconditional transfers to the provinces and would later make massive new investments in a series of new initiatives designed to facilitate research linkages between universities and industry, and increase Canada's research capacity in strategic areas. One could therefore observe that, with perhaps a five-year time lag, Canada's national policies for higher education were heading in roughly the same direction as several of its Anglo peers. In the discussion of globalization and Canadian higher education, it is possible to conclude that there are common themes that link the Canadian response to the policies of other industrialized peers.

While it is easy to find common themes in many respects, it is the variations that become interesting, and as we have demonstrated above, these variations are linked to Canada's historic concerns about American political, economic and cultural domination, the decentralized approach to higher education policy under Canada's federal arrangements, and Canada's highly diverse, multicultural, multiracial population. As former Prime Minister Pierre Trudeau remarked, living beside the USA is like 'sleeping with an elephant', and there is a legitimate fear of sleeping too soundly. Canada has had a long history of cultural protectionism including policies designed to support Canadian media and cultural industries, such as subsidies for scholarly journals and book publishers. Canada's not infrequent constitutional squabbles have been closely related to issues of culture and identity. Canada's bilingual status, and the desire to protect Quebec as a distinct society, have been important factors shaping Canada's cultural and educational policies, and these policies (and the sociopolitical goals that they support) have served to moderate the impact of some globalizing pressures.

Canada has a relatively unusual model of decentralized governance for higher education in comparison with other western countries, and the fact that there is no national higher education department or legislation means that higher education policy is in the hands of the provinces and territories, and there are major differences by jurisdiction in system design, institutional types, and in basic funding and tuition arrangements.

Higher education in Canada is not a 'system' but rather the sum of locally regulated activities, often premised on high levels of university autonomy. Canada's federal government does play a strong role in R&D policy, and the result is a chaotic policy environment with differences in policy approach to higher education by province, and where institutions are pushed and pulled in different directions by federal and provincial policies. The result of the Canadian system's organized chaos is double-edged in terms of its interactions and reactions to the current wave of global influences and pressures: on the one hand, the loosely coupled nature of the various provincial and territorial systems, characterized by robust bottom-up models with strong institutional autonomy, has made many jurisdictions and institutions resistant to the pitfalls of a national, centralized approach or strategy. On the other hand, the lack of a strong central authority has led to a policy environment in which there is no integrated national strategy or strategic planning, where there is an inadequate data and policy research infrastructure, and where there is limited harmonization across provincial systems.

For example, there is no Canadian strategy for the 'internationalization' of higher education policy. This arrangement has allowed the Canadian system to avoid some of the more draconian experiments with standardization and elaborate quality control mechanisms that have emerged in some other jurisdictions, but it also means that the Canadian system has not benefited from the advantages of a national discussion of quality assessment and the related expansion of data-gathering and policy research that have emerged in some countries. Increasing institutional differentiation, including an expanding private sector and the emergence of new degrees offered by non-university institutions, may eventually become the catalyst for a pan-Canadian accreditation or program assessment mechanism.

Finally, Canada's increasingly diverse population is also an important factor in this discussion. In many respects universities and colleges are responding to the pressures of globalization through local, institutional responses to the changing nature of their communities and the changing needs (and demands) of their increasingly diverse student populations. Canada has been a major beneficiary of global labor flows, including academic labor. Canada's rich history of immigration has played a major role in the development of internationally engaged universities. Canada is home to a multiplicity of diasporas that influence Canada's perceptions of the world, but also embody a pool of formal and informal networks with institutions and academics in both the global North and the global South.

REFERENCES

Anderson, D. and R. Johnson (1998), *University Autonomy in Twenty Countries*, Canberra: Evaluation and Investigations Programme, Department of Employment, Education, Training and Youth Affairs, Government of Australia.

Atkinson-Grosjean, J., D. House and D. Fisher (2001), 'Canadian science policy and public research organizations in the 20th century', *Science Studies*, **14** (1), 3–25.

Auriol, L. (2007), *Labour Market Characteristics and International Mobility of Doctorate Holders: Results from Seven Countries* (STI Working Paper 2007/2), Paris: OECD.

Beaudin, Y. (2009), 'International quality provision in cross-border higher education and the internationalization of Canadian degree-granting institutions', in R. Trilokekar, G.A. Jones and A. Shubert (eds), *Canada's Universities Go Global*, Toronto: Lorimer, pp. 297–305.

Brennan, J. and T. Shah (2000), *Managing Quality in Higher Education: An International Perspective on Institutional Assessment and Change*, Buckingham: OECD/SRHE/Open University Press.

Buchbinder, H. (1993), 'The market-oriented university and the changing role of knowledge', *Higher Education*, **26** (3), 331–47.

Burchell, G. (1996), 'Liberal government and techniques of the self', in A. Barry, T. Osborne and N. Rose (eds), *Foucault and Political Reason: Liberalism, Neoliberalism, and the Rationalities of Government*, Chicago, IL: University of Chicago Press, pp. 19–36.

Cameron, D. (1991), *More Than an Academic Question: Universities, Government, and Public Policy in Canada*, Halifax: Institute for Research on Public Policy.

Canada Foundation for Innovation (2008), *2007–2008 Annual Report*, Ottawa: Canada Foundation for Innovation.

Canadian Council of Learning (2007), *Measuring What Canadians Value: A Pan-Canadian Data Strategy for Postsecondary Education*, Ottawa: Canadian Council of Learning.

Careless, J. (1963), *Canada: A Story of Challenge*, Toronto: Macmillan.

Circum Network Inc. and R.A. Malatest (2009), *Evaluation of the Tri-Agency Indirect Costs Program: Final Report*, retrieved 2 January 2009 from http://www.indirectcosts.gc.ca/publications/evaluation_report_e.pdf

Council of Ministers of Education, Canada (2007), *Report of the CMEC Quality Assurance Subcommittee*, Ottawa: CMEC.

Dennison, J. (ed.) (1995), *Challenge and Opportunity: Canada's Community Colleges at the Crossroads*, Vancouver: University of British Columbia Press.

Dennison, J. (2006), 'From community college to university: a personal commentary on the evolution of an institution', *The Canadian Journal of Higher Education*, **36** (2), 107–24.

Duckworth, H. (2000), *One Version of the Facts: My Life in the Ivory Tower*, Winnipeg: University of Manitoba Press.

Falconer, R. (1930), 'American influence on the higher education in Canada', *Transactions of the Royal Society of Canada*, **II**, 23–38.

Fisher, D., K. Rubenson, J. Bernatchez, R. Clift, G. Jones, J. Lee, M. MacIvor, J. Meredith, T. Shanahan and C. Trottier (2006), *Canadian Federal Policy and Postsecondary Education*, Vancouver: Centre for Policy Studies on Higher Education and Training, University of British Columbia.

Harvey, L. (2008), 'Placing Canadian quality assurance initiatives in an international context', 'CMEC Quality Assurance Symposium', Quebec City, Quebec, 27–8 May 2008.

Hodgetts, A.B. (1968), *What Culture? What Heritage? A Study of Civic Education in Canada*, Toronto: OISE Press.

Jones, G. (1997), 'A brief introduction to higher education in Canada', in G. Jones, *Higher Education in Canada: Different Systems, Different Perspectives*, New York: Garland Publishing, pp. 1–8.

Jones, G. (2009a), 'Internationalization and higher education policy in Canada: three challenges', in

R. Trilokekar, G.A. Jones and A. Shubert (eds), *Canada's Universities Go Global*, Toronto: Lorimer, pp. 355–69.

Jones, G. (2009b), 'Sectors, institutional types and the challenges of shifting categories: a Canadian commentary', *Higher Education Quarterly*, **63** (4), 371–83.

Jones, G.A. (2009c), 'Why so little public accountability for quality?', in *Accounting or Accountability in Higher Education: Proceedings from the January 8, 2009 OCUFA Conference*, Toronto: Ontario Confederation of University Faculty Associations, pp. 45–9.

Jones, G. and A. Oleksiyenko (2011), 'The internationalization of Canadian university research: a global higher education matrix analysis of multi-level governance', *Higher Education*, online, March, DOI: 10.1007/s10734-010-9324-8.

Jones, G., T. Shanahan, L. Padure, S. Lamoureux and E. Gregor (2008), *Marshalling Resources for Change: System-level Initiatives to Increase Accessibility to Postsecondary Education*, Ottawa: Canada Millennium Scholarship Foundation.

Knight, J. (2003), 'Report on quality assurance and recognition of qualifications in postsecondary education in Canada', presented 3–4 November 2004 at OECD/Norway Forum on Trade in Educational Services.

Levin, J. (2003), 'Two British Columbia University Colleges and the process of economic globalization', *The Canadian Journal of Higher Education*, **33** (3), 59–86.

Marginson, S. (2006), 'Putting "public" back into the public university', *Thesis 11*, **84**, 44–59.

Marginson, S. (2007), 'University mission and identity for a post post-public era', *Higher Education Research and Development*, **26** (1), 117–31.

Marginson, S. and G. Rhoades (2002), 'Beyond national states, markets, and systems of higher education: a glonacal agency heuristic', *Higher Education*, **43**, 281–309.

Marshall, D. (2004), 'Degree accreditation in Canada', *The Canadian Journal of Higher Education*, **34** (2), 69–96.

Mathews, R. and J. Steele (1969), *The Struggle for Canadian Universities*, Toronto: New Press.

McKillop, A. (1994), *Matters of the Mind: The Ontario University, 1791–1951*, Toronto: University of Toronto Press.

Metcalfe, A. and T. Fenwick (2009), 'Knowledge for whose society?: Knowledge production, higher education, and federal policy in Canada', *Higher Education*, **57**, 209–25.

Networks of Centres of Excellence of Canada (2004), *The Networks of Centres of Excellence Program: 15 Years of Innovation and Leadership*, Ottawa: Networks of Centres of Excellence of Canada.

OECD (1996), *The Knowledge Based Economy*, Paris: OECD.

OECD (2008), *Tertiary Education for the Knowledge Society*, Paris: OECD.

Olssen, M. and M. Peters (2005), 'Neoliberalism, higher education, and the knowledge economy: from free market to knowledge capitalism', *Journal of Educational Policy*, **20**, 313–45.

Ozaga, J. (2007), 'Knowledge and policy: research and knowledge transfer', *Critical Studies in Education*, **48** (1), 63–78.

Picard, F. and D. Mills (2009), 'The internationalization of Quebec universities: from public policies to concrete measures', in R. Trilokekar, G.A. Jones and A. Shubert (eds), *Canada's Universities Go Global*, Toronto: Lorimer, pp. 134–53.

Polster, C. (2007), 'The nature and implications of the growing importance of research grants to Canadian universities and academics', *Higher Education*, **53**, 599–622.

Rajagopal, P. and H. Buchbinder (1996), 'Canadian universities: the impact of free trade and globalization', *Higher Education*, **3** (3), 283–99.

Shanahan, T. and G.A. Jones (2007), 'Shifting roles and approaches: government coordination of post-secondary education in Canada, 1995–2006', *Higher Education Research and Development*, **26** (1), 31–43.

Shubert, A., G.A. Jones and R. Trilokekar (2009), 'Introduction', in R. Trilokekar, G.A. Jones and A. Shubert (eds), *Canada's Universities Go Global*, Toronto: Lorimer, pp. 7–15.

Slaughter, S. and L. Leslie (1997), *Academic Capitalism: Politics, Policies and the Entrepreneurial University*, Baltimore, MD: Johns Hopkins University Press.

Statistics Canada (2009), *Education Indicators in Canada: an international perspective* (Cat. No. 81-604-X), Ottawa: Statistics Canada/Canada Education Statistics Council.

Statistics Canada (2010), *Canada's Population Clock*, retrieved 22 February, 2010 from http://www.statcan.gc.ca/edu/clock-horloge/edu06f_0001-eng.htm.

Stensaker, B. (2007), 'Impact of quality processes', in L. Bollaert, S. Brus, B. Curvale, L. Harvey, E. Helle, H.T. Jensen, J. Komljenovic, A. Orphanides and A. Sursock (eds) (2007), *Embedding Quality Culture In Higher Education: A Selection Of Papers From The 1st European Forum For Quality Assurance*, Brussels: European University Association, pp. 59–62.

Symons, T. (1975), *To Know Ourselves: The Report of the Commission on Canadian Studies*, Volumes 1 and 2, Ottawa: Association of Universities and Colleges of Canada.

Trilokekar, R. (2009), 'The Department of Foreign Affairs and International Trade (DFAIT), Canada:

providing leadership in the internationalization of Canadian higher education?', in R. Trilokekar, G.A. Jones and A. Shubert (eds), *Canada's Universities Go Global*, Toronto: Lorimer, pp. 98–118.

Tudiver, N. (1999), *Universities for Sale: Resisting Corporate Control over Canadian Higher Education*, Toronto: Lorimer.

Välimaa, J. and D. Hoffman (2008), 'Knowledge society discourse and higher education', *Higher Education*, **56**, 265–85.

van Vught, F.A. (1994), 'Intrinsic and extrinsic aspects of quality assessment in higher education', in D. Westerheijden, J. Brennan and P. Maassen (eds), *Changing Contexts of Quality Assessment: Recent Trends in West European Higher Education*, Utrecht: Lemma, pp. 31–50.

van Vught, F.A., M. Van der Wende and D. Westerheijden (2002), 'Globalization and internationalization: policy agendas compared', in J. Enders and O. Fulton (eds), *Higher Education in a Globalizing World: International Trends and Mutual Observations; a Festschrift in Honour of Ulrich Teichler*, London: Kluwer Academic, pp. 103–20.

Williams, G. (2005), *Doctoral Education in Canada*, Ottawa: Canadian Association of Graduate Studies.

Wolfe, D. (2005), 'The role of universities in regional development cluster formation', in G.A. Jones, P. McCarney and M. Skolnik (eds), *Creating Knowledge, Strengthening Nations: The Changing Role of Higher Education*, Toronto: University of Toronto Press, pp. 167–94.

14 Globalization, internationalization and the world-class university movement: the China experience

Mei Li and Qiongqiong Chen

INTRODUCTION

It is now widely noted that globalization is reshaping higher education worldwide. Over the past three decades the higher education system in China has undergone significant developments in response to both international and internal changes in economic and social contexts. Higher educational policies have been deeply affected by these developments, and this can be observed in various ways: the decentralization of national administrative structures; expansion of university autonomy; diversification of the financial resources for higher education institutions; government-promoted merging of existing institutions; the encouragement of private institutions; and the establishing of stronger ties by universities with the international academic community (Yang, 2002; Yoder, 2006; Huang, 2007; Vidovich et al., 2007; Mok and Chan, 2008; Ngok and Guo, 2008; Deem et al., 2008).

These trends reflect international contexts and a rising tide of such notions as 'competition', 'efficiency' and 'accountability' that are vigorously diffused by the processes of globalization (Zha, 2011). As economic growth and global competitiveness are increasingly driven by knowledge and technology, research universities particularly play a key role in accelerating and strengthening their own and their nation's global standing. Therefore their internationalization deserves close examination.

This chapter examines how and with what major strategies government and universities in Mainland China have changed in response to globalization. More specifically the focus is on the building of world-class universities and related policies. The chapter explores how, and in what ways, research universities in China have attempted to benchmark with the best universities worldwide. The first section begins with an overview of changes in the processes of internationalization of higher education in China in three related dimensions: the mobility of students and faculty; cross-border collaboration; and the internationalizing of the curriculum. The second section looks particularly at government's policy priority of developing world-class universities, with a focus on Project 211 and Project 985. The third section discusses how research universities in China are internationalizing themselves to facilitate entry into the world-class university league tables and uses Tsinghua University and Peking University as examples. The final section concludes with a critical reflection on the ongoing 'world-class university movement' in China. Consideration is given to the contributions that Chinese universities might bring to a reshaping of global intellectual culture.

INTERNATIONALIZING HIGHER EDUCATION IN CHINA

The internationalization of higher education is widely regarded as part of a country's response to the impact of globalization (Knight, 1999). In order to compete in the global economy and achieve an advanced academic status worldwide, China has been remarkably open in its approach to internationalizing higher education. The past 30 years have witnessed China as one of the world's largest education-importing countries, sending thousands of students to study abroad, as well as being a fast-growing receiver of students from overseas. Meanwhile China also actively engages in substantial forms of international cooperation, participating in collaborative research projects and international university consortia.

The first remarkable aspect of higher education internationalization in China was the increasing mobility of students and staff around the world. Prior to 1990 the internationalization of higher education in China was fundamentally characterized by sending students and faculty abroad for advanced studies and research (Huang, 2007). From 1978 to 1980 almost all were selected from leading universities and supported with public funds. In 1981 the State Council issued a document *Interim Provisions for Study Abroad with Self-funding*, which permitted students to study abroad at their own expense. Since then the number of overseas Chinese students has increased dramatically, some still under government sponsorship but with many more at their own expense.

Initially Chinese students mainly chose English-speaking countries in which to study, but a recent trend has been towards a greater diversification of destinations, including countries such as Japan, South Korea, Singapore, Russia and Spain (Hayhoe and Liu, 2010). Table 14.1 shows that by the end of 2008 the total number of students studying abroad had risen to 179 800, with 11 400 central-government-sponsored students but with self-financed students totaling 161 600, around 90 percent of the overall numbers (Pan et al., 2009). The number of students under central-government sponsorship was relatively stable at around 3000 to 5000 for around two decades but then climbed to surpass 10 000 in 2008. This leap reflects the government's determination to accelerate the process of internationalizing talents by expanding overseas study scholarships.

Historically Chinese universities have had an international peripheral status for more than a century, sending large numbers of students abroad for higher studies but receiving a relatively small number of international students in return (Hayhoe and Liu, 2010). However, the last three decades have seen Chinese universities seeking a more central place in global academic cultures, with a rising number of incoming international students. From 1979 to 1999 the total number of international students studying in China had reached 342 000 (MOE, no date), but most were short-term students in Chinese language and culture programs. In 2000 the State Council issued the *Rules on Foreign Students' Enrollment in China's Colleges and Universities*, which formulated the principles and policies for recruiting international students, the detailed management work and residential procedures (China Research and Education Network, 2001).

Since then both the quantity and quality of international students has improved significantly. In 2000 the number of international students studying in China was 52 000. By the end of 2007 the total number rose to 195 503, among which degree students accounted for 34 percent (of which 84 percent were undergraduate, 11 per cent masters, and 5 percent in PhD programs) (MOE, 2008). In 2008 there were 3 million interna-

Table 14.1 *Numbers of Chinese students studying abroad*

Year	Number of public funded students			Number of self-funded students	Total
	Funded by central government	Funded by local government and employers	Total		
1980	2124	–	–	4000*	–
1982	2326	–	–	6000*	–
1984	3073	–	–	6877	–
1986	4676	–	–	10000*	–
1996	1905	5400	7305	13600	20905
1998	2639	3540	6179	11443	17622
2000	2808	3888	6696	32293	38989
2002	3500	4500	8000	117000	125000
2004	3500	6900	10400	104300	114700
2006	5580	7542	13122	120700	134000
2008	11400	6800	18200	161600	179800

Notes:
– = data not available.
* = estimated.

Source: Li and Zhang (2010).

tional students worldwide and China ranked as the sixth destination for international students in the world (6 percent), after the US (21 percent), the UK (13 percent), France (9 percent), Germany (8 percent) and Australia (7 percent) (Institute for International Education, 2010). Clearly the attraction of the degree programs of Chinese universities to international students is still largely at the undergraduate level and in the areas of language and cultural programs (69 percent). Yet there are indications of a broadening range of knowledge areas, such as economics (4.5 percent), management (4.3 percent), engineering (3.4 percent), and law (2.4 percent) (MOE, 2009).

The second significant development of recent years has been transnational programs, designed to encourage international linkages and cooperation in the form of joint-degree programs, collaborative research projects and international university consortia. In promoting these practices the Chinese government has implemented varied legislations and documentations, among which two documents need to be noted. These are the *Interim Provisions for Chinese–Foreign Cooperation in Running Schools* launched in 1995 and the *Regulations of the People's Republic of China on Chinese–Foreign Cooperation in Running Schools* promulgated in 2002. These stipulate that foreign organizations are legally permitted to provide education in China but they must partner with Chinese universities and must not seek profit as their objective. They also restrict the levels and forms of the joint programs, excluding compulsory education and those forms of education and training under special provisions by the state (Huang, 2006b; Yang, 2008).

The first joint program was an MBA program started in 1988, operated by Tianjin University of Finance and Economics and Oklahoma City University of the USA (Huang, 2006b). After China joined the WTO in 2001 such programs had expanded to

745 by 2004, among which 169 were qualified to grant overseas degrees (including Hong Kong) (Yang, 2008). These joint programs are identified as an important complementary component of the Chinese higher education system. They not only give Chinese universities the opportunity to cooperate with international counterparts while maintaining the integrity of their own curriculum and degree requirements, but they also give students the chance to gain foreign degrees while doing the majority of their study in China (Hayhoe and Liu, 2010).

At the same time Chinese universities are also actively extending their own programs to an international arena by setting up cooperative branch schools and Confucius Institutes worldwide. The first Confucius Institute opened in South Korea in 2004 and many more have been established in other countries, such as the USA, Germany and Japan. By the end of 2007 there were 226 Confucius Institutes and Centers in 66 different countries and regions (MOE, 2009). These Institutes play an important role in promoting Chinese language and culture, and strengthening educational and cultural exchange between China and other countries.

Last but not least, internationalizing the curriculum is regarded as an essential way of engaging with the processes of globalization (Rizvi and Lingard, 2010). While the idea of the internationalization of the curriculum has become popular, there's no clear interpretation of what it means specifically. The discussion of internationalization in most Chinese universities is inextricably linked to the English language, evidenced in such matters as introducing English-language original textbooks and promoting English or bilingual instruction. In 2001 the Ministry of Education issued a document requiring that 5 to 10 percent of all curricula in the leading universities should be taught in English, especially in the areas of natural science and professional disciplines such as biology, information science, material sciences, economics and business studies (Huang, 2006a). Another way Chinese universities have sought to internationalize the curriculum is by establishing study-abroad programs, which we explore further in case studies of Peking University and Tsinghua University in the next section. Study abroad is considered as a pragmatic, quick and achievable way of internationalizing the curriculum because it does not require significant structural changes to the existing curriculum (Rizvi and Lingard, 2010).

THE QUEST FOR WORLD-CLASS UNIVERSITIES AT GOVERNMENTAL LEVEL: PROJECT 211 AND PROJECT 985

After a brief overview of the process of internationalizing higher education in China, this section looks particularly at the government's policy priorities in relation to building world-class universities. The Chinese government has a clear strategy of developing a small number of universities to reach world standards, with the decision to select 100 for intensive funding under Project 211, then to further focus on a smaller number of top universities and turning them into world-leading institutions under Project 985 (Mok and Chan, 2008; Ngok and Guo, 2008). The quest for world-class universities indicates that the internationalization of higher education in China is no longer confined to issues of mobility and transnational collaboration. Rather it shows that China is trying to build up its own centers of excellence to benchmark with the best universities worldwide (Huang, 2007; Mok and Chan, 2008).

Table 14.2   Funds for Project 211 (unit: billion yuan in renminbi – RMB)

	Total	Source of funding			Funding expense		
		Central government	Local government	University	Overall capacity	Key disciplinary	Public service
First round (1996–2000)	18.63	2.755	10.32	5.56	8.55	6.47	3.61
Second round (2001–2006)	18.75	6	5.97	6.78	5.26	9.79	3.71
Third round (2007–2011)	n.a.	10	n.a.	n.a.	n.a.	n.a.	n.a.

Source: MOE (2008).

Project 211

Project 211 is the Chinese government's great endeavor to strengthen about 100 institutions of higher education and key disciplinary areas as a national priority for the twenty-first century. It was officially implemented in 1995 under the direct guidance of the Central Committee of the Communist Party of China (CCCPC) and the State Council, and with the coordination of the State Planning Commission, Ministry of Education and Ministry of Finance (MOE, 2004). The objective is to train high-level professional manpower to implement a national strategy for social and economic development and to promote some of the key universities and disciplinary areas reaching advanced international standards, so that the international profile of Chinese higher education institutions overall is raised.

Project 211 consists of three major components for development: (1) improving institutional capacity – through efforts to train a large number of academic leaders and competent teachers, enhancing infrastructure and laboratory facilities for teaching and research, and strengthening international exchange and co-operation in higher education; (2) developing key disciplinary areas that can have a significant impact on social and economic development, scientific and technological advancement and national defense; and (3) developing the public service system of higher education through the development of the Chinese Education and Research Network (CERNET), the Library and Documentation Support System (LDSS), and the Modern Equipment and Facilities Sharing System (MEFSS) (China Research and Education Network, 2001; MOE, 2008).

As shown in Table 14.2 with regard to funding, during the first phase of the Project from 1996 to 2000, China invested a total of 18.63 billion yuan, with 2.75 billion yuan coming from central government (US$1 equals around 6–7 yuan). During the second period from 2001 to 2006, the central government alone invested 6 billion yuan and the total investment was 18.75 billion yuan (MOE, 2008). For the third phase (2007–11) of construction, the central government increased its funding to 10 billion yuan, with the emphasis on 'the cultivating of talents and competent faculty'.

By 2008 there were 106 key universities and colleges within Project 211, 6 percent of the higher education institutions in China. However, Project 211 institutions take on the responsibility for training 80 percent of doctoral students, 67 percent of masters' students, and 33 percent of undergraduates. They offer 85 percent of the state's key subjects, hold 96 percent of the key laboratories, and utilize 70 percent of scientific research funding (*People's Daily Online*, 2008). The implementation of Project 211 has also brought a significant growth in enrollment rates at various levels. Moreover, the number of faculty with doctoral degrees and publications in the Standard Citation Index (SCI) has increased five and seven times respectively (MOE, 2008). These figures indicate that Project 211, as the first key national initiative in promoting universities with world-class standards, has made a significant contribution to the quality enhancement of higher education in China (Mok and Chan, 2008).

Project 985

Project 985, aiming at developing several top universities to be world-leading, marked a second step in the quality enhancement of higher education in China (Mok and Chan, 2008). On 4 May 1998 President Jiang Zemin asserted that 'China must have several first-rate universities of advanced international level' (MOE, 1998, p. 2). In 1999 the *Action Plan of Education Promotion for the Twenty-First Century* stressed that within the first two decades of the twenty-first century certain key universities and areas of study should reach a world-class level. Such objectives were formulated under Project 985 (MOE, 2008). This Project reflects a strategy priority to concentrate limited resources on a small group of universities with the greatest potential for success in the international academic marketplace.

In the initial stage of the Project, only the top two universities, Peking University and Tsinghua University, were selected to be intensively funded by the central government and granted 1.8 billion yuan for the first three-year cycle. Given the financial limitations and the pressure from universities, the central government decided to involve local government in the campaign. In 1999 seven more universities were included in the list of budding world-class universities. These were: University of Science and Technology of China; Fudan University; Shanghai Jiao Tong University; Nanjing University; Xi'an Jiao Tong University; Zhejiang University; and Harbin Institute of Technology (see Table 14.3). For example, Fudan University and Nanjing University were granted 1.2 billion yuan respectively, with half from central government and half from local governments (Gong and Li, 2010; Ngok and Guo, 2008).

The second phase of Project 985, launched in 2004, increased the number of included universities to 36. During this period central government alone invested 19.1 billion yuan to enable more universities to achieve world renown (MOE, 2008). In addition to enhancing the effectiveness of existing laboratories, developing new research centers and improving facilities, much of the 985 funding has been used to build international networks, such as holding international conferences, attracting world-renowned faculty and visiting scholars, sending students and faculty abroad, and exploring ways to partner with top institutions around the world (Mok and Chan, 2008). Project 985 entered into the third phase in 2008, and, by 2010, 39 universities were included. These universities have undoubtedly benefited from the Project. With such large sums of extra money they are in a better position to recruit top talent and to improve laboratories and other facilities. Their capacity for teaching and research has been greatly enhanced and their competitive edge in advanced areas has been sharpened.

Table 14.3   Funds received in the first phase of Project 985 (unit: billion yuan in renminbi – RMB)

Higher institutions	Total	Central government	Local government and others
Peking University	1.8	1.8	0
Tsinghua University	1.8	1.8	0
Nanjing University	1.2	0.6	0.6
Fudan University	1.2	0.6	0.6
Shanghai Jiao Tong University	1.2	0.6	0.6
University of Science and Technology of China	0.9	0.3	0.6[a]
Xi'an Jiao Tong University	0.9	0.6	0.3
Zhejiang University	1.4	0.7	0.7
Harbin Institute of Technology	1.0	0.3	0.7[b]
Total	11.4	7.3	4.1

Notes:
[a]   Half from local government and half from the Chinese Academy of Sciences.
[b]   0.4 billion yuan from local government and 0.3 billion yuan from the Commission of Science Technology and Industry for National Defense.

Source: Gong and Li (2010).

Program 111 and the State-Sponsored Graduate Scholarship Program

Both Project 211 and Project 985 place great emphasis on the importance of creating a high concentration of talent, and this has resulted in two important program initiatives: Program 111 and the State-Sponsored Graduate Scholarship Program. The former aims to attract the most qualified professors and researchers to develop advanced teaching and learning, while the latter looks to send excellent students and faculty abroad to learn from their international counterparts. Program 111, also called the Program for Introducing Disciplinary Talents to Universities, was launched by the MOE and the State Administration of Foreign Experts Affairs (SAFEA) in 2006. The objective is to establish 100 world-leading disciplinary innovation bases by gathering 1000 overseas talents from the top 100 universities or research institutions worldwide to enhance the innovation capability and overall competitiveness of China's universities at global level (MOE, 2005). Only universities under Project 985 and Project 211 can be chosen for Program 111. The overseas talents must be world-renowned professors or scholars who are required to work at least one month a year within China. Disciplines covered by Program 111 are mainly science, technology, engineering and management. MOE and SAFEA allocated at least 600 million yuan between 2006 and 2010 for the Program (MOE, 2005).

The State-Sponsored Graduate Scholarship Program for Building High-level Universities was launched in 2007 under the supervision of the China Scholarship Council (CSC). This program, with funds from central government, aims to send excellent students to study in world-class universities. In 2007, 3952 students were selected, with 3549 in joint PhD programs, and 403 in regular PhD programs abroad. A total of 83 percent of the students were from 985 Project universities and 62 percent entered the top 100 world-class universities (CSC, 2008). In 2008 CSC increased the number of students to 4892, of which 2753 were PhD candidates in joint Chinese and foreign institution arrangements and 2139 were pursuing doctoral degrees abroad (CSC, 2009). This indicated that the Chinese government is encouraging more graduate students to pursue PhD degrees abroad and then to return to use their expertise and knowledge to help China's technological, scientific and economic development.

UNIVERSITIES' RESPONSE TO GLOBALIZATION: THE CASES OF TSINGHUA UNIVERSITY AND PEKING UNIVERSITY

With strong support from the government, some top universities are selected and encouraged in the national quest for world-class universities. Peking University and Tsinghua University are used here as cases to explain how major research universities in China are internationalizing as part of a build-up to becoming world-class universities. Peking University, as the first formally established modern national university of China in 1898, has produced and hosted many of modern China's prominent thinkers, scholars and politicians. Tsinghua University, established in 1911, has played an important role in the construction of modernization in China. They are regarded as the top two universities in China by most national and international rankings.

Assigned by the Chinese government to be world-class universities like Oxford, Cambridge, Harvard or Stanford, both Tsinghua and Peking universities have made concerted efforts to internationalize and enhance global competiveness through student exchange programs, collaborative international research projects, hiring Chinese scholars from graduate schools at top universities in developed countries, and inviting foreign scholars to campus to teach and conduct research.

Internationalizing Staff and Students

One key determinant of an excellent university is the ability to attract international professors and researchers. These individual talents can help upgrade existing departments or establish advanced research centers in new areas of competitive advantage (Salmi, 2009). Unfortunately both Peking University and Tsinghua University have had a very low proportion of overseas faculty members. After joining Project 211 and Project 985 they have endeavored to recruit overseas scholars and promising Chinese graduates from world-leading universities. For example, Tsinghua University has launched a recruitment program seeking to attract 100 outstanding scholars as academic leaders in various disciplines and allocated about 200 million yuan in support (Ngok and Guo, 2008). In addition, it has offered incentives, including flexible remuneration and employment conditions, housing, modern laboratories and equipment, and good research terms, to bring them on board. By 2007, 116 promising academics had been recruited under this program. Furthermore, there were 725 overseas experts for short-term and 157 overseas experts for long-term positions (Yuan and Pan, 2009).

The strategies adopted by Peking University involve using national funding under

Program 111, Peking University (PKU) overseas scholar Fellowships, and Deanship Global Hunting to make itself a preferred destination of talents into China. For example among 1882 faculty members with doctorates in 2007, 45.7 percent were Peking University graduates, 23.2 percent were from other universities in China, and 31.1 percent were graduates who had returned from abroad (Hayhoe et al., forthcoming). In order to recruit and retain outstanding academic leaders, Peking University conducted a policy of giving high levels of autonomy to certain units. Under this policy academic salaries and research funding are under the direct control of each unit (ibid.).

Another way to internationalize the campus is to recruit international students. An influx of foreign students can enrich the quality of the learning experience through a multicultural dimension and more generally upgrade the academic level of the student population (Salmi, 2009). Both universities are proactively attracting international students through outreach and promotional activities and by offering scholarships. At Tsinghua University the number of international students has increased significantly over the last decade. The total of 546 in 2000 had, by 2007, increased to 2204 from 87 countries and accounted for 7 percent of the total enrollment number. These comprised 56.53 percent who were degree students (809 pursuing bachelor degrees, 320 masters and 117 in doctorate programs (Yuan and Pan, 2009)).

At Peking University 2780 international students were studying in 2009, 8 percent of the total student number: 70 percent degree students, with 1550 in undergraduate programs, 364 in masters' programs, and 218 in PhD programs (Xia, no date). Although the proportion of international students is still relatively low compared to the top universities in English-speaking countries, there are already indications of considerable progress.

At the same time, both Peking and Tsinghua send increasing numbers of students and staff to study abroad. The number of Tsinghua staff going abroad increased from 2706 in 2004 to 3856 in 2007, while the number of students studying abroad rose from 1018 in 2004 to 1966 in 2007 (Yuan and Pan, 2009).

Building International Networks and Joint-degree Programs

With the support of Project 985 and Project 211, both universities have made efforts to establish international links with top universities overseas through joint-research projects, exchange programs and co-organizing international conferences. Peking University (PKU) has relied most on strategic alliances and partners globally. By 2008 it had established 68 programs with more than 200 universities around the world for academic exchange, as well as 11 school programs (such as Yale Summer School; Munich International Summer School; Auckland Summer School; Summer Institute of Economics, in cooperation with the London School of Economics; Summer Institute in Social Statistics, in cooperation with the University of Michigan), and 20 scholarship programs (for example Wing Ping Scholarships and the Cambridge Harvard–PKU China winter service program) to support their students with options for study abroad.

The most renowned international cooperation programs are: the PKU–Yale joint undergraduate program, which provides the opportunity for Yale and Peking students to study and live together on the PKU campus for a semester; the PKU–Waseda joint program, which enables students to spend two years at Waseda and the other two years at Peking for a degree in international relations (Hayhoe et al., forthcoming). Others include the PKU–Georgia Tech–Emory joint PhD in biomedical engineering; the PKU–Moscow State University joint Graduate School; the University of Michigan–PKU joint Institute; and the European Center for Chinese Studies at PKU.

Like Peking University, Tsinghua University also has impressive networks and partnerships with many overseas universities. In 2007 alone, Tsinghua University signed 580 new international co-research programs and held 72 international conferences (Yuan and Pan, 2009). Tsinghua is particularly enthusiastic about deepening its relationships with Rheinisch-Westfälische Technische Hochschule (RWTH) Aachen University by setting up a joint masters' program; with MIT Management School for a joint IMBA program; and with the Harvard Kennedy School of Government for a joint Public Management program. Through international cooperation both universities are promoting their areas of research excellence and raising their international research profiles.

Internationalizing the Curriculum

Both Tsinghua and Peking universities highlight the importance of internationalizing the curriculum as a way of becoming globally competitive. Most of their initiatives focus on study abroad, intercultural understanding and global competence. As discussed above, both universities are committed to facilitating study abroad and using educational exchange programs to enrich students' multicultural experiences. These programs comprise components of the curriculum with a full transfer of academic credit.

Other strategies for both universities to internationalize the curriculum are by promoting English as the medium of instruction and adopting cross-cultural education to develop their students' skills in intercultural communication. In the academic year 2006–07, Tsinghua University had 87 undergraduate courses that were taught in English while more than 22 schools and departments had adopted bilingual education for 125 courses. In the areas of information science, biology, law, economics and management, 16.1 percent of courses were taught in English and 23 percent of courses used English-language original textbooks (Yuan and Pan, 2009).

In their case study of Peking University, Hayhoe et al. (forthcoming) interviewed faculty about what they were most proud of at Peking from the recent reforms. Many mentioned the efforts to provide bilingual programs, which was regarded as a positive trend and as facilitating greater integration into the world community by providing opportunities for Peking students to interact with international students. In recent years a new summer teaching term has been added to those of autumn and winter/spring in Peking's curriculum in order to provide opportunities for students to be exposed to visiting international scholars as well as giving them greater flexibility for electives (Hayhoe et al., forthcoming). Beyond the formal curriculum Peking University also broadens its students' global experiences through a more informal curriculum, such as its prominent programs in the Beijing Forum, which aims at promoting the study of humanities and social sciences around the world. Students are highly encouraged to be involved in dialog with academic scholars on the broad issues of civilizations and social development.

These pictures of Tsinghua and Peking universities give interesting insights into the experience of two top universities in the move to integrate more internationally.

Their efforts to become world-class universities indicate a strong response to national priorities.

CRITICAL REFLECTIONS ON THE 'WORLD-CLASS UNIVERSITIES' MOVEMENT

With strong policy support from government for the objective of developing world-class universities, the financial positions and basic infrastructures of these selected key universities have improved substantively. However, the question raised is: how far are the '985 universities' still removed from the world-class level? Despite the controversial debates over the credibility of global university rankings, rankings are still widely used as a benchmark for gauging progress in relation to international peers. Recent tables by the Quacquarelli Symonds (QS) Asian University Rankings show that China's research universities continued to lag far behind their counterparts in Hong Kong and Japan (QS Top Universities, 2010). At the same time no Chinese universities were in the list of the world's top 100 universities in the Academic Ranking of World Universities of 2010 by Shanghai Jiao Tong University. It is obvious that the gap between Chinese top universities and world-class universities is still wide. Thus critical reflections are needed on the world-class university movement in China.

First, China's vision of world-class universities focuses almost exclusively on factors such as more buildings, more publications, up-to-date laboratory equipment, star professors and more money (Mohrman, 2005; Salmi, 2009). This vision, coupled with an academic culture that demands quick results ('leaping forward in development'), hampers innovation and long-term research efforts (Salmi, 2009). Mohrman (2005) argues that simply buying laboratory equipment or pushing for more journal articles will not guarantee the kind of intellectual atmosphere that has developed over centuries on European and American campuses. No matter how much money can be thrown at the endeavor, it is unrealistic to expect instant results. Building a world-class university does not happen overnight. It requires many years to create a university culture of excellence and achieve high-quality outputs.

Second, a lack of academic freedom and university autonomy are major constraints facing Chinese universities (Yang et al., 2007; Ngok and Guo, 2008). According to Altbach (2003), academic freedom and an atmosphere of intellectual excitement are central to a world-class university, where professors and students are free to pursue knowledge without fear of sanction by external authorities. Similarly, Salmi (2009) argues that the favorable governance for world-class universities requires institutions to make decisions and manage resources without being encumbered by bureaucracy.

However, China's central government exercises strong regulation and authority over the governance of universities in general and their internationalization in particular. It keeps strict control over the universities politically, financially and administratively (Ngok and Guo, 2008), such as through the political appointment of Party secretaries and university presidents, the allocation of financial resources and the admission of students, the criteria for the award of degrees, the curriculum, and the basic direction of teaching and research, especially in the fields of the social sciences and the humanities. Politically the academic work of universities must follow the Party's fundamental line;

financially universities become more dependent on the government with the increase of the central government budget; and administratively the decisions of universities are under control from government. Although the government makes concerted efforts to increase funding for selected universities, just investing money is not sufficient to build a world-class university. Experiences from the major world universities show that their success is not only due to their wealth but to their relative independence from the state and their ability to conduct academic work autonomously (Salmi, 2009).

Third, this authoritarian state leads to a dilemma in the world-class movement led by China's government. The state designates the list of institutions of Project 985 and Project 211 rather than nurturing a fair mechanism for open competition or allowing more diverse institutions to benefit from government resources.

Fourth, in the process of pursuing world-class and internationalized universities, Chinese universities should be fully aware of variations of excellence among different disciplines, particularly between hard and soft sciences. Chinese research universities could learn much from their counterparts in industrialized countries in the fields of hard sciences by taking international standards as their gauge. Meanwhile they should retain their domestic traditions and independence in the soft sciences (particularly humanities) and avoid the dangers of being externally or self-colonized. Social sciences and humanities are fundamentally culturally bounded and ideologically relevant and should be indigenous rather than internationalized.

Finally, consideration of 'world-class' within China is largely imitative rather than creative (Mohrman, 2005). The vision of 'world-class' in China has been influenced strongly by western standards or ideologies. The introduction of English as the medium of instruction, the adoption of textbooks from the English-speaking countries in Europe and more so the USA, sending students to study abroad, establishing exchanges, together with the quest for the world-class universities as predominantly defined by the western world, have reinforced a western hegemony and created a new culture of dependency (Deem et al., 2008). Thus simply copying the world top universities does not guarantee the successful building of world-class universities in China. What is needed is a creative vision based on specific cultural and political environments, and equal dialogue between Chinese universities and other universities worldwide.

Therefore it is necessary to critically examine, when attempting to internationalize universities for entry into the league table of world-class universities, what it means to be world-class. What constitutes a world-class university? Is there only one international standard or can the standards and practices commonly available in the west be coherently adapted to Chinese traditions and cultures?

The few scholars who have attempted to define world-class universities have identified a number of features, such as highly qualified faculty, diverse student groups, excellence in research, quality teaching, consistent and substantial public financial support, academic freedom and institutional autonomy, a university's contribution to society, as well as well-equipped facilities for teaching, research and administration (Altbach, 2003; Alden and Lin, 2004; Salmi, 2009). Yet despite this list of the key attributes, there is no real agreed definition of what is a world-class university. The paradox of world-class universities, as Altbach (2003, p. 5) has stated, is that 'everyone wants a world-class university. No country feels it can do without one. The problem is that no one knows what a world-class university is, and no one has figured out how to get one.'

In the case of China there is a long tradition of higher education scholarship, yet Chinese literature rarely refers to China's comparative advantage in competing with the top world universities, or to China's contribution to the broader internationalization of higher education. The criteria of world-class universities are weakly related to Chinese culture. Mohrman (2005, p. 22) states that 'it would be quite interesting to learn of a new definition of a world-class university that is not simply an imitation of Harvard but a creative blend of the best of east and west'.

CONCLUSION

In the pursuit of internationalization Chinese research universities should focus on the 'internationalization of the university of China' rather than the 'internationalization of the university in China'. That is, Chinese research universities have to reflect on how to balance and integrate the complexity and significances of localization, nationalization and internationalization.

China still faces the challenges of disequilibrium in its higher education export and import, and also pressing difficulties in the move from the periphery to the center of the world system. So far globalization has not changed the essence of the internationalization of higher education in China (Huang, 2007). A clear indicator is that China still exports more students abroad than it accepts. It imports more foreign educational programs and services than are exported. China is still influenced by English-language products, and maintains its basic character as essentially catching up with advanced countries and current centers of world-class learning that are mostly identified with the English-speaking countries in Europe and, even more so, the USA.

Given the notion that internationalization is an interactive response to globalization, China's response to globalization is both universal and unique. It is universal because, similar to other countries, the Chinese government and universities are concerned with such issues as: providing services abroad, recruiting foreign students, the employability of graduates, and the motivation driving faculty. At the same time the focus is unique. The internationalization of Chinese universities has a very strong image-building element and is associated with the building of world-class universities' policies and funding from central government. Both governmental policies and institutional leaders strongly support the development of world-class universities. Given the revolutionary changes in Chinese higher education over recent decades, it may be optimistic to believe that its blossoming will be only a matter of time.

REFERENCES

Alden, J. and G. Lin (2004), *Benchmarking the Characteristics of a World-class University: Developing an International Strategy at University Level*, London: Leadership Foundation for Higher Education.
Altbach, P. (2003), *The Costs and Benefits of World-class Universities: An American's Perspective*, Hong Kong China: Hong Kong America Center, Chinese University of Hong Kong.
China Research and Education Network (2001), *Rules on Foreign Students' Enrollment in China's Colleges and Universities*. Available at http://www.edu.cn/cooperate_1406/20060323/t20060323_17533.shtml, accessed 20 June 2010.

China Scholarship Council (2008), *CSC Annual Report 2007*, available at http://en.csc.edu.cn/uploads/20080813132840281.pdf, accessed 24 June 2010.

China Scholarship Council (2009), *CSC Annual Report 2008*, available at http://en.csc.edu.cn/uploads/20091014104613465.pdf, accessed 7 August 2010.

Deem, R., K.H. Mok and L. Lucas (2008), 'Transforming higher education in whose image? Exploring the concept of the "world-class" university in Europe and Asia', *Higher Education Policy*, **21** (1), 83–97.

Gong, F. and J. Li (2010), 'Seeking excellence in the move to a mass system: institutional responses and changes in Chinese key comprehensive universities', *Frontiers of Education in China*, **5** (4), 477–506.

Hayhoe, R. and J. Liu (2010), 'China's universities, cross-border education, and dialogue among civilizations', in D. Chapman, W. Cummings and G. Postiglione (eds), *Crossing Borders in East Asian Higher Education*, Dordrecht: Springer, pp. 77–100.

Hayhoe, R., Q. Zha and F. Yan (forthcoming), 'Peking University: icon of cultural leadership', in R. Hayhoe, J. Li, J. Lin and Q. Zha (eds), *Portraits of 21st Century Chinese Universities in the Move to Mass Higher Education*, Hong Kong: Comparative Education Research Centre, University of Hong Kong, pp. 95–130.

Huang, F. (2006a), 'Internationalization of curricula in higher education institutions in comparative perspective: case studies of China, Japan and The Netherlands', *Higher Education*, **51**, 521–39.

Huang, F. (2006b), 'Transnational higher education in mainland China: a focus on foreign degree-conferring programs', in F. Huang (ed.), *Transnational Higher Education in Asia and the Pacific Region*, Hiroshima: Research Institute for Higher Education, Hiroshima University, pp. 21–34.

Huang, F. (2007), 'Internationalization of higher education in the era of globalization: what have been its implications in China and Japan?', *Higher Education Management and Policy*, **19** (1), 47–61.

Institute for International Education (2010), *Global Destinations for International Students at the Post-secondary level, 2001 and 2008*, available at http://www.atlas.iienetwork.org/?p=48027, accessed 7 August 2010.

Knight, J. (1999), 'Internationalization of higher education', in J. Knight and H. de Wit (eds), *Quality and Internationalization in Higher Education*, Paris: OECD/IMHE, pp. 13–28.

Li, M. and Y. Zhang (2010), 'Two-way flows of higher education students in Mainland China in a global market: trends, characteristics and problems', in S. Marginson, S. Kaur and E. Sawir (eds), *Higher Education in the Asia-Pacific: Strategic Responses to Globalization*, Dordrecht: Springer.

Ministry of Education (MOE) (no date), *International Students in China*, available at http://www.moe.edu.cn/english/international_3.htm, accessed 24 June 2010.

Ministry of Education (MOE) (1995), *The Interim Provisions for Chinese–Foreign Cooperation in Running Schools*, Beijing MOE, available at http://www.moe.edu.cn/publicfiles/business/htmlfiles/moe/moe_861/200506/8600.html, accessed 22 March 2011.

Ministry of Education (MOE) (1998), *Kejiao xingguo dongyuanling [The Action of Revitalizing China through Science and Education]*, Beijing daxue chuban she [Peking University Press].

Ministry of Education (MOE) (1999), *The Action Plan of Education Promotion for the Twenty-First Century*, Beijing: MOE, available at http://www.moe.edu.cn/publicfiles/business/htmlfiles/moe/moe_177/200407/2487.html, accessed 22 March 2011.

Ministry of Education (MOE) (2003), *The Regulations of the People's Republic of China on Chinese–Foreign Cooperation in Running Schools*, Beijing: MOE, available at http://www.moe.edu.cn/publicfiles/business/htmlfiles/moe/moe_861/200506/8644.html, accessed 22 March 2011.

Ministry of Education (MOE) (2004), *211 gongcheng jianjie [Introduction to project 211]*, available at http://www.moe.edu.cn/edoas/website18/level3.jsp?tablename=724&infoid=5607, accessed 20 June 2010.

Ministry of Education (MOE) (2005), *Jiaoyubu guojia waiguo zhuanjiaju guanyu gaodeng xuexiao xueke chuangxin yinzhi jihua 'shiyiwu guihua' de tongzhi [Information about introducing disciplinary talents to higher institutions Eleventh Five-Year Plan by MOE and SAFEA]*, available at http://www.moe.edu.cn/edoas/website18/level3.jsp?tablename=1245&infoid=16682, accessed 25 June 2010.

Ministry of Education (MOE) (2008), *211 gongcheng, 985 gongcheng, ji yanjiusheng jiaoyu peiyang jizhi gaige youguan qingkuang [Project 211, Project 985, and the Reforms of Graduate Education]*, available at http://www.moe.edu.cn/edoas/website18/level3.jsp?tablename=1222139707228251&infoid=1223513711350102, accessed 25 June 2010.

Ministry of Education (MOE) (2009), *China Education Yearbook 2008*, Beijing: People's Education Press.

Mohrman, K. (2005), 'World-class universities and Chinese higher education reform', *International Higher Education*, **39**, 22–3.

Mok, K.H. and Y. Chan (2008), 'International benchmarking with the best universities: policy and practice in Mainland China and Taiwan', *Higher Education Policy*, **21**, 469–86.

Ngok, K. and W. Guo (2008), 'The quest for world-class universities in China: critical reflections', *Policy Futures in Education*, **6** (5), 545–57.

Pan, C.G., X.Y. Yang and J. Chang (2009), 'Zongbaogao: woguo liuxue rencai shiye de fazhan yu zhanwang [General report: the development and outlook of Chinese overseas education talents]', in H. Wang (ed.),

Zhongguo liuxue rencai fazhan baogao [The Report of the Development of Chinese Overseas Education Talents], Jixie gongye chuban she [Mechanical Press], pp. 1–37.

People's Daily Online (2008), 'Over 10 billion yuan to be invested in 211 Project', 26 March, available at http://english.people.com.cn/90001/6381319.html, accessed 25 June 2010.

QS Top Universities (2010), 13 May, available at http://www.topuniversities.com/university-rankings/asian-university-rankings, accessed 20 June 2010.

Rizvi, F. and B. Lingard (2010), *Globalizing Education Policy*, London: Routledge.

Salmi, J. (2009), *The Challenge of Establishing World-class Universities*, Washington, DC: World Bank.

Vidovich, L., R. Yang and J. Currie (2007), 'Changing accountabilities in higher education as China opens up to globalisation', *Globalisation, Societies and Education*, **5** (1), 89–107.

Xia, H. (no date), '*The internationalization of higher education at Peking University*', available at http://iehe.mohe.gov.sa/2010/files/The%20Internationalization%20of%20Higher%20Education%20at%20Peking%20University(Final).ppt, accessed 25 June 2010.

Yang, R. (2002), *Third Delight: The Internationalization of Higher Education in China*, New York and London: Routledge.

Yang, R. (2008), 'Transnational higher education in China: contexts, characteristics and concerns', *Australian Journal of Education*, **52** (3), 272–86.

Yang, R., L. Vidovich and J. Currie (2007), 'Dancing in a cage: changing autonomy in Chinese higher education', *Higher Education*, **54**, 575–92.

Yoder, B.L. (2006), Globalization of higher education in eight Chinese universities: incorporation of and strategic responses to world culture, doctoral dissertation, University of Pittsburgh, retrieved from ProQuest Digital Dissertations.

Yuan, B.T. and Y.L. Pan (2009), *Gaodeng Jiaoyu Guojihua Yu Shijie Yiliu Daxue Jianshe: Qinghua Daxue de Anli [Higher education internationalization and the quest for world class universities: A case study of Tsinghua University]*, Zhongguo Jiaoyu Keyan Cankao [Research Reference of Education in China], **9**, 24–9.

Zha, Q. (2011), 'Is there an emerging Chinese model of the university?', in J. Hayhoe, J. Li, J. Lin and Q. Zha (eds), *Portraits of 21st Century Chinese Universities in the Move to Mass Higher Education*, Hong Kong: Comparative Education Research Centre, University of Hong Kong, pp. 451–71.

15 European higher education and the process of integration
Jussi Välimaa

INTRODUCTION

This chapter explores the roles the European Union (EU) plays in the globalization of higher education. It begins by explaining briefly the nature and the political structures of the EU, followed by an analysis of how higher education has become an important policy domain in the EU and, finally, it reflects on how the EU promotes globalization in and for European higher education institutions.

In the field of higher education the EU plays the role of a globalizing regional actor that aims at creating a European Area of Higher Education (EAHE) and European Research Area (ERA) by relying on the Bologna Process and the Lisbon Strategy. Both of these processes aim at strengthening Europe as a knowledge-based economy and society in a global competition with other regions of the world. The influence the EU has on higher education cannot, therefore, be explained as a straightforward policy implementation process; there are many actors in the EU and the nature of the EU is basically a voluntary and often mercurial process of integration. To understand the interplay between the different actors in the EU requires a historical approach to understand the processes of integration between European nations and states.

According to the EU, 'The European Union . . . is not a State intended to replace the existing states, but it is more than just another international organization. The EU is, in fact, unique. Its Member States have set up common institutions to which they delegate some of their sovereignty so that decisions on specific matters of joint interest can be made democratically at European level' (http://europa.eu/abc/european_countries/languages/english/index_en.htm?_en). Traditionally matters that have been problematic include how to define what 'matters of joint interest' are, and how member states are able to delegate 'some of their sovereignty' to the EU. Education, including higher education, belongs to 'matters of joint interest' that have risen to the core of European policies during the 1990s, although they can be dated back to the 1950s. Therefore all current developments in globalizing European higher education can be understood properly in historical perspective. New higher education policy ideas in Europe did not emerge recently out of the blue, but have a longer lineage (Corbett, 2005).

A BRIEF HISTORY OF THE EU AND ITS INSTITUTIONS

The need for European cooperation was generally recognized in Western Europe after the conflict of the Second World War. The aims of cooperation were made public in the so-called 'Schuman Plan', which aimed at creating an organized Europe in order to maintain peaceful relations between European nations. The cooperation was launched by six countries (Germany, France, Italy, The Netherlands, Belgium and Luxembourg), which signed The Coal and Steel Treaty in 1951 to cooperate internationally to run their heavy industries, known to be essential for making weapons and for preparing for war. This initiative took place in the context of the emerging Cold War in Europe. The cooperation was expanded with the Treaty of Rome (in 1957), which created the European Economic Community (EEC), or 'common market', with the aim of enabling people, goods, services and capital to move freely across borders. The EEC Treaty also had political objectives to achieve common policies, in addition to providing the establishment of a common market and a customs union.

The EEC was expanded when Denmark, Ireland and the UK joined in 1973, followed by Greece in 1981, Portugal and Spain in 1986, and the eastern parts of Germany in 1990. The Maastricht Treaty, signed in 1991 and effective in 1993, has been defined as the major EU milestone that advanced the integration process by agreeing on the timetable and criteria for moving to Economic and Monetary Union (EMU), and by creating the conditions for intensified or new EU political cooperation in two fundamental areas of national sovereignty: foreign policy, and justice and home affairs. It was also agreed that the EU become the official name of the Community. The Maastricht Treaty also introduced the principle of 'subsidiarity' to govern 'the distribution of responsibilities and powers between different levels of governance'. In practice this principle means, to take education as an example, that the Commission cannot initiate any action intended to harmonize the member states' education policies or structures without the explicit consent of the member states (Corbett, 2005; Maassen and Musselin, 2009). In 2010 there were 27 countries in the EU, and three new ones were in various phases of the membership negotiation processes.

From the very beginning there have also been two main interpretations of the purposes for European cooperation and integration. Following the line of reasoning suggested by Jean Monnet (who was behind the Schuman Plan), the aim was to unite people not states, whereas Winston Churchill presented a more federal line of reasoning with his idea of creating a version of the United States of Europe. These political tensions over the purposes of the EU shape the political reality even today. The relationship between the European Commission and the nation-states has been a major field of power struggles, with nation-states defending their sovereignty and the Commission promoting European integration. These tensions have also influenced the ways education – including higher education – have been seen and defined in the EU. Traditionally educational policies have been regarded by the member states as a component of national sovereignty rather than a European-level domain. This rationale is rooted in the perception that systems of education play a crucial role in the socialization of citizens into national cultures, societies, labor markets and politics. Systems of education are regarded as the core of activities run by the nation-states (Gornitzka, 2009).

The most recent development of European integration has been the Treaty of Lisbon (initially known as the 'Reform Treaty', or the 'European Constitution'), which came into force on 1 December 2009 following years of controversy. Even though it is far too early to say whether it will make the EU more democratic and efficient – as has been claimed – or more centralized and bureaucratic – as has also been argued – it is clear that it changes the decision-making processes in the EU. According to the Treaty there will be more qualified majority voting in the Council of Ministers and an increased involvement of the European Parliament in the legislative process in cooperation with the Council of Ministers. There will also be a long-term President of the European Council and a High Representative of the Union for Foreign Affairs and Security Policy. This Treaty has also strengthened the role of the EU in the creation of the European Research Area, discussed below.

The process of European integration has involved other European institutions that are not subordinated to the EU, but work in close cooperation with it. The Council of Europe established in 1949, with the objectives to promote European cultural values, human rights and the rule of law, provides a good example of that kind of cooperation. The Council of Europe is a separate organization from the EU, extending geographically over the borders of the EU with its 47 member states (http://www.coe.int/). However, all the present EU member states have been members of the Council of Europe, thus demonstrating shared European values. Similarly with the Bologna Process, for only countries that are members of the Council of Europe are eligible for the membership in the European Higher Education Area that Bologna promotes (Berlin Communiqué, 2003).

THE MAIN TASKS OF THE EUROPEAN PARLIAMENT, THE COUNCIL OF EUROPE AND THE EUROPEAN COMMISSION

To understand the dynamics of the EU requires knowledge of the main European institutions; they have different roles in setting the frameworks of action for higher education too. The main task of the European Parliament is to pass European laws on the basis of proposals presented by the European Commission – and, in principle, it has the power to dismiss the European Commission. Since 1975, members of the European Parliament have been elected every five years by the people of Europe. The Council of the EU (formerly known as the Council of Ministers), which represents the member states, is the EU's main decision-making body. Meetings take place at the level of European ministers. However, when the Council meets as heads of state or at government level, it becomes the European Council, whose role is to provide the EU with political impetus on key issues. The Parliament and the Council also share authority for approving the EU's annual budget (currently €130 billion). The Council of the EU shares with Parliament the responsibility for passing EU laws. It is also in charge of the EU's foreign, security and defense policies, and is responsible for key decisions on justice and freedom issues.

The European Commission (EC) is the executive organ of the EU. It represents and upholds the interests of Europe as a whole and drafts proposals for new European laws, which it presents to the European Parliament and the Council. It also manages the day-to-day business of implementing EU policies. The Commission consists of 27 members – one from each EU country. They are assisted by about 24 000 civil servants, most of whom work in Brussels. The Commission is a unique international organization in the sense that it has the potential to act independently as an executive (Egeberg, 2006). It is structured according to departments known as the Directorates-General (DGs) covering specific policy areas. Originally higher education matters belonged to the DG for Research, Science and Education, whereas now these questions are handled in the DG for Education and Culture (EAC). The administrative capacity in higher education consists of some 550 officials and temporary agents, which is about half the staff working with European research policy. The EC's committee structure is a crucial part of the EU system of governance as it represents the system of expertise that drafts proposals and prepares new policies. It links both the member states' governments, the different levels of administration within the Commission, and various outside partners when putting policies and programs into action (Gornitzka, 2009).

In addition to these European political institutions, the Court of Justice of the EU constitutes the judicial authority of the EU. It was established originally as the Court of Justice of the European Coal and Steel Communities in 1952. Since the Treaty of Lisbon (2009) its mission has been to ensure that the law is observed in the interpretation and application of various European Treaties.

THE EU AND HIGHER EDUCATION

Traditional views hold that the EEC had no involvement with universities, or education in general, before the 1970s. According to Guy Neave (1984), it was 'taboo' because the national governments had not given the Community competence for education when they signed the Treaty of Rome. However, Corbett (2005) notes that this is not necessarily a correct interpretation; higher education was mentioned in the EC treaties as early as the 1950s.

According to Corbett (2005), EU higher education policy can be regarded as comprising three periods, with the treaties as landmarks. The first years (1952–57) marked the creation of three European communities: first the European Coal and Steel Community; then the EEC; and finally the European Atomic Energy Community (Euratom) in 1957. Higher education was, in fact, included in the Euratom Treaty in article 9 (2), which stated that 'an institution of university status shall be established'. This statement finally led to the establishment of the University Institute in Florence in the 1970s. However, the real significance of this article is not the establishment of European higher education institutions, but that higher education was perceived as important for European cultural integration (Corbett, 2005). Nonetheless, during the first decades of the EEC, education policy had a minor role; the key objective was to ease the free movement of labor through the mutual recognition of diplomas and cooperation in vocational education (Saarinen, 2007; Corbett, 2005).

The second period (1958–91) witnessed the growing political importance of education and higher education in the EEC. The ministers of education of the member states began their regular (unofficial) meetings in 1971, and the Council of Ministers defined the first general plan of action, establishing an education committee in 1976. This also gave the basis for European exchange and cooperation programs launched in the 1980s (Erasmus, Comett and Lingua), the creation of the teaching and information network (Eurydice), and the development of a statistical information system in cooperation with Eurostat (Lawn and Lingard, 2002). Important during this phase was the decision (the so-called Gravier judgment in 1985) given by the European Court of Justice, interpreting higher education as also by nature vocational.

This reinterpretation was significant because it opened for the first time an action line for the Commission to promote higher education in the name of the free movement of labor. This led to the decision to establish the Erasmus program in 1986 (effective in 1987) to promote student and teaching staff mobility and broader university cooperation in Europe. It is also significant that the Erasmus decision was the first EC decision in education made under Community rules (Corbett, 2005). Nowadays there are separate mobility programs for vocational education (Leonardo da Vinci), adult education (Grundtvig) and school education (Comenius). The naming of various mobility programs after famous European educators and scholars shows an appeal to a common European cultural heritage.

These mobility policies were and continue to be related to labor policy with the goal of producing a flexible workforce able and prepared to move between the member countries. From the perspective of cultural policy, the mobility programs have been seen to strengthen the integration and the sense of European identity (Corbett, 2005). The preparation of the Erasmus program was strongly supported by the European university rectors. It can be located in a policy continuum originating in the 1950s, when it was realized that the vision of free-market new Europe needed closer links between universities. However, from a critical perspective, Maassen and Musselin (2009) argue that the general trend in the EEC was the fact that the nation-states refused to provide the European Commission with formal competencies on higher education issues. This was one of the reasons why the EC was able to act only on relatively marginal topics like the mobility of students and staff, where its actions were justified by the construction of European labor market or vocational education objectives.

During the third period (since 1991) education entered the core of European policy-making following its inclusion in the Maastricht Treaty. Different levels of the educational system were no longer excluded from Commission competency, and the harmonization of the common educational space in Europe began, covered by the provision that the Community was 'fully respecting the responsibility of the member States for the content of their teaching and the organisation of the education systems and their cultural and linguistic diversity' (article 126). The Maastricht Treaty stipulated Community action to be aimed at: developing the European dimension of education; encouraging the mobility of students and teachers, *inter alia* by encouraging the academic recognition of diplomas and periods of study; and promoting cooperation between educational establishments (Corbett, 2005, p. 206). The Maastricht Treaty thus laid out, for the first time, the conditions under which the EU could intervene to support education. This was further emphasized in the Amsterdam Treaty (2004), which made it an explicit goal of the EU member states 'to promote the development of the highest possible level of knowledge for their peoples through a wide access to education and throughout its continuous updating' (Corbett, 2005, p. 9).

The Lisbon Treaty (2009) has the potential to have a strong influence on higher education because the development of the European Research Area (ERA) has been defined as one of the objectives of the EU. According to the Treaty (article 163):

> The Union shall have the objective of strengthening its scientific and technological bases by achieving a European Research Area in which researchers, scientific knowledge, and technology circulate freely, and encouraging it to become more competitive, including in its industry, while promoting all the research activities deemed necessary by virtue of other Chapters of the Treaties.

Here, once again, the ERA is connected to the mobility of people, a traditional policy objective in the EU. In addition, a step further is taken in article 166, which states that 'as a complement to the activities planned in the multiannual framework program, the European Parliament and the Council . . . shall establish the measures necessary for the implementation of the European Research Area'. In line with these decisions, the EC has already started to create a new EU2020 Strategy, under consultation while this chapter was being written (see below). It remains to be seen what kinds of measures will be taken by the EU and how these measures respect (or conflict with) the principle of subsidiarity. In any case it is clear that higher education is now defined as one of the major policy fields in the EU through the development the ERA.

Two main processes need to be understood in order to see the role played by the EU in the globalization of European higher education. This first is the Lisbon Strategy, which is closely related to the policy objectives of the EU. The other is the Bologna Process, which is not led by the EU for reasons explained below.

THE LISBON STRATEGY

Academic research had emphasized the importance of knowledge as a production factor, seen most famously in the 1970s with the work of Daniel Bell (1973). Subsequently Nico Stehr (1994) developed a social theory of the 'knowledge society' in order to explain social changes and the role knowledge plays in all spheres of society. Another academic tradition rooted in the traditions of neoliberal economic thinking has, in turn, introduced the concept of 'knowledge economy' to the wider public and has been influential in various policy arenas. 'Knowledge economy' has a narrower perspective than 'knowledge society', emphasizing the importance of knowledge in promoting economic activities and innovations (Välimaa and Hoffman, 2008). These concepts and ways of thinking found their way into EU higher education policy domains mainly through the perspectives of global competition and globalization in the 1990s. The main concern was, and is, how to make the EU more competitive in relation to its major competitors, the USA, Japan, and increasingly countries from the East Asian 'tiger economies', such as Singapore, South Korea and, more recently, China, plus India.

In this competitive context the EU has emphasized the importance of knowledge for economic development. In March 2000, at the meeting of the European heads of states (Lisbon European Council), these concerns promoted the declaration that the EU set itself a strategic goal for the forthcoming decade 'to become the most competitive and dynamic knowledge-based economy in the world, capable of sustainable economic growth with more and better jobs and greater social cohesion' (Lisbon European Council, 2000). The Lisbon Strategy rests on three pillars: the economic pillar aimed at development toward a competitive, dynamic, knowledge-based economy; the social pillar focused on modernizing the European social model by investing in human resources and combating social exclusion; and the environmental pillar aimed at ensuring that economic growth is decoupled from the use of natural resources. To reach the objective of becoming a knowledge-based economy, it was asserted that 'Europe's education and training systems need to adapt both to the demands of the knowledge society and to the need for an improved level and quality of employment' (http://ec.europa.eu/employment_social/knowledge_society/index_en.htm).

The Lisbon Strategy has meant that the construction of the ERA was taken on to the agenda of the Commission. The Lisbon Strategy also supported the creation of the European Institute of Innovation and Technology (in 2007) to advance technological development in Europe, the establishment of the European Research Council (in 2005) to allocate research funds, and an increase in the budgets of Framework Programs six (FP6) and seven (FP7). FP7, with a budget of over €50 billion, is the largest public research program ever witnessed (Maassen and Musselin, 2009). It has been suggested that the main underlying reason for the development of the Lisbon Strategy was the Commission's aim to gain control over European universities to develop the European knowledge economy (Giddens, 2006).

However, according to the mid-term review of the Lisbon Strategy in 2004, 'the progress of the Lisbon Strategy has suffered from incoherence and inconsistency, both between participants and between policies' (Kok, 2004, p. 39). Following the report's recommendations and the Commission's proposals, the European Council in 2005 relaunched the Lisbon Strategy by refocusing on growth and employment in Europe. By 2010 it had become clear that the objectives of the Lisbon Strategy had not been achieved.

An important policy innovation flowing from the Lisbon Strategy is the introduction of the Open Method of Coordination (OMC) as a legitimate new policy-making instrument in the EU, after which it has been implemented in other policy areas as well. The classic community method is based on 'command' directive and top-down legal regulation by the EC, whereas the OMC is a more intergovernmental policy-making instrument.

Historically the OMC can be seen as a reaction to the EU's economic integration in the 1990s, which reduced the member states' sovereignty in several fields (Corbett, 2005). It has also been seen as an element creating balance between the perspectives emphasizing pure economic competition and social cohesion respectively (Scharpf, 2006). According to Veiga and Amaral (2009), the Lisbon Strategy required European coordination of policies in areas that the treaties of the Union have reserved for the authority of the member states. Therefore, without the OMC it would normally have needed the acceptance of significant exceptions to the principle of national sovereignty, transferring powers of the member states to the Commission. The European Council (2000, §38) developed the OMC thus:

> A fully decentralized approach will be applied in line with the principles of subsidiarity in which the Union, the member States, the regional and the local levels, as well as the social partners and the civil society, will be actively involved, using variable forms of partnership. A method of benchmarking best practices on managing change will be devised by the European Commission networking with different providers and users, namely social partners, companies and NGOs.

The principles of the OMC rest on 'soft law' (that is, not law-based) mechanisms, such as fixing guidelines when appropriate, designing indicators (qualitative and quantitative), and developing contextualized and tailored benchmarks to compare best practices. These help to translate the European guidelines into national and regional policies (Veiga and Amaral, 2009). There are no official sanctions for those lagging behind because the effectiveness of OMC relies on peer pressure (naming and shaming), and member states normally do not want to be seen as the worst performer in a given policy area. The OMC sets routines for comparisons and organizes a learning process on the European level to promote exchange and emulation of best practices that will help the member states to improve their own policies.

However, the OMC has been criticized because of its fragility in coordinating policies (see Dehousse, 2002), and because of its lack of transparency due to the nature of OMC as an 'insiders' network of networks' (ibid., p. 18), one that is not open to any form of external or public control. A balancing view suggests that the main aim of the OMC is to encourage national reforms and thus the convergence of European higher education policies may be only a by-product of the implementation of commonly defined policies. In principle, the Commission has mainly a monitoring role; in practice, however, it may have a more significant role in helping to set the policy agenda and persuading reluctant member states to implement agreed policies. Furthermore the Commission's central place in the Community machinery makes it a reference point not easily overlooked, especially in the weakly structured national networks, such as found with the Lisbon Strategy (Dehousse, 2002).

There are, however, good grounds for believing that the direction of the Lisbon Strategy has been more important than the quantitative goals it has been set up to achieve. From a Chinese perspective,

> the EU has sent a clear message to the world on developing the EU into 'a global model', and that 'model' may be identified as a dynamic economy with social cohesion . . . Therefore, it matters not much if the quantitative targets of the Lisbon Agenda will not be matched in full by 2010. It matters much, if the Lisbon Agenda is a qualitative success in the sense of generating conceptual and institutional innovations. (Zhou, 2007, p. 365)

THE BOLOGNA PROCESS

The Bologna Declaration of 1999 has its own history. A starting point was the *Magna Charta Universitatum* promulgated by the European University Rectors in 1988. Crucial in this document was the aim to create a unified vision for European universities at a time when Europe was politically divided between communist East and capitalist West. It was also important for the authority of the Declaration that the actors behind it were European university rectors, who aimed at defining a common cultural ground for European universities.

The second important event was the Sorbonne Declaration ('Joint declaration on the harmonization of the architecture of the European higher education systems') by the ministers of education of four big European countries (France, Germany, Italy and the UK). The ministers declared that Europe was not only about economy, but is also 'built upon the intellectual, cultural, social, and technical dimensions of our continent'. The ministers also saw that 'these have to a large extent been shaped by its universities, which continue to play a pivotal role for their development' (Sorbonne Declaration 1998). Other European countries eventually wanted to join this Declaration, for a variety of reasons, ranging from domestic reform needs to the unwillingness to stay outside an important European process.

The main objective of the Bologna Process is to construct the European Area of Higher Education and to promote it worldwide. To reach these objectives the Bologna Declaration (1999) set the following aims:

1) Adoption of a system of easily readable and comparable degrees, not least to promote the employability of European citizens and the international competitiveness of the European higher education system.
2) Adoption of a system essentially based on two main cycles (undergraduate and graduate), where undergraduate studies should last at least three years and be relevant to the European labor market. This objective was extended into three cycles, including doctoral degrees, at the Bergen meeting (in 2005).
3) The establishment of a system of credits (the ECTS system) as a proper means for widespread student mobility.
4) The promotion of mobility by overcoming obstacles to the effective exercise of free movement for students, teachers, researchers, and administrative staff.
5) The promotion of European co-operation in quality assurance with a view to developing comparable criteria and methodologies. In the Berlin meeting (2003) it was agreed that national quality assurance systems should include 'a system of accreditation, certification or comparable procedures', leaving the door open for many different national quality assurance practices to be implemented. This led to the creation of the *Standards and Guidelines for Quality Assurance in the European Higher Education Area* in the aftermath of the Bergen meeting (in 2005) and to the decision to establish the *Quality Assurance Register for Higher Education* at the London meeting in 2007.
6) The promotion of the necessary European dimensions in higher education, particularly with regards to curricular development, inter-institutional co-operation, mobility schemes, and integrated programs of study, training and research.

In addition to these objectives, lifelong learning was taken into one of the objectives in the Prague meeting (2001). In the Bergen and London meetings the social dimension, meaning equality of opportunities in higher education, was accepted as a new theme to be advanced in and through the Bologna Process.

Crucial for the Process is the fact that 31 signatory countries agreed to follow-up meetings and research to take it forward. The Bologna Process thus has a social structure supported by its Secretariat and Bologna Follow-up Group. Follow-up structure has led to Trends reports, which are based on academically inspired follow-up reports, made by the European University Association on the basis of the data delivered by some 900 European universities (Trends V) and Stocktaking reports, which are based on the information provided by the ministries of education to the Bologna Process Secretariat. The aim of these follow-ups is to present the Bologna Scorecard in order to give a 'big picture' overview of progress on priority action lines. In addition, the 'Bologna with Student Eyes', produced by the Student Unions in Europe (ESU), provides another empirically rooted perspective to the Process among many other reports published to support or challenge the Process.

The bi-annual follow-up meetings have also provided a political forum for discussing the process and its objectives, for extending the scope of the Bologna Process and involving new partners in the Bologna Process. In 2010 there were 46 signatory countries of the Bologna Process, one additional member (European Commission) and eight consultative members including representatives of students, business and universities. In addition to the European continent, the Bologna Process has met with growing interest from other parts of the world. Policy dialog and cooperation partnership are the new forms of communication and cooperation with the USA, and Latin American and Asia-Pacific countries. The main aims are to promote and enhance European higher education and its worldwide attractiveness and competitiveness, to intensify policy dialogue, to strengthen cooperation based on partnership, and to further the recognition of qualifications.

Owing to its expanding and complicated characteristics, the Bologna Process has organized itself according to the following Bologna action lines: Qualifications Framework/Three Cycle System; Mobility; Quality Assurance, Employability; EHEA in the global context; Joint Degrees; Recognition; Social Dimension; Lifelong Learning; Stocktaking and Bologna Beyond 2010 (http://www.ond.vlaanderen.be/hogeronderwijs/bologna/). Each action line has its own tasks and duties analyzing the processes and suggesting new actions to be taken in the ministerial meetings.

THE IMPACTS OF THE BOLOGNA PROCESS

Politically the Bologna Process has been a success story because of its popularity and the spread of the three-cycle structure of studies, the implementation of the Diploma Supplement, and with ECTS helping student mobility. It has also influenced the European quality assurance systems and is evidently expanding globally. The Bologna Process is a remarkable European higher education reform process for two main reasons. First, the declaration by the European Ministers of Education in 1999 meant that the European Commission was excluded, even though it was accepted as a partner later. The Bologna Process is not coordinated or led by the EU or by the Commission, even though it is supported financially by the latter and close to the objectives of the EU. Second, the nature of the Bologna Declaration was political. According to one of the signatories, the then Portuguese Minister of Education observed that 'The Bologna Declaration was meant to be a declaration of an exclusively political nature, and all its words were analyzed in great detail to avoid excessive embarrassment to any country. . . . Such a document is both remarkable and vague. What is important is to understand that it is a political declaration, each party having surely its own intentions in its country' (Veiga and Amaral, 2009, p. 135).

This point of departure is important because it indicates that nation-states in Europe continue to exert their sovereignty in the policy arena most resonant to them: national educational policies. Therefore it is hardly surprising that national interpretations and uses of the Bologna Process vary so much. According to a number of studies it is evident that each nation-state has used the Bologna Process for its own purposes (Tomusk, 2006). As regards curricular reforms, Witte (2009, p. 247) notes that 'the reforms of national curricular systems were largely determined by the heritage of national higher education systems and the internal dynamics of their political processes' rather than motivated by the attempts to create European comparability. The same notion is repeated when analyzing the political rhetoric of the national ministries of education. In Finland, for example, the Ministry of Education emphasizes national goals when explaining the Bologna Process to the Finnish citizens. However, when describing the achievements of Finnish higher education to the Europeans, the aim is to show how extremely well Finland has followed the principles of the Bologna Process and how Finland has successfully implemented it in Finland (Saarinen, 2007).

The interesting aspect of the Bologna Process is not the fact that it is proceeding faster than anyone expected (Lourtie, 2001; Haug and Tauch, 1999), but the extent to which it is changing the European landscape of higher education. It has the potential to change the dynamics of national higher education systems because it has introduced alternative and multiple rationales and perspectives to the way in which academic work can be approached (Hoffman et al., 2008). The importance of the Bologna Process lies in the fact that it simultaneously has influenced – and influences – multiple levels of European higher education. National higher education policy-makers have aimed at implementing the reform at the system level, higher education institutions have been developing institutional policies to implement the Bologna Process, and individual academics are occupied with the requirements of adapting curricula changes that can accommodate the idea of the three cycles of degrees. The higher education landscape is changing with the Bologna Process because of the increasing global competitive logic in education, in addition to the fact that it has been a reality in research for decades in some academic fields. The feature the Bologna Process introduces is a structure that enables comparability between higher education systems in a way that forms an instant matrix in which stratification, differentiation and ranking can be carried out.

According to a Finnish empirical study, the Bologna Process may introduce new competitive horizons to basic units in European universities (Hoffman et al., 2008). That is, some basic units were born amid disciplinary and interdisciplinary developments that could be characterized as thoroughly global at the time of their founding. For these units their competitive horizon has never been anything but global. However, some units have enjoyed a long-term legal monopoly on degree-conferring status, which in many cases was an exclusive route to a second national monopoly, that is, certification in the case of schoolteachers or social workers. These units produce students whose education indicated nationally based norms of competence had predominated in their education. There was no compelling reason for the horizon to be anything but national in scope.

The Bologna Process reforms have not fundamentally changed academic work as such by creating 'new' competitive horizons, because these horizons already existed. It is more precise to say that the Bologna Process challenges traditional differentiations mainly because it illuminates them. This is not to say that European higher education is globalizing only because of the Bologna Process, but it is evident that without the deepening of the European perspectives in European universities the processes of globalization would have been slower.

One of the consequences of the Bologna Process is the organization and intensification of European cooperation and networking at the level of higher education institutions. In 2001 two organizations representing the leadership of European universities, European Union Rectors' Conferences and the Association of European Universities, were merged into the European Universities Association (EUA), which represents the voice of the European universities in the Bologna Process. It is remarkable that from the other two groups essential for universities, students and academic staff, only students through ESU (formerly ESIB) are recognized as partners in the Bologna Process, whereas the academic staff are represented only through the partnership of a general teacher organization – Education International – but not by their labor unions.

It should also be mentioned that although the Bologna Process has been initiated by nation-states and supported by European universities, students and staff, it is seen by the European Commission as one of the policy tools for reforming European higher education. The objectives to create standards for quality assurance, to promote student mobility (ECTS and Diploma Supplement), and to construct the European dimension of higher education all support the aims of the EU. The Commission also says very clearly that it is willing to 'help member states and neighboring countries in their modernizing efforts through policy initiatives, discussion papers, and forums, as well as through EU programs such as Erasmus, Tempus, and Erasmus Mundus' (http://ec.europa.eu/education/lifelong-learning-policy/doc62_en.htm). The Commission has also aimed at building a bridge between the Bologna Process, the Lisbon Strategy and the Copenhagen Process, which aims at improving vocational education and training.

STUDENT AND STAFF MOBILITY, AND ERASMUS

Student and staff mobility has been the most traditional policy instrument used by the Commission for developing European identity and for increasing mobility in parallel with the free movement of labor. The Erasmus program mentioned above was established in 1987 by the Commission. Students join the Erasmus program to study from three months to a full academic year in another European country. The Erasmus program also guarantees that the period spent abroad is recognized by their university when they come back and that students do not pay extra tuition fees to the university they visit. They can also apply for an Erasmus grant to help cover the additional expense of living abroad.

Based on official student mobility numbers, the Erasmus program has been called 'a success story' by the EU. There have been about 1 866 000 mobile students between 1987 and 2008, and the student mobility numbers have been growing steadily, so that in 2007/8 their number reached about 183 000. When exchange students are compared with the number of graduates at the bachelor and masters' levels, it can be estimated that about 4.2 percent of European students will participate in the Erasmus program at some stage during their studies. On the basis of official statistics the average duration of Erasmus mobility is 6.2 months, the average student age is 22 years with a slight female overrepresentation (62 percent) as compared with the overall number of European students (of which 55.2 percent are female) (EC, 2010).

There are differences between incoming and outgoing student mobility, even though big countries naturally dominate the numbers. The countries attracting most incoming students include Spain, France, Germany and the UK, and the countries sending most students to other European universities are Germany, France, Spain and Italy. When student participation is compared to the number of graduates, one can see that Greece, Italy, Hungary, Finland and Sweden are the countries that send more outgoing students than the European average.

Teichler (2009) has however pointed out that the consequences of this temporary student mobility differ significantly between European countries. In countries (such as Switzerland, Austria, the UK, Belgium, Germany and France) where the foreign student rate is 10 to 20 percent, it strongly affects the daily life of the universities as compared to those countries (such as Estonia, Italy, Latvia, Lithuania, Poland, Romania, Slovenia, Slovakia and Turkey) where there are only 2 percent or less foreign students. The same applies to countries (Bulgaria, Greece, Ireland, Slovakia, Norway, Austria and Switzerland) that send 5–10 percent of students abroad compared to countries that have less than 2 percent outgoing students.

The Erasmus program for university teachers was launched in 1997. More than 190 000 teachers had participated in this mobility program by the academic year 2007/08. The number has been steadily increasing during the last 11 years, from 7797 in 1997/98 to 27 157 in 2007/08. Annually about 2 percent of academic staff go on a teaching assignment as part of Erasmus, although this includes those who may go more than once. The most active countries with outgoing Erasmus teachers are the Czech Republic (11 percent), Finland (8 percent), and Liechtenstein (6 percent) (EC, 2010).

The Erasmus program also supports the Bologna Process because five of the action lines of the Bologna Declaration are directly related to the Erasmus program. These are: easy readable and comparable degrees (diploma supplement); establishment of a credit system (ECTS); promotion of mobility; quality assurance; and the European dimension in higher education. Furthermore, the impacts of the Erasmus program on the Bologna Process extend beyond the countries participating in the program because the Tempus program supports capacity building in 27 countries, inside and outside the EHEA. Erasmus Mundus has, in turn, opened up double and joint degrees developed under the Erasmus program to students from all over the globe (EC, 2008).

The Erasmus program is one of the major supporters of temporary student and staff mobility in Europe, even though there are other reasons for and channels to study abroad. What do the figures for mobility say about the globalization of higher education in Europe? The first message seems to be quite clear: the EU has been active and rather successful in supporting student and teacher mobility in Europe. This mobility is largely motivated by the aim to create European identity, thus following a different logic from global student mobility, which is motivated largely by economic national policies to attract fee-paying students, especially to Australia, the USA and the UK. Second, it is difficult to measure the cultural, political and social impacts of this globalizing policy. One may, however, assume that it does open wider perspectives to Europe for those students who participate in the exchange programs. Studies also suggest that the experiences of students are normally positive in terms of personal growth and comparative perspectives opened to one's culture and higher education system.

EUROPEANIZATION, GLOBALIZATION AND HIGHER EDUCATION INSTITUTIONS

Europeanization in higher education formally refers to processes that have been initiated at the European level, forced to be implemented at the national level, and monitored by the European institutions (Cowles et al., 2001). In the strictest sense of the concept, neither Bologna nor Lisbon has followed this rather linear policy implementation concept. However, all European national actors have been challenged to translate European processes and change their legislation, policies and practices (Maassen and Musselin, 2009; Witte, 2009). In this sense the Europeanization of higher education is an interactive process, where national-level decisions also influence European-level processes and decisions. Seen this way, the nature of Europeanization is that of a multi-level exchange (as seen, e.g., with the process of agreeing on a quality assurance register).

The European processes of integration are also processes of globalization in the sense that a regional actor, the EU, aims to set norms, procedures and decisions to steer these processes over the heads of the nation-states and higher education institutions. In reality, however, the processes are more those of exchange and interaction than one-way domination. The EU as a globalizing actor is nonetheless a reality, because without the pressure created by the European Commission and the rule of the Community, the Bologna Process, with its strong rooting in nation-states as a counter force to the Commission, and the Lisbon Strategy, which introduced OMC as an alternative implementation and development strategy, would not have been implemented.

The integration of European higher education can also be seen from the perspectives of horizontal and vertical integration. Horizontal integration is represented by the nation-states' intra-governmental cooperation and by cooperation taking place between higher education institutions. The Bologna Process exemplifies this. Vertical integration refers to processes led by the Commission. During the twenty-first century these processes of integration have come closer together; the Commission is using the Lisbon Strategy to influence national higher education policies in the name of the ERA. Maassen and Musselin (2009) note that research and higher education are separated from each other at the European level, whereas they are combined in the same ministry in most European nation-states. This arrangement is seen also at the European level, where the aims to create an EAHE and an ERA stem from different sources. The European integration of higher education has been strengthened both through a supranational process (Lisbon Strategy) and intergovernmental agreement (Bologna Process). A new phase in the globalization of higher education in Europe is beginning with the implementation of a key Lisbon Treaty objective: the creation of an ERA.

THE EU 2020 STRATEGY

According to the European Council (December 2009), 'the Lisbon Strategy has been useful in setting a framework for strengthening European competitiveness and encouraging structural reform'. Yet member states know that 'in order to further improve competitiveness and increase the EU's sustainable growth potential, policies must be refocused towards long-term reforms in an ambitious and revamped new strategy' (EC, 2009).

This revamped strategy is called 'EU 2020'. Supported by the Lisbon Treaty (2009), the Commission has now more authority to influence European higher education through the creation of the ERA. The Commission, however, continues to see the role of the European universities mainly from an economic perspective. In the introduction of the EU 2020 strategy, the motivation for change goes like this:

> Europe has some of the best universities in the world. But our ambition should be to have many more and turn them into a true engine for knowledge and growth. This will not only require investment but also reforms and where necessary consolidation, closer co-operation, including with business, and a more open attitude to change. To assist in this process of change, European universities should be benchmarked against the best universities in the world. (Consultation, 2009)

The Commission also admits that

> An efficient, effective and well-resourced European Research Area is an indispensable part of the EU 2020 vision. The EU needs to increase its research efforts by pooling resources, jointly developing major research infrastructures across the EU and raising research quality to world-leading standards . . . The EU needs to provide more attractive framework conditions for innovation and creativity, including those that are carried out through incentives for the growth of knowledge-based firms. (Ibid.)

This objective is supported by a Council of Europe resolution, which states that there is a need to 'advance in bringing about the modernization of Europe's universities, addressing their interlinked roles in education, research and innovation, as a key element of Europe's drive to create a knowledge-based society and economy and improve its competitiveness' (Council of Europe, 2007).

A crucial question is what is meant by 'modernization' of universities. The Commission is helpful in defining three main fields of reforms. The first is curricular reform, which aims at establishing the three-cycle system, competence-based learning, flexible learning paths, recognition, and student and staff mobility. The second is governance reform, with the focus on university autonomy, strategic partnership (including with enterprises) and quality assurance. The third is funding reform, which aims at diversified sources for university income, better rewards linked to performance, promoting equity, access and efficiency, and the possible role of tuition fees, student grants and loans. The first two are parallel with the objectives and starting points of the Bologna Process. However, the definition of these problems is in itself a radical change in the traditional policies of the EU as the EU has now set political aims to develop European higher education, and the Commission has defined the main objectives of the reforms for higher education institutions and national systems of higher education.

It is evident that the EU 2020 strategy aims to be more than just an updated version of the Lisbon Strategy. Furthermore, the Lisbon Treaty has given the Commission more authority to try to 'modernize' European universities in order to make them economically more efficient and useful globally. At the time of writing this chapter, it is uncertain what the final form of the EU 2020 strategy will be. However, due to political tensions between the Commission and the EU member states, we are quite likely to see new social innovations, and the continuance of problems and tensions between the Commission and the subsidiarity and sovereignty of European nation-states in resolving the forward direction for globalizing European higher education.

REFERENCES

Websites visited in January 2010

http://europa.eu/abc/european_countries/languages/english/index_enhtm?_en
http://www.ond.vlaanderen.be/hogeronderwijs/bologna
http://ec.europa.eu/employment_social/knowledge_society/index_en.htm
http://en.wikipedia.org/wiki/
http://ec.europa.eu/education/lifelong-learning-policy/doc62_en.htm

Documents

Bologna 5th Ministerial Conference in London on 17–18 May 2007 *London Communiqué 2007*: towards the European Higher Education Area: responding to challenges in a globalised world.

CEU (2007). Council of the European Union. *Council resolution 23. November 2007: on modernising universities for Europe's competitiveness in a global knowledge economy.*

Conference of Ministers responsible for Higher Education, Berlin 19 September 2003. *Berlin Communiqué 2003*: Realising the European Higher Education Area.

Conference of Ministers responsible for Higher Education, Bergen 19–20 May 2005. *Bergen Communiqué 2005*: the European Higher Education Area – Achieving the Goals.

Conference of European Ministers Responsible for Higher Education, Leuven and Louvain-la-Neuve, 28–9 April 2009. *Leuven–Louvain-la-Neuve Communiqué 2009*: The Bologna Process 2020 – The European Higher Education Area in the new decade.

Consultation 2009. Commission Working Document. Consultation on the Future 'EU 2020' Strategy. COM (2009)647 final. Brussels 24.11.2009.

EC 2009. European Council Conclusions 2009. http://europea.eu/rapid/pressReleasesAction.do?reference=DOC/09/6&format=HTML&aged=0&language=EN&guiLanguage=en.

Meeting of European Ministers in charge of Higher Education in Prague May 19 2001. *Prague Communiqué 2001*: towards the European Higher Education Area.

Sorbonne Joint Declaration: Joint declaration on harmonization of the architecture of the European higher education systems by four Ministers in charge for France, Italy and the United Kingdom, Paris, the Sorbonne, 25 May 1998.

The Bologna Declaration, 19 June 1999: joint declaration of European Ministers of Education.

Treaty of Lisbon: amending the Treaty on the European Union and the Treaty establishing the European Community (2007/C 306/01). *Official Journal of the European Union*, December 2007, Vol. 50.

Literature

Bell, D. (1973), *The Coming of Post-industrial Society: A Venture in Social Forecasting*, New York: Basic Books.

Corbett, A. (2005), *Universities and the Europe of Knowledge: Ideas, Institutions and Policy Entrepreneurship in European Union Higher Education Policy, 1955–2005*, Basingstoke: Palgrave Macmillan.

Cowles, M., J. Caporoso and T. Risse (eds) (2001), *Transforming Europe: Europeanization and Domestic Change*, Ithaca, NY: Cornell University Press.

Dehousse, R. (2002), 'The Open Method of Coordination: a new policy paradigm?', paper presented at the first Pan-European Conference on European Union Politics: The politics of European integration: academic acquis and future challenges, Bordeaux, 26–8 September.

EC (2008), *The Impact of ERASMUS on European Higher Education: Quality, Openness and Internationalization*, European Commission, DG EAC, Final Report by the consortium of CHEPS, INCHER and ECOTEC at http://ec.europa.eu/education/erasmus/doc/publ/impact08.pdf.

EC (2010), *Statistical Overview of the Implementation of the Decentralised Actions in the Erasmus Programme in 2007/2009*, Brussels: EC.

Egeberg, M. (2006), 'Europe's executive branch of government in the melting pot: an overview', in M. Egeberg (ed.), *Multilevel Union Administration: The Transformation of Executive Politics in Europe*, Basingstoke: Palgrave Macmillan, pp. 1–16.

Giddens, A. (2006), *Europe in the Global Age*, Cambridge: Polity.

Gornitzka, Å. (2009), 'Networking administration in areas of national sensitivity: the Commission and European higher education', in A. Amaral, G. Neave, C. Musselin and P. Maassen (eds), *European Integration and the Governance of Higher Education and Research*, Dordrecht: Springer, pp. 109–32.

Haug, G. and C. Tauch (1999), *Toward the European Higher Education Area: Survey of Main Reforms from Bologna to Prague*, at http://www.ond.vlaanderen.be/hogeronderwijs/bologna/documents/, accessed 5 February 2010.

Hoffman, D., J. Välimaa and M. Huusko (2008), 'The Bologna Process in academic basic units: Finnish universities and competitive horizons', in J. Välimaa and O.-H. Ylijoki (eds), *Cultural Perspectives on Higher Education*, Dordrecht: Springer, pp. 227–44.

Kallo, J. (2009), *OECD Education Policy: A Comparative and Historical Study Focusing on the Thematic Reviews of Tertiary Education*, Jyväskylä: Finnish Educational Research Association (Research in Educational Sciences 45).

Kok, W. (2004), *Facing the Challenge: The Lisbon Strategy for Growth and Employment*, Luxembourg: European Communities.

Lawn, M. and B. Lingard (2002), 'Constructing European policy space in educational governance: the role of transnational policy actors', *European Educational Research Journal*, **1** (2), 290–307.

Lisbon European Council (2000), *Presidency Conclusions*, at http://www.europarl.europa.eu/summits/lis1_en.htm.

Lourtie, P. (2001), *Furthering the Bologna Process: Report to the Ministers of Education of the Signatory Countries*, at http://www.ond.vlaanderen.be/hogeronderwijs/bologna/documents/, accessed 5 February 2010.

Maassen, P. and C. Musselin (2009), 'European integration and the Europeanization of higher education', in A. Amaral, G. Neave, C. Musselin and P. Maassen (eds), *European Integration and the Governance of Higher Education and Research*, Dordrecht: Springer, pp. 3–16.

Neave, G. (1984), *Education and the EEC*, Stoke on Trent, UK: Trentham Books.

Saarinen, T. (2007), *Quality on the Move: Discursive Construction of Higher Education Policy from the Perspective of Quality*, Jyväskylä: Jyväskylä Studies in Humanities, 83.

Scharpf, F. (2006), *Problem Solving Effectiveness and Democratic Accountability in the EU, HIS Political Science Series 107*, Vienna: Institute for Advanced Studies.

Stehr, N. (1994), *Knowledge Societies*, London: Sage.

Teichler, U. (2009), 'Student mobility and staff mobility in the European Higher Education Area beyond 2010', in B. Kehm, J. Huisman and B. Stensaker (eds), *The European Higher Education Area: Perspectives on a Moving Target*, Rotterdam/Boston/Taipei: Sense Publishers, pp. 183–202.

Tomusk, V. (ed.) (2006), *Creating the European Area of Higher Education: Voices from the Periphery*, Dordrecht: Springer.

Välimaa, J. and D. Hoffman (2008), 'Knowledge society discourse and higher education', *Higher Education*, **56**, 265–85.

Veiga, A. and A. Amaral (2009), 'Policy implementation and European governance', in A. Amaral, G. Neave, C. Musselin and P. Maassen (eds), *European Integration and the Governance of Higher Education and Research*, Dordrecht: Springer, pp. 133–58.

Witte, J. (2009), 'Parallel universes and common themes: reforms of curricular governance in the Bologna context', in A. Amaral, G. Neave, C. Musselin and P. Maassen (eds), *European Integration and the Governance of Higher Education and Research*, pp. 227–56.

Hong Zhou (2007), 'A Chinese perspective on the Lisbon Strategy', *Asia Europe Journal*, **5**, 357–65.

16 Neoliberal globalization and higher education policy in India
Sangeeta G. Kamat

INTRODUCTION

> It is important to recognise that there is a quiet crisis in higher education in India which runs deep. The time has come to address this crisis in a systematic and forthright manner . . . because India's future depends on it. (National Knowledge Commission, 2009, p. 73)

Higher education has moved center stage in India's national economic reform process. While higher education was accorded priority in the country's development plans from the early years of Independence, the current sense of a foreboding crisis marks a significant departure from the sense of pride and accomplishment that characterized appraisal of the higher education sector in the early postcolonial period. After all, the historic task of development of a young democracy could hardly be realized without higher education playing a directive and constructive role to produce the requisite scientific and professional class that could build industry, nurture a modern democratic temperament among the public, and expand the numbers of the educated middle classes. Higher education had lived up to its promise on all three counts and especially in comparison with its south Asian neighbors was seen as a success story. In this period of roughly 50 years, it was school education that was the *bête noire* of policy planners and educators, having made minimal and highly uneven progress in ensuring universal schooling even at the elementary level.

There is reason therefore to pause and ask why higher education in India at this moment is seen to be in such a deep crisis that only a complete overhaul of the sector will be able to address it. The repositioning of higher education coincides with a shift in the country's national economic policy in the early 1990s from a state-regulated to a liberalized economy that supports deregulation of the state sector, and expanding the private sector and foreign investment and trade, as the path toward a high-growth economy. In the same period the growth in technology-related services has produced a worldwide shift toward an information-based economy as the new growth sector for investment, trade and employment. It is the articulation of these two shifts, one in the national policy regime and the second in the global economic realm, that have repositioned higher education as the linchpin that will decide India's fate as either suspended eternally between its developing and emerging status or realizing its aspiration to become a developed economy.

Ironically it was not the free market but state policy for higher education in the post-Independence period that provided the foundation for India's success in the information technology sector in the 1990s and which is celebrated as the fulfillment of the dream of modern India. The postcolonial Indian state committed to a development program that prioritized advanced science and technology that would result in large river valley dams and hydroelectric projects that, in Prime Minister Nehru's words, were the 'temples of modern India'. This was an early defining moment in the Indian state's technological imaginary – the new nation was visualized as one where technological miracles in the form of large dams, large public sector infrastructure projects in iron and steel, nuclear fuel, shipbuilding and aeronautics would be the central concerns and the driving force for its modernization project. A second defining premise of the postcolonial state's development vision was its commitment to sovereignty and autonomy that derives from the anticolonial nationalism of the independence movement.[1] The scientific and technical workforce required to build the 'temples of modern India' was to be sourced domestically with minimal reliance on foreign assistance to meet the objectives of self-reliance and self-sufficiency. Thus the success of India's great leap forward occurred through an elite technological workforce supported by a state-subsidized quality public higher education system, which today is declared to be in crisis.

In order to sift through the nature of the crisis, its genesis and the predicament of Indian higher education in an era of globalization, I provide a brief history of higher education in the post-Independence period and the social and economic contradictions that were generated as a result. Leading from a historical overview I examine the current reform efforts and policy prescriptions to restructure higher education to meet the challenges of global economic integration. Here I focus on the recommendations of the National Knowledge Commission (NKC), an expert committee appointed in 2005 that directly reports to the prime minister as the premier policy body charged with outlining a bold new vision for higher education in India. I assess the implications of the NKC's recommendations both in terms of addressing the socioeconomic contradictions produced by the first fifty years of higher education policy, and confronting the challenges of a globalizing economy. My analysis of the history of India's higher education and its emergent reforms illustrates two main arguments. First, globalization theory presumes an opposition between the state and the market that is misleading and is not representative of the higher education reform process in India. Second, the transformations in higher education under globalization do not represent a clean break from the past but integrate existing political–institutional alliances and sociocultural resources. I conclude with some reflections that counterpose the claim in the quote from the NKC: that the future of higher education will depend upon the country's response to the creeping crisis in its economy and polity.

HIGHER EDUCATION IN THE POSTCOLONIAL CONTEXT

Informed by the logic of Nehruvian[2] modernity, India's developmentalist regime operated along two main principles: (1) scientific and industrial development that articulated the aspirations of the national bourgeoisie and the domestic capitalist class; and (2) social development that was responsive to the needs of the vast majority of the country's population. Higher education policy in the post-Independence period is a reflection of the state's efforts to balance these twin objectives, giving rise to the contradictions in the sector that have resulted in a full-blown crisis in the context of globalization. In terms of the first objective, the state provided the infrastructure for building domestic capital's productive capacities, protected its markets from international competition, and ensured a leadership role for the national bourgeoisie in the economic and bureaucratic sectors. The last in particular was accomplished through a highly selective, restricted and heavily subsidized public higher education system that urban upper-caste and middle-class students were able to access far more easily. For the majority of the urban and rural poor, and lower castes and other minority groups, the state instituted a reservations policy in the public sector (equivalent to an affirmative action policy), limited land reforms, employment generation schemes and subsidies in essential commodities.[3]

The hierarchies and dualities in the higher education sector are the combined effects of the two doctrines that mark the Nehruvian period. The national technological education infrastructure, concentrated in a few highly selective institutions, produced an elite engineering workforce that enabled the state to establish public industries in key sectors such as petrochemicals, industrial and consumer goods, telecommunications and energy production.[4] The success of this project, namely the consolidation of state and economic power by upper-caste elites, also discursively established the hegemony of technological modernity in the minds of large segments of the Indian middle and lower castes from rural and urban areas. The reservation policy for certain marginalized caste groups in state universities and colleges has provided limited gains and has largely precluded access to these groups. For example, the reservation policy that allots 22.5 percent of seats for Dalits (scheduled caste)[5] in public and state-aided institutions has been ineffective, and the numbers of Dalit students and faculty in public universities are negligible. A strong urban and upper-caste bias is evident in student success in the national entrance exams, an outcome also of the proliferation of expensive coaching institutes concentrated in the metropolitan regions.

The pent-up demand for high-status degrees in engineering and medicine was channeled toward an expanding private sector in higher education, but one that was organized along caste lines. In the 1980s there was the phenomenon of private engineering (and to a lesser extent medical) colleges that was peculiar to the southern states. These colleges were set up primarily by landowning middle-caste groups that had capital that was internally mobilized to establish colleges and universities with significant state support and subsidies (including in the form of assets such as land at subsidized rates). These caste groups organized themselves into charitable education trusts that provided special scholarships to students from their caste group and charged high fees to students from other caste groups.[6]

The educational success of the three southern states – Tamil Nadu, Karnataka and Andhra Pradesh – is attributed to the anti-Brahmin movements founded in this region in the late-colonial period that gathered momentum after independence (Jaffrelot, 2003; Jeffrey et al., 2002; Omvedt, 1993). The political mobilization of non-Brahmin castes in southern India fueled demand for higher education, especially for professional education (Kamat et al., 2004).[7] These institutions openly proclaimed their caste basis and their caste-specific educational goals.[8] The trend of 'donation engineering colleges' represented an elite strategy of ascendant middle-caste groups to wrest some control from upper castes who dominate at the state level and in the higher education sector.

State policy in higher education therefore largely reproduced the class and caste inequalities that constitute the postcolonial nation. Public higher education remained the preserve of the upper castes – in other words, Brahmins and other allied castes that enjoyed a legacy of higher education even in the colonial period.[9] For the vast majority an optional route to higher education, especially in the high-status fields of engineering and medicine, was made available through private institutions although the caste basis of these institutions favored ascendant landowning middle castes. This allowed the state to contain class and caste conflict, albeit at the expense of a large majority who remained excluded from higher education. With a rapidly expanding private sector, the public sector was allowed to stagnate and this undermined the efficacy of the reservation policy for marginalized groups. The historically specific regional trajectory of private higher education has produced sharp regional imbalances between the northern and southern parts of the country. Also the privileged position of modern science and technology in the state's development mission has exacerbated rural–urban inequalities.

In the 1990s, with the phenomenal growth of the computer and information technology sector in western industrialized countries, the private higher education sector was able to fully realize its potential and has become an influential part of the national and global economy.[10] The successes notwithstanding, the contradictions immanent in the post-Independence period have deepened. As discussed here, higher education policy has contributed to regional, social and economic inequalities. In addition, the sector as a whole is excessively skewed toward a private sector whose investments are in a narrow range of professional and technological fields and has resulted in serious decline and devaluation of the pure sciences, social sciences and humanities. Policy analysts cautioned that in the long term India's share in the knowledge economy would be seriously hurt by its dependence on narrow export specialization of low-value information technology services. More worrisome are the pronounced imbalances generated by the high growth of the software sector in a structurally weak economy that are likely to intensify social and political polarization among the polity and result in endemic conflict. In the following section I critically review the nature of the crisis identified in the NKC's reports, and the proposed reforms that attempt to address the crisis and reposition India in the global economy.

HIGHER EDUCATION'S FUTURE IN A BRAVE NEW WORLD

The appointment of a National Knowledge Commission (NKC) in 2005 to recommend policies and reforms to make India competitive in the knowledge economy inaugurates a unique moment in the history of higher education reform in India.[11] While the NKC reports provide a state-of-the-nation review and suggest reforms for different areas of the education sector, higher education represents a focal area of policy reform. The NKC identifies three objectives that the reforms are expected to address: expansion, excellence and inclusion. The reform agenda for higher education is the most ambitious and far-reaching yet, and has generated energetic debate and discussion among educationists, policy-makers and students.

Baseline Data on Higher Education

A recurring thread that is present throughout the NKC's reports is the Indian state's dismal performance globally, especially in comparison with other developed and emerging economies such as the USA and China. A brief statistical summary of higher education will highlight the problems related to expansion, excellence and inclusion that the NKC seeks to address.[12]

- The gross enrollment ratio (GER) for higher education currently is around 10 percent whereas it is 25 percent for many other developing countries.
- India has about 355 universities and 18064 affiliated colleges. The available number of seats in universities is simply not adequate in relation to the current demand. There are also large disparities in enrollment rates across states, urban and rural areas, gender, caste and poor/non-poor.
- Around 11 million students were estimated to be currently enrolled in Indian higher education. As per the 2001 Census, 31.2 percent of the country, or 337 million, are below the age of 15, an indication of anticipated demand.
- Public expenditure (center and states) on education is only around 3.6 percent of GDP. Government funding of higher education is still below 1 percent of GDP.
- The percentage expenditure on university and higher education to GDP, which was 0.77 percent in 1990–91, showed a gradual decrease to 0.66 percent in 2004–05.
- With high disparities, inclusive education has remained an elusive target. Inter-caste, male–female and regional disparities in enrollment remain prominent. For example, while the GER for people living in urban areas was almost 20 percent, it was only 6 percent in rural areas.
- The GER for scheduled tribes (STs), scheduled castes (SCs) and other backward classes (OBCs) was 6.57, 6.52 and 8.77 respectively, much lower than the all-India figure of 11.
- India has one of the lowest public expenditures on higher education per student at US$406, which compares unfavorably with Malaysia ($11790), China ($2728), Brazil ($3986), Indonesia ($666) and the Philippines ($625).
- The total number of teachers in the higher education system is 480000. Out of the total teaching faculty, 84 percent were employed in affiliated colleges and only 16 percent in the universities and university colleges.

National Knowledge Commission: Proposed Reforms

The NKC's recommendations aim to close the gap between supply and demand and raise expenditure and quality to match those of other competitor economies. In addition to substantial increases in the budgetary allocations for higher education, and increases in the quantum of institutions and teachers that have been welcomed,[13] the NKC recommends a tighter coupling between the public education sector and the market economy, a recommendation that has been criticized by leading educationists and university faculty. Some key recommendations include: autonomy to universities to set student fees as a source of funding, autonomy to use university land for purposes of income genera-tion,[14] salary incentives to faculty who demonstrate productivity, and a closer working relationship with business and industry. The recommendations call for increased state investment in higher education and at the same time for deregulation and autonomy of universities. The NKC acknowledges that these reforms would require changes in gov-ernance policies, regulatory structures, income tax laws and, most challenging of all, in the institutional culture of public higher education itself: 'This requires not only policy measures but also changes in resource allocation, reward systems, and mindsets' (NKC, 2008, p. 57).

The commitment to inclusive development, a legacy from the postcolonial state, is also reflected in the NKC's recommendations. The proposed reforms, however, support a significant revision of the historic reservation policy that has been in place since Independence. While the expert committee concurs that the university should have the freedom to set its own fee norms, it also proposes 'needs-blind' admissions and provision for state funds for scholarships to underprivileged students.

The proposed expansions involve a reorganization of higher education into several different tiers. To increase enrollment proportionate to demand and compete with other emerging economies (mainly China), the NKC recommends founding 50 national universities (10 within the next three years) that would form elite research universities, establishing 1500 universities (that would include public and private institutions and granting certain high-performing colleges university status), and converting a proportion of the 18 064 undergraduate colleges into two-year community colleges.

The NKC emphasizes that these ambitious plans to scale up the higher education infrastructure would be impossible without the continual expansion of the private higher education sector, and expects that at least half of the increase in demand would be met by private providers. The committee concedes that there has 'already been a de-facto privatization of the professional education sector, with more than 80 percent of the engineering colleges being privately funded and managed' (NKC, 2008, p. 73).[15] The state therefore would 'need to recognize the role of the private sector and encourage their participation' (NKC, 2009, p. 187). The NKC also outlines a new approach to regulating standards in higher education that would significantly limit the functions of existing national and state regulatory structures such as the University Grants Commission, the Medical Council of India and the All India Council for Technical Education, and establish a central regulatory authority, the Independent Regulatory Authority for Higher Education (IRAHE) that would be charged with degree-granting authority for all higher education institutions. It would also establish norms for accreditation for all institutions and license private agencies to regulate and monitor these norms for a fee.

To fully comprehend the dramatic turn and extent to which a changed economic environment has reconfigured the place of higher education, it is worth revisiting an earlier moment in Indian higher education when the Third National Planning Commission (1962–66) noted with some concern 'the proliferation of universities and colleges and the problem of the educated unemployed' (http://planningcommission.nic.in/plans/planrel/fiveyr/index9.html).

The Planning Commission was concerned that even with a low GER of 2.9 percent, employment opportunities for college graduates remained slack. The proposal then was that at least half the students completing high school should be diverted to the vocational stream to prepare them for productive employment and reduce pressure on universities. Today the category of the 'educated unemployed' has virtually disappeared from national debate and instead policy experts push for an exponential increase in universities in India, as evident in the NKC recommendations. The new orientation to higher education indicates the historical movement of the Indian economy from a closed national economy to an economy that is closely integrated with the world market. This shift, however, is not without its contradictions for the postcolonial nation-state and the future of higher education. The following section critically evaluates the historical moment currently confronted that underlies the emergent transformations in higher education and their implications for national development and democracy.

NEOLIBERALISM, HIGHER EDUCATION AND THE COMPETITION STATE

In the NKC's comprehensive report to the nation on how higher education should be restructured to be competitive in a global economy, there is a conspicuous lack of any discussion or details on the knowledge economy itself. In contrast to the Third Planning Commission mentioned above, the NKC reveals little if anything at all about the new economy. For example, there is no mention of the projected capacity of the knowledge economy to absorb the increase in numbers of college graduates, professionals and researchers that a vastly expanded higher education system is expected to deliver, a question foregrounded by planning experts in an earlier period of national development. This is especially ironic given that the present reform package is justified in terms of meeting global demand for knowledge goods and information services. The unstated assumption in the report is that the reform of the higher education sector will more effectively prepare graduates for opportunities in the global knowledge economy. I argue here that the global knowledge economy defies the certainty of planning and serves more as a heuristic device, a placeholder for the state as it adapts to global economic transformations. The volatile and unpredictable nature of the global economy makes it impossible for the state to offer any projections about how precisely higher education will contribute to employment and jobs in the new economy, but the heuristic allows the state to lay the groundwork for a radical overhaul of higher education necessitated by the dynamics of neoliberal globalization.[16] To understand the nature of higher education reforms and their implications therefore requires an analysis of neoliberal globalization and the compulsions of the postcolonial state in this changed economic context.

Here I draw on the extensive body of work on neoliberalism as a distinct policy regime that drives the present phase of capitalist globalization (Brenner and Theodore, 2002; Harvey, 2005; Nef and Robles, 2000; Ong, 2006). Rooted in neoclassical economics, neoliberalism is an economic doctrine that provides both a policy roadmap and the intellectual justification for the expansion of the capitalist class globally. The fundamental premise of neoliberalism is that all societies, economies and institutions down to the level of the individual have to adapt, compete and abide by the objective laws of the market. Nef and Robles (2000) summarize the six-point program of neoliberalism as: (i) re-establishing the rule of the market; (ii) reducing public expenditure through cuts in subsidies, reduction in public services and dismantling welfare programs; (iii) reorganizing the tax base by reducing direct taxes such as income and wealth tax, and increasing indirect taxes on goods and services that benefit the investor class and reduce public revenue; (iv) deregulating the private sector; (v) privatizing the public sector; and (vi) doing away with the concept of the commons and the public good. The scholarship on globalization generally marks the 1970s as the period when neoliberalism made significant inroads into state discourse in the developed countries, endorsed by influential political leaders such as Reagan and Thatcher (Harvey, 2005). In India the definitive break from a welfare developmentalist regime to a neoliberal regime occurred in 1991 when the state under-took macroeconomic reform that would over a period of a decade liberalize trade barri-ers, privatize public industries and deregulate markets to promote foreign investment.[17]

The history of neoliberalism debunks the myth that for the market to gain dominance the state must recede, and instead highlights the role of the state as fundamental to creating and enforcing the new architecture of economic reforms. As Marginson (2002, p. 414) astutely observes, the nation-state 'has not disappeared, but has been refocused on position and strategy in a global context'. The state as a central figure in the reform process is most evident in the higher education sector, and the appointment of the NKC represents but one obvious instance of this. In fact I would argue that the intervention-ist role of the Indian state remains fairly continuous with the earlier pre-liberalization phase of economic growth and national development, but is shaped now by new stra-tegic imperatives in response to evolving international conditions. In the developmen-talist period the state intervened at the macro-level, setting monetary, fiscal and other regulatory regimes that insulated certain key elements of higher education from market forces while at the same time promoting certain other aspects of the market in ways that contributed to economic growth and national community. Being able to combine protectionism, welfarism and growth gave the postcolonial development state its legiti-macy, power and social embeddedness. The history of higher education policy in India outlined earlier, where a thriving private market in education was cultivated alongside a protected, highly valued, subsidized public sector suggests exactly the strategies of the state in the pre-liberalization era. With increased external trade, new technologies that allow for transnational production and supply chains, and the power of finance capital, the developmental state is superseded and becomes in Cerny's (1997, p. 259) words, the 'competition state':

> The crisis of the welfare states lay in their decreasing capacity to insulate national economies from the global economy, and the combination of stagnation and inflation which resulted when they tried. The world since then has seen the emergence of a quite different beast, the competition state. Rather than attempt to take certain economic activities *out* of the market, to 'decommodify' them as the welfare state was organized to do, the competition state has pursued *increased* marketization in order to make economic activities located within the national terri-tory, or which otherwise contribute to national wealth, more competitive in international and transnational terms. (Emphasis in original)

The higher education reforms proposed by the NKC symbolize the shift from state devel-opmentalism to a competition state. Taken together, the different elements of the reform program exemplify the characteristics of such a state. For one, the reforms propose to make public higher education responsive to international demands and standards by allowing for fiscal autonomy, flexibility in hiring and firing policies, and encouraging competition among public institutions through special grants and incentives. Second, the reforms seek to create a multi-level, multi-layered flexible institutional context in which public and private institutions of higher education and the corporate sector are required to coordinate to maximize higher education's contribution to an international and trans-national market in education services and knowledge goods. The NKC recommenda-tions indicate a qualitative shift in the interventionism of the state from a commitment to support the sector as a whole as both fundamental and strategic to self-sufficient economic growth and state legitimacy, to a microeconomic flexible approach that imposes market rules on the public sector to promote enterprise, innovation and profitability.

The higher education reform process in India is illustrative of how regional and national histories, political legacies and institutionally specific landscapes combine in new ways to advance certain neoliberal reforms while containing others. One example that is particularly noteworthy here is the Indian state's negotiations on GATS that involve opening the country's higher education sector to foreign providers. The Indian state has consistently faced significant domestic opposition to this agreement and has strategically deployed its emerging power status to postpone and limit the terms of the agreement. Domestic concerns about foreign providers have focused on the dangers of fly-by-night operators and fake universities that are a likely consequence of such deregulation and that would significantly undermine India's credibility and competitiveness in the global economy.[18] After nearly a decade of protracted negotiations at the GATS and WTO meetings, early in 2010 the Indian government drafted the Foreign Educational Institutions Bill for legislation. The Act will permit entry to foreign providers in higher education, with an important caveat that the income earned by foreign providers could not be repatriated to their home countries but would have to be expended within the domestic economy. The expectation here is that this ruling would serve as a disincentive for many foreign investors in higher education and curtail the entry of for-profit foreign providers in the Indian market. The negotiations and final draft of the Bill that opens the domestic market to foreign direct investment can also be understood as an outcome of the state's arrangement with the domestic public and private sector in higher education. This is especially relevant in the case of the domestic private sector in higher education that started out as non-profit trusts organized along caste lines in the 1970s and has expanded into a flourishing for-profit sector over the last two decades (Kamat, 2009; see also Kapur and Mehta, 2004). In other words, the Indian state has to balance the pressure for greater liberalization and deregulation of the higher education sector with the interests of the domestic capitalist class that has significant stakes in higher education as a new investment sector. Public institutions of higher education also opposed the Foreign Educational Institutions Bill, referring to it as a new form of colonialism, posing a challenge, albeit rhetorical, to the legitimacy of the postcolonial state (Altbach, 2010).

Among all the proposed reforms, the policy on reservations (affirmative action) for scheduled castes (SCs), scheduled tribes (STs), and other backward castes (OBCs) in higher education institutions has stirred a great deal of debate among policy-makers and the public alike. While no single policy has been adopted nor consensus reached on the ideal policy framework, the debate on reservations reflects a reworking of class and caste politics in India in the context of globalization. Economic liberalization, the growth of the IT sector, an expanding middle class and a burgeoning youth population have fueled a redistributive backlash that has converged around access to higher education. The debate is constructed in familiar terms of equity versus excellence, with pro-reservation positions arguing for equity in higher education and the anti-reservation voices privileging excellence over equity. While this is not a new debate in India, in the current reform context and the aspiration to global competitiveness the anti-reservation position has become increasingly influential and more widespread, with support from a growing urban professional middle class, policy experts and government officials including the Minister for Human Resource Development, Kapil Sibal, who is also the chairperson of the NKC. The state, while pushing forward market competitiveness in higher education, has struck a compromise position on the issue of reservations, mediating the strong demand for reservations from SCs, STs and OBCs with increasingly strident opposition from an aspiring middle class. In state colleges and universities it has mandated an increase in seats for SCs, STs and OBCs without any reduction in quota for the unreserved category, thereby increasing enrollment, while in public–private partnership institutions and private institutions the state has refused to mandate reservations.

As noted above, private institutions represent a major share of the higher education sector that is only growing in the new economy, indicating that access to underrepresented caste groups (who constitute the numerical majority) remains fairly limited in the current scenario. However, because state institutions continue to be heavily subsidized, especially in comparison to private institutions, and admission into the small number of IITs, IIMs, and state medical colleges is highly coveted, there is a growing public campaign to eliminate reservations altogether (Ghosh, 2006). It is difficult to say with any certainty whether such a campaign will eventually succeed, but worth noting here are the selective efforts at redistribution and equity that help the state retain legitimacy among those who represent the majority of society while also advancing neoliberal reforms across the sector.

EPILOG

India's emphasis on higher education in the postcolonial period has given it a comparative advantage over most other developing nations. The early decades of investment in science and technology, coupled with private enterprise in higher education that capitalized on the unexpected growth of the IT sector, have seen the country ascend from developing country to emerging economy. Seeking to leverage its ascendant status and improve its competitive advantage in the global economy, the state has focused on reforms in the higher education sector. However, the past 60 years of higher education policy have also produced a highly imbalanced higher education sector that mirrors the social and economic inequalities of the nation-state as a whole. Furthermore, the drive towards global competitiveness and the capitalization of knowledge as a high-value commodity provides the rationale for neoliberal reforms to enhance the national and global competitiveness of the higher education sector. In this context higher education is no longer oriented toward national development and building national identity, culture and community. Rather, higher education is subordinated to the needs of a global knowledge economy, however amorphous, ill defined and exclusive such an economy may be. That said, higher education in India remains one of 'the swiftest elevators to the pinnacles of modern Indian (and now global) power and opportunity', and given the demographic trends there is every indication that pressures for access to quality higher education will only increase in the coming decades (Wolpert, cited in Kapur and Mehta, 2004, p. 6). The ambitious reform plans to expand higher education access and improve quality to address these challenges are likely to remain unfulfilled without massive state expenditure, a policy prescription that is at odds with the neoliberal policy regime.[19] Under such conditions of rising demand and unrealized expectations, of heightened competition and unequal opportunity, it would not be too far-fetched to predict that higher education in India will be a site of intense and protracted struggle and contestation.

NOTES

1. India was one of the imitators of the Non-Aligned Movement (NAM) that had its inaugural conference in Bandong, Indonesia in 1955, when 34 Asian and African countries pledged economic cooperation, cultural cooperation, human rights and self-determination, the issue of people in dependent countries, and the promotion of world peace. The guiding principle of NAM was to develop a middle path to social and economic development that would be independent and distinct from western capitalism and Soviet communist models of development.
2. The state-led phase of development is commonly referred to as the Nehruvian period after India's first prime minister, Jawarharlal Nehru.
3. The Nehruvian developmentalist regime was not a unique moment but one that exhibited important continuities with a colonial regime where the trajectory of development was defined by national elites who spoke 'in the name' of the people (Corbridge and Harriss, 2000).
4. The Indian Institutes of Technology (IITs) are the elite science and technology institutes directed by the central government, while the regional engineering colleges (RECs) form the second-tier elite colleges administered at the state level with substantial aid from central government. A specialized and elite cluster of institutions was also established in medicine (the All India Institute of Medical Sciences, the Armed Forces Medical College), management (Indian Institutes of Management – IIMs), and in pure and applied sciences (Indian Institutes of Sciences).
5. 'Scheduled caste' (SC) is the modern administrative term for caste groups that were outside the Hindu caste structure and in the colonial period were referred to as 'untouchables'. The upper castes deemed the hereditary occupations of SCs as polluting and unclean. In the 1960s, scheduled castes accepted the term 'Dalit', which means 'downtrodden' and 'oppressed', as a political identity that symbolizes their struggle for equality and dignity.
6. The 1970s saw the establishment of what came to be dubbed 'donation engineering colleges' – private educational institutions where entering students could bypass the highly competitive public entrance examinations and join engineering and medical colleges by paying a steep 'donation' in order to be admitted.
7. For more extensive discussion of this phenomenon and its concentration in the southern Indian states, see Kamat et al. (2004). Why similar developments did not take place in northern states has yet to be fully explained.
8. For instance, the Kammavari Trust advertises that the Kammavari Sangham . . . has 'diversified its activities to many folds. The Sangham provides scholarships and free hotel facilities to the poor and meritorious students of the Kamma community . . . The Sangham also started the Kammavari Credit Cooperative Society to mobilize deposits, to lend loans for productive purposes, encourage small entrepreneurs and social causes' (cited in Kamat et al., 2004).
9. Admission is limited to approximately 2000 students spread across seven IITs, giving an acceptance rate of only one in 25, compared to graduate admissions rates at Harvard and MIT of one in eight. The narrow selectivity crowds out other equally qualified students, creating a super elite of graduates (*Times Higher Education Supplement*, 2004).
10. The three southern states of Andhra Pradesh, Karnataka and Tamil Nadu account for nearly half of all technical institutions. These states are the main suppliers of software professionals and a significant source of software revenue for the country. All the IITs combined contribute only 3 percent of the workforce for the software industry (D'Costa, 2003).
11. The NKC, appointed by the prime minister, is a six-member experts committee appointed for four years and it has submitted interim reports and a final report in 2009. The Head is the Human Resource Development Minister, an industry person who has several technology patents to his name, and his appointment is widely regarded as reflecting the government's commitment to neoliberal reforms in education.
12. The following summary data and statistics are from the NKC report (2009).
13. The NKC recommends 1.5 percent of GDP, out of a total of at least 6 percent of GDP for education overall.
14. 'Most public universities are sitting on a large reservoir of untapped resources in the form of land. It should be possible to draw up norms and parameters for universities to use their available land as a source of finance' (NKC, 2009, p. 71).

15. The share of private unaided higher education institutions increased from 42.6 percent in 2001 to 63.21 percent in 2006. Their share of enrollments increased from 32.89 percent to 51.53 percent in the same period.
16. By heuristic I do not mean to suggest that the knowledge society is a fabrication or that capitalization of knowledge is not a trend and a profitable one. Apropos Robertson (2005), my argument is that this heuristic helps justify a program of reform that does not necessarily prepare people for a knowledge economy and that may well achieve quite different economic and political objectives given the broader context of neoliberal globalization.
17. The Structural Adjustment Program (SAP) of the World Bank and the IMF imposed neoliberal policies on borrower nations as conditionalities in exchange for loans. Countries in Africa and Latin America had much less negotiating power than for instance India, and the deleterious effects of neoliberal policies or SAP became apparent much sooner in these countries.
18. 'Fake universities' and 'fly-by-night' operators in higher education are already a significant problem in India. There have been several scandals of colleges and degree programs that exist on paper only, or that do not meet even minimal norms of having classrooms or competent (let alone qualified) teachers but that issue certificates and degrees on payment. The most recent scandal that made national news was the state of Chhattisgarh, where 108 private universities sprung up overnight. Dubbed as 'one-room' universities by the media, the University Grants Committee (UGC) declared nearly all illegal. The UGC regularly publicizes a list of 'fake universities' on its website to warn gullible students (see www.ugc.gov.in). While the NKC urges regulation to prevent foreign predators in the higher education market, it does not directly address the problem of domestic predators and how the introduction of private regulatory agencies proposed by the NKC will curb this trend.
19. Altbach (2010) and Kapur and Mehta (2004) arrive at a similar conclusion but make no reference to the neoliberal policy regime. Altbach (2010) calls the reform program of the NKC 'mission impossible'.

REFERENCES

Altbach, P. (2010), 'India's proposed reforms: somewhat half-baked', *Times Higher Education*, 5 August, retrieved 25 October, http://www.timeshighereducation.co.uk/story.asp?storyCode=412793&sectioncode=26.
Brenner, N. and N. Theodore (2002), 'Cities and the geographies of "actually existing neoliberalism"', *Antipode*, **34** (3), 349–79.
Cerny, P. (1997), 'Paradoxes of the competition state: dynamics of political globalization', *Government and Opposition*, **32** (2), 251–74.
Corbridge, S. and J. Harriss (2000), *Reinventing India: Liberalization, Hindu Nationalism and Popular Democracy*, Cambridge: Polity Press.
D'Costa, A. (2003), 'Uneven and combined development: understanding India's software exports', *World Development*, **31** (1), 211–26.
Ghosh, J. (2006), 'Case for caste-based quotas in higher education', *Economic and Political Weekly*, 17 June.
Government of India (1966), *Third Five Year Plan*, retrieved at http://planningcommission.nic.in/.
Harvey, D. (2005), *A Brief History of Neoliberalism*, New York: Oxford University Press.
Jaffrelot, M. (2003), *India's Silent Revolution: The Rise of the Lower Castes*, London: C. Hurst and Company.
Jeffrey, C., R. Jeffery and P. Jeffery (2002), 'Degrees without freedom: the impact of formal education on Dalit young men in north India', *Development and Change*, **35** (5), 963–86.
Kamat, S. (2009), 'Education in emergent India: genealogies of actually existing neoliberalism', paper presented at the Annual Comparative and International Education Society Meeting, Charleston, NC, February.
Kamat, S., Mir Ali Hussain and Biju Mathew (2004), 'Producing hi-tech: globalisation, the state, and migrant subjects', *Globalisation, Societies and Education*, **2** (1), 1–39.
Kapur, D. and Pratap Bhanu Mehta (2004), 'Indian higher education reform: from half-baked socialism to half-baked capitalism', Center for International Development Working Paper No. 108, USA: Harvard University, September, retrieved at www.hks.harvard.edu/var/ezp_site/storage/fckeditor/file/. . ./108.pdf.
Marginson, S. (2002), 'Nation-building universities in a global environment: the case of Australia', *Higher Education*, **43**, 409–28.
National Knowledge Commission (2008), *Towards a Knowledge Society: Three Years of the National Knowledge Commission*, New Delhi: Ministry of Human Resource Development, Government of India, retrieved February 2010 at http://www.knowledgecommission.gov.in/.
National Knowledge Commission (2009), *National Knowledge Commission: Report to the Nation 2006–2009*,

New Delhi: Ministry of Human Resource Development, Government of India, retrieved February 2010 at http://www.knowledgecommission.gov.in/.

Nef, J. and W. Robles (2000), 'Globalization, neoliberalism and the state of underdevelopment in the new periphery', *Journal of Developing Societies*, **16** (1), 27–48.

Omvedt, G. (1993), *Reinventing Revolution: New Social Movements and the Socialist Tradition in India*, New York: M.E. Sharpe.

Ong, A. (2006), *Neoliberalism as Exception: Mutations in Citizenship and Sovereignty*, Durham, NC: Duke University Press.

Robertson, S. (2005), 'Re-imagining and rescripting the future of education: global knowledge economy discourses and the challenge to education systems', *Comparative Education*, **41** (2), 151–70.

17 Globalization and higher education in South Korea: towards ethnocentric internationalization or global commercialization of higher education?
Terri Kim

INTRODUCTION: THE KOREAN BACKGROUND TO GLOBALIZATION

This chapter offers a critical review of the current state of South Korean higher education in the context of economic globalization and examines higher education policy and practice towards internationalization over the last decade or so since the 1997–98 Asian economic crisis. It will, first, review the distinctive characteristics of South Korean development and the ways in which it has met the global challenges of neoliberal market-principled restructuring.

It is argued that, despite the number of higher education reforms in South Korea, assumptions about the university and its pragmatic and subordinate relations to the national government and the *chaebol* (the large conglomerates equivalent to the *zaibatsu* in Japan) have not changed. Given the unique combination of strong governmental regulation and the *chaebol*'s dominance in university governance and management, the direction of higher education development in South Korea is poised between ethnocentric internationalization and global commercialization.

KOREAN COMPONENTS OF THE DEVELOPMENTAL STATE IN THE PROCESS OF GLOBALIZATION

South Korea has achieved rapid and high-level economic growth, rising from the rubble of the Korean War in the early 1950s into present-day membership of the OECD and G20. In 2009 South Korea joined the Development Assistance Committee (DAC) of the OECD, the first time since the establishment of OECD in 1961 that a former aid beneficiary had become a donor (OECD, 2009b). The South Korean economy has been driven by manufacturing goods (such as IT electronics, cars, ships, steel and textiles) oriented towards exports, which account for 50 percent of GDP. It is now the world's ninth-biggest exporter – ahead of the UK, Canada and Russia – and ranked among the 15 largest economies in the world with an advanced economy with GDP per capita of about US$30 200 in 2010 (CIA, 2011; World Bank, 2010).

Despite the ongoing global recession, South Korea's economy expanded 7.6 percent during the first half of 2010. Data from the Bank of Korea show that the figure is a 10-year high since the first half of 2000, when the nation had economic growth of 10.8 percent. Korea is also one of the industrial countries that have continued to boost spending on education despite the global recession, while the USA, the UK and Ireland among others have made substantial budget cuts in (higher) education (*San Francisco Chronicle*, 2010). Overall the South Korean pattern of development has been regarded as a role model for the East Asian 'developmental state' (Woo-Cummings, 1999), in which strong governments' political and economic projects have matched individual practical needs for higher education. As examined in Kim (2000, 2009), most Koreans have used educational credentials and networks as an important conduit for upward social mobility, which can be attributed to both Confucian and Japanese colonial legacies in state–university relations and an examination-based selection of governing elites.

Broadly, government–university relations worldwide tend to be subject to, and conditioned by, the public funding regime. In South Korea, however, well-established governmental regulations persist regardless of changes in funding patterns (Kim, 2008a, p. 558). Nevertheless, higher education has expanded rapidly, led by the private sector, to meet the demands of fast economic development driven by a strong government and the *chaebol*. Links between the *chaebol*, the banks and government in this process have been well established and the government has sponsored the *chaebol* in developing the private sector. Accordingly the *chaebol* – such as Samsung – has dominated the infrastructure of almost all socioeconomic sectors. In the field of education, however, the government has maintained centralized regulations over all educational institutions – both public and private – to make education serve the state's purposeful, utilitarian and technically functional uses of (higher) education (Kim, 2008a, 2009).

This Korean model of development was internationally challenged by the major economic crisis of November 1997. A condition of the International Monetary Fund's (IMF) subsequent rescue package of a record US$58 billion in December 1997 envisaged South Korea undertaking a major restructuring process. A new vision of the future articulated by the government thus had to be in accordance with the reforms of the Structural Adjustment Program (SAP) imposed by the IMF and the World Bank as part of the funding allocation (Kim, 2000, p. 184). The government's restructuring programs included issues such as: the influence of the *chaebol*; reforming the financial and banking sector; the opening of the stock market; a market-oriented macroeconomic policy; privatization; deregulation; trade liberalization; flexibility of the labor market; and the gradual reduction or elimination of government intervention (IFWEA, 1999; Kim, 2000, pp. 185–6). The aim was transparent corporate governance, prudent financial management, cooperative labor relations, and efficient government administration.

Assuming the presidency amid the economic crisis in 1998, Kim Dae Jung proclaimed a new state vision of the future – *A Second Nation-Building* (*Je Yi-ey Kuen Kook*) – to unite the South Korean people in crisis. The patriotic slogan effectively convinced the public of the necessity of the socioeconomic restructuring process for the survival of the nation. As widely reported in newspapers, a nationwide campaign called 'Save the nation' was strongly supported by the public. During the campaign people were selling or donating their rings and jewelry or anything else in their households that contained gold. Despite the condition of a foreign bailout, South Korea's economy even grew 10.7 percent in 1999 and 8.8 percent in 2000, and South Korea eventually paid off all its debts by August 2001 – 2 years and 10 months ahead of schedule. Consequently Korea regained its economic sovereignty (*Asian Economic News*, 27 August 2001).

Overall it was after the Asian financial crisis (1997–98) that neoliberal, market-principled economic globalization began to restructure Korea's economic and social apparatus and eventually led to a real shift in higher education policies. However, the policy rhetoric of economic globalization had started to be incorporated earlier in higher education reforms during the period of the Kim Young Sam government (1992–97), the first civilian government after 20 consecutive years of military regimes (Kim, 2000, pp. 182–3). The civilian government began to put great emphasis on *Segyehwa* (globalization), which was based on popular views at that time, such as the rise of a borderless transnational economy, the new revolution in ICT, and lifelong learning (Kim Young Sam, 1996, pp. 7–16). National opinion supported the political rhetoric and strategic aim for globalization although there seemed to be a lack of awareness about how to achieve it. Nevertheless President Kim Young Sam declared 1994 to be a milestone in its pursuit.

The immediate interest at that time was how to make South Korea a more visible and influential member of international society. The government sought ways to improve the international image of South Korea and its level of international communication. One measure was to strengthen the work of the Korea Foundation overseas. Another was to join, as the second Asian nation after Japan, the OECD in 1996 (Kim, 2000, pp. 182–3). The government clearly intended to reform the earlier model of a state-guided and protected economy monopolized by the *chaebol* and to promote a free-market economy. With hindsight the Kim Young Sam government's initiatives were a precursor of the restructuring program conditioned by the IMF bailout, although that could not prevent the looming economic crisis in 1997–98. The governmental reforms in this period at least disclosed corrupt connections between banks and business borrowers and a lack of transparency. They sought also to implement a deregulation policy and this included the formation of an Education Deregulation Committee to introduce a new contractual relation between the government and individual universities to better ensure institutional accountability. The new scope of governmental funding for individual universities was to be determined by the results of the self-evaluation and the external evaluation of each higher education institution (Byun, 2008, pp. 194–6). Enrollment quotas for private universities were also abolished in 1995 (Kim, 2008a, p. 560).

However, it was not possible to realize the grand policy visions of *Segyehwa* (globalization) in the Kim Young Sam period (1992–97) as the country was consumed by the major Asian financial crisis (1997–98) and the subsequent IMF bailout.

THE NATIONAL IMAGE AND WORLD RANKING

As a nation that was 'used to seeing itself as an underdog, overshadowed by neighbouring China and Japan and all-but ignored by the rest of the world' (*Financial Times*, 2010), the Korean government and its people are alert to global rankings. However, South Korea has not yet been successful in breaking away from being an isolated and closed society. Its general public image outside the corporate realm of South Korea is still linked with the Korean War of the 1950s and North Korea's alleged nuclear weapons, rather than with technologies and economic development (Korea Trade-Investment Promotion Agency, re-quoted from *JoongAng Daily*, 27 April 2010).

Nevertheless the country has at least become quite visible in some of the international indices. For instance, it ranks quite high on the world R&D (6th), which measures expenditures; on the human-capital index (10th), which refers to the percentage of people with college degrees; and on the scientific-talent index (13th), which examines the number of researchers per capita. Above all, its gross enrollment rate (GER) in higher education is the world highest at 96 percent (OECD, 2009a; McKinsey and Company, 2010).

According to the Institute of Management Development (IMD) *World Competitiveness Yearbook 2010*, South Korea has improved its positive scores from the previous year: in the rankings of 58 industrialized nations it was first in patent productivity, third in employee training, fourth in scientific infrastructures, fifth in R&D spending in proportion to GDP, eighth in GDP growth per capita, thirteenth in fiscal policy, and second in higher education achievement assessed by the percentage of the population with higher degrees. In contrast, South Korea's lowest rankings came in labor relations (56th), openness to foreign ideas (52nd), preparation for an aging society (54th), and the extent to which university education boosts economic competitiveness (46th) (Institute of Management Development; re-quoted from *JoongAng Daily*, 20 May 2010).

As these indices show, South Korea has achieved universal participation in its higher education; yet the student population overall is decreasing as a consequence of continuing low fertility. The government is trying to tackle Korea's record low birth rate, one of the world's lowest, coupled with a rapidly aging society, a trend that began emerging shortly after the Asian financial crisis in the late 1990s. On the other hand, the adult population participating in lifelong learning in South Korea is still at a relatively low level: less than 3 percent of 30–39-year-olds and less than 1 percent over 40-year-olds are participating in tertiary education. In comparison, the UK ratios are 5.7 percent and 1.7 percent respectively (OECD, 2009a).

At the same time the number of foreign students studying in South Korea is very low, despite a considerable increase recently. In 2001 the total number of foreign students studying at Korean higher education institutions was just 4682. By 2008 it had increased by 13 times, estimated at 63 952 (including 23 367 enrolled in language and other training programs). Nevertheless the number is still insignificant in comparison with the number of Korean students studying abroad, which was 149 933 in 2001 and 216 876 in 2008 (including 89 865 enrolled in non-degree programs) (Ministry of Education, Science, and Technology – MEST, 2008). South Korea thus has a chronic imbalance between the inbound and outbound mobility of students. As a result of the factors outlined above, an increasing number of higher education institutions in South Korea are having difficulty recruiting enough students to meet higher education enrollment quotas. A similar condition is also found in Japan (Yonezawa and Kim, 2008).

Unlike other indices related to economic advancement and the expansion of higher education, the quality of higher education in South Korea and its ranking in the world university league tables have received less attention worldwide than other neighboring countries, such as Japan, Hong Kong and Singapore – see Table 17.1.

According to the *THE–QS World University Rankings*, in 2009 only Seoul National University and the Korean Advanced Institute of Science and Technology (KAIST) were included among the top 100 universities in the world. They are ranked 47 and 69 respectively. Among the top 200 rankings just two more Korean universities appear: POSTECH (Pohang University of Science and Technology) (134) and Yonsei (151).[1]

Moreover, there is severe gender disparity in the correlation between educational attainment and participation in economic life and political decision-making. While the enrollment rate of females in higher education is now 82.4 percent, exceeding that of

Table 17.1   QS World University Rankings

Country/territory	Number of universities in 2009 top rankings	Top-ranked university (2009)
USA	103	Harvard (1)
UK	51	Cambridge (2)
Germany	42	Technische Universität, München (55)
Japan	35	University of Tokyo (22)
France	29	École Normale Supérieure, Paris (28)
Australia	21	Australia National University (17)
Canada	20	McGill University (18)
Italy	19	University of Bologna (174)
South Korea	16	Seoul National University (47)
China	13	Tsinghua University (49)
Spain	13	University of Barcelona (171)
Taiwan	12	National Taiwan University (95)
Switzerland	8	ETH Zurich (Swiss Federal Institute of Technology) (20)
Hong Kong	5	University of Hong Kong (24)
Malaysia	5	Universiti Malaya (180)
Singapore	2	National University of Singapore (30)

Source: http://www.topuniversities.com/university-rankings/press-coverage.

males (81.6 percent) in 2009, the economic participation rate of females is less than 50 percent (Statistics Korea, 2010).

In 2008 South Korea's global ranking in women's rights fell four points to 68 from its 2007 ranking of 64, based on the 2008 Gender Empowerment Measure (GEM) released in 2009 (McKinsey and Company, 2010). The GEM is produced by the United Nations Development Program (UNDP) to measure the extent of women's participation in economic life and political decision-making in over 100 countries and thus exposes inequality of opportunities in selected areas. Such a fall in ranking may have had to do with the decline in female participation in economic activities in the aftermath of the global economic crisis. The Korea Labor Institute also has reported that among the workers that have been made redundant since November 2008, 98 percent are women (Korea Labor Institute, re-quoted from IPS news 30 June 2010).[2]

The university academic profession is no exception to these gender imbalances. Evidence suggests that the higher the level of education, the greater the gender gap in South Korea: women represent only 13 percent of all R&D personnel, for example. The government has set up a national target of increasing the proportion to 20 percent by 2010 and has established a second 'Basic Plan for Fostering and Supporting Women in Science and Technology' (2009–2013). However, the overall rate of female academics employed in four-year universities in Korea is still less than 18 percent (12.8 percent in the national/public universities and 20.3 percent in the private universities) – very low even compared to the percentage of women in tertiary education studying science, engineering and technology (SET) subjects, which was 30.3 percent in 2008 (Ianchovichina and Leipziger, 2008, pp. 137–8; Lee, 2010, pp. 237–8; *Kyosu Shinmun*, 2009).[3]

Overall the South Korean economy seems at a crossroads, facing some major challenges such as a rapidly aging population, an inflexible, gender-biased labor market, and overdependence on manufacturing exports (CIA, 2010). In the context of higher education these challenges can be linked to:

(1) labor market demand for a new kind of high-skilled workforce in a context of demographic shrinkage of the student cohort;
(2) increasing global pressures to open up the domestic education market for transnational for-profit higher education services under world trade negotiations;
(3) increasing national competition for the recognition of world-class universities and top global university rankings.

Against this background the following section will review distinctive features of Korean higher education (HE) and reforms over the last decade. It will analyze the ways in which the South Korean government has responded to economic globalization and discuss possible ways forward given the longstanding characteristics of Korean higher education development.

DISTINCTIVE FEATURES OF KOREAN HIGHER EDUCATION

One of the major characteristics of Korean higher education is the strong and dominant private sector. The majority (about 85 percent) of higher education institutions in South Korea are private. More precisely, 145 out of a total 172 four-year universities, and 143 out of a total 158 two-to-three-year junior colleges, are private. About 78 percent of university students and 96 percent of professional school students enroll in private institutions (Korean Educational Development Institute – KEDI, 2010).

As indicated earlier, however, the government has kept direct control and close regulation over the higher education system as a whole – regardless of funding patterns. A World Bank Report in 2000 indicates that:

> Although it provides only 4.4 percent of GDP public spending on education, with two-thirds of its education expenditure coming from private sources and with private education institutions constituting 35 percent and 90 percent of schools at the secondary and the tertiary levels respectively, the government's control over the entire operation of the education system has rendered the system highly centralized and inflexible to market needs. The most illustrative example of over-regulation comes from the tertiary education sector. Both the private and public universities lack autonomy in their management and academic affairs as a result of government regulations. (World Bank, 2000, p. 44)

It was only after 1995 that the government for the first time began to subsidize private higher education institutions (HEIs) on a competitive basis. The general direction of higher education in South Korea since then has followed the Anglo-American model of audit mechanisms to promote competition among HEIs and to provide selective support for high-performing institutions (Kim, 2008a, p. 561). The evaluation and accreditation systems have also been used in South Korea to measure a university's ability to provide quality education. About 46 percent of the government's research funding has been allocated to the top 10 institutions – regardless of the public–private sector division. Over the last 15 years public funding for higher education has continued to increase in South Korea and yet the government's overall budget for higher education is still very low. The proportion of government subsidies against the total revenue of universities is limited to 22.7 percent, much lower than the OECD average of 78.1 percent, with the USA at 45.1 percent and Japan at 41.5 percent. Public financial expenditures on higher education as a percentage of GDP are very low at 0.3 percent in South Korea compared to the OECD mean of 1.1 percent, with the UK at 0.9 percent and Scandinavian countries at 1.5 percent. However, when we look just at the total investment in higher education as a percentage of GDP, Korea is one of the three OECD countries that invest more than 2 percent of GDP in tertiary education: Korea 2.5 percent, Canada 2.7 percent and the USA 2.9 percent, although in South Korea it is predominantly through private funding, unlike many other OECD countries (Ministry of Education – MOE – statistics published on 11 May 2006 and reported in the *University News Network*, 12 May 2006; re-quoted from Kim, 2008a, p. 558; *Times Higher Education*, 28 January 2010).

This combination of private funding of tuition and public funding of research and economic growth in South Korea may be attributed to the East Asian Confucian model as analyzed by Kim (2009). Marginson also argues that East Asian higher education in 'the Confucian zone' is on the rise and their success stories are based on commonalities, including that the predominant funding of tuition costs by households enables governments to invest selectively in infrastructure, R&D, and the top universities so as to develop global research capacity (*Times Higher Education*, 27 May 2010).

THE DOMINANCE OF THE PRIVATE SECTOR AND GOVERNMENTAL OVERREGULATION AND UNDERFUNDING

Given the pattern of higher education development framed by governmental direct control, the conventional binary division of 'public' and 'private' becomes somewhat arbitrary in South Korea (see Kim, 2008a). There are no substantial differences between public and private institutions – except in funding. Private HEIs in South Korea are also governed under the government's regulatory framework – on admission procedures, the establishment of new institutions, academic courses, financial allocations and expenditure, and faculty recruitment admission policy.

Broadly, all universities in South Korea have been underfunded and overregulated by the government (Kim, 2008a, p. 562), and as a result there is strong conformity and lack of autonomy with little or no strategic diversification among HEIs. The proportion of four-year general universities producing postgraduate degrees in South Korea is about 75 percent, which is far higher than in the USA (61 percent) and Japan (48.5 percent) (Ryu et al., 2006, p. 26). The World Bank depicts this issue succinctly:

> Although the universities do not receive direct government instructions on curriculum content, the curricula that they actually provide are fairly uniform and many universities simply copy the programs of the top-ranking universities. Consequently the students coming out of this

system tend to have the same knowledge structure and skills. Such a heavily regulated system does not have the flexibility to fulfil the country's growing demand for new types of knowledge workers. (World Bank, 2000, p. 44)

Despite the World Bank report in 2000, there has still been no fundamental change in the Korean higher education system since then. Generally it can be suggested that the government has been a regulator rather than a purveyor of higher education in Korea. Government regulations of the education system as a whole reflect a strong egalitarian motif. To promote the equality of educational opportunity, the Korean government has maintained a standardized primary and secondary schooling system, regardless of the public–private sector division, since 1973. As a result, real competition and selection start only at university entry level. As mentioned earlier, until 1995 the government had strictly regulated university admission criteria and the number of students for each institution (Kim, 2001; Kim and Lee, 2006). Regardless of the changes in the government's regulations over admission criteria, however, fierce competition to enter the best universities has never been loosened in South Korea. There is a steep hierarchical order in which less than 2 percent of high school graduates enter the top three universities. This is because the prestige attached to a university degree is probably the most important surface indicator of social status as well as of future economic prospects. This theme permeates every aspect of social life and networking in South Korea.

Against this background and despite the government's strict and direct regulations over private higher education, the expansion of higher education in South Korea has been led by the private sector. However, unlike the situation in Japan or China, the status of private HEIs in Korea is not necessarily lower than public institutions. The Korean University League Table in 2009, for instance, shows the dominance of private HEIs: among the top 10 only two (KAIST and Seoul National University) are national, and among the top 20 there are just five national universities (see Table 17.2).

The excellence of private universities in South Korea is also attributed to their partnership with the corporate sector, especially the *chaebol*. For instance, conglomerate sponsorship was essential in realizing the Sung Kyun Kwan University's 'Vision 2020', including a Samsung Digital School on campus that provides a specially designed elite education in the field of nanotechnology for the 200 students recruited annually, all of whom are under full scholarships and given free accommodation. All courses are taught in English. *Chaebol* have not only donated development funding to some of the major universities (both public and private), but have also acquired private universities. For example, Chung-Ang University, a private university among the top 15 universities in South Korea, was purchased by the Doosan Group in 2008, and Sung Kyun Kwan University is now operated by Samsung (*JoongAng Daily*, 19 January 2009).[4]

THE VALUE OF HIGHER EDUCATION AND EMPLOYABILITY

The rapid expansion of higher education has led to concerns about the quality of university graduates among business leaders, students and parents. Given the large supply of higher education graduates, their overall quality and employability has come under scrutiny, particularly as the unemployment rate of university graduates has continued

Table 17.2   Top 20 universities in South Korea in the University League Table, 2009

1	Kaist (1)
2	Seoul National University (3)
3	Postech (2)
4	Korea University (5)
5	Yonsei University (4)
6	Sungkyunkwan University (6)
7	Hanyang University (7)
8	Kyung Hee University (10)
9	Sogang University (8)
10	Hankuk University of Foreign Studies (11)
11	Inha University (11)
12	Ewha Women's University (9)
13	Chung-Ang University (14)
14	Konkuk University (16)
15	Pusan National University (13)
16	Kyungpook National University (17)
17	University of Seoul (18)
18	Ajou University (15)
19*	Chonnam National University (23)
	Hongik University (19)

Note: * Two universities ranked in 19th place.

Source: JoongAng Daily Newspaper, 23 September 2009, http://joongangdaily.joins.com/article/view. asp?aid=2910430.
Reprinted with the permission of *JoongAng Daily*.

to increase. Currently over one million university graduates are unemployed in South Korea. In 2008 the employment rate of university graduates was just 70 percent but in 2009 it went further down to 55 percent (*Money Today*, 2 February 2009).[5]

Currently the overall unemployment rate is at its lowest for more than 10 years at 3.2 percent (Trading Economics, 2010), which is attributed to government programs to create public sector jobs. In reality, however, many of the public sector jobs available for new graduates are short-term internships that often do not lead to a permanent contract position.

The South Korean labor market relies on a high proportion of short-term, contract-based irregular jobs. Among the under-30-year-old age cohort, the proportion of irregular employment was 52.1 percent in March 2010, exceeding that of regular employment (47.9 percent). Further, the average salary of temporary contract-based employees with no job security is 46.2 percent that of full-time regular employees, which indicates a widening income discrepancy between the two groups (*Hankook Ilbo*, 11 July 2010).[6]

The higher education sector is similar: part-time, contract-based academics now outnumber the tenure-track academics in universities in South Korea (*Hankyoreh Shinmun*, 10 September 2009). The total number of irregular fixed-term university academics in South Korea is estimated at 135000 and the number of tenured or tenure-track academics at 55000. Almost half of all subjects in Korean universities are reportedly being taught by part-time, fixed-term lecturers who do not have job security and yet whose average salary is just about 5–10 percent of that of their tenure-track counterparts. They can be easily dismissed at any time. In 2009 alone 1219 lecturers out of 10 000 were reportedly laid off without advance notice. Facing hardship and humiliation as a result of irregular employment after obtaining doctorates, seven lecturers have committed suicide since 1998. Recently some of the lecturers in irregular employment in South Korea continued a sit-in protest in front of the parliament and several other major sites for 960 days, requesting the revision of the Higher Education Act and the restoration of the legal status of university teachers (STIP: Status of Teacher for Irregular Professor in Korea, 5 June 2010).

Nevertheless the issues and debate around irregular employment in Korean universities do not include the disadvantages and discrimination that foreign academics experience when they are employed in Korean universities. The overall public discourse – let alone the legal terms and conditions of irregular employment contracts – focuses only on 'Korean' nationals in general, even though an increasing number of foreigners live and work in the society and there is a strong case that there ought to be a universal application of the principle of equal opportunity in employment policy and practice. Generally it has been taken for granted in South Korea that foreign academic faculty are not employed on the same legal terms as local faculty. Academic faculty issues in Korean universities are a serious problem for official internationalization policies and practices in South Korea.

Changes in employment relations – such as the end of lifetime employment, voluntary and compulsory redundancies, the routinization of irregular, short-term and contract-based employment, performance-based payment schemes and so on – came after the Asian economic crisis (1997–98) and were part of the restructuring program as conditioned by the IMF bailout. The surface impression of these changes is that Korea is following the 'Anglo-American' model of neoliberal policies and practices found worldwide – which King (2010) argues has a form of network power that enhances 'policy internationalization' in a more interconnected world (Thatcher, 2007).

In the UK, for example, the casualization of academic labor commenced earlier and academic tenure was abolished in the late 1980s. Throughout the 1990s the position of academic faculty in the UK became progressively less secure. In many research-intensive universities the proportion of academic faculty on full-time permanent contracts is around only 30 percent (Kim, 2010). Subsequently the UCU (University and College Union) set up an Anti-Casualization Committee in June 2007 to help combat such changes (UCU, 2007). In the USA, similarly, the proportion of tenured, or tenure-track, faculty members has also dropped – from 57 percent in 1975 to 31 percent in 2007, and was below one-third by 2009. In other words, the so-called adjuncts – both part-timers and full-timers not on a tenure track – account for nearly 70 percent of professors at colleges and universities, both public and private, in the USA (*The Chronicle of Higher Education*, 4 July 2010; *University World News*, 29 March 2009).

Given these contexts, the value of higher education for 'employability' has been questioned in South Korea. As indicated earlier, the government's egalitarian-principled regulation of the education system has led to limited educational choices. As a result of the strong parental dissatisfaction with university education in South Korea, the number of Korean students studying abroad has continued to increase and the pattern of educational migration has become more diversified, ranging from primary schooling to university undergraduate and postgraduate studies, and including both short-term or frequent study visits and long-term educational migration.

NEW PATTERNS OF KOREAN ACADEMIC MOBILITY AND EDUCATIONAL MIGRATION

According to the OECD (2009a), Korea has the third largest absolute number of students (after China and India) studying abroad. In the USA, South Koreans comprise the largest national group among foreign students, with a total of 115 852 in 2008, followed by India and China (US Government, *2008*; re-quoted from Fulbright US-Education Center, 19 October 2008).[7] Overall, Korea has the world's largest number of students per capita who go abroad for study.

Besides young adults and mature students enrolled at HEIs abroad, an increasing number of primary and secondary school students in South Korea are also opting for foreign education abroad, and this has shaped a new form of educational migration in South Korea. In 1998 the number of Korean children studying abroad was only 1562, but this has rapidly increased since 2000. In 2006 it reached a peak, estimated at 29 511 and then slightly declined in 2008 to 27 349. Elementary students currently take up the largest share, with 12 531 going abroad, compared with 8888 middle-school and 5930 high-school students respectively (Fulbright US-Education Center, 6 November 2009).[8]

Unlike ordinary immigration, however, Korean students' moves are not intended to be permanent. They usually depart abroad alone or with just one parent while the other parent – usually the father – stays behind in Korea to work and send money. The increasing number of these 'wild geese fathers' in South Korea has been a prominent item in media coverage. This new pattern of educational migration is indicative of the dysfunctional schooling process and the failure of the Korean education system as a whole.

THE VALUE OF FOREIGN HIGHER DEGREES AND THE XENOPHOBIC BOUNDARIES OF ACADEMIC CAPITALISM

The Korean pattern of educational migration can also be linked to another very distinctive feature of higher education – the high proportion of foreign, especially US-educated, Korean academics as faculty members in major universities. On the whole there is considerable evidence that the Korean academic profession is already internationalized in terms of the overseas academic experience of its members. For instance, over 90 percent of the academic staff in the POSTECH – a top private institution specializing in science and technology, owned by POSCO/Pohang Iron and Steel Company – took PhDs in the USA. In the so-called 'SKY' universities (Seoul National, Korea and Yonsei among the top universities), the proportion of foreign doctoral degree-holders among the academics in humanities and social sciences faculties was 77 percent (SNU), 80.3 percent (KU) and 81.7 percent (YU) as of July 2010. According to the government's statistical data released in 2010, the overall proportion of academics who gained foreign doctorates at SNU was 50.4 percent, which is 10 times more than that of Tokyo University (5.2

percent). Furthermore, the majority with foreign doctorates have studied in the USA (*University News Network*, 13 July 2010).[9]

In the case of Seoul National University Education Department, where the author worked as a Brain Korea (BK) 21 (see later) contract professor, there were 23 (tenured or tenure-track) faculty members, who were all male, and all but one professor (who was in fact a specialist in the Korean history of education) had gained their doctoral degrees in the USA. The preference for male academics with foreign doctorates, especially US PhDs, has been a longstanding part of the Korean university tradition. When employing academics with Korean PhDs, however, preference has been given to the graduates of elite SKY universities and KAIST or the alumni of recruiting universities (*JoongAng Ilbo*, 22 April 2003).[10]

As discussed earlier, not only have the great majority of university academics in South Korea studied and gained degrees abroad, but also many Korean students have experienced studying in another country for primary and secondary schooling as well as for tertiary education. As Chang comments, it seems that 'no other country of similar stature shows such a severe dependency on foreign education' (Chang, 2008, p. 4). Yet the foreign academic degrees possessed by Korean university academics have not necessarily increased the internationalization of Korean universities and its higher education in general (Kim, 2005). The overall character of university academic culture remains homogeneously and resolutely 'Korean' as the infrastructure of professional, academic and personal relations in Korea is based on highly exclusive alumni networking and academic inbreeding.

Given these distinctive characteristics of Korean higher education, we now examine the patterns of higher education reform in South Korea in the context of globalization during the last decade, including the effects of economic restructuring and the adoption of the new public management (NPM) for public services such as universities after the Asian financial crisis of 1997–98.

HIGHER EDUCATION REFORM IN SOUTH KOREA OVER THE LAST DECADE

After the Asian economic crisis the government felt it necessary to urgently reform its universities and human resources development programs. The government upgraded the Ministry of Education (MOE) to the Ministry of Education and Human Resource Development (MEHRD). In January 2000 the government of President Kim Dae-jung announced a vision for Korea to become an advanced, knowledge-based economy. Only three months later the government put into effect a three-year action plan for implementing the knowledge economy strategy. It consisted of 83 associated action plans in the five main areas of information infrastructure, human resource development, the development of knowledge-based industry, science and technology, and elimination of the digital divide. Following the government's guidelines on its internationalization framework, universities also went through self-initiated reform. A number of South Korean universities have set their sights on creating an Asian education hub like Singapore and Hong Kong in order to retain more Korean students and to attract more foreign students. Some of them have already concluded agreements with American, British and

Australian universities for joint degrees, study abroad programs and faculty exchanges (World Bank, 2010; Kim, 2008b; *Inside Higher Ed.*, 2007).

The government also launched the famous Brain Korea 21 (BK21) project with the aim of bringing selected major university research projects to a 'world-class' level and increasing the competitiveness of local universities. Around US$1.3 billion were invested in 120 institutions to enable 440 projects to be run for seven years (1999–2005). A second round of BK 21 programs (2006–13) subsequently was agreed, emphasizing the areas of technology development in collaboration with industry (Kim, 2008a, pp. 561–2).

The Roh Moo-hyun government (2003–08) kept the strong egalitarian ethos as a policy theme. However, the emphasis on equality and fairness in education perpetuated the standardization of education in Korea and seemed at odds with the new policies of creating a cadre of world-class universities. In line with the previous government's strategy of 'transforming Korea into a knowledge-driven economy', the Roh Moo-hyun government introduced another new 'National Vision and Long-Term Fiscal Strategy' in 2005. Its goals included leapfrogging into the top 10 knowledge-information leaders in the globe, upgrading educational environments to OECD standards, and harnessing the science and technology base to reach the G7 standard (World Bank, 2006).

The new plan also addressed some of the issues where previous government efforts had only limited or moderate success – most notably in educational reform. The Roh Moo-hyun government put emphasis on 'equality and participation' to fight against polarizing trends in Korean society, which had become more visible after the 1997–98 economic crisis and the subsequent neoliberal economic restructuring processes. For instance, the government launched the NURI (New University for Regional Innovation) project in 2004 within which the role of the university was defined as being more tightly linked to the regional/local government's development agenda and to local industry. To achieve regional balance in development, only HEIs located outside the capital region were considered as beneficiaries of the NURI funds. A total of US$1.4 billion was to be invested over a period of five years (2004–09) and aimed at restructuring the HE system around notions of concentration, specialization and diversification in each region through the NURI project (MOE, 2005; Kim, 2008a, p. 564).

The NURI project can be considered as a Korean version of the 'triple helix' model of university–industry–regional government partnerships. At the same time, however, an NPM restructuring process was implemented in the higher education sector, including encouragement of mergers and acquisitions, increasing the level of competition at and between the top universities, establishing professional graduate schools in law, medicine, engineering and business administration, and incorporating the national/public universities, which essentially was benchmarking the Japanese experience.

Neoliberal-principled economic globalization processes have continued to intensify in South Korea through GATS and similar world trade negotiations. Yet, as noted previously, the continuing pattern of the government's regulatory policy-making reinforced conformity in HEIs and limited educational choices. Accordingly Korean students and parents are seeking alternatives abroad and educational migration is a new trend in Korea, pointing to the strong public demand for internationalized higher education at all levels (Kim, 2008a, p. 564).

Given this, and the ongoing pressure from the WTO–GATS, the government has removed restrictions for foreign institutions to provide educational services directly within South Korea. By doing so, the government aims, in legislation enacted in 2002, to attract more foreign direct investment and economic activities in special Free Economic Zones, with tax incentives, fast-track permit processing and similar incentives. Further, in December 2005 the Korean government allowed foreign educational institutions to open at all levels – kindergartens, primary, secondary and high schools, and universities – in the three designated International Free Economic Zones (IFEZs) – that is, in Incheon, Busan-Jinhae and Gwanyang – and in the international visa-free city of Cheju (Jeju). The Special Act on the Establishment and Operation of Foreign Educational Institutions of 2005 has:

- drastically eased restrictions on the establishment of institutions by foreign universities;
- permitted the transfer of surplus assets overseas under certain conditions if a school corporation was liquidated;
- allowed the Korean government to fund foreign-owned universities.

The ultimate goal of South Korea in this process of opening up the domestic higher education market is to make an educational hub of North-east Asia (Kim, 2008a, pp. 564–5; MEST, 2009). At least two American partners, North Carolina State University and the State University New York at Stony Brook, has each received US$1 million funding to help develop undergraduate programs in Songdo City as an initial step to create the Songdo Global University Campus – a collaborative attempt to blend Korean, American and European academic strengths with programs running from 2010. By 2011 the University of Delaware and George Mason University are scheduled to open courses there also (*Chronicle of Higher Education*, 19 June 2009). Overall the local authority aim is to attract 1200 companies domestically and from overseas by 2014 as part of the bid to become an important hub for business and logistics, IT and biotechnology, education, and tourism and culture (*Korea Times*, 8 June 2010).

A free trade agreement (FTA) in educational services is also under negotiation with the USA. The South Korean government expects that the FTA will not only liberalize the education market but also curb the increasing levels of outward educational migration that start well before the tertiary level. If foreign universities enter Korea and ignite competition, this is expected to help Korean universities to develop more competitively and to meet global standards while heightening the marketability and attraction of the local higher education system.

The incumbent government (2008–13) led by President Lee Myung Bak is continuing with neoliberal market-based reforms. The Ministry of Education and Human Resource Development (MEHRD) has been restructured to form the Ministry of Education, Science and Technology (MEST), and a Special Law has been introduced to enhance the public accountability and transparency of university management.

The government has also initiated the World Class University (WCU) Project (in 2008), along with the 'high-risk, high-return' pioneer research project to put public investment into strategically important areas, especially basic research and advanced technology, and in R&D in biotechnology, nanotechnology and brain research. For the WCU project (2008–13) the government has allocated US$617 million to raise the quality of research at 30 selected universities. As a part of the scheme the government has also invited 81 foreign scholars, including nine Nobel Prize winners, who are expected to help transform Korean universities into world-class research institutions. However, sceptics offer rather pessimistic views that such an approach might help to achieve a sustainable world-class research base. Many of the international scholars who have responded may already be past their best work and are required to stay in South Korea for just a semester, or at most two months a year, on a three-year contract (*Chronicle of Higher Education*, 19 June 2009).

To achieve an inbound internationalization of universities in South Korea, there has been a notable increase in the number of English-medium courses, and dual-degree and joint-degree programs with partner universities, mostly in the USA and China. English education is big business in South Korea. The nation spends over US$3 billion a year on various forms of English-language training. South Korea, despite having a population a third the size of Japan's, reportedly spends three times as much as Japan on this activity (*Inside Higher Ed.*, 27 February 2007).

Along with the English language, South Korean universities are also obsessed with the quantitative indices of internationalization – such as the number of publications in refereed international journal articles and with the international rankings established by the THE–QS and other rating bodies. Top-tier private universities – such as Yonsei, Korea and Ewha – have recently established all-English liberal arts colleges to attract both Korean and international students. The condition of international academic faculty has also changed recently. Tenure-track positions are finally open to foreign academics although most foreign academics in Korean universities are still on a short-term contract (Kim, 2008b).

As part of internationalization strategies, Yonsei University has taken an extreme measure in its academic staffing policy for its Underwood International College: only foreign nationals can apply for the full-time faculty positions – as though only foreign passport-holders would guarantee the international standard of the College. No Korean national, however excellent he or she may be as an international scholar, is eligible to apply unless of course they give up their Korean nationality. It could be surmised that this move looks like a counter-discrimination practice against Korean nationality in the name of 'internationalization' (Kim, 2008b), for generally foreign academics are seldom given full tenure and only a limited number of universities offer non-discriminatory rates to their non-Korean faculty.

This apparent discriminatory practice gives few highly qualified foreign professors sufficient motivation to work for any Korean university on a long-term basis (Jambor, 2009). As a result, many of the 'foreign' academics employed in Yonsei Underwood International College are, in fact, Korean returnees from the USA as American citizens (Kim, 2008b). This is not surprising, however, given the unequal terms of employment contracts offered to non-Korean academics in Korean universities. According to the THE-QS World University Rankings, Seoul National University (SNU) was placed 47 in 2009, but when it was measured against the proportion of international faculty SNU was ranked 363 – near the bottom of the league table (*THE-QS World University Rankings*).[11]

According to a government report in 2008 of 172 four-year colleges and universities nationwide, just 4.6 percent of full-time faculty are foreigners in South Korea (*Chosun Ilbo*, 13 September 2008).[12]

Meanwhile the number of foreign students studying in Korean universities has notably increased. Although most international students come with scholarships, their presence makes a fresh change to student profiles. On average more than one-third (more than 40 percent in some universities such as Seoul National and Hanyang) of students who enroll in postgraduate degree courses on Korean language and literature at six major universities in Seoul are international. They are not just from neighboring countries like China and Japan, but also from Thailand, Myanmar, Vietnam, Indonesia, Uzbekistan, USA and so on (*Yonhap News*, 8 July 2010). Such an expansion and diversification of foreign students studying in Korean universities can be attributed to the fruitful result of the government's Study Korea Project and also to an improved image of Korea and its economic significance internationally.

Both the government and universities are eager to recruit more foreign academics and students as a part of internationalization strategies. However, international academic staffing is often considered as a short-term way to meet a policy target in South Korea. Unlike in the UK, USA, Australia or Canada, foreign academics are not employed on the same legal terms as the local staff – as indicated earlier. Overall there is no legal protection for the equality of job opportunities for foreigners in South Korea as yet. This may be a bit similar to the Japanese case, but there is more exclusive ethno-nationalism serving as boundaries of non-inclusion in Korean academic culture (Kim, 2008b). Foreign academics are, in general, excluded from academic management roles and the administrative business of the university in South Korea (Kim, 2005).

CONCLUSION

Having reviewed the distinctive characteristics of government–university relations and HE reforms in Korea, it is suggested that the government's internationalization of HE policy in Korea is not very different from its famous five-year economic development plans in the past, which have been carried out consecutively and successfully as 'the national project' since 1962. Underneath the conventional, neoliberal market-oriented architecture of Korean HE policy, the Ministry of Education remains much the same – its old bureaucratic apparatus and regulatory role have not changed. Since the implementation of the government's deregulation policy in 1995 to emulate neoliberal NPM principles (Byun, 2008), the role of government seems to have become more refined as regulator and assessor, but it has not weakened, nor has it been fundamentally changed – and remains as depicted in the World Bank report over a decade ago (World Bank, 2000), as discussed earlier.

In effect, the relations of government and the university in Korea have never been constructed on 'liberal' premises. The Korean mode of governance has been typically labeled as a 'strong' or 'interventionist' state. These terms capture the authoritarian state's power implemented through a centralized bureaucracy, which can be attributed to the mixture of the Confucian, colonial and military cultural legacy in Korean political history (Kim, 2001).

According to another World Bank report (2001), the South Korean economy has a relatively sophisticated apparatus, giving greater managerial discretion to state-owned enterprises, which are governed by 'performance contracts' with the Department of

Finance. The World Bank praised Korea's 'recently taken steps to move towards international best practice' in terms of accounting, audit standards and practices, and in public sector reforms (World Bank, 2001, p. 5).

However, in the process of higher education policy-making and execution, South Korean government regulations are still as prescriptive as before, although they are now more precisely conditioned by subsequent financial incentives. The government's higher education policy framework itself may look like the result of change but its approach and measures to implement reforms are reminiscent of the strong government-led consecutive five-year economic development plans in South Korea from the early 1960s onwards that made South Korea famous as a typical model of the East Asian 'developmental state' (Goodman et al., 1998).

Although its policy framework and control mechanisms exhibit neoliberal, market-oriented NPM principles (Byun, 2008), given the condition of the unchanging regulatory relations between government and the university, the neoliberal concept of public accountability has not yet been fully incorporated into Korean higher education (Kim, 2008a, p. 567). Who owns and who owes accountability to whom in the Korean higher education sector? The real terms and actual practices of accountability are issues that need to be clarified for the future advancement of higher education in South Korea.

Despite the official emphasis for more than a decade on internationalizing higher education, culturally the internal features of the contemporary university in South Korea are still very local in practice. Internal academic faculty culture draws on Confucian patriarchal relationships and principles. The internal culture of universities and academic communities of practice in South Korea on the whole have not shifted to embrace the consequences of internationalization and entrepreneurial policies, despite the increasing influence of *chaebol* on university governance and management in the private sector.

Korean higher education is now at a crossroads with two signposts: first, ethnocentric internationalization; and second, commercialization in the process of economic globalization. Although there is an increasing number of foreign residents in Korea, there is lack of diversity and intercultural embrace as part of academic communities of practice to attract creative international talents. Universities need to play a major role for the inbound mobility and exchange of global talents. However, if international academics see Korea as an inhospitable environment for their professional and personal aspirations, they will not consider Korea as a possible destination for their academic career development. Furthermore, the challenge is not just limited to attracting 'outside' talent. Korean academics studying abroad also have more diverse career options nowadays, given the new patterns of global academic mobility (Kim, 2008c, 2010).

Despite the strong presence of women studying in higher education, educated women (more than 40 percent) remain an untapped resource for Korea's future growth. Korea is unique in that university-educated women are actually less likely to work than their less-educated sisters. In terms of gender equality, there are only 8.1 women managers for every 100 male managers; the OECD average is close to 30 percent. The wage differential between men and women in Korea is almost twice as high as in the rest of the OECD (*JoongAng Daily*, 27 May 2010).

Also we should be mindful of global commercialization leading to homogeneity and commodification of knowledge by means of nominally multicultural and intercultural higher education marketing. South Korea can boast of its strong tradition of learning and its achievements in both economic and education development, and there is a good chance, given that culture of learning, that the new internationalization in Korean universities may eventually be successful. Only then will South Korea become a cultured member of the global society rather than just one of a group of newly industrialized countries (NICs) in East Asia. This will enhance the long-term international visibility of South Korea, not least within the global mobilities of academics and creative knowledge.

NOTES

1. See http://www.topuniversities.com/university-rankings/world-university-rankings/2009/results.
2. www.ipsnews.net/news.asp?idnews=51994.
3. http://www.kyosu.net/news/articleView.html?idxno=8390
4. http://joongangdaily.joins.com/article/view.asp?aid=2899999.
5. http://stock.mt.co.kr/view/mtview.php?no=2009020209143186144&type=1&outlink=2&EVEC.
6. http://news.hankooki.com/lpage/economy/201007/h2010071122332321540.htm#.
7. http://blog.educationusa.or.kr/category/korean-students-overseas/.
8. http://blog.educationusa.or.kr/category/korean-students-overseas/.
9. www.unn.net/news/detail.asp?nsCode=62787.
10. http://article.joins.com/article/article.asp?Total_ID=157632.
11. http://www.topuniversities.com/university-rankings.
12. http://issue.chosun.com/site/data/html_dir/2008/11/05/2008110500471.html.

REFERENCES

Asian Economic News (2001), 'S. Korea pays back remaining debt to IMF', 27, August, http://findarticles. com/p/articles/mi_m0WDP/is_2001_August_27/ai_78570214/.

Byun, Kiyong (2008), 'New Public Management in Korean higher education: is it reality or another fad?', *Asia Pacific Education Review*, **9** (2), 19–205.

Chang, S. (2008), 'A cultural and philosophical perspective on Korea's education reform: a critical way to maintain Korea's economic momentum', Korea Economy Institute (KEI) Academic Paper Series, March, **3** (2): http://www.keia.org/documents/APS_08Chang.pdf.

Chronicle of Higher Education (2009), 'South Korea moves to make its universities more international', 19 June, http://chronicle.com/article/South-Korea-Powers-Ahead-With/44530/.

Chronicle of Higher Education (2010), 'Tenure, RIP: what the vanishing status means for the future of education', 4 July, http://chronicle.com/article/Tenure-RIP/66114/.

CIA (2010), *The World Factbook*, https://www.cia.gov/library/publications/the-world-factbook/geos/ks.html, accessed 7 July 2010.

Financial Times (2010), 'South Korea is no longer the underdog', 25 February, http://www.ft.com/cms/s/0/10c98f68-21ae-11df-acf4-00144feab49a.html.

Goodman, R., G. White and H. Kwon (eds) (1998), *The East Asian Welfare Model: Welfare Orientalism and the State*, London: Routledge.

Ianchovichina, E. and D. Leipziger (2008), 'How can Korea raise its potential growth rate?', *World Economics*, **9** (4).

IFWEA (International Federation of Workers' Educational Association) (1999), 'Instruments of globalization in the Asia International Study Circles Project', http://ifwea.org/.

Inside Higher Ed. (2007), 'English growth – and backlash – in Korea', 20 February, http://www.insidehighered. com/news/2007/02/20/korea.

Jambor, P. (2009), 'Why South Korean universities have low international rankings', *Academic Leadership Online Journal*, **7** (1), 20 February 2009, http://www.academicleadership.org/emprical_ research/606.shtml.

JoongAng Daily (2010a), 'Korea's image trails Japan, USA and even China', 27 April, http://joongangdaily. joins.com/article/view.asp?aid=2919727.

JoongAng Daily (2010b), 'Retooling the brain power factory', 18 May, http://joongangdaily.joins.com/article/view.asp?aid=2920568.

JoongAng Daily (2010c), 'Korea's competitiveness up: IMD', 20 May, http://joongangdaily.joins.com/article/view.asp?aid=2920716.

Kim, S. and J. Lee (2006), 'Changing facets of Korean higher education: market competition and the role of the state', *Higher Education*, **52** (3), 557–87.

Kim, T. (2000), 'South Korea', in R. Cowen, D. Coulby and C. Jones (eds), *The World Yearbook of Education 2000: Education in Times of Transition*, London: Kogan Page, pp. 181–91.

Kim, T. (2001), *Forming the Academic Profession in East Asia: A Comparative Analysis*, New York and London: Routledge.

Kim, T. (2005), 'Internationalisation of higher education in South Korea: reality, rhetoric, and disparity in academic culture and identities', *The Australian Journal of Education*, Special Issue: International Education, eds S. Marginson, G. Joseph and R. Yang, **49** (1), 89–103.

Kim, T. (2008a), 'Higher education reforms in South Korea: public–private problems in internationalizing and incorporating universities', *Policy Futures in Education*, Special Issue on *University restructuring experiences in East Asia: myth and reality*, eds K.H. Mok and D. Chan **6** (5), 558–68.

Kim, T. (2008b), 'The academic profession in East Asian higher education', in A. Yonezawa (ed.), *Frontier of Private Higher Education Research in East Asia*, Tokyo: Research Institute for Independent Higher Education (RIIHE), pp. 139–61.

Kim, T. (2008c), 'Transnational academic mobility in a global knowledge economy: comparative and historical motifs', in D. Epstein, R. Boden, R. Deem, F. Rizvi and S. Wright (eds), *The World Yearbook of Education 2008, Geographies of Knowledge and Geometries of Power: Framing the Future of Higher Education*, London: Routledge, pp. 319–37.

Kim, T. (2009), 'Confucianism, modernities and knowledge: China, South Korea and Japan', in R. Cowen and A. Kazamias (eds), *The International Handbook of Comparative Education*, Dordrecht, The Netherlands: Springer, pp. 857–72.

Kim, T. (2010), 'Transnational academic mobility, knowledge, and identity capital', in J. Kenway and J. Fahey (eds), *Discourse Journal: Studies in the Cultural Politics of Education, special issue*, **31** (5), October.

Kim, Young Sam (1996), *Korea's Reform and Globalization*, Korean Overseas Information Service, Seoul: The Government Press.

King, R. (2010), 'Policy internationalization, national variety and governance: global models and network power in higher education states', *Higher Education*, forthcoming but on-line 24 February, 1–12.

Korea Herald (2009), 'South Korea's low birth rate', 28 February.

Korea Times (2010), 'Songdon Global Campus has niche clients', 8 June.

Korean Educational Development Institute (KEDI) (2010), *The Yearbook of Educational Statistics in Korea*, Seoul: Korean Educational Development Institute.

Lee, Kong-Ju-Bock (2010), 'Women in science, engineering, and technology (SET) in Korea: improving retention and building capacity', *International Journal of Gender, Science and Technology*, **2** (2), 236–48.

McKinsey and Company (2010), *Korea 2020: Global Perspectives for the Next Decade*, Seoul: Random House Korea.

Ministry of Education (MOE) (2005), *New University for Regional Development (NURI)*, Seoul: Ministry of Education.

Ministry of Education, Science and Technology (MEST) (2008), *Annual Statistics on Student Mobility: The Number of Korean Students Studying Abroad and Foreign Students in Korean Higher Educational Institutions*, Seoul: MEST.

Ministry of Education, Science and Technology (MEST) (2009), *The Plan for Advancing the Education Service Industry [in Korean]*, Seoul: MEST.

OECD (2009a), *Education at a Glance*, Paris: OECD, http://www.oecd.org/dataoecd/40/58/43633897.pdf.

OECD (2009b), 'OECD Development Assistance Committee (DAC) welcomes Korean membership', 27 November, http://washfinance.wordpress.com/2009/11/27/oecd-development-assistance-committee-dac-welcomes-korean-membership/.

Ryu, J. et al. (2006), *Seven Strategies for University Reform*, Seoul: Samsung Economic Research Institute.

San Francisco Chronicle (2010), 'Education cuts may lead to US brain drain' 27 February, http://www.sfgate.com/cgi-bin/article.cgi?f=/c/a/2010/02/26/BU1E1C7S61.DTL&type=business#ixzz0uc7rrwDf.

Statistics Korea (2010), 'Women's lives through statistics in 2010', KOSIS (Korean Statistical Information Service), 7 July, http://kostat.go.kr/eboard_faq/BoardAction.do?method=view&catgrp=eng2009&catid1=g01&catid2=g01b&catid3=g01ba&catid=g01ba&board_id=106&seq=318&num=318.

STIP (2010), 'Why are university lecturers committing suicide in Korea?', website of 'Status of teacher for irregular professors', 5 June, http://stip.or.kr/bbs/board.php?bo_table=Solidarity&wr_id=25

Thatcher, M. (2007), *Internationalisation and Economic Institutions*, Oxford: Oxford University Press.

Trading Economics (2010), 'South Korea unemployment rate', http://www.tradingeconomics.com/Economics/Unemployment-Rate.aspx?Symbol=KRW.

UCU (University College Union) (2007), 'Fixed-term scandals', November, http://www.ucu.org.uk/media/pdf/s/1/ucu_ftscandalcontinues_nov07.pdf.

US Government (2008), *SEVIS by the Numbers Report 2008*, http://www.ice.gov/sevis/numbers/student/country_of_citizenship.htm.

Woo-Cummings, M. (ed.) (1999), *The Developmental State*, Ithaca, NY and London: Cornell University Press.

World Bank (2000), *Republic of Korea: Transition to a Knowledge-based Economy*, Report No. 20346-KO, 29 June.

World Bank (2001), *Special Focus: Public Financial Accountability in East Asia*, http://www1.worldbank.org/publicsector/pe/specialfocus.pdf.

World Bank (2006), *Korea as a Knowledge Economy: Evolutionary Process and Lessons Learned*, WBI Development Studies, http://web.worldbank.org/WBSITE/EXTERNAL/WBI/WBIPROGRAMS/KFDLP/0,,contentMDK:20997709~menuPK:461215~pagePK:64156158~piPK:64152884~theSitePK:461198,00.html.

World Bank (2010), *Case Study: Korea's Transition towards Knowledge Economy – The Story of One 'Vision'*, http://web.worldbank.org/WBSITE/EXTERNAL/WBI/WBIPROGRAMS/KFDLP/O, content MDK: 21014147.

Yonezawa, A. and T. Kim (2008), 'Future of higher education in a context of a shrinking student population: policy challenges for Japan and Korea', in S. Vincent-Lancrin (ed.), *Higher Education to 2030. Vol. 1: Demography/L'enseignement supérieur en 2030. Vol. 1: Démographie*, Paris: OECD, pp. 199–216.

18 The invisible topics on the public agenda for higher education in Argentina
Marcela Mollis

INTRODUCTION

This chapter addresses the invisible topics of the public agenda of Argentine higher education that were not taken into account in the debate on higher education public policy during the recent 'neoliberal' decade that occurred in the context of global educational reforms. Not only are the policies with a public–private orientation described, but they are also compared with the public-oriented policies of the previous welfare state period. The impact of former policies is discussed through the analysis of the higher educational reforms that took place in Argentina in the 1990s. The chapter concludes with a discussion of key points for creating an alternative diagnosis of higher educational reform.

We begin with a discussion of the public policies that have recently had a significant impact on the missions of universities, increasingly turning them into tertiary institutions dedicated to professional training and away from their identity as institutions that create and use knowledge to transform and to socialize a critical citizenry. History shows a tendency to replace the notion of a specific university policy with an all-encompassing higher education policy that homogenizes and – frankly – indiscriminately confuses tertiary (non-university) and university education (Mollis, 2003).

THE INVISIBLE TOPICS OUTLINED

The historical relationship between public policy and higher education emerged during the rise of the nation-state in the nineteenth century, and continued through its consolidation and expansion. Obviously, in western civilization, the nation-states were the main actors in the capitalist modernization of the late nineteenth century, especially in terms of configuring educational systems at all levels. Therefore the first topic in discussing higher education public policy is the model of the capitalist nation-state (here defined as 'dependent' in its political-economic dimension), and the civilizing paradigm it produces. The nation-states of the nineteenth century were the central players in the process of 'social modernization', notably in the role they took in the creation and expansion of national education systems and the application of educational public policy. Building a sense of national integration required the development of a homogeneous conscience and citizenry that could overcome the legitimacy of the so-called *ancien régimes*.

The national education systems were directly linked to the expansion of this nationalistic sentiment, and each education level played a particular function in the process. In Argentina the liberal disposition prevailed in the laws that would regulate basic and higher education, and, as in other Latin American countries, public universities fundamentally attended to the training and other needs of the bureaucratic apparatus of 'modern' political systems and of agricultural export development. Faced with the need to provide certain kinds of services, higher education institutions (HEIs) took on as one of their particular functions the training of professionals that met specific demands in terms of quantity and quality deriving from the economic and political contexts. This did not mean an absence of conflict caused by the adjustments that these new functions brought about. Public universities faced internal pressures from institutional actors representing various power groups (be they students, professors or other institutional members) demanding structural changes to meet particular interests. Therefore we can identify two kinds of conditions that affect the social function of universities: external and internal (Mollis, 1990).

What ideas did Latin American universities embody during the foundational modern stage that coincided with the break from colonial Spain (Mollis, in Rhoads and Torres, 2006)? The Latin American university style of the late nineteenth century was characterized by the kind of professional knowledge that German historian Hans Steger (1974) describes as 'the university of lawyers'. The conception of the professional university bespeaks an institution that is predominantly secular, pragmatic and state-oriented, entrusted with the mission of shaping citizens, professionals and public administrators. This model adapted to relatively static social systems and maintained a close link to the state, which recognized the privileges and rights of the university while financing it, thus becoming the 'teaching state' towards the end of the nineteenth century. The so-called 'teaching states' in Latin America served as the administrators and inspectors of the entire educational system, with exclusive sovereignty over educational matters.

Lawyers graduating from these institutions were professionally and ideologically linked to agrarian property, and as statesmen and public officers they created the instruments of political control within state institutions such as courts, prosecution offices and police headquarters. Through the schools and the press they carried out other activities that allowed them to widen the expression of the hegemonic classes, whether as writers, poets or educators:

> This group gave rise to a bureaucratic elite and a political class with a formalistic and pompous style which adapted perfectly to the interests of the dominant classes. (Canton, 1966, p. 46)

The 'scientific university' arrived in Argentina in the 1960s, boosted by the globally valued image of the researcher–professor, exclusive functions, new laboratories, and the elevating place of research alongside the teaching and service missions. The Humboldtian university model, which emphasizes the leading role of universities as R&D centers, was effectively superimposed on the Latin American Napoleonic model. Risieri Frondizi offers some eloquent insights in this respect:

> Everyone, including lawyers themselves, knows that our countries require increasing numbers of scientists and technicians and fewer lawyers. The process of industrial and economic development is held back, however, because universities are not creating the professionals required by this process. (Frondizi, 2005, p. 22)

Among the events that characterized the University of Buenos Aires in this 'Golden Age' of scientific development, contemporary witnesses mention the recruitment of world-renowned professors, the departmentalization of academics, the issue of a summons to alumni and the creation of a graduate school, as well as the creation of the School of Public Health, hospital units and medical residencies. Alfredo Lanari founded an institute that revolutionized the practice and teaching of medicine, which attracted as patients 'professors, generals and bishops, due to the superior service to that of any other medical establishment, including those in the private sector' (Rotunno and Diaz de Guijarro, 2003, p. 207).

At this point we can agree that public universities in Argentina are the offspring of modern reason, and, consequently, of the confidence promised by the humanities, scientific progress and the professions. The current crisis of modern reason affects the institutional project of traditional institutions. New institutions are responding to this crisis and the short-term nature of the market by turning out 'diploma buyers' in less than five years.

New technologies have replaced previous perspectives regarding the social function of universities. Their participation in the configuration of a democratic citizenry has been left behind in favor of training competent workers for a restricted labor market. Global capitalism is reproduced through weakened post-neoliberal states and their respective western dominant civilizing formulae. The western paradigm currently in use in our higher education policy has been defined by a civilizing doctrine exported from the developed North and defended as such. In this sense it is interesting to reflect on the alternative university models (indigenous, Bolivariana, municipal etc.) emerging in Bolivia, Venezuela and Cuba, respectively, which aim at incorporating a local identity within an institution that is strongly conditioned by, and a condition of, the western paradigm. To what extent are universities open to an alternative identity? To what extent are universities, heirs to western intellectual culture, impervious to radical transformation?

The second topic refers to the dialectic between knowledge and power that is governed by the regime and international map of universities. From the Middle Ages universities began shaping the power that comes with possessing knowledge and, somehow, today we are witness to the power appropriated by those who monopolize knowledge. Those with the power to censor knowledge from the majority, that is, those with the power to dole out knowledge, those with the power to organize the international distribution of knowledge, are also the ones who restrict the knowledge needed to attain autonomy from being diffused more generally in our region.

The crucial dialectic of knowledge and power, however, has been omitted so far as a point of analysis in the creation of higher education policy. De Sousa Santos (2005) considers that the process of transnationalization in universities is a cornerstone of the neoliberal project, produced by the expansion of the university services market, articulated with decreasing public financing, the deregulation of financial markets, and the revolution in information and communication technology (ICT). In this sense, the tremendous growth of the Internet is of particular importance because of the alarming proportion of electronic flows concentrated in the North, even though this is a global development and therefore supposedly 'universal'. The global–universalizing illusion conceals deep differences in terms of users and consumers in Latin American public universities, who are neither producers of communication technologies nor creators of the information that they consume (Marginson and Mollis, 2001). The geopolitics of knowledge is also related to the imposition of a communications paradigm (mass media and the Internet) that reflects the reality of the core Northern countries, whose educational investments are twice those of the automobile industry (De Sousa Santos, 2005).

The geopolitics of knowledge and power divides the world into countries that consume the knowledge produced by the countries that culturally and economically dominate globalization, while the latter assign universities in the periphery to an economic function as producers of 'human resources'. This new condition, in which knowledge is increasingly a factor in resource accumulation, implies questioning the public-good character of the knowledge produced by universities and the right that the broader society has to access this knowledge. One of the rhetorical forms assumed by this argument is the call to academize universities, which allows discrediting all interpretations that recognize the urgent political condition of these institutions. In this case, the goals of university endeavor are imposed as pre-established 'missions' that university actors are merely in charge of executing.

This discussion necessarily leads us to a third topic, the missions of the university. What is a university (Mollis, 2001; Rüegg, 1994)? Why is it necessary to take a step back from higher education and consider the university as an entity? In truth, beginning in the 1990s the Argentine agenda has been oriented towards thinking about higher education after it was decided that the Ministry of Education would be in charge of policy-making for post-secondary learning in general, including both tertiary and university education. From a historical perspective, the legal framework that marked the beginning of the national universities – known as the 'Avellaneda Law' – established the university as the sole higher learning institution, a natural ally of the state and of its national development policies. Tertiary institutions subsequently were created to satisfy the training needs of teachers and technical specializations. The nineteenth-century nation-state adopted the universities as instruments for its scientific, professional and political development.

Definitions

At this point I would like to share three British definitions of a university:

- A place for teaching, specifically a place of teaching universal knowledge (John Henry Newman, 1881)
- 'It is not a place of professional education' (John Stuart Mill, 1867)
- A university may be defined by its particular mission or purpose, which differentiates it from other educational institutions (including tertiary institutions) (Sheldon Rothblatt, 1997).

The first definition is by John Henry Newman, who was one of the founders of the liberal arts colleges in the English Catholic tradition (he converted to Catholicism late in life and was ordained Cardinal of the famous Trinity College at Oxford in 1878). These colleges – the equivalent of the Latin American *facultades* – were designed for a small elite population, for which higher education meant access to a general education that would guarantee acquiring the universal knowledge needed to lead the grand fates of nations (or empires, as the case may be). For John Henry Newman, the university was a place for teaching, where universal knowledge was passed on. The emphasis was on a general culture and, of course, on observing the Catholic values of these colleges.

The second definition, by John Stuart Mill, describes the university by what it is not: it is not a place for professional education. This vision, later taken on by Newman, conceives of universities as spaces for educating the ruling elites through a curriculum heavily oriented towards the liberal arts. It is important to note that this tradition would be adopted by members of the Argentinean Reform Movement of 1918, who believed that general culture was necessary for educating future national leaders. Members of the Movement also defended a university model that would place and keep the best professors in charge of teaching. The idea of hiring the best faculty-teachers (those who teach best, those who best know what they teach) became a code of honor for the University Reform Movement, and years later would lead to the model for hiring new faculty through qualifying exams.

Finally, the third definition is provided by a contemporary English historian, Sheldon Rothblatt (1997). A university may be defined by its particular mission or purpose, which differentiates it from other educational institutions. Rothblatt tells us that we can recognize universities because they do not resemble any other educational institution. This is a broad definition that allows us to think of a university that serves a social or public good, or a university that serves knowledge; a militant university, a committed university, or one that emphasizes culture, education, science and so on. However, something else catches our attention in this definition. Rothblatt also asserts that the university – even when we accept the diversity of missions adopted by it – is not similar to any other institution in the system; he places the emphasis on the characteristics that make these institutions particular and distinctive, and which we can define as the identity of the university.

My hypothesis is that the reformist university identity born during the 1918 Reform became the center of the more recent neoliberal reforms, and was in fact the aim of the neoliberal transformation (Mollis, 2003, 2006, 2008). Not many have recognized this feature, but a quick reading of the main documents published by the World Bank in the 1990s reveals the diagnosis of Latin American universities made by the Bank at the time. This diagnosis (World Bank, 1993, 2000) seeks to discredit the identity of public universities. Why? The World Bank describes the excessive political activity of students, who are not real 'students' because they hold jobs while enrolled at the university; by the same token, professors are 'lazy' and not real professors (because they are exclusively dedicated to teaching). This diagnosis suggests that the 'Latin American identity' must be changed so that universities can be real universities, since students are not real students and professors are not real professors. Neoliberalism modified the social pact between state and education. It modified many other things in the public agenda, but it definitively transformed the pact that existed between education and the welfare state, which adhered to a liberal ideology as promoter, guarantor and provider of public education. Neoliberalism turned the state towards the game of supply and demand, and, in so doing, left higher education at the mercy of mighty market forces, leaving it up to individual institutions to sell services and finance what the nation-state would no longer finance. This is why the fourth topic is 'the institutionalization of international influence'.

This institutionalization has taken place through all agreements signed between the state and multilateral agencies, including the World Bank and other international agencies, whose educational agenda was based on the diagnosis discussed above (Rodríguez Gómez, 2006). This institutionalization took place because the World Bank, as any banking institution, sought to profit from the credit given to local governments. Along with the institutionalization of international influence, an omnipresent culture of measurement also appeared. This culture developed a local-particular profile (especially in Latin America and the post-socialist countries), since it became an end in itself. It is crucial to clarify that the culture of measurement or outcome evaluation is not in question: their omnipresence is.

The fifth theoretical topic, closely tied to the previous one, is 'the privatization of the educational public interest' (Mollis, 2009), represented by the privatizing policies promoted by the neoliberal state. To understand the characteristics born of this tendency, it will be depicted in the following sections and supported by quantitative data.

DEPICTING THE PRIVATIZATION OF THE EDUCATIONAL PUBLIC INTEREST

The Scenario of Higher Education Reforms in Argentina

From 1995 onwards, in Argentina as in Mexico, Brazil, Bolivia, Russia, Bulgaria and Mongolia, among other Latin American and the former socialist countries, an 'international agenda for modernizing HE systems' was implemented, mostly promoted by international credit agencies like the World Bank and the Inter-American Development Bank (Marginson and Mollis, 2001). Essentially this agenda proposed diminishing state subsidies for education and science, a selective control of the state in the distribution of financial resources, the expansion of institutions and private enrollment, the enactment of a Higher Education (HE) Act with implications for assessment and accreditation systems, and lastly, the creation of central bodies or agents to assess and accredit academic institutions (such as Secretary of University Policies, actually called Secretary of HE, and the National Commission for University Assessment and Accreditation, or CONEAU (Mollis, 2001)).

(a)   Diminishing state subsidies for education, science and culture

Argentina is one of the countries within a sample of the OECD with one of the lowest investments in higher education. The percentage invested with respect to gross domestic product (GDP) is lower than other Latin American countries with lower per capita income, such as Chile, Brazil, Venezuela and Mexico. The average of the above sample for HE is 1.3 percent of GDP; Argentina, however, invests only 0.95 percent of GDP. Yet the private sector, unlike that in other industrialized countries, virtually has no involvement in spending on higher education.

Susana Torrado (2001), in a provocative article, says that the discussion on how to rationalize spending for HE is fallacious. Both those that are in favor or against restricting enrollment, or for applying a fee or not, forget that educational strategies are designed by the economic project developed by the Ministry of Economy. Data provided by the author are basic to understanding that the problem of different funding sources does not solve university social reproduction or rather the self-recruitment that the university has been conducting since the immigrants became the second generation of Argentineans. When asked: who has access to education – that is, the probability of individual access or finishing several educational levels as a member of a particular social stratum? – Torrado provides answers that seem obvious, with important consequences for demystifying the problems of financing HE. The Argentinean university recruits itself. This means mostly the children of professionals and who, in turn, are more likely to graduate than others. Changing to alternative financing systems from that of the state does not solve the problem of the beneficiaries of the universities. The social selection within the education system corresponds to that in the economic plan – both leave out the poorest Argentineans.

With regard to investment in R&D, according to an international report recently prepared by the Ibero-American and Inter-American Network of Science and Technology Indicators (RICYT, 2000), Argentina spends less funds (0.24 percent of GDP) than in the 1980s (0.37 percent of GDP), which is less than its neighbors Chile and Brazil, while it is 189 times lower than that of the USA. At the same time Latin America as a whole invests less in R&D than Canada. The efforts of the public and private sectors in the area of scientific and technological development in Argentina can only be described as inadequate and poorly sustained.

Even those who defend the modernizing thesis that the future is only feasible for 'knowledge societies' consider that these indicators highlight the abandonment of investment in basic and applied research by the state and by the private sector. This university divestment is part of the mandate by which globalization leaves the production of innovative knowledge in the hands of highly industrialized countries, namely the universities and companies in the North. In the allocation of global functions of knowledge, Argentine universities are assigned the role of trainers of human resources, which remain human only as economic outputs rather than by being the product of humanistic syllabuses. With this, Britto García's clever phrase becomes real, that 'the place that a society assigns to the university mysteriously coincides with the place that that society has in the world' (1990, p. 78).

(b)   Expansion of private institutions and tuition

The process of privatization has become one of the key mechanisms for the transformation to a capitalist accumulation regime in Argentina and the rest of Latin America. In keeping with this process, state intervention in the economy is modified and the function of controlling state enterprises is abandoned since all are privatized (electricity, telephone, airline, oilfields etc.). Culture is subordinated to market rules; the state is reduced to a series of government measures whose effectiveness is measured by stock market interests.

From the perspective of educational policy-makers, the explosion of the demand for university education in the last five years of the twentieth century encouraged the 1995 Act and several projects to reorient student demand to non-university tertiary institutions, public or private, as well as other proposals aimed at collecting direct taxes from the families of university students. The explosion of postgraduate studies (promoted in part by the HE Act) reflects the demand for more training or expertise at the end of the academic cycle, and in all cases, this provision was for a fee.

(c)   The 1995 HE Act

The Act was issued on 7 August 1995, with great dissent from the student bodies, rectors, academics, and even from some representatives of the legislature. The Act includes HEIs, academic and non-academic, national, provincial or municipal, public and private, all of which are considered part of a national education system. The Act consists of IV Titles, subdivided into chapters and sections with a total of 89 articles. The Act introduces substantive changes with regard to historical concepts of autonomy, government and university funding. For example, it authorizes universities to autonomously develop rules on enrollment, retention and the graduation of their students (in universities with more than 50000 students, the system of admission, retention and promotion can be defined by each faculty); authorizes each university to set its own salaries for teaching and administrative staff, and to assure its own decentralized management of revenues; enables universities to promote the establishment of 'societies, foundations or other forms of civil associations' aimed at supporting financial management and facilitating the relations between universities and/or faculties; makes collegiate bodies responsible for defining policies and control, while those of a sole person have executive functions; modifies the integration of the faculty by authorizing all teachers (including assistants) to be elected as faculty representatives; and finally, increases the number of bodies represented in the collegiate bodies. The spirit of this extensive law is very different from the traditional Avellaneda Act that governed the destinies of the universities for more than 70 years. In the agreements produced for the approval of the law, corporate interests and supporters are recognized who are not intrinsically linked to the desire for excellence for HE.

(d)   Creation of the Secretary of University Policies (SPU) and HE System (SES), and the National Commission for University Assessment and Accreditation (CONEAU)

The 1995 Act created significant change in higher education policy-making. In 1995 the National Commission on Accreditation of Postgraduate Qualifications (CAP) launched an accreditation process of postgraduate careers in which 176 postgraduate degrees of public and private universities were assessed, accredited and scored. The policy of assessment and accreditation of institutions, and degree-level and postgraduate qualifications, was part of the 'policy of promoting quality' driven by the Ministry of Culture and Education. The other two programs that contributed to that effect were:

- the Incentive Program for Teachers–Researchers, which gives additional funds to reward the best performance of academic work; and
- the Funding for the Improvement of University Quality (FOMEC), which since 1995 has allocated funds through contests to financially support reform and quality improvement processes in the national universities.

The greatest impact of the Act occurred with the introduction of centralized mechanisms for universal assessment and accreditation through the National Commission for University Assessment and Accreditation (CONEAU). The Commission has a legal mandate to conduct external assessments, accredit degree programs and postgraduate degrees, assess institutional projects for the creation of new national or provincial universities, and evaluate the development of projects for the subsequent recognition of private universities by the Ministry of Culture and Education. The Act determines that the CONEAU is a decentralized agency within the jurisdiction of the Ministry of Culture and Education. CONEAU consists of 12 members appointed by the national government based on nominations from the following agencies: three members by the Inter-University National Council (CIN), one member by the Council of University Rectors of Private Universities (CRUP), one by the National Academy of Education, three by the Chamber of Deputies, three by the country's Senate, and one by the Ministry of Culture and Education.

These reforms occurred in the context of neoliberal public policies that sustained deregulation and markets in the freedom given to universities to charge fees, pay differentiated salaries and design schemes for admissions (admission tests, introductory courses, quotas etc.), but alongside increased governmental tendency to control and assess the performance of academic institutions (Mollis, 2006). Institutions were free to seek other sources of alternative financing from that of the state, and in turn have their results evaluated by assessment and accreditation bodies such as CONEAU.

ARGENTINE HIGHER EDUCATION STRUCTURE: TWO DISARTICULATED SUBSYSTEMS

HE in Argentina is both a typical and a specific case of a binary system, with the specificity characterized by the greater educational provision of non-university higher-level programs focused on teacher training compared with binary systems elsewhere. Nonetheless the highest concentration of enrollment occurs within public universities. There is great diversity in provision, with significant overlaps between the degrees offered at university and non-university levels, with a visible fragmentation of the whole system consisting of various types of institutions disarticulated from one another. This situation occurs as a result of historical educational policies implemented by various governments and reflecting their own interests, political projects and different economic models for education. As a result, HE offers a variety of institutions that differ in quality and in their specific missions. In this way a costly fragmentation that conspired against the effective functioning of the whole HE level was developed because the sectors that shaped it never established coordination channels between the different types of training that the higher level provided (university and non-university) and never reviewed the educational programs already operating (Dirié and Mollis et al., 2001).

Thus higher education policies can be characterized by a fragmented, costly and inefficient overlapping that in the last decade has been further complicated by consumerism. According to surveys of educational choices, an accelerated growth of new public and private programs can be seen in those urban areas with the highest population density and greatest buying power. There has also been a growth of private institutions in urban regions with the greatest economic and growing provincial political development. At the same time, the weight of HE enrollments (university and non-university) in the total population has grown over the years. The number of students per 10 000 inhabitants grew from 7 in 1914 to 32.4 in 1950, to 106.7 in 1970, and 149 in 1980.

According to data from the *2005 University Statistics Yearbook* published by the Secretary of University Policies (SPU) based on the estimated population between 18 and 24 years, the net university participation rate is 18.3 percent, the gross rate is 33.8 percent, and the overall higher education gross rate is 45 percent. However, in spite of the great expansion and growth in the coverage of HE in Argentina in recent decades, its distribution and characteristics are far from homogeneous in the various provinces and regions.

Problems Arising from the Overlapping and Disarticulation of Provision

The basic organizational principle of different national HE systems, such as the American, Chilean or Finnish, is that they operate as a coherent system or articulated entity. However, the set of Argentinean academic and non-academic institutions do not work as a 'system' with the component parts articulated between each other. The problem is not the 'diversity' of university enrollment and its provision, but the lack of overall planning and coordination between the secondary and post-secondary levels.

The problem of Argentinean HE is not massification in itself but the lack of an adequate infrastructure for higher education amid growing social demand. Therefore it is essential to configure a higher education system articulated with the secondary level that offers various educational tracks that are clearly transparent and linked. If various post-secondary education 'training tracks' were offered to young people in their age cohort, the percentage of university students and consequent graduates probably would rise (as in other industrialized countries) to the extent that the enrollment retention levels would increase in other segments of post-secondary education, too.

Coexistence of different admissions systems in the universities takes place because Argentinean HE as a whole is not homogeneous, but heterogeneous. There is a correspondence between the institutional diversity and heterogeneous admission systems. An admissions system good for one or one type of institution with certain characteristics might not be so for others. Worldwide we tend to find that generally countries with diversified HE systems composed of various types of institutions and missions also tend to have a diversity of admission policies (Dirié and Mollis et al., 2001).

Higher Education Data

The inaccurately described HE 'system' in Argentina is a complex and heterogeneous institutional conglomerate, consisting of more than 1700 establishments at the non-university tertiary level and 102 universities. The non-university education system is made up of teacher-training institutes for different levels of education, specialized schools and institutes with a technical orientation. The state-run institutions depend on the provincial governments for their management and funding, such as the government of the City of Buenos Aires. At the same time, private institutions are funded by fees, although the private teacher-training schools also receive state subsidies when the fees charged are low.

By 2007 the 101 officially recognized academic institutions in the country consisted of 38 national universities, 41 private universities, 6 national university institutes created under the legal regime of provincial universities, 14 private university institutes, and one provincial university, foreign university, and international university respectively. All of them help configure a map whose strongest features are complexity, diversity and a heterogeneous multifunctionality (that is, the same university conducts multiple tasks or functions, such as teaching, training professionals, researching, developing local cultures and selling services).

Table 18.1   State-funded and private academic institutions: number and expansion waves

	Number of institutions 2007		Foundational stage 1613–1970 (357 years)		Expansion and nationalizing stage 1971–90 (19 years)		Private expansion stage 1991–2007 (16 years)	
	N 102	% 100	N	%	N	%	N	%
National universities	38	37.7	10	26.3	19	50	9	23.7
Private universities	41	40.7	11	26.8	12	29.3	18	43.9
National university institutes	6	5.9			1	16.7	5	83.382
Private university institutes	14	13.9			1	7.2	13	92.8
Provincial university	1	0.9					1	100
Foreign university	1	0.9					1	100
International university	1	0.9			1	100		

Source: http://www.me.gov.ar/sp/servicios/autoridades_universitarias/au_listado_de_universidades.htm.

According to Table 18.1, we can recognize the trends towards institutional expansion and privatization that predominated in the 1990s by the number of national and private institutions that were created in that period. The majority of HEIs were created over the past 16 years, including 24 percent of all national universities, 44 percent of private universities, 83 percent of national university institutes, 93 percent of the private university institutes, as well as all the provincial and foreign universities.

The expansion and massification of post-secondary enrollment has occurred since the 1950s. Since then the university has grown in successive waves. As a result of the first expansion, public universities grew to 30 in 1970. A second wave of growth among public institutions between 1971 and 1990 led to the creation of 19 national universities (including some that had been provincial and became nationalized) and 12 private universities in different regions of the country. From 1991 onwards there was a third wave of expansion, of a mixed public–private character but with a clear predominance towards the private sector.

Each of these stages is significant in consolidating policies for HE expansion and the changing trends promoted by governmental bodies. The so-called foundational stage (1970) distinguishes itself by creating universities that helped to cement the university system that had followed from the Reform Movement in Argentina and which included the University of Cordoba (founded in 1613), the University of Buenos Aires (founded in 1821) and the University of La Plata (founded in 1905). Afterwards only another seven universities were subsequently founded to consolidate the public university system.

Table 18.2   New enrollments by management sector, 2005

Institution	State management 2005		Private management 2005		Total new enrollments	
	N	%	N	%	N	%
Universities	289 708	80	73 265	20	362 973	100
University institutes	4249	59.4	2907	40.6	7156	100
Total	293 957		76 172		370 129	

Source: SPU (2005), p. 173.

The second stage, here called 'expansion and nationalization of universities (1971–90)', incorporated the traditional private universities in Argentina. In the third phase, that of 'private expansion' (1991–2007) inaugurated by the 1995 HE Act, were created new public and private universities with an organizational model different from the one of the previous eras.

Thus a highly heterogeneous and diverse institutional framework was taking form where there coexisted traditional and new universities, public and private, Catholic and secular, elite and mass, professional and research. However, public universities captured 83.5 percent of total student enrollment and many of them accomplished the set of missions that the US HE system had assigned to each of its types of institution. At present, universities operate in almost all the country's regions.

While Table 18.1 evidences a trend in the expansion of private universities that exceeds that for the public ones, Table 18.2 nonetheless illustrates that the new enrollment percentage in the private sector in 2005 does not exceed 21 percent, with 79 percent in the public universities. The trend in terms of university institutes is more convergent, since 59 percent are enrolled in public institutes and nearly 41 percent in those that are privately operated.

As for the expansion of higher education as a whole, that is, university and non-university combined, the former continues to dominate the scene with 73.5 percent enrolled compared to 26.5 percent of students at the non-university tertiary level. These quantitative trends are highly significant when compared with Brazil and Mexico, which show the inverse, with public universities that offer postgraduate degrees for elites but with a large number of private tertiary institutions for the majority of the population.

In Table 18.3 it can be seen that the highest annual average growth rate of students between 2001 and 2005 occurs in the private university institutes, with 43.63, although these students accounted for 16.5 percent of the overall total compared with those of the state and privately managed universities, which represent 83.5 percent of the total, as shown in Table 18.4.

From the financial point of view, national universities are free and enjoy autonomy, although the 1995 HE Act introduced changes in this respect. One of the purposes of creating new public universities in the Buenos Aires urban cone, for example (University of Quilmes, founded in 1989; University Tres de Febrero, founded in 1995; University General Sarmiento, founded in 1992; and University General San Martin, created in 1992), was to break with the reformist model of traditional public universities, changing

Table 18.3   Students: annual average growth rate (AAGR) by management sector, 2005

Institution	State management			Private management		
	2001	2005	AAGR	2001	2005	AAGR
Universities	1 200 215	1 273 554	1.49	196 357	244 844	5.67
University institutes	9423	12 071	639	2179	9273	43.63
Total	1 209 638	1 285 625	1.53	198 536	254 117	6.36

Source: As for Table 18.2.

Table 18.4   Student distribution by sector, 2005

Type of institution	National	Private	Total
Number of students	1 285 625	254 117	1 539 742
Rate	83.50	16.50	100

Source: As for Table 18.2.

key performance criteria. Traditional university governance was replaced by a management body committed to obtaining alternative funding resources; unrestricted admission was exchanged for a selective one; fees for students introduced (in the case of the University of Quilmes); assistant teachers were replaced by temporary, contract professors, and part-time professors replaced full-time professors, the latter generally dedicated to teaching and research and with wide extra-classroom responsibilities (such as student follow-up, office schedules, attending consultations and other meetings, and so on). Also introduced were: more differentiated salaries; shorter vocational degrees leading directly to employment; intermediate qualifications; distance learning and the use of virtual technologies; professional programs; and little in the way of basic and applied sciences.

At the end of the first five operational years we find that because of organizational size there exists a more direct or hierarchical relationship between university management and academia (the professor is increasingly supervised by managers); agreements had been made with the municipalities or local governments in the jurisdictions where these universities operate to expand their funding sources and to satisfy community needs; professional postgraduate options were the key to obtaining alternative resources; there are fewer students per teacher for undergraduates; and there is a lower percentage of student dropout due to the impact of the admission tests. Among the weaknesses we might mention: the overlapping of qualifications offered in areas close to other public universities, with so few students available that it did not justify the multitude of choices; few professors of an outstanding caliber; and low investment in library resources (fewer books and scientific journal collections). However, measuring the impact of this 'modernizing' university model on the quality performance of new graduates is still a pending task, as is the broader evaluation of the advantages and disadvantages of adopting models derived from an international reform agenda.

Table 18.5   Faculty by status, 2005

	Total	Professors*	Faculty assistants**
National universities	119 339	49 041	70 298
Percentage	100	41.1	58.9

Notes:
*   Professors: titular, associate and adjunct.
**   Assistant teachers: chief of practical works, 1st and 2nd assistant.

Source: SPU (2005), p. 182.

Table 18.6   Faculty by status and dedication

	Exclusive		Semi-exclusive		Simple		Totals	
	N	%	N	%	N	%	N	%
Professors	9886	20.2	12.42	25.3	26 731	54.5	49 041	100
Assistants	5563	8	13.93	20	50 798	72	70 298	100

Source: As for Table 18.5.

In the period 1982–92 national universities not only doubled their student population but also the number of faculty. Table 18.5 shows that in 2005, 41 percent of academics had the status of professor (adjuncts, associate and titular) and the remaining 59 percent are in the assistant teacher category. Table 18.6 indicates that of the 41 percent of the professors at national universities, 20.2 percent are fulltime dedicated to the tasks of teaching and research with 40 hours per week, 25.3 percent have a semi-full load (20 hours a week), and 54.5 percent have less than 10 hours per week. Among the assistant teachers only 8 percent are fulltime and 20 percent semi-full, while the remaining 72 percent have low contact hours.

From the standpoint of teaching strategies, these indicators suggest that the bulk of classroom time of university students is spent in contact with young teachers with little or no professional or educational experience. The cause is financial: it is cheaper to hire many honorary teachers with low wages to attend to a mass student population than to recruit professionals with expertise, seniority and full-time commitment. There appears a very clear tendency that in those academic units where the teaching responsibility lies with professors rather than with assistants, where there are more full-time teachers with qualifications or postgraduate degrees, then the teaching quality rises. But mass enrollment favors the recruitment of young, inexperienced teachers.

FIVE MYTHS OF THE ARGENTINE UNIVERSITY SYSTEM AND ONE PROPOSAL FOR CHANGE

Despite the shocks to the national public universities, which no longer enjoy their old status as providing the 'foundation of public legitimacy' for the nation-state, which finances it, there exists a crisis of the university institutional model in itself. Today the concept of 'university democracy' is questioned and remains embedded only in the body of 'regular professors' (elected by competition), who represent a minority percentage of the total of university professors. There is a crisis of representation of the collegiate bodies that were associated with the growth of a faculties' structure based on the Napoleonic model, a disconnection with the urgent needs of civil society, and a loss of community identity. The descriptions of the myths that follow are linked to the crisis of the structural model of the public university, which we recognize as an opportunity for fundamental changes in the institutions that are carriers of learning and knowledge-makers in the twenty-first century.

- *Universal access* The massive public universities of direct access developed, in the last decade, enrollment devices that hide the selective mechanisms at stake, whether common initial cycles, summer courses, tutorials and so on. The socio-economic composition of the student body leaves out of the education circuit the children of workers at the lowest levels.
- *Representative and democratic government* The composition of the faculty is misaligned due to the significant number of teachers in lower categories ('assistant teachers') that are outside the collegiate body, which with increasing competition for positions leads to a small percentage of professors as collegial voters and candidates.
- *Place of knowledge edge production* The fierce lack of funding from the state during the last decade, together with the low investment of GDP in R&D, reduces the chances of constructing empirical, basic and cutting-edge scientific research at the public universities.
- *Meritocracy to access contest posts* Faculty post contests in the past decade have turned into devices of political clientelism rather than academic contests; observed juries, challenged opinions and legal presentations highlight the arbitrariness of the new mechanisms.
- *The university community is broken* Instead of a community there is a set of overlapping and conflicting identities within the guild actors, with ultra-individualistic subjects and high disenchantment. There is the absence of a committed institutional membership that encourages them to innovate.

The public Argentinean and Latin American universities, fascinated by the illusion of a global, homogeneous identity, have distorted their historic social functions. The academic community, heir to the medieval community tradition, has vanished in the face of faculty ultra-individualism. The heterogeneity of the body of university professors is expressed in a range that goes from the motivated research professor (representing 18 percent of the national population of university professors in Argentina) to the newly graduated professor (which represents a significant majority of the population of the university teaching staff). The identity of the professors of public universities is in transition from the academic to the international consultant because prestige and fees come from other funding sources such as bank agencies (national or international) or the central government.

Thus, for all these reasons, public universities that lie at the leading edge of the changes promoted by globalization, face the biggest challenge since their founding stage, including that of survival itself.

A TRANSFORMING DIAGNOSIS

To survive and recreate the original foundational sense, it is necessary to agree on a description of urgent priorities. Where to start? There will be a need to diagnose effectively in order to change: to recognize the education deficit of the syllabuses that train professors who have taught at other levels of the education system; to recognize the need to rebuild institutional mission(s) and the value of knowledge; to recognize the crisis of the representative collegiate bodies and the dysfunctions of the management structure; and to project research towards the satisfaction of local cultural and social issues and promoting the formation of political leaders with public awareness and social ethics. Finally, there is a need to philosophize about the meaning, mission and praxis of the university to conquer a sovereign project supported by a social epistemology of local knowledge.

Recognizing this identity crisis implies consolidating and building the sensibility of higher education actors towards a new reality. This idea expresses something rather general and very complex at the same time. The institutional identity crisis has to do not only with the discomfort and uneasiness we feel when the university does not reflect ourselves, when the university is not what we want it to be. The contextual crisis on the one hand has been imposed by the dominant Anglo-Saxon paradigm and its global agenda coming from outside the institution, as mentioned above. Yet, on the other hand, there is a crisis inherited from the local history of Latin American and Argentine universities that emerges in a context where the nation-state is no longer the main provider and guarantor of the educational structure. It is urgent to create a transforming diagnosis in order to recognize the existence of an identity crisis that entails a crisis of empathy with significant others. Who are the meaningful others in the building of institutional identity in universities? Who are the significant others for building consensus and empathic communication? It bears mentioning that each of these 'institutional others' seeks to satisfy their own corporative interests, and therefore they are not the significant others for building common identity. There is an urgent need for community but there is an absence of community and of institutional cohesion. It is difficult to find actors who define themselves as members of the university; rather, each defines himself or herself from their own position, based on particular interests that prevail above the institutional identity.

The absence of community resides with a certain incompatibility between regulations oriented to universities, the new governmental state, and the solutions being proposed to build a legitimate identity for the university. There is a kind of neo-clientelism dominating the scenarios at the expense of the university mission in terms of its relationship to knowledge. For our Reformist leaders of Córdoba in 1918, professors were at the core of the transformation; it was imperative to look for new faculty members with new voices who would, in turn, create the new man. As we can observe according to the present bureaucratic requirements on university faculty, there is a relative incompatibility between them and the historical demands of the institutional identity of nineteenth-century universities.

It is urgent to recognize that historical missions of the university have been denaturalized. If we believe in teaching, service and knowledge production aims, we must consider to what extent teaching and learning processes are taking place in higher education institutions. We should not put the responsibility on students or professors, but rather acknowledge that a denaturalizing process has deepened over time. Unfortunately, turning educational rituals into theatrical performances is common currency: professors simulate teaching and students simulate learning, that is, we all behave as if the university made sense. We need more actors on the path of transformation, of change and projects, actors more concerned with the institution itself than with the spoils of office.

Immanuel Wallerstein (2001, p. 8), a most critical and lucid social scientist, asserts that we find ourselves in a moment between capitalism and post-capitalism. This places us as historical subjects of the world and not merely as subjects of globalization. He states that 'there are three aspects in a period of systematic transition: it will be long, it will be chaotic and the outcome will be ultra unknowable. We cannot predict it but we can influence it.' In this context the role of intellectuals is to contribute to reducing the confusion.

REFERENCES

Britto García, L. (1990), 'Dime cómo enseñas y te diré quién eres', *Nueva Sociedad*, no. 107, Mayo–Junio.
Canton, D. (1966), *El Parlamento Argentino en Épocas de Cambio: 1816–1916–1946 [The Argentinean Parliament in Times of Change: 1816–1946]*, Buenos Aires: Editorial Instituto.
De Sousa Santos, B. (2005), *La Universidad en el Siglo XXI [The University in the 21st Century]*, Buenos Aires: Laboratorio de Políticas Públicas (LPP) y Miño y Dávila.
Dirié, C. and M. Mollis et al. (2001), 'Mapa de la oferta de la Educación Superior en la Argentina', paper prepared for the National Commission for Improvement of University Quality, Buenos Aires: Ministry of Culture and Education of Argentina (pdf version).
Frondizi, R. (2005), *La Universidad en un mundo de tensiones: misión de las universidades en América Latina [Universities in a World of Conflict: The Mission of Latin American Universities]*, Buenos Aires: EUDEBA (primera edición 1971).
Marginson, S. and M. Mollis (2001), 'The door opens and the tiger leaps: theories and reflexivities of comparative education for a global millennium', *Comparative Education Review*, **45** (4), 581–615.
Mollis, M. (1990), *Universidades y estado Nacional. Argentina y Japón entre 1880 y 1930*, Buenos Aires: Editorial Biblos.
Mollis, M. (2001), *The Comparative History of Universities [A Comparative History of Universities]*, Visiting Scholars Report, Berkeley, CA: Center for Studies Higher Education (CSHE), State University of California at Berkeley Press.
Mollis, M. (2003), 'Un breve diagnóstico de las universidades Argentinas: Identidades Alteradas' [A brief diagnosis of Argentinean universities: altered identities], *Las Universidades en América Latina: Reformadas o Alteradas? La Cosmética del Poder Financiero*, Buenos Aires: Editorial CLACSO, pp. 203–16.
Mollis, M. (2006), 'Geopolítica del saber: biografías recientes de las universidades latinoamericanas' ['The geopolitics of knowledge: recent biographies of Latin American universities'], in U. Teichler (ed.), *Reformas de los Modelos de la Educación Superior*, Buenos Aires: Facultad de Filosofía y Letras –Universidad de Buenos Aires and Miño y Dávila Editores, pp. 357–75.
Mollis, M. (2008), 'Las huellas de la reforma en la crisis universitaria argentina' ['Reform footprints in the Argentinean university crisis'], in E. Sader, H. Aboites and P. Gentili *La Reforma Universitaria, Desafíos y Perspectivas*, Buenos Aires: CLACSO Libros, pp. 86–104.
Mollis, M. (ed.) (2009), *Memorias de la Universidad, [Memories of the University]*, Buenos Aires: Centro Cultural de la Cooperación and CLACSO.
Red de Indicadores de Gencia y Tecnología Iberamericana/Interamericana (RICYT) (2000), *El Estado de la Gencia. Principales Indicadores de Gencia y Tecnología*, Buenos Aires: RICYT.
Rhoads, R. and C. Torres (eds) (2006), *The University, State and Market. The Political Economy of Globalization in the Americas*, Stanford, CA: Stanford University Press, pp. 203–20.
Rodríguez Gómez, R. (2006), 'Cooperación académica versus comercio transfronterizo. ¿Hacia la con-

figuración de una doble agenda en el proceso de internacionalización de la universidad contemporánea?' ['Academic cooperation versus transnational trade: towards the creation of a double agenda in the internationalization of contemporary universities?'], presented at the la Reunión Conjunta de los Grupos de Trabajo de CLACSO: Tratados de Libre Comercio, Espacio Público y Derecho a la Educación en América Latina, Antigua, Guatemala, 28 February–2 March.

Rothblatt, S. (1997), *The Modern University and its Discontents: The Fate of Newman's Legacies in Britain and America,* New York: Cambridge University Press.

Rotunno, C. and Díaz de Guijarro, E. (2003), *La Construcción de lo Posible: la Universidad de Buenos Aires de 1955 a 1966 [Creating the Possible: The University of Buenos Aires from 1955 to 1966],* Buenos Aires Libros del Zorzal.

Rüegg, W. (ed.) (1994), *Historia de la Universidad en Europa,* Vol. I [*A History of Universities in Europe*], Bilbao; Editor Hilde de idder-Symoens.

SPU (2005), *University Statistics Yearbook,* Buenos Aires: SPU.

Steger, H.A. (1974), *Las Universidades en el Desarrollo Social de América Latina,* Mexico City: Fondo de Cultura Económica.

Torrado, S. (2001), 'Mitos y verdades sobre la universidad argentina', *Diario Clarín,* sección Opinión, Buenos Aires, jueves 12 de Abril, 14.

Wallerstein, I. (2001), *The End of the World As We Know It: Social Science for the Twenty-first Century,* México DF: Siglo XXI Editores.

World Bank (1993), *Argentina: From Insolvency to Growth,* Washington, DC: World Bank Country Study, p. 89.

World Bank (2000), *Higher Education in Developing Countries. Peril and Promise,* Washington, DC: World Bank and Task Force.

19 Globalization, a knowledge-based regime and higher education: where do Mexican universities stand?
Alma Maldonado-Maldonado

INTRODUCTION: MEXICO'S STANDING IN A GLOBAL WORLD

This chapter discusses the complex relationships between globalization, a knowledge-based economy and higher education in Mexico. The first two sections review the concept of globalization, internationalization and a knowledge-based economy. The third section discusses Mexico's position in the knowledge-production race. The fourth section analyzes the discourses and policies of 25 Mexican higher education institutions (HEIs) on globalization and internationalization. The fifth section suggests ways to analyze the current situation of Mexican universities facing globalization and the challenges on the international knowledge regime. The last section provides concluding remarks.

In a recent article, Cantwell and Maldonado-Maldonado (2009) discuss the differences in meaning between the globalization of higher education and internationalization of higher education. One of their main criticisms is the lack of agency implicit in the concept of internationalization of higher education that most experts in the higher education field use (Altbach, 2004; Altbach and Knight, 2006; de Wit, 1999; Knight, 2004; van der Wende, 2001; van Vught et al., 2003). Defining internationalization as the higher education response to globalization constrains the possibility that universities have to be more than a passive recipient and contribute more in shaping what globalization means. As an attempt to enrich the debate, here we suggest that the topic of the knowledge-based economy brings a dimension in which universities can play a role directly influencing globalization.

According to Waters (1995, p. 5), 'Globalization is a social process in which the constraints of geography on economic, political, social and cultural arrangements recede, in which people become increasingly aware that they are receding and in which people act accordingly.' This definition is pertinent because it describes the different elements comprising globalization, and also considers the importance of individuals and organizations to the process. As part of the four structural shifts that define globalization, Mills and Blossfeld (2005, p. 2) include:

(1) the swift internationalization of markets after the breakdown of the east–west Cold War divide;
(2) the rapid intensification of competition based on deregulation, privatization, and liberalization within nation-states;

(3) the accelerated diffusion of knowledge and the spread of global networks that are connecting all kinds of markets on the globe via new information and communication technologies (ICTs); and,
(4) the rising importance of markets and their dependence on random shocks occurring somewhere on the globe.

It seems that there is a consensus about the role played by knowledge on the global stage today. As Paasi (2005, p. 772) notes, 'Knowledge is a major element in the forces of production and an increasingly significant part of internationalization, competition, and the governance and regulation of globalization in most countries.' Globalization implies the concept of the globe as a unity, but as many authors have discussed from different approaches, this idea is not conveyed that simply (Appadurai, 2000; Beck, 2001; Castells, 2000; Held et. al., 1999; Marginson and Rhoades, 2002; Robertson, 2006; Sassen, 2000; Stiglitz, 2003). Very few current issues are really spatially global (in scope and dimension), perhaps none as much as the recent economic crisis and global warming. We have to think of both global benefits and global disparities, and the picture of a fair and equal globe is far from perfect.

An example to illustrate the global paradoxes associated with knowledge is the use of information and communication technologies (ICTs). While one-third of the world population has never made a telephone call, yet, 'with only 18 percent of the world population, Organization for Economic Co-operation and Development (OECD) countries contain nonetheless 79 percent of the world's internet users' (Women's Learning Partnership for Right Development and Peace, 2010). The best example to illustrate country disparities in knowledge production is the USA:

> The USA accounts for 40 percent of the world's total spending on scientific research and development, employs 70 percent of the world's Nobel Prize winners, is home to three-quarters of the world's top 40 universities, and invests 2.6 percent of its GDP on higher education (compared to 1.1 percent in Japan and 1.2 percent in Europe). (UK/US Study Group, 2009, p. 6)

Besides global income distribution, reported since 1992 when the UNDP showed that the richest fifth received 82.7 percent of total world income and the poorest fifth received only 1.4 percent (UNDP, 1993), another major global disparity has to do with human mobility. It is reported that 'more than three-quarters of international migrants go to a country with a higher level of human development than their country of origin' (UNDP, 2010, p. 2). With globalization most movement occurs within regions and in proportion to its inhabitants, while Europe is where most mobility occurs given its geographical and political proximity. At the same time Europe is the region that sends more remittances to other regions (ibid., pp. 24, 73). The UNDP also suggests that 'people in poor countries are the least mobile: for example, less than 1 percent of Africans have moved to Europe' (ibid., p. 2).

The KOF Index, published by ETH University, Zurich, Switzerland, which ranks countries based on the level of globalization, helps explain these data. The Index comprises three areas: economic, social and political. In the case of economic globalization there are two main criteria: actual flows (trade, foreign direct investment, stocks, portfolio investment and income payments to foreign nationals) and restrictions (hidden import barriers, mean tariff trade, taxes on international trade and capital account restrictions). However, there are three criteria for social globalization: personal contact (telephone traffic, transfers, international tourism, foreign population and international letters); information flows (Internet users, televisions and trade in newspapers); and cultural proximity (number of McDonald's restaurants, IKEA stores and trade in books). The indicators for political globalization are based on embassies in the country, memberships in international organizations, participation in the UN Security Council, and international treaties. The KOF Index provides evidence of three key aspects of globalization. First, most globalized countries are among the richest worldwide. The top 25 countries in the Index are OECD members except for Singapore and Cyprus. Second, globalization as a phenomenon is mostly located in Europe. The top 24 countries are European (or Eurasian) except for Australia, Canada and Singapore. Third, the position of the USA in the Index is surprising. Some authors have equated globalization with 'Americanization' or even 'McDonaldization' (Ritzer and Stillman, 2003), given the enormous influence of the USA globally. Nevertheless the USA is not among the top 25 most globalized countries in the KOF Index; it is 27th. The USA may be an influential source in globalization processes, but it does not mean that this is reciprocated. Therefore the USA is not one of the top globalized nations, at least according to the KOF Index.

As previously stated, globalization cannot be considered an inevitable phenomenon and it is not necessarily static, inclusive, one-dimensional or unproblematic (Cantwell and Maldonado-Maldonado, 2009; Maldonado-Maldonado and Cantwell, 2010). On the contrary, it is an uneven process with winners and losers. So the question is: what is the globalization situation for a country such as Mexico? According to the 2010 KOF Index of Globalization (2010), Mexico is 71st on a list of 156 countries, which means Mexico, a middle-income economy, is located in the range of being medium-globalized. Economically and socially, Mexico is ranked 81st while politically it is 80th. Among the OECD countries Mexico is located furthest from the top 25 globalized nations. Comparing Mexico with other countries in the KOF Index is revealing. Mexico's position (71st) should be compared with other Latin American countries. For example, Chile is 34th, Panama 48th, Costa Rica 49th, Uruguay 53rd, Peru 61st and Honduras 62nd. Surprisingly, given their recent economic, social and political achievements, Brazil and Colombia are ranked after Mexico, although not far from it (75th and 78th respectively). The KOF Index position for Mexico does not look too promising. Although the country is considered to be an emerging economy, it is far from being considered a rich country. Its geographical location is far from Europe, where most mobility takes place. Mexico's northern neighbor is the most influential country in terms of worldwide globalization, and yet it is not one of the top 25. How do these elements affect the country in terms of higher education globalization?

GLOBALIZATION AND THE ESTABLISHMENT OF A KNOWLEDGE-BASED REGIME

'Knowledge economy' and 'knowledge society' are two terms that have recently been used extensively. A quick Google search will provide about 1.25 million links for 'knowledge economy' and about 696 000 for 'knowledge society'. A search of the US Library of Congress results in about 539 titles with 'knowledge economy' and 987 titles including the words 'knowledge society'. In 2000 the Library of Congress reported only 25 books published with the phrase 'knowledge economy' and the same for 'knowledge society'. There was an increase for each in 2007, with 52 titles including 'knowledge economy' and 84 with 'knowledge society', but in 2009 they declined to 40 and 60 respectively. The peak for publishing books written in English on these subjects occurred only three years ago.

The idea of knowledge economy, or more precisely 'knowledge-based economy' and society, refers to knowledge production driving economic and social activities in countries. Factors such as human capital, ICTs and networks play a key role in national development. According to Stiglitz (1999, p. 310), 'knowledge is one of the five global public goods, along with international economic stability, international security (political stability), the international environment, and international humanitarian assistance'. Knowledge is considered a public good because 'the use of a piece of knowledge for one purpose does not preclude its use for others' (Mas-colell et al., 1995, p. 359) and 'there is zero marginal cost from an additional individual enjoying the benefits of the knowledge' (Stiglitz, 1999, p. 309). Clearly, knowledge possesses a symbolic value in current societies; if knowledge once was a conventional and ordinary economic input, this is no longer the case (OECD, 2006).

However, the notion of a knowledge-based economy is problematic because there are forms of knowledge that can be appropriated. This is possible mainly through intellectual property regimes (patents, copyright, and so on). Such issues have become increasingly important in the last decades. The World Intellectual Property Organization (WIPO), in charge of developing a balanced and accessible international intellectual property (IP) system, counts 184 states as members (WIPO, 2010). Often knowledge is usually taken for granted and there are few discussions about different types of knowledge. Measuring the impact of knowledge and the analysis of its externalities is challenging given its symbolic nature. In fact, there are many assumptions about the importance of knowledge but few empirical data on how much knowledge production really contributes to economic development.

Gürüz (2008, p. 6) points out that 'knowledge, and those possessing knowledge, are the main drivers of growth and the major determinants of competitiveness in the global knowledge economy'. That is, 'education and labor-force experience become the most important type of human capital' (Mills and Blossfeld, 2005, p. 9). However, clarification on what type of knowledge is relevant would help to understand what type of human capital is needed to be competitive in the new global economy. According to the OECD there are four types of knowledge: know-what (facts); know-why (scientific knowledge); know-how (skills or the capability to do something); and know-who (involves information about who knows what and who knows how to do what) (OECD, 2006, p. 12).

The production and use of knowledge also serves to classify countries:

> It now appears that the world is moving in a direction where there are three groups of countries. The first group, largely led by the United States, comprises the countries that create knowledge and knowledge-based technologies; they are the 'knowledge producers'. China is emerging as the manufacturing hub and India as the service hub of the global knowledge economy, both countries taking on increasingly central roles in global supply chains. China and India are currently leading the so-called 'knowledge users'. The third group includes countries that either are passive users of knowledge or 'technologically disconnected'. (Gürüz, 2008, p. 12)

Higher education institutions are integral to knowledge production and dissemination, taking an active role in a knowledge-based economy. It has been noted that 'higher education has entered an unprecedented period of globalization – western universities are opening branch campuses abroad and at the same time attracting ever-growing numbers of international students to their home campuses; students from the USA and UK increasingly view time in another country as an essential component of their educations; nations around the world are investing vast sums of money into creating and building their own higher education (HE) sectors' (UK/US Study Group, 2009, p. 2).

According to the OECD (2006) factors to consider when measuring knowledge production are: national R&D spending (public and private); number of researchers; number of patents registered by countries (and within the countries by sector); number of patents relevant to industry; number of high-tech exports; diffusion of information technologies; relevance of industries that use high-tech (aerospace, computing, pharmaceutical, electronics–communications, and so on); and new innovations based on recent academic research by industry. Nearly all of these are within the realm of HEIs.

Gürüz (2008, p. 17) summarizes how HEIs are being scrutinized and called on to change:

1. Institutions should not be insular to the world of business and academic research should produce commercial activities.
2. Access should be broadened and teaching should produce a workforce with an entrepreneurial attitude, capacity to learn, intercultural skills, and the skills that are necessary to adapt to the new ways of using knowledge and organizing work to produce goods and services internationally.
3. Traditional institutions should change the way they are organized so that they can efficiently, effectively, and preferably profitably compete with each other and the new providers of postsecondary education for students, scholars, and resources in the global higher education market.

Of course the socioeconomic disparities previously discussed do impact on how countries participate in knowledge production. For example, OECD countries, with 14 percent of the world's people, accounted for 86 percent of the patent applications filed in 1998 and 85 percent of the scientific and technical journal articles published. Also, 'firms in developed countries currently account for the 96 percent of royalties from patents or \$71 billion a year' (Women's Learning Partnership for Right Development and Peace, 2010). Other examples of how globalization disparities are reflected in the higher education spaces are the global university rankings, the geographical concentration of student mobility, and the central role of the USA in academic collaboration. According to Marginson (2007), instruments such as global rankings function as mechanisms to position universities and highlight the existing stratification among universities globally, where prestigious universities from the USA and the UK dominate. The rules that determine these rankings appear designed to strengthen the division between universities of the top 25 from the rest.

In terms of student mobility, the top five countries that have received the largest concentration of international students traditionally are the USA, the UK, Germany, Australia and France (Lee et al., 2006). India and China have been the largest senders of degree-seeking international students. Most of the international students who go to the UK and France come from their former colonies. In the case of the student mobility of non-degree students, given the high costs of this mobility the region of Europe is by far the most active. As part of EU initiatives (van der Wende, 2000; Wächter, 2004), it has developed the Erasmus program in order to enhance student mobility among European countries (but not exclusively). This program is a vivid example of the possibilities of higher education collaboration and it is considered the most ambitious of its type worldwide. No other region has developed a similar program in terms of flow and scope (Teichler, 1999, 2001).

In order to manage its global influence, the overwhelming geopolitical and cultural power of the USA does not facilitate reciprocity with other countries. In the case of higher education, most scholars around the world want to establish any type of collaboration with the USA, but still very few US institutions or faculty are interested (Altbach and Lewis, 1996; Finkelstein, 2009).

MEXICO JOINING THE KNOWLEDGE-BASED ECONOMY RACE

Two of the most important characteristics of Mexico are its inequalities and contradictions. As mentioned earlier, according to the KOF Index, Mexico is a medium-globalized country. Mexico represents 'an intriguing case study for understanding individual responses to globalization because its population has experienced growing uncertainty both on a macro and micro level' (Parrado, 2005, p. 328), as well as illustrating interesting collective responses to globalization processes given its geopolitical, economic and cultural paradoxes (Ordorika, 2006). For instance, the wealthiest man in the world is Mexican, according to *Forbes* magazine (Kroll and Miller, 2010), while there are approximately 11.2 million Mexicans living in extreme poverty and 36 million living in moderate poverty, according to the National Council for the Evaluation of Policies on Social Development (Enciso, 2009).

According to some of the main indicators of a knowledge-based economy, Mexico has:

- Fewest households (22 percent) with access to a home computer among OECD countries, except for Turkey. In contrast, in Greece and the Czech Republic more than 40 percent of households have access to a home computer, while the top five countries (Sweden, Denmark, Japan, Netherlands and Iceland) have more than 82 percent (OECD, 2010).
- With respect to Internet connectivity, Mexico has 7.62 Internet subscribers per 100 inhabitants, close to the world average of 7.64. Mexico also has 21.71 Internet users per 100 inhabitants, which almost reaches the world average of 23.44 (International Telecommunications Union, 2009). Comparatively, these numbers position Mexico in an acceptable place. However, when other indicators are taken into consideration, it is a different story.
- The percentage of school computers connected to the Internet in Mexico was 47 percent in 2007, according to the Economic Commission for Latin America and

the Caribbean (ECLAC). In comparison, the OECD's average was 84 percent and Brazil 65 percent (Peres and Hilbert, 2009, p. 231).

- In 2009 the Mexican government reported that about 10 percent of public higher education institution libraries are not connected to the Internet, although the goal is to have 100 percent connected by 2012 (Gobierno Federal de los Estados Unidos Mexicanos, 2009).
- In terms of Mexico exporting ICT equipment, the country is located in the top seven. According to the OECD, in 2007 Mexico exported about US$53.3 million worth of value. However, when Mexico's position is compared with other major exporters, the differences are notable. For example, China is the top exporter with US$355.5 million, the USA is the second country with more than US$160 million, and Japan, located in third position, is almost double Mexico's ICT exports with roughly US$120 million (OECD, 2010).
- Triadic patent families are a series of corresponding patents for the same invention and filed at the European Patent Office (EPO), the US Patent and Trademark Office (USPTO) and the Japan Patent Office (JPO). In 2006 Mexico had 0.2 patents per million inhabitants and its position was only one above India, the lowest country reported, with only 0.1 registered. The top five countries are Finland (64.7), Germany (74.9), Sweden (93.3), Japan (111.1) and Switzerland (114.8) (OECD, 2010).
- The number of researchers per thousand employed in Mexico was only 1.2 in 2007, ranked just above India with 0.3 and below Brazil with 1.3. Mexico was also relatively close to South Africa (1.5), China (1.8) and Turkey (1.9). In comparison, the top five countries are Denmark (10.4), New Zealand (10.5), Japan (11.1), Iceland (13.4) and Finland (15.7) (OECD, 2010).
- The gross domestic expenditure on R&D as a percentage of the GDP of Mexico is the lowest of the countries reported by the OECD with 0.46, ranked just below the Slovak Republic (0.47), Poland (0.56) and Greece (0.57). Other middle-income countries ranked above Mexico are South Africa (0.95), Brazil (1.02), and China (1.49). The top eight countries are Austria (2.56), the USA (2.68), Iceland (2.77), Switzerland (2.9), Korea (3.22), Japan (3.39), Finland (3.47) and Sweden (3.63) (OECD, 2010).

Most of these factors reveal that Mexico is struggling to find its place in a global knowledge-based economy. However, these numbers may not offer a complete vision of the current situation in Mexico. There are other aspects that need to be taken into consideration. One of the most shocking issues concerns the young adult population in the country. Recently there has been a national discussion about referring to this demographic as *ni-nis*, which is slang using the two first letters in Spanish for the phrase 'neither studying nor working'. It has been estimated that there are 7 million young people who fit into this category (Avilés, 2010). Many Latin American countries share this unemployment problem; it is estimated that there are approximately 42 865 000 *ni-nis* in Latin America (Maldonado-Maldonado, 2009). The Mexican paradox is that millions of young adult Mexicans are 'available' to work, but unfortunately the nation does not have the capital to educate or employ them.

According to the Mexican government, between 2008 and 2009 approximately 27.6

percent of the total population in the 19–23 age group were enrolled in higher education, including both traditional and non-traditional forms of education. If the high-school dropout rate is about 15 percent, then the dropout rate for higher education is thought to be even higher, although these numbers are not included in the official data (Gobierno Federal de los Estados Unidos Mexicanos, 2009). The peak of unemployment is among those between 20 and 24 years old. There are some differences between the numbers of unemployed men and women, depending on the age group. Two other age groups with high unemployment are those between 15 and 19 years and those aged 25 to 29. For example, in 2008 the rate of unemployment was 23.7 percent for those aged 20 to 24; 15.9 percent for those 25 to 29; and 17.3 percent for those 15 to 19 years. Thus 56.9 percent of all unemployed Mexicans that year were between 15 to 29 years old (International Labor Organization, 2010). The Instituto Nacional de Estadística y Geografía (INEGI) reports that between 2006 and 2009 unemployment for those with a higher education degree has almost doubled. The International Labor Organization (2010) reports that in 2008 about 19.3 percent of the unemployed population was at the first stage of tertiary education in academic programs defined as 'theoretically based', in contrast to programs that were more 'practically oriented'. In other words, an important percentage of those unemployed were able to attend HEIs under programs that were 'theoretically based', which are the majority in the country, but are unable to get a regular job. Even beyond the lack of opportunities for the young population in Mexico, the consequences of these social problems are crystallizing in the increase in social violence linked to drug trafficking. The illegal drug industry has increasingly become an alternative for more Mexicans between 15 and 30 years old.

MEXICAN HIGHER EDUCATION DISCOURSES AND PRACTICES ON GLOBALIZATION

For the purposes of this chapter, official documents posted on 25 university websites were reviewed to offer a better sense of the current discourses and practices regarding globalization in Mexican universities. A variety of documents was reviewed, including university development plans, university presidents' reports and yearbooks. As context, Mexico has approximately: 45 public universities (enrolling 52 percent of undergraduate students and 48 percent of graduate students nationally); 147 HEIs forming the technological education subsystem; 976 private institutions (enrolling 27 percent of undergraduate students and 36.5 percent of graduate students nationally); 357 teacher-training colleges; and another 110 institutions with specific purposes, such as military schools (Casanova-Cardiel, 2006).

The 25 universities selected for this research were chosen from the north, south and center of the country. Twenty-one schools are public and four are private, reflecting the broad categorization in the sector. A university's discourses regarding globalization highlight its approach to this phenomenon, revealing metaphors, definitions, emphasis, and perhaps contradictions. There appear to be four general tendencies that the 25 universities use to approach globalization. One group considers globalization to be a challenge as well as an opportunity; a second group assumes it is something that just occurs and is mostly positive; a third group considers globalization to be a threat; and finally there is a group that does not express any real opinion about globalization.

The most interesting aspect about the first group is that some of the universities that consider globalization to be a phenomenon with both positive and negative attributes are positioned well in terms of size and quality. These schools seem to realize that globalization brings disadvantages but also offers opportunities. The Universidad de Guadalajara (2010) refers to globalization positively as a dream and negatively as a nightmare. For this group of universities to become internationalized is a goal that will take them to being part of the knowledge society. A university in this group says that globalization is the general ambition, so becoming internationalized is one step to getting there. The main activities identified by universities as part of the internationalization process are: academic mobility; international cooperation; establishing international agreements; growing distance education and use of ICTs; and improving the social contribution of universities, including helping increases in productivity and supporting sustainable development. However, this group of universities is aware of the risks from these processes such as the tendency to commercialize higher education services (Universidad Nacional Autónoma de México, 2010) or aspects such as 'brain drain' that draw the most talented from developing to developed countries (Universidad Autónoma del Estado de México, 2010).

The second group similarly is characterized by being well established in terms of size and quality. However, it differs from the first group in assuming that globalization just occurs from outside fairly neutrally but is able to bring positive effects to universities eventually. The Universidad Autónoma de Coahuila (2010) implies an unproblematic idea of globalization in that 'globalization means no national borders of capital, technology, and information'. The Universidad Autónoma de Yucatan defines globalization as 'a social space of meaning, actions, and interactions', whose challenges to education include 'changing work organization, improving the quality of educational systems, the virtualization of education, and increasing networks'. The universities in this group also assume that internationalization is the necessary response to globalization. The Instituto Politécnico Nacional (2010) even mentions creating an 'internationalization culture' throughout the institution. For the Universidad Autónoma de Nuevo León (2010) the aspiration is to become a 'world-class university'.

Interestingly, the four private universities reviewed are in this group. The Instituto Tecnológico y de Estudios Superiores de Occidente (2010) remarks on the importance of training its students in 'global competences' and the Instituto Tecnológico de Estudios Superior Monterrey (2010) endorses 'promoting the international competence of companies and business through knowledge, innovation, technological development, and sustainable development'.

The third group believes that globalization is an overall threat and a process full of risks. One of the problems observed by these universities is that the market economy dominates all the other aspects of nations. The Universidad Autónoma de Nayarit (2010) uses the term 'capitalist globalization' to refer to this phenomenon. The Universidad de Chapingo (2010), which specializes in agriculture, goes beyond that and presents an analysis of the impact globalization has on Mexican agriculture, expressing concerns about issues related to the environment, agricultural trade unfairness, global warming, and a decrease in the quality of life for farmers in Mexico. This group also states that strategic international cooperation could help alleviate the negative effects of globalization. The University Veracruzana (2010) affirms that universities must play the role as a 'mitigating factor' against the negative effects of globalization.

The final group basically does not acknowledge globalization, and includes the Universidad Autónoma de la Ciudad de México, which was created in 2001. In the case of the Universidad Autónoma de Oaxaca (2010), the university assumes there are complications to reaching a global level and prioritizes local necessities above the need to establish other goals. According to its Institutional Development Plan, the Universidad Autónoma de Campeche's (2010) main goal is to become a competitive, high-quality, pertinent university for the sustainable development of the state of Campeche, and avoids mentioning national or international scales.

It is interesting to notice that the majority of universities acknowledge the connection between globalization and the use of ICTs. In fact, some institutions do not define globalization but take the use of ICTs as synonymous with globalization (Universidad Autónoma de San Luis Potosí, 2010; Universidad de Guadalajara, 2010). Universities such as UNAM (2010) include the 'expansion of advanced technologies' as one of globalization's components, together with 'academic mobility, flexibility, international cooperation, and academic exchange'. The universities that fall in each group do tend to share similarities such as size and educational capacity-building. However, almost all institutions refer to globalization issues in official documents, recognizing its effects and visualizing its challenges. Still, the institutional responses are different.

According to Van Dijk (1998, p. 27), 'The discourse is a social practice' and, following this, Cantwell and Maldonado (2009) raise the question of 'how do concepts about higher education globalization lead to particular practices in the field by individuals and groups of actors?' They consider the notion of social practices as too broad a concept for operationalization purposes and thus university policies were chosen as a more concrete manifestation to review, to help answer their question and to examine the impact and results of such policies.

The first challenge in studying Mexican higher education is to find accurate data for policies. General data on the internationalization processes of Mexican HEIs are very rare, since internationalization is not a main policy axis. For example, to answer the simple question of how many Mexican students go to the USA for an academic degree compared to how many American students go to Mexico, it was necessary to review 33 websites and almost 70 databases. The problem is that many Mexican sources are irregular and inconsistent (Maldonado-Maldonado et al., 2010). For this chapter, yearbooks, presidents' annual reports and institutional development plans were reviewed for each of the 25 universities. Naturally some institutions have more material available than others.

A second challenge is to find out how globalization practices and, more importantly, policies materialize in HEIs. Given the hegemonic tendency in the field of higher education, the closest materialization seems to be in reference to internationalization policies, but even finding information about these policies was complicated. Some of the indicators found pertaining to the level of globalization or internationalization of Mexican universities are: international cooperation agreements; data on English as a second language; international student exchange; and academic exchange participation.

However, a problem occurs when the question arises regarding the participation of Mexican HEIs in a knowledge-based economy. It is never simple to find empirical data on what actions they are following in response to it. One example is the Benemérita Universidad Autónoma de Puebla (2001), which affirms that part of its teaching curriculum includes the desire to 'become entrepreneurial'. What indicators should be examined to determine how they have accomplished this goal? Should the number of spin-offs or businesses created by its graduates before and after the incorporation of that goal be examined? Unless such statements are supported by solid data, it is very difficult to consider when it is a matter of a university's broad desires or actual policies.

INTERNATIONAL COOPERATION AGREEMENTS

There seems to be a wide range of possibilities for international cooperation agreements. Some of them only refer to agreements that create student exchange programs. Other agreements include collaborations such as faculty exchange, or research, teaching, service and dissemination activities. Finally a further type of agreement includes very specific projects or clearly labeled activities. Some universities only report reciprocal university collaboration agreements, while others report all that they have, even if they are only one-sided. In the case of the Universidad de Guadalajara (2010), the university distinguishes between ordinary agreements (reporting 525 international and 322 national) and collaboration agreements (58 international out of a total 149). It is not clear what the main differences are between the two.

There is a growing tendency to subscribe to international agreements, which raises questions about their relevance. Another aspect that has not been addressed yet is the effectiveness of these agreements because their number does not correspond to the number of students who participate in international exchanges. Among the 25 universities reviewed, the group with fewest international agreements includes the Universidad Autónoma de Nayarit (2010). This institution appears to have about 563 collaboration agreements, but all are international. The other universities report between seven and 18 international agreements. In the case of the Universidad Autónoma de Querétaro (2010) it reports that seven international and 128 total (including national) agreements have been signed.

A second group reports between 38 and 73 international agreements. In this group it is interesting to note the larger number of international agreements in comparison to national agreements. For example, the Universidad Autónoma de Chihuahua (2010) reports 38 international agreements and 28 national, while the Universidad Autónoma del Estado de México (2010) claims 48 international and only 16 with other Mexican universities. In the case of the National Polytechnic Institute (2010) there are 73 cooperation programs with international universities and only 11 national.

The third group presents the largest number of international agreements. The Universidad Anáhuac (2010) reports 104 international and just 14 national, the Universidad Nacional Autónoma de México (2010) has 122 international, Universidad Autónoma de Nuevo León (2010) has 183, and the Benemérita Universidad Autónoma de México (2010) has 243 agreements (the information about the national agreements for the last three universities was not available). The majority of international agreements among the Mexican universities reviewed are with Spanish universities, and there are reasons to believe that this could be generalized to most Mexican institutions. Most likely this is due to the postcolonial relationship between Mexico and Spain and the fact that residents of both countries speak the same language and share many cultural characteristics. These factors matter greatly in the context of student mobility, faculty mobility and second-language acquisition.

STUDENT EXCHANGE PROGRAMS ABROAD

According to the *Atlas* of *Student Mobility* (2010), produced by the Institute of International Education (IIE), about 0.95 percent of the students enrolled in Mexican HEIs have had an international education experience (see Table 19.1). In terms of international students as a percentage of the total global enrollment, only 0.11 percent go to Mexico. Unfortunately, of the 25 institutions reviewed, only nine include more precise information regarding the mobility of their students, further evidence of the lack of accurate information about this issue. Consequently simple questions cannot be answered, including: how long did they study abroad, what type of universities and programs did they attend, and what impact is it having on their education or on the education of their classmates?

Table 19.1   Number of students going abroad in selected universities in 2009

University	Total enrollment (only graduate and undergraduate)	Number of students in an exchange program abroad	Percentage of students going abroad
Universidad Autónoma de Coahuila	24 354	33	0.13
Universidad Nacional Autónoma de México	196 300	423	0.21
Universidad de Guadalajara	86 792	341	0.39
Universidad Autónoma de Yucatán	12 419	51	0.41
Universidad Autónoma del Estado de México	37 680	194	0.51
Universidad Autónoma de Nuevo León	69 100	365	0.52
Benemérita Universidad Autónoma de Puebla	49 544	109	0.56
Universidad Autónoma de Baja California	45 104	368	0.81
Universidad Autónoma de Aguascalientes	11 770	126	1.07

Source: Official university websites.

Table 19.2   Number of faculty going abroad in selected universities (between 2008 and 2009)

University	Total faculty members (only graduate and undergraduate)	Number of faculty members going as a visiting faculty abroad	Percentage of faculty members going abroad
Universidad Autónoma de Nuevo León	3754	89	0.29
Universidad Autónoma del Estado de México	5200	35	0.67
Universidad Nacional Autónoma de México	29 733	220	0.76
Universidad Autónoma de Coahuila	2040	18	0.88

Source: Official university websites.

FACULTY MOBILITY

The information on academics going abroad is even more limited (see Table 19.2). The percentages are relatively low but it is important to take into consideration the raw numbers.

The same questions about the type of student mobility and its impact also apply to faculty mobility. It is a topic that also needs further research and examination.

ENGLISH AS A SECOND LANGUAGE

Despite the fact that more institutions are discussing the importance of learning English, it seems that English-language acquisition is still a pending issue in most Mexican HEIs, even those located near the Mexico–US border (Maldonado-Maldonado and Cantwell, 2008). The importance of English is observed in most official university documents; for example, the University of Coahuila (2010) reports that the number of students studying abroad had doubled. However, there are very interesting disparities regarding English learning. While some institutions are looking to diversify and add languages, such as the Universidad de Quintana Roo (2010), which has incorporated Mandarin Chinese, most institutions consider English as a key language for globalization. The Universidad Autónoma de Querétaro (2010) is just now looking to translate its website into English while other institutions have translated their websites into five or six languages (respectively the Universidad Nacional Autónoma de México and the Universidad Autónoma de Nuevo León).

OTHER POLICIES LINKED TO GLOBALIZATION RESPONSES

The creation of academic or administrative departments specifically for establishing national and international collaborations has been very common in the last decade.

However, tracking that information, even when there were only 25 universities to consider, is very difficult. In the majority of the 25 universities, at least one such unit was detected. Another factor mentioned is the development of ICT infrastructure within institutions. The Universidad Autónoma de Chihuahua (2010) recognizes its lack of ICT infrastructure and most universities mention the urgency to update their ICT. Other universities go beyond this and more explicitly consider that ICT expertise is part of the competences they need to teach (Instituto Tecnológico de Estudios Superiores Monterrey, 2010; Universidad Autónoma de Aguascalientes, 2010; and Universidad Autónoma del Estado de México, 2010).

Most of the 25 universities recognized the necessity to adapt their curriculum and, even further, to create new academic programs. However, very few acknowledge that much has happened as yet. The Universidad Autónoma de Yucatán (2010), however, refers to the creation of virtual academic programs as one response to globalization. In the case of creating double-degree programs, while only two public universities seek to establish them with international higher education institutions (Universidad Autónoma de Querétaro, 2010 and Universidad Autónoma de Baja California, 2010), all the private universities seem very active in promoting these (Instituto Tecnológico y de Estudios Superiores de Occidente, 2010; Instituto Tecnológico de Estudios Superiores Monterrey, 2010; Universidad Anáhuac, 2010; Universidad del Valle de México, 2010).

Another university policy linked to their response to globalization is the increase of more accredited programs (international but also national). The most concrete example is the Instituto Tecnológico de Estudios Superiores Monterrey (ITESM) which is accredited by the US Commission on Colleges of the Southern Association of Colleges and Schools to award bachelors', masters' and doctoral degrees. Other universities only mention the importance of improving the number of accredited programs nationally and internationally but they did not provide evidence about efforts undertaken (such as the Universidad Autónoma de Campeche, 2010 and the Universidad Autónoma del Estado de México, 2010).

IS MEXICAN HIGHER EDUCATION MISSING THE OPPORTUNITY?

Once the complexities of globalization, internationalization and the knowledge-based economy with relation to Mexican HEIs have been discussed, it is imperative to assess the implications for policy-making and the worldwide debate on globalization and higher education. During the 1990s evaluation policies drove reforms in Mexican HEIs. The effectiveness of these reforms was linked to funding rewards (Mendoza Rojas, 2003; Díaz Barriga et al., 2008). However, with internationalization policies it is important to know how some practices become accepted without these financial incentives. Obtaining international research and other prestige has been a goal of evaluation programs in Mexico but there is no similar objective for becoming internationalized. There are important criteria for academic evaluation and discussion of relevant academic work, including publishing in international journals, publishing in another language (preferably English), joining international associations, attending international conferences and so on. However, there are no financial incentives for such factors as the number of students or faculty with an international experience, the enrollment of international students, the role of second-language acquisition, and the number of international cooperation agreements.

For many years at the National System of Researchers (Sistema National de Investigadores, or SNI), the number of times an academic was published (mostly in journals) was the standard used to evaluate academic productivity. This practice continues today despite the fact that the SNI has modified some of the evaluation criteria to consider other aspects such as teaching activities, forming academic networks, and training future researchers. Looking for elements to add to the discussion of the impact of knowledge at the national level involves establishing criteria that go beyond using classical standards to measure academic productivity. As discussed earlier, some of these criteria may consider the number of patents and actual application in industries; R&D spending (public and private); relevance of industries that use high technology (aerospace, computing, pharmaceutical, electronics–communications, for example); or new innovations based on academic research by industry. If the question is about how indicative these evaluation policies are of the status of the country in relation to the knowledge-based economy, the answer is obvious: they are not very indicative at all.

After reading the discourses and policies connected to globalization, one general impression is that internationalization at this moment is something very positive to boast about, particularly within university presidents' reports. Activities aimed at the internationalization of higher education have been emphasized in most of the universities reviewed. On the other hand, it seems clear that very few institutions have been able to highlight actual policies related to a knowledge-based economy.

Before concluding this section, it is very important to mention at least two main limitations. The first is that this analysis is based only on the official discourses provided by university officials and not evidence by faculty, students or administrative personnel. More in-depth analysis and additional research is needed for this. The second limitation is related to the complexities in seeking to analyze how higher education policies respond to globalization and their impact in the Mexican context. It is not only problematic to find available information on the concrete policies established by HEIs that were recognized as institutional responses to globalization, but it is even harder to have sufficient elements to help to analyze these policies. For example, who actually substantiates and implements universities' discourses about globalization and internationalization? How do institutions adapt theses discourses officially? What part do power, politics and negotiations play in implementing these policies? How do we gauge when universities have a genuine interest in these issues or not? These are pending but important questions that need further research.

CONCLUSION

The examination of how Mexican higher education is facing globalization provides interesting elements for comparison with other developing countries. Besides the OECD and European nations, there is an important group of countries that share the same challenges and paradoxes as Mexico. Globalization implies the notion of the entire planet being included, but whether it is truly worldwide in scope is under scrutiny. It is not clear for how long globalization will be valid as a social concept among social scientists, but for now, there are no signs that it will stop being used to describe key current worldwide phenomena.

As part of the debate on globalization and higher education, there are two other important terms: internationalization and knowledge-based economy. Both terms have very different uses in the field of higher education. Internationalization describes an HEI's policies in response to globalization. The concept is problematic because it misses the agency of these institutions in many ways. Examples of these policies are: student exchange programs; faculty mobility; establishing international collaboration agreements with international HEIs; becoming members of international networks and consortia; joining international accreditation systems; transforming academic programs to have more international profiles; establishing modalities such as double-degree programs; and establishing overseas branch campuses, among others. In countries such as Mexico the available information to aid analysis is inconsistent.

The varying definitions of knowledge-based economy are more problematic within the field of higher education. Some authors see it as synonymous with globalization. Others assume that being part of the knowledge-based economy should be the main goal of HEIs. Others may consider the term only at the rhetorical level. The work by international organizations on the different indicators to measure the position of national higher education systems regarding a knowledge-based economy are contributions that help to clarify the concept. Currently the debate seems to be progressing at the level of national higher education systems but not in terms of how to fully understand the participation of individual universities reaching the goal of being agents within the knowledge-based regime.

In the case of Mexico it seems that the country does not have too many options. The nation can do everything possible to transcend its place as an eternal knowledge-user in a knowledge-based economy and take a different position. But the challenge seems difficult, nationally and institutionally. The test for the country is that transforming its position as knowledge-user and perhaps becoming more active as a service hub of the global knowledge economy, as have such as China and India, might be the best and only chance to reduce the socioeconomic gap that exists between Mexico and the developed countries. Therefore higher education internationalization (establishing international cooperation agreements or promoting academic international mobility) may be just one of the steps towards transforming the national higher education system into an actor within a knowledge-based economy. One of the main problems observed after looking at how Mexican universities understand globalization and their possible role with such processes is that most of the 25 universities considered here seem to perceive internationalization as the main destination, not as one of the steps for going further.

After presenting all the empirical data on where Mexico is positioned in this knowledge race, it is imperative to ask whether or not it has the necessary conditions, resources and visions to achieve this goal. Although Mexico fulfills these conditions, the rules of this race seem too restrictive. In some ways, the rules are already established to make sure the winners always win and the losers always lose. So a relevant question may have to do with how much of a role politics will play in the international community to help developing countries in this race, thus reducing the gap. Perhaps it is important to pay attention to what Sen discusses in his most recent book on the idea of justice. He says,

'The question that we have to ask here is: what international reforms do we need to make the world a bit less unjust?' (Sen, 2009, p. 25). In this case, the questions should go to the most important international organizations involved with knowledge and education, as well as the most dominant countries in the game of knowledge production. By doing so it will help determine how things can change, at the global, national and local levels, to make sure countries such as Mexico will be able to succeed in becoming part of the knowledge production race and not lag behind. The idea of debating global governance in this and other areas makes more sense than ever.

Finally, answering the question of where Mexican higher education stands in this global race, it is clear Mexican universities are stuck in the attempt to become 'international', but are far from taking part in the knowledge-production race. It does not mean that there should not be a national discussion on whether the country should join this race or not; the real problem is that not even that discussion is taking place. Without a national debate on where to go and the political will of the powerful actors within the current knowledge-based regime to compensate current disparities, who knows if reacting later would be too late for Mexico and countries under similar circumstances? Time will tell.

ACKNOWLEDGMENT

Grateful thanks are due to Nicta-Ha Dzib Soto for her research assistance in gathering data from the 25 university websites for this chapter.

REFERENCES

Altbach, P. (2004), 'Globalization and the university: myths and realities in an unequal world', *Tertiary Education and Management*, **10**, 3–25.
Altbach, P. and J. Knight (2006), 'The internationalization of higher education: motivation and realities', *The NEA Almanac of Higher Education 2006*, 2–11.
Altbach, P. and L. Lewis (1996), 'The academic profession in international perspective', in P. Altbach (ed.), *The International Academic Profession: Portraits from 14 Countries*, Princeton, NJ: Carnegie Foundation for the Advancement of Teaching, pp. 3–50.
Appadurai, A. (2000), 'Grassroots globalization and the research imagination', in A. Appadurai (ed.), *Globalization*, Durham, NC: Duke University Press, pp. 1–13.
Avilés, Karina (2010), 'Suicidio y narco, "opciones" de jóvenes por el fracaso educativo', *La Jornada*, (12 January).
Beck, U. (2001), *What is Globalization?*, Cambridge: Polity Press.
Cantwell, B. and A. Maldonado-Maldonado (2009), 'Agency and power in four stories: confronting contemporary ideas about globalization and internationalization in higher education', *Globalisation, Societies and Education*, **7** (3), 289–306.
Casanova-Cardiel, H. (2006), 'Mexico', in J. Forest and P. Altbach (eds), *International Handbook of Higher Education*, Dordrecht: Springer, pp. 881–98.
Castells, M. (2000), *The Rise of the Network Society*, New York: Blackwell.
De Wit, H. (1999), 'Changing rationales for the internationalization of higher education', *International Higher Education*, **15**, 2–3.
Díaz Barriga, Ángel, Concepción Barrón Tirado and Frida Díaz Barriga Arceo (2008), 'Impacto en la evaluación en la educación superior Mexicana', México: UNAM, ANUIES, Plaza y Valdés.
Enciso, Angélica (2009), 'Sólo 18 por ciento de mexicanos tienen ingresos suficientes para vivir: Coneval', *La Jornada*, (11 December).
Finkelstein, M. (2009), 'The changing personal characteristics, career trajectories and sense of identity/

commitment of academics in mature higher educational systems: the USA case', paper presented at the Council for International Higher Education Forum at the 34th Annual Conference of the Association for the Study of Higher Education, Vancouver, British Columbia, Canada, (4 November).

Gobierno Federal de los Estados Unidos Mexicanos (2009), *Tercer informe de gobierno*, México: Gobierno Federal, retrieved from http://www.informe.gob.mx/informe/.

Gürüz, K. (2008), *Higher Education and International Student Mobility in the Global Knowledge Economy*, Albany, NY: State University of New York Press (SUNY).

Held, D., D. McGrew, D. Goldblatt and J. Perraton (1999), *Global Transformations: Politics, Economics and Culture*, Stanford, CA: Stanford University Press.

Institute of International Education (2010), Atlas of Student Mobility, retrieved from http://www.altas.iienetwork.org/page/97988/.

International Labor Organization (2010), LABORSTA Internet. 'Topic: Unemployment by age group', retrieved from http://laborsta.ilo.org/STP/.

International Telecommunications Union (2009), *Internet Indicators: Subscribers, Users and Broadband Subscribers*, retrieved from http://www.itu.int/ITU-D/ICTEYE/Indicators/Indicators.aspx#.

Knight, J. (2004), 'Internationalization remodeled: definition, approaches, and rationales', *Journal of Studies in International Education*, **8**, 5–31.

KOF (2010), Index of Globalization, retrieved from http://globalization.kof.ethz.ch/.

Kroll, L. and M. Miller (2010), 'The world's billionaires', *Forbes*, retrieved from http://www.forbes.com/2010/03/10/worlds-richest-people-slim-gates-buffett-billionaires-2010_land.html?boxes=Homepagetop specialreports.

Lee, J., A. Maldonado-Maldonado and G. Rhoades (2006), 'The political economy of international student flows: patterns, ideas and propositions', *Handbook of Higher Education*, Dordrecht. Springer, pp. 545–90.

Maldonado-Maldonado, A. (2009), 'Latin American higher education: hope in the struggle?', in D. Palfreyman and T. Tapper (eds), *Structuring Mass Higher Education: The Role of Elite Institutions*, New York and London: Routledge Taylor & Francis, pp. 73–94.

Maldonado-Maldonado, A. and B. Cantwell (2008), 'Caught on the border: a study of university collaboration along the Mexican–American border', *Comparative Education*, **44**, 317–31.

Maldonado-Maldonado, A. and B. Cantwell (2010), 'Agency in university collaboration: the case of international students in a global and borderland context', paper in preparation for publication.

Maldonado-Maldonado, A., B. Torres-Olave and M. González Canché (2010), *Mexico–US Graduate Student Mobility: Current Trends and Future Issues to Study*, report for the US–Mexico Commission for Educational and Cultural Exchange (COMEXUS), Mexico: COMEXUS.

Marginson, S. (2007), 'Global position and position taking: the case of Australia', *Journal of Studies in International Education*, **11** (1), 5–32.

Marginson, S. and G. Rhoades (2002), 'Beyond national states, markets, and systems of higher education: a glonacal agency heuristic', *Higher Education*, **43**, 281–309.

Mas-colell, A., W. Michael and J. Green (1995), *Microeconomic Theory*, New York and Oxford: Oxford University Press.

Mendoza Rojas, J. (2003), 'La evaluación y acreditación de la educación superior mexicana: las experiencias de una década', Ponencia presentada VIII Congreso Internacional del CLAD sobre la Reforma del Estado y de la Administración Pública, Panamá; 28–31 de octubre.

Mills, M. and H. Blossfeld (2005), 'Globalization, uncertainty and the early life course: a theoretical framework', in H. Blossfeld, E. Klijzing, M. Mills and K. Kurz (eds), *Globalization, Uncertainty and Youth Society*, London and New York: Routledge, pp. 1–25.

OECD (2006), *The Knowledge-Based Economy: General Distribution*, Paris: OECD.

OECD (2010), *OECD StatExtracs*, OECD Official website, retrieved from http://stats.oecd.org/Index.aspx?DataSetCode=CSP2009.

Ordorika, I. (2006), 'Educación superior y globalización: las universidades públicas frente a una nueva hegemonía', *Andamios*, **3** (5), 31–47.

Paasi, A. (2005), 'Globalization, academic capitalism, and the uneven geographies of international journal publishing spaces', *Environment and Planning*, **35**, 769–89.

Parrado, E. (2005), 'Globalization and the transition to adulthood in Mexico', in H. Blossfeld, E. Klijzing, M. Mills and K. Kurz (eds), *Globalization, Uncertainty and Youth Society*, London and New York: Routledge, pp. 327–48.

Peres, W. and M. Hilbert (2009), 'La sociedad de la información en América Latina y el Caribe: desarrollo de las tecnologías y tecnologías para el desarrollo', Santiago: CEPAL/ IDRC/ EuropeAid.

Ritzer, G. and T. Stillman (2003), 'Assessing MacDonaldization, Americanization and globalization in global America', in U. Beck, N. Sznaider and R. Winter (eds), *The Cultural Consequences of Globalization*, Liverpool: Liverpool University Press.

Robertson, S. (2006), 'Absences and imaginings: the production of knowledge on globalization and education', *Globalisation, Societies and Education*, **4** (2), 303–18.

Sassen, S. (2000), 'Spatialities and temporalities for the global: elements for a theorization', in A. Appadurai (ed.), *Globalization*, Durham, NC: Duke University Press, pp. 260–78.

Sen, A. (2009), *The Idea of Justice*, London: Allen Lane.

Stiglitz, J. (1999), 'Knowledge as a global public good', in I. Kaul, I. Grunberg and M. Stern (eds), *Global Public Goods: International Cooperation in the 21st Century*, New York: Oxford University Press, pp. 308–25.

Teichler, U. (1999), 'Internationalization as a challenge for higher education in Europe', *Tertiary Education and Management*, **5** (1), 5–23.

Teichler, U. (2001), 'Changes to Erasmus under the umbrella of Socrates', *Journal of Studies in International Education*, **5**, 201–27.

United Kingdom/United States of America Study Group (2009), *Higher Education and Collaboration in Global Context: Building a Global Civil Society. A private report to Prime Minister Gordon Brown*.

United Nations Development Program (UNDP) (1993), *Human Development Report 1992: Global Dimensions of Human Development*, New York: Oxford University Press.

United Nations Development Program (UNDP) (2010), *Human Development Report 2009: Overcoming Barriers: Human Mobility and Development*, New York: Oxford University Press.

van der Wende, M. (2000), 'The Bologna Declaration: enhancing the transparency and competitiveness of European higher education', *Higher Education in Europe*, **25** (3), 305–10.

van der Wende, M. (2001), 'Internationalization policies: about new trends and contrasting paradigms', *Higher Education Policy*, **14**, 249–60.

van Dijk, T. (1998), *Ideology: A Multidisciplinary Approach*, London: Sage Publications.

van Vught, F. et al. (2003), 'Globalisation and internationalisation: policy agendas compared', in J. Enders and O. Fulton (eds), *Higher Education in a Globalizing World: International Trends and Mutual Observation. A Festschrift in Honour of Ulrich Teichler*, Dordrecht: Kluwer Academic Publishers, pp. 103–20.

Wächter, B. (2004), 'The Bologna Process: developments and prospects', *European Journal of Education*, **39** (3), 265–73.

Waters, M. (1995), 'A world of difference', in M. Waters, *Globalization*, London: Routledge, pp. 1–25.

Women's Learning Partnership for Right Development and Peace (2010), retrieved from http://www.learning-partnership.org/.

World Intellectual Property Organization (2010), Official Website. Retrieved from http://www.wipo.int/portal/index.html.en.

University Websites

Benemérita Autónoma Universidad de Puebla (2010). Cuarto informe del rector, 2009. Retrieved from: http://www.buap.mx/

Instituto Politécnico Nacional (2010). Página oficial. Retrieved from: http://www.cca.ipn.mx/

Instituto Tecnológico de Estudios Superior Monterrey (2010) Página oficial. Retrieved from: http://www.itesm.edu/wps/portal?WCM_GLOBAL_CONTEXT=/migration/ITESMv22/Tecnol_gico+de+Monterrey/Profesional/Estudia+en+el+extranjero/Programas+en+el+extranjero/

Instituto Tecnológico y de Estudios Superiores de Occidente. (2010) Página official. Retrieved from: http://portal.iteso.mx/portal/page/portal/Dependencias/Rectoria/Dependencias/Direccion_de_Relaciones_Externas/Dependencias/Oficina_de_relaciones_institucionales/Intercambio_academico/Alumnos_del_ITESO

Universidad Anáhuac (2010). Página official. Retrieved from: http://www.anahuac.mx/intercambios/archivos/Convenios_internacionales_intercambio_09.pdf

Universidad Autónoma 'Benito Juárez' de Oaxaca (2010). Primer informe del Rector. Retrived from: http://www.uabjo.mx/docs/rtvPrimerInforme.pdf

Universidad Autónoma de Aguascalientes (2010). Informe del rector 2009. Retrieved from: http://www.uaa.mx/rectoria/informe2009/

Universidad Autónoma de Baja California (2010). Página official. Retrieved from: http://www.uabc.mx/cciia/internacional/indextrue.html

Universidad Autónoma de Campeche (2010). Página official. Retrieved from: http://www.uacam.edu.mx/identidad/documentos

Universidad Autónoma de Chapingo (2010). Página oficial. Retrieved from: http://portal.chapingo.mx/rectoria/?modulo=informes

Universidad Autónoma de Chihuahua (2010). Página oficial. Retrieved from: http://www.uach.mx/institucional_y_juridica/convenios/2008/04/23/internacionales/

Universidad Autónoma de Coahuila (2010). Segundo Informe de Actividades del Rector. Retrieved from: http://www2.uadec.mx/pub/pdf/SegundoInformeActividades.pdf

Universidad Autónoma de la Ciudad de México (2010). Página oficial. Retrieved from: http://www.uacm.edu.mx/

Universidad Autónoma del Estado de México (2010). Informe del Rector 2008. Retrieved from: http://www.uaemex.mx/rector/2008/informe/InfRec09_II2.html

Universidad Autónoma del Estado de Morelos (2010) Página oficial. Retrieved from: http://www.uaem.mx/

Universidad Autónoma del Estado de Nuevo León (2010). Retrieved from: http://www.uanl.mx/transparencia/informes/archivos/2009/Informe_Rector_2009.pdf

Universidad Autónoma de Nayarit (2010). Página official. Retrieved from: http://www.uan.edu.mx/

Universidad Autónoma de Querétaro (2010). Informe del Rector. Retrieved from http://www.uaq.mx/rectoria/infomes_rector.html

Universidad Autónoma de San Luis Potosí. (2010). Página official. Retrieved from: http://www.uaslp.mx/Spanish/Rectoria/Documentos/Paginas/default.aspx

Universidad Autónoma de Yucatán (2010). Informe del Rector 2007. Retrieved from: http://www.uady.mx/pdfs/InformeUADY2007.pdf

Universidad de Guadalajara (2010) Segundo Informe de Actividades 2009–2010. Retrieved from: http://www.rectoria.udg.mx/

Universidad del Valle de México (2010). Página official. Retrieved from: http://www.uvmnet.edu/intercambios/licenciatura.asp

Universidad de Quintana Roo. (2010). Informe del Rector. Retrieved from: http://www.uqroo.mx/index.htm

Universidad Nacional Autónoma de México (2010). Agenda 2009. Retrieved from: http://www.planeacion.unam.mx/Agenda/

Universidad Veracruzana (2010). Página official. Retrieved from: http://www.uv.mx/universidad/doctosofi/menuindex.html

20 Globalization in the USA: the case of California
William G. Tierney

INTRODUCTION

Globalization is a highly complex process that has impacted multiple national and international arenas. Sometimes the term has been employed as a synonym for American imperialism as if the term simply refers to the extension throughout the world of American power and culture. Although the rationale for such an assertion is understandable, such an assumption makes it appear that the USA is not influenced by globalization, as if the country is simply on a unidirectional trajectory and globalization is the next logical stage in the country's development.

In this chapter I shall argue, however, the opposite point of view. My reasoning will be twofold. First, I intend to suggest that the USA has been deeply affected by globalization and second, I wish to underscore the point that there is no static logic or trajectory to the idea that makes globalization's impact a foregone conclusion. Although citizens have certainly been influenced by definitions and reactions to globalization, it is within our reach to determine the paths we choose rather than simply having to go down a predetermined avenue. I shall work through this argument by way of a discussion of higher education in California.

Globalization is a difficult term to come to grips with, especially when we consider a country as large and diverse as the USA. A diversified economy and vastly differing cultural and population centers make generalizations difficult if the discussion is focused on abstractions. Issues of trade and immigration, for example, have been influenced by globalization, but their effect on a large urban city such as Los Angeles, which is near the Mexican border is quite different from that on Bozeman, Montana, which is closer to Canada.

Even an abstract discussion about tertiary education in the USA is weakened insofar as a small state such as Vermont struggles with the effects of globalization in very different ways than does California. American higher education is a diversified system where the states have had more impact and control than the federal government with regard to the structure, purpose and functions of colleges and universities. To a certain extent, accrediting bodies have played a regulatory role; even accreditation in the USA, however, is broken down by region rather than having one system based at the national level.

Accordingly, I shall discuss California's post-secondary system in order to demonstrate how globalization has impacted students, post-secondary structures and the state's role in higher education. As I elaborate below, the system is a microcosm of issues that are being played out on a national level, albeit frequently in different ways from state to state. California also has the largest post-secondary system in the country; its 50-year-old 'Master Plan' has been hailed as a model for a state's post-secondary framework; and the state's economy has been roiled by the recession and governance issues that have deeply affected public funding in a manner similar to other states.

I begin with a discussion of the meaning of globalization. I discuss the changing nature of how higher education in the USA has been thought of as a public good. I then turn to a discussion of the state and higher education and focus on five key areas: (1) 'public' higher education; (2) inequality and access; (3) privatization; (4) regulation; and (5) knowledge-based economies and research. California then serves as a case study for these ideas. I consider what we have done in each area, and how the impact of globalization has changed our interpretations of these five areas. I conclude with a brief overview of what lies ahead for higher education in the USA and various decisions that need to be made.

GLOBALIZATION AND THE PUBLIC GOOD

I shall use the term 'globalization' to refer to practices that extend beyond national borders even though they are frequently enacted in local and national contexts. Globalization has come about and is spread by capital, migration and, most importantly for the discussion here, technology. The result is greater integration across sectors and countries and an increase in cross-border goods, services and capital. Because globalization refers to transnational actions, it is often difficult to see how local practices are impacted. I concur with Gerald Gutek (2006, p. 100), however, that globalization 'as a general process needs to be considered in terms of contextual settings', particularly when we are discussing education. It is the nation-state (and in the USA when we discuss higher education, particularly the state itself) that frames processes and goals. Education is a useful example of the breadth of globalization insofar as education's reach transcends one or another category: education is transformed by globalization, but, as knowledge-producing organizations, schools, colleges and universities also transform globalization. At one point, however, the impact of globalization on education was in dispute, but as Mok (2005) notes, in the twenty-first century it has become clear how far-reaching globalization's reach is and how much it has impacted education. Discussions often center around, for example, globalization's impact on economics, trade or culture. Education cuts across virtually all of these categories. The result is that education in general and higher education in particular in the USA is undergoing changes that are as significant as at any time in the last century, in large part because globalization assumes a knowledge-based economy and at least in the USA until recently the major purveyor of knowledge has been the post-secondary institution.

Lester Thurow (2000) has observed that the definition of a country's economy now exceeds simple geographic boundaries. Communication and transportation technologies enable companies to transcend borders in ways unimaginable only a generation ago. The same may be said of tertiary education (Findlay and Tierney, 2010). Where one takes classes and how one takes them and who teaches these classes – indeed, even what we mean by a 'class' – are being unalterably changed in remarkably quick ways.

The assumption has been that in part because of globalization the USA needs a better-educated workforce. If the USA is to remain competitive, it needs more people participating in higher education; specifically, the Obama Administration has called for a million more people a year to be added to higher education in the USA for the next decade. Higher education's 'product' gets defined as equipping individuals with the skills necessary to compete in a global economy. Numerous reports such as that by McKinsey (2009) highlight that the USA faces an achievement gap in comparison with other industrialized countries, and there is a severe economic impact if nothing is done. The result is a renewed focus on improving primary and secondary education, increasing participation in tertiary education, and speeding up time to degree in colleges and universities.

Similarly, because of the compression of time and the force of technological change, how higher education in the USA has been structured is being reconsidered (Walker, 2009). As Judith Walker has observed, academics now face a '"time crunch" where everything has become more time sensitive – to absorb more information in a limited amount of time; to publish more; to serve on more committees . . . Time becomes a limited resource' (ibid., p. 497). The result is that the assumption that a course equals a specific number of credit hours, and that when one accumulates a set number of credits one may graduate, is likely to change. Seat time – a student sitting in classes on defined days and set time periods for an academic term – is being challenged by courses offered in cyberspace whenever the student wants to log on. Rather than wait for an end-of-term exam, the potential now exists to challenge a course with specified learning outcomes that a student has to master. If students are able to master the material in a matter of weeks rather than a full academic term, then so be it. These sorts of changes are being considered now because technology enables us to consider them; the leisurely pace of academic life seems anachronistic in the twenty-first century. Furthermore, an increased demand for higher education has outstripped the capacity of traditional campuses to offer traditional courses at conventional times. The definition of a 'traditional' student also has changed insofar as the full-time 18–21-year-old is now a minority of the college-going population and the part-time working adult student is now the norm.

All of these changes, or proposed changes, go to the core of how the USA should define a public good. Until recently the country has had a quite traditional definition. As Kaul et al. (1999) have pointed out, a private good is excludable and rival in consumption, whereas a common (public) good has benefits that are nonrivalrous in consumption and nonexcludable. The typical example of a public good is a traffic light or lighthouse. The use by one individual of the traffic light or the lighthouse does not detract from the use by others, and the cost and benefit is similar for all.

We have thought of primary and secondary education as a public good, created by the public in the form of organizations where everyone can be educated. Until recently, if a parent wanted his or her child to attend a private institution (such as a Catholic school), that parent received no public support and needed to continue to pay taxes toward the public good. As with other public goods in the USA – national defense, potable water, safety, fire prevention and the like – the public was the provider through public agencies. If individuals wanted their own security or a private road on private land, then that was within their rights, but they had to pay for it – and they had to pay taxes toward the public good.

Higher education has had a mixed history. Until the late nineteenth century the country did not think of higher education as a public good. Attendance at colleges and universities was largely the prerogative of those who were wealthy or religious. The wealthy attended private institutions such as Harvard University or Yale University, and the religious attended the literally hundreds of small colleges that trained people in a particular religion. The passage of the Land Grant Act during America's Civil War created public higher education for the working class. For the better part of a century every state had public colleges and universities that were largely free and primarily concentrated on training individuals for professional jobs. The assumption was not that everyone needed to attend a post-secondary institution, but when people did they did not need to pay fees. Further, the role of land-grant institutions was to help the largely agricultural sectors of the country improve their output. Again, if a student wanted to attend a private institution, he or she could do so, but even with federal support the assumption was that tuition fees were the responsibility of the individual.

A central derivative of globalization has been a rethinking of what we mean by a public good. This redefinition cuts across many areas, but includes education. The consequence has been circular. Dissatisfaction with inadequate police protection, for example, has led to the rise of private security firms that the individual has paid for, which has made the individual less willing to support taxes for public security. The assumption that traditional public goods, such as national parks, museums and civic events, should be supported by the taxpayer has been replaced by fees for service and a need to raise money from private philanthropy. Public television receives a fraction of what it once received from the federal government as private companies have arisen on cable, the Internet and other outlets. On the one hand, individuals argue that technology has made what is offered on public television superfluous, and on the other is the argument that taxpayers should not support services that are also offered in the private sector. And in education individuals can attend a variety of schools that may not be 'public' but instead are charter schools. Although the assumption in education is still that education is a public good, rather than an organization – public schools – we now fund individuals to go wherever they desire.

The result in higher education has been a movement in the same direction. Public higher education has slowly been defunded at the state level, and private institutions, known as for-profits, have seen a rise. Rather than fund the organizations – public colleges and universities – the trend has been to try to fund the consumer (student). At the same time, rather than have the public pay for the cost of higher education, greater responsibility for the cost has switched to the consumer. All of this has occurred at a faster pace not simply because of technological changes but also because of the ideology of capitalism that is at globalization's core (Slaughter and Rhoades, 2004). The driving assumption is that the organization needs to be more efficient and productive.

I mentioned that the first wave of globalization was simply the movement of students across borders. The number of students in the Asia-Pacific, for example, moving overseas for their university education almost doubled between 1999 and 2006 (Tierney and Findlay, 2008). To be sure, such increases will continue. The new wave of globalization, however, includes not merely teachers on the move but also programs, degrees and institutions. And 'movement' is not simply geographic travel but also participation enabled by improvements in technology and communication. The underlying ethos is one of competition; the World Trade Organization has estimated that the global market for education is well over US$30 billion. The Organization for Economic Co-operation and Development (OECD) estimates that there are now over 150 million students in tertiary education – a number that has doubled in ten years.

THE STATE AND HIGHER EDUCATION

Public Higher Education

A local state's role in higher education has been relatively straightforward until recently; the states had different kinds of institutions for different kinds of students. All states have three tiers of higher education institutions – community colleges, colleges/universities and elite research universities. We also have seen institutional isomorphism occur throughout the twentieth century such that a state teacher's college became a state college and then a state university and then a research university. Two-year community colleges eventually offered four-year degrees and the like. One challenge of the twentieth century was to differentiate the different sectors so that all institutions were not similar; at the same time, given that the institutions frequently catered to local clientele, there was a push for institutions to offer a full array of courses and degrees.

The primary job of these institutions has been to educate individuals, and that has been defined by the attainment of a degree. The idea of education as a socializing agent or as a way to instill civic values in individuals has largely been overlooked for at least a generation. Community colleges always have offered certificates for working-class jobs (such as plumbing) but they also frequently have been criticized because of their perceived large drop-out rates, non-completion rates, and low transfer rates to four-year institutions. The second-tier state universities have also offered master's degrees and the research universities have focused on graduate education. Most states have had a medical complex devoted to the training of physicians; this has contributed to the health and economic welfare of a state. Research, as an economic engine for a state, has varied significantly, with California particularly concerned about research and a state such as Mississippi showing virtual disregard for university-based research.

Although variations have occurred across states, the general principle throughout most of the twentieth century was that the state funded public institutions and a relatively small portion of a post-secondary institution's budget was dependent upon tuition or other revenue. Trends also varied by sector: virtually all of a community college and state university's budget derived from state support, whereas the elite public research universities have a history of attracting federal research dollars, primarily for science, and foundation support for a variety of research areas.

Over the last generation public institutions also have become involved in capital campaigns in much the same way as private universities have done in order to generate revenue from alumni and wealthy philanthropists. It is important to remember, however, that even in 1990 a majority of public research universities had never embarked on a capital campaign. When Pennsylvania State University announced at that time that it was going to have a $100 million capital campaign, it was the largest such campaign ever embarked on by a public institution; today, such a campaign would be thought of as trivial. Thus the sorts of activities that occur today are relatively new and a result of reduced revenue on the part of the state and increased demand for services by the university.

Inequality and Access

Although public higher education has in large part existed to aid those who could not afford private universities, an overt emphasis on lessening inequality and increasing access to higher education has not always been a specific force for public policy. For much of the first half of the twentieth century public higher education officials had a *laissez-faire* attitude toward using public colleges and universities as a vehicle for overcoming economic inequality. And in some states, especially in the south, there was an overt emphasis on keeping African-American students out of college. In general, however, the assumption was that if students found their way to campus, then they were educated. Those that did not make it to campus were not educated. The responsibility for applying to college largely rested with the individual and it was not the obligation of the state or institution to help the individual get to university.

Eventually the approach to who should go to college and whose responsibility it was to help people prepare for and apply to college changed. Although higher education was not yet seen as imperative, enough studies were done that pointed out the benefits of a well-educated workforce and the unfair advantages that existed for the economically better off that the state directed public institutions to take a more proactive stance toward inclusion. The GI Bill increased the participation of veterans returning from the Second World War, for example, and a variety of federal and state initiatives has occurred since the 1960s. Affirmative action, a policy designed to increase representation of people of color in higher education, had some success in enabling more faculty and students of color to be represented.

The strategy taken with most initiatives frequently was to make the benefit available to everyone. Financial policies, tuition benefits and the like were available to all citizens and not simply those who needed them. Thus, even though some private and public universities offered equivalent curricula with equally qualified faculty, tuition at the public institutions was dramatically discounted – not only for those who were unable to pay full tuition, but for the middle and upper classes as well. Again, the philosophy had been that the cost of tuition, as a public good, was the same regardless of income or location just as the cost of clean drinking water or protection from unsanitary conditions was the same.

Affirmative action was the exception to the rule. The underlying assumption of affirmative action was that a public good existed – higher education – that not all individuals could make use of in large part because students of color were underprepared. From the 1960s until the end of the twentieth century this policy was hotly debated by those who felt it provided unfair advantage for students of color, even though African Americans and Latinos were significantly underrepresented in higher education. By the beginning of the twenty-first century the policy had largely been downplayed in most states (such as Michigan) and eliminated in others (such as California). Although sharp discrepancies remained in college participation and graduation rates between the poor and the wealthy and among African-American, Latino, Anglo and Asian-American students at the end of the twentieth century, it is also true that significant participation and graduation increases had occurred, especially over the last half-century.

States currently pursue a schizophrenic policy toward access and equity. On the one hand, policies such as affirmative action have been defeated by proponents who argue that the state should have no role in what critics believe is social engineering. Admission to an institution, they claim, should be on the merits of one's test score, and the economic hardship that a person has faced or any racial discrimination that has occurred should nevertheless not affect admission policies. On the other hand, others argue that it is in the state's interest to find ways to improve achievement in a state's worst public schools; thus an increase in college-going among the poor and largely underrepresented students of color will occur.

Privatization

The shift from the idea that an organization should be the provider of a public good has opened the door to a significant increase in private providers and the privatization of public institutions. Currently the fastest-growing sector in higher education in the USA is for-profit colleges and universities (FPCUs) (Tierney and Hentschke, 2007). Although FPCUs have existed for over a century in the USA, until recently they were relatively small companies that offered one specific skill or trade such as cosmetology or welding. However, the largest institution in the USA is now the for-profit University of Phoenix. These institutions all have a similar funding model. They outsource the vast majority of their services (such as admissions) and standardize their curricula, teaching and learning across campuses. Courses are offered in areas that are convenient to students, such as shopping malls, and the courses are offered at convenient times for the working adult – evenings and weekends. Faculty are part-time; in general they do not receive health or retirement benefits, and they will be dismissed if there is a drop in enrollment in the classes that they teach or if their teaching evaluations are not excellent.

FPCUs rely largely on their ability to fill out paperwork for a student to apply for grants and loans from the federal and state governments. The result is that over 90 percent of the institution's income is generated from the fee-paying student, and the student's fees derive from the government. Ironically, then, the most private of our institutions thrive with, and most likely could not survive without, public funding. The difference, of course, is that these private for-profit companies pay taxes to the government and generate revenue for the owners or corporate boards. Students also graduate with greater debt loads than at comparable public and private non-profit institutions, the retention and graduation rates tend to be lower than at comparable institutions, and default rates on loans have been a significant issue.

The argument for for-profits has been made succinctly by Weisbrod et al. (2008, p. 4): 'Services that can be sold profitably do not need public subsidies.' From this perspective, education, defined as preparation for the job market, is a good that can be sold and a for-profit college can do it as well as or better than a publicly subsidized institution. The alternative argument, of course, is that education is more than vocational training and that the purpose of a public university is more than simply the selling of a service.

There is a vigorous debate about whether public institutions are receiving less revenue from the state government, or if these institutions are growing in areas that are irrelevant to the state, which makes it appear that the institution is receiving significantly less revenue when actually they are receiving stable funding for core activities. Regardless, whereas public institutions at one point relied almost entirely on the state government for their revenues, these same institutions now have diversified revenue streams – the state, donors and philanthropy, research grants from federal, state, local governments and foundations, extramural activities and tuition. Some public institutions receive less than 25 percent of their operating expenses from the state government. Occasionally a governor of a state, or a president of a public institution, has floated the idea of letting these institutions become entirely private, but no one has yet acted on the idea. More commonly a state has allowed a public institution to set its own tuition rates, purchase items without going through the state bureaucracy, or receive funds outside of the state system.

Nevertheless the public landscape is significantly different at the end of the first decade of the twenty-first century than it was a half-century ago. Privatization also has had an impact on the working conditions of the institutions. The USA now hires more non-tenure-track faculty than tenure-track; part-time faculty are more common in many institutions than full-time (tenure- or non-tenure-track) faculty. Because public institutions still rely on a part of their revenue from the state when the economic crisis of 2008–09 erupted, public institutions had more significant problems than private non-profit institutions and especially for-profit colleges and universities. Many faculty at public institutions were furloughed, as were public employees, which resulted in a loss in many states of about 10 percent of a professor's salary.

Private institutions had similar problems. However, because their losses were largely restricted to endowment income, they did not face a crisis with regard to their operating revenue. Because for-profit institutions have a low set cost for personnel, they were not impacted. None of the institutions faced a decrease in applicants; the result was that those institutions that relied on tuition revenue – for-profit and private non-profits – did better than those institutions that still existed in part through public funding. As I shall discuss, because of the loss of operating revenue, public institutions are now considering downsizing their enrollment whereas for-profits are gearing up for growth.

A consequence of privatization is greater managerial power and decision-making authority. Although private universities also function under the academic model of shared governance, it is fair to say that the diminution of the 'public' nature of an institution increases the voice of administrators and reduces that of the academic staff. As Douglass (2009, p. 9) has observed, the consequences of globalization are 'broader authority for university presidents, including greater authority in budget management and administrative authority'. Democratic principles of decision-making are not so much eschewed or reputed but simply overlooked in the rush to make decisions so that the organization is more efficient.

Regulation

One might think that a decrease in funding makes a public institution less dependent on state demands, but as state funding has decreased as an absolute percentage of overall revenue, state regulatory control has increased – for public institutions. However, state regulation of for-profit institutions has been relatively weak and it has been subject to effective lobbying efforts by their industry.

Until recently the state had been relatively uninvolved in the regulation of post-secondary institutions. Regulation had been ceded to accrediting bodies – both institutional and professional. What a college or university offered and how quality was defined had been granted to the institution in general and in particular the faculty. Regional accreditation, although critically important, simply demonstrated minimal levels of institutional competence. Without accreditation an institution's degree was relatively worthless, although many institutions, especially for-profit institutions, have existed without it. The lack of accreditation, however, meant that the students could not receive federal or state loans and grants, and that if they wished to transfer to another institution, their degree and institutional credits would not be accepted.

Although state legislatures always have taken on 'hot-button' curricular issues from time to time – queer theory, Afro-centric literature, women's studies and the like – in general the state has stayed away from regulatory control. Presidents created budget requests and the legislature approved all or some portion of it. Line-item vetoes or oversight of a particular course offering was generally not done. To be sure, at times special requests occurred. The state may have decided that a particular focus was important, or a legislator simply wanted some particular center or institute at the post-secondary institution in his or her political district, but the overarching assumption was that the post-secondary institutions knew best how to lead their institutions.

Over the last generation that assumption has gradually changed. Accreditation has come under attack as being too weak and too slow, and technological changes have challenged geographically based accrediting agencies. If a public, private or for-profit institution is based in Nebraska but has an online master's degree that students in New York are taking, from which region of the country should the degree be given accreditation? If someone wants to be a veterinarian, is it more important for the institution to have accreditation from a state agency or one with broader reach, possibly beyond national borders? As Duderstadt and Womack (2003, p. 76) have pointed out, 'Higher education is breaking loose from the moorings of physical campuses, even as its credentialing monopoly begins to erode.' The result is that, on the one hand we are seeing the market replace regulatory control, while on the other the state is asking for greater oversight of those diminishing public dollars that they provide.

Higher education, then, is evolving like other deregulated industries such as healthcare, where we see public and profit-making hospitals; we also experience all the strengths and weaknesses of the market and deregulation, such as we have recently experienced in the banking and housing industries. The general winner of deregulation is for-profit companies that have viewed accrediting bodies as exclusionary gatekeepers. Critics charge, however, that precisely at the time that the state is adding regulatory burdens to public institutions they are weakening their oversight capacity of other institutions and as a result putting the consumer at risk.

The shift away from the creation, sustenance and support of a public good reflects shifts with other goods and services for the state such that the state no longer sees itself as a purveyor of public goods. A consistent, and radical, line of thinking is that the state federal government's regulatory role should also be negligible. The housing crisis and sub-prime mortgage loans in the USA reflect a philosophy that says for capitalism to flourish, markets need to be unregulated. FPCUs have made the same sort of argument, and have largely succeeded. They would argue, as most proponents of such arguments argue, that there is still too much regulation. Their argument is that if problems exist, they will fix the problems, and do not need regulation to hamper their efforts. The consumer (student) only buys 'good' products, so it is in the organization's interest to police the quality of the product. Although there is some truth to such an assertion, it does not take into account a history of malfeasance by companies that have shown little regard or concern for the customer.

Ironically public institutions have faced a twofold problem. They have been criticized as the opposite of consumer-friendly. Because they presumably receive a steady stream of revenue that is impervious to consumer demands, the argument has been made that they are out of touch and exist to support the academic staff rather than the students. Because of this perception, steps have been taken to regulate them and to make demands with regard to admissions, retention, graduation, time to degree and a host of other issues.

An additional point worth mentioning relates to transnational agreements and the like. Discussions about Bologna, GATS and other similar protocols have been of some importance in Europe, Australia and Asia (Hartmann, 2008). International rankings such as those of Shanghai and Times Higher Education also account for a good deal of commentary and analysis outside of the USA. Although there has been some discussion about Bologna – either as a dire warning that the country had best pay attention, or rather that something can be learnt from the processes (Adelman, 2009) – in general transnational regulations and evaluations continue to play a relatively minor role in post-secondary deliberations in the USA. To be sure, rankings are important – but the rankings that Americans obsess about have to do with US-based institutions in *US News and World Report*, not with international rankings. Institutions may worry about federal regulations or try to weaken accreditation, but Bologna remains relatively unimportant.

KNOWLEDGE-BASED ECONOMIES AND RESEARCH

The country's approach to research is odd insofar as the majority of the revenue derives from federal agencies – the National Institutes of Health, the National Science Foundation and the like – but those agencies distribute monies to state agencies or to institutions located in states. Some states have been more aggressive in creating a research policy for the state (such as Texas), whereas other state efforts have been negligible (for example, North Dakota). Because of the economic downturn, states and cities also have adopted what to some is a short-sighted approach where either they can reduce revenue to public research universities (such as Arizona) when all budgets need to be cut, or they have considered taxing post-secondary institutions (for example, Pittsburgh).

One of the dilemmas of American research policy is that it is state-based and generally institution-based. Research goes hand in hand with the concomitant activities of any university – teaching and learning, outreach and the like. Thus states rarely decide issues of research need without related discussions about upsizing or downsizing its post-secondary system. The creation of more community colleges, for example, may serve the needs of a local community with regard to serving additional students, but it has nothing to do with the state's research capacity. Similarly, adding a state university may increase the bachelor's degree production of the state but it will have little direct impact on its research infrastructure.

The addition of a research university presumably should have something to do with an increased research capacity; more often than not, however, such an addition has to do with creating another elite institution for a state where full-time traditionally aged students may attend. Because research universities have doctoral education and other institutions do not, they are generally more expensive to staff. Academic staff teach less than their colleagues at state universities and community colleges, classes are smaller, and more monies go to support a research infrastructure. Although a state may be well advised to increase the number of research universities that exist, or to enable a state university to become a research university, such decisions generally have little to do with any decision about whether the state's research infrastructure is adequate to meet the needs of the state's strategic plans.

CALIFORNIA AND THE STATE OF GLOBALIZATION

Throughout much of the twentieth century California was looked on as the state with the best higher education system in the country (University of California – UC). Its research universities, especially UC Berkeley and UC Los Angeles, were thought of as among the best post-secondary institutions in the world. The California State University system served more students and produced more bachelor's degrees than any other state system in the country. The community college system was elaborate and served all potential students throughout the state so that anyone had geographic access to higher education. California had private universities that were consistently ranked in the top 100 – Stanford, California Technology, the University of Southern California. The state also had more universities than any other state that were members of the AAU – the country's elite association of premier research institutions. California also had many small elite liberal arts colleges with storied traditions – the so-called Claremont colleges.

Because of the elaborated post-secondary system, a state government that viewed research as part of an economic engine, and the wealth and size of the state, California received a significant amount of research funding from the federal government and foundations. Silicon Valley succeeded in part because of its proximity to post-secondary institutions, most importantly Stanford University. Perhaps what is most remarkable in all of this is that the state rose to eminence in a relatively short time period. Few post-secondary institutions existed in the 1880s, and not until after the Second World War could the state begin to boast of a successful system of colleges and universities.

Most point to the state's Master Plan as the progenitor of excellence. The Master Plan is a half-century old and focused exclusively on access to higher education for the state's citizens. The assumption was that an educated citizenry benefited the state and, regardless of income, individuals should be allowed to gain a post-secondary degree in one of the three state systems – community college, state university or research university. The Master Plan made no comment on the state's need for a research infrastructure or the role of private colleges and universities, much less that of for-profit institutions.

Although the Master Plan clearly had shortcomings, the assumptions in it were clear and it worked relatively well up until the last decade. Universities have been bound by size constraints, however, and as the state's population grew, the system struggled with how to expand. Although explicit forms of discrimination did not exist, the poor and minority communities had a much higher participation rate in community colleges than in the system's best institutions. Sustained and systemic transfer from the community college to four-year institutions never succeeded. By the start of the twenty-first century a much higher percentage of high-school students aspired to go to college than had in 1960, and working adults also wanted additional educational services but they were also less prepared than their predecessors. For-profit higher education became the fastest-growing sector in the state but its growth was largely ignored by the legislature – both to help alleviate the overcrowding in the public system and to regulate alleged practices that short-changed the consumer.

How the state responded to the enrollment crisis, however, was to build more campuses. And the creation of new campuses occurred not only in growth areas but also in locations that met the needs of the state's politicians, but not necessarily higher education. Nevertheless the assumption remained that the obligation of the state was to continue to provide a public good to the citizenry, and the manner in which that good was to be delivered was via a public organization. Although tuition had been implemented by a verbal sleight-of-hand known as 'fees', the cost of attending a public post-secondary institution was among the lowest in the country. Private non-profit and for-profit institutions were able to set their costs to whatever the market allowed, but public institutions provided below-market cost and the state subsidized the costs of the institution.

Research as a post-secondary function remained important, if not more so, but the focus had less to do with research policy than with political and fiscal imperatives. That is, the state created a new research university but it placed the institution in a remote part of the state to meet political needs rather than to enhance the state's research capacity. As state funding slowed, the importance of attracting external funding via research also increased. Whether the state actually needed to increase its research capacity was divorced from how the post-secondary system responded to the more pressing needs of enrollment expansion and fiscal contraction.

Although some of what I have outlined above remains as a state obligation, what is currently being experienced in California is something new, and I attribute it to the impact of globalization as an economic, cultural and social force. The state has moved away from the assumption that it is the state's obligation to fund post-secondary institutions and instead is moving toward funding individuals in much the way as in primary and secondary education. The result is that through a confluence of forces the state has significantly increased the cost of higher education – approximately 50 percent over the last 12 months. The cost is likely to increase even further as state revenues continue to decrease and the costs of the public institutions continue to increase.

Academic staff have made minimal use of technology to radically alter their style of teaching. As opposed to the manner in which an individual conducts his or her research, which has been significantly impacted by technology, professors teach their classes in much the same manner as a decade ago, even though class size has increased. Classes begin and end according to an academic calendar. Summer is still a time for students and staff to leave the campus. Courses are more similar in their temporal nature than different, and graduation continues to revolve around the accumulation of credits. In short, the public post-secondary system has not adapted to technological changes that the consumer increasingly desires.

For-profit higher education, however, has adapted and the result is that it is increasing its market share and waging a relatively effective campaign that the higher education market needs to be opened up rather than constrained. Curiously, the state maintains a desire to increase access to higher education, but how access gets defined is changing.

California is rapidly increasing the number of charter schools students may attend and they are providing funding for students to attend non-public schools that were unheard of a generation ago. Because the public higher education system is being privatized and students may use funds to attend private non-profit and for-profit post-secondary institutions, there is also an assumption that students should and can take on increased debt burdens when they complete their degrees. The state has moved from providing grants to students to making available low-interest loans.

In large part the state maintains an ideology that higher education should be available for its citizens, but the underlying philosophy is that the state's role is not to provide those organizations but instead to assure that a panoply of types of organizations exists in the marketplace. Rather than an organization as a public good we now have that public good functioning within a market by private providers, and the role of the state is to enable the consumer with some sort of funding, and to regulate those providers in some fashion.

Those who have been most upset with this shift are not the consumers but the providers – academic staff and the administrations of the public universities. Public employees have seen their wages decrease and their numbers decline. Pension plans, once thought of as untouchable, are likely to be reduced or even eliminated for academic staff. Insofar as healthcare is not mandatory for temporary staff and casual workers, the costs for healthcare are increasingly shifted from the organization to the individual. Many divisions and departments of the universities have felt increasing pressure to pay for the unit's employees; department chairs try to endow their departments by way of gifts from wealthy donors. Basic services such as telephones and janitorial services have been eliminated or dramatically cut back at public universities. Class sizes have increased and some classes have been eliminated.

The largest concerns with privatization are that the university is becoming a glorified trade school where business programs, computer science degrees and the like attract external support at the expense of the humanities and poorer professional schools. Further, when donors 'buy' departments through naming rights, there is also a concern that academic freedom has been compromised. The ability of the university to be a critic of societies becomes compromised when academic survival depends upon those who will bankroll the organization.

One may reasonably ask if all of these changes are due to globalization. Because the term is so porous and multiple actions get attributed to it, doesn't everything fall under its umbrella? Such a question is certainly fair, but consider for a moment if the opposite trends were occurring. Assume, for example, the following was happening in California:

> Tuition was still non-existent and the state paid all costs for an elaborated public post-secondary system. The regional accrediting association acted in a manner to keep for-profit providers from entering. The purpose of a degree was as much concerned with enhancing citizenship and the love of learning as preparation for the workforce. Academic staff taught classes at a time and format that was standardized and students took four years to gain a degree.

Such a sketch is from another time in history and seems outdated today. Although we might claim that such a portrait is what should happen, it is impossible to envision in large part because of globalization's philosophical and practical force. Consider two taxation policies and their result. The state has moved toward a stance that rejects higher taxes in favor of the individual retaining more of his or her income. California also has a regressive tax code that does not place burdens on those who can most afford it – the upper class. The result is that the state is currently unable to meet its fiscal obligations. One of those obligations is a healthy public system.

If the state simply took in the same percentage of sales revenue that it made in 1968, we would not have a deficit and would be able to fund higher education. Why have the state's sales revenues plunged? It is not because we are selling fewer goods, but rather that consumers are free to buy products and services over the Internet and pay no sales tax. In the USA, if an individual buys a book online, for example, he or she pays no sales tax; if the consumer bought that book in a Los Angeles bookstore, he or she would pay a 10 percent sales tax. The result is that consumers have fled local businesses in favor of online shopping. Further, since 1994 the citizens, spurred on by conservative politicians, have repealed tax after tax; the primary beneficiary has been the wealthy. If we still had every tax in place that we had in 1994, we would be able to balance the budget and envision a different post-secondary system.

Similarly, if technology had not made learning possible in radically different formats and modalities, then staple pedagogies might have sufficed. But globalization has speeded up the temporal nature of learning and enabled students to learn in manifold manners and not simply by way of a seat in a classroom. The impact of free trade agreements on the USA in general, and California in particular, is that a vocational trade or simply a high-school degree will no longer suffice to ensure a livable wage. The state also has to import workers from other countries (primarily China and India) and other states to fill professional jobs in science and engineering. The result is that higher education is a growth industry. The public system no longer can be the sole primary provider, and in its stead will be a largely privatized system with multiple providers. Such a system suggests a dramatically different role for the state from what has gone before.

The state changes from being the protector and provider of a public good to that of a player in a market. The state may be a significant player in that market, but so are Microsoft and Google. In part the state tries to regulate in a manner akin to the country's Food and Drug Administration or Environmental Protection Agency. And yet even seemingly neutral agencies that are supposed to protect the public against dangerous foods or a hazard in the environment have different regulatory stands based on the political party that is in power. The same will be said of the state's regulatory role with regard to higher education. Indeed, during the current Republican Administration in California the state's law on how to regulate for-profit higher education lapsed for a year and then, when a new bill was approved, it lacked any strength other than to monitor what is taking place and to make recommendations. The legislation did not provide any agency with the ability to curtail and sanction those for-profit companies that were in violation of state rules and policies.

THE FUTURE OF HIGHER EDUCATION

If the portrait that I have painted is true, then we are on a particular trajectory that has clear implications. Participation in higher education is likely to increase although students will go to multiple types of institutions and incur greater debt. Learning will take place in multiple formats and not be tied down to a specific timeframe. Vocational and professional training will rise in importance and liberal learning will fall even further in demand. States are likely to have a circumscribed strategic plan for research to be conducted by a narrow band of institutions rather than having research done by multiple actors in multiple organizations. The state will see its role as more closely aligned with modest regulation rather than with being a purveyor of a public good.

In turn, fewer academic staff will be full-time and tenure-track. Faculty will have differentiated roles based on institutional type, and the demand for graduate-level training will decrease. The lessening of the social role for universities and academic staff suggests that universities will play less the role of social critic of the state and instead be more closely aligned with consumer demands and trends. Academic freedom will be less, and in turn academic staff will be less likely to speak out on issues crucial to a democracy. To a critic of these changes, the university will have become more commercial and its core purposes will have been corroded such that training will be substituted for education. To a supporter of the changes, the university will be more entrepreneurial, more focused and more efficient.

Whether these trends are ultimately good or bad for a democracy remains to be seen. But it is apparent that they are happening, so we should at least make some sort of decision that we want them to happen rather than simply drift along either as an unthinking advocate for reform or as a naysayer romantically recalling the days before globalization came into our lexicon.

REFERENCES

Adelman, C. (2009), *The Bologna Process for US Eyes: Re-learning Higher Education in the Age of Convergence*, Washington, DC: Institute for Higher Education Policy.

Douglass, J. (2009), *Higher Education's New Global Order: How and Why Governments are Creating Structured Opportunity Markets*, Berkeley, CA: Center for Studies in Higher Education.

Duderstadt, J. and F. Womack (2003), *The Future of the Public University in America: Beyond the Crossroads*, Baltimore, MD: The Johns Hopkins University Press.

Findlay, C. and W. Tierney (eds) (2010), *Globalization and Tertiary Education in the Asia Pacific: The Changing Nature of a Dynamic Market*, Singapore: World Scientific.

Gutek, G. (2006), *American Education in a Global Society: International and Comparative Perspectives*, Long Grove, IL: Waveland Press.

Hartmann, E. (2008), 'Bologna goes global: a new imperialism in the making?', *Globalisation, Societies, and Education*, **6** (3), 207–20.

Kaul, I., I. Grunberg and M. Stern (1999), 'Defining global public goods', in I. Kaul, I. Grunberg and M. Stern (eds), *Global Public Goods*, New York: Oxford University Press, pp. 2–19.

McKinsey and Company (2009), *The Economic Impact of the Achievement Gap in America's Schools*, New York: McKinsey.

Mok, K.H. (2005), 'Globalization and educational restructuring: university merging and changing governance in China', *Higher Education*, **50** (1), 57–88.

Slaughter, S. and G. Rhoades (2004), *Academic Capitalism and the New Economy: Markets, State, and Higher Education*, Baltimore, MD: Johns Hopkins University Press.

Thurow, L. (2000), 'Globalization: the product of a knowledge-based economy', *Annals of the American Academy of Political and Social Science*, **570**, 19–31.

Tierney, W.G. and C. Findlay (2008), *The Globalization of Education: The Next Wave*, Singapore: Pacific Economic Cooperation Council and the Association of Pacific Rim Universities.

Tierney, W.G., and G. Hentschke (2007), *New Players, Different Game: Understanding the Rise of For-profit Colleges and Universities*, Baltimore, MD: Johns Hopkins University Press.

Walker, J. (2009), 'Time as the fourth dimension in the globalization of higher education', *The Journal of Higher Education*, **80** (5), 483–509.
Weisbrod, B., J. Ballou and E. Asch (2008), *Mission and Money: Understanding the University*, New York: Cambridge University Press.

21 The strange death of the liberal university: research assessments and the impact of research
Mark Olssen

INTRODUCTION

The changes to higher education inaugurated in the UK in the early 1980s as a result of the election of Margaret Thatcher's Conservative government ushered in a sea-change in how the public sector was to be managed, and of the role of government in relation to public spending. The broad faith in the state's grandmotherly role of 'guidance and governance', typified in the economic sphere by Keynesian demand management, was replaced by a range of new economic, financial, administrative and political perspectives whose central common assumptions can be seen as constituted by a particular strain of liberal thought referred to most often as 'neoliberalism' (Burchell et al., 1991, 1996; Rose, 1993, 1996). The central defining characteristic of this new brand of liberalism was based on an application of the logic and rules of the market to the public sector. While it bore some similarities to the central tenets of classical liberalism, particularly classical economic liberalism, it was also different from it.

Indeed, understanding the differences between neo- and classical liberal discourse provides an important key to understanding the distinctive nature of the neoliberal revolution as experienced throughout much of the western world in the last three decades. Whereas classical liberalism represents a negative conception of state power in that the individual was taken as an object to be freed from the interventions of the state, neoliberalism has come to represent a positive conception of the state's role in creating the appropriate market by providing the conditions, laws and institutions necessary for its operation. In classical liberalism the individual is characterized as having an autonomous human nature and can practice freedom.

In neoliberalism the state seeks to create an individual who is an enterprising and competitive entrepreneur. In the classical model the theoretical aim of the state was to limit and minimize its role based upon postulates that included: (1) universal egoism (the self-interested individual); (2) invisible-hand theory, which meant that the interests of the individual are also the interests of society as a whole; and (3) the political maxim of *laissez-faire*. In the shift from classical liberalism to neoliberalism, then, a further element is added, for such a shift involved a change in subject position from *homo economicus*, who naturally behaves out of self-interest and is relatively detached from the state, to 'manipulatable man', who is created by the state and who is continually encouraged to be 'perpetually responsive'. It is not that the conception of the self-interested subject is replaced or done away with by the new ideals of 'neoliberalism', but that in an age of universal welfare the perceived possibilities of slothful indolence create necessities for new forms of vigilance, surveillance, performance appraisal, accountability, and new forms of professional monitoring and control. Traditional ideas of professional autonomy, for doctors, health professions, as well as academics and others are checked as the state takes it upon itself to keep us all up to the mark. The state will see to it that each one of us makes a 'continual enterprise of ourselves' (Gordon, 1991) in what seems to be a process of 'governing without governing' (Rose, 1993).

As Graham Burchell (1996, pp. 23–4) puts this point, while for classical liberalism the basis of government conduct is in terms of 'natural, private-interest-motivated conduct of free, market-exchanging individuals', for neoliberalism 'the rational principle for regulating and limiting governmental activity must be determined by reference to artificially-arranged or contrived forms of free, entrepreneurial, and competitive conduct of economic-rational individuals'. This means that for neoliberal perspectives the end goals of freedom, choice, consumer sovereignty, competition and individual initiative, as well as those of compliance and obedience, must be constructions of the state acting now in its positive role through the development of the techniques of auditing, accounting and management. It is these techniques, as Barry et al. (1996, p. 14) put it:

> [that] enable the marketplace for services to be established as 'autonomous' from central control. Neoliberalism, in these terms, involves less a retreat from governmental 'intervention' than a re-inscription of the techniques and forms of expertise required for the exercise of government.

One of the major neoliberal theories concerned to extend market approaches to the restructuring of the public sector, including higher education, is public choice theory. The school of public choice advocates the application of economic theories to public sector institutions in the interest of making public organizations subject to the same costs and benefits as operate in the private sector. In part this was aimed at rendering academics accountable. In this, public choice theory (PCT) represents an application of economic models and theories to politics on the assumption that economic behavior (that of *homo economicus*) describes the true state of human nature and thus is applicable to all aspects of life.

The central figure in the 'economics of politics' is James Buchanan, who from 1969 was Professor of Economics and Director of the Center for Study of Public Choice at the Virginia Polytechnic Institute, Blacksburg, Virginia. A member of the Mont Pelerin Society and of the Institute of Economic Affairs advisory council, Buchanan describes PCT as 'the application and extension of economic theory to the realm of political or governmental choices' (1978, p. 3). In Buchanan's view, economics could not be independent of a theory of institutional politics. By this was meant that economics must also take on board the institutional framework of rules and procedures that are responsible for the governance of human relationships and formulate theories as to how these should operate.

A major influence on Buchanan's distinctively institutional approach to economics and politics, and especially his dissatisfaction with public finance theory, was the nineteenth-century Swedish economist Knut Wicksell. In addition he was influenced by the political theories on voting behavior of Duncan Black (especially his work on committees) and Kenneth Arrow (on social welfare). Impressed by Arrow's argument that a consistent social welfare function for a society could not be derived from individual preferences, Buchanan came to accept his view that any coherent social welfare approach must inevitably entail the imposition of will of some members or groups over others.

Hence he effectively denied the efficacy or utility of the concept of the 'public interest'. In analyzing how public goods were supposed to emerge from individual self-interested behavior, Buchanan's achievement was to abolish any notion of the public interest or public good altogether, claiming that it could not be derived from the disaggregated self-interests of individuals.[1]

Central to the abolition of notions of the public interest, or public good, are several interrelated arguments and ideas concerning the relationship between economics and politics. At the most general level is the application of neoclassical analysis to non-market situations by which the public sector was redescribed as an economic market. In what can only be described as a supreme arrogance of economists during the postwar era, economic rather than political models were utilized to explain and account for political society and political conduct. As Buchanan and Tullock (1962, p. 250) explain:

> One of the great advantages of an essentially economic approach to collective action lies in the implicit recognition that political exchange, at all levels, is basically equivalent to economic exchange.

With Hayek and Friedman, Buchanan characterizes economics as a process of 'catallaxy'; that is, of the voluntary exchange of goods and services between competing individuals. Lying behind such an analysis is a strong normative commitment to free market individualism, which for Buchanan provides a common rationality linking the economic and political worlds. Political action is represented as being governed by the same interests and motivation that govern the market. This libertarian quality of Buchanan's work is reflected also in his deeply individualist approach to public affairs. As far as political prospects were concerned, only those that resulted from the subjective choices of individuals were acceptable. Collective entities such as a 'society' or 'the public interest' were held not to exist because they were reducible to individual experiences. This 'methodological individualism' was fundamental to Buchanan's reduction of collective entities such as the public good to the dispositions and motivations of individuals and their reconceptualization in market terms. In *The Calculus of Consent*, for example, 'the whole calculus has meaning only if methodological individualism is accepted' (Buchanan and Tullock, 1962, p. 265). PCT is ruled by the imperative of a strict methodological individualism in which 'all theorizing, all analysis, is resolved finally into considerations faced by the individual person as decisionmaker' (Buchanan, 1975, p. ix).

It is on this basis that PCT attacks as 'myth' the idea that government or public service is able to serve the public good. Influenced by William Niskansen's work on 'bureaucratic growth', Anthony Downs's pioneering work on 'political parties', Mancur Olson's work on 'interest groups' and Gordon Tullock's writing on 'rent-seeking' behavior, it asserts the view that the notion of the public good is a fiction that cloaks the opportunistic behavior of bureaucrats and politicians as they seek to expand their bureaux, increase their expenditures and maximize their own personal advantages. In *The Limits of Liberty* (1975), Buchanan maintains that a coincidence of interests between the civil servant's private interests and their conception of the public interest ensues, such that 'within the constraints that he faces the bureaucrat tends to maximize his own utility' (ibid., p. 161).

If preferences are inherently subjective, then they cannot be known and transferred into a collective value judgment, such as a public good, for such a notion neglects the rights of consumers, whose interests the public service and politicians are meant to serve, but do not. In *The Calculus of Consent* (1962), Buchanan and Tullock continue the theme, arguing that as public officials have neither the desire nor knowledge to further the public interest, it is foolish to establish policy on the basis that they will do so. Because they act selfishly, they bend public purposes to their private interests, and on this basis public officials cannot be trusted with public power. Buchanan and Tullock (1962, p. 317, note t) cite Wicksell, who stated that 'it is easy for capable but unprincipled politicians to exploit the party constellations of the day for the purpose of swelling public expenditure far beyond the amount corresponding to the collective interest of the people'.[2] Acting in the public interest is therefore, they claim, always wasteful. In Chapter 10 of *The Calculus of Consent* (1962) they claim that for farmers to act collectively to build and repair roads results in double the expenditure than if they each acted individually to pay only for the roading that each wanted.

Repeatedly throughout *The Calculus of Consent* Buchanan and Tullock claim that the public interest does not exist; that public authorities do not in fact promote it; and that claims to do so disguise mechanisms for advancing private interests. In their book the usual forms of public action are replaced by disaggregated individual interests represented as private. In this, as Brian Barry argues, in his influential book *Political Argument* (1990, p. 256), Buchanan and Tullock 'aim to destroy a whole tradition of political theorizing'. Essentially, 'the public has no place in their world'. This is the tradition that recognizes the existence and 'promotion of widely-shared common interests – public interests – the most important reason for the existence of public authorities'.

Characteristic of Buchanan's neoliberal approach is a distrust of *laissez-faire* on the condition that free markets would reach some form of equilibrium. Although the classical liberal tradition stressed the role of markets as 'self-regulating' and was supported by arguments based on the freedom of the individual from the state, Buchanan so distrusted the view that the required efficiency gains would emerge through automatic mechanisms of the market that he supported efficiency achievements through a tightening of state control. As he says (1975, p. 194n) in his criticism of Hayek:

> My basic criticism of F. A. Hayek's profound interpretation of modern history and his diagnosis for improvement is directed at his apparent belief or faith that social evolution will, in fact, ensure the survival of efficient institutional forms. Hayek is so distrustful of man's explicit attempts of reforming institutions that he accepts uncritically the evolutionary alternative.

In this, Buchanan introduced a major shift from liberal to neoliberal governmentality – from a naturalist faith in markets to an anti-naturalistic thesis that expresses a much greater faith in conscious political action to legitimate the 'long over-due task of institutional over-haul' (see Reisman, 1990, p. 74). It was on this ground that he opposed Hayek's naturalist faith in markets as spontaneous self-ordering systems. In Buchanan's view the state should increase accountability of individuals and institutions in order to promote efficiency in market terms. This insufficiently recognized element of neoliberalism gives us a poignant insight into the state-directed nature of public sector reforms throughout the western world from the 1980s.

In disputing that civil servants served the public interest, Buchanan thus sought to develop quasi-market procedures to render such institutions efficient based on the classical economic model of individuals as 'self-interested appropriators'. Essentially this meant structuring institutions in terms of incentives and performance targets in order to appeal to their selfishness as individuals. Such performance targets were introduced in all areas of the public sector in the UK and the USA from the 1980s. There was of course considerable popular support for such policies. Indeed, denying the existence of the public good and appealing to models of the free market to structure public institutions was possible only because of a widespread view among the population at large, exploited and possibly promoted by Thatcher, that the public sector was characterized by inefficiency, incompetence and corruption.

At the operational or policy levels, then, PCT suggests redesigning public institutions to make them reflect more accurately the preferences of individuals. This involves counteracting the possible forms of 'capture' that serve to deflect the interests of public officials from the public's real needs. To do this, PCT advocates a variety of quasi-market strategies, such as contracting out services to the private sector, increasing competition between units within the public sector, placing all potentially conflicting responsibilities into separate institutions, separating the commercial and non-commercial functions of the state, separating the advisory, regulatory and delivery functions into different agencies, as well as introducing an assortment of accountability and monitoring techniques and strategies aimed to overcome all possible sources of corruption and bias, particularly those arising from the pursuit of self-interest. It is on this basis, too, that public sector reforms relating to health, security or education have sought to restructure the basis of accountability through notions tied to individually attached incentives and targets, and through periodic monitoring and assessment through audits.

RESEARCH ACCOUNTABILITY IN THE UK AND NEW ZEALAND

PCT and other neoliberal theories were adopted in the UK with the election of the Thatcher government in 1979. In the domain of higher education one of the first major new external mechanisms introduced to increase accountability was in the area of research. The UK government asked the UK funding councils to devise a means to assess research output and quality. One of the primary reasons given was to inform funding council allocations of the grant for research. The first Research Assessment Exercise (RAE) was implemented in 1986, just seven years after Margaret Thatcher achieved power. Prior to this higher education had operated much in the way that Philip Auger (2000) saw 'gentlemanly capitalism' operating: that is, according to ideas of 'public duty' and 'professional autonomy' that were largely immune from accountability, surveillance or competition of any sort. Jokes and rumors about academics who exploited the conditions of their tenure, or even of reasonable credibility, kept many a journalist gainfully employed.[3]

The idea that some form of individualized accountability was necessary had been debated for some considerable time. When Margaret Thatcher invited James Buchanan to London, he talked freely about public servants and academics as freely exploiting the conditions of their offices while hiding behind notions of 'public duty' or 'professionalism', and as indulging repeatedly in 'rent-seeking behavior'. Anecdotal 'evidence' of shirking, free-riding, slothfulness or corruption led many to agree that an increased level of accountability was warranted (Curtis, 2007).

The UK's Research Assessment Exercise (RAE) became a model to be followed by many other countries, including Australia and New Zealand. The RAE in the UK was first implemented in 1986 and then in 1989, 1992, 1996, 2001 and 2008. In Australia there have been two major phases: first the Research Quality Framework (RQF) initiated by the (Conservative) coalition government under John Howard from 2004 to 2007, followed by the Excellence in Research for Australia (ERA) strategy from 2008 by the Labor government. In New Zealand the Performance Based Research Framework (PBRF) was introduced first in 2003 and has subsequently been implemented in 2006.[4] The main elements assessed include quality evaluation (60 percent), degree completions (25 percent), and external research income (15 percent).

The main difference between the RAE and the PBRF is the unit of analysis. Whereas for the RAE it is the 'unit of assessment' (UoA), for the PBRF it is the individual academic researcher. While both counted individual researcher outputs, the RAE was more 'thematic' and it was not possible to identify individual researchers within particular UoAs.[5] Although these mainly correlated with 'disciplines', universities maintained some flexibility in terms of how their submissions were organized, and could take more disparate groups of academics, perhaps from a variety of fields, and enter them in a suitably generic UoA (such as European Studies).The PBRF, by contrast, by focusing on individual researchers rather than on departments or institutions, had greater significance in relation to individual researcher careers. Beyond this important difference the methods employed were similar: both sought to assess local/national and international impacts; both assessed student degrees awarded and postgraduate research activity and supervisions; and both assessed external research funding, esteem indicators and research outputs. Both operate centralized funding models and adopt a systematic appraisal of research within a defined geographical domain in order to determine and legitimize the competitive allocation of money on performance-based criteria.

The RAE was implemented in order to survey the quantity and scope of research conducted in UK universities, to provide data for the distribution of funding through the funding councils. When initially introduced the stated purposes related to accountability and efficiency, to gauge resource allocation and improve decision-making, and to assist with governance generally. Later RAEs maintained essentially similar aims and rationales. The process was managed and implemented by the agencies responsible for funding UK higher education. Each UoA supported a panel of reviewers comprising expert peer reviewers from across the disciplinary areas. Academics were 'returnable' based on four pieces of research, self-nominated and published over the six years (2000–2007 for the 2008 RAE) proceeding the RAE assessment. The criteria used by the panels included originality, significance and rigor. In later RAEs work was also codified in terms of 'quality', 'excellence', 'international' and 'robustness'.

Accountability and efficiency meant a system of justification for expenditures and decisions based on the results from research. It was argued by its supporters that such a centralized system provided a criterion of cost-effectiveness for expenditure on higher education at the national level, at the level of institutions, at the level of universities, university faculties, and departments, and at the level of individual researchers. It assessed research outputs, research grants, research projects or programs, individual departments, or faculties as well as institutions, disciplines and policies. It also provided a standard for resource allocation, in order to attract further resources by institution and a justification for the allocation of scarce resources. It thus established a criterion or standard for national priority-setting, a competitive basis for the allocation of funding, and a system whereby the value or benefits of research could be quantified and future improvement could be assured. In this sense assessment served as a central mechanism for the 'knowledge economy'. In terms of learning and knowledge, the purposes were both formative (improved research, better research) and summative (a quantitative overview of research and its quality for the purposes of funding).

It was also argued that the RAE sharpened the quality and the focus of research (Gordon, 2005; Currie, 2008), led to improved management of research (Elton, 2000), increased the quality and quantity of journal article placements (Hare, 2003), and made research more internationally competitive (Currie, 2008). Such assessment thus enables a quantitative expression of value for money spent compared to other areas of state spending. In this sense, such assessment techniques served as mechanisms enabling the establishment of quasi-market processes for the public sector. In the modern global economy few today would argue that this is not important. While institutions were allowed and even encouraged to preserve their distinctiveness, this would not cancel the possibility of common descriptors being applied across all institutional and disciplinary units.

Notwithstanding a general consensus as to the need for accountability, criticisms of the particular approach employed or the way such processes are carried out also abound. As Brian Finsden (2008, p. 65) notes, the peer reviewers that constitute the expert panels mean essentially a system of

> subjective judgements and this subjectivity can change depending on who is making the judgement. Hence, who gets to read the actual individual pieces and make recommendations to the next level above can heavily influence the outcome.

That subjective valuations could make particular individual rankings unreliable became evident during the 'dummy runs' that individual universities organized as a practice before the final submission. Although in this sense one must be skeptical of particular individual attributions of research quality, it could be argued in defense that broader classifications, applying to whole departments, or to the more significant grading categories (pass/fail; <2 or >2) are less arbitrary, and less prone to error. (Therefore they are likely to have greater validity and reliability.)

Another criticism relates to the effect of national assessment monitoring on the internal work life and culture of higher education institutions. That such external accountability systems – based on peer assessments that seek to rank academics on a scale – substantially increase anxiety has been well documented (Barnett, 2000; Bates, 2003; Currie, 2008; Coryn et al., 2007; Sharp, 2004). Clearly, where individual assessments are the end result, as in the PBRF in New Zealand, this will be even more the case. The competitive nature of the process, together with the complexity of compliance at the university, faculty, department and individual level, will not only affect anxiety and stress but also research productivity itself. Arguably it places too much emphasis on productivity and performativity, encourages dubious research tactics and strategies for maximizing publications, citations and team-based research, and from the individual researcher's viewpoint encourages conformity to the system of external expectations concerning research.

Because such systems of assessment are regarded, even by their perpetrators, as contingent, that is, most likely subject to change next time round, it could be argued that they encourage norms that are transient and not of enduring benefit to anyone involved. The phenomenon of 'shifting goal posts' can already be seen in the pre-RAE emphasis on 'original publications', which in many universities gave way after the process to a new dominant concern with 'funded applications for research'. Such shifting concerns spread like a system of 'Mexican waves' across the sector, as academics everywhere responded to external levers. Similar reactions could be heard in the plaintive cries and anxieties as universities were forced into restructuring following the post-RAE funding allocations. What was apparent in the UK was that RAE assessments did not always appear to correlate with eventual funding to institutions.

The resultant effects on the internal life of academia, so closely paralleling the external decisions that caused them, are amplified even further by other external levers such as the National Student Survey (NSS). Again, while the evaluation of teaching is important, the way that the NSS is organized, as a national system, whereby disciplines from each university are ranked and compared, further engenders competition, as each individual department, faculty and university 'run[s] fast to stand still'.[6]

Clearly the way external auditing processes are organized impacts on the internal cultures of universities, and on the competitive ethos that now characterizes the relations between staff. As Craig Ashcroft and Richard Smith (2008, p. 50) note, research in such a model is fast becoming an 'academic production-line privileging certain types of activities, thereby reconstituting academic identities'. In his own doctoral research Ashcroft found that academics in New Zealand were overwhelmingly cynical about the process, promoting a new conformity and undermining academic freedom and autonomy. Indeed, the way such auditing is organized contributes to undermining the traditional autonomy and independence academics have traditionally had over selection and organization of their research. It also is radically altering the nature of academia as a career. As the Nobel laureate Harold Kroto (2010) states, '[t]oday in the UK young researchers often spend several years on research fellowships worrying about their future and how they will be able to continue to support their families if they do not make the grade'.

These are some of the ways that the academic career is being deprofessionalized. What it essentially amounts to is that a change in the system of accountability can be seen to impact strongly on the academic career. For Alis Oancea (2008, p. 157), 'the RAE model contributed to the routinization of formal, bureaucratic accountability, and hindered democratic dialogue among the research, practice and policy communities concerned'. She cites Stewart Ranson (2003, p. 460), who describes it as a 'revolution in accountability to preserve public trust'. Ranson (ibid., pp. 463–4), as she also notes (p. 157), distinguishes five types or modes of accountability:

- Professional, based on professional judgment and expert knowledge;
- Consumer, based on market competition and market choice;
- Contract, based on tendering and efficiency;
- Performative, based on public inspection and standards; and
- Corporate, based on business plan and profit.

While 'professional' constitutes a pre-neoliberal, more traditional, internal method of accountability, the remaining types all constitute forms of 'neoliberal' accountability. In my own previous work (Olssen, 2002a, 2002b), I distinguished between 'bureaucratic–professional' and 'consumer–managerial' models based on a model initially put forward in New Zealand by the State Services Commission (New Zealand State Services Commission, 1992). Under the consumer–managerial forms of accountability, 'the assumption is that academics must demonstrate their utility to society by placing themselves in an open market and accordingly compete for students who provide the bulk of core funding through tuition fees. If academic research has value, it can stand up to the rigours of competition for limited funds' (ibid., p. 15). From the neoliberal perspective, however, professionalism is distrusted in that it generates conditions for opportunism, free-riding, shirking, sets self-serving standards, and is prone to what neoliberals call 'provider-capture'. Yet, in theory, there is nothing to stop the state (through the funding councils) together with the universities and the rest of the higher education sector producing a professional–bureaucratic model, based on agreed standards, which exposes free-riding, shirking and incompetence, but which is administered by the sector itself, and which avoids the externally imposed bureaucratic nightmare that is associated with the last RAE.

If some form of accountability on research (and teaching) is necessary, which most would concede to be the case, then some form of assessment that does not adversely impact on the internal lives and careers of academics in relation to stress, competition, anxiety, conformism and compliance is badly needed. It may well be that accountability assessments could be organized on 'internal' rather than 'external' lines, where suitable procedures could be designed by the government (or their funding bodies) and implemented by the universities themselves according to nationally agreed standards and categorizations. Why a system of quality enhancement that does not ratchet up competition in an endless cycle could not be designed, based on reasonable measures of quality assurance, which does not cause a cultural and social revolution, while at the same time conflicting with the traditional norms of academia, such as academic freedom, academic autonomy and professionalism, needs to be addressed. Such concerns, as I shall argue below, is of especial importance today. For while centralized, national systems of auditing have professed in the past to be concerned with funding formulas and decisions, in recent times they have shown a tendency to extend their control to affect academic production more generally, to deprofessionalize academics as a socioeconomic category, and to extend control over the content and nature of academic research. While partly these are concerned with issues of funding, wasted spending and value for the taxpayer, they are also mixed in with typical neoliberal concerns related to questions such as the relevance of research to society, whether academics do a fair day's work (shirking, free-riding) or even whether the country can afford an autonomous university system, where academics choose and select their own issues of interest for research, in a time of deficits and recession.

FROM BAD TO WORSE: THE RESEARCH EXCELLENCE FRAMEWORK AND THE IMPACT OF RESEARCH

There were many other criticisms of the RAE. Some concerned the complexity and cost of the process; some were made by the funding councils themselves. Academics on the whole were also skeptical. It was claimed that the process benefited some universities over others. As Sharp (2004, p. 202) notes: 'The RAE is essentially an "old" universities exercise designed to give more to the already well-off and to deny opportunities for newer institutions.'[7] It was claimed by others that the RAE caused a shift in what was to count as research, demoting the importance of the 'book', or 'monograph', traditionally important in the social sciences and humanities, in preference for the 'journal article' (Lingard, 2008, p. 180). Issues identified for measurement quickly began to function as objectives, with transformative effects on university cultures at every level. It was claimed also that such accountability processes downgraded the professional work of many departments and schools, especially in disciplines such as education, nursing or social work, where there was a practice and policy focus (ibid.).

Due to cumulative criticisms of the RAE, the government announced in March 2006 that the 2008 RAE round would be the last one, and that it would be replaced by the Research Excellence Framework (REF) as the new system for assessing the quality of research in the UK. While the initial aim was to devise something simpler and cheaper, it would still serve to determine the overall distribution of funding across the higher education sector. In addition to informing 'the selective allocation of research funding to HEIs', the Higher Education Funding Council for England (HEFCE) website states that it will also 'provide benchmarking information and establish reputational yardsticks' as well as 'provide accountability for public investment in research and demonstrate its benefits' (HEFCE, 2010a).

The REF is in many ways similar to the RAE. As with the RAE, HEFCE (2010a) states that 'through the REF, the UK funding bodies aim to develop and sustain a dynamic and internationally competitive research sector that makes a major contribution to economic prosperity, national wellbeing and the expansion and dissemination of knowledge'. As with the RAE, also, the REF will be a process of expert review. Although the use of metric-based indicators and especially citation information to inform the reviews of outputs was originally envisaged to be considerably greater, recent reports suggest a retreat from this position.[8] Other aspects are also much the same. Although HEFCE envisages that expert sub-panels will be retained, it is proposed that the new framework will operate with fewer and broader subject divisions than the RAE.

As with the RAE, also institutions will be invited to make submissions to each unit of assessment (UoA). It is here in relation to the nature of these submissions, however, that a major difference becomes evident. While the 'quality of research outputs . . . will continue to be the primary factor in the assessment' and 'the quality of research outputs will be assessed by the expert panels against international standards of excellence' (HEFCE, 2010a), it is expected that research will also be assessed in relation to its wider impact on the 'economy, society, public policy, culture and quality of life as well as the vitality of the research environment' (ibid.). The relative weightings in the overall assessment will be 60 percent (quality of research); 25 percent (impact) and 15 percent (environment).

The issue concerning the impact of research has especially created controversy and unease, for what is provisionally at least meant by 'impact of research' is not the influence of research or researcher(s) on their colleagues within their discipline, or even on teaching (and relatedly textbooks) but to the 'wider impact' of research on 'the economy, society, public policy, culture, the environment, international development or quality of life' (HEFCE, 2010a). This clearly pertains to the demonstrated influence that a researcher or team of researchers has had outside academia. In the September 2009

Second Consultation document, HEFCE (2009d) states that the aim is to 'identify and reward the impact that excellent research carried out within UK higher education is already achieving'. The aim is to 'assess historical impacts, not attempt to predict future impacts'. They will 'assess impact in terms of complete submissions covering a body of activity, not at the level of individual researcher'. Hence impact statements will represent a particular unit or sub-group within a unit rather than be made by each individual. This would mean that there could be one or several impact statements for each UoA, which will be assessed by the expert panels comprising both discipline specialists and 'lay' members.[9] They will keep 'the burden on institutions of providing evidence to the minimum necessary to enable panels to make robust assessments'. Although both the Roberts (2003) and Lambert Reports had criticized the 2001 RAE on the grounds that it failed sufficiently to recognize the relevance and impact of research for industry, it is only with the proposals for the REF that impact becomes an explicit and separate element. Panels will now be required to assess impact separately, and 25 percent allocated for impact will contribute to the final score that forms the basis on which university funding will proceed.

In a presentation titled 'Impact and the REF' (HEFCE, 2009c), David Sweeney, the Director of Research, Innovation and Skills, utilizes the example of Louis Pasteur in order to demonstrate the way impact will work. A three-pronged schema will distinguish 'world-leading outputs' (Pasteur proved that micro-organisms cause fermentation and disease and originated the idea of vaccines); the 'economic and social impact' (Pasteur saved the beer, wine and silk industries, and saved the life of Joseph Meister); and an assessment of the 'right environment' (Pasteur developed a custom-built laboratory of physiological chemistry at the École Supérieure in 1867). What is being talked about is not academic impact, but 'economic, social, public policy, cultural and quality of life impact', says Sweeney. The impacts evaluated will be 'those operating during the REF period 2008–12 underpinned by research over a longer time frame'. Expert panels will 'assess rather than measure' impacts based on a 'narrative supported by indicators' plus a possibility of 'third-party verification' with 'expert panels to judge the credibility of the evidence'.

The effects of assessing impact signal a revolutionary new emphasis in neoliberal technologies: no longer concerned solely with demonstrating productivity and the quality of research outputs in all disciplines across the UK in order to inform the UK funding bodies' allocation of money for research, but what now appears as a new concern – to 'sanction' research selection over the types of research being undertaken in terms of the contribution and significance for the wider society. Indeed, as Sweeney admits, impacts will be assessed on a 'proforma' as well as 'case studies', and 'expert panels' will assess evidence in terms of both 'reach' (breadth) and 'significance' (depth) of the impacts.

Stephan Collini has documented some of the possible consequences of this approach to academia in an article 'Impact on humanities' in the November 2009 issue of *The Times Literary Supplement*. One important problem he identifies relates to the effect of such an approach on the humanities, which he believes will have a seriously distorting effect on research. He starts by noting the deleterious effects of trying to hierarchize research according to a four-point scale, and notes that the 'three-star' category calls for judgments that identify research that is 'highly innovative (but not quite groundbreaking)' (drawn from HEFCE, guidance on REF 2009: see HEFCE, 2009a). He conjectures the difficulty of classifying a book on Victorian poetry in such a way, and envisages a situation where, despite being viewed by peers as 'one of the best books in the field', it scores 'zero impact' for research.

Putting aside the issue as to whether having a high impact makes one's research any better, or should be required, it is likely to 'marketize' research in a chillingly new way, for it will constitute a 'structural selectivity' or 'pressure' forcing every academic into hustling and hawking their wares to the media, and into fervent 'networking' to 'end-users' in society. As Collini (2009) puts it:

> Not only do a variety of uncontrollable factors determine the chances of such translation into another medium, but there is also no reason to think that the success of such translation bears any relation to the quality of the original work. If anything, meretricious and vulgarizing treatments (which concentrate on, say, the poet's sex life) will stand a greater chance of success than do nuanced critical readings.

Not only this, but of course scholars will be pressured to select their areas and topics of research according to the potential market impact as foreseen. Departments, Collini suggests, will become 'marketing agents'. In addition, one can surmise, based upon the vast administrative requirements ushered in as part of the cultural revolution that took hold of UK higher education in preparation for the last RAE, there will be a substantial administrative reorganization at every level of the university. To some extent this has already started as Research Council UK (RCUK) already requires 'impact statements' on all research funding applications. Now, with the REF, we can see this idea spreading: there will be 'impact committees' at university, faculty, school and department level; forms will stipulate specifying the 'impact potential' for all sabbatical leave applications – indeed, for every sort of application. And as with esteem indicators, academics will quickly learn to manipulate 'impact' and to see their work as 'jacked up' through the helpful behavior, including mutual citations, by those in networks. Experienced researchers will obviously find this easier to operate than younger, less experienced ones. Moreover, certain actions and links will be seen to represent the impact to be targeted, while others will be seen as to be avoided.

In addition to turning every academic into an entrepreneur of him/herself, or, in Collini's words, 'to become accomplished marketing agents', the sheer epistemic difficulty of assessing impact seems to have blithely escaped the attention of all involved. For, as Collini expresses it, in order to assess impact they will need to 'become implausibly penetrating and comprehensive cultural historians'. He wonders (ibid.):

> Has anyone really thought about what this could involve where ideas are concerned? An experienced cultural or social historian, working on the topic for years, might – just might – be able to identify the part played by a particular piece of academic research in long-term changes in certain social practices and attitudes, but it would require a highly detailed study and could probably only be completed long after the event and with full access to a wide range of sources of different kinds. Yet every department in the land is going to have to attempt something like this if they are to get credit for the 'impact' of their 'excellent' research.

Of course, in practice, they will not be able to do it. What is to count as impact, like the question who decides what has impact, will be operationalized according to standard functionalist criteria. To settle on a single criterion (the proposal is to award a grade for 'impact' in a way similar to 'quality of research', on a four-star scale) can only be done if a single criterion of usefulness, or benefit, or relevance or 'impact' is devised. Someone will have to decide what this is, that is, what is to count as impact. In order to dissolve the infinite task of cascading judgmental uncertainty and squabbling between rival paradigms or ideologies, operationalization will reside in expert panels that assess narratives with the (possible) assistance of metric indicators. Rival paradigms will no doubt succumb to decisions as to outcome by vote. Whatever is decided, it is likely to give rise to endless and irresolvable controversy about what impact is, or even whether it can be measured or assessed. As only present impact is to be assessed, relying inevitably on past research reputation, or present existing appeal, what about contemporary scholars seeking presently to develop new positions, new arguments, new paradigms and perspectives that they might hope one day will have impact but which do not yet as determined by the panel charged with defining the situation for a particular discipline?

We can extend this example and imagine even more difficult cases. Imagine a scholar who accepts a role for themselves as critic and conscience of society, in perhaps the spirit of Adorno or Foucault, of revealing to the society its own historical, political and ideological unconscious in order to create a terrain on which deeper conceptions of life and justice could take root. What if they see as an important criterion of success the extent to which they prick the sensibilities of their colleagues, or society, and of arousing irritation, in the way, perhaps, that Friedrich Nietzsche tried to do, or that Marxists might presently try to do. Does their work have impact? Will it have 4*, or 3*, or 2* or 1*? Could assigning impact unknowingly perform the function of scapegoating? Can one be certain that the multiple effects and possible interpretations concerning the impact of research be so precisely and unidimensionally ranked? And is the panel in question competent to decide?

There are problems too with the stipulation by HEFCE that only present impact will be assessed, underpinned by a longer period of research. This can hardly suit new or young researchers. In this sense, the very notion of impact is gerontocratic and becomes in effect the means by which older researchers assert their hegemony. It also ignores much research that is very important for society and perhaps is oriented to transforming society, but lies dormant for years (zero impact!) and only has a social impact years later, when social conditions are 'ripe'. In this sense the methodological obstacles to assessing impact are huge.

Think of the research in science where discoveries of huge importance have lain dormant for years, sometimes until well after the researcher has died because nobody recognized its relevance. In every discipline numerous researchers have battled tirelessly for decades as marginalized lonely academic isolates whom hardly anyone takes seriously until suddenly, some decades later, the importance and relevance of their work are recognized. Will HEFCE retrospectively correct mistakes? One can imagine a letter from Mrs Thatcher to Friedrich Hayek: 'Dear Professor Hayek, We regret that your work has been recorded as having zero impact for the first twenty years of your research. We now recognize that this was wrong, and we will be retroactively changing the scores to full 4* on all years.' Or think of Wilhelm Conrad Roentgen, the discoverer of X-rays, whose pioneering paper 'On a new kind of rays' was published in an undistinguished non-refereed journal and had no immediate impact. Think also of Peter Mitchell,

Nobel Laureate in Chemistry in 1978, whose 'chemiosmotic process in 1961 [was] arguably the most important biological-sciences discovery of the twentieth century . . . It led to the notorious "ox-phos" wars' (University and College Union (UCU), 2010). Mitchell's work was received with considerable hostility. Or think of Max Perutz and John Kendrew, Nobel Laureates in Chemistry, 1962, who worked on the problem of haemoglobin structure for 25 years, making for most of the time only 'modest progress' (UCU, 2010).

As Collini also concludes, no one disputes that academics should not seek to explain the significance of what they do to the wider public, to policy-makers, and specialist groups who may be interested. Yet it is not this that is being proposed in the UK in proposals on the impact of research. It is, I shall argue, an extension of the neoliberal project from accountability to control. What is being proposed by the REF is 'the uptake of research by external users' (that is, industry). It constitutes a new definition of research and of what is allowed, and is dangerously open to interpretation by the hegemony of dominant and powerful groups.

> Instead of proposing that 'impact' of this kind is a desirable social good over and above the quality of the research, the exercise makes the extent of such impact part of the measurement of the quality of the research. In terms of this exercise, research plus marketing is not just better than research without marketing: it is better research. (Collini, 2009)

If HEFCE has been unsettled by the amount of criticism and controversy generated by the REF proposals, it has not shown it.[10] Indeed, in 2009 it has proceeded apace with two main forms of action: first, it established an impact pilot exercise in order to 'test and develop the proposals' (HEFCE, 2009b). The exercise, completed in 2010, will seek to 'inform decisions on the assessment of impact and its weighting within the framework that will be taken in the light of the consultation exercise and the pilot outcomes'. Second, as part of the consultation exercise, in February 2009 it commissioned RAND Europe, a not-for-profit policy think tank based in Cambridge, UK to review approaches to evaluating the impact of research as part of their wider program to develop the fine detail of the new framework. The 72-page report surveys the use of impact assessment in other countries and attempts to draw lessons that HEFCE could learn from these. The report views the work of the Australian RQF Working Group on Impact Assessment as providing the most promising basis for developing an impact approach for the REF.

The Research Quality Framework (RQF) was initiated by the Australian coalition government in 2004 but never adopted due to a change of government. The approach taken to assessing impact is very similar to that HEFCE is now proposing in the UK. It emphasizes a case-study approach, consisting of unit-based narratives plus conformity to pre-set indicators;[11] proposes 'to direct funding to research that generates impact' (RQF, 13); recommends 'that high impact institutions would receive proportionately more funding' (ibid.); and that impact would be determined by Expert Panels comprising 'end-user' or 'stakeholder' representatives. Each Research Grouping could submit a number of Impact Statements of up to ten pages. Each Statement would seek to address four questions: (1) how the Research Grouping is engaged with end-users to address community problems; (2) what new products, policies, legislation, paradigms, attitudes, outlooks, and so on have been adopted, implemented, and/or taken up as a result of the research; (3) what economic, social, environmental, and/or cultural benefits of the research have been adopted by the end-users; and (4) what is the magnitude of the extent of benefits to end-users as a result of the research (p. 9).

Many of the proposals appeared to constitute a radical reconfiguration of research as traditionally understood, and from the perspective of 'blue-skies' academics appears ominous. Rather than collect evidence themselves as part of the compilation of their submission, HEIs were to provide names of end-users who could be approached for evidence independently by the Expert Assessment Panel (EAP). Significant attention is devoted to the issue of incorporating end-users in the assessment process, as part of the EAPs, and how practical difficulties of time and money could be overcome. RAND Europe concludes that the 'RQF provides an obvious basis to develop an impact module for the REF' (p. 17).[12]

Although RAND focuses on the RQF as a promising model, it has neglected to emphasize several important differences and criticisms that distinguish the RQF from what is proposed in the UK. One feature not proposed for possible adoption in the UK was the possibility in the Australian RQF that research groups could 'make a claim for exclusion from the impact assessment', should they consider that their research is not suited to impact assessment 'because of the intrinsic nature or stage of development of their research' (Department of Education, Science and Training, 2007, p. 20).[13] This alone would seem to constitute a rather crucial difference between the RQF and what is proposed by RAND and HEFCE. Other factors neglected by RAND include the severe criticisms directed at the RQF, and especially the proposals to assess impact, from a new Labor government. Although they acknowledge that due to the change of government the pilot trials were never conducted, this rather crucial point is not made enough of and they do not seek to present the views of academics or the debates that appeared in the media. Indeed it is fair to say that their report for HEFCE gives inadequate expression to the intensity of the debate and the hostility expressed by many in Australia to the impact assessment proposals in the RQF. One of the first acts of the new government was to abolish the scheme. According to the new Minister for Innovation, Industry, Science and Research, Kim Carr, 'The RQF is poorly designed, administratively expensive, and relies on an "impact" measure that is unverifiable and ill-defined' (Carr, 2007).[14]

While the RAND Report for HEFCE concludes that impact can be assessed, in later comments the President of RAND Europe, Jonathan Grant, questions 'whether the burden is worth it'.[15] While good models are in use elsewhere, matters relating to the 'undesirable perception' and 'excessive workloads' need careful consideration.[16] They recommend further consultation. Undaunted, HEFCE continues to plan to assess impact. Meanwhile, a survey of 589 professors by the University and College Union (UCU), released in the first week of January 2010, claims that a third of professors would consider taking jobs elsewhere than the UK if plans to assess impact were implemented. Some two-thirds of those polled opposed proposals to assess the impact of research.[17] In addition, six Nobel Prize winners are among 18 000 people who have signed a petition opposing the plans.[18]

NEW FORMS OF CONTROL AND THE END OF THE LIBERAL UNIVERSITY

While neoliberal technologies of accountability and individualized incentives and performance targets introduce the always-present dangers of engendering a work environment of uncontrolled spiraling competition, many conceded that they also checked the dangers of what Buchanan and Tullock (1962) call 'rent-seeking behavior' and introduced much-needed mechanisms of accountability and auditing. Recent events such as the MPs' 'expenses scandal' at Westminster, and frequent jokes concerning academics who took advantage of the generous conditions of their tenure,[19] have underscored the need for sensible measures to be in place. In that these were limited to preventing free-riders and ensuring that academics all contributed an honest day's work, or to guiding decision-making and justifying public expenditure on higher education, they served a sensible and positive function. Very few today would defend conditions of academic professionalism that were based on lifelong tenure and unscrutinized professional autonomy.

Yet impact goes well beyond the initial reasons provided for introducing systems of accountability. When the RAE was introduced in 1986, the aims and purposes were: accountability and efficiency in relation to taxpayer money; to facilitate resource allocation; to improve decision-making; to assist governance; to justify expenditures, decisions, and results from research; and to justify cost-effectiveness. A concern to assess 'impact' goes beyond straightforward accountability in financial terms and starts to exert control on the content or substance of what is to be researched. In that it does so, it comes perilously close to contradicting academic freedom.

Although it could be said that researchers are still free to research what they like, with no interference, the fact that some academics' or departments' work might be graded as having no impact constitutes at least indirect pressure on what should be researched. Will a university be prepared to continue to employ a researcher whose work is judged by panels of their peers as having no or little impact? And is not this really a none-too-clever form of pressure directed at academics, departments, schools, faculties and universities as to what topics, discipline subjects and areas they should be researching? Will mathematics or theoretical physics need to 'get into bed with' music, or engineering, or education, in order to have impact? In the early 'guidance' on the REF, HEFCE appreciated that such a situation, where a discipline like mathematics teamed up with one like engineering, was 'closer to the market and thereby had greater economic impact'. The seemingly unconscious alignment of all research impact with the market leads Collini (2009) to refer to this extract in the HEFCE REF document as 'a rather chilling paragraph'.[20]

To the extent that the assessment of 'impact' on a four-point scale indirectly coerces certain types of research, it could be argued to conflict with a long tradition of academic freedom, whereas the statement embodied in the 1988 Education Act presently seeks to protect the rights of individual researchers in terms of that which is researched. The existing legislation on academic freedom is framed and worded by Lord Jenkins, a former Chancellor of Oxford University, who put forward an amendment to the Education Reform Act of 1988 that defined academic freedom as: 'The freedom within the law to question and test received wisdom, and to put forward new ideas and controversial and unpopular opinions without placing themselves in jeopardy of losing their jobs or privileges they may have at their institutions.'

In the light of such a definition, one could be forgiven for thinking, or wondering, whether the assessment of 'research impact' will not insidiously direct the nature or areas of permissible research endeavor, and thus further diminish the autonomy of academics and subject them to increased external control. Will heads of department start to divert their staff from their preferred areas to areas where likely impact is seen to be high? This seems, in fact, to be explicitly understood by HEFCE (2009d, p. 8), which announces that 'We will be able to use the REF to encourage desirable behaviours at three levels: . . . the behaviour of individual researchers within a submitted unit . . .'.[21] The previous RAEs, it can be argued, already did this but did not trespass into directing the substance of research, or demand that research undertaken have certain specific effects (impacts), or be seen in a certain light.

EFFECTS OF NEOLIBERAL HIGHER EDUCATION ON DEMOCRACY: TOWARD A MACRO-POLITICAL ANALYSIS

However, the erosion of individual researcher autonomy and control and the increased constraints exerted over professionalism are perhaps not the only serious issue here. For the REF, like the old RAE, and the PBRF in New Zealand, erodes the autonomy of universities as an independent sector within the larger political society. There is a sense in which supply-side funding is being increasingly used to exert political control over universities. Whereas until the REF these have tied universities into control through financial accountability in order to justify expenditure and inform decision-making, now, with the REF, there is a new shift from accountability over finances to control over substance and the content of what is researched. Possibly this constitutes an important qualitative break in that it represents an extension of the neoliberal project from accountability to control. Having trodden the path of increased financial accountability for some three decades, and conditioned the suspecting but powerless academics along the way, HEFCE now sees itself as a rightful custodian of universities in England on behalf of industry and society generally. It has expanded a concern with marketization and accountability, which surfaced under Thatcher administrations, to a new concern over the nature and production of knowledge and the relevance of universities to the wider society.

In that the REF signals a growing centralism, there are parallel indicators at the political/regulatory level. In a recent *Times Higher Education* article by Melanie Newman, titled 'Funding council seeks powers to eject vice-chancellors' (Newman, 2010), she summarizes new proposals by HEFCE in a consultation document addressed to all universities in England on 'Regulating higher education institutions as charities', issued in December 2009 (HEFCE, 2009f). The new plans have been developed in the wake of a financial crisis involving London Metropolitan University, which had over-claimed student fee entitlement from the government leading to demands for a claw-back from the institution of millions of pounds. Given difficulties with removing the vice chancellor, a new memorandum between HEFCE and universities proposed to give HEFCE powers to remove the 'accountable officer' (usually the vice-chancellor) of the institution. The consultation document also proposed changes to the charity regulation provisions of the 2006 Charities Act (most UK universities are 'exempt charities'[22]) that would give

HEFCE new powers from 2010 to assume an increased role as one of several 'principal regulators'[23] of HEIs as charities. This would enable HEFCE to extend the powers it has over institutions to collect previously uncollected information, and to intensify the accountability system over both financial data and serious incident reporting to ensure institutional compliance with charity-law principles.

That HEFCE has perhaps exaggerated its powers can be seen in the context that many universities are only partially funded from the government purse.[24] Although many universities are registered as 'exempt charities', the fact that they are largely autonomous from the state as far as their funding bases are concerned possibly weakens HEFCE's case. On issues like the REF, as all universities want as much government funding for research as is on offer, there is little option but to conform. What can be clearly seen on both fronts, in relation to the changes in the regulatory framework, as well as the proposals for the REF, is an increase in the confidence and powers of central control.

The consequence of this increasing central control is that it slowly but surely erodes two of the central roles of the liberal university. First, as a consequence of the increase of pressure over the nature of what is researched, the resulting decline of academic freedom (that is, of researchers to creatively choose to research a subject of their interest) alters the nature of knowledge production. When it is insisted that research be evaluated according to its impact on 'end-users' (industry), the separation of universities and higher education from the market is further undermined. This inserts an additional commercial driver that undermines important traditional academic principles based on disinterested academic research, open enquiry, and intellectual curiosity and discovery. It is what John Ziman, the physicist, terms 'post-academic research' based on a model of 'instrumental research driven by market forces' (Ziman, 2000).

The rise of neoliberalism thus signals the death of liberal values of individual rights and freedom, and makes these notions subservient to responsiveness to market forces as the criterion of usefulness to society. Not only will this militate against 'blue-skies' research in preference for short-run research objectives that can demonstrate impact, but it also neglects the fact that most research of value is contributed after many years of activity, comprising modest returns, false starts and blind alleys.

Research of real benefit to society proceeds from trial and error and is 'curiosity-driven'. What is not understood by the policy-makers is that impact on society is in an important theoretical sense unforeseeable. Whether in science or social science or humanities, serendipity, luck, long-term perseverance and commitment have been central to outcomes, and these cannot always be predicted from the standpoint of the present. There is a danger that in trying to second-guess good research by assessing and funding it in terms of impact, where the indicators are shaped at the central levels of society, the very preconditions of discovery and innovation that are central to our futures and our conceptions of ourselves as free liberal beings are being undermined. Good research is not only unpredictable, but it can also take an inordinately long time. John Rawls reputedly took seven years to write *A Theory of Justice*, and one may be excused for wondering whether the REF will be able to accommodate such an endeavor. And, of course, many writers whose work has had impact have produced very little in quantitative terms during their lives. Ludwig Wittgenstein, one of the great philosophers of the twentieth century, published only one book during his lifetime, and that numbering only 70 pages.[25]

Second, what is also eroded through neoliberal reforms is the political autonomy of the university, which constitutes a traditional foundation of the democratic polity, and which was central to its role of offering objective, detached and informed policy advice, as well as critical insights to the government of the day. From being autonomous centres of power – the fifth estate, as it were – which, like the media, could both inform and criticize government, universities have had that autonomy curtailed. This was a central role of the very first universities, emerging in Bologna in the ninth century, Paris in the twelfth century, and at Oxford and Cambridge in the thirteenth century. As Max Weber (1921) argued, the independence of universities from the state served an important political function as it ensured the separation of knowledge and its production from those who exercised political rule. In this sense, the separation of universities was similar to the separation of powers as formulated by John Locke and Baron de Montesquieu in the seventeenth and eighteenth centuries.

The doctrine of the 'separation of powers' was a central structural girder of democracy, and was based on the desirability of keeping the various estates of society – legislature, judiciary, executive – apart from each other in order to ensure countervailing checks and to safeguard people against the possible corruption of – or even the over-zealousness of or carelessness of – their rulers. It suggests that power should be dispersed, and that the idea of criss-crossing or overlapping centres of influence, both within society and within institutions, itself functions as a bulwark of democracy and support for legitimate governance. This is why trade unions and professional associations are so important in the workplace, for they subject management and leadership decisions and conduct to scrutiny. It is also the case that the mass media should also be separate from political control in order to ensure the independence of news production. It was in this sense too, that John Stuart Mill believed that power should be dispersed throughout the institutions of civil society for the very purpose of ensuring a system of 'checks and balances' so that no one group could exploit its power.

In the UK it has been long understood that the liberal university performed such a role. Its critical independence from the state was jealously guarded. Such was presumed in the institution of the 'university constituency', for instance.[26] Although Labor politicians criticized such a system as elitist,[27] the system did enable the dispersement of power and in a peculiar way exemplified the model of the liberal university as being semi-autonomous from the state. It is this system that has lost its independence with the onset of supply-side funding from the 1980s and the calls for greater accountability. The RAE and REF constitute but two forms of these. Added to these are many others – the new tendency to recruit to councils from business expertise outside the university has in some cases displaced academics from effective control and governance; the erosion of the powers of Senate and the establishment of executive boards; the abolition of tenure and the importation of systems of line management, and the frequent and widespread use of restructuring – that seriously threaten academic professionalism, institutional autonomy and academic freedom today. The control of financial resources through either research funding via RCUK or other providers, and by the funding councils, through the RAE and the REF, further increase the pressures and contribute to a process of deprofessionalization of academic staff at the same time as the traditional autonomy of the university is undermined by subjecting it to market forces.

Such processes, it must be concluded, have been deliberately engendered and have seen university and higher education generally increasingly managed and governed by expertise from outside academia. Just as some universities are now managed by either non-academics or by academics who regard themselves as 'managers', it is no great surprise to learn from George Monbiot (2009) that the Medical Research Council is run by an arms manufacturer, the Natural Environment Research Council is run by the head of a construction company, and HEFCE is headed by the chairman of a real-estate company. Although non-academic expertise can certainly lend important skills and knowledge to university governance and management, it is important that academics are not themselves displaced from decision-making and control of their own institutions. There is a need to restore a balance. What must occur, to use the language of Kofi Annan, is that 'we, the academics', must recapture the governance and management to restore the autonomy of the estate. One cannot do better than to cite (below) an extract from the 1997 UNESCO Recommendation on the Status of Higher Education Teaching Personnel as a place for this chapter to end, and for the process of the reprofessionalization of academics to start.

B. Self-governance and collegiality

31. Higher-education teaching personnel should have the right and opportunity, without discrimination of any kind, according to their abilities, to take part in the governing bodies and to criticize the functioning of higher education institutions, including their own, while respecting the right of other sections of the academic community to participate, and they should also have the right to elect a majority of representatives to academic bodies within the higher education institution.
32. The principles of collegiality include academic freedom, shared responsibility, the policy of participation of all concerned in internal decisionmaking structures and practices, and the development of consultative mechanisms. Collegial decisionmaking should encompass decisions regarding the administration and determination of policies of higher education, curricula, research, extension work, the allocation of resources and other related activities, in order to improve academic excellence and quality for the benefit of society at large.

NOTES

1. Buchanan develops these themes in all his writings, but see 1954a and 1954b for his early enthusiasm for Arrow's insights.
2. The source for Wicksell's statement given by Buchanan is Musgrave and Peacock (1958).
3. The television programmes *Yes Minister* and *Yes Prime Minister* were, as Adam Curtis (2007) documents, inspired by public choice theory and contributed to the general perception of the public sector as characterized by wastage and incompetence. Another journalist who adopted a satirical approach specifically concerned with academics was Laurie Taylor, whose columns in the *Times Higher Education* made Poppleton University appear a fit institution for reform. Poppleton was founded in 1979.
4. The 2006 round was a partial round. The next full round will be in 2012.
5. This changed to some extent in 2008 when the percentages of the submissions with each number of stars was published, which meant, in the case of a small unit, calculating the number of papers that were internationally excellent, and being able to guess in most cases which papers they were.
6. The NSS surveys students from each discipline from across the country on their assessments of their teaching. It then ranks each university on a scale. Individual departments that get bottom, or near the bottom, have been subject to newspaper feature articles. The heads of department, staff generally, or the future of the department itself, are placed in jeopardy.
7. Ball (1997) also argues that the RAE separates the 'old' from the 'new' universities. Hence the first 59 are almost all 'old' universities, while 60–111 are predominantly 'new'.

8. Corbyn (2010) reports that citations may be dropped as a means to assess the quality of research. If this happened, the differences between the REF and the RAE would be greatly reduced.
9. While all of the details are at the time of writing provisional, in that consultations are still under way, the recommendation of appointing lay members of panels has already been suggested by HEFCE. This parallels the Warry Report recommendation to RCUK on the efficiency and effectiveness of peer review that an individual competent on the economic impact of research should be accommodated on each panel, when deliberating on research grant bids. The incorporation of impact statements for research grant bids can in an important sense be seen as a precursor for their incorporation into the REF. In a submission by the Russell Group on the Warry Report to RCUK, it was stated that 'There is no evidence to date of any rigorous way of measuring economic impact other than in the very broadest of terms and outputs. It is therefore extremely difficult to see how such panel members could be identified or the basis upon which they could be expected to make their observations' (see Russell Group, 2007).
10. There is evidence that, while academics are against the impact agenda, many business and university managers are for it. On 5 November 2009 the *Times Higher Education* reported that resistance to the plans (for impact assessment) is also causing frustration amongst universities and funders. A policy round table (in November 2009), hosted by the 1994 Group of small research-intensive universities and the British Library, asked 'How can we maximize the impact of the UK's research base to meet national priorities?' The report stated that 'Amongst the twenty-five attendees, there was growing frustration with those who think impact is a "dirty word"' (see Corbyn, 2009).
11. A list of these indicators appears on p. 13 of the Recommended RQF Report (Department of Education, Science and Training, 2007). They include such items as 'Reduced pollution', 'Regeneration or arrested degradation of natural resources', 'Lives saved', 'Repeat business', 'reduced treatment time and cost', 'increased literacy and numeracy rates', 'increased cultural awareness', 'royalties', 'increased employment', 'spin-off companies', 'new products and inventions', 'licences', 'citations in Government reports, Hansard, and so on', 'community awareness of research', and suchlike.
12. RAND Europe was also a consultant on certain matters for the RQF.
13. It is somewhat strange that this possibility is not referred to at all in the entire 72-page report by RAND. Indeed, somewhat disingenuously they recommend in the executive summary that 'Within a single approach [the RQF is] . . . adaptable to apply to all disciplines' (RAND Europe, 2009, p. iv). They later say, under the heading 'Additional Technical Aspects', that the RQF is 'intended to apply across all research areas' (p. 16). This claim sits uncomfortably with the 'exclusion' provision that I have noted in the RQF. RAND's failure to refer at any stage to this possibility in the RQF also calls into question the extent they can be held to have performed the first task set for it: 'To review international practice in assessing research impact.'
14. These failings could possibly suggest that RAND has failed to perform adequately the second task set for it: 'To identify relevant challenges, lessons and observations from international practice' (RAND Europe, 2009, p. iv).
15. Cited from Sattary (2010).
16. Ibid.
17. Ibid. Also cited in newspaper report by Graeme Paton (2010).
18. Cited in Paton (2010). There have been a number of petitions. *Times Higher Education* of 5 November 2009 states that 'more than 2300 academics have signed a petition to the Prime Minister requesting the reversal of both research council and HEFCE policies to direct funds to projects whose outcomes are determined to have a significant impact'. It cites particular concerns for the humanities and social sciences. Further, it states that 'almost the entire philosophy sub-panel from the 2008 RAE writes voicing "deep concern" about HEFCE's proposed use of impact as a measure of research quality in the REF'.
19. Laurie Taylor in his column in the *Times Higher Education* perhaps promoted such views.
20. See the article by Art Laptev (2009), where he documents the dramatic decline in research funding for fundamental mathematics applications, especially the EU Framework Programme and EPSRC in the UK.
21. I am indebted to Alexandre Borovik (18 November 2009) for this insight, who says it in response to 'Peter Cameron's Blog' on 'Responses to Impact'. Online at: http://cameroncounts.wordpress.com/2009/11/16/impact/, accessed 6 May 2010.
22. An 'exempt charity' is defined, although expected to comply with charity law, as exempt from registration with the Charity Commission and as currently outside the scope of the Charity Commission's regulatory powers.
23. Principal regulators will be expected to promote compliance with charity law. From 2010 HEIs will be subject to the Charity Commission's regulatory powers.
24. The average funding by HEFCE for HEIs as a percentage of total income is 34.6 percent. Some 24 of 156 HEIs receive below 30 percent, and 9 receive below 20 percent, however, making it questionable as to how much control HEFCE can realistically exert (see *Times Higher Education*, 18–24 March 2010, 39–43).

25. This was the *Tractatus Logico-Philosophicus*. In addition, it can be noted that he had considerable help with it. Russell wrote the foreword, Ogden provided the translation, and Keynes helped find the publisher (see Peters and Olssen, 2005).

26. University constituencies can be traced in their origins to Scotland, where the earliest universities held representation in the unicameral Estates of Parliament. England adopted the same system in 1603 as the basis of its Parliament, with the accession of James VI to the throne. In the eighteenth century the system was continued in the Parliament of Great Britain and the United Kingdom Parliament until the mid-twentieth century, as well as in Ireland. The central feature of a university constituency resides in the basis of representation to Parliament of the land as residing in the university rather than in a geographical area. In some university constituencies a system of plural voting enables residents to vote once on the basis of the university and once on the basis of a geographical area. Cambridge and Oxford were given two seats in Parliament from 1603; Edinburgh and St Andrews in the eighteenth century; London from 1868 until 1950; Glasgow and Aberdeen from 1868 until 1918; and the University of Wales from 1918 until 1950. The year 1918 saw an increase in the numbers of universities represented in Parliament, with the addition of Queen's University in Belfast and the National University of Ireland, and an extension of enfranchisement of two seats each to many universities in England. In each constituency the university could elect members. It was held that as the universities were affected by decisions, and could inform decision-making, they ought therefore to have representation in it. Among the members for the university constituencies were notables such as William Pitt the Younger, Lord Palmerston (Cambridge), Robert Peel (Oxford), William Gladstone (Oxford) and Ramsay MacDonald (Combined Scottish Universities) (sources: Pugh, 1978; http://en.wikipedia.org/wiki/Combined_English_Universities_(UK_Parliament_constituency), accessed 18 March 2010.

27. It was held by socialists and others on the political Left that possession of a degree should not confer greater electoral rights.

REFERENCES

Ashcroft, C. and R. Smith (2008), 'Give me your four best papers: the privileging ethos of research accountability systems from an Aotearoa/New Zealand perspective', *Access: Critical Perspectives on Communication, Cultural and Policy Studies*, **27** (1–2), 49–60.

Auger, P. (2000), *The Death of Gentlemanly Capitalism*, London: Penguin Books.

Ball, D.F. (1997), 'Quality measurement as a basis for resource allocation: Research Assessment Exercises in United Kingdom universities', *R&D Management*, **27** (3), 281–9.

Barnett, R. (2000), *Realising the University in an Age of Supercomplexity*, Ballmoor, Buckinghamshire: Open University Press.

Barry, B. (1990), *Political Argument: A Reissue with a New Introduction*, New York and London: Harvester/ Wheatsheaf.

Barry, B., T. Osborne and N. Rose (eds) (1996), *Foucault and Political Reason: Liberalism, Neo-liberalism and Rationalities of Government*, Chicago, IL: University of Chicago Press.

Bates, R. (2003), 'Phelan's bibliometric analysis of the impact of Australian educational research', *The Australian Educational Researcher*, **30** (2), 57–64.

Buchanan, J. (1954a), 'Social choice, democracy, and free markets', *Journal of Political Economy*, **62** (2), 114–23.

Buchanan, J. (1954b), 'Individual choice in voting and the market', *Journal of Political Economy*, **62** (3), 334–4.

Buchanan, J. (1975), *The Limits of Liberty: Between Anarchy and Leviathan*, Chicago, IL: University of Chicago Press.

Buchanan, J. (1978), 'From private preferences to public philosophy: the development of public choice', in J. Buchanan (ed.), *The Economics of Politics*, London: Institute of Economic Affairs.

Buchanan, J. and G. Tullock (1962), *The Calculus of Consent: Logical Foundations of Constitutional Democracy*, Ann Arbor, MI: University of Michigan Press.

Burchell, G. (1996), 'Liberal government and techniques of the self', in A. Barry, T. Osborne and N. Rose (eds), *Foucault and Political Reason*, Chicago, IL: Chicago University Press, pp. 19–36.

Burchell, G., C. Gordon and P. Miller (1991), *The Foucault Effect: Studies in Governmentality*, Chicago, IL: Chicago University Press.

Carr, K. (2007), 'Cancellation of research quality framework implementation', media release, 21 December. Online at: http://wwwarc.gov.au/media/releases/media_26feb08htm, accessed 24 September 2009.

Collini, S. (2009), 'Impact on humanities', *Times Literary Supplement*, **13**, November, accessible at http://entertainment.co.uk/tol/arts_and_entertainment/the_tls/article6915986.ece.

Corbyn, Z. (2009), 'Managers and scholars divided as resistance grows to impact agenda', *Times Higher Education*, 5 November.

Corbyn, Z. (2010), 'Nervous HEFCE "edging out" of REF citations', *Times Higher Education*, 1 April.

Coryn, C., J. Hattie, M. Scriven and D. Hartman (2007), 'Models and mechanisms for evaluating government funded research: an international comparison', *American Journal of Evaluation*, **8**, 437–57.

Currie, J. (2008), 'Research Assessment Exercises and some negative consequences of journal rankings and citation indices', *Access: Critical Perspectives on Communication, Cultural and Policy Studies*, **27** (1–2), 27–36.

Curtis, A. (2007), *The Trap*, Television documentary in three parts, Part I: *Fuck You Buddy* (11 March); Part II: *The Lonely Robot* (18 March); Part III: *We Will Force You To Be Free* (25 March), London: BBC Television.

Department of Education, Science and Training (2007), *The Recommended RQF: Research Quality Framework – Assessing the Quality and Impact of Research in Australia*, Australian Government, Canberra: Department of Education, Science and Training. Online at http://www.education.monash.edu.au/staff/research/rqf/docs/recommended-rqf-14nov2007.pdf, accessed 24 September 2009.

Elton, L. (2000), 'The UK Research Assessment Exercise: unintended consequences', *Higher Education Quarterly*, **54** (3), 274–83.

Finsden, B. (2008), 'The RAE in Scotland: a Kiwi participant-observer in an ancient university', *Access: Critical Perspectives on Communication, Cultural & Policy Studies*, **27** (1–2), 61–72.

Gordon, C. (1991), 'Governmental rationality: an introduction', in G. Burchell, C. Gordon and P. Miller, *The Foucault Effect: Studies in Governmentality*, Chicago, IL: Chicago University Press, pp. 1–52.

Gordon, C. (2005), 'The human dimensions of the Research Agenda: supporting the development of researchers throughout the career life-cycle', *Higher Education Quarterly*, **59** (1), 40–55.

Hare, P. (2003), 'The United Kingdom's Research Assessment Exercise: impact on institutions, departments, individuals', *Higher Education Management and Policy*, **15** (2), 43–62.

Higher Education Funding Council for England (HEFCE) (2007/34), *Research Excellence Framework: Consultation on the Assessment and Funding of Higher Education Research post-2008 (November)*. Online at http://www.hefce/pubs/hefce/2007/07_34/, accessed 2 June 2010.

Higher Education Funding Council for England (HEFCE) (2009a), *Guidance Notes for the REF*. Online at http://www.hefce.ac.uk/research/ref/, accessed 2 June 2010.

Higher Education Funding Council for England (HEFCE) (2009b), 'The Research Excellence Framework: a brief guide to the proposals (October)'. Online at http://www.hefce.ac.uk/research/ref/resources/REF.pdf, accessed 24 May 2010.

Higher Education Funding Council for England (HEFCE) (2009c), *Impact and the REF*, presentation by David Sweeney, Director of Research, Innovation and Skills at the Higher Education Funding Council for England (HEFCE) (22 October). Online at http://www.hefce.ac.uk/news/hefce/2009/ref.htm accessed 30 May 2010.

Higher Education Funding Council for England (HEFCE) (2009d), *Research Excellence Framework: Second Consultation on the Assessment and Funding of Research (38/2009)*. Online at http://www.hefce.ac.uk/pubs/hefce/2009/09_38/, accessed 24 May 2010.

Higher Education Funding Council for England (HEFCE) (2009e), *Report on the Pilot Exercise to Develop Bibliometric Indicators (39/2009)*. Online at http://www.hefce.ac.uk/pubs/hefce2009/09_39, accessed 24 May 2010.

Higher Education Funding Council for England (HEFCE) (2009f), *Regulating higher education institutions as charities: Consultation on HEFCE's information requirements as principal regulator (December 2009/45) (45/2009)*. Online at http://www.hefce.ac.uk/pubs/hefce/2009/09_45, accessed 24 May 2010.

Higher Education Funding Council for England (HEFCE) (2009g), *Consultation on Changes to the Funding Agreement between HEFCE and Institutions (December 2009/46)*. Online at http://www.hefce.ac.uk/pubs/hefce/2009/09_46, accessed 24 May 2010.

Higher Education Funding Council for England (HEFCE)/RAND (2009), *Capturing Research Impacts: A Review of International Practice*, Report prepared by RAND Europe (HEFCE DB-578). Online at http://www.hefce.ac.uk/pubs/rdreports/2009/rd23_09/, accessed 24 May 2010.

Higher Education Funding Council for England (HEFCE) (2010a), *Research Excellence Framework*. Online at http://www.hefce.ac.uk/research/ref/, accessed 30 May 2010.

Higher Education Funding Council for England (HEFCE) (2010b), *Research Excellence Consultation Outcomes* (HEFCE Circular letter 04/2010). Online at http://www.hefce.ac.uk/pubs/circlets/2010/c104_10/, accessed 24 May 2010.

Kroto, H. (2010), 'A story about an almost extinct species', *Left Field Science*. Online at http://www.csc.liv.ac.uk/~leslie/impact/LeftFieldScience.pdf, accessed 3 June 2010.

Laptev, A. (2009), 'Mathematics and its interfaces with science, technology and society', *EMS Newsletter*, September.

Lingard, B. (2008), 'Globalising Research Accountabilities', *Access: Critical Perspectives on Communication, Cultural and Policy Studies*, **27** (1–2), 175–88.

Monbiot, G. (2009), 'These men would have stopped Darwin', *Guardian*, 11 May. Online at: http://www.csc.liv.ac.uk/~leslie/impact/impact.html.

Musgrave, R. and A. Peacock (1958), *Classics in the Theory of Public Finance*, London: Macmillan.

New Zealand State Services Commission (1992), 'Governance of Tertiary Institutions', paper submitted to the Taskforce on Capital Charging of Tertiary Institutions, Wellington: Government Printer.

Newman, M. (2010), 'Funding Council Seeks to eject Vice-Chancellors', *Times Higher Education*, 28 January.

Oancea, A. (2008), 'Performative accountability and the UK Research Assessment Exercise', *Access: Critical Perspectives on Communication, Cultural and Policy Studies*, **27** (1–2), 153–73.

Olssen, M. (2002a), *The Neoliberal Appropriation of Tertiary Education Policy in New Zealand: accountability, research and academic freedom*, Wellington: New Zealand Association for Research in Education State of the Art Monograph Number 8.

Olssen, M. (2002b), 'The restructuring of tertiary education in New Zealand: governmentality, neoliberalism, democracy', *McGill Journal of Education*, **37** (2), 57–88.

Paton, G. (2010), 'Warning over academic "brain drain"', *Telegraph*, 7 January. Online at: http://wwwtelegraph.co.uk/education/6943360/Warning-over-academic-brain-drain.htm, accessed 1 June 2010.

Peters, M. and M. Olssen (2005), '"Useful Knowledge": redefining research and teaching in the learning economy', in R. Barnett (ed.), *Reshaping the University: New Relationships between Research, Scholarship and Teaching*, Buckingham: Society for Research in Higher Education and Open University Press, pp. 37–48.

Pugh, M. (1978), *Electoral Reform in War and Peace 1906–1818*, London: Routledge and Kegan Paul.

RAND Europe (2009), *Capturing Research Impacts: A Review of International Practice*, Jonathan Grant, Philipp-Bastian Brutscher, Susan Kirk, Linda Butler and Steven Wooding, Documented Briefing 578 HEFCE, Cambridge, UK.

Ranson, S. (2003), 'Public accountability in the age of neoliberal governance', *Journal of Education Policy*, **18** (5), 459–80.

Reisman, D. (1990), *The Political Economy of James Buchanan*, College Station, TX: Texas A & M University Press.

Roberts, G. (2003), *Review of Research Assessment: Report to the UK Funding Bodies*. Online at http://www.ra-review.ac.uk/reports/roberts.asp, accessed 24 May 2010.

Rose, N. (1993), 'Government, authority and expertise in advanced liberalism', *Economy and Society*, **22** (3), 283–300.

Rose, N. (1996), 'Governing "advanced" liberal democracies', in A. Barry, T. Osborne and N. Rose (eds), *Foucault and Political Reason*, Chicago, IL: Chicago University Press, pp. 37–64.

Russell Group (2007), *RCUK Consultation on the Efficiency and Effectiveness of Peer Review*. Online at: http://www.csc.liv.ac.uk/cmsweb/downloads/rcuk/research/peer/russell.pdf, accessed 4 June 2010.

Sattary, L. (2010), 'HEFCE takes more hits over impact', *Chemistry World*, January, Royal Society of Chemistry.

Sharp, S. (2004), 'The Research Assessment Exercises 1992–2001: patterns across time and subjects', *Studies in Higher Education*, **29** (2), 201–18.

Smith, R. (2008), 'Introductory editorial: The politics of research assessment exercises and accountability, an international overview', *Access: Critical Perspectives on Communication, Cultural and Policy Studies*, **27** (1–2), 1–8.

Taylor, L. (2009), 'How big is your impact?', *Times Higher Education*, 30 July. Online at: http://wwwtimeshighereducation.co.uk/story.asp?sectioncode=26&storycode=407611, accessed 24 May 2010.

University and College Union (UCU) (2010), 'Discoveries that would not survive the REF'. Online at http://www.ucu.org.uk/media/pdf/0/s/ucu-notsurvivingtheREF.pdf, accessed 2 June 2010.

Weber, M. (1921), *Economy and Society*, Totowa, NJ: Bedminster.

Ziman, J. (2000), *Real Science*, Cambridge: Cambridge University Press.

PART III

GLOBAL GOVERNANCE

22 Introduction to Part III
Roger King

In Part III the authors examine the various aspects of the governance and steering of higher education in the global era. More specifically the contributions examine the interplay of various levels of governance, of the national and the transnational, and the governmental and the non-governmental.

In the opening chapter, Simon Marginson observes that universities and higher education systems operate in global, national and local dimensions simultaneously – they are 'glonacal' organizations. Yet the global grows ever more important. The three key world imaginaries of world market, global status competition, and open source knowledge and networks increasingly influence university presidents and higher education policymakers. The chapter examines particularly the global strategizing that follows such imaginings but that takes place for actors within structures of constraint and opportunity, and that are strongly influenced by conceptions of the self and the availability of resources. The interplay is of a world that is structured as 'out there' and one in which 'structure' is experienced more immediately and hermeneutically as being more or less constraining.

Yet not all these world imaginaries are resonant with global higher education and research. Marginson points to only the partial cross-border relevance of a universal global market imaginary for global higher education. He instances the failure of electronic-only universities that ignore the continued relevance of place and nation for university identities and attractiveness for students and other clients. Rather it is the worlds of status competition and open source and other networks that appear to count for more, and both are symbiotically and perhaps somewhat diametrically related to each other. Without global openness and networks, the worldwide engagements necessary for knowledge and organizational competitiveness tend to shrivel. Yet rankings and similar forms of status competition imply closure as well as opportunity, especially for those excluded from the top reaches of such rankings.

Consequently we see the global governance of higher education as a largely informal affair, governed not so much by sovereign rules as by peer pressures and emulation. Most global initiatives follow mimicry rather than being genuinely radical and path-breaking, in strong part reflecting the risk-averse tendencies propelled by heightened forms of competitiveness in global higher education. Yet this informal world of regulatory governance also implies rather more scope for the imaginings and actions of agents than is found in more constrained national settings, although national settings are not only necessary for organizational identity purposes but also for the resources necessary for global wanderings and strategies.

David Dill, in Chapter 25, examines particularly the growth of academic quality assurance organizations as both a national response to globalization and as reflected in regional and global institutions. The question is posed whether a 'rational design' theory of institutions is an appropriate explanation for these developments, namely that as transnational exchanges grow in higher education, transnational institutions and entities are generated to help reduce national transaction costs.

Consequently his chapter undertakes three tasks. First, it describes the processes of globalization that generate incentives for the construction of international organizations and regimes for assuring academic standards, not least as there is a worldwide emphasis on maintaining or improving student learning outcomes. The Bologna Process, for example, has located quality assurance at the centre of its mechanisms. Second, the chapter explores the strengths and weaknesses of the new global institutional framework for assuring academic standards, including both transnational networks of national quality assurance agencies and non-governmental entities such as the accreditation bodies in Business Studies and other subjects, as well as the proliferation of mainly privately constructed university rankings. Third, Dill examines the legitimacy of these developments and wonders whether some form of professional 'capture' may be at work that thwarts a global public interest in these matters.

In part these concerns arise from two developments that feature throughout this collection, namely the rise of commercialization in transnational higher education, and the requirement for softer forms of governance in the global sphere as a consequence of the absence of the legal and other sanctions found in the more command-and-control regulatory systems of national states. These two developments make it essential that adequate quality assurance is in place to safeguard institutional standings and the mobility of student qualifications based on notions of equivalence. But, generally comprising higher education 'insiders', quality assurance and accreditation processes may also lead to temptations to only 'lightly' and inadequately conduct such processes of assessment in order not to reduce the reputations of both national systems and individual universities in a world of increased competitiveness.

Dill doubts that the self-regulatory approaches found in transnational quality assurance properly sustain the public interest (the saving of professional reputational skins is too developed an instinct in such circumstances), while rankings appear to display little valid knowledge of education programs and possibly even run counter to market forces that rely on adequate consumer information to work effectively. Based almost exclusively on research reputation and performance, such rankings possibly debilitate academic quality.

Rather pessimistically, Dill wonders whether the assurance of standards in global higher education can really deliver the goods when so many self-interests are involved. National states are anxious to obtain worldwide acknowledgment for their education qualifications, quality assurance professionals seek to have their essentially self-regulatory agencies widely legitimized, the producers of commercial university rankings have a strong stake in promoting their products as part of successful business strategies, while academics are often not slow to collude to help secure the reputations of their universities and programs. All this may limit the effectiveness of global efforts to assure and improve academic standards in the public interest.

A primary requirement is how to secure the public acceptance of these worldwide attempts to assure the quality of academic standards. Dill concludes by arguing that legitimate global institutions do more than simply satisfy the consent of participating states and must develop some notion of the 'global public good'. He suggests that open-minded and evidence-based deliberation in quality regulation, overseen by 'supreme audit agencies' covering a range of public services and not just higher education that are found in many national states, is a possible solution.

Musselin, in Chapter 26, examines the extent to which national higher education systems are becoming more similar as a consequence of the isomorphic tendencies generated by globalization and policy internationalization. She suggests that both divergences and convergences in steering tertiary sectors may be found, and that the emphasis on one or the other is often the outcome of the level of analysis that is brought to bear. Undoubtedly the state is changing its role and its governing instruments across many sectors, and is increasingly influenced by the activities of international organizations such as the OECD and the EU. But this is more an internationalization of the national than a supplanting of the national by transnational organizations. Effectively, however, both converging and diverging tendencies in national higher education systems may be found.

Undoubtedly Musselin believes that we can detect across many systems some common characteristics: the changing role of the state from micro-manager to broader regulator; the growth of private funding and supply; the development of networks and public–private alliances in sector policy-making; the creation of at least quasi-independent agencies, not least to take on responsibilities devolved from central governments, and including the quality assessment and evaluation bodies that Dill describes in his chapter; the notion of universities as organizational actors capable of establishing their strategic directions and undertaking contracts from both the state and commercial sectors; the growth of competition, quasi-markets and a strong regulatory oversight at the central level; benchmarking among peers both in formal governmental exercises such as research assessment and 'world-class excellence' initiatives, and more informally within university consortia or similar like-minded collections of universities where membership is determined often on the basis of positions and reputation emanating from university rankings; the emergence of employer–employee relations in place of more collegial understandings and processes within institutions; and the growth of institutional stratification and a move away from ideas of egalitarianism and a small reputational range of universities in national systems.

Yet, despite such processes of worldwide policy convergence, higher education systems remain quite national, with divergent steering mechanisms often reflecting particular historical biographies and path-determining critical junctures. In part, national divergence is a manifestation of policy implementation. Much comparative higher education research reveals, for example, that academic departments are capable of remaining somewhat immune to the corporatization occurring above them. However, the broader macro-level indicates distinctive national characteristics too. Levels of state micro-intervention, and the areas for such activism, can vary quite strongly, while ideas of a 'new public management' contain a variety of models and standards that lend to differential adoption and implementation in countries. Moreover, national systems of public services reflect levels of compatibility between various sectors and reflect important national subsystems, such as the economic. These institutional complementarities between sectors may form important sources of global advantage (and distinctiveness) for countries. Importantly, however, convergence and divergence should not be regarded as binary concepts but as related, for both are found in higher education systems.

King, in Chapter 24, argues also that convergence and divergence are not necessarily opposed tendencies: national customizations ('divergences') of global templates may actually strengthen universalism by allowing for wider and more extensive processes of diffusion. Moreover, certain models, such as those associated with the new public management, can reach thresholds of adoption that result in a subsequent snowballing effect, not necessarily on merit-based or rational evaluation grounds but because current non-adopters feel powerful influences to go with the crowd or else be penalized by becoming marginalized in key policy networks.

In discussing global science as a form of predominantly self-regulating global governance, King argues that the spread of the communications revolution in the last two decades or more allows for collaborations on research across national borders largely outside the gaze of state supervision. Rather, global science is an emergent social system that severely challenges the dominant model of state-directed scientific nationalism and highlights the vitality of curiosity-driven, status-seeking research by scholars as a vital element in scientific progress. Moreover, science's standards and rules are constituted and used by scientific actors in processes of structuration in which agency and structure are conjoined in ways that reproduce the system of global science. Furthermore, scientific collaborations and communities worldwide are formed in processes of sociability, rather than directed by forms of nation-state sovereignty; they seem to consist of loose connections between scientists rather than tightly integrated social capital networks. It is the former – loose connections rather than tight community or solidly cohering social capital – that conduce the scientific creativity necessary for advance and innovation.

The emergent global system of science raises important issues for well-established theories linking so-called 'open societies' and national capacities for innovation and creativity. For many years congressional and liberal democratic societies have been seen as generating the necessary sociopolitical conditions for preserving the openness and civic tolerances within which critical scientific cultures flourish without fear or favor (thus leading to scientific progress), and as also reflecting the way in which innovative and high-quality science itself was organized. There was, and still is, a strong commitment to Popperian notions of scientific falsification that require very open and democratic scientific processes in order to test hypotheses in the determined and replicating ways that help distinguish good science from dogma and similar forms of traditionalism. Yet the loose ties of global science seem to escape the constraints (and even facilitations) of national sociopolitical conditions and lead to more self-regulatory and open forms of scientific collaboration than before.

Consequently King raises the issue of whether the state and Party commands and controls found, for example, in China will mean that universities there will reach levels of scientific innovation short of those found in the west. That is, will China's universities and their gradual rise up global university rankings eventually plateau short of 'world-class' standings? King suggests that participation in global scientific networks provides the key and that, alongside recent increased autonomies for China's leading research universities, this form of transnationalism may enable research progress to continue. Moreover, many of China's leading universities are strongly science- and technology-based, and it may be that the open society is less critical here for research creativity than it is for the social sciences (which are largely underdeveloped and undernourished in contemporary China).

Enders and Westerheijden, in Chapter 27, analyze three particular issues: the political success of Bologna as a project; implementation and adoption of Bologna nationally and institutionally; and, finally, the recent development of 'Bologna going global' and attracting interest from other parts of the world and whether this offers a promising route for some form of normative leadership for European higher education in a globalizing and increasingly competitive market.

Enders and Westerheijden suggest that it is rather a surprise that an intergovernmental reform agenda that is Bologna could actually emerge and become quite well diffused. The explanation lies predominantly in a political process of soft governance where national policies are gelled at the European level but national governments remain responsible for the implementation process and its transformation into national contexts. The agreements arising out of the Bologna Process are formally voluntary and without the legal sanctions found in more conventional EU processes of supranational authority and hierarchical direction. Yet, although such processes allow the autonomy and integrity of national decision-makers to be preserved, the peer pressures for compliance are quite compelling nonetheless and work very effectively in securing intergovernmental progress.

Furthermore, intergovernmental agreement on Bologna from its very inception has always proved rather useful for national decision-makers. When confronted by the need to reform domestic higher education systems, not least in the face of strong resistance and reform blockages, the ability to point to Europe as the villain is remarkably tempting. Enders and Westerheijden argue that Bologna does not simply address issues of structure and institutional governance frameworks, but reaches into the hallowed ground of curriculum and the nature of academic degrees, the very center of the academic production process. It is clear that a system of soft but quite powerful governance has been necessary to make progress in a policy domain that for long has been jealously protected as almost exclusively a matter for national authority. Reporting, benchmarking, stocktaking, naming, shaming and blaming are mechanisms that effectively move voluntary national participation at the European level to one of 'monitored coordination' as a result of powerful socialization impacts.

Finally, Enders and Westerheijden suggest that Bologna was formed, in part at least, to ensure the global competitiveness of those higher education institutions (HEIs) in the broader European region. Whether this is being secured is difficult to measure. Yet the Bologna 'brand' has attracted attempts at emulation worldwide and fears that it may confer market advantage on European institutions to the detriment of those elsewhere in the world. Hence we see increased efforts by other regions to see if they can achieve a similar form of regional integration.

Lauder and Brown, in Chapter 28, argue that globalization is leading to the development of a hierarchy of 'circuits' in higher education systems based on global reputation. Moreover, these circuits impact differently on the types of education that the universities provide, not only in the classroom and in the positional-goods nature of the qualifications gained, but also in the individual character formation that is engendered. This latter point is especially important as the large multinational corporations in the global knowledge economy see character traits as key indicators of creativity, innovation and leadership qualities that they scour the globe for in their graduate recruitment policies.

There is thus a correspondence between the global division of labor and the global division of university reputation that is in part reinforced by global university league tables. Despite the often-found association of the 'knowledge society' and requirements for the advanced theoretical knowledge formed by university education, there is also a fragmentation of knowledge work as recent digital revolutions become more routinized in business practices. Global employers require potential corporate leaders wherever they may be found from the global university elite institutions, but they also require graduates with more standardized knowledge of the kind transmitted in non-elite universities – to carry out the increasing standardization of knowledge work. These standardized work processes are associated with what Lauder and Brown describe as 'digital Taylorism' and correspond to the standardized learning processes (modularization, bite-sized curricula and often pre-packaged learning) found increasingly in mass higher education.

Although Lauder and Brown accept that their idea of a correspondence between the top levels of the global labor market and the worldwide reputational circuits of the top universities needs further testing, they argue that employers, nonetheless, increasingly demand university outputs to be benchmarked so that judgments can be made about the comparability of degrees between universities. Thus they remark that 'benchmarking and standard-setting is a focal element of global networks between universities'.

Consequently the top-ranked universities have little need to promote the 'consumerism' found in the mass higher education providers. The rather mechanistic and procedural forms of learning and assessment found in the latter are not where the university elite gain their advantages. These lie more in the peer-generated character formation of their students rather than the possession of standardized skills by their graduates. And in such broader capabilities and social characteristics – among graduates from the top universities worldwide – are found the sources of innovation and initiative. These are not attributes that can be taught through standardized learning and codified quality assurance processes.

As a result, Lauder and Brown argue that transnational companies are globalizing their recruitment strategies and focusing on the top universities across national borders. These are the institutions that are believed to have graduates with the appropriate behavioral dispositions – not technical skills – to assume leadership positions and to empathize and develop global corporate cultures. Moreover, such graduates have the potential to adapt corporate cultures to the variety of local cultures within which transnational companies increasingly find themselves operating.

This segmentation of knowledge work is reproduced in the rankings of national and international universities. According to Lauder and Brown, there is a genuine 'correspondence' at work as the mutual 'buying and selling' of top graduates reinforces the reputation of both the elite universities and the major transnational employers.

Ellen Hazelkorn, in Chapter 29, notes a global magnetism with university rankings in recent years, one that 'has reached almost fever pitch'. Hardly any stakeholder appears immune. University presidents, faculty staff, many students and their parents, employers, governments and the media all give almost continuous attention to positions and movements up and down the various hierarchies. Increasingly, and perhaps worryingly, government policies appear not only shaped by rankings but often incorporate them as proxies, such as in the determination of which students to support with scholarships for studying abroad (at only, say, the top 100 universities in the major global rankings).

Yet such rankings are published by a range of governmental and non-governmental entities alike, including higher education, research and commercial organizations, and major media bodies. There is powerful emerging evidence that universities also construct or modify their strategies to be in alignment with the models and outcomes of the major rankers. As Hazelkorn notes, 'what began as a consumer-oriented guide for students and parents has been transformed into a rapidly expanding global intelligence information business'. She estimates that by 2011 there were 11 different global rankings, and over 50 national rankings, of universities.

In this sense we see in university rankings a global phenomenon in two senses. One is that national rankings or league tables of colleges and universities have become globally diffused as a characteristic of higher education systems. And, second, the emergence of global rankings, or the construction of hierarchies relating and comparing universities from around the world, appears increasingly influential for government leaders, not least in widening efforts at introducing funding and other policies to support the growth of 'world-class universities' in their territorial domains, the success or otherwise of such policies being gauged by positions in the global rankings.

Hazelkorn argues that the growth of university league tables in the last decade or so can be traced to four central and interrelated reasons. First, the widespread acceptance that global economic competitiveness for nations depends on high-value knowledge and innovation, of which higher education is an important contributor. Governmental decision-makers and others need to know how they are doing in world science and in attracting international talent, and they perceive global university rankings as helping to provide such measures. Second, demographic and other pressures in a number of countries are producing soft and weakening domestic student demand that needs to be replaced or compensated for by increased international recruitment. Good league table performance increases the attractiveness of home institutions. Third, league tables help to inform views about value for taxpayers' money, productivity and efficiency. And, finally, students as well as governments are demanding greater transparency about performance from universities in a more consumer-focused and privately funded sector; the more formalized information sources in the shape of league tables appear to be taking the place of informal and primarily exclusive, national networks.

23 Strategizing and ordering the global
Simon Marginson

INTRODUCTION

Universities and other higher education institutions operate in the global, national and local dimensions simultaneously. They are 'glonacal' organizations (*glo*bal + *na*tional + lo*cal*). Within this mix the global element grows more important. All the cross-border moves of higher education institutions and systems taken together sum up to the global dimension of action. This is formed by a combination of global imagining, global strategizing and global ordering. Chapter 2 of Part I introduced the global dimension and looked at global 'imaginings', in the context of space-time compression, space-making by institutions and systems, the world imaginaries drawn on by global subjects (the economic market, the world of status comparison and competition, and the world of networks and open source knowledge), and discussed global subjects themselves and their agendas and transformations.

The present chapter, the second of Part III on governance and also the pair of Chapter 2, focuses on how those global imaginings, with their sense of what might be possible in higher education, play out in the global positioning strategies of institutions and systems; and the implications of these strategies for the formal and informal ordering and governance of the higher education sector. Like Chapter 2, the present chapter is generic in character. It is preliminary to Part III's more specific studies of aspects of governance.

The chapter begins with the coordinates of the strategic setting. How do global subjects conceive that setting and position themselves within it? What creates the scope for and the limits of action? In part the possibilities are controlled by global subjects themselves in their strategies for managing and reinventing higher education space. But there are limits to space manipulation in higher education; and some global subjects have more options than others. The chapter returns to the three principal world imaginaries (global pictures) that shape thinking in higher education – the market, status, and networks and knowledge – and examines the manner in which they play out in the main global strategies: comparisons and rankings, WTO–GATS market reform, higher education export, capacity-building in research, global 'hubs' and knowledge cities, transnational campuses, partnerships and consortia, global 'e-Universities' and cross-national regionalization. It considers which global strategies work best, and why; which world imaginaries are most appropriate to global conditions, and why; and summarizes the strategic imperatives of global positioning. The chapter then moves to the implications of globalization for formal and informal regulation. It discusses the pronounced role of informal regulation in the global setting, the potency of global standardization and the scope for diversity, the dynamics of global inequalities, and the continuing tension between national and global goals and perspectives.

STRATEGIZING THE GLOBAL

Global strategic thinking is an active interplay of, respectively, the 'world out there', the world as it is perceived, and the sense of self – all of which are changing. Global strategy is shaped by the oscillation between localized identity and mobile knowledge, the antinomy foundational to the university as an institution (see Introduction to Part I). But in this more global era movement between localities is no longer confined to a small number of traveling scholars. Many global subjects – whether individuals, higher education systems or whole national systems – are now mobile within the circuits of knowledge; and all travel in the virtual sense. This continually multiplies visions, strategies, global connections and activities.

The strategies of global subjects are a mix of path dependence, imitation and novel departures. There is continuing tension between, on one hand, resource limitations and local pragmatism, and, on the other, the imagining of bold cross-border initiatives. 'Can we afford to invest in this?' 'Is this core business?' It is not surprising that global initiatives are mostly imitations. Competition generates risk-averse strategies of follow the leader: if everybody fails, no one loses relative position; and if a new initiative succeeds, it is fatal to be left behind. 'Can we afford to miss out?' Thus some prototypes spread rapidly, such as consortia and e-Universities in the 1990s, and hub strategies in the 2000s (for a detailed description of each global strategy, see Chapter 2). Genuine innovation creates risk: if a bold new initiative fails, the unhappy first mover loses ground. Despite this, new vistas can be compelling – and from time to time there are original acts of global creation. Consider the first transnational campuses in South-east Asia, which pioneered a new kind of multiple provision across borders spanning two different national regulatory spaces and cultural settings. Consider the Singapore Global Schoolhouse, the first and best hub, and the global outreach of the National University of Singapore. Consider the Shanghai Jiao Tong rankings group, which has gained a global authority to shape the field of performance comparison and university hierarchy. Consider the dual identity and governance structures evolving in Europe, a novel mix of regulation plus advanced voluntarism, which works; and the fecund excitement and wave of innovation that Europeanization has opened up. All of these moves opened up new global positions and scope for new positioning strategies.

The 'Space of Possibles'

How do changing and self-changing global subjects navigate the global setting? What creates the scope for and limits of action? That which individuals, nations and institutions can achieve is determined by what Bourdieu calls 'the space of possibles' in conjunction with their own resources and attributes. In *Distinction* (1984), Bourdieu argues that subjects compete for resources, status and other objects of interest. Perhaps he underestimates the capacity for flat collaboration in the global setting. For example, research and knowledge dissemination combine hierarchical status with horizontal open source flows. This is the mix of competition and cooperation found in both higher education and gift economies. Nevertheless, whether competing or cooperating, subjects must position themselves within the relational setting. Bourdieu models the interplay of the positional strategies of subjects, which are conditioned by their prior positions, and the overall framework or system of positions in which they find themselves.

> Every position-taking is defined in relation to the *space of possibles* which is objectively realized as a *problematic* in the form of the actual or potential position-takings corresponding to the different positions; and it receives its distinctive *value* from its negative relationship with the coexistent position-takings to which it is objectively related. (Bourdieu, 1993, p. 30, emphasis in original)

Position-taking is the 'space of creative works' (ibid., p. 39). It is not an open-ended free-wheeling creativity. Only some position-takings are possible, identified by agents as they respond to changes in the settings and the moves of others in the game. Agents have a number of possible 'trajectories', the succession of positions occupied by the same agent over time, and employ semi-instinctual 'strategies' to achieve them. Agents respond in terms of their '*habitus*', their acquired mix of beliefs and capabilities. In particular their 'disposition' mediates the relationship between position and position-takings (ibid., pp. 61–73).

Bourdieu's schema is consistent with some evidence on the decisions of university executives as they strive for relative advantage (see, e.g., Marginson and Considine, 2000, pp. 68–95). Concepts of positioned/position-taking can be readily applied in situated case studies of the strategies of universities (Deem, 2001). Likewise specific national trajectories can be identified in, say, China, Singapore, Germany or Australia (Marginson, 2007b, 2008a). Nevertheless the strategies of some systems and institutions are so novel as to be difficult to explain in these terms, such as the Singapore Schoolhouse. Bourdieu's schema raise questions about the room left for self-determining agency; in particular, how much the positions of subjects are fixed in advance. In the global setting, where the map of possibilities is in flux, with new subjects, strategies and positions continually emerging, there is an enlarged scope for new trajectories.

It seems that in the global dimension there are more possibilities, and possibilities are less fixed. Partly disembedded from national government regulation, individuals and institutions enjoy a greater negative freedom (freedom from constraint) than in the national setting. Here the half-formed, open character of global rules and relations comes into play. Global higher education is a different kind of regulatory space from national higher education. At the same time global action also entails positive freedoms (capacities for self-determining action). Here the broader scope for imaginative strategy comes into play. Bourdieu is right to argue that our conditions and histories affect our perceptions, choices and desires. But we can alter our fate, within limits, when we have the resources to do so. In part these resources are material: money, infrastructure, global connections. In part they are mental: the imagination. The global dimension offers a remarkable scope for invention.

MANAGING AND REINVENTING SPACE

One way in which new global positioning becomes possible is by reinventing space. Global subjects respond to the spatial settings in which they find themselves, and also develop and exploit the de-severed spatiality opened up by globalization. They open spaces, block spaces, make spaces more multiple, and make new kinds of spaces. Global space is plastic to a wide range of interests and strategies, although all space-making strategies have their limits. Sometimes, but not always, space-making strategies change the 'space of positions' itself.

We saw in Chapter 2 that globalization imposes a glonacal spatiality on governments and institutions. They deal with global systems in their own terms and with the effects of those systems in the national and local dimensions. It is easier for governments, which largely remain within the shelter of the national domain and treat global systems and forces as external, than for university presidents who are *bona fide* global actors (part of the time at least). The difficulty is that global, national and local are often heterogeneous in their agents, relationships, drivers, behaviors and resources. Executive leaders must work with fluency and sureness of judgment across all three dimensions. These are the skills of polyphony, which requires the artist to concentrate on two or more strands of music at once. Three strands are more difficult than two. It is the most challenging of musical forms.

The compensating factor is the vast new possibilities opened up by de-severing, as the strategies listed in Table 23.1 suggest. De-severing and synchrony are the heart of voluntary networks. De-severing suggests audacious hub strategies, in which outliers such as Qatar or Mauritius seek to position themselves at the center of attention. De-severing and desires for synchrony strong enough to overcome centuries of war underpin Europeanization in higher education (van der Wende, 2008). Where de-severing is present but desires for synchrony are fractured, then regionalization is slow, as in East Asia. De-severing is integral to global research collaboration and open source knowledge. It is wholly essential to virtual learning. De-severing carries those strategies not dependent on fixed national locations such as e-University delivery; and those strategies that render national identity of institution more ambiguous or multiple, such as transnational education (Ziguras and McBurnie, 2006).

Yet de-severing is not the whole of the story. Global strategies vary spatially in the manner in which they combine place and mobility. Together they offer a flexible toolbox. Some strategies focus on building place-bound strength within the volatile global setting so as to capture a share of the mobile traffic going past: capacity-building in research; global hubs and knowledge cities; and national education export industries, a strategy begun in the Westminster countries and then extended to Malaysia, Singapore and China. Other strategies exploit not fixedness but mobility (transnational campuses), or de-severed instantaneous movement (the e-Universities). A third kind of spatial move is about moving between the fixed concentrations of status and resources, for example partnerships and networks. Regionalization also combines place-bound concentration with external linkages.

Spatial Limits

Space management has two limits. The first limit is conjured by absolute de-severing in which place and identity are lost. The second limit is when place is used to block mobility. The early e-Universities such as NYU (New York University) Online and Cardean University assumed all distances – geographical, modal and cultural – had been abolished. All places had been rendered equivalent – which is to say there was no

*Table 23.1   Global strategies in higher education: what they tell us about space-making,
global imaginings and glonacal effects*

Strategy	Glonacal dimensions	Spatial strategies and implications	World imaginaries of higher education
Global comparisons of institutions, and research performance	Models higher education as a single world, emphasizes global systems like research metrics. Affects national positioning strategies, and the local status and practices of institutions.	Becomes possible because of (1) universal knowledge, especially quantifiable science, and (2) advanced de-severing in a more globalized higher education sector. Once geo-culturally distant universities are almost local for purpose of comparison.	University status competition always had an international dimension and readily translates into an ecological imaginary. Networked links and web visibility of institutions confirm this. Idea of global economic competition reinforces status competition and provides some of its language.
WTO-GATS negotiation of global system of free trade in educational services	Negotiation between nations to create global higher education trading space (world market). Deregulates national dimension, changes pattern of local activity.	Paradoxical strategy in glonacal terms. Goal is one world system, but to be fulfilled by nation-states that have little incentive to dismantle barriers, and would continue unchanged once the global market is put in place.	Unrealistic vision. Too easy neoliberal assumption of one global market subsuming nation-state and national political economy. Must fail: higher education too state-heavy for this, and much of its output not tradable – especially in research.
Capacity-building in research	National action to strengthen system in global dimension. Wave of mimetic national investments triggered. Stimulates local activity in selected sites.	Depends on and reinforces nation as place, affecting global flows both ways – by drawing global resources and status to nation, and by magnifying its global competitiveness and cross-border impacts.	Higher education's role in knowledge creation/ dissemination at centre of nation as 'competition state'. Draws on both global status competition imagining (the source of national benefits), and networked open source imagining always part of research.
Remaking of nation/city as a 'global hub' of education and research activities	National action to strengthen system in global dimension by building global activity and centering more on nation. Stimulates local activity and cooperation.	Rests on global de-severing, convergence, synchrony while making nation stronger within knowledge-based competition. Shapes global sector by drawing flows, resources, status to nation. Prone to de-severing errors.	Positions knowledge-intensive nation as competition state in globalizing world. Stimulates global education markets and also knowledge flows. Growth of education catalyzes other industries. Two signs of success: economy, and university rankings.

Table 23.1 (continued)

Strategy	Glonacal dimensions	Spatial strategies and implications	World imaginaries of higher education
Knowledge cities	National action to strengthen system and city/locality in global dimension by centering more global activity in locality. Stimulates local activity and cooperation.	Depends on and reinforces nation and city/locality as place. Rests on global de-severing, convergence, synchrony; and on intensive local networks. Shapes global sector by drawing flows, resources, status to city/ locality.	Similar to hub strategy: uses global networks and knowledge flows to fulfill imaginaries of both economic market and status competition. Less explicitly national in form and intent. Two signs of success: economic indicators, and university rankings.
Commercial export of education	Builds export capacity of national system to attract global student flows. Changes national policy, regulation, funding; and also local activity.	Nation-centered. Little change in spatiality except fostering of cross-border student flows, and bilateral trade negotiation. Little realized potentials for global or multilateral regulation.	The global market imaginary in its most developed practical form. Also rests on the imaginary of status competition, especially in research, which helps to shape demand – and is facilitated by university networks.
Regionalization in higher education and research	Meso-level between global and national. Positions region as global player, relativizes nation. Drives modernization of nation and local, and intra-region networking.	Combines concentration of place-based strength with networked external comparisons and linkages. Creates new place (geographical) identity. Rests on de-severing and multiplicity. But external wall against global.	Contents of regionalization are (1) global economic competition against USA and Asia, (2) status competition in higher education, (3) networked collaboration in Europe underpinned by knowledge function, less national conflict, common public good.
Transnational campuses	Local university in global space, while subject to two systems of national regulation, two cultures. Potential transformative effects in both nations and both localities.	Rests on mobile students and institution, global de-severing/ convergence. Pluralized locality, regulation – evades full control by either nation. Can be multiple in identity, culture. De-severing errors occur if home link weak.	All three imaginaries at play here. Rests on economic market in students; networked higher education sector especially local-foreign provider partnership dealings; status ranking affects economic market, and shapes host country invitations.
Partnerships between universities	Global network around institution as node, some	Rests on global convergence, de-severing, synchrony.	Foregrounds universal knowledge (research central to much networking and

Table 23.1   (continued)

Strategy	Glonacal dimensions	Spatial strategies and implications	World imaginaries of higher education
	nodes thicker than others. Transmits effects directly between global and local, without nation-state.	Moves and relations across fixed localities accumulate as a global spatiality. Bypasses national regulation, fosters university autonomy.	the main beneficiary). Draws on open source networked imaginary, while status and market economic potential enter networking decisions.
University consortia	Selective networks; facilitate global flows of people and knowledge. Transmits effects directly between global and local, without nation-state.	Rests on global convergence, de-severing, synchrony. Moves and relations across fixed localities accumulate as a global spatiality. Bypasses national regulation, fosters university autonomy.	Foregrounds universal knowledge (research central to much networking and the main beneficiary). Draws on open source networked imaginary, also economic and status potentials: consortia also exclusion devices.
Global 'e-Universities' (e-Us)	Global dimension alone. Virtual institutions are pure cyber-creations, or shadow 'brick' locals. No local effects (except lost resources). Parallel world of virtual locals. Bypasses national.	In 1990s e-Us, ultra de-severing without producer/consumer synchrony, no local and cultural variation. Failed. But e-Us that shadow 'brick' institutions gain referred local identity – have better prospects, especially if nuanced for consumer variety.	The 1990s e-Us were world market imaginary writ large – abstract neoliberal economy *sans* states or local variation, realized as real virtual universe. Strategy also drew on imaginary of global network of local universities as conjured by institutional websites.

longer any place – in a networked world where 'brick' and 'click' universities were one and identity was created not by history and geography but by marketing and branding. E-Universities reached out to the whole world as a single classroom learning the same lesson. Low-teaching-intensity institutions operating in global English would build a massive market in China as the webpage flickered into life on a million screens. Yeah, right. With dreams like these the e-Universities were doomed before the first prospectus was out. They attracted a handful of students. The extreme nature of this imagined de-severing gave the virtual universe its oddly normative character. Advocates of the 1990s e-Universities were convinced that face-to-face education would soon be obsolete. Because the 'brick' university was going to disappear bridges between 'click' and 'brick' were irrelevant. When the e-Universities failed, the 'brick' world was left as default. There is a vacancy for imaginings of virtual higher education that situate e-institutions alongside and within 'brick' institutions rather than against them (OECD, 2005).

'Knowledge villages' erected in the desert at the edge of Gulf State cities, connecting with students and universities worldwide but with weak local presence (the local population remains insulated from foreign cultural influence), reflect the same hubris. Likewise the quality of transnational education falters when the franchised institution spins away from the parent university. The common error is absolute de-severing, the identity of 'here and there', sustained by global communications and 'world-market' ideology. When de-severing becomes absolute there is no need for local embeddedness – and the historical antinomy of place and mobility is lost. Universities can live in more than one place; and place is more and also less than geography. The global dimension is built by global strategies that extend or augment place on the global scale, such as networks, hubs, and the most innovative of all, transnational education. The place/mobility antinomy essential to the university is changed, and perhaps rendered more complex – but not abolished. All global strategies that rest on extreme de-severing have failed. No institution without a place-based identity can function.

Openness and Closure

Global subjects create both openness and closure. At times they push each strategy to extremes. They also do both together. WTO–GATS created an open space for cross-border trade. It also fixed a hierarchy of economic benefits, benefiting rich trading nations with strong English-language education systems. The comparison and rankings world creates one open setting for the institutions in the top 500 – and sets a firm closure against the universities left outside. Partnerships open a wider world for partners – and close it to non-partners.

By no means all actions by global subjects are designed to enlarge our common freedoms. The global dimension is cluttered with projects that exploit its openness by turning selected spaces into monopolies for exploitation. In going global, companies and universities try to seize first-mover advantage via status systems (university rankings), market values (intellectual property) or nation-state decisions (securing favored foreign-provider status in a national system, for example Malaysia) that create enclosures. Then they work to turn first-mover advantage into something more permanent. Global enclosures are also a means of defending national system coherence and identity, and a means of cultural reproduction and standardization. Global communications and knowledge spread the role of English and make a one-world culture by occluding other tongues. The one-way Americanization of research creates an enclosure that advances US interests abroad while protecting the hegemon from global difference at home. But large powers can postpone full global engagement. This opens a space for the small and nimble – the Singapores, Hong Kongs, Switzerlands – to create new opportunities for themselves out of global openness.

All strategies embodying global closure are designed to protect the subject against global contingency through an act of will, a smaller contingency pushed up against the larger. Such maneuvers are always limited. No strategy holds for all times and places. The global setting changes quickly. Few can evade global contingency for long. Even strong US institutions need global talent. Sooner or later each successive closure is exploded. The danger of global enclosures, for subjects that perpetrate them, is that in blocking free entry from outside they truncate their own global engagement. In the end, openness, connection, responsiveness, flexibility and ease of movement are essential. To step outside the flows, even partly, is to retard the speed of learning and narrow the range of action. It is to reduce the potential partners. It is to miss options not as opportunity costs but through ignorance. It is to court irrelevance. All global strategy rests in some way on place as identity. This is the final limit of global openness and mobility. But global closures are too place-bound.

WORLD IMAGINARIES IN STRATEGY

Table 23.1 summarizes the main global strategies in terms of the world imaginaries they fulfill. Of the three imaginaries – the world market, global status competition, and open source knowledge and networks – only the last two are fully apposite to the development of global higher education and research. The world market locks onto only parts of the sector.

The Market Economy

Economic visions shape government policies, and neoliberal language frames the agenda of institutions even with other ends in view. This sustains the differing imaginaries of higher education as a WTO-supervised market of commodity-producer institutions, and higher education as an 'arms race' between states in education and research. The latter also has older roots in nineteenth-century competition between nation-states (Bayly, 2004). The limitations of the market vision are obvious, in the failure of both e-Universities and WTO–GATS, and the swing to open science in research policy. But the market imaginary survives. It is entrenched in NPM (new public management) organization; and reproduced by global markets in intellectual property (IP) and education exports. Commercial export is managed in the disciplines of economics, business strategy and marketing. Here national systems are competing brands on the world scale. The export market flips over normal relations between, on one hand, economic goals, and on the other, university prestige and its handmaiden, knowledge. Normally prestige is the primary goal and its foundation is research. In the export market research morphs from an end in itself to a means for securing market share, channeling demand and determining price. Unlike the national education of elites in a status market, in which the scarcity of places determines their value, full fee-paying international education is driven by the logic of capitalist expansion. The growth of the global for-profit sector, centered on the USA, confirms the economic vision. Here the economic imaginary also underpins hub strategies, partnerships and transnational campuses where these dovetail with export strategy.

For national government the economic imaginary creates the need for policies and regulatory frameworks that facilitate market transactions, such as the consumer protection of international students. For institutions it sustains marketing, recruitment, pricing, and the administration of financial transactions and service contracts. In export nations like the UK and Australia there has been more development of these areas than teaching and learning specific to international students, such as intercultural education (Marginson et al., 2010). But the lesson of the last two decades is that the economic imaginary has purchase in global higher education only under limited conditions. It works when centered on commodifiable activities – international, but not domestic, education. It works when centered on real places and aligned with national political economies and not against them. This cuts off the potential for the ultra-globalism imagined by 1990s neoliberalism. The e-Universities work only when coupled to a 'brick' institution of the same name, and not always then. They also need to approximate the benefits of geo-located higher education. Absolute de-severing and abstract global markets cannot drive commodity production.

As a result, culture and knowledge have proven to be more universalizable in higher education than is the market economy. Why did the two big economic ideas – GATS and the e-Universities – fail? Both are the product of mainstream economics and, more specifically, business management notions. Business management thought has yet to evolve a satisfactory understanding of global higher education. The WTO–GATS vision lacks purchase because commercial production is largely marginal to education in public sectors and non-profit private sectors across the world. It has less purchase in research given the public-good nature of knowledge (Samuelson, 1954). The market imaginary works only for the minority of activities where commercial trade is important, notably full-fee international education. It misses most of the global dealings of universities, in which their 'economy' is status competition and the gift economy, or morphs into open source knowledge relations that are not an economy at all. The one big open global market is also impossible because national political economies survive. The notion of an unfettered world market is an ideological artifact of neoliberalism – and one that has never been pursued consistently in neoliberal doctrine where the anti-statist rhetoric disguises the central commitment to nation-state control. Neoliberalism confers the largest freedoms only on powerful market actors; and even they can be impacted by national regulation. The state has not disappeared from higher education systems. It will not, unless it is a global state (and perhaps not then).

Neoliberal marketization strategies, for all their globalist and anti-statist rhetoric, work better at national than global level. Far from securing the disappearance of the state, the quasi-market in higher education is possible only because of the state. At global level the status and network imaginaries work better than does the economic market imaginary. And the status and network imaginaries frame themselves without the need for a state.

Networks and Knowledge

Networks are integral to almost all global imaginings in higher education, and every-where else. There is no global equivalent of the bounded, centralized, identity-heavy nation-state. So networks roll out unfettered. The global dimension lacks an intrinsic boundary or enclosure. Yet the ecological imagining is weak. Global subjects are strongly conscious of national differences, which fragment world imagining. In this context the binding qualities of networks have become crucial to imagining and organizing the global dimension.

Networks arise naturally out of global communications, the mobility of information and ideas, and the 'flat' character of open source knowledge. The many online systems are all network-based. Strategies of research capacity-building and global hubs, used by nations and institutions to position themselves in global competition, are also turned to horizontal exchange. Transnational education – the quintessentially global extension of the university form that rests on both de-severing and the pluralization of place – is even more flexible. It plays into the economic imaginary. It also augments networking, research collaboration and knowledge exchange. Similar points can be made about education exports, which augment not just people mobility but synchronous networks. International students maintain contact with home families and friends while engaging with the country of education. As they struggle to survive and change in the new country, they draw the world closer together. International education makes money for its producers. It all builds a one-world ecology.

Incidental outcomes? The unexpected consequence of global markets? No. These outcomes in knowledge flows and networked relations should not be seen as spin-offs from more practical, economically verifiable activities supported by policy. On the contrary, the relationship is reversed. The autonomous role of institutions of higher education within larger circuits of knowledge confers on them universal functions in both teaching/learning and research. It is this that makes global strategies possible – as was always the case in cross-border work – including strategies fostered by economic policy. There would be no trade reform, no export sectors, no competitive capacity-building, no hubs and knowledge cities, no partnerships, no transnational education, and no comparative mapping of global higher education without the essential knowledge-bearing role of institutions. Likewise cross-border networks provide necessary conditions for most global activities, including relations between partners, transnational education and exports. Branch campuses founded offshore rest on networking and open source logics as well as economic logics. Some generate export receipts. Others do not. Many are beachheads for partnerships and research collaboration. Transnational education is a hybrid not only in governance (across two nations) and pedagogy (potentially multicultural), but mission (both cultural and economic). Both functions rest on the bedrock of teaching and research, which are both means and end.

We find a similar synergy at work in the relations between status and knowledge. Hub and knowledge-city strategies position the nation or city to attract global flows of students, research talent and capital, and to build markets: education exports, IP and industrial applications of research-based knowledge, and associated activities in construction, human services, tourism, property and retail. The hub vision rests on the logic of concentration in a global status market and it models open-ended global flows as resources to secure and exploit. It sees global status and wealth as mutually reinforcing. It is a hybrid imagining. But all this rests on whether the hub or city has a *bona fide* presence in the circulation of knowledge.

Arguably the quality of education and research in Singapore – and the brilliant manner in which it uses the hub strategy to continually improve quality – enables the Singapore hub to function effectively while Malaysia's hub cannot. The universal character of knowledge enables it to play the broad enabling role in higher education that abstract economic forms cannot. At the same time the universal role of knowledge allows specific economic markets to develop. These in turn have feedback effects, generating further networking and further potentials for the flow of knowledge. Knowledge is universal; its locations are not. As has been repeatedly argued here, the knowledge-bearing role of higher education rests on its location in real institutions in real places. In fact the hub strategy is strongest in cities within primary zones of global economic, demographic and cultural passage such as Paris, Shanghai or Los Angeles. Singapore just makes this list, but then the Straits of Malacca have long been an important passage for trade. Mauritius does not.

Summarizing, this argument suggests the conditions of effective global strategies in higher education are thus: they are founded in the production/dissemination of knowledge; and those knowledge-related functions are grounded in real institutions in real places.

Status Competition

The reach of performance comparison, rankings and hierarchies of value is undeniable. The hierarchical vision, arbitrary and problematic as it is, has great influence on practical thought in higher education, in the manner that distasteful strategic imperatives (such as the need to use force to defend ourselves) become compulsory in war. In one way it strongly supports the neoliberal vision while also taking higher education to another place. Through the processes of global comparison and ranking, status competition gives form to a global economic market in higher education. The ranking of systems and institutions, via 'best university' lists and in research performance, advances the practice of higher education as a competitive market. It defines the field of competition, standardizes performance criteria, and sets institutions and nations directly against each other. Yet classification and ranking also provide data that facilitate mutual recognition and collaboration – although ranking hierarchies tend to marginalize institutions with lesser resources, and subordinate systems where the main language is not English.

Many strategies set out to accumulate status and draw positional advantage from it. They include all capacity-building, especially in research. Knowledge cities and hubs are designed to build a mass of status sufficient to attract global talent and investment money, especially in R & D. Meanwhile institutions carry prestige-maximizing behaviors at work in the national dimension into the global setting. Partners can secure referred status, especially when networking up to the strongest members of the consortium. Strong export performance can generate status up to a point – although when higher education exports reach a mass education level, universities can be trapped at the wrong Bourdieuian pole.

Another way to garner prestige is research on problems of global public good such as epidemic disease and climate change. Global public goods can be hybridized like most kinds of knowledge and rendered ambiguous in purpose; turned to self-interest and fed into the maw of global status competition – without ceasing to create global public benefits. Researchers exchange knowledge in the form of gifts. As in the classical gift economy, giving (academic publishing) confers power and prestige on the giver. Gift economies speak to both self-interest and the collective interest. Research behaviors are common, open and meritocratic – and fiercely hierarchical. They make closures and slopes too steep to climb. Research systems often reinforce the hegemony of the old imperial nations and their leading institutions. This system of power is more conservative and reproductive than economic competition. It is certainly less contestable. Yet open source flows undermine it.

The normative implications of these two imaginaries – on one hand status competition, on the other knowledge and networks – are profoundly different. Network imaginaries encourage openness and enjoin us to connect. Rankings and performance hierarchies are tougher. They create the firm binaries (big/small, strong/weak, winner/loser) used to create exclusions. They push us hard towards differentiation. Yet it is no coincidence that the two imaginaries make a pair. First, the two imaginings can be fitted to each other because both hybridize readily and creatively. They coexist not only with each other but with many institutional, political and ideological positions. Networks constantly evolve new and stronger connections. Rankings systems engage in a continuing conversation about techniques and effects. New rankings appear all the time. These are fecund domains. They are also spatially flexible. Flat networks and ordering hierarchies are mixed in a wide range of ways. Second, global networks and rankings taken together – horizontal and vertical – provide a full set of vectors of social organization. They provide conceptual resources for visualizing internal relations in organizations, visualizing relations between organizations, and understanding those relations as a 'field' (Bourdieu, 1993).

Networks hold the field together. The rankings imaginary provides boundaries to the field. This is one of its principal attractions. Here systems of comprehensive classification of institutions of higher education, already existing in North America and China and being developed in Europe, are especially useful. They provide the whole map: horizontal lines, vertical lines and outer borders. Classifications inform universities that want to build consortia of like-minded parallel players and set the rules for universities that want to move up and network up.

It is striking how the horizontal network imaginary and the vertical status imaginary achieve symbiosis in higher education – and more so at global than at national system level. Open source flows and networks bring modernity to the old hierarchy. They do not destroy the hegemony of the Ivy Leagues, which gain a larger reach, but these are shaken up. In the process the global symbiosis has more room for new universities than in national systems of preferment. It finds earlier openings for rising systems. And it draws every university old and new into the whirlwind of continuous rapid change from which there is no shelter.

THE GLOBAL SELF

Globalization requires its subjects to combine two heterogeneous qualities. Without holding both objects in the air it is impossible to be fully effective. The first is active engagement, including the capacity to learn and, where necessary, to change. The second quality is the sense of one's own project and capacity to hold to it, even while the project changes. Only agents with both qualities can shape global relationships (subject to resource limits) as well as become shaped by them. Remain broadly connected and keep one's options open – while maintaining self-determined identity, strategic coherence and a crisp development trajectory with an eye on long-term goals. Again we find the antinomy between place and mobility, between self and engagement with the other. The global presses inwards with greater intensity. Openness to the other threatens to overwhelm the self. The distinction between 'us' and 'others' is fragmented more readily than in the past. Identity must bend and become more complex, without ceasing to be itself. The old ivory tower retreat into remote and bounded locality, the standard move for preserving the university in difficult (or just noisy) times, is gone. The old antinomy is both more essential and more difficult to achieve.

What sustains strategic coherence? A strong sense of one's own project. Non-dependency. Strength of will. Executive capacity and internal controls that point the different parts of the institution or system in the same direction. Objectives that evolve on a reflexive basis – or plans become too rigid and break, or become irrelevant to the real agenda. What sustains strategic flexibility? Loose networking, porous borders, de-coupled systems with scope for faculty initiative, facility in common languages, multiple identities on site so as to maximize potential networks, the willingness to break with path dependence and innovate. All this rests on capacity, especially in research, and executive leadership.

ORDERING THE GLOBAL

Every presence creates an absence. Dark matter is interspersed with light. The global strategies of universities and national systems, with their soaring visions and wide open prospects, become turned into systems and structures that make some positions and 'possibles' while closing off others. A familiar pecking order emerges with the leading American universities on top. Yet it is a global order less stable and predictable than it was.

The global actions that together create this pattern of openness and closure constitute a form of informal ordering and regulation. Because there is no global state, most acts of global ordering are informal. Because the one-world ecological sense is under-formed, most global ordering is unreflexive. Although national regulation is one ordering function at play, the nation is no longer the final arbiter in higher education – and less so in research and knowledge, which always spilled beyond it. In one sense the move from global openness and imagining, to global strategizing, to global ordering, is a long passage from freedom to constraint. But even ordered as it is the global higher education space offers new liberties.

Informal Order

The absence of a global state, and the modest role of multilateral forums in higher education, mean that the space for formal global governance and regulation is largely vacant. Only Europe exhibits an advanced level of cross-national negotiation (see the chapters by Välimaa (Chapter 15) and Enders and Westerheijden (Chapter 27) in this volume, and Marginson and van der Wende, 2009). In other parts of the world there are bilateral negotiations between governments in the recognition of institutions and qualifications, and the exchange of quality assurance data, to facilitate the mobility of students, graduates and qualifications. There are many instances of government-supported international collaboration, especially in research. All of this takes embryonic regional form in Southeast Asia and South Africa, and to a lesser degree in East Asia and Africa. That is as far as it goes. Meanwhile de-severing facilitates informal regulation; and de-severing and synchrony ensure that there are always ways beyond and behind formal national regulation. The absence of formal regulation in global matters is more than necessity; it is also choice.

But it has costs. Higher education creates common global public goods and benefits that spill over borders (Kaul et al., 1999), especially in research. But they are under-recognized and under-measured. There is no regime for managing shared global goods (or for sharing the cost of global public 'bads' in higher education, such as brain drain). Thus global public goods are under-produced and not optimally distributed (Marginson, 2007a). This may be surprising given the wide reach of the ecological imaginary, the sense of interdependency (Marginson, 2010a), and given also the mobile character of knowledge. It is a sign of the extent to which higher education is still identified with national systems.

Informal regulation shows itself primarily in two ways. The first is the systems of institutional classification, comparison and ranking (Marginson, 2009; chapters by Hazelkorn (Chapter 29) and King (Chapter 22) in this volume). Comprehensive global information is increasingly potent – nothing is more effective in defining global higher education than the metrics of comparison. Outside Europe higher education rankings are not primarily instigated by government, although governments play a larger role in classification systems. However, governments are among the active users of these data. Comparative data have become a driver of modernization reforms and investment programs on a nation-by-nation basis. Thus the Shanghai Jiao Tong rankings were explicitly cited in the decision of France to invest in a large-scale merger program (Salmi, 2009). It is an example of the growing role of non-government regulation in modern societies and the manner in which the formal and informal domains intersect, especially in global matters (Marginson et al., 2010). Scholars working with concepts developed by Michel Foucault (1980) describe rankings as a 'disciplinary' technology (Sauder and Espeland, 2009). 'Discipline' has a dual meaning: bounded knowledge and subordination to authority. Ironically, governments often rail against rankings when 'their own' universities are subordinated, while initiating steps to improve the position. This is a sign of the lock-in that rankings have created.

The other manifestation of informal regulation is policy borrowing, transfer and adaptation between national jurisdictions (see chapters by King (Chapter 22), Dill (Chapter 25), Musselin (Chapter 26) and others, and also King, 2009; Rizvi and Lingard, 2010). This is not new. Bayly (2004, p. 10) notes that modernity has been characterized by 'a process of emulation and borrowing' on a national scale since the birth of the modern nation-state in nineteenth-century Europe, Japan and North America. Nations are habitually conscious of global patterns and changes, and of each other (ibid., p. 4). But amid communicative globalization, policy borrowing is now faster and more insistent. It extends beyond single programs and mechanisms to include holistic institutional models and system design. As noted, all of the explicit moves that redesign higher education at world level – WTO–GATS, the virtual universe of e-Universities, the world of status comparison – imagine the global dimension as a world market. Each also constitutes a radical homogenization of higher education, imposing one set of values on all others.

The templates for institutional reform are based on reified, idealized versions of Anglo-American higher education, underwritten by American practical domination (Marginson, 2008a). Most nations want comprehensive science-oriented universities of the type that dominates research rankings: the 'world-class university' (SJTUGSE,

2010), or 'global research university' (Ma, 2008; Marginson, 2008b). They want these universities to be academically excellent, 'entrepreneurial' (Clark, 1998) and closely connected to industry. They should be selective in their student intake, financially autonomous and globally competitive. The model has growing ascendancy even in systems with very different traditions; for example European nations with high-status vocational sectors, and Latin American systems led by mega-universities with a very broad social role. There is also a second template, the for-profit vocational university. This model institution focuses on training for business, computing and the mass professions. It is marketing-driven and customer-focused; relentlessly expansionary in students, sites and market share; and spare and efficient with no 'frills' such as research, libraries or academic freedoms. In the ideal neoliberal system these two kinds of institutions occupy opposing ends of the spectrum. This imagined ideal system, with its polarity between autonomous high-status research universities and heteronymous mass colleges, is exactly as described by Bourdieu (1993).

STANDARDIZATION AND DIVERSITY

Are tendencies to standardization and homogeneity uppermost in relation to national and cultural diversity? Does global convergence multiply encounters with difference, cross-fertilization and plurality? Or is it making systems and institutions the same? Which aspects of higher education are becoming common on a global basis – and which remain locally nested with greater scope for self-determined variations? What is the scope for smaller nations and subsystems to follow their own paths? Is there only one line of development and one possible university? Are all becoming branches of a world system? Or are they both parts of a world system *and* regionally/nationally/locally variant at the same time? These issues are much debated in the literature.

Observation conducted exclusively at the synthetic global level tends to suggest that homogenization is uppermost. This derives in part from the globalist bias in perspective. By definition the global is about commonality. This is its virtue: global systems of knowledge bring a great part of human wisdom within reach of all. On the other hand studies conducted in the local and national dimensions bring greater divergence and specificity into the frame (Musselin, 2005). A full exploration of the dynamics of standardization and diversification in higher education would require a program of situated empirical studies (Deem, 2001) carried out on a comparative basis.

The networked and knowledge-bearing character of universities sustains powerful tendencies to standardization. Knowledge is increasingly a matter of one-world publication in English. Work in other languages is losing status. Science is a unitary republic, not a polyglot empire. It reaches everywhere but expects all its practitioners to dance to the same tune, or at least in the same tonal system. Evolutionary biologists remark that in the natural world, when biologically independent regions are brought together, species diversity is reduced, as happened when North and South America were joined at Panama: 'The more biotic provinces, the greater the total global biodiversity' (Erwin, 2006, p. 44). The spread of non-native species around the world is a second form of biotic homogenization. The generic character of organizational design and management practices is another form of homogenization. NPM methods can be attached to a wide range of interests and projects and are often varied by locality – as noted, this facility in local hybridization helps to give the NPM its purchase – but all over the world HEIs have been at least partly NPM'd. Here the organizational sociology of universities is converging with other complex organizations (Meyer et al., 2006, pp. 259–65). The spread of neoliberal ideas and NPM forms is not driven from a global centre but proceeds via mimetic global cultural flows, sustained by policy borrowing. These shape the global sector according to dominant and often neo-imperial norms more surely than could any imperial command.

But while contents and forms are becoming more homogeneous, there is a growing plurality of global subjects. The NPM favors autonomous universities that create their own responses to strategic global opportunities; and worldwide higher education and research capacity are becoming more plural. New centers of higher education power are rising, especially in East Asia and Singapore, and through the Europeanization project.

There are three main zones of R & D each accounting for roughly one-third of activity: North America ($393 billion in 2007), Europe ($313 billion), and Asia and the Pacific, including West Asia ($351 billion) (NSB, 2010, 4.33–34). East Asian research is developing very rapidly. National investment in R & D in 2007 was 3.5 percent of GDP in Korea, 3.4 percent in Japan, and 2.6 percent in Taiwan and Singapore. In China R & D investment doubled in a decade to 1.5 percent of GDP. From 1995 to 2007 China increased published science papers by an average 16.5 percent per year (UNESCO, 2010; World Bank, 2010; NSB, 2010). At the same time, Eastern Asian nations and Singapore have rapidly increased student numbers. In China between 1990 and 2007 the gross rate of enrollment in tertiary education rose from 4 to 23 percent. Meanwhile Project 985 created a layer of global research universities. East Asian nations are able to sharply increase student numbers and research at the same time because households pay for a high and growing proportion of tuition. Private tertiary investment exceeds public investment by three to one in Korea and Japan. In China the public share of tertiary funding fell from 96 percent in 1978 to 45 percent in 2005 (Zha, 2009, p. 46; Rong, 2009). This formula allows China to keep increasing investment in research as long as high economic growth is sustained. The 'Confucian Model' of higher education system is another blueprint for emerging nations, although few can replicate the necessary levels of economic growth and nation-state control.

GLOBAL INEQUALITIES

Globalization creates an enhanced potential for freedoms and an uneven capacity to use them. It is associated with three structural forms of inequality in higher education (Naidoo, 2010). First is the structure of inside/outside. Globalization fosters a binary divide between institutions and nations with global mobility and power of attraction, and those de-linked from global circuits. Higher education in the poorest nations such as Cambodia and Papua New Guinea has little global connectivity. Second is the structure of hierarchy inside the global sector. Among those connected to global circuits, operating capacity is unequal. Strong research universities provide scholarships for international doctoral students. In some other nations leading universities cannot buy academic journals (Marginson and Sawir, 2006). Institutions experience not just inequalities of resources but inequalities in operational liberty. Some are constrained or marginalized in the global setting by national regulation. The global strategies of others are fostered by governments, for example in Singapore. Third is the structure of cultural difference. Global convergence is often problematic for non-English-speaking institutions. Language barriers tend to weaken engagement, the subordination of national culture is galling, and at worst there is potential for fractured identity – although many non-English-speaking systems manage cultural plurality more effectively than does higher education in the English-speaking world.

Status competition and traditional hierarchies, reinforced by global rankings with their performance templates that few systems can meet, maintain all three forms of inequality. The challenge for emerging systems is to be open within the global dimension, while maintaining control over their identity and the shaping of their global projects. Market competition might appear to offer a meritocratic path out from under the dead weight of status hierarchy, but this is largely an illusion. In the global setting the power of institutions and systems to compete in economic markets is closely correlated to their global status and to primary elements such as resources and research performance that drive status. There is no alternative to building capacity in the connective and knowledge-related functions integral to the university *qua* university. This will be slower in most nations than in East Asia. But flat networking offers potential additional resources. So does the imagination.

NATIONAL AND GLOBAL

The focus of this chapter on the global dimension of higher education imposes a 'globalist' bias on the argument. Global phenomena and relations stand out too much. But the higher education world is vectored by not one but two sets of cross-border relations. The first is the global dimension of action. The second is the international dimension of action, the world as it is perceived from the vantage point of the bounded and separated nation-state.

'International' literally means inter-national, meaning relations between separate nations. 'Internationalization', the process of enhancing relations between nations, is a product of the modern nation-state. It presupposes cross-border relations in which nations, their authority and identity, are essentially unchanged. Likewise multilateralism rests on the premise of national sovereignty, first established in the Treaty of Westphalia in seventeenth-century Europe. It scarcely acknowledges global systems except as spaces for inter-national bargaining. The United Nations (UN) is the ultimate expression of a benign multilateralism. It is a forum for talk between zero-sum nation-states, not an independent global agent designing the world of the future. The UN has been partly sidelined by globalization, which corrodes all forms of Westphalian authority. Globalization punches holes in sacred borders. Its systems cut across them. Imaginings of the nation-state remain potent and central to higher education. But the tides are not commanded by sovereignty or ideology. Globalization does not eliminate the nation, any more than it eliminates region, locality or self. It relativizes them. It undermines all claims to absolute authority at the national level. Sovereignty and internationalism are being imploded by globalization in a long-drawn-out process.

Meanwhile both nation-state and globalization are strong in this era, and they can make competing claims. When university leaders imagine globally, they are at cross-purposes with their states. University presidents must be adept in both ways of seeing – national and global. The national dimension provides resources – from government and from students, alumni and industry. Yet the global dimension is where most research is conducted, and opportunities to build status and activity are more open than in regulated national settings. Both state and university focus on the world competitive position, but this has differing meanings. For government the issue is the rewards the nation can extract from international dealings, such as fee revenues from foreign students, or better research capacity. But it wants to augment research universities only to the extent that they generate status for the nation and innovations captured by the national economy. For their part, research universities care about national and local standing; they want to embed themselves locally by recruiting high-quality students; and their national mission is crucial to their funding base. Yet their position in the global circuits of knowledge matters more (for universities outside the USA, at least). Government sees this as grandstanding irrelevance. It is likely that nation-states will become more frustrated by the lack of fit between their objectives and university agendas. Many of the fruits of research, on entering the global domain, leak to industry outside the creator nation – to the competition. Governments could ask 'how do *we* benefit from funding basic research?' This could drive a crisis in the research university.

The global research university has become the dominant form of higher education on a worldwide basis. Yet it nurses a growing tension within itself (Marginson, 2010b, 2010c, 2011). As its global mission becomes more potent – as global imaginings and strategy-making become more and more central to it – this unbalances the old antinomy, which threatens to become a fracture in global governance. The research university is a national project whose field of operation is often global. The global and national dimensions are heterogeneous in form and purpose. In the national dimension the purpose is the nation as an end in itself. The global dimension has no purpose. There the university is its own purpose. In the global setting it flourishes, translating its long role in mobile and universal knowledge into an astonishing flowering of activity powered by an advanced sense of the world as a whole – while securing the status (and sometimes the revenues) globalization brings. Its global activity serves more than itself, however. In reality the connectedness of higher education is a boon to the place-bound administrations that regulate it. Paradoxically, unless the university is in some measure *disloyal* to the nation – by placing global relationships and global good above and if necessary against the felt interests of the nation – the university cannot give the nation what it needs, which is the continuous flow of intelligence gleaned from global engagement. But governments and media publics rarely understand this.

The unstable balance between national and global imaginings varies from nation to nation. It also varies between different types of institution. Of all the institutions of the modern nation-state, the research university is the most global in its imagining. This places universities, along with global agencies and information companies, in the forefront of the slow but discernible movement towards world society. Inevitably this agenda will take them further beyond the bounds of the nation-state that is their funder and regulator.

REFERENCES

Bayly, C. (2004), *The Birth of the Modern World 1780–1914: Global Connections and Comparisons*, Oxford: Blackwell.

Bourdieu, P. (1984), *Distinction: A Social Critique of the Judgment of Taste*, trans. R. Nice, London: Routledge and Kegan Paul.

Bourdieu, P. (1993), *The Field of Cultural Production*, ed. R. Johnson, New York: Columbia University Press.

Clark, B. (1998), *Creating Entrepreneurial Universities: Organizational Pathways of Transformation*, Oxford: Pergamon Press.

Deem, R. (2001), 'Globalization, new managerialism, academic capitalism and entrepreneurialism in universities: is the local dimension still important?', *Comparative Education*, **37** (1), 7–20.

Erwin, D. (2006), *Extinction: How Life on Earth Nearly Ended 250 Million Years Ago*, Princeton, NJ: Princeton University Press.

Foucault, M. (1980), *Power/Knowledge: Selected Interviews and Other Writings, 1972–1977*, ed. C. Gordon, New York: Pantheon Books.

Kaul, I., I. Grunberg and M. Stern (eds) (1999), *Global Public Goods: International Cooperation in the 21st Century*, New York: Oxford University Press.

King, R. (2009), *Governing Universities Globally: Organizations, Regulation and Ranking*, Cheltenham, UK and Northampton, MA, USA: Edward Elgar.

Ma, Wan Hua (2008), 'The University of California at Berkeley: an emerging global research university', *Higher Education Policy*, **21**, 65–81.

Marginson, S. (2007a), 'The new higher education landscape: public and private goods, in global/national/local settings', in S. Marginson (ed.), *Prospects of Higher Education: Globalization, Market Competition, Public Goods and the Future of the University*, Rotterdam: Sense Publishers, pp. 29–77.

Marginson, S. (2007b), 'Global position and position-taking: the case of Australia', *Journal of Studies in International Education*, **11** (1), 5–32.

Marginson, S. (2008a), 'Global field and global imagining: Bourdieu and relations of power in worldwide higher education', *British Journal of Educational Sociology*, **29** (3), 303–16.

Marginson, S. (2008b), '"Ideas of a University" for the Global Era', paper for seminar on 'Positioning university in the globalized world: changing governance and coping strategies in Asia', Centre of Asian Studies, The University of Hong Kong; Central Policy Unit, HKSAR Government; and The Hong Kong Institute of Education, 10–11 December 2008, The University of Hong Kong, http://www.cshe.unimelb.edu.au/people/staff_pages/Marginson/Marginson.html, accessed 5 December 2009.

Marginson, S. (2009), 'University rankings and the knowledge economy', in M. Peters, S. Marginson and P. Murphy, *Creativity and the Global Knowledge Economy*, New York: Peter Lang, pp. 185–216.

Marginson, S. (2010a), 'World', in P. Murphy, M. Peters and S. Marginson, *Imagination: Three Models of Imagination in the Age of the Knowledge Economy*, New York: Peter Lang, pp. 139–65.

Marginson, S. (2010b), 'University', in P. Murphy, M. Peters and S. Marginson, *Imagination: Three Models of Imagination in the Age of the Knowledge Economy*, New York: Peter Lang, pp. 167–223.

Marginson, S. (2010c), 'Nation', in P. Murphy, M. Peters and S. Marginson, *Imagination: Three Models of Imagination in the Age of the Knowledge Economy*, New York: Peter Lang, pp. 225–325.

Marginson, S. (2011), 'Global perspectives and strategies of Asia-Pacific universities', in N. Liu, Q. Wang and J. Salmi (eds), *Paths to a World-Class University*, Rotterdam: Sense Publishers, pp. 3–27.

Marginson, S. and M. Considine (2000), *The Enterprise University: Power, Governance and Reinvention in Australia*, Cambridge: Cambridge University Press.

Marginson, S. and E. Sawir (2006), 'University leaders' strategies in the global environment: a comparative study of Universitas Indonesia and the Australian National University', *Higher Education*, **52**, 343–73.

Marginson, S. and M. van der Wende (2009), 'Europeanisation, university rankings and faculty mobility: three cases in higher education globalisation', in OECD, Centre for Educational Research and Innovation, *Higher Education to 2030, Volume 2: Globalization*, Paris: OECD, pp. 109–72.

Marginson, S., C. Nyland, E. Sawir and H. Forbes-Mewett (2010), *International Student Security*, Cambridge: Cambridge University Press.

Meyer, J., G. Drori and H. Hokyu (2006), 'Conclusion', in G. Drori, J. Meyer and H. Hwang, *Globalization and Organization: World Society and Organizational Change*, Oxford: Oxford University Press, pp. 258–74.

Musselin, C. (2005), 'European academic labor markets in transition', *Higher Education*, **49**, 135–54.

Naidoo, R. (2010), 'Global learning in a neoliberal age: implications for development', in E. Unterhalter and V. Carpentier (eds), *Global Inequalities and Higher Education: Whose Interests are we Serving?*, London: Palgrave Macmillan, pp. 66–90.

National Science Board, NSB, United States (2010), *Science and Engineering Indicators 2010*, http://www.nsf.gov/statistics/seind10/, accessed 18 April 2010.

Organization for Economic Co-operation and Development (OECD) (2005), *E-learning in Tertiary Education: Where do we Stand?*, Paris: OECD.

Rizvi, F. and B. Lingard (2010), *Globalizing Education Policy*, London: Routledge.

Rong, W. (2009), 'Reforms and consequences in the higher education system in China', paper presented to 'Reforms and consequences in higher education system: an international symposium', Center for National University Finance and Management, National Center of Sciences, Hitotubashi Chiyoda-ku, Tokyo, Japan, 26 January.

Salmi, J. (2009), *The Challenge of Establishing World Class Universities,* Washington, DC: World Bank.

Samuelson, P. (1954), 'The pure theory of public expenditure', *Review of Economics*, **36** (4), 387–9.

Sauder, M. and W. Espeland (2009), 'The discipline of rankings: tight coupling and organizational change', *American Sociological Review*, **74**, 63–82.

Shanghai Jiao Tong University Graduate School of Education, SJTUGSE (2010), *Academic Ranking of World Universities*, http://ed.sjtu.edu.cn/ranking.htm, accessed 21 August 2010.

UNESCO Institute for Statistics (2010), *Data on Education*, http://www.uis.unesco.org/ev.php?ID=2867_201&ID2=DO_TOPIC, accessed 17 April 2010.

van der Wende, M. (2008), 'Rankings and classifications in higher education: a European perspective', in J. Smart (ed.), *Higher Education: Handbook of Theory and Research,* Dordrecht: Springer.

World Bank (2010), data and statistics, http://web.worldbank.org/WBSITE/EXTERNAL/DATASTATISTICS/0,,contentMDK:20798108~menuPK:64133152~pagePK:64133150~piPK:64133175~theSitePK:239419,00.html, accessed 17 April 2010.

Zha, Q. (2009), 'Diversification or homogenization: how governments and markets have combined to (re)shape Chinese higher education in its recent massification process', *Higher Education*, **58**, 41–58.

Ziguras, C. and G. McBurnie (2006), *Transnational Education: Issues and Trends in Off-shore Higher Education*, London: Routledge.

24 Governing knowledge globally: science, structuration and the open society

Roger King

INTRODUCTION

This chapter explores the increasing global governance of knowledge systems, focusing particularly on science. Science is defined as the systematic pursuit of knowledge through recognizable and publicly accepted social institutions (which are defined as structured collections of norms). It is characterized by self-regulatory and collaborative processes that stretch across time and space and that we characterize as 'networks'. Prominent elements of globalization can be understood as the growth of shared forms of social coordination as the world reconstitutes itself around a series of networks – increasingly interlinked – that are strung around the globe on the basis of advanced communication technologies. A 'network' refers to an interconnected group of people linked to one another in a way that makes them capable of beneficial collaboration (such as through the exchange of goods in markets, or the exchange of ideas). The concept of 'structuration' is also introduced to account for the actions that reproduce such social coordination. By 'structuration' we mean the interplay of agent and structure in the accomplishment of social practices, including the tensions between autonomy and constraint for agents (Giddens, 1995).

Notions of 'standards' and 'network power' define the particular ways in which networked actors (such as scientists) are connected and constituted through norms as standards of appropriate behavior. 'Standards' as behavioral norms regulate the interactions of independent agents in the absence of formal hierarchy. As with the protocols governing access to the Internet, standards are necessary to enable people to interact. Without such standards there is no network, and while actors are free to stay outside networks, those that do may face marginalization. That is, power operates through exclusion rather than through hierarchical coercion.

'Network power' characterizes the 'pulling' power of universalizing or dominant models or standards (Grewal, 2008). That is, some norms may reach levels of adoption by a critical mass of actors, particularly in the global age, such that a 'tipping point' is reached and widespread agreement to follow by current non-adopters quickly ensues (Finnemore and Sikkink, 1999). However, such 'snowballing' of adoption requires explanation as to its dynamics, particularly that of 'power', or, more specifically, 'network power'. Consequently notions of power as well as social coordination are central concepts in the following analysis of networks.

GLOBALIZATION STRUCTURES

In globalization it is useful to distinguish between broad systemic notions of social structure – the macro and meso patterns of institutional properties (occupational or healthcare systems, for example, or the global division of labor) – and a hermeneutic interpretation where structure is conceived as the medium for, and outcome of, autonomous actor practices. In the latter we find that social structures – comprising norms and resources – are experienced as memory senses by knowledgeable individual agents. That is, such structures do not exist 'objectively', or as 'agent-free' causal factors, but become manifest and produced in action, such as in scientific practices or through the act of speaking made possible by languages (Giddens, 1995; Stones, 2005).

For our analysis two assumptions are important. First, such ontological notions of 'structure' are designed to be trans-situational (or 'virtual'), as capturing the essential metaphysics of being. They refer to the inherent character of social entities, and concepts apply to the widest possible set of circumstances. In this sense institutions or normative arrangements are codified and 'disembedded' from particular contexts. Social practices at this (ontological) level are conceptualized as potentially diffusing across vast reaches of time and space. Such prototypical or rather abstract approaches are an important part of analyses of global governance processes, as we shall elaborate later. Nonetheless, while the very generalizability and transposability of such models and structures allow solutions to similar problems worldwide, they undergo specific critiques and nuanced modifications of form and content in processes of diffusion and substantive application. That is, real people – 'situated agents' at a concrete level – accomplish outcomes that rest on a view of their capabilities and resources to resist, shape or regulate globalizing schemas or models. Effectively, in this piece, we are looking at ontology 'in action'.

Second, hermeneutic or interpretative structures 'nest' within the wider meso or macro structures of distributed economic and political power, and within sedimentary cultural significations or ideologies. These wider structures generate differential opportunities for agents to draw upon and be influenced by normative rules and to achieve their interests. In this – macro – view, 'structural constraint' refers to the 'objective' existence of structural properties (in a systemic sense) that individual agents (hermeneutically) feel either unwilling or unable to change. They limit the breadth of options available to an actor. These limitations are accepted with greater or lesser levels of habituation or criticality, although modernity generally expands criticality as a normative system (Giddens, 1995).

In accepting the utility of both senses of 'structure', we should note then that systemic, or 'objectively' constraining macro structures, always have phenomenological implications as these external structures are experienced as independent causal influences. They are also produced and reproduced by socially situated agents. Researchers tend to 'bracket', or hold in some form of methodological suspension, these different notions of structure – following one approach rather than the other – in the light of the issues that they investigate (Stones, 2005). Nonetheless, analytical interplay of the two ideas of 'structure' is to be preferred wherever possible.

WORLDWIDE SOCIAL COOPERATION

Structures, such as standards and similar normative frames, help to constitute the social cooperation worldwide made possible by the technological and communicative compression of space over recent decades. But some normative frames become more influential than others in globalization. Following Grewal (2008), we note an increasing tendency for certain standards and governance models, such as those in public services provision that we may collectively refer to as the 'new public management' (NPM), to possess a 'pulling' or network power that generates their increasing global dominance. These tend to displace competing and incompatible models as means of accessing social networks (such alternative models as, say, strong state-interventionist and micro-directed public administration).

This process of 'snowballing' or a magnetizing 'pulling' effect for a model gathers pace once a certain critical mass of network participants coming to share the defined norms of practice (standards) associated with a particular model has been reached. After such a threshold of adoption, the 'spread' of universalizing standards to previous non-adopters may be as much for extrinsic reasons (the sheer weight and/or influence of the network's users) as for intrinsic judgments (the merits of a particular standard). Nonetheless, universalizing models over time can also demise when they face reactions to the anti-innovative conformism that is often engendered by triumphant models and orthodoxies. This occurred, for example, during the first part of the twentieth century with the collapse of the almost universal Gold Standard for regulating currencies once the point was reached when it was perceived by policy-makers as restricting the growing need for innovation and local autonomy in the management of national economies.

While individuals, including policy-makers, ontologically are always 'free' to choose to act other than the way they do, in reality they frequently feel that they have few, if any, options. Although the power of structures is not necessarily experienced in an oppressive way by agents (even though regarded as exercising a form of dominance), certain models are able to settle the terms of access to important global networks in a manner that seems outside the direct influence of those participating, or wishing to participate, in such networks (Grewal, 2008). Science provides a good example.

Global Science

Global science is based on a universalizing set of standards that mediates the social coordination of scientists worldwide. This both constrains and facilitates researchers seeking access to the network of research and collaboration that is constituted by such normative frames. Scientific norms display what Giddens (1995) famously has described as the 'duality of structure'. They are both the medium and the outcome of research practices. In producing valued research outcomes by using accepted scientific conventions, an individual also contributes to that structure's reproduction through time and space (although unintended consequences of course may also follow and be a source of change).

Scientists in their investigative practices draw upon, and thereby reproduce, not necessarily intentionally, the globalizing rules and resources associated with scientific standards. Convergence on global research standards is therefore created and reproduced through an accumulation of many decentralized and individual choices. While these decisions are made autonomously, they are also strongly constrained, reflecting the power of scientific networks and scientific standards to influence such choice-making.

Global science occurs largely behind the back of the nation-state, despite powerful political rhetoric espousing the competitive economic necessity of scientific nationalism in the knowledge economy. The standards and conventions of science provide a form of globalization through their facilitation of worldwide communication and cooperation by scientists. Dominant scientific models exert a powerful pull on researchers who seek access to the forms of worldwide research cooperation mediated by such structures.

Levels of exclusivity in science nonetheless do not appear particularly weakened by global ties. Classifications, such as global university rankings and disciplinary reputations, reassert and bind traditional research standings, in higher education at least, in this period of considerable diversity in scientific locales and knowledge explosion. Resources and relationships appear to be subject to forms of cumulative inequality and preferential attachment that benefit elite scientists through traditional processes of reproductive hierarchy (Wagner, 2008). Yet such 'closures' appear at variance with the well-established notion of science as a republican polity (Polanyi, 1962), and with the related notion of the 'open society' as the necessary sociopolitical condition for safeguarding science as a deliberative and critical democracy. The view that science requires an 'open society' for the production of high-quality knowledge indicates an important mechanism for the continued reproduction of science as a form of self-generating global governance.

SCIENCE AND THE OPEN SOCIETY

Scientists (and others) claim that there is a close connection between the governance of so-called 'open societies' – liberal parliamentary or congressional democratic systems – and the governance of research. That is, liberal democratic societies are regarded as safeguarding the institutional autonomies and civic tolerances that provide the protected spaces necessary for creative activity, not least in universities, and whose political processes also correspond to how science itself is best governed – in a self-organizing, free, and openly critical manner (Altbach, 2007; Hayek, 1960; Merton, 1942; Popper, 1945, 1963; Polanyi, 1962).

This raises an important question. Where political systems are not pluralistic and competitive, as in China and in some other parts of Asia, for example, do sociopolitical constraints (the lack of autonomous and protected research cultures and spaces) place a ceiling on the extent to which universities and other research institutions can contribute high-quality and innovative basic research? As a consequence, will universities in such countries be limited in the degree to which they can rise up global research-based rankings (such as the Shanghai Jiao Tong University or THE tables)? How far are they able to contribute to governmental objectives of developing a 'world-class university system' based on the emerging global model of the research university (Mohrman et al., 2008)?

Arguably we may still find high-level research in political systems other than liberal democracies where other factors compensate for the absence of political pluralism. High levels of public expenditure in science and university research (in China and other so-called East Asian 'tiger societies' currently and perhaps also in the former Soviet

Union) could help override the absence of a strongly developed culture of institutional autonomy and individual freedom. After all, most liberal democracies tend also to be quite wealthy, and it may be that the causal connection with high-level science is with resource rather than democratic variables.

Asian Universities

Marginson (2010) describes how many of the 'Confucian' nations, notably those in East Asia, are helping to make the Asia Pacific a global force in higher education as student numbers and research grow dramatically to match those levels found in the region's leader – Japan – and elsewhere since the 1970s. Particularly striking is the mixture of private investment in tuition-fee and other student costs (reflecting an old Confucian tradition of belief in individual development through education and competitive hard work) and high public investment in research, the latter in part made possible by the strong private expenditure by families on securing higher education participation. Although academic freedom and autonomy are constrained by the Party-led state, raising doubts about the ability of countries such as China and Singapore to generate cultures of openness and criticality, nonetheless Marginson notes the striking expansion in scientific output in the Confucian systems in recent years.

A number of major Asia-Pacific countries, such as China, Singapore, Taiwan, Hong Kong and South Korea, appear to have taken the view that resources, rather than type of sociopolitical system, count for more in facilitating quality research, although as we shall see some forms of 'openness' and NPM reforms have become noticeable recently. Following Marginson's analysis, there may be a belief within (and outside) Confucian systems that they are superior to western liberal democratic forms in generating the funds for long-term scientific development.

Nonetheless Altbach and Balán (2007), in considering Asian universities, argue that many of these organizations have not established the high levels of academic and institutional freedom that are necessary if research universities are to develop successfully and to enable a globally respected research culture to become established. The OECD (2008) notes, too, that while South Korea, for example, has one of the highest levels of student participation in tertiary education among all OECD countries, with high completion rates and significant student achievements in literacy, mathematics and science, the governmental aim of creating world-class research universities requires more than the large public allocations of research funding. Rather the factors the OECD stresses as important (and currently missing, as Terri Kim's Chapter 17 in Part II highlights), are the granting of enhanced autonomy to institutions, including a capacity to offer more differentiated salaries, and the creation of an entrepreneurial culture and visionary leadership. Kim in her chapter notes the strong reluctance of governments in South Korea to let go of important areas of institutional decision-making, despite repeated promises to do so.

In China, despite high state investment in research, universities have some way to go in establishing such a culture of institutional and individual research autonomy. The influence of the Communist Party-led state remains strong, not least in appointments to senior administrative positions, including university presidents, and in the authorization of institutional evaluation plans, funding allocations, curricula and faculty size (McGregor, 2010). Publications and research activities can be closely inspected by the state, and institutional student enrollment numbers by institution and discipline are fixed. In China, 'shared governance' between academics and university leaders is weakly practiced in comparison with other countries (Cummings et al., 2010).

Mohrman (2008) notes nonetheless that the 'emerging global model' of the research university provides the blueprint for China's government leaders' plans for developing a top echelon of institutions to rank with the best in the USA and Europe. Ranking systems, such as the Shanghai Jiao Tong University's global league tables, were established to help the government measure how far China's universities have still to travel to fulfill such objectives and to establish the criteria for success. Moreover, the central government has initiated a number of programs to encourage prestigious international scholars and institutions to come to China, as Mei Li and Qiongqiong Chen's earlier case study in Part II (Chapter 14) indicates. A number of China's leading academics also have spent considerable time abroad on their higher education, suggesting a significant cadre of staff in China's universities that may chafe at inhibitions on freedoms of the kind that they enjoyed in universities abroad.

Undoubtedly China's higher education development in recent years is not remarkably different from that found in many other countries, including liberal democracies. That is, mass expansion accompanied by privatization, decentralization and institutional concentration has been the order of the day (Liu and Wang, 2010). Nonetheless, although central government in China is moving away from strict command-and-control of its leading research universities and towards utilization of some of the meta-evaluations and accountabilities found in the new public management (NPM) forms of governance associated with the west, particular difficulties are presented in responding to demands for institutional autonomy and academic freedom within a system that traditionally has been strongly Party-controlled. Moreover, swapping state control for the managerial direction associated with the NPM may not provide the conditions for scientific freedom desired by many academics in China. Nor may it necessarily overcome the strong tradition of rote-learning pedagogy still prevalent in virtually all the Confucian higher education systems.

University leaders in China may also struggle to move to more consultative strategies. A recent study of managerial attempts to introduce performance-based accountability for staff at Peking University indicates strong opposition to the reform, not least from those in the humanities and social sciences (Yang, 2010). Although regional governments and individual universities are exercising more self-determination in areas of decision-making (such as, for some institutions, over study abroad opportunities for staff and students), continued strong interventionist modalities may hamper achievement of the official governmental objective of developing truly 'world-class' research universities. And, of course, increased organizational autonomy is not the same as expanded academic or scientific freedom.

Interestingly, however, the growing production of world-class research in the natural sciences and engineering in China and other East Asian countries suggests that socio-political constraints may exercise disciplinary variation in their consequences for research creativity and innovation by being a less necessary context in the natural sciences and engineering than for, say, the social sciences and humanities. This may aid highly placed positioning in global university ranking systems and assist policies aimed at creating world-class universities based on such tables. Such subjects count for more in the methods employed by such rankings, which generally diminish the impact of outputs in the arts and social analysis.

Moreover, many of the leading Chinese universities among those selected by the government for support to world-class status have a strong 'polytechnic' or science and engineering provision, stemming from the era of strong Soviet influence in the 1950s (Hayhoe and Zha, 2010).

Although an explicit governmental goal in China has been to make China's universities and research organizations directly supportive of national economic growth over the last three decades or so, as in many western liberal democracies and other countries, this has not resulted in notably improved innovatory capacity. Proportionate reductions in governmental funding for research until recently, and the comparative rise of industrial and corporate sponsorship with the emphasis on applied research, have resulted in industry providing around half the source of research funds. Yet rather than the move to business funding being in part liberating, the hangover of strong Party planning and the lack of institutional autonomy have prevented the higher education system from turning these new market circumstances to the universities' financial and creative advantage and for increased innovative outcomes to be achieved (Lan Xue, 2008).

Yang et al. (2008) note similarly that rising R&D funding has not significantly improved the innovative capacity of China's universities. Governmental policy over recent decades rather has moved the institutional priority of universities towards low-level technological diffusion and the commercialization of technologies to benefit industry immediately (and to achieve short-term funds for the universities to compensate for any shortfall in governmental funding). Such an approach has enabled a diversification in university funding overall but has not particularly expanded basic indigenous research capacity, not least blue-skies academic creativity. Imported technologies and the innovative capacity of foreign companies in China fill the gap.

Although state policy in China since 2006 seeks to address these issues, with strategies to strengthen the research and independent innovation abilities of the universities through enhanced expenditure on infrastructure such as equipment, the weakness is less the hardware than the 'software' and the institutional conditions influencing a country's innovative capacity. Implementation is commanded from on high and is task-based. Moreover, the systems of rewards and incentives become distorted by the mixing of economic benefits, academic achievement and political promotion as sources of merit within China's innovation system.

Several East Asian countries have invested high levels of state expenditure in public research and related innovation systems in a similarly directive manner, rather than relying on private, competitive and self-determining actions by more autonomous agents. Nonetheless, as we have noted, this may not matter to the same extent across all disciplines. It is arguable that the sociopolitical and cultural conditions necessary for conducing radical imaginings may matter less in some subjects than in others, and that it is mainly the arts and social sciences that may require genuinely critical and highly contestable contexts in order to be genuinely innovative.

We cannot be certain that the economic development paths taken by countries will continue with the same trajectories and policies as found currently. To take China, continued high growth rates almost certainly will ensure a level of economic disorderliness in the years to come. As well as Confucian traits, high public investment in science and research recently is made possible by large foreign earnings based on low labor costs and an undervalued, export-focused currency, and on quite high taxation levels on companies in the context of a taxation system for individuals with low rates and which is widely avoided. If economic growth falters, then the conditions for maintaining such high levels of state investment in universities may also change. Furthermore, the 'wise', merit-selected state official of Confucian repute who attracts considerable popular support and relative autonomy of decision-making that allows strong bureaucratic sources of power, is an ideal not immune to the consequences of economic faltering. The case of Japan recently demonstrates a rapid decline of bureaucratic status and influence as the economy has confronted a prolonged and major slowdown since the 1990s (Emmott, 2009).

PHILOSOPHICAL AND HISTORICAL ACCOUNTS OF SCIENTIFIC 'DEMOCRACY'

The view that the 'open society' of liberal democracy is regarded as providing the optimal social conditions for creativity has longstanding philosophical and sociological credentials. Popper (1945, 1963) most notably in the twentieth century viewed scientific knowledge from the perspective of a philosopher and regarded it as distinguished from other forms of tradition in that it was always open to empirical testing and therefore to potential falsification. Unlike Marxism and psychoanalysis, for example, whose theories of underlying and hidden causal structures he believed foreclosed on empirical refutation, scientific advance was made possible through the factual testing of hypotheses and the elimination of false explanations. An 'open society' was thus required in both society and science – where no dominant ideology held sway over the social order. Rather basic freedoms allowed critical encounters between many different ideas and policies, and allowed the rational evaluation of these competing claims to flourish. Philosophy and democracy became conjoined in this interpretation.

Popper rejected the view of many conventional scientists that induction – the movement from observation and experimentation to scientific law – distinguished science from non-science. There was no logical way of constructing general theories from particular observations and instances. Rather the process of empirically testing deduced hypotheses proceeded on the basis that such experimentation should seek their falsification, not their verification, as the latter was impossible and always likely in time to be confounded by the discovery of counterfactuals. Scientific statements thus never can be 'concluded' but always should be subject to continuous and rigorous testing. The best that we can hope for with consistent empirical scrutiny is to move closer to some approximation of a correct explanation. Scientific theory consequently is always an explanatory claim that must be open to empirical challenge from any quarter. This is where, for Popper, the problem lay with Marxism, for example. It was not the absence of confirming empirical evidence that damaged its scientific credentials but rather that it was a closed and self-explanatory system not open to refutation by factual testing.

More recently, in the aftermath of the Second World War, Popper, along with Merton (1942/1996), starkly contrasted 'totalitarian' regimes based on pseudo (non-refutable) science – Nazi and Soviet especially and their suppression of respectively 'non-Aryan' and 'non-socialist' science – with the more pluralistic societies of parliamentary and congressional political systems (as found in the USA and the UK, for example). For both Merton and Popper this contrast illustrated historically the affinity between the critical rationalism ('organized skepticism' and 'disinterestedness', according to Merton) that underpins both well-conducted science and the processes of a properly functioning democracy.

As a sociologist, Merton regarded science predominantly as a social institution. It involves recognized methods and accumulated knowledge, but above all it comprises interacting individuals and networks reproducing norms and standards. These norms appear in the form of principles for what is allowed and what is not, and as rules for what actions and procedures are desirable and which are to be discarded. These become legitimized in institutional values. That is, scientists form a moral community with an agreed outlook as to appropriate behavior.

Particular types of (macro) social structure are more conducive to world-class science than others in this view. Specifically Merton asserts that the conditions of individual freedom, institutional autonomy, and scientific and other forms of pluralistic self-regulation that constitute key value systems in liberal democracies, are functional for producing high-quality science. The market as well as the state, if both become overly intrusive and prescriptive, can threaten the ideal of normative self-regulation. The role for commercialized 'intellectual property' is quite limited here. Rather, secrecy and non-public disclosure potentially violate the scientific norm of openness that sustains the pursuit by individual scientists of reputation and esteem through their wide and timely dissemination of findings. These views have come to assert a powerful hold on scientists globally and help to mediate scientific coordination on a wide scale.

For Popper (1963), however, the explanation for the correlation between good science and democracy lay as much in the nature, or the philosophy, of the scientific method as in science being a protected and self-reproducing social institution, important though the latter was. Conjecture and refutation based on the deductive mode of reasoning enabled scientific progress; the ideal scientific community is quite democratic in order to allow the full blossoming of the scientific method. This permits anyone to propose an idea for experimental or other testing, and allows the fullest freedom possible to criticize it in a productive way.

The required scientific community for both Merton and Popper resembles what Polanyi (1962) calls the political system of 'republics'. That is, it is not subverted or cramped by over-intrusive state regulation or by commercialization and private objectives. Rather, scientific authority is determined by the mutual, self-regulatory association of scientists. Professional standards provide the focal points to enable the social coordination of autonomous and interdependent agents to form the most efficient and effective organization of science (paralleling similar processes found in capitalist markets). Although scientific work is conservative in that its methods and integrity with established knowledge are principles adhered to strongly by scientists, the demands for originality spearheaded by reputation-enhancing individual researchers enable science also to be progressive and vital (Philips, 2007). The dynamic in the system of scientific social reproduction, accomplished through autonomous actors drawing upon and thus reproducing existing standards and resources in forming their social practices, is the individual motivation for reputation and esteem that comes from producing path-breaking discovery. Rather than portraying science within a model of static functionalism, for Merton science as a social institution always requires the energy and innovation that come from ambitious and career-enhancing researchers.

GLOBAL SCIENCE AS AN OPEN SOCIETY

Undoubtedly the notion of science as an open society retains remarkable influence not least within the scientific community. But policy-makers take it seriously too, even when situated in political systems other than liberal democracies. In China, despite the difficulties in providing relatively unambiguous self-governing contexts for universities and other research institutions, nonetheless there have been increased moves recently to enable at least the top-ranked universities to exercise more autonomy and with more emphasis on third-party research funders other than governmental. China appears to take the 'open society' theory as sufficiently important to be focusing more on increasing the independent innovation ability of research-oriented universities than relying on state command and expenditure alone. In Singapore, too, recent large public investments in the arts, as well as formal decentralization of some aspects of university decision-making, indicate recognition that some forms of openness are necessary for the underpinning of creativity (and for attracting high-value researchers from the west).

The notion of openness as necessary for innovation and as requiring key sociopolitical freedoms has taken organizational, geographical and globalized turns in recent years. Schumpeter (1951) early on wrote of the dampening effect of large organization on creativity. Florida (2002) in similar vein argues that the rise of the 'creative class' in the USA and other advanced societies in the last two decades or so, particularly that class's higher echelons that include scientists and university professors, requires environments of openness, tolerance and diversity within which to flourish. These 'creative ecosystems' are places open to new ideas and people, where networking and promoting radical ideas are easy, and which are not stifled by too much regulation from 'above'.

Stiglitz (1999) similarly argues that the experimentation essential for knowledge economies necessitates a type of openness that is inimical to closed societies. As summarized by Peters (2009, p. 61), Stiglitz asserts that this requires in the political realm 'institutions of the open society such as a free press, transparent government, pluralism, checks and balances, toleration, freedom of thought, and open public debate'. For Peters himself the open society is best interpreted culturally as much as organizationally, for free scientific exchanges depend upon trust, reciprocities and sharing. However, such cultures (what we would term 'institutions') may be expressed differently in the various regions and state forms worldwide.

Peters' perspective on the 'open society' as a cultural rather than a specifically sociopolitical formation is highly suggestive. It raises the possibility that the increasing global interdependence of scientists, socially coordinated by processes of trust, reciprocity and commitment to general scientific standards, may be becoming more important for high-quality research than national sociopolitical conditions. In an Internet-driven world of global private communicability and informal scientific collaboration, which occurs largely out of the gaze of supervisory authorities, sociopolitical conditions in countries may not matter quite so much for behaviors of many sorts as they did in the preceding age of more strongly contained national borders. As such we could surmise that creative knowledge production may be found outside strictly liberal-democratic forms, mainly because such forms may be having less impact on scientific habitats than before. The global social coordination of interdependent, increasingly collaborative but autonomous researchers, through the utilization and worldwide reproduction of powerful scientific standards for accomplishing scientific practices, may be more important. This is a world of sociability rather than sovereignty (Grewal, 2008).

CREATIVITY, ORGANIZATIONAL OPENNESS AND WEAK TIES

What we may describe as the organizational turn in interpreting the conditions for creativity and innovation appears to support a view that the 'meso' or organizational level may be at least as important a variable as the sociopolitical configurations of the national state, although clearly these levels do interpenetrate. Moreover, organizational contexts and the ideas influencing their constructions and authority relations have become particularly transnational. The command-and-control and hierarchical patterns of twentieth-century bureaucracies, public and private, are increasingly regarded by policy-makers and regulators worldwide as inimical to free-thinking, path-breaking discovery in knowledge economies. Foucault's notion of power operating as a disciplinary but also as a productive and not necessarily oppressive force throughout a range of social structures and practices outside the state has strikingly influenced practitioners and observers of regulatory governance on a global scale (Foucault, 2000; King, 2007, 2009).

The move away from command-and-control hierarchical governance, including such steps in Confucian East Asia, is reinforced by growing recognition that the production of a stream of innovatively designed models and products that generate high value is crucial for contemporary economic wellbeing. Murphy (2009), for example, argues that the effect of the dominance of 'Fordist' organizational forms and their vertical hierarchical integration in twentieth-century corporate life, particularly in the USA, although it may have increased efficiency, nonetheless confounds aesthetic–technological design innovation, a key driver of economic competitiveness. Command structures in Fordist organizations impose significant costs on intellectual capital development.

Moreover, in a point we pick up later in discussing worldwide science, in the current global age intellectual capital tends to develop through 'weak ties' or peer relations 'at a distance', and this further undermines the attention given by twentieth-century thinkers to national sociopolitical formations. Unlike the 'thick' social relationships associated with 'social capital' and based on localism and close family ties, which are regarded as facilitative of democratic institutions in territorial states (Putnam, 2000), 'scientific and artistic creation is accompanied by transactions over long distances between creative figures who correspond with others about problems of mutual interest' (Murphy, 2009, p. 32; see also Florida, 2002; Granovetter, 1973; Wagner, 2008).

Networks of collaborating peer-related strangers rather than those characterized by close, long-standing and immediate association appear to innovate most when it comes to generation of the ideas and similar intellectual assets found in the knowledge society. Weak ties, not least those found over the relatively anonymous Internet, bring new and more 'chaotic' knowledge with little of the high-maintenance social baggage found in closer relationships. Loose-tie networks are less insular and distrustful of new ideas and strangers than the more intense social and locally based communities that tend to exhibit high levels of normative uniformity.

Yet even weak-tie networks require some level of 'working social capital' in the form of trust and expectations of appropriate behavior, including, in science, adherence to the values of the scientific community. But it is a normative trust founded on professional rather than close-knit social relationships. Interaction is based more on a periodic sharing of the excitement of intellectual dialog and discussions than through the social intensity of more integrated relationships. 'Weak-tie' relationships or networks are not market-based or bureaucratically commanded, but rather take the form of voluntary collective action.

Global science is increasingly characterized by the technologically aided collaboration of researchers over vast distances who share weak ties that leave them relatively free to focus on scientific productivity around a specified project or series of projects. Nonetheless, this transnational cooperation requires standards, conventions, rules and other 'focal points' to mediate it (Schelling, 1960). Scientists look for ways to access important scientific networks – 'places to meet', as Grewal (2008) describes it – in the absence of global sovereignty. Their social coordination requires frames of reference – standards – to facilitate exchange. Increasingly, certain standards of the scientific community have assumed a dominance that confronts individual researchers. They exercise a form of network power that is not easily shrugged off if access to critical scientific resources and researchers is desired. The choice whether to accept powerful network standards or not – and autonomous agents have free if increasingly involuntary choices on these matters – may be between access to the global scientific community or exclusion from it.

THE OPEN SOCIETY AND ITS DIFFICULTIES

Before exploring the emergent system of global science further and illustrating why previous state-centric accounts linking scientific creativity to particular sociopolitical national formations may require revision in the Internet-driven world of the twenty-first century, it will be useful to consider some other problems with the open society theory.

First, the scientific community is not as 'open' as is sometimes claimed and its 'public goods' are not easily accessed. Although science networks reinforce the idea of global governance more generally as containing strong elements of private or self-regulatory authority, and although patterns of coordination are largely non-governmental, neither are they random. They follow clearly recognizable patterns and rules, and are based on normative association. That is, tacit modes of social coordination are achieved through standards that exercise closure and network power.

Moreover, quite long processes of scientific apprenticeship, qualification-building and interpersonal contacts help to develop this tacit knowledge that is necessary for scientific understanding. Without the reflexively generated and generally unstated knowledge that is constituted within science's 'invisible colleges', it becomes difficult for outsiders to replicate experimentation by following published and formally codified processes alone.

Globally networked science, despite becoming more publicly accessible than before, is not necessarily a model for the 'open society'. It operates by rules which, although not controlled by any specific organization or state agency, are not easily perceived by outsiders. As Kealey (2009) and Wagner (2008) note, the expense of forming a transnational research network can be large and participation can be costly. Participants must share valued information or provide another resource – funds or experience, for example – and as a network matures, the cost to new members rises accordingly. Moreover, there is a distinct system of cumulative inequality at work. Those that have high reputations, extensive collaborators, many citations, and relatively easy access to research funds and to the most talented younger scientists tend to attract even more. A law of 'preferential attachment' appears to operate in which highly creative and productive people attract other such individuals (Florida, 2008, p. 64). The global science network operates with, at best, limited openness.

Of course, much of this would have been familiar to Merton and even applauded. That is, cumulative advantage and levels of exclusivity could be justified within the terms of the open society as continuously changing its composition and reflecting always temporary outcomes that are quickly challenged by the relatively open competition, merit and reasonable equality of opportunities found in scientific communities. Yet normative processes may be as 'closed' to outsiders as are state power and commercial markets, and may not be quite so illustrative of meritocracy as Merton, Popper and others assumed.

Second, despite the claimed affinity for the methods and procedures of innovative science and liberal democracy, politics is more about the interplay of values and how we live together than finding out how the world works (the main preoccupation of science). Moreover, there are also marked divergences between Popper's prescription for scientific inquiry and some well-known descriptions of how scientists actually behave. The method of falsification, which appears so neat and logical as a way of resolving the problems of induction, is less concise and orderly when applied to the analysis of real-world scientific processes and the evaluation of theories. Kuhn (1962), for example, in his history of science shows that very little falsification is undertaken. Radical hypotheses are often frowned upon, young scientists have to undergo an apprenticeship before being allowed to be inventive, and 'normal science' is mostly 'gap-filling'.

Popper's notion of a decisive moment (of falsification) does not seem intuitively how scientists operate in practice. It is rare for a theory to be rejected simply because its predictions have not worked out on particular occasions. More usually scientists will keep on testing to see how it all works out in the long run. For Kuhn the characteristic pattern of development in the natural sciences – 'normal science' – involves testing propositions within established paradigms. (This may be why scientific progress in places such as China may not be as hindered by sociopolitical constraints as often assumed.) Revolutionary change, when it happens and when a new paradigm supersedes the current shared model, occurs periodically (and in the global age quickly diffuses to all manner of political systems within which scientists operate).

For Kuhn, 'normal science' is a prerequisite for scientific advance. Constantly seeking to change a paradigm debilitates the focus on well-articulated issues that is necessary if science is to progress. Rather than permanent scientific revolution through falsification, actual scientists, quite desirably, get on with the job. The often gradual accumulation of anomalies within normal science itself enables paradigmatic change.

An anthropological study of Australian medical scientists by Charlesworth and colleagues (1989) comes to similar conclusions. Postgraduate students and postdoctoral fellows are sent off on global sojourns to other laboratories to pick up new but conventional methods, techniques and contacts before becoming accepted as full-blown scientists. Their scientific papers at this stage in their careers are designed less to be read than to be published. Nowotny et al. (2001) also observe that science is not especially democratically organized and scientific careers and rewards are often highly gendered and unequal in distribution.

Third, a further difficulty with the open society theory are the consequences following the dissemination of the NPM globally as a more competitive, market-based, corporately organized and managerial way of running universities than traditional collegiality. This has made contemporary notions of academic freedom and university autonomy somewhat ambiguous in many countries, not least in liberal democracies where the NPM has come to predominate as a mode of control and external accountability. Marginson (2008) suggests that the NPM is not necessarily incompatible with academic freedom as a whole, as it involves heightened senses of individual freedom from sometimes stiffly professorial and similar collegiate influences, although it does increase external control, accountability and agenda-setting (commercially and by public agencies). Moreover, governmental and even some commercially specified research priorities and funding for universities still tend to be accompanied by conventional mechanisms of allocation based on peer review and academic excellence.

Nonetheless, academic autonomy and entrepreneurialism sit uneasily alongside external accountability and recent state strategies for funding research. Within a number of European societies, science and research funding has become subject to an explicit framework of national research priorities with a policy focus on national economic competitiveness. In the UK, for example, the research councils have become more strongly governmentally steered in the last two decades, with increased programmatic (rather than individual–response mode) funding, the introduction of the commercial users of research into peer-review processes, and increased requirements that academics make explicit the anticipated 'impact' or real-world relevance of their research outcomes in advance of funding. Yet university researchers believe great breakthroughs begin with the curiosity of the scientist not at the imperative command of government, while commercial and industrial applications can take many years to appear.

Continental European countries display similar processes. In The Netherlands, for example, third-party and contracted funds have grown for universities since the early 1980s, while governmental funding has declined (de Boer et al., 2005). A previous longstanding and convenient coalition between state officials and local disciplinary guilds at chair level (with academic self-governance on academic matters complementing state regulation on non-academic matters) has given way to more collective academic processes and stronger corporate and managerial governance. Research coordination has become shared between state officials, academics and institutional managers. The governmental science budget emphasizes selectivity and concentration, external accountability, business, social relevance and value for money.

University researchers feel that research agendas have become increasingly externally controlled, diminishing the creativity and serendipity they regard as essential for high-quality basic science. Yet the levels to which the NPM constrains or encourages innovative research nonetheless remain largely unexplored. There is some evidence that the impact varies by discipline. Leisyte (2008) found, perhaps not unsurprisingly, that medieval historians had greater difficulty than biotechnology researchers in adapting to the need for more diverse sources of funding and the forging of private sector–academic partnerships. Occasionally, however, both subject groups (who nonetheless continue to value basic, risky, and cutting-edge research and who treasure their professional autonomy) often are able to satisfy both personal and external agendas respectively, through the 'strategic' writing of research proposals according to the requirements of the funders while still investigating topics of their own curiosity.

Research by stealth and maneuver appear more commonplace strategies than before to protect the open space considered necessary for blue-skies research. How sustainable such tactics are for preserving curiosity-driven research in the face of strong external agenda-setting is unclear. The loss of issue choice and control over their research agendas by university researchers is felt most keenly as the major deprivation. Henkel (2005), in a comparative study of scientists, found that academic freedom based on the primacy of discipline is generally understood by academics and researchers as 'control over one's work' and the 'ability to construct one's own research agenda', but they feel that this is gradually slipping away.

More generally there is less academic self-determination over the contents of the research itself than previously (Marginson, 2009). The OECD (2008), in a wide-ranging survey of countries, concludes that recent NPM reforms may be limiting academic autonomy, intellectual freedoms and the capacity to innovate in favor of short-term, less risky and applied projects. The liberal-democratic capacity for creating an 'open society' that enables curiosity- and individually driven quality knowledge formation may, at best, have become attenuated in recent years. However, as we shall see, the recent growth of global, individually collaborative science offers considerable scope for researchers to pursue their research interests outside the stricter confines of scientific nationalism.

Fourth, and finally, a persisting problem with the open society theory for innovative science is that relatively 'closed' and 'insider' associations of scientists enjoying high influence are not easily reconciled to notions of wider democratic and public accountabilities. How best is the 'public interest' to be discharged by elected governments in the face of networks that are by no means 'open' and fully accessible but which operate by informal and self-regulatory processes? And is this possible without damaging the conditions for creativity and path-breaking discovery that 'open society' theorists, with some justification, argue is based on maximum levels of individual freedom and institutional autonomy?

The dominance of the view that forms of 'open society' are necessary for research creativity and innovation, which is shared by governments to a greater or lesser extent in diverse sociopolitical configurations, guards against over-intrusiveness by governments, despite recent moves by such decision-makers to make science more publicly accountable and steered. This helps to sustain a form of national, but particularly global, governance of science that remains essentially 'self-reproductive' and 'self-regulative'. Systemic macro-structures on the one hand, and situational-agent structural reproduction on the other, essentially reinforce each other.

Reflexive, de-centered and responsive governance is likely to be best for national and global systems of science rather than politicians constraining it through direct command or tightly drawn national borders. The objective is to find ways of guiding networks, influencing and facilitating access to them, in ways that preserve their essential dynamics.

Such issues take us to more specific consideration of the network power and standards of globalizing science.

GLOBAL SCIENCE'S NETWORKS AND STANDARDS

Emergent global science enhances the opportunities for researchers to undertake collaborative projects across territorial boundaries outside the direct control of national governments. A feature of global forms of governance is often their private and self-regulatory nature. In science, global networks and their associated processes of standardization have begun to exceed the power of governmental scientific nationalism. While the latter regards scientific outcomes as national assets to benefit a country's economic and military objectives – an approach that emerged strongly in the decades after the ending of the Second World War in 1945 – global science is characterized by a self-governing and self-reproducing form of coordination that is highly unequal in its national consequences. It has developed strongly in the last two decades or so, not least with the ending of the Cold War between the USA and the Soviet Union (including their respective allies) and the widespread communicative use of the Internet.

The use of network theory as a framework for gaining insights into the essentially self-regulating world of twenty-first-century science has been well exemplified by Caroline Wagner in her work *The New Invisible College* (2008). She suggests that in the sixteenth and seventeenth centuries as well as now, scientific coordination and discovery are characterized by scientists exchanging ideas as part of a shared search for knowledge. However, in the current age networks have a technical dimension (the World Wide Web) as well as a social one. Moreover, government exercises less control over science now than a few decades ago, when high-cost 'big science' dominated. Rather, a renewed and networked model of science in the current century is a more open system and based on individual collaboration.

A preponderance of worldwide scientific joint ventures is formed by person-to-person projects rather than by trans-ministerial agreement. Mainly these are arranged collectively by individuals through well-established professional and disciplinary linkages. The objective is to create a research project of discovery founded on complementary capabilities and shared curiosities. Finance, however, is usually derived from national and similar public funding agencies that are unable or unwilling to exercise too strong a constraint on who is enrolled to work on the project, especially when elite scientists are involved, once projects have been approved. National priorities set by governments also appear to aid networked global science of a more informal kind in that national research and innovation agendas display a remarkable convergence around a few areas, such as biochemistry, nanotechnology, genetics and the environment, rather than reflecting local concerns and circumstances, thus facilitating worldwide scientific 'clustering'.

One interpretation of these developments is to argue that the necessary affinity between high-quality science and the open society associated with liberal democracy has taken a globalized turn. Fukuyama (2008, pp. 1–2), for example, maintains that most research in basic science 'can develop only in an atmosphere of free and open exchange', and that this helps to explain the strong internationalization of scientific collaboration in recent years. Despite governmental rhetoric (and funding) that views science through a national prism, underpinned by strong beliefs connecting scientific development to national well-being, globalizing science 'can be understood only as the by-product of a horizontal process of social collaboration in which merit and results trump any consideration of national origin or jurisdiction' and whose outcomes are largely public rather than proprietary goods. Modern science is thus an emergent transnational system (it reproduces itself through the interdependence of countless individual actions rather than by sovereign direction). It generates complexity in an unplanned and unpredictable way through the interactions of autonomous agents.

Wagner (2008, p. 1) provides considerable evidence to support the view that the focus of science has moved from the national to global level and that 'self-organizing networks that span the globe are the most notable feature of science today'. Scientists are collaborating across the globe not because they are ordered by governments to do so but because this is often the best way to utilize differing perspectives, resources and knowledge to conduct the high-quality science that satisfies both individual curiosity and the career desire for esteem, reputation, and also scientific autonomy.

Such a picture contrasts sharply with the dominant paradigm for knowledge and innovation in most of the advanced countries in the second half of the twentieth century, which Wagner terms 'scientific nationalism' and where science is conceived as both governmental and national property. In the USA, Europe and Japan, large federal and regional agencies came into existence after 1945 to manage the relationship between the scientific and political communities. Publicly funded programs to help the economic application of scientific results also developed. The scientifically advanced countries contributed to scientific governance by introducing regulations, standards, funds and institutions to develop and capture the advantages of science. Wagner (2008, p. 23) notes that 'science, technology and state institutions co-evolved into mutually helpful entities'. Even now the connectivity between national sciences and governmental technology policies remains a highly observable element of the system of science worldwide.

The recent movement to a globally based, networked science is controlled effectively by researchers rather than by governments. Global science is self-reproducing in that its structure is formed by interacting and communicative researchers who use such structures as the basis for their own action as autonomous agents and who, through their scientific collaborations founded on worldwide views as to the 'morality' of science and its methods and conventions, thereby simultaneously sustain such structures. The global alliances of scientists, like university league tables, provide reputational and informational shortcuts within a world of exploding knowledge and potential contacts. They are 'status-signaling' devices, creating a basis of trust that facilitates confidence in exchanging information on the foundation of common norms.

Global science is thus both open and bounded. Reputation provides a heuristic to 'order' rapidly growing knowledge, and disciplinary and institutional rankings help do this by reinforcing existing worldwide patterns of scientific opportunity and inequality. Although scientific networks remain collegiate, insider-understood and protected (Kealey, 2009; Wagner, 2008), and while obscure processes and the high levels of tacit knowledge found in scientific experimentation and outputs continue to maintain strongly exclusionary tendencies, these are not the only mediating characteristics. Strong notions of autonomy, objectivity, testability and peer judgment provide key standardizing features across the global scientific network. Moreover, not only do scientific normative models provide 'ordering' and coordination across researchers' networks, they also operate as forms of power.

NETWORKS

As we have noted, the network of global science has been described as 'emergent' in that, rather like an ecosystem, it develops unpredictably on the basis of free individual exchanges (Wagner, 2008). In our conceptualization, actor exchanges freely entered into are subject to processes of structuration in which actors use and maintain (and modify) structures through their decisions that in turn both enable (constitute) and constrain their actions. Scientific structuration involves the utilization and reproduction of key standards, and these characterize the particular manner in which the members of scientific networks are interconnected. These standards are shared norms of practice that enable members to gain access to each other, and thus generates cooperation (Grewal, 2008).

Such standards serve to coordinate the network, including through notions of correct operational methods, but they also act as entry or membership tests for the network. That is, their acceptance as mediating standards is a requirement for accessing the network itself. While membership standards more generally may require explicit collective regulation and policing by a network, mediating standards in science tend to be tacit and individually self-enforcing.

In the same way that we use language – its grammar, vocabulary and rules – as a resource to communicate with fellow language speakers (or through a process of translation into another language with similarly understandable rules), and thus, through our utterances and actions, contribute to the language's continued reproduction across time and space, so scientists use scientific standards as a medium of social coordination and through their practices contribute to the reproduction of these standards. Changes to standards clearly do occur, in some cases as a result of exogenous factors outside the scientific world, such as governmental or economic actions, and, in others, as endogenous or internally created adaptations. More especially, change occurs as a result of strategizing by actors in the context of differential power resources associated with dominant network standards.

CONCEPTUALIZING NETWORKS

Global science networks may best be described as 'networks as structures'. In this conception, relational structures in a network systematically influence the actions of its members and generate recognizable outcomes. That is, network structure is an existing resource for actors and is reproduced by decentralized and autonomous agent choice-making in social practices. Thus, although created by agents' decision-making, network structure is not the deliberate result of conscious and purposeful action designed to produce such a goal. Rather, the focus of our interest is on the effects of such networks – as structures and resources – for the individual actors and groups who comprise them.

An alternative perspective is to conceptualize 'networks as actors', which does refer to deliberative collective action in order to achieve particular objectives (Kahler, 2009). Often operating to influence governments, networks as actors are political entities frequently found within the sphere of sovereignty, while networks as structures turn our attention more to processes of sociability.

Both network concepts – as structures and as purposeful actors – tend to become intermingled in concrete situations: networks tend to normatively constrain actors as well as forming the basis for collective associations to take up the cudgels to promote the ideas and interests of members. Yet both refer to rather distinctive notions of power. 'Network power' flows from networks as structures, while 'networking power' reflects the purposeful actions of the network as a collective agent, or network as actor (Kahler, 2009). Global science is characterized especially by 'network power' and by standards that impact strongly on individual agents. More particularly, the spreading network power of scientific models is aided by quite high levels of their incompatibility with any alternative scientific standards. Such incompatibility tends to drive the dominance of already powerful networks governed by distinctive norms of practice, and moves towards the universalization of a single model. The network's size is progressively increased and leads to the decline of alternatives. As with telecommunication networks, fewer members or subscribers of a network reduces the efficacy of alternatives and raises their relative cost to users.

Scientists (and proto-scientists) experience global science as a given structure that shapes their behavior – and it is also the outcome of the actions of scientists. This structure comprises standards, including 'scientific methods', that as they stretch over time and space attract 'network power' properties based on global normative influence. Alternative models and networks (such as those found in 'totalitarian' societies characterized by state-withering constraints over individual and institutional autonomy, in the name of, say, advancing overriding political objectives) increasingly lack credibility and influence. That is, they lack power as standards (Grewal, 2008).

'Networking power', however, attaches more to individual agents – to scientific 'stars' – through such processes as 'preferential attachment' and cumulative advantage. Here new members (doctoral and postdoctoral students, for example) disproportionally attach to individuals (network nodes) that are already densely connected to other nodes. As Kahler (2009) and Wagner (2008) respectively note, global science is a scale-free network in which connections exhibit a power-law distribution so that a large number of scientists possess few network links while a small number display many.

Generally, network forms of organization allow actors to maintain their freedoms (they allow exit options) and this is perceived as highly desirable by scientists who value their intellectual freedom (although a consequence of exercising the exit option may lead to marginalization in global science). Moreover, scientific autonomy and creativity are furthered enhanced by the 'distant' connections between practitioners that characterize global science and creative innovation more generally.

CONVERGENCE AND DIVERGENCE

As various standards compete for global attention as solutions to the many demands for access to socially coordinated networks, we are likely to find various types of accommodative outcomes. Although there is a general tendency towards the universalization of standards as part of globalizing processes, and as the network power of key models exerts strong magnetisms over users of other models in other networks, convergence on the same standard is subject to a range of contextual conditions. Grewal (2008), for example, notes that strict incompatibility of standards and their equal intrinsic value tends to produce universalization of one or other as network power propels convergence on a single standard. However, where such conditions do not obtain – if the intrinsic merits of competing models are regarded as differing greatly, for example – forms of coexistence will endure. Levels of availability (openness to others) and malleability (capability of being revised, including by taking on elements of competing network standards) are also variables that determine the universal dominance or pluralistic existence of network models and standards.

More particularly, too, the universalizing of network models is subject to national and similar processes of adaptation and revision as they become 'domesticated'. Such modifications generally enhance universalization rather than hinder it. Standards are rather abstract and generic models. Expert systems decontextualize models and prototypes to enable widespread, codified diffusion as solutions to common problems. This sustains their legitimacy and also their network power by appealing to potential users. Standards as rational designs provide a means of communication that allows the articulation of locally varying relations to such models and discussion on how far harmonization and standardization should go (Demortain, 2009).

Sociological accounts of knowledge as context-bounded tend to value processes of dialogue and deliberation for the effective adoption of standards. Unlike more mechanical or prescriptive approaches to the application of standards, sociological versions place greater weight on local collective agreement, respecting local traditions, and allowing actors to feel comfortable with standards for models to 'stick'. There is recognition, too, that contemporary nation-states are less unified than before, often comprising a number of relatively autonomous subsystems, and that governmental and other decision-makers are confronted with a range of often competing internal perspectives and interests (Whittington, 1997). This generates a softer process of standardization that gives scope to agents to understand and explain their arrangements, not least in comparison with other adaptations. If taken too far, of course, the language of a standard may simply be appropriated to preserve, codify and defend alternative and substantially different local choices. 'Universalization' in such cases becomes ritualistic or a form of mock compliance. The key point, therefore, is that global forces, including those of standardization, work together with local structures.

Standardization through processes of structuration is not a rigid process. It allows for processes of local deliberation and adaptation to local 'path histories' – indeed, sociologists and others accepting of a dialogistic approach to standardization would view such a process as necessary for successful diffusion – within a nonetheless strong 'pull' towards dominant, but relatively abstract, globalizing models. Governance models globally diffuse, in this view, through mechanisms affording elaboration and flexibility while retaining the overall coda of a new institutional arrangement. However, with increasing global standardization, the 'structure' in 'structuration' tends to become more compelling for non-adopters than agency autonomy as a consequence of a model's increasing network power.

In higher education, for example, under the standardizing influence of global university rankings can be detected worldwide governmental 'follow-my-leader' ambitions to develop selected domestic entities as 'world-class universities'. We have noted also how national strategic investment policies for science and research appear eerily similar. Rather than being linked distinctively to local capacities and requirements, they comprise an almost generic list of the sectors identified for such support by countries (OECD, 2008). The European Union meanwhile is creating the structural conditions for a European Research and Higher Education Area, implying not only stronger forms of policy coordination across nation-states but also heightened peer pressures for emulation.

CONCLUSION

In this chapter we have examined processes of standardization as key governance and social coordination mechanisms in the global age. Moreover, we have suggested that the sphere of sociability – and the accumulation of decentralized agent choices – is at least as important as that of sovereignty in understanding how individuals make history but not quite as they please. That is, notions of structuration and their inherent patterns of power, including the network power of standards – the 'pulling' and universalizing factors of certain model solutions to the problem of accessing other people in networks – are important concepts in explaining global governance in higher education too. It is the reproduction and modification of governance patterns in situations of free but constrained choice for actors that offers an important area of empirical inquiry for higher education and scientific policy-making more generally.

REFERENCES

Altbach, P. (2007), 'Globalization and forces for change in higher education', *International Higher Education*, **50**, 2–3.
Altbach, P. and J. Balán (eds) (2007), 'Introduction', in *World Class Worldwide: Transforming Research Universities in Asia and Latin America*, Baltimore, MD: Johns Hopkins Press.
Charlesworth, M., L. Farrall, T. Stokes and D. Turnbull (1989), *Living Among the Scientists: An Anthropological Study of an Australian Scientific Community*, Melbourne: Oxford University Press.
Cummings, W., W. Locke and D. Fisher (2010), 'Faculty perceptions of governance and management', *International Higher Education*, **60**, Summer, 3–5.
De Boer, H., L. Leisyte and J. Enders (2005), 'The Netherlands: steering from a distance', in B. Kehm and U. Lanzendorf (eds), *Reforming University Governance: Changing Conditions for Research in Four European Countries*, Bonn: Lemmens.
Demortain, D. (2009), 'Discourses that standardize', *Risk and Regulation*, Winter, 6.
Emmott, B. (2009), *Rivals: How the Power Struggle between China, India and Japan will Shape our Next Decade*, London: Penguin Books.
Finnemore, M. and K. Sikkink (1999), 'International norm dynamics and political change', in P. Katzenstein, R. Keohane and S. Krasner (eds), *Exploration and Contestation in the Study of World Politics*, Cambridge, MA: MIT Press.
Florida, R. (2002), *The Rise of the Creative Class*, New York: Basic Books.
Florida, R. (2008), *Who's Your City? How the Creative Economy is Making where to Live the Most Important Decision of Your Life*, New York: Basic Books.
Foucault, M. (2000), *Power*, ed. J. Fabio, New York: New Press.
Fukuyama, F. (2008), 'Foreword', in C. Wagner, *The New Invisible College: Science for Development*, Washington, DC: Bookings Institution Press.

Giddens, A. (1995), *Politics, Sociology and Social Theory*, Cambridge: Polity Press.

Granovetter, M. (1973), 'The strength of weak ties', *American Journal of Sociology*, **78** (6), 1360–80.

Grewal, D. (2008), *Network Power: The Social Dynamics of Globalization*, New Haven, CT and London: Yale University Press.

Hayek, F. (1960), *The Constitution of Liberty*, London: Routledge.

Hayhoe, R. and Qiang Zha (2010), 'The polytechnic universities in China's transformation', *International Higher Education*, Summer, 11–13.

Henkel, M. (2005), 'Academic identity and autonomy in a changing policy environment', *Higher Education*, **49** (1–2), 156–7.

Jian Liu and Xiaoyan Wang (2010), 'Expansion and differentiation in Chinese higher education', *International Higher Education*, Summer, 7–8.

Kahler, M. (2009), 'Networked politics: agency, power and governance', in M. Kahler (ed.), *Networked Politics: Agency, Power and Governance*, Ithaca, NY and London: Cornell University Press.

Kealey, T. (2009), *Sex, Science and Profits*, London: Vintage Books.

King, R. (2007), *The Regulatory State in an Age of Governance: Big Sticks and Soft Words*, Basingstoke: Palgrave Macmillan.

King, R. (2009), *Governing Universities Globally: Organizations, Rankings and Regulation*, Cheltenham, UK and Northampton, MA, USA: Edward Elgar.

Kuhn, T. (1962), *The Structure of Scientific Revolutions*, Chicago, IL: University of Chicago Press.

Lan Xue (2008), 'China's evolving innovation system – the role of universities', in H. Vessuri and U. Teichler (eds), *Universities as Centres of Research and Knowledge Creation: An Endangered Species?*, Rotterdam: Sense Publishers.

Leisyte, L. (2008), 'The effects of the NPM on research practices in English and Dutch universities', in H. Vessuri and U. Teichler (eds), *Universities as Centres of Research and Knowledge Creation: An Endangered Species?*, Rotterdam: Sense Publishers.

Liu, J. and X. Wang (2010), 'Expansion and differentiation in Chinese higher education', *International Higher Education*, **66** (Summer).

Marginson, S. (2008), 'Academic creativity under new public management', *Educational Theory*, **58** (3), 269–87.

Marginson, S. (2009), 'Intellectual freedoms and creativity', in M. Peters, S. Marginson and P. Murphy, *Creativity and the Global Knowledge Economy*, New York: Peter Lang, pp. 91–124.

Marginson, S. (2010), 'Confucian values', *Times Higher Education*, 17 June.

McGregor, R. (2010), *The Party: The Secret World of China's Communist Rulers*, London: Penguin.

Merton, R. (1942/1996), *On Social Structure and Science*, Chicago, IL: University of Chicago Press.

Mohrman, K. (2008), 'The emerging global model with Chinese characteristics', *Higher Education Policy*, **21**, 29–48.

Mohrman, K., W. Ma and D. Baker (2008), 'The research university in transition: the emerging global model', *Higher Education Policy*, **21**, 5–27.

Murphy, P. (2009), 'Defining knowledge capitalism', in M. Peters, S. Marginson and P. Murphy, *Creativity and the Global Knowledge Economy*, New York: Peter Lang, pp. 23–50.

Nowotny, H., P. Scott and M. Gibbons (2001), *Re-thinking Science: Knowledge and the Public in an Age of Uncertainty*, Cambridge/Oxford: Polity/Blackwell.

OECD (2008), *The Thematic Review of Tertiary Education: final draft*, Paris: OECD.

Peters, M. (2009), 'Introduction: knowledge goods, the primacy of ideas, and the economics of abundance', in M. Peters, S. Marginson and P. Murphy, *Creativity and the Global Knowledge Economy*, New York: Peter Lang, pp. 1–22.

Philips, P. (2007), *Governing Transformative Technological Innovation*, Cheltenham, UK and Northampton, MA, USA: Edward Elgar.

Polanyi, K. (1962), 'The republic of science: its political and economic theory', *Minerva*, **1**, 54–74.

Popper, K. (1945), *The Open Society and its Enemies*, London: Routledge.

Popper, K. (1963), *Conjectures and Refutations: The Growth of Scientific Knowledge*, London: Routledge and Kegan Paul.

Putnam, R. (2000), *Bowling Alone: The Collapse and Revival of American Community*, New York: Simon and Schuster.

Rui Yang (2010), 'Peking University's personnel reforms', *International Higher Education*, Summer, 10–11.

Schelling, T. (1960), *The Strategy of Conflict*, Cambridge, MA: Harvard University Press.

Schumpeter, J. (1951), 'Economic theory and entrepreneurial history', in R. Clemence (ed.), *Essays on Economic Topics of Joseph Schumpeter*, New York: Kennicat Press.

Stiglitz, J. (1999), *Knowledge for Development: Economic Science, Economic Policy and Economic Advice*, Washington, DC: World Bank.

Stones, R. (2005), *Structuration Theory*, Basingstoke: Palgrave Macmillan.

Wagner, C. (2008), *The New Invisible College: Science for Development*, Washington, DC: Brookings Institution.

Whittington, R. (1997), 'Putting Giddens into action: social systems and managerial agency', in C. Bryant and D. Jary (eds), *Anthony Giddens: Critical Assessments, Vol. 4*, London: Routledge.

Yang C., R. Sanders and J. Wang (2008), 'The commercialization of Chinese universities and its effects on research capacity', in H. Vessuri and U. Teichler (eds), *Universities as Centres of Research and Knowledge Creation: An Endangered Species?*, Rotterdam: Sense Publishers.

Yang, R. (2010), 'Peking University's personnel reforms', *International Higher Education*, **66** (Summer).

25 Governing quality
David D. Dill

Academic quality assurance, historically a national concern, has been evolving rapidly over the last several decades in reaction to the forces of globalization. The first response was the development in many countries of new national models for assuring academic quality in the context of the adoption of mass systems of higher education (Brennan and Shah, 2000; Dill and Beerkens, 2010), which itself was a national reaction to the economic impacts of increased global economic competition. More recent responses include the development of regional and increasingly international organizations and regimes for academic quality assurance as a consequence of the globalization of the higher education industry itself (King, 2009; Santiago et al., 2008a). This development of international institutions of academic quality assurance appears to be consistent with the 'rational design' theory of institutions (Koremenos et al., 2001). This would predict that as transnational exchanges involving students, faculty, services and university-produced knowledge grow, international institutions will emerge to help reduce the associated transaction costs of these exchanges, including bodies for making and enforcing necessary agreements.

Practices for assuring quality are relevant to all the traditional academic activities of universities, including the quality of services such as academic consultancy and knowledge transfer, the quality of basic research and of teaching and student learning. While there have been significant new national policies designed to assure the quality of research (Dill and van Vught, 2010), the primary attention of academic quality assurance efforts at the national, regional and now global level has been on confirming and improving academic standards (Dill and Beerkens, 2010), which is the focus of this chapter. By academic standards is meant the specific level of knowledge, skills and abilities that students achieve as a consequence of their engagement in a particular academic program. As such, this definition of academic standards reflects the growing worldwide concern with assuring and improving the quality of student learning (Santiago et al., 2008a).

The immediately following sections explore first the forces of globalization that provide incentives for the development of international organizations and regimes for the assurance of academic standards. In succeeding sections the emerging global institutional framework for assuring academic quality is outlined and the strengths and weaknesses of these arrangements are explored. The concluding section will examine the issue of the legitimacy of these emerging global academic quality assurance institutions (Buchanan and Keohane, 2006).

ACADEMIC QUALITY ASSURANCE INSTITUTIONS AND GLOBALIZATION

Global economic forces have influenced the emergence of both national and international policies governing academic quality (Dill and Beerkens, 2010; Santiago et al.,

2008a). However, while national policies of academic quality assurance have received increasing attention, the institutional framework of international quality assurance is still developing and is less well understood. The primary reasons for the adoption of new national policies on academic quality assurance over the last several decades have been the 'massification' or expansion of access to higher education and the associated rapidly rising expenditures in many countries, both arousing policy-makers' concerns about maintenance of academic standards and value for money in universities. If, as is increasingly apparent, massification and national concerns about academic standards are in turn responsive to global pressures affecting the economic viability of citizens and states, so also the more recent emergence of international agencies and regimes of academic quality assurance has been motivated primarily by global economic competition. International student mobility has risen quite dramatically over the last three decades, with the number of foreign students doubling since 1995 (Santiago et al., 2008b) as students around the globe seek a competitive economic advantage through the nature and provenance of their academic degrees. The adoption of English as the language of international commerce and the rapid development of the Internet have provided further momentum for international student flows as well as for the development of a new industry in the cross-border provision of academic degrees by publicly funded, private and newly developed for-profit universities. These increasing global transactions have fostered the recent development of international agencies and regimes designed to address the uncertainties of assessing academic quality in this new world of academic commerce. As in other international spheres of governance, such as the environment, health and finance, the hierarchical or command-and-control forms of regulation often favored by national governments have proven less politically feasible and 'softer' forms of governance appear more prominent (King, 2009).

The OECD (2004) has outlined the national motivations for the growing internationalization of higher education. These rationales include the traditional goal of enhancing mutual understanding, but also increasingly reflect economic concerns such as revenue generation for universities. In the case of developing nations, internationalization is motivated also by the desire to develop human capital in a cost-effective manner by supporting student study abroad and encouraging foreign higher education providers domestically. The economic rationale for internationalization in higher education was graphically illustrated in 1989 when the University of Reading became the first (but not the last) university in the UK to win the Queen's Award for Export Achievement. In addition, most nations desire to ensure that the quality of their academic programs is appropriately recognized so that their citizens can compete effectively for positions in the global marketplace. Developed nations also desire to attract highly skilled migrants, especially in research doctoral programs that have been shown to contribute to the technical innovation critical to maintaining national economic competitiveness (Dill and van Vught, 2010). These latter economic rationales have been significantly influential in supporting the emergence of global institutions and regimes for academic quality assurance.

The competitive economic nature of this national motivation in support of global mechanisms governing academic quality, however, also suggests one of the underlying weaknesses of these institutions. Both nations and their universities may be well served if the international institutions for academic quality assurance confirm the reputations respectively of a country's academic institutions and programs. But the global public interest is best served only if these international institutions verify or help assure the actual academic standards of a country's universities and academic programs as previously defined. This distinction between reputation and academic standards is a key factor in assessing the strengths and weaknesses of the evolving global institutions and regimes for assuring academic quality.

INTERNATIONAL INSTITUTIONS FOR ASSURING ACADEMIC QUALITY

The international institutional framework for assuring academic quality is composed of a complex and growing web that includes:

(a) intergovernmental agencies such as the European Commission (EC), the Organization for Economic Co-operation and Development (OECD), the United Nations Educational, Scientific and Cultural Organization (UNESCO), the World Bank (WB) and the World Trade Organization (WTO);
(b) networks of national academic quality assurance agencies such as the European Association for Quality Assurance in Higher Education (ENQA) and the International Network for Quality Assurance Agencies in Higher Education (INQAAHE);
(c) institutions of civil society including voluntary and professional organizations engaged in academic quality assurance activities such as the Centre for Higher Education development (CHE) and the Accreditation Board for Engineering and Technology (ABET); and
(d) commercial organizations such as *The Times Higher Education Supplement* (*THES*), now *Times Higher Education* (*THE*), and *Financial Times* (*FT*) that provide international rankings of universities and selected academic programs.

One high-profile example of an intergovernmental institution for international academic quality assurance is the Bologna Process. While nominally a voluntary activity of the Ministries of Education of the 46 cooperating states that lies outside the formal institutional framework of the European Union, the process has been effectively driven behind the scenes by the European Commission, which first articulated publicly many of its core ideas, provides financial support for Bologna activities, and most recently sponsored the independent evaluation of the process (Balzer and Rusconi, 2007; Westerheijden et al., 2010). Although the Bologna Process has a number of goals, including the restructuring of academic degrees and the expansion of student mobility within the 'European Higher Education Space', the recent evaluation argues that academic quality assurance 'has proven to be the at the heart' of the process (Westerheijden et al., 2010, p. 29). The key quality assurance institutions and regimes implemented as part of the Bologna Process are the *Standards and Guidelines for Quality Assurance in the European Higher Education Area* (ESG) developed by ENQA (2009), the *European Quality Assurance Register* for Higher Education (EQAR), which lists quality assurance agencies that substantially comply with the ESG, and the *Framework for Qualifications of the European Higher Education Area*

(QA-EHEA, 2005) listing generic descriptors of learning outcomes and competences for the three degree cycles of higher education (that is, bachelor, master and doctoral degrees). In addition to these more top-down mechanisms, the Bologna Process has helped to institutionalize the Tuning Process as a means of improving academic quality (Westerheijden et al., 2010). The Tuning Process is designed to enhance academic quality at the subject level by developing reference points for curricula in all three cycles based upon competences and learning outcomes articulated collectively by faculty members drawn from subject fields.

Global membership organizations such as the OECD, UNESCO, the WB and the WTO also play an increasing role in the international framework for academic quality assurance. Over the last 20 years the OECD has changed its approach to education policy, shifting from individual in-depth country studies to a focus on rankings and ratings of member countries, utilizing carefully developed measures of educational performance. This 'comparative turn' (Martens, 2007) of the OECD has created new and influential peer pressure among the participating developed and cooperating emerging countries for reforms in education. By systematically improving its measures and data-gathering of educational performance and by creating its own independent measures, as with the Programme for International Student Assessment (PISA) (the worldwide evaluation of 15-year-old schoolchildren's scholastic performance), the OECD has markedly increased its reputation and influence for helping assure and improve educational quality.

With regard to academic quality, the OECD has focused on producing comparative studies of national best practices in quality assurance as well as suggested guidelines derived from related research. In response to the growing global concern with assuring academic standards, the OECD (2009) has also embarked on the International Assessment of Higher Education Learning Outcomes (AHELO) project to assess learning outcomes on an international scale through the creation of measures that would be valid for all cultures and languages. These new measures would then permit construction of national rankings of academic performance similar to those that have proven so influential with the PISA assessments. Similarly, the World Bank (2002) has provided comparative reports drawn from the experience of the Bank's constituent states, primarily developing countries, which attempt to provide global standards and guidelines for national quality assurance policies.

UNESCO and the WTO have also played the role of global standardizers for academic quality assurance (King, 2009). UNESCO (1993) has developed a *Recommendation on the Recognition of Studies and Qualifications in Higher Education,* which it employs to lessen transaction costs in higher education by guiding the development of recognition conventions – legal accords among countries designed to recognize academic qualifications among the signatories. UNESCO also promulgated in collaboration with the OECD (2005) *Guidelines for Quality Provision in Cross-border Higher Education*, and in association with other international organizations published the *Berlin Principles on Ranking of Higher Education Institutions* (IHEP, 2006) as a global standard for the design of academic league tables. The WTO, through its General Agreement on Trade in Services (GATS) process, also plays a role in global academic quality assurance (Scherrer, 2007). Countries participating in GATS must consent to apply similar national quality assurance mechanisms and standards to all higher education providers, public and private, national and international. These international trade agreements have also stimulated cooperative efforts among professional bodies such as accounting, architecture, engineering and law societies in different countries to develop mutually acceptable standards and criteria for licensing and certification, which may, like the Tuning Process, eventually inform the articulation of similar learning outcomes around the globe for academic degrees in these professional fields.

International networks of national quality assurance agencies such as ENQA and INQAAHE have published standards and guidelines for the conduct of external quality assurance activities, such as academic audit, accreditation and subject assessments. Based upon the experiences of member quality agencies in over 65 countries, the INQAAHE (2007) has set out in *Guidelines of Good Practice in Quality Assurance* the best practices it believes should be adopted globally by all quality agencies. As with most professional associations, these best practices are implemented though the socialization and educational activities of INQAAHE. In contrast, the similar guidelines developed by ENQA form the basis of the ESG adopted by the ministerial participants in the Bologna Process and therefore these guidelines are reinforced by related policies implemented by these ministers in the participating countries, and by the independent evaluations and judgments necessary to be listed in the EQAR established as part of the Bologna Process.

In addition to these international networks composed of national quality assurance agencies, there are other voluntary, non-governmental organizations of civil society that play an influential role in the global institutional framework for academic quality assurance. These include specialized voluntary accreditation agencies that attempt to assure minimum academic standards in particular subject fields or programs worldwide by applying a common external quality assurance approach, such as the Association to Advance Collegiate Schools of Business International (AACSB) and the Accreditation Board for Engineering and Technology (ABET), both based in the USA, as well as the European Quality Improvement System (EQIS) accrediting process of the European Foundation for Management Development (EFMD). The university rankings of the Centre for Higher Education development (CHE) and the Shanghai Jiao Tong University (SJTU) also have made important contributions to the public provision of information on academic quality by systematically designing cross-national rankings of first-level academic subjects in the case of the CHE and the Academic Ranking of World Universities (ARWU) in the case of the SJTU. The CHE initiated its rankings of bachelor-level programs in Germany, then extended them to other German-speaking countries, and is now developing a listing of 'excellence' subjects at the first-degree level across Europe. The SJTU has had a significant impact on the debates of national policy-makers about quality in higher education by developing a global ranking of universities based primarily upon their research activity.

Finally the commercial organizations of the market, such as newspaper and magazine publishers who produce university league tables, have become an increasingly visible and influential part of the institutional framework affecting academic quality in many countries (Dill and Soo, 2005). With the recent development of international academic league tables such as the Global MBA Rankings of the *Financial Times* and the World University Rankings by the *Times Higher Education* (*THE*, previously *THES*), commercial organizations have now also become an important component of the emerging global framework governing academic quality.

STRENGTHS AND WEAKNESSES OF THE GLOBAL INSTITUTIONAL FRAMEWORK

Given the emerging global framework for assuring academic quality described above, what are the strengths and weaknesses of these institutional arrangements? In assessing this framework several obvious limitations of global governance must be acknowledged (Keohane, 1998). The fact that there is literally no overarching global government alters the relative effectiveness of the legal, financial and informational policy instruments traditionally favored by national governments (Van Vught, 1994). Because international governance requires the concurrence of nation-states and as such represents negotiated agreements among volunteer participants, the legal policy instruments of command-and-control, obligation and prohibition, by which national governments have traditionally asserted their formal authority and regulated higher education, are less feasible in global governance. Similarly the 'power of treasure', the financial instruments of direct support, grants, contracts and subsidies national governments utilize to steer higher education is not practicable at the international level. Instead, as noted above, the global governance of higher education quality relies heavily on informational policy instruments or 'soft law' (King, 2009) such as guidelines, codes of best practice, recommended standards and rankings. These international mechanisms depend less on the legal sanctions and financial power employed by national governments and more on the influence of socialization, peer pressure and reputation that is characteristic of voluntary organizations. In this complex global framework for governing academic quality, international rankings of universities play a significant role. However, similar to the weaknesses of international bond-rating agencies discovered during the financial crisis of the first decade of the twenty-first century, these rankings appear to distort market forces rather than help them operate more efficiently in the public interest.

The experience to date of the Bologna Process suggests that efforts to globally define learning outcomes of academic programs, using common national qualifications frameworks and the collective efforts of academic staff at the subject level through mechanisms such as the Tuning Process or the activities of professional associations stimulated by the GATS, will make a modest but important contribution to assuring international academic standards (Westerheijden et al., 2010). While some policy-makers have hoped and some academic staff have feared that these types of effort could become an effective regulatory device for assuring the fitness of purpose of academic degrees, the impacts of these instruments appear more limited. The evidence from the Bologna Process reinforces the insights from equivalent national mechanisms, which have had a limited influence on assuring academic standards (McInnis, 2010; Williams, 2010). The increasing specialization of academic knowledge and the rapid development of new interdisciplinary fields of study in the university sector tend to compromise attempts to prescribe academic content. The impact of the qualifications frameworks adopted in a number of countries, as well as the collegially defined Subject Benchmarks program implemented in the UK, have proved more broad and general, and more formative and developmental, than regulatory. The more significant benefit of qualifications frameworks and subject standards appears to be changing national policy debates about academic standards from a focus on course content to one of student learning outcomes. Collectively developed subject-level standards similarly have helped alter the traditional orientation of academic staff and proven particularly useful in some universities in the planning of new courses of study.

The effectiveness of the standards, guidelines and best practices for governing academic quality developed by global networks of academic quality professionals such as ENQA and INQAAHE, and/or in association with intergovernmental efforts such as the Bologna Process or international organizations such as UNESCO, is more debatable. One obvious problem with self-regulatory approaches, again clearly illustrated by the experience with bond-rating agencies in the recent financial crisis, is that professional academic quality assurance agencies possess their own interests and therefore may attempt to 'capture' (Laffont and Tirole, 1991) or shape the regulatory process to ensure agency survival and prosperity rather than maximize the public interest in assuring academic standards. For example, although a stated main goal of the Bologna Process is 'promotion of European cooperation in quality assurance with a view to developing comparable criteria and methodologies' (Westerheijden et al., 2010, p. 29), the ENQA *Report to the Bologna Ministerial Anniversary Conference of March 2010* stresses the diversity among political systems, national higher education arrangements and cultures. Consequently ENQA states 'this makes a single monolithic approach to quality, standards, and quality assurance in higher education inappropriate' (ENQA, 2010, p. 1). As ENQA then makes plain, its primary concern is legitimizing fellow professional agencies: 'There is little point in adopting a "hard line" position in respect of compliance with the ESG if, by doing so, trustworthy and credible agencies are prevented in gaining Full membership of ENQA . . .' (ibid.). This concern with diversity so influenced the ESG that as the independent Bologna evaluation observed, 'there are no [ESG] criteria that directly affect actual education, that is, academic standards' (Westerheijden et al., 2010, p. 32).

As the Bologna evaluators further noted, all participating national quality assurance agencies are now required to undergo an international evaluation of their conformance with the ESG. Of the 44 agencies reviewed by ENQA as of 2009 by teams composed primarily of fellow quality assurance professionals, all were judged positively. In contrast, the parallel process for approving national agencies for a listing on the *European Quality Assurance Register* for Higher Education (EQAR), which evaluates agencies that operate in Europe and have proven their credibility and reliability against the ESG, rejected one ENQA-approved agency and saw three other approved agencies withdraw their applications. The Bologna evaluators observed that on the basis of the same ESG and similar review processes, different bodies reach different conclusions and this variation does not enhance the public's faith in the regulatory process. The evaluators concluded that the ESG reviews by ENQA vary so much in their methods and processes (see also Stensaker et al., 2009) that they do not help build international trust; therefore greater attention needs to be given in the future to achieving the Bologna goal of compatible quality assurance practices (Westerheijden et al., 2010).

An earlier evaluation of a mutual recognition experiment conducted among Nordic quality assurance agencies also suggested that evaluations primarily by quality assurance professionals may limit the incentives for the development of methodologies that more effectively assure academic standards (Dill, 2002). Although the recognition evaluations carried out by the quality assurance professionals revealed some variations among the respective agencies in the rigor and scientific approach of their quality assurance processes, these differences were given little weight in the recognition process, and mutual acceptance of agencies appeared to trump concerns with the validity of the respective quality assurance methodologies. As a consequence, all the participating agencies were recognized and the process appeared to provide little motivation for the adoption of the more demanding processes of the stronger agency.

Similarly, in a series of informative papers on the best practice guidelines and quality assurance agency evaluations developed by international networks and organizations, Blackmur (2007a, 2007b, 2008a, 2008b) raises a number of important challenges regarding the effectiveness of self-regulation. At both the national and global level the common answer to the question 'who guards the guardians' of academic quality assurance (Blackmur, 2008b) has been to require public evaluation of national agencies. But these evaluations, like those in the Bologna Process, are most often designed and carried out by the agencies themselves in cooperation with associations of agency professionals and/ or selected representatives of those regulated. Blackmur (2008b) argues that this type of evaluation lacks independence, fails to employ a suitably relevant and robust method of validation, and generally ignores the critical issue of value for money. As suggested above, this type of collegial review may provide insufficient incentives for the development of the 'science' of external quality assurance, which as noted in independent studies of national academic audits, subject assessments and accreditation processes, appears to exhibit substantial variations in objectivity and rigor (Dill and Beerkens, 2010).

The guidelines of good practice published by international organizations and international professional networks may suffer from similar weaknesses (Blackmur, 2007a, 2007b). For example, the *Berlin Principles on Ranking of Higher Education Institutions* (IHEP, 2006) were developed by UNESCO in cooperation with an expert group that included commercial providers of ranking information such as the *Times Higher Education Supplement* (*THES*) (now *THE*) and *US News and World Report* (*USNWR*). Reflecting their interests, the standards avoid addressing a number of important methodological factors in the design of more valid and reliable university rankings. These methodological points have been clearly identified by not-for-profit and scholarly organizations that produce academic rankings such as CHE in Europe and the National Academy of Sciences in the USA, as well as in research on league tables and student choice (Beerkens and Dill, 2010; Dill, 2009; Federkeil, 2009; Dill and Soo, 2005; Marginson, 2009). This collective literature emphasizes that student choice is best informed by information on subject fields and academic programs, not by the commercially popular university institutional rankings that offer little positive – if not negative (see below) – benefit to the public interest in assuring academic standards. Further, there is a need to present ratings information as ranges rather than rankings because the differences between the ranks in most league tables are not statistically significant, and to avoid the use of reputational surveys as a basis for rankings because it is clear that such raters have little valid knowledge of educational programs (Federkeil, 2009; Ostriker and Kuh, 2003). But such design considerations are not directly addressed in the Berlin Principles because '[w]hat could have been a restrictive set of guidelines was headed off by the ranking organisations, which argued that unrealistic principles would be ignored' (Jobbins, 2006). Thus the development of global guidelines and standards such as the Berlin Principles provides a further example of the means by which self-regulatory processes may be captured by those supposedly regulated (Laffont and Tirole, 1991).

An increasingly significant institution for the governance of academic quality is national university rankings or league tables, which were initially developed by commercial publications as a means of informing student choice. At the global level, influential world rankings of universities and some subject fields such as MBA programs have now been developed by the Shanghai Jiao Tong University, the *Times Higher Education Supplement* (*THES*, now *THE*), and the *Financial Times*. The justification for the publication of most university quality rankings is the economic argument that better-informed students will be able to make more effective educational choices, that competition for these better-informed students will in turn lead universities to improve academic quality, and these overall efforts will increase the efficiency of the higher education system (Teixeira et al., 2004). But as Gormley and Weimer (1999) suggest, information provision is likely to influence academic standards only if quality rankings utilize measures linked with societally valued educational outcomes, students use this information in their choice of subjects, and institutions respond to student choices by improving relevant academic programs.

The collected research on national university rankings suggests instead that commercially produced university rankings not only fail to produce the expected efficiency benefits but likely so distort the forces of the competitive market that they encourage inefficiency (Dill and Beerkens, 2010). The challenge and cost of developing valid indicators of educational outcomes are significant and commercial publications have little motivation to make such investments. Instead they enjoy substantial sales and influence among opinion leaders, high-achieving students and even university personnel by focusing on the production of league tables utilizing reputational surveys, input measures such as student test scores and financial resources, and indicators of research quality, all of which have questionable validity as predictors of effective student learning (Pascarella and Terenzini, 2005). The students most influenced by national university rankings are those of high ambition, achievement and social class (Dill and Soo, 2005), many of whom are most interested in obtaining the private benefits of higher education and therefore may be satisfied with reputational ratings rather than valid measures of societally valued educational outcomes. While there is evidence that some universities have been motivated by the existing national academic quality rankings to improve their internal data-gathering (Locke et al., 2008), since the commercial league tables are not based on any testable theory or model of university educational performance it is not clear that this investment in information leads to institutional actions that actually improve the educational quality of academic programs.

The more common response by universities is to try to improve their reputation, as reflected in their relative position in the rankings, by 'gaming' the system, 'cream skimming' high-achieving student applicants, increasing expensive investments in activities associated with research reputation, as well as developing more sophisticated institutional marketing (Dill and Soo, 2005). The pernicious effect of this competitive pursuit of reputation, which affects all universities, not just research-intensive institutions, is an increasingly costly zero-sum game that diverts resources as well as administrative and faculty attention away from the collective actions within universities necessary to actually improve student learning outcomes (Kuh and Pascarella, 2004). These negative impacts of national commercial league tables have motivated the creation of a number of more valid rankings by not-for-profit groups such as the CHE in Europe and the

National Survey of Student Engagement (NSSE) in the USA, as well as by the US government which supports the respected research doctoral rankings of the National Academy of Sciences (Dill and Beerkens, 2010). It is hoped that these more valid academic rankings will better aid responsible student choice and motivate real improvements in the academic standards of universities.

The early research on the impacts of the global university rankings reaches similar conclusions as studies at the national level (King, 2009; Locke et al., 2008; Marginson, 2009), except that the world rankings are even more influential than national rankings on the academic choices of foreign students. The global rankings also probably influence the decisions of foreign governments supporting students who study abroad as well as the recruiting activities of international employers. Among the two major world rankings, The *THES/THE* adopts the student choice rationale for its justification, suggesting that the rapidly growing global mobility of students and increasing international competition among universities requires a trustworthy, vigorous and transparent guide to the world's universities. By contrast, the researchers producing the Academic Ranking of World Universities (ARWU) at the Shanghai Jiao Tong University wished to produce an indicator of the relative standing and progress of the Chinese university system. Although pursuing different purposes, the approach of these two world league tables is quite comparable: both place the heaviest emphasis on research prestige as measured by quality of faculty, amount of university resources and publication citations. The *THES/THE* also includes a reputational survey, the significant limitations of which have been previously noted (and which have been addressed in recent reforms to its methodologies). For these reasons there are comparable concerns at the global level that these world university rankings may undermine the assurance of academic quality. In an effort to correct the distortive effects of the current system of global university rankings, the European Commission (2009) has funded a Consortium for Higher Education and Research Performance Assessment (CHERPA) to develop a world ranking system to overcome the noted limitations of the Shanghai Jiao Tong and the *THES/THE* schemes.

A continuing challenge to the effective regulation of academic quality at both the national and global level is the problem of developing valid and reliable measures of educational outcomes that can both help inform student choice and, perhaps more importantly, guide academic efforts within universities to assure and improve academic standards (Dill and Beerkens, 2010). At the national level, surveys of the student experience have been developed in Australia, the UK and the USA as a means of academic quality assurance, and are now spreading to other countries. The Australian Course Experience Questionnaire (CEQ) (Harris and James, 2010) and the similar UK National Student Survey, both of which are supported by the national government, provide graduates' perceptions of teaching quality and skills learned as well as their satisfaction with their academic program. The US National Survey of Student Engagement (NSSE) (Ewell, 2010) asks currently enrolled students to report on experiences in their educational program known to be associated with effective learning. While they are generic instruments, these surveys are based upon systematic research on effective teaching and student learning and therefore offer more valid and informative indicators of academic quality for potential students as well as academic staff. Both the Australian and UK governments also support destination surveys that provide information on the labor market outcomes of recent graduates, including the nature of graduates' employment, their average salaries and their further education. At the global level a recent comparative analysis of national quality assurance experiences by the OECD (Santiago et al., 2008a) suggests that an appropriate global standard would be: public provision of data on student retention; student progression; and graduate destination outcomes by subject field for all institutions of higher education.

In addition to these indicators, both Australia (Graduate Skills Assessment – GSA) and the USA (Collegiate Learning Assessment – CLA) are experimenting with value-added measures of generic skills for first-level students. Great interest has been expressed also in the announced OECD (2009) attempt to create global measures of academic learning outcomes through its Assessment of Higher Education Learning Outcomes (AHELO) project. This project aims to assess learning outcomes on an international scale by creating valid measures for all cultures and languages. The AHELO feasibility study now under way is attempting to measure generic skills using an adaptation of the CLA instrument developed in the USA, discipline-specific competencies in the sample fields of engineering and economics, as well as indicators of the educational context. When implemented, the AHELO project will represent a voluntary form of regulation but, as with the OECD PISA project, it will probably exert significant influence on the global governance of academic quality because of the direct involvement of national governments, the stature of the nations participating in the OECD, and the proven power of peer pressure among the OECD nations.

In summing up the role of information in the governance of educational quality at the national and global level, it is clear that valid and reliable information for assuring academic standards will be underprovided by the market and that the more valid academic quality information designed by not-for-profit organizations cannot be effectively produced or utilized without the intervention of government to secure necessary university cooperation. In this sense, valid and reliable information to help assure and improve academic standards at the national or global level is best understood as a pure public good that will be undersupplied and underused unless supported, subsidized or provided by governments.

The complex web of institutions and regimes that compose the framework conditions for the global governance of academic quality has a number of strengths and weaknesses. This review suggests that while several international mechanisms and innovative efforts offer promise, the interests of states in obtaining recognition of their academic credentials, of academic quality professionals in legitimizing their agencies, of commercial rankings providers in continuing their profitable activities, and of academics in securing the reputations of their programs and universities may limit the effectiveness of global efforts to assure and improve academic standards. What additional steps might therefore be taken to better achieve the public interest in the global governance of academic quality?

THE LEGITIMACY OF THE GLOBAL GOVERNANCE OF ACADEMIC QUALITY

The weaknesses and limitations of the emerging international framework for academic quality assurance outlined above raise questions about the legitimacy of these institutions and regimes. As in other areas of global governance such as trade, finance and the environment, the ability of institutions to function effectively depends on whether they have the support of citizens, affected organizations and ultimately of states (Buchanan and Keohane, 2006). A presumptive condition for legitimacy, therefore, is whether international agreements possess the ongoing consent of democratic states. But state consent, while a necessary condition, is often insufficient. As noted, voluntary mutual recognition processes may help secure the reputations of the universities and academic degrees of participating nations, but may do little to assure or improve academic standards overall. For this reason truly legitimate global institutions must seek to satisfy more than the consent of the participating states. They must be designed to achieve some conception of the 'global public interest'. How might this global public interest be defined in the case of academic quality assurance?

Critics of the legitimacy of global institutions have often argued that these arrangements must achieve, in addition to the consent of the participants, some standard of accountability and transparency (Buchanan and Keohane, 2006). With regard to global academic quality assurance organizations, transparency has most often been interpreted as requiring that they have public membership on their boards of control and/or that they make public their guidelines, procedures and assessments. In turn, accountability has been interpreted as requiring that these agencies undergo regular external evaluations that also are published. However, the arcane nature of academic quality assurance procedures and language may create an information asymmetry problem in which published quality assurance guidelines and assessments are comprehensible only to insiders – the self-interested professionals and academic constituencies and organizations directly affected by the processes. Outsiders such as citizen groups or even policy-makers may have great difficulty assessing the real comparative benefits or relative gains from global quality assurance institutions and regimes. Similarly, as previously noted, the mandated external evaluations are most often carried out by professionals in other academic quality assurance agencies who thereby have a vested interest in maintaining the status quo. Consequently the standards applied in these evaluations may be too forgiving or low.

An additional suggested criterion for establishing legitimacy is the 'epistemic–deliberative' quality of international institutions (Buchanan and Keohane, 2006). That is, does the institution or regime function in such a way as to facilitate principled, factually informed deliberation about the terms of accountability? This emphasis on fair-minded, evidence-based deliberation is often associated with the legitimacy and respect earned by national and international legal tribunals such as the International Court of Justice, but the idea of rigorously established objective evidence informing public policy choices among alternative regulatory approaches is now being advanced under the concept of 'evidence-based policy' (Davies et al., 2000). An interesting example of this approach is the significant role the non-partisan Congressional Budget Office (CBO) played in the approval by the US Congress of sweeping health policy reform in 2009. The CBO's influence was based upon its non-partisan structure and demonstrated scientific expertise in 'scoring' the financial impacts of various regulatory alternatives.

Studies of the global governance of academic quality similarly emphasize that the degree of influence of various institutions is a function of their perceived political independence, their scientific knowledge and the compelling authority of their expertise (King,

2009). As previously noted, the recent increase in influence over global education policy of the OECD is attributed to its strategic shift from conducting qualitative evaluations of individual countries to developing quantitative-based comparative studies such as the PISA Project and comparative education indicators such as the publication *Education at a Glance* (Martens, 2007). The OECD is becoming a more respected global governance institution because its legitimacy rests upon the objective scientific processes of its analyses and the careful deliberations of its expert researchers. Correspondingly, the academic rankings with the greatest legimacy are those developed by institutions of civil society such as the CHE in Germany or the National Research Council in the USA, which have systematically applied relevant research and scholarly methods to the design and development of more valid and reliable league tables (Dill, 2009). Policy analyses of external quality assurance processes such as academic audits, subject assessments and accreditation processes similarly suggest that the most influential on assuring and improving academic standards have been those such as the Teacher Education Accreditation Council (TEAC) in the USA, the Danish Evaluation Institute (EVA) and the General Medical Council in the UK, which have developed rigorous evaluation methodologies that conform to social-scientific standards of evidence (Dill and Beerkens, 2010).

This perspective suggests some possible directions for improving the effectiveness of the emerging global governance of academic quality. Consistent with the trend toward evidence-based policy deliberation noted above, many nations have established 'supreme audit' agencies (INTOSAI, 2006) to evaluate the efficacy of various regulatory institutions and regimes. National examples include the Government Accountability Office in the USA, the Australian National Audit Office, the German Federal Audit Office, and the UK National Audit Office. While initially created to conduct financial audits of government organizations and agencies, these institutions over time have also developed the capacity to carry out independent, objective, evidence-based evaluations of the effectiveness of public agencies and policies. Since all regulatory activities, including governmental and non-governmental mechanisms for governing academic quality, produce both positive and negative impacts, the ability to assess objectively the social benefits and associated social costs of regulatory laws, agencies, guidelines and information is important to both the public and to the universities that will be directly affected. At the national level, therefore, the public interest in effective and efficient regulation of academic quality in the university sector is likely to be better served if existing guidelines, standards, as well as national agencies, are publicly evaluated by established and respected national evaluation or audit agencies. The public and policy-makers will thereby be provided with more truly independent, objective, evidence-based and expert assessments of the extent to which current institutions and regimes for academic quality assure or improve academic standards, and academic quality professionals will gain greater insights into means of improving their methodologies and practices. Similarly, transnational institutions and regimes for the governance of academic quality, such as ENQA, ESG and EQR, or guidelines and standards produced by global-level organizations such as UNESCO and INQAAHE, should be subject to external evaluations, not only by academic quality assurance professionals, but by truly independent international organizations such as the European Court of Auditors, the OECD or the World Bank, which possess the expertise to better assess the social benefits and social costs of these regulatory approaches.

CONCLUSION

Universities are organizations dedicated to gathering, comprehending and conveying information and knowledge to students and to the larger society. They are also institutions that are particularly attentive and responsive to valid information about their own academic performance, quality and reputation. The emergence of a truly global academic industry over the last decades warrants the development of international institutions and regimes for governing academic quality. Given the known complexities of effectively measuring higher education learning outcomes and of assuring academic standards, regulatory processes that reflect the universal academic values of objectivity, rigor and a scientific approach to understanding are most likely to be deemed legitimate by society and the universities as well as to best protect academic quality.

REFERENCES

Balzer, C. and A. Rusconi (2007), 'From the European Commission to the member states and back: a comparison of the Bologna and the Copenhagen process', in K. Martens, A. Rusconi and K. Leuze (eds), *New Arenas of Education Governance: The Impact of International Organizations and Markets on Educational Policymaking*, Basingstoke, UK: Palgrave Macmillan, pp. 57–75.

Beerkens, M. and D.D. Dill (2010), 'The CHE university ranking in Germany', in D.D. Dill and M. Beerkens (eds), *Public Policy for Academic Quality: Analyses of Innovative Policy Instruments*, Dordrecht: Springer, pp. 61–82.

Blackmur, D. (2007a), 'A critical analysis of the UNESCO/OECD guidelines for quality provision of cross-border higher education', *Quality in Higher Education*, **13** (2), 117–30.

Blackmur, D. (2007b), 'The public regulation of higher education qualities: rationale, processes and outcomes', in D. Westerheijden, B. Stensaker and M. Rosa (eds), *Quality Assurance in Higher Education: Trends in Regulation, Translation and Transformation*, Dordrecht: Springer, pp. 15–45.

Blackmur, D. (2008a), 'A critical analysis of the INQAAHE guidelines of good practice for higher education quality assurance agencies', *Higher Education*, **56** (6), 723–34.

Blackmur, D. (2008b), 'Quis custodiet ipsos custodes?: the review of the Australian universities quality agency', *Quality in Higher Education*, **14** (3), 249–64.

Brennan, J. and T. Shah (2000), *Managing Quality in Higher Education: An International Perspective on Institutional Assessment and Change*, Buckingham, UK: OECD, SRHE and Open University Press.

Buchanan, A. and R. Keohane (2006), 'The legitimacy of global governance institutions', *Ethics and International Affairs*, **20** (4), 405–37.

Davies, H., S. Nutley and P. Smith (2000), *What Works?: Evidence-based Policy and Practice in Public Services*, Bristol, UK: The Policy Press.

Dill, D.D. (2002), 'Through the looking glass: comments on the Nordic pilot project on mutual recognition', in T. Lindeberg and D. Kristoffersen (eds), *A Method for Mutual Recognition: Experiences with a Method for Mutual Recognition of Quality Assurance Agencies*, Helsinki: European Network for Quality Assurance in Higher Education (ENQA), pp. 21–9.

Dill, D.D. (2009), 'Convergence and diversity: the role and influence of university rankings', in B. Kehm and B. Stensaker (eds), *University Rankings, Diversity, and the New Landscape of Higher Education*, Rotterdam: Sense Publishers, pp. 97–116.

Dill, D.D. and M. Beerkens (2010), *Public Policy for Academic Quality: Analyses of Innovative Policy Instruments*, Dordrecht: Springer.

Dill, D.D. and M. Soo (2005), 'Academic quality, league tables, and public policy: a cross-national analysis of university ranking systems', *Higher Education*, **49** (4), 495–533.

Dill, D.D. and F. van Vught (2010), *National Innovation and the Academic Research Enterprise: Public Policy in Global Perspective*, Baltimore, MD: Johns Hopkins Press.

ENQA (2009), *Standards and Guidelines for Quality Assurance in the European Higher Education Area*, http://www.enqa.eu/files/ESG_3edition%20%282%29.pdf, accessed 18 May 2010.

ENQA (2010), *Report to the Bologna Ministerial Anniversary Conference of March 2010*, http://www.enqa.

eu/files/Project%204%20-%20ENQA%20Report%20to%20the%20Anniversary%20Bologna%20ministe-rial%20meeting%20of%20March%202010_final_with EClogo.pdf, accessed 18 May 2010.
European Commission (2009), *Report on Progress in Quality Assurance in Higher Education*, http://ec.europa.eu/education/higher-education/doc/report09_en.pdf, accessed 18 May 2010.
Ewell, P. (2010), 'The US national survey of student engagement (NSSE)', in D.D. Dill and M. Beerkens (eds), *Public Policy for Academic Quality: Analyses of Innovative Policy Instruments*, Dordrecht: Springer, pp. 83–98.
Federkeil, G. (2009), 'Reputation indicators in rankings of higher education institutions', in B. Kehm and B. Stensaker (eds), *University Rankings, Diversity, and the New Landscape of Higher Education,* Rotterdam: Sense Publishers, pp. 19–34.
Gormley, W. and D. Weimer (1999), *Organizational Report Cards*, Cambridge, MA: Harvard University Press.
Harris, K.-L. and R. James (2010), 'The course experience questionnaire, graduate destinations survey, and learning and teaching performance fund in Australia', in D.D. Dill and M. Beerkens (eds), *Public Policy for Academic Quality: Analyses of Innovative Policy Instruments*, Dordrecht: Springer, pp. 99–120.
INQAAHE (2007), *Guidelines of Good Practice in Quality Assurance*, http://www.inqaahe.org/admin/files/assets/subsites/1/documenten/1231430767_inqaahe---guidelines-of-good-practice%5B1%5D.pdf, accessed 18 May 2010.
Institute for Higher Education Policy (IHEP) (2006), *Berlin Principles on Ranking of Higher Education Institutions*, http://www.ihep.org/assets/files/publications/a-f/BerlinPrinciplesRanking.pdf, accessed 18 May 2010.
INTOSAI (2006), *The International Organization of Supreme Audit Institutions*, http://www.intosai.org/en/portal/about_us/, accessed 18 May 2010.
James, R., G. Baldwin and C. McInnis (1999), *Which University? The Factors Influencing the Choices of Prospective Undergraduates*, Canberra: Australian Government Publishing Service.
Jobbins, D. (2006), 'Change in rankings as expert group sets principles', *Times Higher Education*, 9 June, http://www.timeshighereducation.co.uk/story.asp?storyCode=203645&sectioncode=26 her, accessed 18 May 2010.
Keohane, R. (1998), 'International institutions: can interdependence work?', *Foreign Policy*, **110**, 82–96; 194.
King, R. (2009), *Governing Universities Globally: Organizations, Regulation and Rankings*, Cheltenham, UK and Northampton, MA, USA: Edward Elgar.
Koremenos, B., C. Lipson and D. Snidal (2001), 'The rational design of international institutions', *International Organization*, **55** (4), 761–99.
Kuh, G. and E. Pascarella (2004), 'What does institutional selectivity tell us about educational quality?', *Change*, **36** (5), 52–8.
Laffont, J. and J. Tirole (1991), 'The politics of government decisionmaking: a theory of regulatory capture', *Quarterly Journal of Economics*, **106** (4), 1089–127.
Locke, W., L. Verbik, J. Richardson and R. King (2008), *Counting what is Measured or Measuring what Counts? League Tables and their Impact on Higher Education Institutions in England*, Bristol, UK: Higher Education Funding Council for England.
Marginson, S. (2009), 'Global university rankings: some potentials', in B. Kehm and B. Stensaker (eds), *University Rankings, Diversity, and the New Landscape of Higher Education*, Rotterdam: Sense Publishers, pp. 85–96.
Martens, K. (2007), 'How to become an influential actor: the "comparative turn" in OECD education policy', in K. Martens, A. Rusconi and K. Leuze (eds), *New Arenas of Education Governance: The Impact of International Organizations and Markets on Educational Policymaking*, Basingstoke, UK: Palgrave Macmillan, pp. 40–56.
McInnis, C. (2010), 'The Australian qualifications framework', in D.D. Dill and M. Beerkens (eds), *Public Policy for Academic Quality: Analyses of Innovative Policy Instruments*, Dordrecht: Springer, pp. 141–56.
OECD (2004), *Internationalization and Trade in Higher Education: Opportunities and Challenges*, Paris: OECD.
OECD (2005), *Guidelines for Quality Provision in Cross-border Higher Education*, http://www.oecd.org/dataoecd/27/51/35779480.pdf, accessed 18 May 2010.
OECD (2009), *The Assessment of Higher Education Learning Outcomes (AHELO)*, http://www.oecd.org/dataoecd/3/13/42803845.pdf, accessed 18 May 2010.
Ostriker, J. and C. Kuh (2003), *Assessing Research-Doctorate Programs: A Methodological Study*, Washington, DC: National Academies Press.
Pascarella, E. and P. Terenzini (2005), *How College Affects Students: Vol. 2, A Third Decade of Research*, San Francisco, CA: Jossey-Bass.
QA-EHEA (2005), *Framework of Qualifications of the European Higher Education Area*, http://www.bologna-bergen2005.no/EN/BASIC/050520_Framework_qualifications.pdf, accessed 18 May 2010.
Santiago, P., K. Tremblay, E. Basri and E. Arnal (2008a), *Tertiary Education for the Knowledge Society, Volume I*, Paris: OECD.

Santiago, P., K. Tremblay, E. Basri and E. Arnal (2008b), *Tertiary Education for the Knowledge Society, Volume II*, Paris: OECD.

Scherrer, C. (2007), 'GATS: commodifying education via trade treaties', in K. Martens, A. Rusconi and K. Leuze (eds), *New Arenas of Education Governance: The Impact of International Organizations and Markets on Educational Policymaking*, Basingstoke, UK: Palgrave Macmillan, pp. 117–35.

Stensaker, B., L. Harvey, J. Huisman, L. Langfeldt and D. Westerheijden (2009), 'Are European quality assurance agencies reviewed according to the European Standards and guidelines?', Paper presented at the 31st Annual EAIR Forum, 23–26 August.

Teixeira, P., B. Jongbloed, D. Dill and A. Amaral (eds) (2004), *Markets in Higher Education: Rhetoric or Reality?*, Dordrecht: Kluwer.

UNESCO (1993), *Recommendation on the Recognition of Studies and Qualifications in Higher Education*, http://portal.unesco.org/en/ev.php-URL_ID=13142&URL_DO=DO_TOPIC&URL_SECTION=201.html, accessed 18 May 2010.

Van Vught, F.A. (1994), 'Policy models and policy instruments in higher education', in J. Smart (ed.), *Higher Education: Handbook of Theory and Research*, 10, New York: Agathon Press, pp. 88–126.

Westerheijden, D. et al. (2010), *The Bologna Process Independent Assessment: The First Decade of Working on the European Higher Education Area, Volume I*, http://ec.europa.eu/education/higher-education/doc/bologna_process/independent_assessment_1_detailed_rept.pdf, accessed 18 May 2010.

Williams, G. (2010), 'Subject benchmarking in the UK', in D.D. Dill and M. Beerkens (eds), *Public Policy for Academic Quality: Analyses of Innovative Policy Instruments*, Dordrecht: Springer, pp. 157–82.

World Bank (2002), *Constructing Knowledge Societies: New Challenges for Tertiary Education*, Washington, DC: World Bank.

26 Convergences and divergences in steering higher education systems
Christine Musselin

INTRODUCTION

We could discuss at length whether higher education systems and the ways they are steered are converging or not. On the one hand, world polity theorists like Meyer (Drori et al., 2006) or Ramirez (Ramirez, 2006) would stress that the diffusion and worldwide adoption of scripts such as 'a common logic of mass education suggesting [universities] become broadly inclusive, socially useful and flexible organizations' (ibid., p. 225) clearly show that isomorphism processes play a driving role in the sector. On the other hand, most of the many comparative books dealing with the transformation of higher education (e.g., among many others, Gornitzka et al., 2005; Kehm and Lanzendorf, 2006; Paradeise et al., 2009), while stressing in their introduction or in their conclusion that countries are experiencing common evolutions, are never structured around these common points but are organized around 'national chapters' in which each of the authors starts describing the national landscape, the specific problems and the related policies that have been adopted in the country under study. Schwarz and Westerheijden (2004), for example, provide a wonderful example of the general development of evaluation/ accreditation/assessment devices in the 20 countries they cover, but each and every chapter shows how differently each country understood these notions, created its own institutional responses and developed its own way.

Above all, the levels of analysis are the best explanation for these divergent visions of current governance processes in higher education. Convergences are generally stressed by authors interested in discourses and political orientations and looking at actors or policies at the macro level, that is, transnational bodies, governmental actors and so on. By contrast, authors interested in concrete practices and looking at actors at the meso level (higher education institutions) or at the micro levels (academic identities or academic tasks, for instance) are concerned with the variations they can observe as well as with the existing decoupling between the ideas informing the policies and the concrete implementation of these policies. In the comparative book written by Kogan et al. (2000) on the transformation of the higher education systems of Norway, Sweden and the UK, the four authors clearly stress the converging trends they observed at the macro level (that is, the governmental actors and the co-opted academic elites) but remark that the diffusion and the influence of the reforms decrease when one goes closer to the individual actors within the universities.

Both perspectives will therefore be successively developed in this chapter. I begin by observing that higher education systems are experiencing two main evolutions that are common to many other sectors in which public authorities have a steering role. First, it will be argued that the role of the state in steering higher education systems has evolved towards more regulative than control interventions, towards more procedural than substantive policies, and towards framing rather than ruling. Then, in a second section, the emergence of transnational and infra-national actors as allies, counterweights or even opponents of national states will be discussed. Subsequently, because some convergences are more typical for this sector than for others, a third section tackles the specific and convergent conceptions that prevail about higher education systems. Finally, the last section will be dedicated to divergences and aims at explaining why higher education systems remain very national despite these general trends and suggesting that the way that they are steered is still quite divergent.

CONVERGENCES IN THE TRANSFORMATION OF STATE STEERING

Claiming that states have undergone dramatic transformations in democratic countries is almost a truism nowadays. These transformations are multiform. They first concern the general conception of what the state is and should be. Up to the recent economic and financial crisis, modest states that focused primarily on fundamental and traditional functions (collecting taxes, waging wars, guaranteeing the security of the citizens, administering justice and so on) had become the normative model to attain and some countries (the USA, the UK and New Zealand, for example) have become notable exemplars. Transformations further concern the blurring relationships between the state and society and can lead to dedifferentiation processes. These concern the declining role of collective actors such as the political parties or the unions, and more broadly an increasing distrust in representative democracy that leads to a redefinition of what politics is and means. New actors (such as non-governmental organizations – NGOs) have emerged while forms of deliberative democracy are developing and are welcomed by many authors (Bohman and Rehg, 1997; Elster, 1998; Przeworski et al., 1999). Finally, these transformations impact on the construction, the content and the implementation of public policies. Here the role of the state in such processes is described as less important and less influential than in conventional or more traditional accounts (Hassenteufel, 2008), and notions of governance or networks of governance often have replaced the idea of government and steering. In the higher education sector as in others, such common trends have been observed during the last decades and have affected how public policies are developed, what they are supposed to do, and on what they are expected to act. Although in some sectors public services such as energy and transport have been privatized in countries where they developed as a public mission, in higher education public authorities are still expected to play a role but they are expected to play it differently. Three main trends can be identified.

First, the quasi-monopolistic relationships most national states had developed with their higher education systems since the Second World War have opened up. This can be traced in two ways. On the one hand the public character of higher education has been put into question. In many countries (Portugal and most East European countries, Russia, but also China and others), private higher education institutions have expanded as public authorities considered that they could not financially support the necessary expansion in higher education training. They thus delegated the development of supplementary training programs to for-profit or not-for-profit private actors. Almost everywhere, too, private support has been solicited in order to fund public institutions. Claiming that they cannot and should not be the sole funders of higher education and research, public authorities have asked private actors (firms but also families when tuition fees have been introduced or increased) to take over part of the financial burden (Ward and Douglass, 2006). Such trends are less observable in many European countries (CHINC Project, 2006; Lepori, 2008), but there is a general discourse on the budgetary crisis of the state and the need to find complementary funding.

On the other hand, access to decision-making about higher education has widened 'up' and the network of actors engaged in steering higher education has increased in size. Aust (2004), for instance, shows that the number of actors involved in determining the construction of new university buildings in the 1960s in France was rather restricted. It consisted of some individual academics at the local level, and the ministry and DATAR (an agency created in the 1960s in France to equalize imbalances between the regions) at the central level. In the 1990s, if DATAR did not play any role, the ministry was still very active but had to negotiate with its own local representative (the *recteur*), the presidents of the concerned universities, the regional administrative and political actors, and the administrative and political staff of the town where the building was to be located. The network of actors involved is also frequently more hybrid than it was in the past, and stakeholders are solicited and intervene in decisions for matters from which they were excluded before. The use of conference consensus on scientific issues is certainly a good example of this trend, as well as the participation of non-academic and non-state actors in the British research councils (Henkel, 2005).

A second important trend consists in the type of policies displayed by public authorities. While higher education is very high on the public agenda of almost all countries and while many governments consider it is a major strategic issue that they must influence, the way the latter is perceived and exercised has evolved. While many countries used to develop very substantive policies that detailed what should be done and how, with precise and prescriptive rules, they now have recourse to more procedural policies that set the frame and the principles within which higher education actors can operate but without specifying the processes and details. This trend is not only common in higher education policies in most countries but is linked to a general transformation of state intervention and has been described by many authors in other sectors too, especially the environmental sector (Lascoumes and Le Bourhis, 1997; Howlett, 2000). Many examples could also be drawn from higher education, but the implementation of the Bologna Process in France – a country well known for its centralistic character and the command-and-control style of its public administration – is quite spectacular from this point of view. Not only was the implementation of Bologna's two-tier scheme of bachelor and master's not compulsory for French universities (which may explain why they all adopted it very quickly!), the definition of the content of the new programs was rather open as the national guidelines (*maquettes*) that previously existed had been suppressed (Witte, 2006; Musselin, 2006b, 2009).

Finally, the third and more critical trend certainly concerns the instruments used to steer higher education systems. Again it is important to notice that this is not specific to this sector and that the same tools are observed in many other sectors. In many countries (Paradeise et al., 2009) they resulted from the influence of the new public management

(NPM) narrative on the public sector, but they can also be observed in countries where this narrative has been much less successful (Bezes, 2009; Musselin and Paradeise, 2009). Three main families of instruments are widely exhibited by this last development.

A first family consists in the creation of agencies. This of course includes the national research councils in charge of allocating grants to specific research projects, but the latter had long been an important component of the higher education landscape in many countries for some time (such as the USA, Germany and Switzerland). Nevertheless this instrument of funding has generalized and can now be found almost everywhere. Furthermore, less classical forms of agencies also developed and received responsibilities that were previously in the hands of the higher education ministries. Missions linked to evaluation, assessment and accreditation, for example, have often transferred to specific agencies: the AERES (Agence d'Evaluation de la Recherche et de l'Enseignement Supérieur) in France (strictly speaking a consolidation of previously dispersed functions and agencies), the diverse Akkreditierungsagenturen in Germany, the NVAO (Netherlands–Flemish Accreditation Organization), the QAA (Quality Assurance Agency) in the UK, and so on. In fewer countries agencies have been created to allocate public funding to the universities. In Sweden no fewer than nine agencies are attached to the government to steer the Swedish higher education system.

Contracts between the public authorities and each higher education institution (HEI) constitute a second family or set of instruments that have diffused. On the one hand, they promote and introduce a new way of allocating budgets by linking specific amounts of funding to university objectives and strategies, and engaging in negotiation on these objectives and the means by which they would be supported. On the other hand, they encourage universities to construct regular strategic plans and to identify specific priorities.

A third family of instruments centres on the incentives frequently used by public authorities to obtain from higher education actors the adoption of specific behaviors. As shown by Naidoo (2008), the UK government has been quite partial to these kinds of tools. Incentives are used, for example, to push universities to open access to less privileged students, while information is provided on the performance of HEIs in order to lead students to choose their study programs in the way consumers do for every other product. A combination of increased central bureaucracy and market incentives is certainly particularly common in the UK (Le Galès and Scott, 2008), but is widely used elsewhere too. In Germany, for instance, many *Länder* (regions) transformed the way they allocated public budgets by introducing funding formulas whose parameters and components aimed at incentivizing HEIs to take into account factors they did not care about previously, such as the drop-out rates or the number of students getting their degree on time (Orr et al., 2007).

Finally, a fourth set of instruments used more frequently by public authorities comprises the use of competition (although not necessarily the use of markets; see Musselin, 2010), and benchmarking between universities. As will be argued below, national higher education policies increasingly tend to push for differentiation between institutions. Instruments are developed, allowing public and private comparison of institutions (sometimes down to departmental or even faculty levels), but also obliging institutions to look at what they are achieving, comparing one with another, and providing publicized information to higher education stakeholders (students, their parents, future employers, firms looking for research partners and so on). The UK RAE (Research Assessment Exercise) is probably one of the best examples of this kind of instrument. But public authorities also use highly competitive devices in order to sort out a few 'best' places to be funded. The German *Exzellenz Initiative* is typical of funding competitively a race by universities for 'excellence' and 'world-class' standing. A small number of institutions, doctoral schools or scientific clusters have been identified through a selective peer-review process and have received substantial extra funding. This was a completely new departure for a country where to that point all were considered equal (in theory at least).

In the late 1980s Neave and van Vught (1991) described the transformation in the steering of higher education as a drift from control states to evaluative states. But this was only one aspect (and, in a way, the first step) of the ongoing changes. The latter show that interpreting the emergence of evaluative states as a form of disengagement of the state or as a trend towards a declining – or at least a less directive – role of public authorities on the higher education systems was probably misleading. The instruments described above on the contrary testify that evaluative states are simultaneously more constraining – and steering in the strong meaning of the term – in many respects than what went before. In order to discipline behaviors – in the Foucaldian sense – the new tools look much more efficient than creating micro rules and multiple detailed interventionism and control.

CONVERGENCES ABOUT THE EMERGENCE OF NEW LEVELS

A second convergent trend affecting democratic states in general and the steering of higher education consequently is linked to the emergent influence of supra- and infra-national actors, leading to what is sometimes called the 'hollowing out of the state' (Ferlie et al., 2008). This trend towards multilevel governance is of course part of the de-monopolization of the relationships between the state and the diverse components of higher education systems, but it is also a process of de-nationalization of these systems and a potential weakening of the nation states.

The Increasing and Irresistible Influence of Local Actors

On the one hand, the transformation of the role of governmental actors in the steering of higher education allowed or fostered the involvement of infra-national actors and local public authorities. In countries like Germany, where the *Länder* were already in charge of most higher education issues, their prerogatives increased quite considerably and the possibility for differentiation among them was reinforced. In other countries like Spain or the UK, devolution of competencies over higher education has been granted to infra-national entities that may have quite different policies between one another. The introduction of higher tuition fees in England, for instance, was not followed by Scotland. Furthermore, in some countries like France, where regional actors have not been given competencies over higher education by the successive decentralization acts, local authorities nevertheless became more and more involved in higher education issues and have become inescapable partners for HEIs (Aust, 2004, 2007; Manifet, 2004; Filâtre, 2003).

Whatever way it took, and there were strong variations in the competencies of infra-national actors between countries, there clearly exists a trend towards political decentralization and/or administrative devolution in many countries. Central as well as federal states often are challenged by these local actors with whom they have to conduct their policies and develop partnerships.

The Increasing and Irresistible Role of Supranational Actors

The emergence of supranational actors is particularly visible in European countries where the construction of the European Union (EU) led to various measures aimed at creating the European Higher Education Area (mostly through the Bologna Process, an intergovernmental process led by the individual states (Ravinet, 2007) and the European Research Area (a policy developed by the European Commission)). If, in theory, higher education formally is not a competence of the European Commission, it has since the beginning (Corbett, 2005) always been an issue for the European bodies. This led to decisions such as the creation of the European University Institute in Florence, but also to the development of measures aimed at promoting mobility and vocational training in Europe (two domains on which the European Commission can make decisions). These include the Erasmus program for inter-country student mobility, the promotion of lifelong learning, and the creation of ECTS, a credit recognition and transfer scheme (to facilitate the recognition of degrees in different countries). The influence of the three latter examples on each European country has been variable but cannot be completely ignored. For instance, the current general discourse about international students and staff and the need for national students to have an international experience cannot be solely attributed to the Erasmus program, but the latter and the rhetoric developed around it certainly reinforce the current belief in the benefit of internationalization.

The impact of European research policy is at the same time clearer and more visible on the national steering of research activities than for higher education. Research funding allocated by the EU has become a rather common source for many academics in Europe. Successive Framework Programs were developed from 1984 in order to foster the development of research in Europe but also to promote collaborations among research teams from different EU countries and to produce research relevant for society. EU funding did not simply 'top up' national resources but also pushed for scientific orientations that were not always at the forefront of the EU members' national policies, and fostered cooperation across the territorial boundaries of Europe. The pursuit of purely national research goals becomes more and more difficult to achieve, and issues such as coordination between the objectives of the European Framework Program, the European Research Council (created in 2005 to reward the best research and focused especially on basic investigations), and the national research councils have emerged. Increasingly national levels have to take into account decisions made in Brussels or try to influence the decisions taken there through the many existing networks (Gornitzka and Sverdrup, 2008).

The Bologna Process provides another interesting case for supranational forces. Undoubtedly the national states behave as leaders in this process, which started in 1998 at the Sorbonne with a first declaration signed by four countries (France, Germany, Italy and the UK) and led in 1999 to a second Declaration signed by 29 countries, many of them beyond the borders of the EU. By doing so, the governments constructed a supranational roadmap even if its implementation was not very compelling. Arguably the Bologna Process has a weak constraining character, but Ravinet (2007) demonstrates the strong normative pressure on the signatories despite the absence of overt sanctions. Almost all the signing countries now offer training programs that follow the bachelor–master scheme. Many studies show that the Bologna Process should nevertheless not be understood as an inhibition imposed on the signing countries, but much more as an opportunity that countries used in order to lead to the reforms that they had intended to implement (Gornitzka, 2006; Witte, 2006). As a result, the Bologna Process is as much a case of Europeanization of national steering in higher education as a demonstration of how initiatives at the European levels are being renationalized (Musselin, 2009).

This shows the complexity of a process that is simultaneously soft and constraining, and both European and national, and that aims at building a European Higher Education Area, but also going far beyond the frontiers of the EU, and other dilemmas. Nevertheless, and despite the dual character of this process, it is almost impossible for national governments in the EU and in Europe and beyond (Adelman, 2009) to ignore it. Moreover, although the European Commission has not been a leader of the Bologna Process itself despite continuous efforts to become involved in such a capacity (Ravinet, 2007), Bologna allowed the Commission the opportunity increasingly to express its views on European higher education systems and the ways they should be managed. The publication of communications on higher education in 2005 and 2006 (European Commission, 2005, 2006) was quite new and clearly exposed the orientations that the Commission wished to push forward.

The influence of such publications on national governmental actors, their representations, goals and policies, is often more assumed than demonstrated. The same holds true for the studies and publications of OECD, UNESCO, the World Bank and similar international organizations. All these supranational institutions aim to shape the debates about higher education and to develop solutions and recommendations. But they are probably more influential when they use 'name-and-shame' devices. Producing comparative figures that show the bad performance of a specific country on this or that indicator may sometimes have more effect than more direct actions.

From this point of view, the publication of the Shanghai Jiao Tong University rankings has a similar impact on universities as the PISA study led by the OECD on secondary schooling. While it is overstated to understand the ongoing reforms within each and every national country as the direct result of these supranational bodies or international rankings, national governments cannot operate as if these publications, representations and recommendations did not exist. They at least use them as a threat to impose their own views. In France the idea to regroup universities located in the same territory existed before the first Shanghai rankings were published (seen in the promulgation of an act in 2003 that subsequently failed to pass) but it became much easier to 'sell' after the first Shanghai rankings. Becoming more globally visible and prestigious quite quickly were aims for the higher education sector used as a leitmotiv by the Ministry.

At an even more global level, some may argue that transnational norms are developing and imposing their rationale on national states (Djelic and Sahlin-Andersson, 2006). The transformation of higher education systems (or at least part of them) into an industry (Gumport, 2000) based on an international market for training and for research, whose rules and norms are defined beyond nation-states, may lead some institutions to loosen their national belonging and to lose the orientations and missions set by their national public authorities.

CONVERGENCES IN THE CONCEPTIONS OF WHAT A HIGHER EDUCATION SYSTEM OUGHT TO BE

The best evidence displayed by those arguing that a convergent model is being diffused by imitation and emulation (Simmons et al., 2007) or by mimetic, normative and coercive isomorphism (DiMaggio and Powell, 1983), relies on the strong similarities that may be observed in the discourses and solutions held by governments on higher education.

It is probably impossible nowadays to find a policy statement on higher education that does not start with a sentence close to 'In a globalized world governed by knowledge societies, higher education plays a crucial role in the economic development of our nation.' The idea that globalization prevails, that knowledge drives modern economies, and that higher education is a central player as a producer and a diffuser of knowledge, is almost never contested. This is also true about the idea that more highly qualified manpower will be needed for advanced economies. In governmental statements, getting a higher proportion of the population with a university degree is a positive result and a key objective.

Another generalized assumption that, like the previous one, is neither demonstrated nor questioned consists in assuming that HEIs are more efficient if they are autonomous and self-managed. As a result, new governmental acts often increase the formal decision-making domains on which HEIs can decide. In Asian countries authors (Oba, 2006; Mok, 2007) often use the expression 'incorporation' to describe the process by which public authorities devolve more autonomy to these institutions and expect them to behave more like firms than like public administrations. Organizational theorists such as Brunsson and Sahlin-Andersson (2000) describe this process as the construction of universities (and public services in general) as organizations, characterized by identity, hierarchy and rationality. This process has been encouraged in many public university systems (Musselin, 2006a; Krücken and Meier, 2006; Boer et al., 2007; Whitley, 2006).

As a widely shared consequence of these developments, the nature of the relationships between academics and their university is expected to change. First, institutional rules have developed and are competing (or conflicting with) academic professional regulations. The possibility for institutions to directly manage their staff and positions has been recognized in many countries, thus leading to the emergence of more employer–employee kinds of relationships between academics and senior managers of HEIs and to the development of more equipped internal labour markets (Doeringer and Piore, 1971; Musselin, 2005). While this mostly occurred through the devolution of these responsibilities from government ministries to the universities – accompanied in some places (e.g. Japan and Austria) by a shift for academics from civil servant status to an 'ordinary' employment contract – some governments developed peer-review processes on which institutions can rely in order to assess the activity of their staff and at the same time guarantee a certain homogeneity or evenness of performance.

Higher education policies also engaged in a quite radical move in continental European countries over the last decade. They shifted from policies aiming at developing rather balanced and non-differentiated systems to policies for excellence aimed at recognizing and improving the vertical and horizontal stratification of each system. The policy of 'balanced policies' admittedly never really succeeded in homogenizing higher education systems. Even in France, where institutions, training programs and staff were supposed to be equivalent and where centralized accreditation processes and input-formula-based allocations of budget were supposed to serve this objective, these equivalences were more theoretical than real. But 'equivalence' and non-differentiation were official government policy. This is no longer the case. Building on earlier ideas of individual universities having specific, different and prioritized contracts with government, over recent years a new discourse has emerged that stresses the variety in performance output and, without notions of inequality being prevalent, argues that performance should pay. Whether this could increase the level of differentiation among institutions no longer is an issue, or is less an issue than to recognize 'the best of the best' (the politically correct expression is 'the excellent') and to support them. The development of rankings and benchmarking instruments described above directly results from this representation of higher education systems as stratified arenas within which competition prevails and which should produce more differentiation.

This competition is of course not limited to the national scene but is international in scope. Even if in many countries the international mobility of academics remains modest, discourses about attracting the best teachers and the best students from other countries have become the norm. The percentage of international staff (and students) is seen as a sign of excellence (and some accrediting agencies regard a proportion of such as a requirement for accreditation), while inbreeding is systemically associated with a low profile and is condemned.

According to the three perspectives developed up to now in this chapter, evidence sustains the view of convergence between higher education systems. As a traditional public sector, higher education first of all experiences the same evolutions as other traditional public sectors and is affected by the ongoing recomposition of the role of the state, which has been quite common to all welfare states since the end of the 1970s. It is also affected by the trend toward multilevel governance resulting from the role regional actors are expecting to play on the one hand and the increasing influence of supranational actors, forces and norms on the other. Finally, the content of the policies generated by the national authorities in this context seems rather similar and oriented towards the same objectives.

When we look at this in a macro way, the nuances that could be introduced among the different countries disappear behind an overall convergent picture. Two questions must nevertheless be raised. First, is this convergence new or would the same observation have been made 40 years ago? In other words, are we going from various diversified pictures toward a common one or are we moving from one convergent picture to another? Answering this question seriously would need further investigation and more refined empirical work, but a quick overview of the situation in the 1970s suggests that the second option should not be overlooked. At that time the role of the state in higher education was considered as legitimate, the relationships between the state and the higher education system were mostly monopolistic, and many universities were adopting a participative form of governance. Rather than a new phenomenon, convergence would appear to be more longstanding, although the content has changed.

A second question to be raised deals with whether the convergences observed in terms of the role of the national government, the emergence of multilevel governance and the content of the policies have the capacity or not to reduce divergences at the meso and micro levels in terms of concrete practices, relationships and values. Many studies looking at these issues point to the persistence of national profiles and emphasize the national appropriation of the same solutions and ideas across sectors. Summarizing and listing the diverging issues highlighted by these studies would be fastidious and very long because it cannot be done without going into details and describing different national systems. I therefore choose to identify in the next section the mechanisms and theories that explain how convergence forces are limited by re-differentiation processes.

STILL VERY NATIONAL SYSTEMS: POTENTIAL EXPLANATIONS

As shown in the three previous sections, there are rather strong convergences in the way higher education systems are steered, in the emergence of supra- and infranational actors competing with national states in the governance of these systems as well as in the main orientations, beliefs and assumptions driving public authorities in charge of higher education systems. Some authors argue that this should lead us to compare institutions or regions rather than countries, and that the comparison of national systems no longer make sense. For example, two institutions/regions in the same country may reveal more divergences than two others belonging to different countries. While this certainly leads to innovative results, as demonstrated by Clark (1998) in work on entrepreneurial universities, national comparisons, whatever the theoretical approach they mobilize, generally point to remaining divergences prevailing among countries.

For historical neo-institutionalists this is no surprise. For years they have explored why countries confronted with the same problems and looking at the same kind of solutions finally do not come to the same conclusions, and may even develop completely different models. When comparing the construction of national health systems for the UK and the USA (but also in Canada), Hacker (1998), for instance, shows that the two countries were confronted with roughly the same problems at the same time, but while the two considered support for social coverage of ill workers, only the UK adopted it in 1911 and went on to introduce universal coverage after 1945. Two main explanations are raised by Hacker that can both be applied to higher education systems.

First, the national settings in which solutions are developed are more or less favorable. The political regime in the UK (an alliance between the Labour Party and the Liberals), the existence of a central administration, and the precarious financial situation of British doctors allowed Lloyd George to introduce a National Insurance Act. By contrast, the federalist regime of the USA and the absence of a strong central administration, as well as the quite wealthy situation of doctors in that country at that time, led to the failure of the campaign directed by Theodore Roosevelt and the AALL (American Association for Labor Legislation) for similar measures. This explanation in terms of 'national institutional settings' is close to the one developed by Europeanists (see, e.g., Cowles et al., 2001) when they claim that the chances for a European policy to be adopted at the domestic level are greater when the national settings are favorable (when there are no veto points, for instance).

This kind of explanation can be very useful in understanding why variety still prevails among training programs in Europe after the Bologna Process (Mangset, 2009). The slow implementation of this reform in Germany can for instance be explained by the federal structure of this country (each *Land* is in charge of the implementation) and the previous organization of the training programs. The bachelor level did not exist at all before, and has had to be introduced from scratch in the university training programs and also imposed on German employers. By contrast, the French case was much easier (at least in universities) as students already received a degree at the end of the third year, while implementation has been led centrally by the national ministry.

Second, following Hacker (but also many other authors in this vein and in particular Pierson, 1994), national institutional situations result from critical junctures that at a particular point engage a country on a certain path. Once this path is taken and the longer the country follows it the more difficult it is to divert and take another one. Path dependence (Pierson, 2000) thus prevails. Hacker shows that the failure of Roosevelt and the AALL at the beginning of the twentieth century blocked all further reforms as it institutionalized a situation in which private insurances developed and became allied to the doctors in order to develop a very expensive health system. This can again be applied to higher education reforms. It is, for instance, difficult to understand the demonstrations that happened in France at the beginning of 2009 without remembering that the creation of the imperial university in 1806 led France down a path where disciplines (or the academic profession) and not universities were the core components of the French higher education system.

Important shifts in this path have already occurred since the recreation of universities in 1968, the reforms of the beginning of the 1990s (Musselin, 2004 [2001]), and the recent Pécresse Act of 2007. But the reluctance of many French faculty members to accept autonomous universities and the (successful) claims not to leave the evaluation of the individual faculty member to the universities but to a discipline-based national body (the CNU, Conseil National des Universités), which were heard by the beginning of 2009, are typical of the persisting dependence on the Napoleonic conception of the French higher education system.

A further explanation for the persistence of divergences is suggested by the sociological neo-institutionalist perspective. Although they observe the scripts and common logics weighing on the organizational fields they study, adherents suspect that decoupling processes will increase between these scripts and the concrete practices (Meyer and Rowan, 1977), or/and that organizational hypocrisy prevails (Brunsson, 1989). In a way, the more convergent the levels of analysis developed in the three first points of this chapter, the less convergent the operational level is, and the more decoupling there is!

A third explanation focuses more on the very process through which the same ideas or solutions are differently adopted. This can be linked to the differences in national settings mentioned above, but also to the specific ways by which an idea will be diffused, translated and interpreted. The strength of an idea itself, its degree of clarity and specification then play a role, as well as the cognitive processes to which it is submitted. The (finally successful) 'misunderstanding' of the German model by the American academics who developed the US research universities around departments and not '*Lehrstuhle*' reveals the limit of transfers of solutions from one situation to another and the creative process that develops on such occasions.

Finally, another explanation relies on the level of interdependence of a national higher education system and other national systems in the same country. The reception of new insights by a national higher education system does not so much depend on the institutional characteristics of this system (or organizational field in the neo-institutionalist vocabulary) but on the overall characteristics, arrangements and institutionalized relationships prevailing at the level of a national country between different systems. What is at stake here is the autonomy of the higher education sphere *vis-à-vis* the other spheres and their interdependencies. When Whitley (2000) argues that innovation strategies vary according to market economies, and when he applies this kind of analysis to the field of teaching and research in management studies, he points at the links between science and economic organization. Recently a similar perspective has been developed by authors (Graf, 2009; Regini et al., forthcoming; Powell and Solga, 2010) trying to bring higher education into the analytical framework of the 'varieties of capitalism' approach (Hall and Soskice, 2001) – which up to now has considered only vocational training but not higher education. They thus consider each higher education system 'as a complementary subsystem within the national model of capitalism' (Graf, 2009, p. 4). Pechar and Andres (2009) have undertaken a quite similar approach but use the Esping-Andersen (1991) typology of welfare states to differentiate higher education systems.

Whatever the theoretical perspective, there are thus many reasons to believe that the overall convergent environment within which higher education systems evolve and are steered cannot constrain the development of local and specific understandings, implementations and adaptations, thus recreating variety within standardization.

CONCLUSION

The aim of this chapter has been to review the main perspectives developing on the evolution of higher education systems, particularly their steering and governance. Two opposed conceptions have been exposed. In the first part of this chapter three main domains on which convergences prevail, according to the literature, have been explored. The examination shows that recent evolutions have to be understood in the overall context of the global transformation of contemporary nation-states and the recognition that higher education public policies are quite comparable in terms of content and orientations.

Rather than concluding from this first array of work that divergences in steering higher education are reducing, I then took seriously the still-numerous studies that consider the national perimeter as a pertinent one and observe variances at the meso and micro levels of analysis from one country to another. Instead of listing these variances, nuances, or even oppositions and differences, I looked at the explanations that might justify the persistence of divergences and how they are theoretically informed and promoted.

Three main arguments justify this absence of choice between two contradictory points of view. First, as mentioned in the Introduction, these apparently conflicting conclusions can to a large extent be explained by the fact that opponents on the issue do not look at the same levels and objects. Second, taking seriously both perspectives shows that rather than regarding convergence and divergence as being binary processes, it seems more fruitful and compatible with the empirical data to consider their relationship. There are levels or issues on which convergences can be observed but, at the same time, within this rather global evolution, there is much room for idiosyncrasies (as for educational systems more generally; see Green et al., 1999). This allows national higher education systems to develop their own way and to keep many of their singularities. There are simultaneously convergences and divergences, or to put it another way, differentiation as well as re-differentiation processes occur, as exemplified by Segrestin (1997), who showed that international norms about quality assurance both standardize and differentiate firms.

REFERENCES

Adelman, C. (2009), *The Bologna Process for US Eyes: Relearning Higher Education in the Age of Convergence*, USA: Institute for Higher Education Policy.

Aust, J. (2004), *Permanences et mutations dans la conduite de l'action publique. Le cas des politiques d'implantation universitaire dans l'agglomération lyonnaise (1958–2004)*, PhD in Political Science: Université de Lyon 2.

Aust, J. (2007), 'Le sacre des présidents d'université. Une analyse de l'application des plans Université 2000 et Université du 3ème millénaire en Rhône-Alpes', *Sociologie du Travail*, **49** (2), 220–36.

Bezes, P. (2009), *Réinventer l'État. Les réformes de la bureaucratie française (1962–2008)*, Paris: PUF.

Boer, H. de, J. Enders and L. Leisyte (2007), 'Public sector reform in Dutch higher education: the organizational transformation of the university', *Public Administration*, **85** (1), 27–46.

Bohman, J. and W. Rehg (eds) (1997), *Deliberative Democracy*, Cambridge, MA: MIT Press.

Brunsson, N. (1989), *The Organization of Hypocrisy: Talk, Decisions and Actions in Organizations*, Chichester: John Wiley and Sons.

Brunsson, N. and K. Sahlin-Andersson (2000), 'Constructing organisations: the example of public reform sector', *Organisation Studies*, **21** (4), 721–46.

CHINC Project (2006), *Changes in European Higher Education Institutions' Research Income, Structure and Strategies (CHINC Report)*, Seville: Institut de prospective technologique.

Clark, B. (1998), *Creating Entrepreneurial Universities: Organizational Pathways of Transformation*, Oxford: Pergamon–Elsevier Science.

Corbett, A. (2005), *Universities and the Europe of Knowledge: Ideas, Institutions, and Policy Entrepreneurship in European Community Higher Education Policy, 1955–2005*, Basingstoke: Palgrave Macmillan.

Cowles, M., J. Green, T. Caporaso and W. Risse (2001), *Transforming Europe: Europeanization and Domestic Change*, Ithaca, NY and London: Cornell University Press.

DiMaggio, P. and W. Powell (1983), 'The iron cage revisited: institutional isomorphism and collective rationality in organizational fields', *American Sociological Review*, **48** (2), 147–60.

Djelic, M.-L. and K. Sahlin-Andersson (2006), *Transnational Governance: Institutional Dynamics of Regulation*, Cambridge: Cambridge University Press.

Doeringer, P. and M. Piore (1971), *Internal Labor Markets and Manpower Analysis*, Lexington, DC: Heath Lexington Books.

Drori, G., J. Meyer and H. Hwang (eds) (2006), *Globalization and Organization*, Oxford: Oxford University Press.

Elster, J. (ed.) (1998), *Deliberative Democracy*, Cambridge: Cambridge University Press.

Esping-Andersen, G. (1991), *The Three Worlds of Welfare Capitalism*, Cambridge: Cambridge University Press.

European Commission (2005), 'Mobilising the brainpower of Europe: enabling universities to make their full contribution to the Lisbon Strategy', Communication from the Commission, Brussels.

European Commission (2006), 'On the Modernisation Agenda for Universities: education, research and innovation', Communication from the Commission to the Council and the European Parliament, Brussels.

Ferlie, E., C. Musselin and G. Andresani (2008), 'The steering of higher education systems: a public management perspective', *Higher Education*, **56** (3), 325–48.

Filâtre, D. (2003), 'Les universités et le territoire: nouveau contexte, nouveaux enjeux', in G. Felouzis (ed.), *Les Mutations Actuelles de l'Université*, Paris: PUF, pp. 19–45.

Gornitzka, Å. (2006), 'What is the use of Bologna in national reform: the case of the Norwegian quality reform in higher education', in W. Tomusk (ed.), *Creating the European Area of Higher Education: Voices from the Peripheries*, Dordrecht: Springer, pp. 19–41.

Gornitzka, Å. and U. Sverdrup (2008), 'Who are the experts? The informational basis of EU decisionmaking', ARENA Working Paper Series: 14/2008.

Gornitzka, Å., M. Kogan and A. Amaral (2005), *Reform and Change in Higher Education: Analysing Policy Implementation*, Dordrecht: Springer.

Graf, L. (2009), 'Applying the varieties of capitalism approach to higher education: comparing the internationalisation of German and British universities', *European Journal of Education*, **44** (4), 569–85.

Green, A., A. Wolf and T. Leney (1999), *Convergence and Divergence in European Education and Training Systems*, London: Institute of Education, University of London.

Gumport, P. (2000), 'Academic restructuring: organizational change and institutional imperatives', *Higher Education*, **39** (1), 67–91.

Hacker, J. (1998), 'The historical logic of national health insurance: structure and sequence in the development of British, Canadian, and US medical policy', *Studies in American Political Development*, **12** (1), 80–130.

Hall, P. and D. Soskice (eds) (2001), *Varieties of Capitalism: The Institutional Foundations of Comparative Advantage*, Oxford: Oxford University Press.

Hassenteufel, P. (2008), *Sociologie politique: l'action publique*, Paris: A. Colin.

Henkel, M. (2005), 'Academic identity and autonomy in a changing policy environment', *Higher Education*, **49** (1), 155–76.

Howlett, M. (2000), 'Managing the "hollow state": procedural policy instruments and modern governance', *Canadian Public Administration*, **43**, 412–31.

Kehm, B. and U. Lanzendorf (eds) (2006), *Reforming University Governance: Changing Conditions for Research in Four European Countries*, Bonn: Lemmens.

Kogan, M., M. Bauer, I. Bleiklie and M. Henkel (eds) (2000), *Transforming Higher Education: A Comparative Study*, London and Philadelphia, PA: Jessica Kingsley Publishers.

Krücken, G. and F. Meier (2006), 'Turning the university into an organizational actor', in G. Drori, J. Meyer and H. Hwang (eds), *Globalization and Organization*, Oxford: Oxford University Press, pp. 241–57.

Lascoumes, P. and J. Le Bourhis (1997), *L'environnement ou l'administration des possibles, la création des directions régionales de l'environnement*, Paris: L'Harmattan.

Le Galès, P. and A. Scott (2008), 'Une révolution bureaucratique britannique: une autonomie sans contrôle ou "freer markets, more rules"', *Revue Française de Sociologie*, **49** (2), 300–330.

Lepori, B. (2008), 'Options et tendances dans le financement des universités en Europe', *Critique internationale*, **39** (2), 25–46.

Mangset, M. (2009), *The Discipline of Historians. A comparative study of historians' constructions of the discipline of history in English, French and Norwegian universities*, PhD in Sociologie, Sciences Po (France) and University of Bergen (Norway).

Manifet, C. (2004), *Gouverner par l'action: le cas des politiques universitaires de La Rochelle, Albi, Rodez*, PhD in Sociology, Université de Toulouse le Mirail.

Meyer, J. and B. Rowan (1977), 'Institutionalized organizations: formal structure as myth and ceremony', *American Journal of Sociology*, **83** (2), 340–63.

Mok, K.H. (2007), 'Questing for internationalization of universities in Asia: critical reflections', *Journal of Studies in International Education*, **11** (3–4), 433–54.

Musselin, C. (2004), *The Long March of French Universities*, New York: Routledge (translation of *La Longue Marche des Universités*, Paris: PUF, 2001).

Musselin, C. (2005), 'European academic labor markets in transition', *Higher Education*, **49** (1–2), 135–54.

Musselin, C. (2006a), 'Are universities specific organizations?', in G. Krücken, A. Kosmützky and M. Torka (eds), *Towards a Multiversity? Universities between Global Trends and National Traditions*, Bielefeld: Transcript Verlag, pp. 63–84.

Musselin, C. (2006b), 'Les paradoxes de Bologne: l'enseignement supérieur français face à un double processus de normalisation et de diversification', in J.-P. Leresche, M. Benninghoff, F. Crettaz von Roten and M. Merz (eds), *La Fabrique des Sciences*, Lausanne: Presses polytechniques et universitaires romandes, pp. 25–42.

Musselin, C. (2009), 'The side effects of the Bologna Process on national institutional settings: the case of France', in A. Amaral, G. Neave, C. Musselin and P. Maassen (eds), *European Integration and the Governance of Higher Education and Research*, Dordrecht: Springer, pp. 181–206.

Musselin, C. (2010), 'Universities and pricing on higher education markets', in D. Mattheou (ed.), *Changing Educational Landscapes: Educational Practices, Schooling Systems and Higher Education – A Comparative Perspective*, Dordrecht: Springer, pp. 75–90.

Musselin C. and C. Paradeise (2009), 'France: from incremental transitions to institutional change', in C. Paradeise, E. Reale, I. Bleiklie and E. Ferlie (eds), *University Governance: Western European Comparative Perspectives*, Dordrecht: Springer, pp. 21–49.

Naidoo, R. (2008), 'L'État et le marché dans la réforme de l'enseignement supérieur au Royaume-Uni (1980–2007)', *Critique Internationale*, **39** (2), 47–65.

Neave, G. and F. van Vught (1991), *Prometheus Bound: The Changing Relationship between Government and Higher Education in Western Europe*, Oxford and New York: Pergamon Press.

Oba, J. (2006), 'Incorporation of national universities in Japan and its impact upon institutional governance', paper to the conference 'University reforms in Eastern Asia: Incorporation, privatisation, and other structural innovations', Hiroshima University, January.

Orr, D., M. Jaeger and A. Schwarzenberger (2007), 'Performance-based funding as an instrument of competition in German higher education', *Journal of Higher Education Policy and Management*, **29** (1), 3–23.

Paradeise, C., E. Reale, I. Bleiklie and E. Ferlie (eds) (2009), *University Governance: Western European Comparative Perspectives*, Dordrecht: Springer.

Pechar, H. and L. Andres (2009), 'Higher education policies and welfare regimes: theory and evidence', Porto, 22nd CHER Conference.

Pierson, P. (1994), *Dismantling the Welfare State? Reagan, Thatcher and the Politics of Retrenchment*, Cambridge: Cambridge University Press.

Pierson, P. (2000), 'Path dependence, increasing returns, and the study of politics', *American Political Science Review*, **94** (2), 251–67.

Powell, J.W. and H. Solga (2010), 'Analyzing the nexus of higher education and vocational training in Europe: a comparative–institutional framework', *Studies in Higher Education*, **35** (6), 705–21.

Przeworski, A., S. Stokes and B. Manin (eds) (1999), *Democracy, Accountability and Representation*, Cambridge: Cambridge University Press.

Ramirez, F. (2006), 'The rationalization of universities', in M.-L. Djelic and K. Sahlin-Andersson (eds), *Transnational Governance: Institutional Dynamics of Regulation*, Cambridge: Cambridge University Press, pp. 225–44.

Ravinet, P. (2007), '*La genèse et l'institutionnalisation du processus de Bologne*, PhD in Sociology, University of Sciences Po, Paris.

Regini, M. (with G. Ballarino, S. Colombo, L. Perotti and R. Semenza) (forthcoming), 'Il mutamento dei rapporti fra università e sistema economico', in R. Moscati, M. Regini and M. Rostan (eds), *Torri d'avorio in frantumi? Dove vanno le università europee*, Bologna: Il Mulino.

Schwarz, S. and D. Westerheijden (eds) (2004), *Accreditation and Evaluation in the European Higher Education Area*, Dordrecht: Kluwer Academic Publishers.

Segrestin, D. (1997), 'L'entreprise à l'épreuve des normes de marché: Les paradoxes des nouveaux standards de gestion dans l'industrie', *Revue française de sociologie*, **38** (3), 553–85.

Simmons, B., F. Dobbin and G. Garrett (2007), *The Global Diffusion of Markets and Democracy*, Cambridge: Cambridge University Press.

Ward, D. and J. Douglass (2006), 'Higher education and the spectre of variable fees: public policy and institutional responses in the United States and United Kingdom', *Higher Education Management and Policy*, **18** (1), 1–28.

Whitley, R. (2000), 'The institutional structuring of innovation strategies: business systems, firm types and patterns of technical change in different market economies', *Organization Studies*, **21** (5), 855–86.

Whitley, R. (2006), 'Understanding differences: searching for the social processes that construct and reproduce variety in science and economic organization', *Organization Studies*, **27** (8), 1153–77.

Witte, J. (2006), *Change of Degrees and Degrees of Change: comparing adaptations in European higher education systems in the context of the Bologna Process*, PhD, CHEPS/UT, Twente and CHE, Gütersloh.

27 The Bologna Process: from the national to the regional to the global, and back
Jürgen Enders and Don F. Westerheijden

INTRODUCTION

European higher education has shown itself to be no stranger to change: for the better part of three decades the sector has been included in much broader reforms of public sectors and political systems in western, central and eastern Europe. Since the late 1990s the rate of change has accelerated to unprecedented levels, largely on the shoulders of two European political key agendas: the Bologna Process, whose objectives are to create a European Higher Education Area and to make European higher education more competitive and attractive in a globalizing world, and the European Union's (EU) growth and innovation strategies (formerly the Lisbon Strategy), which seeks to reform the continent's higher education and research systems into a more powerful motor for the European knowledge economy. The 'Modernization Agenda' of the European Commission (EC) could be added as the third key development, bringing together the reform agendas of the Bologna Process and the Lisbon Strategy and linking them up with a new public management (NPM)- inspired agenda for the modernization of higher education institutions (HEIs).

In the following, our main focus will be on the Bologna Process and its links to other major reform agendas for European higher education and research. In analyzing Bologna, three issues will be addressed. First, we focus on the undeniable success story of Bologna as a political project. Certain theoretical strands mainly derived from political studies will be used to shed further light on the dynamics of the Process and the reasons for success. Second, we shall look at the state of the art of the national adoption, and implementation of Bologna. A recent assessment of Bologna shows mixed performance as regards its adoption, and this calls for further explanations within and beyond the perspectives of policy implementation studies. Third, the recent trend of 'Bologna going global' and reaching out to other parts of the world will be addressed. We look at Bologna as a promising brand or script within the context of political regionalism and the competition for normative leadership in a globalizing market for higher education.

BOLOGNA AS A EUROPEAN POLITICAL PROJECT: A SUCCESS STORY

The Bologna Process as a European political project has unfolded a surprising dynamic with many special characteristics, among them its expanding geographical scope and thematic outreach. The Sorbonne Declaration of 1998 constituted the first signal from major European countries (France, Germany, Italy and the UK) that they perceived a need for intergovernmental coordination to move towards a more compatible and comparable set of European higher education systems while upholding the ideal of the rich diversity of teaching, learning styles and higher education cultures across Europe. In Bologna, a year later, 25 other European countries joined the original four. At each biannual ministerial follow-up conference since (see the Follow-Up Group), more countries have joined and by 2007 the total number of countries had reached 46. Nowadays Bologna encompasses 47 countries and reaches far beyond the EU member states to include, for example, Albania, Georgia, Russia and Turkey. Bologna thus generated enormous international dynamics and geographical outreach across Europe even beyond the EU.

The Bologna Process also has constantly broadened its thematic scope, agenda and political reform goals. Bologna has raised many issues and sought the establishment of a European Higher Education Area by 2010. While the signatory countries have interpreted the Bologna Declaration in their own way, the Process rapidly achieved its own momentum. Focusing at first on reforming study programs into a two-cycle 'bachelor–master' structure, concerns about comparability soon pushed quality assurance (such as through accreditation) and degree recognition issues firmly onto the agenda. Bologna's perspective broadened at the Berlin Follow-Up Group gathering in 2003 with the inclusion of a third cycle (PhD), and in linking the European Higher Education Area to the European Research Area. The doctoral stage was discussed again in Bergen (2005) as part of the explicit reference to the importance of higher education in further enhancing research, and to the significance of higher education research in underpinning the economic and cultural development of societies and for social cohesion. A subsequent London communiqué (2007) stressed the steps to be taken towards more student-centered higher education, to increased mobility between cycles, and to the international dimension. Moves were also taken towards establishing a European Qualifications Framework and a European Register of Quality Assurance Agencies.

It is perhaps surprising that such a growing reform agenda could emerge within a process of intergovernmental negotiation and agreement. Bologna as a political process of horizontal integration is based on soft governance, where national policies are coordinated by agreement at the European level but national governments try to remain in full control of the decision process, transformation into national contexts and implementation. The cooperation of countries in the Bologna Process is, formally speaking, voluntary and not binding, and thus without the legal consequences of conventional EU processes of supranational steering or hierarchical direction.

The policies described above are in many ways influencing the development of higher education policy at the national level. They lead to initiatives that go beyond the formulation of traditional internationalization policies, which used to be characterized as marginal, add-on activities and mainly focused on the international mobility of students and teachers. Instead, they lead to more structural measures that aim to influence higher education systems more profoundly (Enders, 2004). Bologna does address institutional framework conditions and settings of national higher education systems like many other previous reforms. But Bologna also reaches out into the very academic heartland of universities and other higher education providers by addressing curriculum issues and the nature of academic degrees, and thus the production processes and products of higher education itself (Musselin, 2005).

In addition, more general reform waves in European higher education go even further and deeper than the Bologna changes, and European policies have provided an important 'ice-breaker function' for national transformations (Enders, 2004). In many countries Bologna is used to introduce reforms that are not actually prescribed by the Bologna Process. Although many higher education legislative acts were passed in the 1980s and the 1990s, since then they have been amended, with the Bologna Process used as a reason for 'spring cleaning' (Reichert and Tauch, 2005) national reform agendas. Bologna has not only provided a European role model for national changes but also a powerful legitimating framework for reforms that are, at best, loosely coupled with the Bologna agenda. In some countries this convenient misunderstanding of Bologna by national policy-makers had a boomerang effect as massive (student) protests tended to demonize Bologna as the mother of all evils.

Bologna as a political process is, however, a success story. It stands out as one of the biggest and most far-reaching reform experiments in international higher education. How could the Bologna Process generate such a dynamic, and how could international convergence be achieved in a policy field that was characterized by a strongly protected national diversity? Various perspectives that are not mutually exclusive but rather complementary shed further light on Bologna as a successful political accomplishment.

The overall objectives of the European aim of building a politically, legally, economically, socially and culturally more integrated Europe certainly has generated pressure for the inclusion of education in general, and higher education in particular, as part of this strategic endeavor. Traditionally education was neither high on the European political agenda nor an easy field for European policy-making, given the strong feelings of national culture, identity and political authority involved. In Europe, universities have played an important role in the making of modern nation-states, including the building of a national heritage and identity, the formation and reproduction of national elites, the preparation and selection of the governmental and administrative workforce, and the provision of research for national economic and social development. For long, (higher) education and research were thus supposed to be national affairs, making it difficult to institutionalize European-level responsibilities and policies in this domain, even though particular initiatives can be traced back to the 1950s.

Since the late 1960s the EU has managed, however, to establish some political influence in the field of education. Political authority and influence were 'borrowed' from related though different policy fields such as labor market policies and policies for lifelong learning that allowed these to link up with educational policy. Pollack (1994) introduced the term 'creeping competence' for this process of growing EU influence in domains long regarded as strongly protected national areas of political competence.

Ironically, the conflict between efforts on the part of the EC to constantly extend its field of action, and national governments' aim to keep the Commission out of the core of higher education, triggered a European policy of grass-roots internationalization (Teichler, 1998). Facilitating student mobility (and to some extent academic staff mobility) became the first key instrument of internationalization for the EC. Mobility relates to the free movement of people and goods that forms a core aspect of the Treaty of Rome, and mobility became a key instrument for the EC in developing administrative executive capacities in the area of higher education, an area of relevance as well to the EC's economic policies.

The Joint Study Programs inaugurated in 1976 aimed to stimulate temporary study at a partner department, teaching staff exchange and joint developments of study programs on a small experimental basis. About a decade later the Erasmus program was launched (and followed up by Socrates). It focused on student mobility and included various other means of cooperation. The program was clearly the core activity that addressed higher education in the EU and was accompanied subsequently by a number of other such initiatives. On the basis of various evaluation studies (Enders, 1998; Teichler, 1998; Barblan et al., 2000), we can conclude that such programs caused a breakthrough by bringing a European scope of teaching and learning into a regular and normal element of study at most institutions of higher education, even if international student mobility remained limited to less than 10 percent of the student population. The major effect of the program was not to provide international experience to some 10 000 students, but to challenge the substance and modes of teaching and learning in national systems through comparatively small financial instruments.

Previous activities of the EC provided some 'ideational ground' for intervention in a highly sensitive political field (Balzer and Rusconi, 2007) and for intergovernmental approaches. The mobility programs introduced certain issues to European higher education that became core to the Bologna Process, such as mutual exchange, comparability and recognition. The idea of some kind of European Credit Transfer and Accumulation System (ECTS) was also already discussed in the context of European mobility programs. Thus 'European policies have given nation states both the idea that a solution to national problems must be searched for at the international level, as well as that such a solution must entail at least a certain degree of convergence between single education systems' (Balzer and Rusconi, 2007, p. 59). The Commission had also been very active in the emergence of a European discourse on higher education and research in the knowledge society and economy – a discourse that became important to Bologna subsequently. Bologna is certainly novel and ambitious in many ways, but some of its key agendas are not original but continuous with previous activities of the EU in the field of higher education (Amaral and Neave, 2009).

The governments that initiated the Bologna Process and many of those who subsequently joined up would not, however, have agreed to coordinate their agendas in line with common political goals and instruments without hoping for a benefit to themselves arising from intergovernmental policies for higher education reform. Using Europe as a lever for national reforms is a well-known strategy, and Bologna now is no stranger to the mobilization of international arguments for national political purposes (see Ravinet, 2008). Bologna could thus generate its surprising dynamic because of the prevailing view in some countries that they had major unsolved problems in their higher education systems accompanied by a reform blockage. As regards the four signatory countries, Bologna provided a Trojan horse for the French, German and Italian governments, 'bringing together politicians for substantial short-term and strategic long-term goals: outmaneuvering domestic institutional barriers to specific education reform goals involved changing the distribution of competencies for education in the long run. The UK supported the initiative because its education system was the reference model, so it could bear no costs of reform' (Martens and Wolf, 2009, p. 89).

At an early stage, Bologna was indeed strictly intergovernmental and formally excluded participation by the Commission. Yet the EC soon realized that Bologna was not only in line with some previous European policies for higher education, but was going in promising future directions for EU policies. The Commission actually paid for most of the preparatory work in the initial phase of the Bologna Process and was involved in the drafting of the Bologna Declaration, even though kept at arm's length. In 2001 the Commission became an official member of the Process and is nowadays also included in the Bologna Follow-Up Group. Horizontal integration in the Bologna Process thus opened a window of opportunity for the EC to insert elements of vertical integration and to intervene in intergovernmental policies that were originally meant to avoid growing supranational competence in this field. This political dynamic gave Bologna further momentum that further developed with the advent of the EU's Lisbon Strategy and related policies for higher education and research.

In 2000 the EU committed itself in the Lisbon Strategy to the ambitious objective of becoming the most competitive and dynamic knowledge-based economy in the world, capable of sustainable economic growth with more and better jobs and greater social cohesion. European policy-makers' intentions took on a more concrete form in 2003 when the more operational goal of raising EU countries' investments in R&D to 3 percent of GDP was outlined. In 2004 a mid-term report indicated that the Lisbon goals were likely to be very difficult to reach, partly due to weak economic growth in the larger member states, and because the design and the implementation of the policy actions relied on the member states and industry. Another mid-term review on a similar note reported a gap between the political rhetoric about the knowledge society and the realities of political financial priorities. The Lisbon Strategy was thus restarted with the New Lisbon Partnership for Growth and Jobs (EC, 2005a) in which 'knowledge and innovation for growth' was identified as one of the three main areas for action.

In this context, the EC has increasingly emphasized the role of universities in contributing to the knowledge economy. Thus 'Europe must strengthen the three poles of its knowledge triangle: education, research, and innovation. Universities are essential in all three' (EC 2005b, p. 152). Lack of competitiveness has been one of the major challenges for European universities noted by the Commission since 2003. Stressing education, research and innovation as the pillars of the Lisbon Strategy, the resolution echoes other EC communications. See EC (2002, 2003, 2005b, 2006, 2007). In 2007 the Council of the EU adopted a new resolution on 'Modernizing universities for Europe's competitiveness in a global economy'. As universities are increasingly seen as an important part of an overall innovation system, their contribution (or lack of contribution) to the innovation system is identified as critical.

Clearly these aims reach far beyond the core Bologna agenda and are much more derived from an economic competitiveness agenda that is not at the heart of the Bologna texts, even if it is also mentioned there. The Bologna Process provided, however, a window of opportunity for EU policies to broaden their influence on universities within the triangle of higher education, research and innovation. In turn, Bologna became part and parcel of a powerful political discourse in the name of the knowledge economy and society that fuels the political process (Nokkala, 2005; Fejes, 2005). This discourse gives higher education a new role and puts it high on the regional European agenda for global competitiveness. As one of the defining elements of this competitiveness, higher education must thus be reformed to be more efficient and effective in contributing to economic development and social welfare. Horizontal integration in the Bologna Process as well as vertical integration within the Lisbon agenda thus becomes intertwined, and both are impacting on the European higher education and research landscape.

Last but not least, the success story of Bologna can also be understood in the light of the study of soft governance in public policy and European governance (Ravinet, 2008; Martens and Wolf, 2009). In its mid-term stage, Bologna developed methods and mechanisms for monitoring horizontal political integration that resemble the more general EU Open Method of Coordination (OMC) developed in the context of the Lisbon Strategy – even though the Bologna approach has its own roots and mechanisms for the management of coordination of national policies. What is comparable, though, is that a system of soft but potentially powerful governance instruments is put in place in policy fields that have proven to be difficult when it comes to European vertical integration and hierarchical control. Reporting, benchmarking and stocktaking; and naming, blaming and shaming, can impose enormous pressure on national policy-makers that are formally speaking participating in an unbinding political process based on voluntary agreement. The stocktaking exercises of Bologna that provide a synthetic, easily readable and widely distributed overview of what has been achieved and not achieved in all participating countries signal a competitive turn in the political management of the Process. This move 'from voluntary participation to monitored coordination' (Ravinet, 2008) creates effects of socialization, imitation and shame that lent further support to the political success story of Bologna.

THE ADOPTION AND IMPLEMENTATION OF BOLOGNA: GREAT EXPECTATIONS AND MIXED PERFORMANCE

There is no doubt that in 'political terms, the Bologna Process is clearly a success. It has become the broadest policy forum on higher education so far' (Zgaga, 2007, p. 23). Bologna has potentially far-reaching consequences for the European higher education landscape. Efforts to create convergent patterns of study programs and degrees in Europe in order to facilitate intra-European mobility and global competitiveness are intrinsically aimed at keeping differences in quality between sectors and organizations within limits. The Process stimulates new opportunities for overlaps in the functions of universities and other higher education providers and for convergence of these types; nonetheless, intra-institutional diversity may be increased (Enders, 2009). There are important indirect effects on the organizational level and certain issues (such as degree recognition, credit transfer and quality assurance) have become much more important elements on the national higher education policy agenda of European governments.

The consequences of the recent Bologna reforms are, however, not yet clear. The 'way to Bologna' is a long one, with options for local interpretations and manifold pathways. Neave (2006, p. 29) argues, for example, that there was an 'utter absence of any prior assessment into the capacity of national systems to adapt to the Bologna principles and even less whether the dateline set was itself on any basis other than hunch and ad-hocracy'.

Various studies have addressed the adaption and implementation of the Bologna Process. National case studies in Amaral et al. (2009) show, for example, that 'translation or accommodation' (Maassen and Musselin, 2009, p. 12) dominates the national implementation of Bologna across Europe. Many differences in terms of timing, scope and depth of national policies responding to the Bologna Process could be detected. Only a few countries more or less neglected Bologna (among them England), although no country showed a clear-cut adoption of all aspects of the Process, while in the majority of countries Bologna unfolded in substantially different ways.

The most recent and encompassing assessment of the first decade of the Bologna Process (see Westerheijden et al., 2010a, 2010b) provides a similar though more differentiated conclusion:

> Overall higher education across the 46 EHEA [European Higher Education Area] countries looks substantially different from 10 years ago – perhaps with the exception of the social dimension. Most architectural elements of the EHEA, that is, those involving legislation and national regulation, have been implemented in most countries. The impact of the established architecture on substantive goal achievement at the level of higher education institutions and study programs is still wanting. (Westerheijden et al., 2010a, p. 5)

According to this study, most of the 46 countries have adopted new higher education legislation to introduce and regulate elements of the Bologna Process. Many countries have allocated additional funds for implementation. The EC has also supported projects for the introduction of reforms. There is, however, a large difference in the speed of implementation between individual countries. While some countries have shown considerable progress in implementing almost all action areas, other countries have still to start on some. This creates a European Higher Education Area of different speeds of implementation and varying levels of commitment. Even countries in an advanced stage of implementation have to struggle with certain elements of Bologna: there is no case of full adoption. Newcomer countries (17 countries joined between 2001 and 2005, mostly in the east and south-east of the Bologna region) had to struggle to catch up with changes that were more advanced in countries that joined Bologna early on. The countries participating in the Bologna Process faced different challenges in their higher education systems, ranging from inefficiencies (such as high drop-out rates and low participation) to limited systemic flexibility and the need to upgrade quality during periods of rapid expansion. These different starting points, coupled with different management and governance arrangements, meant that the implementation of national reforms deviated from Bologna intentions. Divergence has been strengthened by the fact that key actors in different countries interpreted elements of the Bologna reform agenda somewhat variably.

The study by Westerheijden et al. (2010a, 2010b) provides a fine-grained view of the Bologna Process. In the following we make reference to its findings on degree and curriculum reform, international student mobility, quality assurance and qualification frameworks, policies for recognition and policies for widening participation.

Degree and Curriculum Reform

All Bologna countries have adopted a bachelor–master structure while some countries are still in the process of transition from traditional degree systems towards a two- or three-cycle degree system. A '3+2 years' system for bachelor and master programs has emerged as the most prominent model in Europe, while there is flexibility to accommodate variations of the model such as, for example, four-year bachelor or one-year master programs. Overall there has, however, been convergence towards a more standardized model, at least in terms of a two-stage degree structure, in the associated labeling and formal length of programs, and in the establishment of credit points that aim to allow for greater comparability.

All the Bologna higher education systems use the European Credit Transfer and Accumulation System (ECTS), are in transition towards it, or use ECTS-compatible systems. This goal has been substantially achieved at the level of regulation, but the study shows as well that the degree of use of ECTS in institutions and programs differs substantially. Linking allocation of credits to student workload and learning outcomes has been attained only in a few of the higher education systems. The degree of modularization of study programs that should allow for more flexibility and mobility varies substantially between the Bologna countries as well as within them. No common understanding of the concept of modularization as a tool to foster mobility, flexibility and transferability has so far been achieved.

International Student Mobility

According to Westerheijden et al., student mobility within the EHEA did not increase substantially in the period up to 2007 (the latest year for which comparable statistics were available). The main change between 1999 and 2007 was from short-term credit mobility (by 'free movers' and learners moving within the framework of European, national or regional programs) to longer-term degree mobility (by students moving to other countries, institutions or programs for further studies after having completed a degree). There was an absolute rise of intra-European student mobility of 39 percent and a relative increase of 4 percent (relative increase takes the growth of the overall student population into account). Most recent data available show that only 2 percent of EHEA students pursue a degree in another EHEA country. There is also an east-to-west imbalance of student mobility within Europe that may call the sustainability of student mobility into question.

Mobility from other parts of the world towards the EHEA has increased substantially and faster than international mobility has grown worldwide. In 2007 the EHEA countries attracted 30 percent of the world's foreign learners. Yet for internationally mobile learners the EHEA has little reality; they choose to study in particular countries and institutions without considering if these are part of the EHEA. Equally the EHEA is not seen as an area providing a uniform level of higher education degrees, and the USA remains the most prestigious destination, attracting the top tier of learners.

Quality Assurance and Qualification Frameworks

The European Standards and Guidelines (ESG) for quality assurance have been adopted (2005), and the Register of Quality Assessment Agencies (EQAR) has been established and operative since 2008. All countries except one apply internal and external quality assurance on a system-wide scale. The extent to which these quality assurance systems (and those within the HEIs) substantially comply with the ESG is, however, an open question and the assessment study by Westerheijden et al. recommended an evaluation of national and institutional practices.

An overarching framework of qualifications for the European Higher Education Area (QF-EHEA) was adopted in 2005. By 2010, eight higher education systems have self-certified national qualification frameworks; other countries are preparing qualification frameworks, and the original deadline for the establishment of qualification frameworks (2010) has had to be extended to 2012.

Recognition

All Bologna countries except two have signed or ratified the Lisbon Recognition Convention (LRC); five have signed and ratified it but their legislation is not in compliance with the LRC; 39 countries have signed and ratified the LRC and their legislation complies with its provisions. This progress in (almost) achieving the official adoption of the LRC has shifted the discussion within the Bologna Process from signing agreements to one of realizing the impacts intended by the measures. The notion of equivalence applies unless there are 'substantial differences', but there are different interpretations of what this might mean as regards programs and degrees as well as with respect to other terms and practices around recognition, in particular the use of learning outcomes as a determinant for recognition.

A Diploma Supplement, a support instrument of the LRC, is issued automatically and without charge in most HEIs in 30 out of 46 Bologna countries. While there is thus room for improvement in around one-third of the Bologna countries, the study also pointed to the need for improving awareness of the existence and meaning of the Diploma Supplement among students as well as among employers.

Widening Participation

Policies suitable for widening participation and the successful completion of studies, such as recognition of prior learning, flexible study modes, counseling for learners and financial aid are available to varying degrees in a number of Bologna countries. Based on few available data, the study could not conclude that these policies have been introduced with the aim of improving inclusion of underrepresented groups, or have been effective in this regard. There were very few signs of the 'social dimension' being seen as a priority area in most Bologna Process countries.

In sum, the story of the implementation of Bologna is one of variable performance compared to great expectations. Given the mixed bag of what has been achieved and what has not been achieved, it is not surprising that some observers and analysts tend to take a critical view, emphasizing the uneven implementation and shortcomings, while others highlight mid-term achievements and praise Bologna as a motor of reform across Europe. In addition, much more attention has so far been paid to the instrumentation of political reform than to substantial goal achievements. In other words, the means for reform (and their achievement) have tended to become goals in themselves. One of the major recommendations by Westerheijden et al. stresses this point: 'Attention in the second decade of the Bologna Process needs to turn to the achievement of the substantive, strategic goals more than to further refinement of the architecture' (Westerheijden, 2010a, p. 9).

Obviously Bologna is no stranger to well-known problems addressed in the classical study of policy implementation (Pressman and Wildavsky, 1973; Cerych and Sabatier, 1986). Big reforms tend to build a political agenda that is likely to promise more than can reasonably be expected to be achieved. Political actors might be well aware of the likely discrepancy between 'big talk' and 'expected action'. Creating great expectations seems, however, unavoidable in order to be able to mobilize political will and resources to get 'something' done at all. What has been functional in the stage of policy formation thus turns later out to become a problem at the stage of policy assessment, thus contributing to the 'institutional hypocrisy' of talk, decision and action (Brunsson, 1989).

Moreover, 'the causal chain from political intention and declarations to implementation can easily be broken or weakened' (Olsen and Maassen, 2007, p. 20). There is a long way to go in the multi-level and multi-actor chain of Bologna from policy formulation on the intergovernmental level to policy-making and instrumentation at the national level, and then policy implementation by institutions. Federal structures and responsibilities may also make implementation more complex.

Last but not least, such a policy chain provides ample opportunity for translation and thus for the transformation of policies within national, federal and institutional contexts. Ideas change while they travel, and get interpreted according to context, conditions, fitness for purpose and political preferences. The international export and import, the transfer and borrowing, of educational policies has certainly intensified (Enders and Fulton, 2002; King, 2009) and is actively encouraged by Bologna. Common political agendas do not necessarily, however, lead to common implementation practices and policy outputs.

Further explanatory insight is thus gained by adding an actor-centered perspective to the study of policy implementation, with a focus on actors' capabilities, preferences, constellations and interactions in the political process within a given institutional context (Scharpf, 1997). Witte (2006) applies this perspective in comparing adaptations of European higher education systems in the context of the Bologna Process among four countries (England, France, Germany and The Netherlands). A quite diverse picture as regards the degree of policy change (policy formulation and policy implementation) emerges. The strong impact of the inherited national institutional frameworks impact on the different degree of adaptations of national degree structures achieved so far.

This analysis shows that while perceptions by policy actors of the changing European context supported national policy change, they did so only in conjunction with domestic political preferences. Bologna provides a strong European role model and a powerful legitimating framework, yet the entire change was mainly driven by national reform interests. It is thus not surprising to note that national higher education systems so far have not converged more clearly around a common model.

BOLOGNA GOES GLOBAL: REGIONALISM AND THE COMPETITION FOR NORMATIVE LEADERSHIP

Bologna and the move towards a European Higher Education Area form part and parcel of a more general process of globalization in higher education. Strictly speaking it is one of its non-economic features, but economic rationales for the Europeanization of higher education have certainly gained in importance. One of the main aims of the European

Higher Education Area is to increase the competitiveness of European higher education and to strengthen its role and attractiveness in a globalizing higher education field. From an early stage, European cooperation in the Bologna Process has among other motivators been driven by the perception of certain weaknesses in European higher education that need to be overcome to strengthen the contribution of higher education to the European knowledge economy in global competition – a discourse that has been reinforced in importance as a result of the innovation agenda of the EU's Lisbon Strategy. National policies for the internationalization of higher education also increasingly emphasize the economic benefits involved. A growing range of European countries are aware of the international competition in higher education and have formulated economic rationales for their higher education policies.

In order to strengthen European higher education competitiveness, Bologna has looked to leading models and practices worldwide to establish its own political agenda. The main source of policy borrowing has been from Anglo-Saxon systems. These have been influential in European norm-making in the restructuring of higher education systems, particularly the two cycles (bachelor and master), the translation of the two cycles into credits, and the introduction of quality assurance (Hartmann, 2008). Bologna has thus partly been built on copying the success stories of normative leaders and role models in global higher education. Such processes of mimetic isomorphism contribute to the further diffusion of templates or scripts for success that increase global standardization in higher education (King, 2009).

At the same time, common European standards have been introduced with a view to strengthen European higher education in the global rivalry for innovation, talent and students (perceived as consumers) (Naidoo and Jamieson, 2006), and to establish a European model as a synonym for high quality in the competition for normative leadership. Political regionalism in European higher education thus has a Janus head with two faces. On the one side, regionalization can be understood as a process of growing regional cooperation or even integration on equal terms, involving mutual cooperation and horizontal interaction – in other words, a benign regional version of internationalization processes between nation-states. On the other side, political regionalization in higher education forms part and parcel of a globalization process, establishing cooperation among neighbors in order to counteract pressure from other parts of the world, and to reach out to other countries and regions worldwide.

A Bologna advantage is that it provides European policy-makers (and the Commission in particular) with a brand that promotes the idea of an attractive European higher education system to a global market. In recent years Bologna has developed a more proactive approach in reaching out to other parts of the world and has emphasized more an external dimension (Zsaga, 2007; Marginson, 2009) where 'interaction with domestic restructuring and nascent regional projects beyond Europe provides a platform for normative leadership by Europe as a region and for Europe to advance, and in turn, act in a state-like way' (Robertson, 2010, p. 28).

This external dimension has been instrumentalized and supported in various parallel ways by Bologna and the EU. The Erasmus Mundus Program is, for example, intended to recruit student talent from around the globe to teaching programs collaboratively constructed between different European universities. Erasmus Mundus reaches out beyond the traditional intra-European mobility programs and incorporates in its second phase not only master but also PhD programs. Additionally, the 'Tuning Educational Structures in Europe' project has been incorporated into the Bologna Process in order to establish mechanisms for the translation of curricula from diverse institutional and national settings into equivalents, enabling more comparability and mobility.

In 2003 the Tuning Group launched its Latin American venture 'Tuning America Latina'. It involves 18 countries (including Argentina, Bolivia, Cuba, Mexico and Venezuela) and 180 universities. The subject areas covered include education, history, medicine, geology, physics and mathematics. The venture has involved surveying the views of students, employers and universities on learning outcomes and competencies in the specified subject area, and then assembling these competencies so as to develop a tool of translation within the Latin American region, and in relation to the EU (see Robertson, 2008).

Other countries outside Europe have been included in such cooperation agreements, and international as well as interregional dialog with other parts of the world has been facilitated by various means, such as through the European Commission's Asia-Link program. Further activities in reaching out to other countries are organized by European academic exchange and international agencies, such as EduFrance (France), DAAD (Germany), Nuffic (The Netherlands) and the British Council (UK). A related though different step concerns an EC-funded feasibility study to develop a European university ranking system that could be applied globally in order to challenge the biases and the dominance of the Shanghai Jiao Tong and the *Times Higher Education* ranking systems in relation to European interests (see www.u-multirank.eu).

No doubt Europe is still far from being able to take over normative worldwide leadership and to create a globally competitive higher education. But there is growing interest and Bologna is 'now viewed as a potential threat (USA, Australia), a model for domestic restructuring (Brazil, China), or the basis for new regional projects around the globe (Africa, Latin America, Southeast Asia)' (Robertson, 2008, p. 5). A number of countries of the Association of South-east Asian Nations (ASEAN) have, for example, begun to discuss the creation of a Bologna-type process in their region and to consider the challenges and opportunities that could be provided by a harmonization of higher education in South-east Asia. Their aspirations mirror some of those in the Bologna Process – to promote higher education quality and to build ASEAN identity through the free movement of scholars around the region. In 2007, agreements were made to focus on five action lines, namely a quality framework and curriculum development; student mobility; leadership in higher education; e-learning and mobile learning; and research clusters.

In Africa, groupings of countries with different colonial histories and related higher education traditions are organizing regional meetings to promote collaboration and higher education reforms inspired by the Bologna Process. Bologna is also stimulating closer university collaboration between Latin-American and European institutions, particularly Spanish and Portuguese universities, in an effort to stimulate Ibero-American student and faculty exchanges. And Bologna provides a political stimulus for Latin America's current debate on curricular reform and higher education competitiveness. Brazil and China have announced their interest in scanning the Bologna Process as one role model for reforming their higher education systems. In the USA, Adelman (2008) has raised concerns about the potential of Bologna as a globally diffusing model and of the related competition from Europe. In 2007, Australia and the EU signed a joint declaration to reinforce collaboration in the fields of education and training (Figel and Bishop, 2007), and some Australian universities have adopted certain elements of Bologna (such as a Diploma Supplement) as a response to concern at the potential threat of losing part of its very sizeable share in the international student market.

As a political process, Bologna is thus reaching out globally irrespective of implementation problems back home. Two characteristics of the Bologna Process seem to be the focal points of attractiveness as well as of concern. First, Bologna as a political process provides a success story of political regionalism via horizontal integration that becomes a model for other regions in the world looking for regional collaboration and national reform strategies. Second, the Bologna reform agenda provides a very broad and sufficiently vague menu for reform in other parts of the world while allowing for local selection, interpretation and variety. Like other templates or scripts that travel around the world (not only in higher education), some diffuseness is useful in global policy standardization.

CONCLUSION

Traditionally, education research was not at the center of political science, while political science was not at the heart of education research. This is surprising given the important role of education for the making and transformation of modern nation-states. It is even more surprising given the manifold perspectives recent political reforms of education as a field of real-life experiment in Europe and beyond has to offer (Enders, 2010). The Bologna Process stands out as one of the biggest and most challenging political reform projects in international education, and the Bologna story is not yet over.

Bologna is a most fascinating journey between the national, the regional and the global, and back again, and with manifold interactions, intersections and translations between the different levels. As we have shown, the dynamics of Bologna as a success story of European policy-making in higher education can best be understood by looking at the policies and their instrumentation as well as by looking at the politics, the actors and their interactions. It all began with horizontal intergovernmental coordination by four governments that were concerned about national reform while already being inspired by previous internationalization policies at the EU level and an emerging worldwide discourse around higher education in a competitive and globalizing world. Subsequently Bologna has developed an impressive expansionist motor in terms of geographical outreach and thematic scope, looking at leading models in other countries as role exemplars as well as sources of rivalry. Interest in national reform as well as the fear of being left behind has made more and more countries join Bologna based on the assumption of participating in a non-binding, voluntary intergovernmental political process that would keep hierarchical integration by the EU at arm's length. Very soon Bologna provided, however, a window of opportunity for regulatory capture by European policy-makers that furthermore fueled Bologna by linking it up to the more economically driven processes of vertical integration within the European innovation agenda. Coercive power within these processes was on the one hand exerted by the peer pressures of the Open Method of Coordination within the EU, and on the other by the move of Bologna from voluntary participation to monitored coordination. Instruments of soft governance can create powerful effects through socialization, imitation and shame, and these influences made the Bologna Process more binding than national governments might have thought.

Bologna as a European political process is obviously a success story while the adoption at the national and institutional level is much more of a mixed bag. Many differences in terms of timing, scope and depth in national policies responding to the Bologna Process can be observed. Uneven implementation as well as a focus on the instrumentation and architecture of Bologna, partly neglecting substantial goals, is the rule not the exception.

Bologna is no stranger to problems of policy implementation, including the institutional hypocrisy of talk, decision and action; the distortion of the agenda in a long and multi-layered implementation chain; and the translation and transformation of European policies in manifold national and institutional contexts. Such aspects were acute given the international multi-level and multi-actor character of the Process and the dominant role of national preferences and capabilities in the selective interpretation and fruitful misunderstanding of Bologna for national policy agendas.

Notwithstanding such problems, the success story of Bologna as a political process provides European politics and higher education with a very much needed and welcome brand label in the context of political regionalism and the struggle for normative leadership in a globalizing higher education field. Bologna is proactively reaching out to other parts of the world, promoting Europe as a role model for regional collaboration in higher education reform and challenging other dominant powers in international higher education. Certainly, Europe still has a long way to go to challenge traditional leaders in international higher education and to compete more successfully on the global higher education market. But Rome was also not built in a day; we are just at the beginning of the second decade of the Bologna Process.

REFERENCES

Adelman, C. (2008), *The Bologna Club: What US Higher Education Can Learn from a Decade of European Reconstruction*, Washington, DC: Institute for Higher Education Policy.

Amaral, A. and G. Neave (2009), 'On Bologna, weasels, and creeping competences', in A. Amaral, G. Neave, C. Musselin, and P. Massen (eds), *European Integration and the Governance of Higher Education and Research*, Dordrecht: Springer, pp. 281–300.

Amaral, A., G. Neave, C. Musselin and P. Massen (eds), *European Integration and the Governance of Higher Education and Research*, Dordrecht: Springer.

Balzer, C. and A. Rusconi (2007), 'From the European Commission to the member states and back: a comparison of the Bologna and the Copenhagen Processes', in K. Martens, A. Rusconi and K. Leuze (eds), *New Arenas of Education Governance: The Impact of International Organizations and Markets on Educational Policymaking*, Basingstoke: Palgrave Macmillan, pp. 57–75.

Barblan, A., M. Reichert, M. Schotte-Kmoch and U. Teichler (2000), *Implementing European Policies in Higher Education Institutions*, Kassel: Centre for Research on Higher Education and Work (*Werkstattberichte*: 57).

Brunsson, N. (1989), *The Organization of Hypocrisy: Talk, Decisions and Actions in Organizations*, Chichester, UK: John Wiley and Sons.

Cerych, L. and P. Sabatier (1986), *Great Expectations and Mixed Performance: The Implementation of Higher Education Reforms in Europe*, Stoke on Trent: Trentham Books.

Enders, J. (1998), 'Academic staff mobility in the European Community: the ERASMUS experience', *Comparative Education Review*, **42** (1), 30–45.

Enders, J. (2004), 'Higher education, internationalization, and the nation-state: recent developments and challenges for governance theory', *Higher Education*, **47** (3) 361–82.

Enders, J. (2009), 'The mission impossible of the European university: institutional confusion and diversity', in

A. Amaral, G. Neave, C. Musselin and P. Maassen (eds), *European Integration and the Governance of Higher Education and Research*, Dordrecht/Heidelberg/London/New York: Springer, pp. 159–80.

Enders, J. (2010), 'Political science and educational research: windows of opportunity for a neglected relationship', in A. Jakobi, K. Martens and K. Wolf (eds), *Education in Political Science: Discovering a Neglected Field*, London and New York: Routledge/ECPR Studies in European Political Science, pp. 205–17.

Enders, J. and O. Fulton (eds) (2002), *Higher Education in a Globalizing World: International Trends and Mutual Observations*, Dordrecht/Boston/London: Kluwer Academic Publishers.

European Commission (2002), *The European Research Area: An Internal Knowledge Market*, Luxembourg: Office for Official Publications of the European Communities.

European Commission (2003), *The Role of the Universities in the Europe of Knowledge*, COM (2003) 58, Brussels: European Commission.

European Commission (2005a), *Working Together for Growth and Jobs: A New Start of the Lisbon Strategy*, COM (2005) 24, Brussels: European Commission.

European Commission (2005b), *Mobilizing the Brainpower of Europe: Enabling Universities to Make their Full Contribution to the Lisbon Strategy*, Brussels: European Commission.

European Commission (2006), *Delivering on the Modernisation Agenda for Universities: Education, Research and Innovation*, COM (2006) 502, Brussels: European Commission.

European Commission (2007), *The European Research Area: New Perspectives*, COM (2007) 161, Brussels: European Commission.

Fejes, A. (2005), 'The Bologna Process: governing higher education in Europe through standardization', in T. Halvorsen and A. Nyhagen (eds), *The Bologna Process and the Shaping of the Future of Knowledge Societies*, Bergen: University of Bergen, pp. 219–31.

Figel, J. and J. Bishop (2007), *Joint Declaration between the European Union and Australia. European Commission and the Government of Australia wish to reinforce co-operation in the fields of education and training*, Brussels: European Commission.

Hartmann, E. (2008), 'Bologna goes global: a new imperialism in the making', *Globalisation, Societies and Education*, **6** (3), 207–20.

King, R. (2009), *Governing Universities Globally: Organizations, Regulation and Rankings*, Cheltenham, UK and Northampton, MA, USA: Edward Elgar.

Maassen, P. and C. Musselin (2009), 'European integration and the Europeanisation of higher education', in A. Amaral, G. Neave, C. Musselin and P. Maassen (eds), *European Integration and the Governance of Higher Education and Research*, Dordrecht: Springer, pp. 3–16.

Marginson, S. (2009), 'The external dimension: positioning the European Higher Education Area in the global higher education world', in B. Kehm, J. Huisman and B. Stensaker (eds), *The European Higher Education Area: Perspectives on a Moving Target*, Rotterdam: Sense Publishers, pp. 297–322.

Martens, K. and K. Wolf (2009), 'Boomerangs and Trojan horses: the unintended consequences of Internationalizing education policy through the EU and OECD', in A. Amaral, G. Neave, C. Musselin and P. Maassen (eds), *European Integration and the Governance of Higher Education and Research*, Dordrecht: Springer, pp. 81–108.

Musselin, C. (2005), 'Is the Bologna Process a move towards a European Higher Education Area?', in T. Halvorsen and A. Nyhagen (eds), *The Bologna Process and the Shaping of the Future Knowledge Societies*, Bergen: University of Bergen, pp. 22–32.

Naidoo, R. and I. Jamieson (2006), 'Empowering participants or corroding learning? Towards a research agenda on the impact of student consumerism in higher education', *Journal of Education Policy*, **20** (3), 267–81.

Neave, G. (2006), 'The evaluative state and Bologna: old wine in new bottles or simply the ancient practice of "Coupage"?', *Higher Education Forum*, **3**, 27–46.

Nokkala, T. (2005), 'Knowledge society/knowledge economy discourse in the internationalization of higher education: a case study in governmentality', in T. Halvorsen and A. Nyhagen (eds), *The Bologna Process and the Shaping of the Future of Knowledge Societies*, Bergen: University of Bergen, pp. 94–117.

Olsen, J. and P. Maassen (eds) (2007), *University Dynamics and European Integration*, Dordrecht: Springer.

Pollack, M. (1994), 'Creeping competence: the expanding of the agenda of the European Community', *Journal of Public Policy*, **14** (2), 95–145.

Pressman, J. and A. Wildavsky (1973), *Implementation: How Great Expectations in Washington are Dashed in Oakland*, Berkeley, CA: University of California Press.

Ravinet, P. (2008), 'From voluntary participation to monitored coordination: why European countries feel increasingly bound by their commitment to the Bologna Process', *European Journal of Education*, **43** (3), 353–67.

Reichert, S. and C. Tauch (2005), *Trends IV: European Universities Implementing Bologna*, Brussels: European University Association.

Robertson, S. (2008), 'The Bologna Process goes global: a model, market, mobility, brain power, or state-building strategy?', paper to ANPED's Annual Conference, October 2008, Brazil.

Robertson, S. (2010), 'The EU, "regulatory state regionalism", and new modes of higher education governance', *Globalisation, Societies and Education*, **8** (1), 23–37.

Scharpf, F. (1997), *Games Real Actors Play: Actor-centered Institutionalism in Policy Research*, Boulder, CO: Westview Press.

Teichler, U. (1998), 'The role of the European Union in the internationalization of higher education', in P. Scott (ed.), *The Globalization of Higher Education*, Buckingham: Open University Press, pp. 88–99.

Westerheijden, D. et al. (2010a), *The First Decade of Working on the European Higher Education Area: The Bologna Process Independent Assessment (Executive Summary, Overview, and Conclusions)*, Enschede: Center for Higher Education Policy Studies, University of Twente.

Westerheijden, D. et al. (2010b), *The First Decade of Working on the European Higher Education Area: The Bologna Process Independent Assessment. Volume I: Main Report*, Enschede: Center for Higher Education Policy Studies, University of Twente, accessible at *http://ec.europa.eu/education/higher-education/doc/bologna_process/independent_assessment_1_detailed_rept.pdf*.

Witte, J. (2006), *Change of Degrees and Degrees of Change: Comparing Adaptations of European Higher Education Systems in the Context of the Bologna Process*, Enschede: Center for Higher Education Policy Studies, University of Twente.

Zgaga, P. (2007), *Looking Out: The Bologna Process in a Global Setting: On the External Dimension of the Bologna Process*, Oslo: Norwegian Ministry of Education and Research.

28 The standardization of higher education, positional competition and the global labor market
Hugh Lauder and Phillip Brown

INTRODUCTION

This chapter examines changes to global higher education and its relationship to research, innovation and the education of graduates for the global labor market. The chapter outlines the factors that lead to the development of a hierarchy of 'circuits' of higher education institutions (HEIs) based on global reputation. It is argued that the circuits provide different forms of education with respect to curriculum, credentials and character formation. These circuits correspond to changes in the division of labor within the global labor market, particularly in relation to transnational companies. Key to understanding the emergence of these circuits and their relationship to the global division of labor is the idea of standardization in higher education (HE).

THE STANDARDIZATION OF KNOWLEDGE IN THE HIGHER EDUCATION SECTOR

There are at least three factors that have combined to standardize pedagogy, credentials and the formation of character for a particular set of HEIs. These are first the global movement of students between institutions; second the construction of international consumer markets for higher education; and third the introduction of global league tables. While it can be argued that these factors have combined to create a tendency towards standardization in the ways we describe below, there is a fourth factor that is the major focus of this chapter: the restructuring of graduate occupations within both the domestic and global labor markets leading to the fragmentation of 'knowledge' work. The 'correspondence' between these changes in the labor market and the standardization of knowledge in many HEIs should be seen as a hypothesis that requires further theoretical and empirical work. However, this 'correspondence' is arresting and, having described it, we consider the possible types of causation that could link changes in the labor market to higher education.

Marginson (2006) has documented the rapidly increasing proportion of students who are now studying overseas. For western universities, particularly those in the USA, the UK and Australasia, a significant proportion of the income in the higher education sector is derived from foreign students. These universities have proved attractive because of their reputations, and because English, currently the *lingua franca* of globalization, is the medium of instruction. However, we should note that the picture of western dominance in the HE market is rapidly changing as, for example, nations like Singapore scale up their HE sector and India and China invest heavily in elite HEIs.

In order for the global market in higher education to operate effectively, standards need to be benchmarked. This is to enable those purchasing higher education to know what they are paying for and that judgments can be made about the comparability of degrees between institutions. The latter is especially important if students are seeking to transfer to a higher degree.

In a little remarked upon but prescient paper, Room (2000) examines the processes of standard-setting or benchmarking between universities across the globe. Having examined how global networks between universities are being created, in which benchmarking is a focal element, he makes two points. First, 'cross-national learning . . . has been shaped by the global networks of cultural influence, based on former imperial connections and the more recent cultural dominance of the United States' (2000, p. 109). Second, policy importation or learning between universities is part of this process. Here issues to do with quality assurance are of particular relevance since they also relate to standard-setting.

There are also regional pressures towards standard-setting. The Bologna Process in Europe has given impetus to EU initiatives for cross-university degrees, including a Euro doctorate, while according to Young (2009), the European Qualifications Framework sees the HE sector as integral to its structure. However, it is almost inevitable that standard-setting will not just rest on approximate judgments about comparability, but that the form and content of knowledge may also be standardized.

CONSUMERISM AND STANDARDIZATION

Naidoo and Jamieson (2006) have sought to examine the impact of consumerism on higher education, exploring both the field of higher education in Bourdieuian terms and the impact on teaching and learning in relation to where an institution is positioned within the field. They report that the North American literature suggests that students who see themselves as consumers are more likely to see learning as a commercial transaction. In turn, the student-consumer identity views education as an entitlement (Sacks, 1996) with educational success being viewed as a 'right'. Naidoo and Jamieson comment that 'These new identities and rationalities . . . have the potential to transform learning into a process of picking up, digesting and reproducing what students perceive of as an unconnected series of short, neatly packaged bytes of information' (2006, p. 879). They place the emergence of these new student-consumer identities within the context of the 'field' of HE (Naidoo, 2004). As such, they argue that those from privileged backgrounds who have the appropriate cultural capital will be attracted to and will be recruited by elite universities.

Marginson (2006, p. 895) notes that 'The production of positional goods necessarily combines competition with oligopoly and market closure . . . In elite institutions, the more intense consumer competition for entry is, the less the elite institutions are required to court the consumer in a conventional manner.' The combination of the position of the elite universities and the type of privileged students they attract means that they operate more or less as they have always done – that is, providing a traditional university education.

Given this context, Naidoo and Jamieson (2006) argue that lower-ranked universities are more likely to engage in pre-packaged learning materials, for example through e-learning-type strategies and forms of assessment and pedagogy that narrow the tasks that students need to accomplish. In turn the knowledge that is 'transmitted' will be pre-packaged and divided into modular form. It is precisely this pre-packaged modular form of knowledge 'delivery' that is more easily standardized and assessed.

Global League Tables

A further development in the global economy of higher education is the emergence of global league tables of HEIs. Lindblad and Lindblad (2009) note, following Marginson (2009), that rankings may have a significant impact on higher education policy and governance in the way that they come to define 'quality'. But they also note that there are competing league tables that have been compiled in different ways. Hence these tables not only reflect the relative standing of universities, but also the global standing of those sponsoring different methods of ranking. In a sense they argue that this is a form of soft global power but that it can easily turn into the hard power of what are assumed to be 'facts' about university performance. From our perspective, the significance of these league tables is the influence they may have on elite universities in relation to the recruiting strategies of transnational companies (TNCs).

MODES OF STANDARDIZATION

Clearly, from the discussion above there are various forms of standardization. However, here we focus on those relating to pedagogy, the curriculum and assessment. On the one hand they lie at the heart of judgments about comparability between university programs and 'standards', but on the other they also specify the classification and framing of knowledge (Bernstein, 2000) in such a way as to delimit modes of thinking and creativity, which for our purposes are crucial. In this context the key to standardization is not the formal knowledge that is taught but the way that it is taught and assessed. Here we would point, as Naidoo and Jamieson do, to pre-packaged modular forms of delivery accompanied by forms of assessment where criteria for success in tests or assignments are narrowly specified.

Assignments or tests are, for example, often posted on websites so that students can practice or imitate what constitutes a good assignment or test. In essence what students are required to undertake are rather mechanical forms of learning for which no 'permission to think' is required. In part this can be seen as ensuring 'quality standards' within universities. Doing the best for students now means the codification of the university experience, including assessment. Hence the emphasis is on following appropriate procedures, clearly defined assessment criteria and so on that are intended to ensure the predictability (quality) of the university product.

However, if a university education is about character as well as competence, then the processes of socialization that accompany pedagogy and the curriculum must also be considered. Standardization is as much about the education of character as it is about learning processes. If creativity and exploration of ideas are secondary to assessment and certification, then in turn character formation is about following routines rather than the risk-taking associated with initiative and innovation.

It should be emphasized that this does not mean that some students will not be very creative in their thinking, for what is taught and what is learned are quite different. It does mean that students do not have to be creative in order to succeed. And, of course, it is in the interests of some universities, as we shall see, to specify pedagogy, the curriculum and assessment in a standardized form because it means that they provide, in principle, a standardized reliable 'product'. For the purposes of this argument, standardization, including knowledge 'delivered' and assessed in bite-size 'chunks', denotes an education into a particular mode of thinking that can be certified as competent within a predefined sphere of learning. This analysis dovetails with what we consider to be an emergent and significant force in the development of standardization. This has to do with the demands of the global labor market, to which we now turn.

THE GLOBAL LABOR MARKET FOR HIGH-SKILLED WORKERS/GRADUATES

Brown et al.'s (2011) research on the global skill strategies of TNCs raises two points of direct relevance to our argument. First, TNCs are globalizing their recruitment strategies. This often involves extending their recruitment from elite universities within specific nation-states to recruiting from elite universities across national borders. Our research suggests that the globalization of elite recruitment is closely related to the fragmentation of professional and managerial occupations. TNCs are increasingly drawing a distinction between top talent who will continue to have 'permission to think' and those for whom 'knowledge' work now requires an ability to engage in the routines relating to what we call 'digital Taylorism'. Moreover, despite the congested market for graduates as a result of mass higher education, TNCs typically subscribe to the view that they are in a war to engage the most talented graduates.

Second, this research also shows that character as well as technical competence is crucial to the way that companies judge 'talent' and behavioral skills. With the expansion of higher education in both developed and emerging economies, companies are increasingly recruiting from elite universities, not only because they can be assured of a high level of technical competence but because those who attend such universities are believed to have the appropriate 'character'. The growing importance of character alongside academic credentials or qualifications requires some background on the development of the global labor market.

Changes in the demand for educated labor and the recruitment practices of TNCs need to be considered if we are going to understand the creation of a global labor market for high-skilled workers. The United Nations estimates that currently there are around 64 000 TNCs, a rise from 37 000 in the early 1990s. These TNCs comprise parent enterprises and foreign affiliates, which vary in size and influence. The foreign affiliates generated approximately 53 million jobs around the world (UNCTAD, 2005). General Electric had the largest foreign assets in 2003 with 330 enterprises in the USA and over 1000 foreign affiliates.

The key role that these firms play in shaping the global economy is reflected in the fact that a third of global trade is due to intra-firm activities where components, products, services and software are sold between affiliates within the same company. Equally it is estimated that over 60 percent of the goods exported from China in 2005 came from foreign-owned firms that had moved manufacturing plants there to increase profit margins. This extraordinary expansion is central to the global labor market for the recruitment of graduates. In what follows we use the findings from our study of the skill strategies of TNCs to develop an understanding of the changing demand for graduate workers (Brown et al., 2011).

THE STUDY

The study comprises 190 interviews with senior managers in 30 TNCs in three sectors – automotive, financial services and electronics/telecoms – across seven countries. Where possible, interviews within companies were triangulated between head office and a company's operations in other countries, especially those in China and India. The timing of the interviews is important because it enabled us to gauge what has turned out to be very rapid change within TNCs over the period 2004–07. Sixty-five interviews were also conducted with policy-makers in the seven countries within which these TNCs operated. This enabled us to examine differences in national skill formation strategies and how they relate to the approaches now being adopted by TNCs. This was of particular interest because we wanted to understand the impact of the globalization strategies of TNCs for national systems of education and training.

THE DIVISION OF LABOR IN TNCs

Our argument is that the global demand for 'knowledge' workers is in part due to the way that the division of labor within TNCs is being restructured in the light of their global reach, facilitated by advances in new technologies. Instead of having a career ladder, it is clear that corporations are distinguishing between those they consider the 'talented', who are typically fast-tracked into senior managerial positions, and those that are considered worthy, loyal and committed but who do not have the key ingredients for leadership positions. Beneath these are workers who engage in routine work. There are two reasons for these changes. The first concerns the ideology of the 'war for talent' in which corporations seek to identify outstanding talent because it is claimed that global corporations now need a range of skills in leadership positions that were not in demand when corporations were embedded in national economies (Brown and Hesketh, 2004). These new skill sets that only a small minority of 'talented' are deemed to have are therefore highly rewarded in contrast to those considered 'worthy' or subject to the routines of 'digital Taylorism'.

Digital Taylorism

One of the major errors made by policy-makers in considering the idea of the knowledge economy is that all those who ascend the credential ladder to become graduates will have interesting and well-rewarded jobs awaiting them. But this fails to understand the nature of capitalism. Throughout its history, innovation has been followed by standardization (Brint, 2001). The particular form of standardization that has accompanied the electronic revolution is that of 'digital Taylorism'.

Historically, productivity has not come from giving people permission to think but from imposing barriers to individual initiative and control through a detailed division of labor. While the management of knowledge workers poses problems for human resources professionals, there is also a major shift to 'digital Taylorism' (Brown et al., 2008, 2011). If the era of Fordism, characterized by 'mechanical Taylorism', involved the transformation of craft work through 'scientific management' (Taylor, 1911; Braverman, 1974), today we are witnessing the translation of knowledge work into working knowledge.

'Digital Taylorism' enables innovation to be translated into routines that might require some degree of education but not the kind of creativity and independence of judgment that is often associated with the knowledge economy. In order to reduce costs, companies have to move from knowledge work to working knowledge: that is, from, on the one hand, the idiosyncratic knowledge that a worker has and applies, to, on the other, working knowledge where that knowledge is codified and routinized, thereby making it generally available to the company rather than it being the 'property' of an individual worker.

There are many ways in which 'digital Taylorism' can be applied. For example, a leading company producing and selling software for handling credit card transactions and credit rating expanded very rapidly over the last decade both within the UK and abroad, mainly through acquisitions. In an interview with the chief executive officer (CEO) in 2006 he defined the company's major problem as that of how to encourage his staff (mostly university graduates) to be innovative. He thought this was essential for the continued success of the business as they developed products for new markets and customers. Today the problem has changed dramatically. The company has achieved an annual growth rate of 25 percent and opened offices across the developed and developing world, including China, India and Bulgaria. There has been a change in CEO and the major issue in no longer defined as innovation but of how to align business processes and roll out software products to a global market. The creative work in producing new platforms, programs and templates has been separated from what the company calls routine 'analytics'. Permission to think is restricted to a relatively small group of knowledge workers in the UK, while the more routine work (customizing products to different markets and customers, also referred to as the 'grunt work') is offshored to offices in Bulgaria (where graduates can be hired at a third of the cost in the UK) and India.

Two related factors lie behind these changes in the division of labor. The first is cost. The intense nature of global competition and the impact of economic recession have placed a premium on cost reduction. The shift from knowledge work to working knowledge has been identified as an important way of achieving more for less. The second is that TNCs have the resources to place their human capital where it is most effective and at the cheapest price. Standardization of processes and platforms enables production of high- as well as low-value goods or services to be located in emerging economies, including China and India.

For those not considered among the 'talented', TNCs now have a variety of standard-ized procedures for recruitment. In effect, just as goods and processes are being standard-ized, so are judgments about the workers they recruit. Yet the 'war for talent' ideology emphasizes the importance of elite graduates because they are seen as leading the future global development of TNCs. However, the key to the most 'talented' lies not only in their technical competence but in their character.

THE RECRUITMENT OF CHARACTER

The human resource (HR) executives whom we interviewed identified a number of core competencies as crucial to recruitment into fast-track and senior managerial positions, which applied across diverse industries. These were firmly rooted in the importance of 'soft skills' such as interpersonal and communication skills, teamworking, personal resilience, business awareness and experience of cultural diversity. Such requirements are neatly encapsulated in an interview with HR managers at an electronics TNC in Korea:

> To be a global manager [requires] being a kind of a cultural translator. I think this really requires a lot of the softer skills that have not been a traditional focus of Korean management. And I think that is something that we have to become more sophisticated about, you know, being a little bit more nuanced in your interactions, just being more aware and again being more flexible. You hear the old adage to treat others as you would like to be treated. It is treating others as they want to be treated . . . it is not just going to a country and being the tourist, but really you know empathising.

In order to be able to relate to multiple national cultures, it was apparent that the culture and identity of the TNC was of fundamental importance. This was reflected in attributes sought in staff such that they could engage with multiple cultures while maintaining a commitment to the distinct culture of the corporation. This was explained similarly in an interview with a global bank in Beijing:

> This kind of person is not only very capable with the softer skills for leadership, communi-cation, interpersonal, and something like that, but also the people who know very well our company and our culture because for [X bank] it has already 140 years' history and why we can run so smoothly is because we have the core culture inside.

An HR executive for a leading electronics TNC also commented that 'X is really a company with a very strong culture globally. It doesn't mean you are US, or UK, or China; we have this consistent culture.'

Another electronics HR manager spoke of the common values that were necessary: 'You can't have a different set of value systems or a code of conduct in India different from Europe; it's the same across the globe.' An HR manager employed by a TNC in financial services spoke in similar terms: 'The organization is attempting to fuse together cultures . . . hopefully they'll absorb the best of each.'

As Alvesson (2001) has noted, there is considerable ambiguity in both the quali-ties that are required for knowledge work and a considerable amount of impression management in judgments made about such workers. Moreover, while at one level it is surprising that HR managers seek the same qualities and skills despite different cultural locations, there may nevertheless be different cultural interpretations of what these qualities and skills mean in practice. Nevertheless, however these terms are understood, these data point to the search within TNCs for professional workers with a new cultural identity and forms of cultural competence, a consequence of a new form of global commercial organization.

This analysis shows how companies are trying to standardize the recruitment, labor process and performance of a greater range of technical and managerial tasks at the same time as continuing to rely on 'character' and other intangible indicators of leadership when recruiting 'top talent'. This segmentation of knowledge work is reproduced in their ranking of national and international universities, and in the recruitment practices of most of the companies we interviewed that targeted 'top' universities in search of 'top' talent.

REPUTATION AND ITS IMPACT ON GLOBAL HIGHER EDUCATION

We should not see the changes in the university sector as emanating solely from the labor market. Far from it: we are witnessing rather a reciprocal beauty competition between TNCs and elite universities. In the war for talent the reputation of the TNC is enhanced by recruiting from elite universities just as elite universities' reputations are enhanced by the prestigious 'destinations' of their graduates.

Moreover, a hierarchy of global university circuits is emerging that is defined by the social class of the students attending. This has a direct bearing on the processes of standardization in higher education. But before turning to an analysis of these global circuits, some observations prompted by Strathdee's (2009) analysis are apposite. He notes that it is difficult to identify the source of a university's reputation, and moreover that it is not necessarily the case that elite universities contribute to the advantage that their already privileged student body possesses.

There are three points to make here. First, when he was writing, Strathdee was skeptical of the premium that attending an elite university could attract. However, more recent work on elite universities in the UK and the USA makes it absolutely clear that the premiums reflect rent-seeking behavior by the social groups involved. In the UK, Hussain et al. (2008) calculate that those from elite universities earn twice the wages of those from lower-ranked institutions. Goldin and Katz (2008) found that Harvard students enjoy a significant income premium and for those that enter financial occupations it is 195 percent of the average graduate income in the USA. These findings suggest that reputation and rent-seeking are two sides of the same coin! Where Strathdee has a point is in his emphasis on understanding the underlying fields that enable HE premiums to be gained in some sectors (such as finance) but not in others.

However, with respect to the TNCs, it is clear that they have at least two considerations in fishing in small national ponds when recruiting the 'talented': they save on the transaction costs of a wider search for talent by targeting elite universities, which they justify because these institutions are believed to offer a reliable source of 'talent' who are expected to 'perform' from day one given global competitive pressures.

GLOBAL HIGHER EDUCATION CIRCUITS

Elite Universities

There is a circuit of elite universities comprising Oxbridge, a few of the US Ivy League and best state colleges, INSEAD in Paris and Singapore, some of the high-class management and technical schools in India, and two or three of the top universities on the eastern seaboard of China. These universities are unlikely to pay more than lip service to forms of standardization because it is precisely their refusal to engage in the standardization of knowledge and pedagogy that distinguishes them. At the same time, they gain their reputation not directly from teaching but from their research. Nobel Prize winners and leading-edge research hold one of the keys to reputation. In this respect, whatever the synergies between research and teaching, and they have been much debated, for elite universities the bridge between them is constructed through building and maintaining 'reputation capital'.

Standardized Universities

Beneath this circuit we can hypothesise other circuits characterized by the standardization of knowledge. Earlier we suggested that one of the important motivations for digital Taylorism was that it enabled business processes to be offshored precisely because they were cast in a standardized form. It can be argued that a process similar to this is now taking place in non-elite universities so as to enable students to be mobile across them and to facilitate access criteria for students on the basis of past performance. The significance of these lower circuits is a rough correspondence between what is taught/delivered and the demand for knowledge 'demonstrators' and 'drones' (Brown et al., 2011) who will undertake the work of digital Taylorism. We are not suggesting that the current drive towards standardization can be explained simply in terms of changes in work organization, international student mobility or the global labor market, but that these are factors that need to be taken into consideration alongside market reforms and quality standards as issues that have been leading to change, especially in less prestigious universities.

However, this raises the question of whether there is a new correspondence between the demands of digital Taylorism and the training received in standardized HEIs, based on the provision of the kinds of skills and dispositions towards knowledge required for this kind of work. If this is the case, then it also raises the question put by Michael Young (2007) on the distinction between 'knowledge of the powerful' and 'powerful knowledge'. The former refers to the knowledge that dominant groups impose on others to their advantage, while the latter is the knowledge that is needed in order for individuals to develop an understanding of the world and is potentially emancipating. The implication of this position is that the knowledge of the powerful and powerful knowledge are found in the elite institutions, which by and large are dominated by the most privileged in society. It is in the elite institutions that powerful knowledge is taught and the pedagogy that is practised enables considerable freedom of expression and creativity.

To what extent can this hypothesis be applied to all HE systems? Is there likely to be a convergence towards these HE circuits? Here it is important to note that not all national university systems are modeled on those in the UK, the USA or indeed China, where are found clearly identifiable elite institutions that would lend themselves to this kind of analysis. Some countries have had highly egalitarian university systems – Germany and New Zealand are examples, although in both cases attempts are being made to differentiate universities by various measures of performance and according to reputation (Kupfer, 2010).

THE EFFECTS ON POSITIONAL COMPETITION

The consequence of the hypothesis outlined above would be a class-based intensification of positional competition. Both UK and US higher education systems are differentiated by institution and social class. The advent of the global auction for high-skilled jobs has the effect of intensifying the competition for access to elite universities because it is only those that gain entry to them (the 'talented') who can avoid a reverse (Dutch) auction for knowledge work (Brown et al., 2011). Recent figures for the socioeconomic profile of UK universities show that those from the upper end of the socioeconomic scale dominate elite universities. For example, the university with the highest percentage of students from top socioeconomic backgrounds (bands 1, 2 and 3) in 2006/7 was Oxford with 90.2 percent, followed by Cambridge with 88.5 percent (HESA, 2008).

A similar story applies in the USA. Bowen et al. (2005) have documented the inequalities in participation in higher education in the USA. There are several reasons for this, but they include the preferential treatment given to alumni of the elite universities, along with high costs. In 2000 the cost of a year at the big three universities, Harvard, Yale and Princeton, had reached $35000, an amount that less than 10 percent of US families could afford. By 2004 this had risen to $40000. While there was some assistance for less well-off students, the majority paid full fees. Even then better-off families seemed to have captured the scholarships available. At Harvard the majority of scholarship recipients had a family income of over $70000, with a quarter having an income of over $100000. When this is translated into the share of family income that goes on tuition fees, even though there is a reduction for low-income families, they still pay an estimated 49 percent of family income. In contrast, the proportion of family income paid in tuition fees for unaided students, those that come from wealthy families, is 21 percent.

Not surprisingly, among the dominant classes in the USA there is overrepresentation in terms of degrees, and especially from the elite universities. David Rothkopf (2008), writing of the new super-class, notes that among the CEOs of the USA's leading corporations, 30 percent attended one of only 20 elite universities, led by Stanford, Harvard and Chicago. He estimates that 91 percent have an undergraduate degree and 47 percent a postgraduate degree, which makes them far better educated than the general population. He shows how these elite universities provide the basis for forging networks between students and alumni, listing the number of high-profile CEOs who graduated from the Harvard Business School.

IS THERE A NEW CORRESPONDENCE BETWEEN HIGHER EDUCATION AND THE GLOBAL DIVISION OF LABOR?

In the correspondence principle articulated by Bowles and Gintis (1976), it is not enough that various factors are considered to provide a correspondence, as it were by coincidence, but that the changes in education are caused by changes in the economy. Are there causal factors that we can identify in this case? In contrast to the original correspondence principle, these are difficult to identify. Clearly there is a connection between what the TNCs demand in terms of talent and what elite universities can supply with respect to both competencies and character. But equally we noted above that there was a reciprocal relationship, posed as a beauty contest, between the interests of the elite universities and TNCs. It could be argued that the underlying common causal factor is the market competition that confronts both companies and universities. However, when it comes to the standardization of pedagogy and assessment in non-elite institutions and the rise of digital Taylorism in the corporate sector, more specific causal mechanisms other than common technologies are more difficult to establish. What we present here are no more than initial observations that point to a tantalizing coincidence between changes in the HE sector and changes in the technical division of labor of TNCs that requires further investigation.

We also note that there is a major contradiction between the means and ends of higher education in terms of student expectations. While the means may be standardized and there may be growing evidence of some kind of correspondence, it contradicts the ends of a university education as understood by students. Although they may be fed on a diet of bite-sized modules, they continue to expect graduate credentials to lead to interesting and rewarding jobs.

CONCLUSION

The hypothesis presented here points to emerging global circuits of higher education that in key respects map onto changes in the global labor market, especially to the restructuring of the division of labor within TNCs. A key element of global HE circuits is the development of both technical competencies and character. The highest elite circuit is based on reputation for research and innovation, as well as for the students who attend these universities. Such students are targeted by TNCs because they are believed to have technical competence that enables them to think creatively as well as the 'character' required for future leadership positions. Beneath elite circuits are others in which technical competence is framed by the limiting of thought as well as of creativity and character. It is clear that the processes described in this chapter presage fundamental changes in the nature and structure of university systems, particularly the standardization of degrees awarded, quality assurance and the curriculum. Some of these changes are linked to the interests of TNCs for research and innovation, as well as to their demands in relation to skill and character in the labor market.

REFERENCES

Alvesson, M. (2001), 'Knowledge work: ambiguity, image and identity', *Human Relations*, **54** (7), 863–6.

Bernstein, B. (2000), *Pedagogy, Symbolic Control and Identity*, Oxford: Rowman and Littlefield.

Bowen, W., M. Kurzwell and E. Tobin (2005), *Equity and Excellence in American Higher Education*, Charlottesville, VA: University of Virginia Press.

Bowles, S. and H. Gintis (1976), *Schooling in Capitalist America*, London: Routledge.

Braverman, H. (1974), *Labour and Monopoly Capital*, New York: Monthly Review Press.

Brint, S. (2001), 'Professionals and the "knowledge economy": rethinking the theory of post-industrial society', *Current Sociology*, **49** (4), 102–32.

Brown, P. and A. Hesketh (2004), *The Mismanagement of Talent; Employability and Jobs in the Knowledge Economy*, Oxford: Oxford University Press.

Brown, P., H. Lauder and D. Ashton (2011), *The Global Auction: The Broken Promises of Education, Jobs and Prosperity*, New York: Oxford University Press.

Goldin, C. and L. Katz (2008), 'Gender differences in careers, education and games: transitions career and family life cycles of the educational elite', *American Economic Review*, **98** (2), 363–9.

HESA (2008), *Higher Education Statistics for the United Kingdom*, London: HESA.

Hussain, I., S. McNally and S. Telhaj (2008), *University Quality and Graduate Wages in the UK*, London: Centre for Economic Performance, London School of Economics.

Lindblad, S. and R. Lindblad (2009), 'Transnational governance of higher education: on globalization and international university ranking lists', in F. Rivzi and T. Popkewitz (eds), *Globalization and Education*, Chicago, IL: NSSE (National Society for the Study of Education), pp. 180–202.

Marginson, S. (2006), 'National and global competition in higher education', in H. Lauder, P. Brown, J.-A. Dillabough and A. Halsey (eds), *Education, Globalization and Social Change*, Oxford: Oxford University Press, pp. 893–908.

Marginson, S. (2009), 'University rankings, government, and social order: managing the field of higher education according to the logic of present-as-future', in M. Simons, M. Olssen and M. Peters (eds), *Re-reading Educational Policy: Studying the Policy Agenda for the 21st Century*, Rotterdam: Sense Publishers.

Naidoo, R. (2004), 'Fields and institutional strategy: Bourdieu on the relationship between higher education, inequality, and society', *British Journal of Sociology of Education*, **4** (25), 457–72.

Naidoo, R. and I. Jamieson (2006), 'Empowering participants or corroding learning? Towards a research agenda on the impact of student consumerism in higher education', in H. Lauder, P. Brown, J.-A. Dillabough and A.H. Halsey (eds), *Education, Globalization and Social Change*, Oxford: Oxford University Press, pp. 875–84.

Room, G. (2000), 'Globalisation, social policy, and international standard-setting: the case of higher education credentials', *International Journal of Social Welfare*, **9**, 103–19.

Rothkopf, D. (2008), *Superclass: The Global Power Elite and the World they are Making*, New York: Little Brown.

Sacks, P. (1996), *Generation X Goes to College: An Eye Opening Account of Teaching in Postmodern America*, Chicago, IL: Open Court.

Strathdee, R. (2009), 'Reputation in the sociology of education', *British Journal of Sociology of Education*, **30** (1), 83–96.

Taylor, F.W. (1911), *Principles of Scientific Management*, New York: Harper and Brothers.

UNCTAD (2005), *The World Investment Report: Transnational Companies and the Internationalisation of Research and Development*, New York: UNCTAD.

Young, M. (2007), *Bringing Knowledge Back In*, London: Routledge/Falmer.

Young, M. (2009), 'Learning outcomes and educational reform: some lessons from the UK's NVQs', paper given at the UK Forum for International Education and Training Conference, Oxford, September.

29 Measuring world-class excellence and the global obsession with rankings[1]

Ellen Hazelkorn

PUTTING RANKINGS INTO CONTEXT

The obsession with global rankings has reached almost fever pitch in recent years. Politicians, university leaders, students, business leaders and media headline-writers alike monitor rankings; conferences on rankings are held around the world, attracting delegates from many countries; hundreds of academic and newspaper articles and opinion pieces, blogs and commentary have been published; and many governments and higher education institutions (HEIs) have redrafted their strategies to conform to the indicators identified by rankings. The language of rankings has entered public discourse and impregnated policy documents and statements drafted by a wide array of international, national, regional and local stakeholders. What began as a consumer-oriented guide for students and parents has been transformed into a rapidly expanding global intelligence information business. By 2011 there will be 10 different global rankings, and over 50 national rankings. Few corners of the globe appear immune from the frenzy that university rankings have created.

Published by, *inter alia*, government and accreditation agencies, higher education, research and commercial organizations, and the popular media, rankings have become ubiquitous. The number of different rankings has risen sharply and, arguably inevitably, since 2003 for four main interrelated reasons.

First, it is now widely recognized that knowledge is the cornerstone of economic growth and national security; it is the new crude oil. This has driven the transformation of economies and the basis of wealth production from those based on productivity and efficiency to those based on higher-valued goods and services innovated by talent. In a globalized world, nations increasingly compete on the basis of their knowledge and innovation systems (Slaughter and Leslie, 1997). Because higher education is an important producer of new knowledge, its contribution to economic growth is very significant. It is rightly regarded as 'the engine of development in the new world economy' (Castells, 1994, p. 14). Accordingly, measuring and comparing higher education has become a vital sign of a country's capacity to participate in world science and attract international talent and investment capital.

Second, at a time when countries are dependent upon talent, many are under demographic pressure. This has arisen for a combination of reasons, including the graying of the population and retirement of professionals combined with the end of the 'baby-boomer' bubble and decline in the number of students. The share of young people in developed countries is expected to fall from 13.7 percent of the population to 10.5 percent by 2050 (Bremner et al., 2009, pp. 2, 6). This will affect the pool of secondary students, ultimately challenging government strategies for growing knowledge-intensive

497

sectors of their economies. Hence most countries are now embarked on a strategy to attract international students, especially postgraduate research students.

Third, as higher education has been transformed from a social expenditure to an essential component of the productive economy, public and policy questions have been asked about how higher education is governed and managed. There has been increasing emphasis on issues of value for money, productivity and efficiency, and ensuring investor confidence. The European Union (Europa, 2006) has stated that 'Universities should be funded more for what they do than for what they are, by focusing funding on relevant outputs rather than inputs.' Put more succinctly, it 'isn't enough to just go around telling ourselves how good we are – we need to measure ourselves objectively against the world's best' (Carr, 2009).

Fourth, international evidence continues to show strong correlation between higher qualifications and graduate outcomes with career opportunities, salaries and lifestyle. As the cost of higher education rises, this is also driving a more consumerist approach; students assess institutions and programs as an opportunity cost. Accordingly there is a growing demand for greater transparency and accountability, not just from governments but also from students (and their parents). In the absence of institutionally generated comparative material, rankings have arguably and controversially become an accountability and transparency instrument. While domestic undergraduate students may rely upon their own networks and intelligence to learn about different HEIs, this process is wholly inadequate for internationally mobile students.

Thus rankings have emerged in response to the pressures and challenges of globalization and the drive for increased information, accountability and transparency. They are a manifestation of what has become known as the worldwide battle for talent and excellence. They are perceived and used to determine the status of individual institutions, assess the quality and performance of the higher education system, and gauge global competitiveness. Rankings have become a more powerful tool in the post-2008 global financial crisis (GFC) era due to the tendency to measure outputs in order to ensure value for money; measuring performance gives the 'appearance of scientific objectivity' (Ehrenberg, 2001, p. 1). Despite the fact that there are over 15000 HEIs worldwide, rankings have encouraged a fascination with the standing and trajectory of the top 100 universities.

This chapter will provide a state-of-the-art summary of the debate around rankings. It will initially illustrate how rankings work, and what they measure. It will then examine how higher education and its stakeholders are responding to the growing influence of rankings, drawing upon international data and experience. The final section will consider some of the wider policy implications and speculate on their legacy.

WHAT DO RANKINGS MEASURE?

Global rankings have become an international phenomenon since 2003, although the origin of rankings dates back to James McKeen Cattell, whose 1910 version of *American Men of Science* in 1910 'showed the "scientific strength" of leading universities using the research reputation of their faculty members' (Webster, 1986, pp. 14, 107–19). Early rankings used several 'dimensions of quality', *inter alia,* faculty expertise, graduate success in later life, and academic resources such as faculty/student ratio or volumes in the library, while later formats have relied more on reputational indicators, using the *Science Citation Index*, 1961 and annually thereafter, and the *Social Sciences Citation Index*, 1966 and then yearly. *US News and World Report* Best College Rankings (*USNWR*) in 1983 marked a second defining moment. Its rise to prominence coincided with the ideological and public 'shift in the Zeitgeist towards the glorification of markets' (Karabel, 2005, p. 514). Today, as indicated, there are a growing number of other national rankings of which the CHE–HochschulRanking, developed in 1998 by the German Centre for Higher Education Development, is one of the most influential.

A third era is marked by the arrival of global rankings with the Shanghai Jiao Tong Academic Ranking of World Universities (ARWU) in 2003. Despite being developed to highlight the position of Chinese universities *vis-à-vis* competitor universities, this ranking has effectively become the 'gold standard'. It was followed by *Webometrics* (produced by the Spanish National Research Council), and *THE-QS World University Ranking* (*THE-QS*) in 2004, the Taiwan *Performance Ranking of Scientific Papers for Research Universities* (HEEACT) in 2007, and *USNWR's World's Best Colleges and Universities* in 2008. *The Leiden Ranking* (2008), developed by the Centre for Science and Technology Studies (CWTS) at the University of Leiden, uses its own bibliometric indicators to assess the scientific output of over 1000 universities worldwide, while *SCImago* (2009) uses the Elsevier *Scopus* database. The Russian *Global University Rankings* (2009) uses data from a questionnaire sent to universities around the world. The *THE-QS* partnership split in 2009, resulting in *QS World University Rankings* (2010) (which retains its relationship with *USNWR*), and *THE*-Thomson Reuters *World University Ranking* (*THE-TR*) (2010), the latter representing a significant entry into the market by the producer of one of the major bibliometric databases. The EU has commissioned *U-Multirank* as a companion to its U-Map classification; variously described as a feasibility or pilot study, it was launched in June 2011.

Rankings' popularity is largely related to their simplicity. They compare HEIs using a range of indicators, which are weighted differently according to 'some criterion or set of criteria which the compiler(s) of the list believe . . . measure or reflect . . . academic quality' (Webster, 2001, p. 5). The scores are aggregated to a single digit in descending order, with universities scoring best given the lowest score, for example first or second place, while institutions considered less good are ranked as high as 500+. Due to this format, differences between institutions are often statistically insignificant. Rankings are essentially one-dimensional, since each indicator is considered independently of the others, whereas in reality 'multicollinearity is pervasive' (ibid., p. 236); for example, older well-endowed private universities are more likely to have better faculty/student ratios and per student expenditure compared with newer public institutions. Rankings focus primarily on whole institutions, although there is an increasing focus on sub-institutional rankings at the field-of-science level (natural science, mathematics, engineering, computer science, social sciences, for example) or by discipline or profession (such as business, law, medicine, graduate schools and so on). The latter are often captured by commercial publishers or websites, such as the *Financial Times, Business Week, US News and World Report, Good University Guide* UK or http://www.premedguide.com/ and http://www.llm-guide.com/. Ultimately the choice of indicators and weightings reflects the priorities or value judgments of the producers. There is no such thing as an objective ranking.

Rankings draw their information from three main sources (Usher and Medow, 2009, p. 6), each with advantages and disadvantages. Independent third-party sources, for example government databases, hold an array of data on higher education performance, primarily in statistical format, and often in response to regulatory reportage by the institutions. While government data are considered the most accurate, they are not usually in the format that organizations require for comparative purposes. Moreover, definitional and contextual differences make cross-jurisdictional comparisons particularly problematic. Bibliometric and citation data are usually supplied by Thomson Reuter's Web of Science or Elsevier's Scopus, but there is also a growing number of electronic formats, such as Google Scholar. HEI sources, such as published data from the institutions, are often provided by way of questionnaires or data surveys. This is the richest source of information but can be open to significant distortion or manipulation, as there is 'no guarantee that institutions will actually report the data to the ranker on a consistent basis', even if there is a standard set of questions being asked (Usher and Medow, 2009, p. 7). Finally, survey data of students, peers, employers or other stakeholders, for example questionnaires, focus groups or student satisfaction surveys, capture valuable stakeholder opinion about a wide range of issues and measure esteem. However, these formats can be susceptible to bias, self-perpetuating views of quality, and 'gaming'.

No matter which ranking system is used, there has been considerable debate within the literature about the underlying methodology, the choice of indicators and weightings, the quality of the data and their reliability as an international or institutional comparator of performance, and whether it is possible to measure and compare complex and diverse HEIs possessing different missions and contexts (Tight, 2000; Bowden, 2000; Turner, 2005; Dill and Soo, 2005; Usher and Savino, 2006, 2007; Sadlak and Liu, 2007; Marginson and van der Wende, 2007; Saisana and D'Hombres, 2008; Usher and Medow, 2009).

Each ranking system purports to measure quality and rank institutional performance differently. For example, while several rankings give preferential weight to research, such as HEEACT (100 percent), ARWU (100 percent), *THE*-TR ranking (65 percent), the choice of the dataset can vary significantly. At the global level, research is principally measured using bibliometric and citation data, while at the national level a wider array of data sources is available (Hendel and Stolz, 2008). This illustrates that there is no universally agreed definition of higher education quality.

Despite the different data sources discussed above, there is a serious lack of consistency in data definition, sets, collection and reporting that makes it difficult to make simple and easy comparisons. Because of these problems, rankings rely on that which can be (easily) measured rather than that which might be most appropriate. Bibliometric and citation data are most commonly used precisely because they are readily available due to the fact that Thomson Reuters and Scopus collect these data. Thus the availability of internationally comparable data has implications both for the methodology and, critically, for the results. This latter point is often overlooked or underestimated.

To get around these issues, measurements are rarely direct but generally comprise proxies. Student-entry scores are often used to gauge the 'quality' of the student; publications, citations, the number of Nobel or other prize winners and research income are all used to measure academic quality; the size of the budget and expenditure equates with the quality of the infrastructure, including the library; graduate employment rates measure the quality of the program and the employability potential of graduates. But is the choice of proxy a worthy and appropriate measurement for the underlying feature?

Different rankings also assign different weightings to the indicators, and thus an HEI's position can change considerably depending upon the weight ascribed to the particular criteria. Aggregating the scores into a final rank ignores the fact that some institutions might score higher in some domains than others, or vice versa. It also leads to inconsistency across the rankings but it also highlights the arbitrariness of the weightings. Most of the movement occurs within the middle ranking, where small statistical changes can make large numerical differences to an institution's position. Grewal et al. (2008, p. 6) claim that 'a highly-ranked university gets more leverage from growing financial resources while lower-ranked universities get more leverage from improvements in academic reputation'.

Commentators commonly point out that rankings are unable to measure the full breadth of higher education activity, for example, with teaching and learning the 'added value' that each HEI contributes to the student's learning over and beyond the student's entry level; the full spectrum of research knowledge, technology transfer activities, engagement and third mission; and social and economic impact. There have been attempts to normalize for these factors by controlling for institutional size or age, focusing on field of science or using questionnaires or stakeholder surveys to capture impact beyond the academy – but each of these methodologies has its own limitations. These lacunae also demonstrate the degree to which rankings can dramatically diverge from and counterpoise public policy objectives – an issue that will be discussed in the conclusion.

To paraphrase Einstein, a wider question to be asked of rankings is whether they measure what counts or count what can be measured. Here are five brief examples (Hazelkorn, 2011, pp. 59–77).

1. The education level of entering students is generally considered a good proxy for student ability on the basic assumption that a roughly similar range of performance can be expected throughout his/her higher education career. This forms the basis on which many higher education systems and institutions select students. But do entry scores and standardized testing simply reflect socioeconomic advantage? 'Many colleges recruit great students and then graduate great students [but is] that because of the institution, or the students?' (Hawkins, 2008).

2. One of the most noticeable changes in how higher education is funded is the shift from inputs to outputs. Financing the number of students who actually complete and graduate within the determined timeframe is seen as a good measure of quality. But measuring graduation rates may be disadvantageous to lower socioeconomic, ethnically disadvantaged groups, or mature students whose life or family circumstances disturb 'normal' study patterns. It may undermine institutions that are working hard to widen participation, and disincentivize access/two-year programs because students often transfer to other universities which then get the credit for their completion. For example, 40 percent of US seniors begin their studies at another institution and almost half of students at masters and doctoral institutions were incoming transfers (Kuh, 2003, p. 29).

3. National rankings often measure the level of resources as a proxy for the quality of the learning environment. Usually what is being measured is the size of the budget or the library collection. To illustrate the significance, Aghion et al. (2007) argue that there is a strong positive correlation between the university budget per student and its research performance in the ARWU ranking. But expenditure per student can penalize 'institutions that attempt to hold down their expenditures' (Ehrenberg, 2005, p. 33), and it provides 'little or no information about how often and how beneficially students *use* these resources' (Webster, 1986, p. 152) or, in the case of library resources, 'the adequacy of the holdings' (Lawrence and Green, 1980, p. 28).

4. Counting peer publications and citations has become the most common way to measure institutional/individual academic research productivity and quality, but it is hugely controversial. While bibliometric databases identify a significant number of peer-reviewed articles (around 9000 in Web of Science and 18 000 in Scopus), this is just a proportion of what is published. The main beneficiaries of this methodology are the physical, life and medical sciences because these disciplines publish frequently with multiple authors. In contrast, the social sciences and humanities are likely to have single authors and to publish in a wide range of formats (monographs, policy reports, translations and so on), whereas the arts produce major art works, compositions and media productions while engineering focuses on conference proceedings and prototypes. Other important sources or publication formats such as books and conference proceedings, technical standards, policy reports, electronic formats or open source publications are ignored by this method. Likewise new research fields, interdisciplinary research or ideas that challenge orthodoxy can find it difficult to get published or are less likely to be published in high-impact journals. Yet low-impact journals can contain valuable research papers, and papers may be cited as examples of scientific errors rather than quality. In addition, authors are most likely to reference other authors whom they know or are from their own country. It also assumes that journal quality is a proxy for article quality.

5. Rankings seek to measure the reputation of a university using the academy's gold standard: peer review. Information is usually gathered by a survey to academic peers, students or industry stakeholders, and respondents are asked to identify institutions that they consider meet the criteria being sought. However, reputational surveys are prone to being subjective, self-referential and self-perpetuating; rater bias occurs when respondents are asked to either identify the top universities they know or choose from a pre-selected list. This process tends to benefit older institutions in developed countries and global cities with which there is an easy identification. It also begs the question: reputation among whom and for what?

This discussion has highlighted the underlying methodological challenges that rankings pose. Yet this has not halted the proliferation of rankings. It is often said that the more rankings the better, as a way of showing there are many ways to measure quality. Nevertheless the fundamental flaws remain. Yet, as the next section illustrates, their sphere of influence extends far beyond the academy. Rankings have acquired popularity due to their simple and easily understood format. Is this the fault of the rankers – many of whom are commercial enterprises and use every opportunity to promote the universality of their product – or those who use and overinterpret the results?

THE IMPACT OF RANKINGS ON HIGHER EDUCATION AND ITS STAKEHOLDERS

Rankings are part of the growing trend for more transparency, accountability and comparability, such as college guides or handbooks, accreditation, evaluation and assessment, and benchmarking. However, rankings have introduced a competitive dynamic into global and national higher education systems. Users of rankings extend beyond students and their parents to include, *inter alia*, policy-makers, employers, foundations and benefactors, potential collaborators and partners, alumni, other HEIs and many other stakeholders. They have also caught the imagination of the public. Around the world the impact of rankings on higher education displays a number of well-documented characteristics. The next subsection provides an overview of how rankings are impacting, influencing and incentivizing the behavior, decisions and opinions of HEIs and their myriad stakeholders.

Impact on HEIs

There is a strong belief among HE leaders – borne out by international evidence – that rankings are influencing key stakeholders in ways that were unanticipated: good students use rankings to 'short-list' university choice, especially at the postgraduate level; rankings often influence policy decisions; external stakeholders use rankings to influence their own decisions about funding, sponsorship and employee recruitment; and other HEIs use rankings to help identify potential partners, assess membership of international networks and organizations, and for benchmarking. The mere inclusion of an HEI within rankings is perceived as granting an important level of national and international visibility, even for lower-ranked institutions. Thus rankings can provide branding and advertising value. Doing well in rankings helps to maintain and build institutional position and reputation – essential elements in a competitive marketplace.

On the other hand, because rankings appear to provide a simple 'quality mark', HE leaders fear that key stakeholders may draw sweeping conclusions to either justify or refuse funding, collaboration or accreditation. After students and parents, government is believed to be most strongly affected by rankings; this has the knock-on effect of influencing higher education policy, the classification of institutions, and the allocation of funding, specifically research funding. HE leaders variously say that 'Benefactors don't want to help or be associated with losers' (senior administrator, pre-1945 private research-informed university, Mexico) or that employers respond positively to 'degree holders from universities with good reputations' (senior administrator, pre-1945 public research-intensive university, Germany), as these examples drawn from Hazelkorn (2011) highlight.

Given this scenario, it is not surprising that 58 percent of HE respondents to a 2006 survey were so disappointed with their current rank that 93 percent and 82 percent wanted to improve their national, or international, position, respectively. And, notwithstanding the mathematical impossibility of it, 70 percent expressed their desire to be in the top 10 percent of HEIs nationally, and 71 percent wanted to be in the top 25 percent internationally (Hazelkorn, 2007). HE leaders believe 'rankings are here to stay' and they have little alternative but to take them 'into account because others do'. Several surveys show that HE leaders follow rankings, and that institutional strategies, policies and operations have often been altered in order to bring institutions into line with ranking indicators. A 2001 survey of US college presidents indicated that 76 per cent thought *USNWR* rankings were somewhat/very important for their institution; 51 percent had attempted to improve their rankings; 50 per cent used rankings as internal benchmarks; and 35 percent announced the results in press releases or on the web. Four percent of university presidents had established a task force or committee to address rankings (Levin, 2002). These results compare favorably with a survey of international HE leaders, of whom 56 percent said they had a formal process for reviewing their institutional position; this was usually undertaken by a committee chaired by the Vice Chancellor/President (56 percent) but in some cases it is undertaken by the governing authority (14 percent). As a result, 63 percent said they had taken strategic, organizational, managerial or academic action. Only 8 percent had taken no action (Hazelkorn, 2007). Forty-seven percent of Japan's national universities refer to world-class rankings as generating explicit management objectives (Yonezawa et al., 2009). Similarly, in a 2010 survey, 40 percent of HE leaders said 'analytic comparisons' were 'extremely/very useful' while a further 45 percent said they were 'somewhat useful' (Adams and Baker, 2010).

While few universities admit to being directly influenced by rankings, others are more forthright about the benefit.

> The fact that you can link an international student driver and a domestic research driver and a government agenda and a philanthropist all through the one mechanism is quite a powerful tool in the arsenal of management and so I actually think it's been good for the sector in being able to drive change and create a vehicle or a discussion point that then gives management more impetus. (Senior administrator, public post-1945 research intensive university, Australia, in Hazelkorn, 2011, p. 97)

Put another way by a research-intensive university in the UK, 'as a manager, it is useful to have different league tables with different methodologies coming out at different times, because one can occasionally use them as levers, which is not unhelpful, although it is not what they are intended for' (Locke et al., 2008, p. 39).

There are four broad types of institutional responses: (1) rankings form an explicit institutional goal; (2) rankings are an implicit goal; (3) rankings are used to set targets with the indicators being rolled into the strategic plan; and (4) rankings are used as a measure of achievement or success (Hazelkorn, 2011, pp. 97–9). For example, many strategic plans make specific reference to rankings, with targets often oriented toward gaining or maintaining positions within certain tiers. Statements are often made by national and institutional leaders, usually seeking to identify with being within the top 20, 50 or 100 in a regional, national or global ranking as the key ambition and confirmation of being within the 'top league' or 'the pantheon of world elite institutions' (Georghiou, 2009, p. 48). In other cases, rankings are used not as a strategic action to raise ranking position but to motivate and to improve the quality of education. Finally, rankings may be used to validate particular strategies or actions.

HEIs have variously established task forces or fully resourced institutional research, strategic planning or policy units. The formalization of information-gathering and data analysis to underpin strategic planning, recruitment strategies, financial assessment, budgeting and so on has been a key component of most US universities but has been a relatively recent addition elsewhere. Its growth and increasing importance is not only a response to rankings but to the audit culture more broadly. Rankings have taken the function of data collection and analysis out of the back office and placed it at the centre of strategic decision-making and performance measurement. HEIs are also hosting workshops or seminars with experts, including the people from the major ranking organizations, or hiring consultants to penetrate their methodological subtleties and thus enable institutions to both benchmark and improve performance.

Some HEIs have adopted an interventionist approach, purposely setting out to change their rank by revising class sizes and raising academic salaries, using the indicators to set departmental targets or to engage in restructuring their institution. Actions might include merging disciplines and departments, incorporating external organizations within the domain institution or, on the contrary, separating undergraduate and post-graduate activity through the establishment of graduate schools. At the organizational level, whole institutions within the same region or city might merge. The objective is to create better synergies or efficiencies, but it is also about professionalizing and improving administration and support services. Fundamentally, the aim is to create larger units with more students and faculty producing higher output and earnings – because size matters.

Rankings provide the evidence for tough decision-making, introducing change, speeding up reform or pursuing a particular agenda. This includes using rankings to inform resource allocation; bonuses have been promised to university presidents as well as to faculty who excel. Some universities are altering the balance between teaching and research, between undergraduate and postgraduate activity, and between disciplines. Resources are redirected towards fields and units that are likely to be more productive, have faculty who are more prolific, especially at the international level, and that are more likely to trigger (upward) changes in the appropriate indicators. The establishment of research centers and institutes, and graduate schools, are some of the most visible manifestations of this rapidly expanding trend. This is not a new phenomenon; Trow described extensive changes at the University of California Berkeley in response to a decline in the rankings of the National Research Council in 1982 (Dill and Soo, 2005, pp. 517–18), while similar stories are told about Cornell University in the 1990s (Ehrenberg and Hurst, 1996).

Almost 50 percent of international HE leaders say that they use their ranking for publicity purposes, with 63 percent saying that they are especially useful for student recruitment. In all cases HE leaders admit highlighting (positive) results on their web page, in speeches, at new faculty or student orientation, at international meetings or when lobbying government – usually 'ignor(ing) less favorable ones, unless they put the university ahead of other rival universities' (Hazelkorn, 2011, p. 104). One of the most noticeable additions has been the development or expansion of a professionalized year-round international office. Many HEIs now spend considerable time and energy sending promotional material to each other to coincide with the peer-reviewing exercise undertaken by various rankings.

Impact on the Academy

Rankings are putting academic staff under pressure. Around the world, faculty say they are 'being pushed into publishing more and more' and 'publishing internationally'

(Hazelkorn, 2011, p. 114). An academic's publication record can affect the way resources are distributed within the department. Rankings also affect morale. When the university's ranking is considered 'good', faculty feel upbeat about themselves. Conversely, rankings can divide; those who are viewed as good performers are seen to benefit.

From a management viewpoint, rankings can accelerate changes in academic work practices. Where autonomy permits, it has supported the introduction of market-based salaries with merit or performance pay and attractive packages to reward and woo high-achieving scholars. Recruitment strategies target faculty from high-ranked universities (Jaschik, 2010) or 'capacity-building professors' who can help improve rank. As a key performance indicator, rankings are used to distinguish between teaching and research-focused faculty. But faculty are not innocent victims. There is plenty of evidence to suggest that they are quick to use rankings to boost their own professional standing and are 'unlikely to consider research partnerships with a lower ranked university unless the person or team was exceptional' (Hazelkorn, 2011, p. 115).

Impact on Peer-to-peer Interaction and Stakeholders

Rankings affect the way peers assess an institution's reputation 'because the rankings and tier placements are so legitimate that they alter the inter-assessments of reputation made by college leaders' (Bastedo and Bowman, 2011). Over 76 percent of international HE leaders say they monitor the performance of peer institutions in their country, and almost 50 percent said they monitor the performance of peers worldwide. Almost 40 percent consider an institution's rank prior to forming strategic partnerships, 57 percent said rankings were influencing the willingness of other HEIs to partner with them, while 34 percent said rankings influenced the willingness of other HEIs to support their institution's membership of academic or professional organizations. It would appear that all institutions want to partner with strong and successful organizations, for it is perceived to assist with accreditation and raising resources. On the other hand, a poor showing (sometimes only relative to expectation) can have the opposite effect. African universities say they have been told, 'usually by universities in Europe or Australia seeking to improve their images internationally, that they cannot work with our institution, because it does not have adequate status in global-university rankings' (Holm and Malete, 2010).

Because rankings act as a register of status, there is mounting evidence that 'major corporations tend to allocate their scarce recruitment dollars to institutions with academic reputations (tiers 1 and 2), and tend to shun those colleges and universities perceived to be inferior (tiers 3 and 4)' (Webster, 2001, p. 240). Those companies that sponsor research put more value on international reputation that is also expressed in rankings (Employers' Association, Germany; see Hazelkorn, 2011). Similarly, Boeing says it intends using performance data to influence its 'choice of partners for academic research and . . . decisions about which colleges . . . to share in the [USD]100-million that Boeing spends . . . on course work and supplemental training' (Baskin, 2008). A UK study found that 25 percent of graduate recruiters interviewed 'cited league tables as their main source of information about quality and standards' (HEFCE, 2006, pp. 80, 87–92). Alumni, particularly recent graduates, are also influenced by institutional prestige, and their contributions are correlated positively with rankings; in other words, when an institution does well, contributions increase (Webster, 2001).

Impact on Student Choice

In many cases, rankings were conceived as a guide for students as consumers about the quality and potential 'private benefits' of university qualifications, including lifestyle and occupational/salary premiums. Institutional and program status and prestige are important factors, as students balance the costs against benefits. While undergraduate students are most likely to choose an institution near home and be influenced by family and friends, graduate students reflect concerns of 'early adulthood' and associated tasks, such as career (Kallio, 1995, p. 120). As international student mobility has risen sharply in recent decades, students have struggled to find information about institutions outside their own intelligence network. In the absence of clarity about quality standards, students and parents turn to rankings as a perceived independent source. As such, international students have become a primary target audience and user of rankings.

US studies have consistently found rankings to be important for high-ability and second-generation undergraduate students, especially those from Asian (or non-US citizen) backgrounds wanting a doctoral, medical or law degree. Studies suggest that the influence of rankings on student choice is growing. Students who have the financial ability to self-finance are more likely to attend higher-ranked colleges (even those ranked higher by just a few places) than grant-aided students, who appear less responsive to rankings. There are also differences between students enrolling at private or public institutions: for the former, 'reputation trumps costs by a healthy margin', while for the latter, 'reputation trumps costs – just barely – and costs trumps location by almost a two-to-one factor' (Lipman Hearne, 2009, p. 26). There is also evidence of strengthening usage among lower-income groups (McManus-Howard, 2002, p. 112).

In 1999, only 3 percent of UK respondents considered electronic media an important source of information and none mentioned rankings; by 2006, 63 percent of students said they consulted websites and 52 percent looked at league tables. Similarly, 61 percent of UK students referred to rankings before making their choice, with 70 percent considering them important or very important (Roberts and Thompson, 2007, pp. 19–20). In Germany, 60 percent of prospective students 'know rankings and use rankings as one source of information among others' (Federkeil, 2007, p. 357). Students taking profession-focused programs are more likely to use such information in contrast to students taking a traditional 'academic' program; likewise students pursuing engineering, business or science programs, which are among the most attractive fields of study to international students, are more likely to refer to rankings than arts, humanities or social science students (HERI, 2007; Roberts and Thompson, 2007, p. 26). No studies discovered any significant gender differences.

The relationship between ranking and institutional reputation presents a complicated, synergistic and sometimes contradictory picture. If rankings help establish reputation, does reputation influence rank? While students are reluctant to identify rankings as the key factor shaping their choice, they overwhelmingly identify reputation as pivotal. Admissions and international officers confirm that prospective students regularly inquire as to institutional rank. Students are especially sensitive to the publicity surrounding rankings; 44 percent of UK students said institutional reputation, based on tangible status characteristics, such as the age of the institution and entry scores, and intangible criteria, for example the extent to which the name of the institution is publicly recognized, was important (Scott, 2006).

Impact on Student Recruitment

Because 'changes in rank [can] have a significant influence on the applications and enrolment decisions of students . . .', particularly among top students, institutions actively seek to influence these factors (Monks and Ehrenberg, 1999, p. 10). Meredith (2004, p. 459) similarly found that 'moving in or out of the first quartile, and hence the first page of the rankings, had a particularly large impact on admission outcomes'. Institutional reputation may be resilient to small or annual changes, but this may be less true for well-established universities than newer ones; in other words, 'the former has a stronger history and hinterland and thus its image is not shifted so much by a change in any one year' (Roberts and Thompson, 2007, pp. 25–6). There are benefits to such changes. An institution whose rank improves can accept a smaller percentage of its applicants and thereby increase its selectivity index or the student entry indicator. Because the selectivity index is a key metric used by some (national) rankings, HEIs have sought to influence the number of applicants they receive or the type of student (e.g. probationary, part-time). Winston (2000, p. 10) suggests that HEIs may seek to limit class or cohort size because 'a larger class means dipping further down in a school's applicant pool and thereby reducing average student quality'. For these reasons, HEIs feel compelled to manipulate their matriculation rate and admissions rate data, where it is possible for them to do so (Avery et al., 2005, p. 1).

Examples of managing student entry grades and numbers are not confined to the USA; such practice is evident even in countries where equity and open recruitment have been the norm. Universities that improved their rank by 10 or more places were likely to experience a rise in the academic quality of students admitted in the following cycle (Roberts and Thompson, 2007, p. 5). University prestige in Japan is also strongly correlated to student selectivity, with 25 percent of all universities using these criteria to achieve 'top-level' status worldwide, and 73 percent adopting this measure in pursuit of international standards (Yonezawa et al., 2009, p. 133).

Because of the perceived correlation between high tuition and reputation or status, Bowman and Bastedo (2009, p. 19) claim that 'colleges have increased tuition substantially in their efforts to become elite institutions', because 'lowering one's tuition relative to one's competitors may be perceived as signally lower quality'. Universities may seek to affect 'less visible price discounts', such as through grants, scholarships or loans, 'in an attempt to attract additional students from their declining applicant pool' (Monks and Ehrenberg, 1999, p. 49). This has led to the allegation that HEIs are choosing to skew the allocation of financial aid away from students with the greatest need to using merit aid to 'purchase talent'.

Impact on Government Policy

The arrival of global rankings, in 2003, triggered alarm bells around the world. Supranational organizations, such as the EU, and policy-makers interpreted the ranking of universities as a comment on national and economic sovereignty. As a consequence, they have embarked on significant restructuring and reshaping of their higher education and research systems. Common policy keywords are international comparability and benchmarking, quality and excellence, transparency and accountability, and (measurable) performance.

Policy-makers have made a simple correlation between rankings, (elite) higher education and global competitiveness. In many instances, significant investment has followed. In other instances, governments are concerned about underinvestment relative to their competitors. Because size matters, many governments are concerned about their institutions' lack of critical mass or visibility, either because (i) they are too small and rankings emphasize quantification measurements, (ii) their research is not included in the calculation due to institutional status, such as French *grandes écoles,* or German Fraunhofer or Max Planck institutes, which are not considered universities, (iii) the disciplinary range is too specialized, for example a medical school which performs well against rankings, or focus solely on the social sciences and thus cannot score high enough against the bibliometric criteria, or (iv) a combination of all of the above (Hazelkorn, 2011, p. 158). These realizations are leading many countries to restructure their higher education and research systems, and prioritize some universities. France, Germany, Russia, Spain, China, South Korea, Taiwan, Malaysia, Finland, India, Japan, Singapore, Vietnam and Latvia – among many other countries – have all launched initiatives with the primary objective of creating 'world-class' universities, using indicators promoted by rankings to define excellence. Individual US states have also sought to build or boost flagship universities, elevating them to what are known as Tier One status, a reference to *USNWR* college rankings.

Rankings are affecting other policy decisions. For example, Zhe Jin and Whalley (2007) attribute an increase in state expenditure of 6.5 percent per student to *USNWR* exposure. In February 2008, Macedonia introduced Article 159 of the Law on Higher Education (no. 35/2008), which automatically recognizes degrees from the top 500 universities listed in the *THE–QS*, ARWU or *USNWR* without going through otherwise complex recognition processes. Mongolia, Qatar and Kazakhstan restrict scholarships to students admitted only to highly ranked (top 100) universities, while Dutch immigration law (2008) targets 'foreigners that are relatively young and received their Bachelor, Master or PhD degree . . . from a university . . . in the top 150' of ARWU or *THE–QS* (Beerkens, 2009); Danish law (2010) introduced tighter criteria. Singapore has introduced the status of foreign specialist institute, which only grants permission to 'high-quality' institutions, unofficially spoken of as universities ranked in the top 100 of the *THE–QS*, to collaborate with local universities or polytechnics. The strictness of the criteria is illustrated by the fact that a prominent UK university reportedly missed out by a few points. In some US states, governing boards have benchmarked presidential salaries against improvements in rankings (Florida and Arizona, for example), while others (including Minnesota, Indiana and Texas) have 'folded in' rankings into their own performance measurement systems (Sponsler, 2009, pp. 10–13).

IMPLICATIONS AND LEGACY

Global rankings coincided with and exploited fundamental shifts in the global economy and, in particular, underscored the fact that human and knowledge capital formation had become the key barometer of global competitiveness. The intensification of competition between nations for a piece of the global marketplace has, especially in the post-GFC world, increased pressure on higher education to meet more societal and economic needs – some with fewer, but others with much-enhanced, resources. This is producing tectonic shifts in the world order and the international division of knowledge: between attractive and less attractive nations and institutions; between selective and recruiting (or more accessible) institutions; and between research-intensive universities – branded as world-class – and the rest. Few countries or HEIs have been left unaffected by this juggernaut (Hazelkorn, 2011).

This chapter has argued that rankings have had a profound impact and influence on higher education and its key stakeholders, beyond the wildest dreams of their progenitors. The international evidence might still be limited and at times contradictory, but at the macro level, both national and global, HEIs and nation-states have introduced strategic and policy changes that meet the (changing) norms of rankings, sometimes in contradiction with other policy objectives. In some instances, this has drawn attention to the inadequacy of existing funding regimes while others have chosen to shift resources to areas that shape prestige. At the same time, by their focus on measuring educational quality, rankings have helped drive up institutional performance, thus providing some degree of public accountability and transparency. In addition, they have prompted a wide-ranging debate about how the value and contribution of higher education to society and the economy can be better and more fairly assessed, measured and made more visible. At the institutional and individual level, 'striving' for status and reputation has been accompanied by the accelerated transformation of institutional culture and academic behavior. Because of correlations between rankings and the 'status system', students, academics and other stakeholders have all been active consumers and advocates of ranking products. Thus the overall impact is varied and multi-faceted, positive and perverse.

Senior HE 'administrators consider rankings when they define goals, assess progress, evaluate peers, admit students, recruit faculty, distribute scholarships, conduct placement surveys, adopt new programs, and create budgets' (Espeland and Sauder, 2007, p. 11). According to Levin (2002, p. 14), US university presidents identified specific indicators that could impact positively on their ranking: 88 percent identified retention rates; 84 percent alumni giving; 75 percent graduation rates; 71 percent entry scores; 63 percent faculty compensation; and 31 percent student–faculty ratio. More than 25 percent sought to improve educational expenditure, by effecting greater selectivity, increasing faculty salaries, creating new and better programs, improving funding and use of resources, changing the hiring or promotional procedures, and improving marketing (Espeland and Sauder, 2007, pp. 25–7). A more recent survey found that two-thirds of institutions had developed strategies designed to support 'strong/robust/higher' positions in global rankings, and that the remaining third had set clear targets to improve their rankings (Anon, 2010). These results confirm the view that rankings have 'changed the behavior, even the strategy, of institutions, not to become more effective, but to perform well against arbitrary ranking criteria' (Adams and Baker, 2010, p. 7).

At the national level, while some governments have remained skeptical, others have been content to let rankings drive change and accelerate competition at the system level, and a third group has embedded rankings directly into decision-making. If higher education is one of the last remaining sectors of the economy to be restructured (Duderstadt, quoted in Fischer and Wilhelm, 2010), rankings have arguably played an important role in this process. There are three key trends (Hazelkorn, 2011, pp. 194–9).

1. *Accountability and transparency.* At a time of increased public interest and scrutiny around issues of quality and productivity, rankings have sharpened discussion on assessment and the measurement of higher education performance at both the institutional and individual academic level. Because rankings ignore national and institutional contexts, they promote different definitions of educational quality based upon the choice of indicators and weightings. As such they function as a commercially-driven international standards-setting body for higher education. In many instances governments have directly adopted or 'folded-in' the indicators used by rankings into their own performance measurements or used rankings to set targets for system restructuring. Their influence extends far beyond their initial objective and their target audience, encouraging and underpinning the trend towards policymaking by numbers.

2. *Internationalization and the battle for talent.* Recognition that human capital is a prerequisite for success in the global economy has coincided with significant demographic changes in many countries. The battle for talent is now on a par with other geopolitical struggles for natural resources. This emphasis on talent has encouraged an over-emphasis on particular types of academic performance that are easily collected and measured globally via bibliometric and citation databases. This has resulted in refocusing higher education away from research-informed teaching towards research in its narrowest sense. At a time when society requires interdisciplinary solutions to global challenges, rankings prioritize ivory tower Mode 1 over Mode 2 knowledge (Gibbons et al., 1994). And, because rankings have the 'capacity to shap[e] academic careers at the point of hiring and promotion' (Marginson, 2008, p. 17), those who rise to the top of the academic league table have a vested interest in retaining 'research power' and the rewards that come with it.

3. *World-class excellence.* According to Mohrman et al. (2008, p. 21), an emerging global model (EGM) of a world-class university is being created by governments and institutions seeking to adopt or ape the characteristics of the top 20, 50 or 100 universities. For many governments this model has become the panacea for ensuring success in the global economy, whereby a few institutions dominate within a hierarchically-differentiated system. This type of restructuring was initially thought desirable but has now been shown to have many disadvantages, especially for smaller (and less wealthy) countries. Concentrating resources and research activity in a few places is at best counterproductive and at worst could undermine national economic capacity. Given the costs of developing and maintaining a world-class university, a strategy of 'selective excellence' (Barrow, 1996) requires a consistent policy of high-level investment over the long term. This is leading to greater economic stratification and inequality between elite research and mass teaching institutions and their students, with uncertain implications for social and national solidarity and development. The public policy imperative has been lost in the (self-interested) belief that elite research universities have a bigger impact on society and the economy, or have higher quality.

These experiences provide important lessons for both institutions and governments, as well as for other stakeholders. Rankings *per se* may be a phenomenon of the moment, but cross-national comparisons are 'here to stay'.

Any alternative method should embrace a system-focused methodology, using an agreed set of sophisticated accountability and transparency instruments that: (i) highlights and accords parity of esteem to diverse institutional profiles in order to facilitate public comparability, democratic decision-making and institutional benchmarking; (ii) identifies what matters and assesses those aspects of higher education, rather than be influenced by the availability of the data; and (iii) enables diverse users and stakeholders to design fit-for-purpose indicators and scenarios customized to individual requirements – but without the capacity to engineer hierarchical ordinal rankings. Comparability is not the same as rankings. It is also vital that institutional and national assessment and evaluation processes embed methodologies that recognize, incentivize and reward the full spectrum of higher education's endeavors across teaching, research and engagement. Finally the collection and control of the data and verification of the methodological processes should not be the remit of private/commercial providers or self-appointed auditors (Hazelkorn, 2011, pp. 204–5).

Higher education must respond in a constructive manner to the debate about quality and performance, because political and societal support for higher education can only be maintained by quality profiling, performance enhancement and value for money that provides (public) investor confidence. At the national level, the stakes are even higher. Aligning systems to indicators set by others for commercial or other purposes threatens the very foundations of national sovereignty and society. Rather than ranking world-class universities, governments should focus on developing world-class systems, on the basis that 'a university system has a much broader mandate than producing hordes of Nobel laureates or cabals of tenure and patent-bearing professors' (Ederer et al., 2008, p. 6). This approach offers the best strategy for understanding and learning why some societies provide the best opportunities and benefits.

NOTE

1.   This chapter is based on Ellen Hazelkorn (2011).

REFERENCES

Adams, J. and K. Baker (2010), *Global Opinion Survey – New Outlooks on Institutional Profiles*, Thomson Reuters. Accessed 27 March 2010, from http://science.thomsonreuters.com/m/pdfs/Global_Opinion_Survey.pdf.

Aghion, P., M. Dewatripont, C. Hoxby, A. Mas-Colell and A. Sapir (2007), 'Why reform Europe's universities?', *Bruegel Policy Brief,* September, 4. Accessed 30 April 2010 from http://www.bruegel.org/uploads/tx_btbbreugel/pbf_040907_universities.pdf.

Anon (2010), 'Higher and higher: lofty positions, beneficial outcomes', *Times Higher Education,* 1 July. Accessed 1 July 2010, from http://www.timeshighereducation.co.uk/story.asp?sectioncode=26&storycode=412246&c=1.

Avery, C., M. Glickman, C. Hoxby and A. Metrick (2005), 'A revealed preference ranking of US Colleges and Universities', NBER Working Paper No. 10803, December.

Barrow, C.W. (1996), 'The strategy of selective excellence: redesigning higher education for global competition in a postindustrial society', *Higher Education,* **41**, 447–69.

Baskin, P. (2008), 'Boeing to rank colleges by measuring graduates' job success', *Chronicle of Higher Education,* 19 September. Accessed 22 June 2010, from http://chronicle.com/article/Boeing-to-Rank-Colleges-by/9954.

Bastedo, M. and N. Bowman (2011), 'College rankings as an interorganizational dependency: establishing the foundation for strategic and institutional accounts', *Research in Higher Education,* **52**, forthcoming.

Beerkens, E. (2009), 'What if I graduated from Amherst or ENS de Lyon . . .' Beerkens' Blog: higher education, science and innovation from a global perspective, 6 January. Accessed 4 June 2010, from http://blog.beerkens.info/index.php/2009/01/what-if-i-graduated-from-amherst-or-ens-de-lyon/.

Bowden, R. (2000), 'Fantasy education: university and college league tables', *Quality in Higher Education,* **6** (1), 41–60.

Bowman, N. and M. Bastedo (2009), 'Getting on the front page: organisational reputation, status signals, and the impact of US News and World Report on student decisions', *Research in Higher Education*, **50** (5), 415–36.

Bremner, J., C. Haub, M. Lee, M. Mather and E. Zuehlke (2009), *World Population Prospects: Key Findings from PRB's 2009 World Population Data Sheet*, Population Reference Bureau, United Nations, Washington, DC. Accessed 26 April 2010, from http://www.prb.org/pdf09/64.3highlights.pdf.

Carr, K. (2009), Speech by Federal Minister for Innovation, Industry, Science and Research to Universities Australia Higher Education Conference, Australia. Accessed 30 March 2009, from http://minister.innovation.gov.au/Carr/Pages/UNIVERSITIESAUSTRALIAHIGHEREDUCATIONCONFERENCE2009.aspx.

Castells, M. (1994), 'The university system: engine of development in the new world economy', in J. Salmi and A. Vespoor (eds), *Revitalizing Higher Education*, Oxford: Pergamon, pp. 14–40.

Dill, D.D. and M. Soo (2005), 'Academic quality, league tables and public policy: a cross-national analysis of university ranking systems', *Higher Education*, **49** (4), 495–537.

Ederer, P., P. Schuller and S. Willms (2008), *University Systems Ranking: Citizens and Society in the Age of Knowledge*. Accessed 27 March 2010, from http://www.lisboncouncil.net/publication/publication/38-university-systems-ranking-citizens-and-society-in-the-age-of-knowledge.html.

Ehrenberg, R. (2001), 'Reaching for the brass ring: how the *US News and World Report* rankings shape the competitive environment in US higher education', *The Review of Higher Education*, **226** (2), 145–62.

Ehrenberg, R. (2005), 'Method or madness? Inside the *US News and World Report* college rankings', *Journal of College Admission*, 29–36.

Ehrenberg, R. and P. Hurst (1996), 'A hedonic model', *Change*, **28** (3), 46–51.

Espeland, W. and M. Sauder (2007), 'Rankings and reactivity: how public measures recreate social worlds', *American Journal of Sociology*, **113** (1), 1–40.

Europa (2006), *Delivering on the modernisation agenda for universities: education, research and innovation*. Communication to the Council and the European Parliament, (COM) 2006 208 final, European Commission, Brussels. Accessed 11 August 2009, from http://www.madrimasd.org/proyectoseuropeos/documentos/doc/education_research_and_innovation.pdf.

Federkeil, G. (2007), 'Rankings and quality assurance in higher education', Proceedings of 3rd Meeting of the International Ranking Expert Group (IREG-3), Shanghai.

Fischer, K. and I. Wilhelm (2010), 'Experts ponder the future of the American university', *Chronicle of Higher Education*, 21 June. Accessed 1 July 2010, from http://chronicle.com/article/Experts-Ponder-the-Future-of/66011/.

Georghiou, L. (2009), 'Strategy to join the elite: merger and the 2015 agenda at the University of Manchester', in M. McKelvey and M. Holmén (eds), *Learning to Compete in European Universities: From Social Institution to Knowledge Business*, Cheltenham, UK and Northampton, MA, USA: Edward Elgar, pp. 48–64.

Gibbons, M., C. Limoges, H. Nowotny, S. Schwartzman, P. Scott and M. Trow (1994), *The New Production of Knowledge. The Dynamics of Science and Research in Contemporary Societies*, London: Sage Publications.

Grewal, R., J. Dearden and G. Lilien (2008), 'The university rankings game: modeling the competition among universities for ranking', *The American Statistician*, **62** (3), 1–6.

Hawkins, D. (2008), 'Commentary: Don't use SATs to rank college quality', CNN. Accessed 27 March 2010, from http://edition.cnn.com/2008/US/10/17/hawkins.tests/index.html.

Hazelkorn, E. (2007), 'Impact and influence of league tables and ranking systems on higher education decision-making', *Higher Education Management and Policy*, **19** (2), 87–110.

Hazelkorn, E. (2011), *Rankings and the Reshaping of Higher Education: The Battle for World-class Excellence*, Basingstoke: Palgrave Macmillan.

HEFCE (2006), *Needs of Employers and Related Organizations for Information about Quality and Standards of Higher Education*, Report, Higher Education Funding Council of England, UK. Accessed 1 July 2010, from http://www.hefce.ac.uk/pubs/rdreports/2006/rd20_06/.

Hendel, D. and I. Stolz (2008), 'A comparative analysis of higher education ranking systems in Europe', *Tertiary Education and Management*, **14** (3), 173–89.

HERI (2007), 'College rankings and college choice: how important are college rankings in students' college choice process?' Research Brief, California: Higher Education Research Institute, UCLA. Accessed 14 July 2010, from http://www.heri.ucla.edu/PDFs/pubs/briefs/brief-081707-CollegeRankings.pdf.

Holm, J. and L. Malete (2010), 'Nine problems that hinder partnerships in Africa', *Chronicle of Higher Education*, 13 June. Accessed 20 June 2010, from http://chronicle.com/article/Nine-Problems-That-Hinder/65892/.

Jaschik, S. (2010), 'Rank hiring', Inside Higher Ed. Accessed 12 October from http://www.insidehighered.com/news/2010/10/12/cnu.

Kallio, R. (1995), 'Factors influencing the college choice decisions of graduate students', *Research in Higher Education*, **36** (1), 109–24.

Karabel, J. (2005), *The Chosen: The Hidden History of Admission and Exclusion at Harvard, Yale and Princeton*, Boston, MA and New York: Houghton Mifflin.

Kuh, G. (2003), 'What we're learning about student engagement from NSSE', *Change*, March/April, 26–7.

Lawrence, J. and K. Green (1980), *A Question of Quality: The Higher Education Ratings Game*, Report No. 5, American Association of Higher Education, Washington, DC.

Levin, D. (2002), 'Uses and abuses of the US News Rankings', *Priorities*, Fall, Association of Governing Boards of Universities and Colleges, Washington, DC.

Lipman Hearne (2009), *Five Great Colleges Want Her: How Will she Decide? Report on High-achieving Seniors and the College Decision*. Accessed 21 January 2010, from http://www.lipmanhearne.com/Libraries/Resources%20Documents/Lipman%20Hearne%20High-Achieving%20Seniors%20Study%20 2009.sflb.

Locke, W., L. Verbik, J. Richardson and R. King (2008), 'Appendix A: research methodologies', *Counting What is Measured or Measuring What Counts? League Tables and the Impact on Higher Education Institutions in England*, Report to HEFCE by the Centre for Higher Education Research and Information (CHERI), Open University, and Hobsons Research, UK. Accessed 11 June 2010, from http://www.hefce.ac.uk/Pubs/HEFCE/2008/08_14/.

McManus-Howard, M. (2002), *Student Use of Rankings in National Magazines in the College Decision-Making Process*, EdD Thesis, University of Tennessee, Knoxville.

Marginson, S. (2008), 'The knowledge economy and the potentials of the global public sphere', Paper to the Beijing Forum, 7–9 November. Accessed 8 October 2010, from http://www.cshe.unimelb.edu.au/people/staff_pages/Marginson/Beijing%20Forum%202008%20Simon%20Marginson.pdf.

Marginson, S. and M. van der Wende (2007), 'To rank or to be ranked: the impact of global university rankings', *Journal of Studies in International Education*, **11** (3–4), 313–18.

Meredith, M. (2004), 'Why do universities compete in the ratings game? An empirical analysis of the effects of the *US News and World Report* college rankings', *Research in Higher Education*, **45** (5), 443–61.

Mohrman, K., W. Ma and D. Baker (2008), 'The research university in transition: the emerging global model', *Higher Education Policy*, **21** (1), 5–27.

Monks, J. and R. Ehrenberg (1999), 'The impact of US News and World Report College Rankings on admissions outcomes and pricing policies at selective private institutions', Working Paper Series, National Bureau of Economic Research, Cambridge, MA.

Roberts, D. and L. Thompson (2007), 'University league tables and the impact on student recruitment: reputation management for universities', Working Paper Series 2, Leeds, Cambridge and Brisbane: The Knowledge Partnership.

Sadlak, J. and N. Liu (eds) (2007), *The World-Class University and Ranking: Aiming Beyond Status*, Bucharest: Cluj University Press.

Saisana, M. and B. D'Hombres (2008), *Higher Education Rankings: Robustness Issues and Critical Assessment: How Much Confidence Can We Have in Higher Education Rankings?* Centre for Research on Lifelong Learning (CRELL), European Communities, Luxembourg.

Scott, J. (2006), 'Why am I here? student choice in the Biosciences', *BioScience Education*, BEE-j 7, May. Accessed 12 April 2010, from http://www.bioscience.heacademy.ac.uk/journal/vol7/beej-7-4.aspx.

Slaughter, S. and L. Leslie (1997), *Academic Capitalism, Politics, Policies and the Entrepreneurial University*. Baltimore, MD: Johns Hopleins University Press.

Sponsler, B. (2009), *The Role and Relevance of Rankings in Higher Education Decision-Making*, Washington, DC: Institute of Higher Education Policy.

Tight, M. (2000), 'Do league tables contribute to the development of a quality culture?' *Higher Education Quarterly*, **54** (1), 22–42.

Turner, D. (2005), 'Benchmarking in universities: league tables revisited', *Oxford Review of Education*, **31** (3), 353–71.

Usher, A. and J. Medow (2009), 'A global survey of university rankings and league tables', in B. Kehm and B. Stensaker (eds), *University Rankings, Diversity, and the New Landscape of Higher Education*, Rotterdam: Sense Publishers, pp. 3–18.

Usher, A. and M. Savino (2006), *A World of Difference: A Global Survey of University League Tables*, Toronto, Educational Policy Institute. Accessed 19 January 2009, from http://www.educationalpolicy.org/pdf/world-of-difference-200602162.pdf.

Usher, A. and M. Savino (2007), 'A global survey of rankings and league tables', *College and University Ranking Systems – Global Perspectives American Challenges*, Washington, DC: Institute of Higher Education Policy.

Webster, D. (1986), *Academic Quality Rankings of American Colleges and Universities*, Springfield, IL: Charles C. Thomas.

Webster, T. (2001), 'A principal component analysis of the *US News and World Report* tier rankings of colleges and universities', *Economics of Education Review*, 20.

Winston, G. (2000), 'The positional arms race in higher education', Discussion Paper 54, Williams Project on the Economics of Higher Education, Williams College, Massachusetts. Accessed 15 July 2010, from http://econpapers.repec.org/paper/wilwilehe/54.htm.

Yonezawa, A., H. Akiba and D. Hirouchi (2009), 'Japanese university leaders' perceptions of internationalization: the role of government in review and support', *Journal of Studies in International Education*, **13** (2), 125–42.

Zhe Jin, G. and A. Whalley (2007), *The Power of Information: How do US News Rankings Affect the Financial Resources of Public Colleges?*, Cambridge: National Bureau of Economic Research Working Paper Series.

Index

ABET (Accreditation Board for Engineering and Technology) 440, 442
academic community 320, 321
academic culture 366, 367, 368, 371, 510
academic employment
  Argentina 318, 319, 320
  Canada 224
  China 248–9
  India 277
  South Korea 290, 294–5, 300, 301, 302
  USA 351, 356, 357
  see also academic employment contracts; academic recruitment; 'brain drain'
academic employment contracts 184, 294–5, 297, 318, 399, 461
academic freedom
  Erasmus 268
  higher education in South Africa 207, 217
  higher education in the USA 356, 358
  neoliberalism impacts 378–9
  research assessment impacts 368, 375–6, 377, 378
  rights 375–6, 379
  world class science 423
academic freedom deficits 193, 251–2, 418, 419–20, 428, 429
academic misbehavior 362, 364, 368, 375
academic mobility 242, 248–9, 259, 260, 296–7, 300, 302, 336, 420, 471
academic quality assurance institutions
  globalization 438–40
  international institutions 440–42
  legitimacy of the global governance of academic quality 448–50
  strengths and weaknesses of the global institutional framework 443–8
academic recruitment 72, 307–8, 319, 503, 504–5, 506, 510
academic standards *see* academic quality assurance institutions; quality/quality assurance; standards
academic work practices 505–6
accountability
  global rankings 498, 503, 510, 511–12
  globalization 203, 241
  higher education in Canada 235
  higher education in South Africa 204, 207, 208, 209–10, 215–16, 218

higher education in South Korea 288, 299, 301
  neoliberalism 367–8, 375
  new public management 199, 215
  public choice theory 361, 363, 364
  quality assurance 198, 199, 201, 231–2, 449
  teaching 367, 368
  types 367–8
  see also quality/quality assurance; research assessments and the impact of research
accreditation 231–6, 237, 278, 291–2, 311, 313–14, 337, 351–2, 356
actors, higher education steering 456
  see also international actors
Africa 45, 47, 53–4, 130, 132, 136, 139, 141, 144, 480, 506
  see also South Africa; South African higher education reform; Sub-Saharan Africa
agencies 457
  see also intergovernmental academic quality assurance agencies; international organizations; national academic quality assurance agency networks
AHELO (Assessment of Higher Education Learning Outcomes) 106–7, 441, 448
Altbach, P. 50, 117, 124, 150, 152, 155, 157, 160, 180, 251, 252, 281, 284, 324, 329, 418, 419
Amaral, A. 51, 262, 265, 472, 474–5
American higher education model 3, 46, 326, 401, 408–9
Appardurai, A. 11, 35, 52, 198, 325
Argentina 48, 51, 132, 480
  see also public agenda for higher education in Argentina
arts 80, 81, 116, 182, 185, 310, 421, 424, 505, 507
Asia 3, 45, 180, 419–22, 507
  see also Asia-Pacific; Asian financial crisis 1997–98; Asian values; Confucian model; East Asia; South-east Asia; *individual countries*
Asia-Pacific 119, 125, 179–80, 181, 265, 347, 410, 419
  see also individual countries
Asian financial crisis 1997–98 187, 287–8, 295, 297, 298
Asian values 48

Printed and bound by CPI Group (UK) Ltd, Croydon, CR0 4YY

16/04/2025

14658392-0005